FOURTH EDITION

All Children Read

Teaching for Literacy in Today's Diverse Classrooms

Charles Temple
Hobart and William Smith Colleges

Donna Ogle
National-Louis University

Alan Crawford
California State University, Los Angeles

Penny Freppon
University of Cincinnati

PEARSON

Boston • Columbus • Indianapolis • New York • San Francisco • Upper Saddle River
Amsterdam • Cape Town • Dubai • London • Madrid • Milan • Munich • Paris • Montreal • Toronto
Delhi • Mexico City • São Paulo • Sydney • Hong Kong • Seoul • Singapore • Taipei • Tokyo

Vice President, Editor-in-Chief: Aurora Martínez Ramos
Acquisitions Editor: Kathryn Boice
Development Editor: Bryce Bell
Editorial Assistant: Michelle Hochberg
Executive Marketing Manager: Krista Clark
Production Editor: Janet Domingo
Editorial Production Service: Cenveo® Publisher Services
Manufacturing Buyer: Linda Sager
Electronic Composition: Cenveo® Publisher Services
Interior Design: Denise Hoffman
Photo Researcher: Poyee Oster
Cover Director: Diane Lorenzo
Cover Illustrator: Steve Morrison

Credits and acknowledgments borrowed from other sources and reproduced, with permission, in this textbook appear on the appropriate page within the text.

Printed in the United States of America

10 9 8 7 6 5 4 3 2 1

PEARSON

ISBN-10: 0-13-306682-7
ISBN-13: 978-0-13-306682-1

About the Authors

● **CHARLES TEMPLE** is a professor of education at Hobart and William Smith Colleges in Geneva, New York, where he teaches courses on literacy, children's literature, peace studies, and storytelling. He has written books on emergent literacy, invented spelling, writing instruction, language arts, diagnosis and remediation of reading disabilities, and children's literature. Along with Alan Crawford and Jean Gillet, he authored the *Developmental Literacy Inventory*, an assessment system for literacy, K–12. With Jim MaKinster, he co-authored *Intervening for Literacy*, a supplemental handbook for Jump Start, the early intervention project. Temple taught as a senior Fulbright Scholar in Portugal and Romania, and was a founding director of the Open Society Institute's and the International Reading Association's Reading and Writing for Critical Thinking Project, which has served more than 100,000 teachers in 40 countries in Europe, Asia, Latin America, and Africa. He co-directs Critical Thinking International, Inc., a non-profit organization that develops materials and fields mid-career professionals for teacher training projects around the world. He has published books for children, and he is currently working with teachers and authors in Liberia, Sierra Leone, and Tanzania to develop indigenous literature for children.

● **DONNA OGLE** is Emerita Professor of Reading and Language at National-Louis University (NLU) in Chicago, Illinois, and is active in research and professional development projects. She served as senior consultant to the Chicago Striving Readers Project, co-directs the Reading Leadership Institute and for eight years was Co-Director of the Literacy Partners Project, collaboration among the Chicago Public Schools, NLU and the Chicago Community Trust. Donna also serves as a literacy consultant internationally: as part of the Reading and Writing for Critical Thinking Project she worked primarily in Russia and Romania, for the U.S government she has worked in Peshawar, Pakistan (for an Afghan Education Project), in Latin America and in Austria; and currently is part of Critical Thinking International and Grupo SM in Latin America. She is currently on the editorial review boards of the *Reading Teacher* and the *Journal of Adolescent and Adult Literacy*. Donna is a past-president of the International Reading Association (IRA) and an elected member of the Reading Hall of Fame. She also conducts research on visual literacy, vocabulary, and content comprehension, having developed both the K-W-L and PRC2 (partner reading in content, too) frameworks. She is the author of many books, book chapters, professional articles, and curriculum materials and is currently coordinating editor for a series of books on the CCSS being published by Pearson Education.

● **ALAN CRAWFORD** is Emeritus Professor of Education at California State University, Los Angeles. He has served as President of the California Reading Association, a Fulbright Senior Scholar in Ecuador and Morocco, and a Researcher in Residence at the American Embassy in Baku, Azerbaijan. He has done extensive teaching, consulting, and writing on teaching reading in the elementary school, especially for second language learners. Alan has written curriculum for teaching reading in Spanish and served on the Editorial Review Board of *Lectura y Vida*. He served as IRA's representative to UNESCO for many years and was a Senior Literacy Specialist at UNESCO in Paris during International Literacy Year (1989–90). He is currently a director of Critical Thinking International. He frequently presents workshops on a volunteer basis for international development projects in Latin America, Europe, Asia, and Africa.

● **PENNY FREPPON** is Emerita Professor of Literacy at the University of Cincinnati, where she taught undergraduate and graduate courses in reading and writing and directed a Literacy Center serving urban children. Federal, state, and university grants supported her research. Her publications appeared in nationally and internationally refereed journals. She has served on Review Boards for Language Arts (LA) and Research in the Teaching (RTE) of the National Council of Teachers of English, *Research Reading Quarterly* (RRQ) and the *Reading Teacher* (RT) of the International Reading Association, *Journal of Reading Behavior* (JRB), the Yearbook of the National Reading Conference (Literacy Research Association), and *Literacy, Teaching and Learning: An International Journal of Early Literacy* of the Reading Recovery Council; she has also won the Distinguished Research Award in Teacher Education. Freppon has written and co-written research and practice-based articles, book chapters, and a book on "what it takes to be a teacher." The state of Ohio and federal funds supported a Literacy Specialist workshop-based and literature-rich program, of which she was field-faculty member. She was a member of the RWCT Team in Uzbekistan, the Liberian Team in Kakata, and the RWCT IC Team in Zambia, and is a member of Critical Thinking International and is a RWCT IC International Trainer.

Brief Contents

Contents

CHAPTER **3**

What Reading Teachers Need to Know About Language   66

PART TWO

Aspects of Reading

CHAPTER **4**

Emergent Literacy 94

CHAPTER **5**

Phonics and Word Knowledge   122

CHAPTER **6**

Helping Readers Build Fluency and Vocabulary   146

CHAPTER 7

Reading Comprehension, Part I: Making Sense of Literature   180

CHAPTER **8**

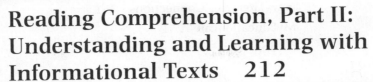

Reading Comprehension, Part II: Understanding and Learning with Informational Texts 212

CHAPTER **9**

Critical Thinking and Critical Literacy   252

CHAPTER **11**

Assessing Literacy   322

CHAPTER **14**

Putting Effective Literacy Instruction into Practice: Grades 6 to 8   438

CHAPTER **15**

Models and Strategies for Teaching ESL and for Teaching Reading in the Mother Tongue   476

Features

Developmental Milestones

Integrating Across the Curriculum

CCSS

Teach It!

The World of Reading

ASSESSMENT

DIFFERENTIATED INSTRUCTION

SIOP®
Sheltered
Instruction
Observation
Protocol®

Being a Professional Reading Teacher

For English Language Learners

Preface

New to This Edition

The fourth edition of *All Children Read: Teaching for Literacy in Today's Diverse Classrooms* expands upon the strengths our readers have found in previous editions of our book. We have added a number of new elements to this edition that respond to significant developments in the literacy field.

The fourth edition includes:

- *An emphasis on the Common Core State Standards (CCSS) throughout the book,* highlighted by icons in the margins alongside content that aligns with these Standards, as well as boxed features.

- A *strengthened chapter on teaching the comprehension of informational text* that reflects the CCSS requirement that reading instruction stress reading for information at all grades, especially from third grade and beyond.

- *Emphasis is provided throughout the book on teaching English language learners,* along with a dedicated chapter on teaching students with low English proficiency.

- *Expanded emphasis on teaching reading comprehension in the lower primary grades,* in response to the Common Core State Standards' insistence that children from the earliest grades be able to understand literary elements of stories as well as the structure of informational texts.

- *Strengthened explanations of concepts about language* prepare teachers to teach foundational concepts for reading as called for in the Common Core State Standards, or CCSS. They also help students develop the language skills specified in the standards.

- *Chapters are correlated with Common Core State Standards* in Appendix A: Addressing the Common Core. This appendix pinpoints which chapters correspond to which Standards, and identifies what students should know and be able to do.

- *An expanded focus on Response to Intervention (RTI)* further explores this important initiative in practical ways.

Carried over from the previous edition are:

- *An entire chapter, Chapter 9, Critical Thinking and Critical Literacy,* that provides explanations of critical thinking and critical literacy and discusses their importance at all levels. The chapter explores ways of teaching students to conduct critical discussion of fictional and informational texts, and also the special and urgent challenges of applying critical thinking to electronic texts.

- *Elaborate coverage of new literacies throughout the book* that provides information about the impact of technology on the teaching of reading and writing. This content is highlighted by a margin note icon.

- *A Developmental Milestones feature* that appears in Chapters 3 and 4. The Developmental Milestones feature provides at-a-glance summaries of typical behaviors in children's development of emergent literacy and phonological awareness.

- *A feature on Integrating Across the Curriculum,* that appears in Chapters 12–14. The Integrating Across the Curriculum feature provides concrete examples of curriculum integration at each of the three levels: K–2, 3–5, and 6–8. This feature shows how integrated curriculum addresses state learning standards while providing needed context for literacy instruction and freeing up valuable class time for instruction in other content subjects.
- *Additional opportunities for readers to apply text concepts.* Accompanying the book is an exciting online resource, MyEducationLab, which provides readers with opportunities to apply the text concepts and build their teaching skills.

We have also updated each of our existing chapters to reflect the newest developments and research findings in the literacy field.

- *Chapter 1: Approaches to Teaching Reading* chronicles recent major changes in the field, including a trend toward integrating instruction across the curriculum, that are affecting classroom practice. Response to Intervention (RTI), the federal initiative to support readers with a range of needs, is introduced in Chapter 1.
- *Chapter 2: The Social and Cultural Contexts for Teaching All Children to Read* includes regulations and implementation guidelines about the federal Response to Intervention (RTI) initiative and insights about teaching reading and writing to children whose home language is African American Vernacular English. A classroom vignette about Getting Parents and the Community Involved is included, as well as a section on creating a professional portfolio.
- *Chapter 3: What Reading Teachers Need to Know About Language* includes careful treatments of the sounds of the English language, vocabulary, morphology or word structure, syntax (grammar), text structure, and varieties of language, including dialects and different kinds of discourse.
- *Chapter 4: Emergent Literacy* includes practices based on current research on assessing and teaching for emergent literacy, including teaching the alphabet and teaching phonological awareness.
- *Chapter 5: Phonics and Word Knowledge* now has a section on Teaching the "Meaningful Word Parts" or Morphological Reader (Grades 3 and 4), which includes structural analysis and word journals.
- *Chapter 6: Helping Readers Build Fluency and Vocabulary* has been updated. It includes an Assessment box feature, Charting Students' Word Learning.
- *Chapter 7: Reading Comprehension, Part I: Making Sense of Literature* includes more teaching strategies to boost the comprehension of younger students, and a general update of major concepts.
- *Chapter 8: Reading Comprehension, Part II: Understanding and Learning with Informational Texts* provides reliable suggestions for teaching students to comprehend and learn from informational text. It is rich with suggested Web and computer-based resources. One section introduces teachers to the importance of helping students learn to use the basic structure of Web sites and identifying the sources of the sites.
- *Chapter 10: Teaching Children to Spell and Write* has been reorganized to provide updates of research-supported practices for assessing and teaching spelling, including the work of Donald Bear, Robert Schlagal, and Richard Gentry. The chapter also includes writing supports for English language learners.
- *Chapter 11: Assessing Literacy* explains the many kinds of assessments of reading and their purposes. It includes a section on administering the Informal Reading Inventory and subsections on scoring and interpreting the outcomes.
- *Chapter 12: Putting Effective Literacy Instruction into Practice: Grades K to 2* provides updated information about research-based approaches to teaching students at grade levels K–2. The chapter includes a feature on Integrating Across

the Curriculum, introducing the use of learning centers to achieve integration across the curriculum. Chapter 12 also includes information about the important relationship between oral language development and written language. References to the Common Core State Standards are made throughout the chapter.

- *Chapter 13: Putting Effective Literacy Instruction into Practice: Grades 3 to 5* provides information about research-based approaches to teaching students at these grade levels. Curriculum integration is introduced through the use of a complete CCSS curriculum map, and references to the Common Core State Standards are made throughout the chapter.

- *Chapter 14: Putting Effective Literacy Instruction into Practice: Grades 6 to 8* provides information about research-based approaches to teaching students at these grade levels. Curriculum integration is introduced through the use of thematic units, with an example provided. The chapter includes a section with current information on the status of NAEP results, the *Reading Next* report from the Carnegie Foundation, and an introduction to the *Doing What Works* Web site sponsored by the U.S. Department of Education. A section on Web-based inquiry through ThinkQuest shows how technology is being used productively; and, again, the Common Core State Standards are referenced throughout the chapter.

- *Chapter 15: Models and Strategies for Teaching ESL and for Teaching Reading in the Mother Tongue* is our anchor chapter on teaching students with limited English proficiency. The chapter introduces research and information about legal policies for English language learners, as well as a section of Building Vocabulary with Read-Alouds. Suggestions for teaching English language learners are included throughout the book, with an opening discussion in Chapter 2 on sociocultural factors in teaching reading, Chapter 3 on the English language, and then in subsequent chapters on assessing and teaching reading and writing.

- The *Teach It!* lesson plan booklet, written by Professor Codruţa Temple of SUNY Cortland, appears as an Appendix containing a wide variety of ready-to-use, classroom-tested activities for teaching critical concepts in Literacy Education. All activities are correlated to lessons in the text itself.

Our Rationale for This Book

Teaching all children to read is a central responsibility of our elementary and middle schools. This book shares the knowledge and skills needed to do that work well. What kind of skills? Many of them could be called "traditional." There are things good teachers of reading have done successfully for a long time: student-centered teaching, immersing children in good literature—both fiction and nonfiction, and combining reading and writing, to name a few. We will pass on the best of those practices here. Traditional teaching won't take us far enough, though, because the circumstances of teaching have changed and are still changing.

We are facing enormous pressure to educate better. Changes in society beyond the classroom are insisting that every student learn to read and think critically—every student. There are fewer and fewer places in our society for the undereducated. By law, children with special needs are guaranteed the right to be educated in the least restrictive environment, and all teachers are invited to team together to plan and carry out instruction that helps every child learn. All of us are educating all or nearly all of the children.

460. That is the number of different languages children in our classrooms speak at home. 14,000,000 is the number of English language learners in our schools. North Carolina, South Carolina, and Indiana are some of the states that have recently seen 200% to 300% increases in English language learners. But 55% is the share of Spanish-speaking children who entered Los Angeles County schools last year. Most teachers at one time or another

will teach a child who doesn't have strong English ability, and a large number will teach many English language learners every year.

A few years ago, teachers could complain of working in a lonely profession: When they closed the door in the morning they were alone all day with the kids. The Response to Intervention Initiative (RTI) is asking teachers who teach reading to work in teams with fellow teachers and other educational professionals in the school, sharing data and ideas and finding solutions to learning problems together.

When teachers plan together, they often speak of ways to combine or integrate the teaching of many subjects. As long as students are reading for comprehension and writing to learn, it makes sense to focus reading and writing some of the time on social studies, science, and mathematics. Integrating curriculum makes good use of teaching time. Also, with the greater attention being paid to reading instruction, integrating curriculum buys more teaching time for social studies and science.

Not long ago, teaching students to understand what they read was the pinnacle of reading instruction. Now we must go further and teach students not only to understand what they read but also to make sure it is credible and to examine it for biases and manipulation. Critical literacy is taking its place alongside reading comprehension.

The technology affecting what students read, how they read it, and how we should teach has been changing so rapidly that literacy educators now refer to the "new literacies," acknowledging that as students continue to encode and decode messages, and store and search for information, the technologies that they use to do these things will have a profound effect on the skills they need.

Finally, as this new edition was being prepared, the Common Core State Standards for the English Language Arts were adopted with dramatic suddenness by 45 states and the District of Columbia. The CCSS call on teachers to understand and be able to teach the details of the English language, to teach children to read for literary details, and to read and learn from informational texts. Fortunately, all of these topics had been addressed for years in previous editions of *All Children Read*. Those explanations are greatly strengthened in this fourth edition.

How This Book Is Organized

All Children Read is organized in three parts. Part One helps you develop a broad understanding of the processes by which students learn to read and write and the important factors such as culture, diversity, and the structure of language that we must understand in order to teach reading. Part Two looks in depth at the different aspects of reading and writing, from emergent literacy to critical literacy, and including comprehension, fluency and vocabulary, word knowledge, comprehension, writing, and assessment. Finally, Part Three describes, level by level, how to put all of this information together into an effective reading program that helps all children become readers and writers.

Part One: The Processes of Literacy

The three chapters in the first section of the book set the stage for teaching reading and writing. Chapter 1, "Approaches to Teaching Reading," describes aspects of literacy that must be taught and stages of reading development before discussing the main approaches to literacy instruction. The chapter includes a discussion of the Common Core State Standards. Chapter 2, "The Social and Cultural Contexts for Teaching All Children to Read," carefully describes the cultural and linguistic diversity of America's students, and lays out guidelines for making literacy instruction work for all of them. Chapter 3, "What

Reading Teachers Need to Know About Language," provides a background in the sounds, rules, and meanings of the English language, so the reader can successfully help learners navigate its challenges.

Part Two: Aspects of Reading

The chapters in Part Two of the book focus on the key aspects of literacy. Chapter 4, "Emergent Literacy," details the early concepts about language and print that lay the basis for learning to read and write. There are many ideas, systematically arranged, for helping children get off to a successful start in literacy. Chapter 5, "Phonics and Word Knowledge," covers assessing and teaching children to decode and recognize words. The chapter begins by exploring what children need to know in order to read words and the phases through which that knowledge develops. It then presents a host of strategies for teaching children to read words and build sight vocabularies. Chapter 6, "Helping Readers Build Fluency and Vocabulary," summarizes our current understanding of reading fluency, what had been called the "neglected skill" in reading, and then presents best practices in teaching children to read fluently. The chapter uses the same theory and practice approach for teaching vocabulary. Chapter 7, "Reading Comprehension, Part I: Making Sense of Literature," explores the nature of reading comprehension and response to literature, and then helps the reader build a repertoire of teaching techniques that work with fictional texts. Chapter 8, "Reading Comprehension, Part II: Understanding and Learning with Informational Texts," extends the discussion of comprehension to teaching students to understand and learn from informational texts. Chapter 9, "Critical Thinking and Critical Literacy," explores ways of having students think hard about what they read, examine messages for their credibility, and especially think critically about technologically mediated texts. Chapter 10, "Teaching Children to Spell and Write," presents the components and phases of the writing process and then explains the writing workshop approach as well as other approaches to teaching writing in many genres. The methods include those that offer support to beginning writers, as well as to English language learners. Chapter 11, "Assessing Literacy," explains a host of procedures that can be used in four "moments" of assessment: screening, diagnosing, monitoring, and outcomes-based assessment.

Part Three: Organizing and Managing the Literacy Program

The last section of the book weaves together the concepts and strategies that were presented earlier and shows how to organize instruction for different levels of learners. All of these chapters point out ways to meet the Common Core State Standards. Three chapters in this section share approaches to teaching reading in different grade level spans, and the fourth shows how to work with English language learners at all levels. Chapter 12, "Putting Effective Literacy Instruction into Practice: Grades K to 2," explains how to set up and manage a literacy program for emergent and beginning readers, including suggestions for working with English language learners. Chapter 13, "Putting Effective Literacy Instruction into Practice: Grades 3 to 5," shows how to build reading and writing fluency and how to help children in the upper elementary grades read for meaning and learn from texts, again with suggestions for working effectively with English language learners. Chapter 14, "Putting Effective Literacy Instruction into Practice: Grades 6 to 8," continues with middle school students and adds a strong emphasis on reading and writing to learn. Chapter 15, "Models and Strategies for Teaching ESL and for Teaching Reading in the Mother Tongue," demonstrates how to set up instructional programs in ESL, reading, and writing for English language learners.

Special Features

Throughout the book, special features focus on issues of recurring importance to reading teachers and extend understanding of key concepts in reading instruction.

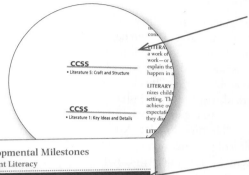

CCSS
• Literature 5: Craft and Structure

CCSS
• Literature 1: Key Ideas and Details

- **NEW! Common Core State Standards (CCSS) features** illustrate chapter content that aligns with Common Core State Standards.

Developmental Milestones
Emergent Literacy

Stages of Literacy Development	Developmental Milestones	Teaching Strategies
Exploring Print (Beginning Kindergarten)	• May tap out syllables in most words, but not phonemes. • Holds a book the right way up and can point to the front. • May know that print "talks" and not pictures. • May recognize some letters and may be able to write a few of them. • Writing shows no relation between letters and sounds. P2X = "little." • After memorizing a short text, cannot voice-point to the words accurately. • When listening to stories, some will respond to parts of them with movements and chants; others will follow the plot with displays of expectation, suspense, and relief. • Can make up a story while paging through a familiar picture book. • May draw pictures and tell you about the scene he or she is describing. • May write captions to pictures or other compositions, using invented symbols and random letters.	• Read-alouds—teachers read daily to children, thinking aloud and emphasizing plot structure (who the characters are, what the problem is, what they do to solve the problem, what happens, how things are at the end). The same story is reread several times and children are later invited to pretend-read it themselves. • Sing-alongs and rhyming games. • Morning message: The teacher asks children to take turns helping introduce and write up the day, date, month, day and weather, as well as the day's activities. Rebus symbols are used for weather and names of activities. • Assignment charts: Children's names printed on tagboard are divided among slots in a pocket chart according to their tasks and center assignments for the day. • Shared reading—the teacher carefully points at large print while pronouncing words. The teacher carefully names aspects of reading—"letters," "words," "direction," "top of the page," "bottom of the page," and calls attention to individual letters and words that are repeated. • Teaching the alphabet. • Incorporating print in play activities—post office, grocery store, etc. • Writing Workshop: Children have opportunities to communicate with pencils and colored pencils; encouragement to write captions; opportunities to share what they have drawn and written.
Becoming Familiar with Print (Late Kindergarten) Logographic Reading	• Can begin to tap out phonemes. • Can provide rhyming words. • Still can't confidently voice-point at	• Read-alouds—teachers continue to read two or three times daily to children, thinking aloud and inviting the children's comments and predictions. At least

- **Developmental Milestones features** provide at-a-glance summaries of typical behaviors in children's development of emergent literacy, phonological awareness, and word knowledge.

Integrating Across the Curriculum
Endangered Dolphins and Other Cetaceans: A Common Core Curriculum Standards Map for Grade 5

Overview
This four-week Common Core Curriculum Standards map for the fifth grade explores novels, stories, poetry, informational text, media, magazine articles, music, and videos about the life of dolphins and related cetaceans. They relate realistic fiction to informational texts about dolphins and other cetaceans, as well as to gathering information from poems, labels on cans in supermarkets, songs, art, and other Internet sources. Based on attitudes and emotional points of view gained from the narrative sources and information gained from expository texts, they draw conclusions and form opinions about the value of dolphins and cetaceans in our lives. They develop the means to share those conclusions and express those opinions through writing and other media. This exemplar map is based on models from Common Core (2012).

Focus Standards
The focus standards for this unit are from the Common Core State Standards, Grade 5, California State Department of Education, August, 2010. <www.scoe.net/castandards/agenda/2010/ela_ccs_recommendations.pdf>

Reading—Literature
• Determine a theme of a story, drama, or poem from details in the text, including how characters in a story or drama respond to challenges or how the speaker in a poem reflects upon a topic; summarize the text.
• Describe how a narrator's or speaker's point of view influences how events are described.

Reading—Informational Text
• Describe the connection between a series of historical events, scientific ideas or concepts, or steps in technical procedures in a text.
• Compare and contrast the most important points presented by two texts on the same topic.

Reading—Foundational Skills
• Read with sufficient accuracy and fluency to support comprehension.

Writing
• Write opinion pieces on topics

• Conduct short research projects that use several sources to build knowledge through investigation of different aspects of a topic.

Speaking and Listening
• Summarize the points a speaker or media source makes and explain how each claim is supported, by reasons and evidence, and identify and analyze any logical fallacies.

Language
• Demonstrate command of the conventions of standard English capitalization, punctuation, and spelling when writing.
• Demonstrate understanding of figurative language, word relationships, and nuances in word meanings.

Selected Student Objectives
• Compare and contrast the main characters of *Island of the Blue Dolphins* and *Moby Dick*; describe how both characters were developed by the authors as they met major challenges.
• Research the controversy of dolphin protection from the point of view of fishermen and of environmentalists on the Internet; write a rationale for either point of view and defend it.
• Describe how dolphins, porpoises, and whales are more like dogs and cats than sharks and salmon; illustrate and label one cetacean, any fish, and any four-legged mammal.
• Research the importance of whale oil 150 years ago, and make an oral presentation about it.

Selected Sample Lesson Activities That Focus on

- **Integrating Across the Curriculum features** provide concrete examples of curriculum integration at each of the three levels: K–2, 3–5, and 6–8. These features show how integrated curriculum addresses state learning standards while providing needed context for literacy instruction, which frees up valuable class time for teaching other content subjects.

Assessment... Reading Inve...

Language and Diversity

What is the effect of language and dialectical differences on the interpretation of oral reading errors in the informal reading inventory?

- Central to this text are six **overriding themes** interwoven throughout the book that are critical in reading instruction today: Language and Diversity, Family Literacy, Writing and Reading Connections, Struggling Reader, Phonics and Phonological Awareness, and New Literacies. Special marginal icons call your attention to points in the text that specifically address these themes. Critical thinking questions attached to each icon help you extend and enhance your understanding of text concepts.

- **Graphic Organizer and Anticipation Guide** at the start of each chapter provide readers with an overall perspective of the chapter and the opportunity to assess their level of understanding prior to reading the chapter.

- Every chapter begins with a narrative **Classroom Story** that shares a reading teacher's experience in an active classroom. Each vignette models key concepts from the chapters and demonstrates the challenges of today's classrooms and considerations for addressing children's needs.

- **The World of Reading** boxes investigate a wide array of subjects as they pertain to the field of reading.

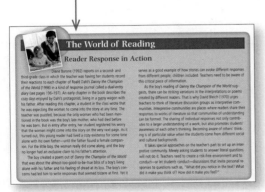

- **Being a Professional Reading Teacher** activities help future teachers explore their own thoughts about teaching.

- **Teach It!** boxes provide readers with ready-made teaching tips for skill development, as well as for introducing new approaches to the teaching of literacy. Teach It! margin icons identify correlating activities from the Teach It! appendix that can be used to teach the concepts discussed.

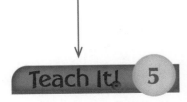

Language Experience with Authentic Children's Literature

- **Differentiated Instruction** features highlight ways to differentiate instruction so that all students are engaged positively and productively, acknowledging the increasing diversity of today's students. Several of these features also include a Sheltered Instruction Observation Protocol—SIOP component, high-lighting ways to differentiate reading instruction for English language learners.

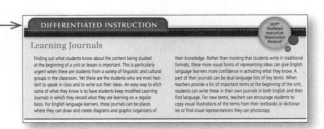

- **Assessment** features highlight practical aspects of assessment approaches related to chapter topics.

- **For Review** sections conclude each chapter and offer a convenient study tool in the form of a brief recap of the most important topics covered.
- **For Your Journal** sections offer ideas for using material learned in each chapter to inform development of a personal teaching journal.
- **Taking It to the World** exercises challenge readers to apply chapter material to authentic classroom situations.
- **New Literacies Connections** offer a selection of relevant Web sites and advice for using them to benefit professional development.

- Did you know this book is also available as an enhanced Pearson eText? The affordable, interactive version of this text includes 3–5 videos per chapter that exemplify, model, or expand upon chapter concepts. Look for the play button in the margins to see where video is available in the affordable enhanced eText version of this text.

To learn more about the enhanced Pearson eText, go to www.pearsonhighered.com/etextbooks

MyEducationLab™

- MyEducationLab is an online homework, tutorial, and assessment product designed to improve results by helping students quickly master concepts, and by providing educators with a robust set of tools for easily gauging and addressing the performance of individuals and classrooms.

- MyEducationLab engages students with high-quality multimedia learning experiences that help them build critical teaching skills and prepare them for real-world practice. In practice exercises, students receive immediate feedback so they see mistakes right away, learn precisely which concepts are holding them back, and master concepts through targeted practice.

- For educators, MyEducationLab provides highly visual data and performance analysis to help them quickly identify gaps in student learning and make a clear connection between coursework, concept mastery, and national teaching standards. And because MyEducationLab comes from Pearson, it's developed by an experienced partner committed to providing content, resources, and expertise for the best digital learning experiences.

In *Preparing Teachers for a Changing World*, Linda Darling-Hammond and her colleagues point out that grounding teacher education in real classrooms—among real teachers and students and among actual examples of students' and teachers' work—is an important, and perhaps even an essential, part of training teachers for the complexities of teaching in today's classrooms.

In the MyEducationLab for this course educators will find the following features and resources.

ADVANCED DATA AND PERFORMANCE REPORTING ALIGNED TO NATIONAL STANDARDS Advanced data and performance reporting helps educators quickly identify gaps in student learning and gauge and address individual and classroom performance. Educators easily see the connection between coursework, concept mastery, and national teaching standards with highly visual views of performance reports. Data and assessments align directly to national teaching standards, including the Standards for Reading Professionals (IRA), and support reporting for state and accreditation requirements

STUDY PLAN SPECIFIC TO YOUR TEXT MyEducationLab gives students the opportunity to test themselves on key concepts and skills, track their own progress through the course, and access personalized Study Plan activities.

The customized Study Plan is generated based on students' pretest results. Incorrect questions from the pretest indicate specific textbook learning outcomes the student is struggling with. The customized Study Plan suggests specific enriching activities for particular learning outcomes, helping students focus. Personalized Study Plan activities may include eBook reading assignments, and review, practice, and enrichment activities.

After students complete the enrichment activities, they take a posttest to see the concepts they've mastered or areas where they still may need extra help.

MyEducationLab then reports the Study Plan results to the instructor. Based on these reports, the instructor can adapt course material to suit the needs of individual students or the entire class.

ASSIGNMENTS AND ACTIVITIES Designed to enhance students' understanding of concepts covered in class, these assignable exercises show concepts in action (through videos, cases, and/or student and teacher artifacts). They help students deepen content knowledge and synthesize and apply concepts and strategies they have read about in the book. (Correct answers for these assignments are available to the instructor only.)

BUILDING TEACHING SKILLS AND DISPOSITIONS   These unique learning units help students practice and strengthen skills that are essential to effective teaching. After examining the steps involved in a core teaching process, students are given an opportunity to practice applying this skill via videos, student and teacher artifacts, and/or case studies of authentic classrooms. Providing multiple opportunities to practice a single teaching concept, each activity encourages a deeper understanding and application of concepts, as well as the use of critical thinking skills. After practice, students take a quiz that is reported to the instructor gradebook.

CHILDREN'S AND YOUNG ADULT LITERATURE DATABASE   The Children's and Young Adult Literature Database offers information on thousands of quality literature titles, and the associated activities provide experience in choosing appropriate literature and integrating the best titles into language arts instruction.

LITERACY PORTRAITS   Year-long case studies of second graders—complete with student artifacts matching each video clip, teacher commentary, and student and teacher interviews—track the month-by-month literacy growth of five second graders. Students will meet English learner Rakie, struggling readers Rhiannon and Curt-Lynn, bilingual learner Michael, and grade-level reader Jimmy, and travel with them through a year of assessments, word study instruction, reading groups, writing activities, buddy reading, and more.

A+RISE ACTIVITIES   A+RISE activities provide practice in targeting instruction. A+RISE®, developed by three-time Teacher of the Year and administrator, Evelyn Arroyo, provides quick, research-based strategies that get to the "how" of targeting instruction and making content accessible for all students, including English language learners.

A+RISE® Standards2Strategy™ is an innovative and interactive online resource that offers new teachers in grades K–12 just in time research-based instructional strategies that:

- Meet the linguistic needs of ELLs as they learn content
- Differentiate instruction for all grades and abilities
- Offer reading and writing techniques, cooperative learning, use of linguistic and nonlinguistic representations, scaffolding, teacher modeling, higher order thinking, and alternative classroom ELL assessment
- Provide support to help teachers be effective through the integration of listening, speaking, reading, and writing along with the content curriculum
- Improve student achievement
- Are aligned to Common Core Elementary Language Arts standards (for the literacy strategies) and to English language proficiency standards in WIDA, Texas, California, and Florida.

GRAMMAR TUTORIAL   The Grammar Tutorial provides content extracted in part from *The Praxis Series*™ *Online Tutorial for the Pre-Professional Skills Test: Writing*. Online quizzes built around specific elements of grammar help students strengthen their understanding and proper usage of the English language in writing. Definitions and examples of grammatical concepts are followed by practice exercises to provide the background information and usage examples needed to refresh understandings of grammar, and then apply that knowledge to make it more permanent.

COURSE RESOURCES   The Course Resources section of MyEducationLab is designed to help students put together an effective lesson plan, prepare for and begin a career, navigate the first year of teaching, and understand key educational standards, policies, and laws.

It includes the following:

- The **Lesson Plan Builder** is an effective and easy-to-use tool that students can use to create, update, and share quality lesson plans. The software also makes it easy to integrate state content standards into any lesson plan.
- The **Certification and Licensure** section is designed to help students pass licensure exams by giving them access to state test requirements, overviews of what tests cover, and sample test items.

The Certification and Licensure section includes the following:

- **State Certification Test Requirements:** Here, students can click on a state and be taken to a list of state certification tests.
- Students can click on the Licensure Exams they need to take to find:
  - Basic information about each test
  - Descriptions of what is covered on each test
  - Sample test questions with explanations of correct answers
- **National Evaluation Series™** by Pearson: Here, students can see the tests in the NES, learn what is covered on each exam, and access sample test items with descriptions and rationales of correct answers. Students can also purchase interactive online tutorials developed by Pearson Evaluation Systems and the Pearson Teacher Education and Development group.
- **ETS Online Praxis Tutorials:** Here students can purchase interactive online tutorials developed by ETS and by the Pearson Teacher Education and Development group. Tutorials are available for the Praxis I exams and for select Praxis II exams.
- The **Licensure and Standards** section provides access to current state and national standards.

The **Preparing a Portfolio** section provides guidelines for creating a high-quality teaching portfolio.

- **Beginning Your Career** offers tips, advice, and other valuable information on:
  - *Resume Writing and Interviewing:* Includes expert advice on how to write impressive resumes and prepare for job interviews.
  - *Your First Year of Teaching:* Provides practical tips to set up a first classroom, manage student behavior, and more easily organize for instruction and assessment.
  - *Law and Public Policies:* Details specific directives and requirements needed to understand under the No Child Left Behind Act and the Individuals with Disabilities Education Improvement Act of 2004.
- The **Multimedia Index** aggregates resources in MyEducationLab by asset type (for example, video or artifact) for easy location and retrieval.

Visit www.myeducationlab.com for a demonstration of this exciting new online teaching resource.

Support Materials for Instructors

The following resources are available for instructors to download on www.pearson highered.com/educators. Instructors enter the author or title of this book, select this particular edition of the book, and then click on the "Resources" tab to log in and download textbook supplements.

- **Instructor's Resource Manual and Test Bank (0-13-336200-0)**
  The Instructor's Resource Manual and Test Bank includes suggestions for learning activities, additional Experiencing Firsthand exercises, supplementary lectures, case study analyses, discussion topics, group activities, and a robust collection of test items. Some items (lower-level questions) simply ask students to identify or explain concepts and principles they have learned. But many others (higher-level questions) ask students to apply those same concepts and principles to specific classroom situations—that is, to actual student behaviors and teaching strategies.

- **PowerPoint Slides (0-13-336194-2)**
  The PowerPoint slides include key concept summarizations, diagrams, and other graphic aids to enhance learning. They are designed to help students understand, organize, and remember core concepts and theories.

- **MyEducationLab Correlation Guide (0-13-337463-7)**
  This guide connects chapter sections with appropriate assignable exercises on MyEducationLab.

- **TestGen (0-13-336193-4)**
  TestGen is a powerful test generator that instructors install on a computer and use in conjunction with the TestGen testbank file for the text. Assessments, including equations, graphs, and scientific notation, may be created for both print or testing online.

  TestGen is available exclusively from Pearson Education publishers. Instructors install TestGen on a personal computer (Windows or Macintosh) and create tests for classroom testing and for other specialized delivery options, such as over a local area network or on the Web. A test bank, which is also called a Test Item File (TIF), typically contains a large set of test items, organized by chapter and ready for use in creating a test, based on the associated textbook material.

  The tests can be downloaded in the following formats:

  > TestGen file - PC
  > TestGen file - MAC
  > TestGen - Blackboard 9
  > TestGen - Blackboard CE/Vista (WebCT)
  > Angel
  > D2L
  > Moodle
  > Sakai Test Bank

Acknowledgments

We would like to thank the reviewers who took time out from busy schedules to share with us their support and expertise and provided us with the valuable feedback that helped to shape this project: Rebecca S. Anderson, University of Memphis; Diane Barone, University of Nevada-Reno; Marian S. Beckman, Edinboro University of Pennsylvania; Vidya Bhat, Anne Hutchinson Elementary School; Charlotte Black, California State University, San Bernardino; Tarsha Bluiett, University of Montevallo; Melise Bunker, Palm Beach Atlantic College; Margaret Bell Davis, Eastern Kentucky University; Deborah Doty, Northern Kentucky University; Mary Ann Dzama, George Mason University; Callie L. Fortenberry, Texas A&M, Texarkana; Nancy L. Kelly, Sierra Nevada College; David Landis, University of Northern Iowa; Linda H. Lord, SUNY Oswego; Darlene Michener, California State University, Los Angeles; Michael Moore, Georgia Southern University; Kathleen R. Murphy, Clarion University of Pennsylvania; John Savage, Boston College; Corlis Snow, Delta State University; Kim Truesdell, State University College at Buffalo; Marion P. Turkish, William Paterson University; Debra Whitaker-Volturo, Ocean City School District; Clairin DeMartini Wilson, Nevada State College; Valerie Wright, Saint Leo; James Zarrillo, California State University, Hayward.

Charles Temple wants to thank his colleagues and students at HWS for good cheer at all hours, the International Reading Association, the Open Society Institute, and CODE-Canada for all their support over the years, and his extended family.

Donna Ogle wants to thank her husband, niece, and colleagues for their contributions to this book. Bud has provided incredible support for this project and is a model "critical reader." Kjersten Kuhlman, who directs a 21st Century Project in Massachusetts, helps Donna stay current and suggested the ThinkQuest feature for this book. The teachers with whom Donna works in the Chicago area and in international contexts energized her to share their ideas. Special thanks to colleagues in CLIP and the faculty at NLU.

Alan Crawford thanks his colleagues and students in the public schools of East Los Angeles and Cal State Los Angeles for inspiration over the years; the teachers with whom he's worked—in California, Latin America, Central Asia, Central Europe, and Africa; good friends at UNESCO, the International Reading Association, and the Open Society Institute; and of course, Linda.

Penny Freppon wishes to thank her co-authors and the teachers with whom she has worked and from whom she has learned so much. She thanks Dr. Jill Dillard and Linda Headings, and Dr. Lisa Campbell for their friendship and professional guidance. She also thanks the Open Society Institute for supporting her international work. In addition, she thanks her family and extended family, and in particular, Don Gustafson, her late husband and intellectual partner, who was all she ever wanted long before she ever knew him.

Last but not least, a special thank you to everyone at Pearson for working so hard to create this beautiful book out of our humble parts and for remaining so steadfastly cheerful and encouraging throughout: Vice President, Editor-in-Chief, Aurora Martínez; Senior Production Editor, Janet Domingo, for her project coordination; Sara Holliday for her assistance with the standards correlations, and to Kathy Smith for her good eye and detailed oversight.

Approaches to Teaching Reading

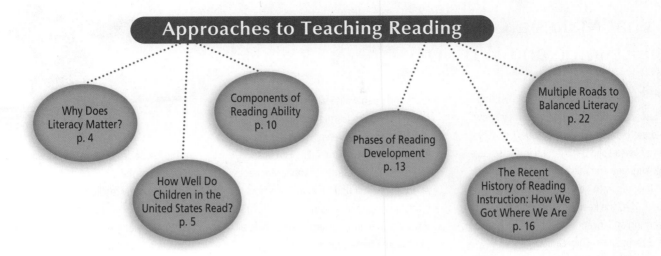

Approaches to Teaching Reading

- Why Does Literacy Matter? p. 4
- How Well Do Children in the United States Read? p. 5
- Components of Reading Ability p. 10
- Phases of Reading Development p. 13
- The Recent History of Reading Instruction: How We Got Where We Are p. 16
- Multiple Roads to Balanced Literacy p. 22

Anticipation Guide

The following statements will help you begin thinking about the topics covered in this chapter. Answer *true* or *false* in response to each statement. As you read and learn more about the topics mentioned in these statements, double-check your answers. See what interests you and prompts your curiosity toward more understanding.

____ **1.** Literacy makes you smarter because the vocabulary, the information, and the habit of learning from text make you better able to learn new things.

____ **2.** Among adults, there is little correlation between people's reading ability and their income level.

____ **3.** American children read fairly well. Nine-year-olds scored in the top third in the world on one recent international comparison of basic reading skill.

____ **4.** Most reading disabilities are caused by malfunctions of the brain, and children with reading problems need a wholly different kind of teaching from that provided to normally developing readers.

____ **5.** Research shows that more than 86 percent of the children who get a poor start in learning to read do not catch up with their peers.

____ **6.** Differences in the amount of reading children do are not significant. What matters in teaching reading is the skill.

____ **7.** Giving parents ideas for helping their children at home with literacy experiences makes a considerable difference in the children's success in school.

____ **8.** Reading ability develops through stages in this order: beginning reading, emergent literacy, reading to learn and for pleasure, building fluency, and mature reading.

____ **9.** The debate between advocates of phonics instruction and advocates of whole-word instruction began in the 1980s in the United States, during the Reagan Administration.

____**10.** Because the U.S. Constitution leaves the governance of education up to the states, standards for education, including reading, vary widely from state to state.

A Classroom Story

What Makes a Good Teacher of Reading and Writing?

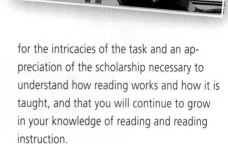

Good teachers of reading and writing are multitalented people. They know a great many teaching methods, but they also have a solid background in the science of language and literacy, and they manage to keep up with new developments in their field. They are keen observers of children's learning and inventive designers of lessons and techniques. They can connect with children, and children of all backgrounds like them, trust them, and are inspired by them. They make unusual efforts to connect with their students' families and help the families feel comfortable with the school environment and process. Good teachers of reading and writing love to read and write, and they gladly demonstrate their enthusiasm and share their knowledge with their students.

Good teachers of reading and writing are everywhere—in classrooms from Los Angeles to New York City, from the Rio Grande Valley to the fields of Saskatchewan, and all around the world. Some work in carpeted classrooms equipped with gleaming rows of computers, but just as many make cheerful places out of storage rooms, hallways, or even tropical shelters with rattling tin roofs and open walls—always thoughtfully orchestrating the learning of an individual child or of many different children. You will find them teaching in English, Spanish, French, Tagalog, Arabic, or many languages at once. You will find them in the offices of school principals and district-wide administrators, pondering the best ways to help all the children make progress in reading; you will also find them huddled in deliberations with a parent and a school psychologist, trying to unlock the puzzle of a child's reading difficulty. You will find them in a school or community library, sharing just the right book with a child who is on the threshold of becoming a reader. You will find them in a classroom in any one of scores of developing countries, creating a lesson without books or paper for children whose parents never knew the craft of literacy, or in a committee room at the United Nations, strategizing to help spread literacy to all of the children in the world.

The authors of this book hope that you will share with those good teachers a passion for bringing the gift of literacy to young people, that you will have a fascination for the intricacies of the task and an appreciation of the scholarship necessary to understand how reading works and how it is taught, and that you will continue to grow in your knowledge of reading and reading instruction.

Teaching every child to read and write is the most important mission of the elementary and middle school teacher. Science, mathematics, and social studies; art, physical education, and vocational preparedness; anti-drug abuse and conflict resolution education; civic education and education for self-awareness—all contribute to the making of the well-rounded child. But teaching children to read and write and to use the thinking processes that accompany literacy prepare them to learn their other school subjects and to educate themselves for the rest of their lives. The skills of literacy are centrally important for other reasons, too: Being able to read and write makes children smarter and ultimately makes their lives better.

Why Does Literacy Matter?

Teaching children to read not only gives them access to knowledge from print, but also makes them better able to use that knowledge. Children who read store up background knowledge about the things they read about, whether it be nature, science, history, current events, or geography (Stanovich, 1992). This knowledge helps them make sense of the new things they read (Anderson & Pearson, 1984). Children who read gain bigger vocabularies, too (Smith, 1997), and having bigger vocabularies enables them to notice things (Brown, 1955) and to make finer distinctions in their perceptions of the world (Beck, McKeown, & Kucan, 2002).

Literacy helps children to think in more sophisticated ways. Studies have shown that reading proficiency makes profound differences in people's reasoning, their awareness of language, their understanding of themselves, and even their ability to formulate questions and learn about things they didn't know (Luria, 1976). Children who read and talk about books with others show greater self-awareness and critical thinking (Almasi, 1995), tend to engage ideas more deeply (Eeds & Wells, 1989; Goatley, Brock, & Raphael, 1995), and are more likely to perceive themes in stories; that is, they are more likely to get the message (Lehr, 1991).

Among adults, literacy is associated with better health, greater job opportunities, and higher incomes (policyalmanac.org, U.S. Department of Health and Human Services, 2006). Surveys show that people who can read and write well tend to have a wider range of options in life. This fact is important to teachers of the lower grades, because students' early experiences as readers often have a determining effect on their eventual success or failure to learn to read and write.

Those of you who are fortunate enough to be teachers are in a privileged position to make sure your children have better choices available to them. You can teach them to read and write. But be aware that people with limited literacy do not usually see themselves as having a literacy problem (National Center for Education Statistics, 1993). The task of a teacher of reading, then, will not only be to teach, but also to motivate. Even though reading ability is a ticket to a better future for all students, they might not know that, and their families might not know it either. Teachers have to make special efforts to encourage every child to *want* to be a reader.

Because literacy is associated with better health and better socioeconomic standing, English as a Second Language (ESL) programs for adults are important services in all communities.

How Well Do Children in the United States Read?

For years, the media have clamored about the poor state of reading in American schools. But the critics have mostly gotten it wrong. They have missed both the considerable achievements as well as the most serious challenges in our nation's efforts to teach all children to read (Klenk & Kibby, 2000). In a nutshell, two things are true about the way children read in the United States:

- In comparison to children in other countries, American students in elementary school do fairly well at basic reading. According to the latest international comparison of reading achievement, the PIRLS (Progress in International Reading Literacy) 2006, American fourth graders scored 11th in the world—in the top third of the participating countries. American 15-year-olds scored 17th in the world—in the top fourth of countries that participated in the PISA (Programme for International Student Assessment) study in 2009.

- Success in reading among American students is spread unevenly, however. Our most successful students do well in basic literacy tasks, but there are many students who do not. For example, the National Assessment of Educational Progress (NAEP) defines a fourth grade "basic reading level" this way:

    Fourth-grade students performing at the Basic *level should be able to locate relevant information, make simple inferences, and use their understanding of the text to identify details that support a given interpretation or conclusion. Students should be able to interpret the meaning of a word as it is used in the text.* (National Center for Education Statistics, 2009).

In 2009, two thirds of all U.S. fourth graders could read at this basic level, but it is troubling that a third of all fourth graders could not. Slightly less than half of black and Hispanic fourth graders in the United States could read on a basic level.

There are also sizable differences in reading levels among the states. The state with the lowest scores had 49 percent of fourth graders reading below the basic level in

2009 and only 18 percent at the proficient level, compared to 20 percent below basic and 47 percent proficient in the state with the highest reading scores at fourth grade.

English language learners (ELLs) are defined by the NAEP as "[S]tudents who are in the process of acquiring English language skills and knowledge." In 2009, 71 percent of the English language learners in the United States scored below the basic reading level, and only 6 percent scored at the proficient level (see Figure 1.1).

At the eighth grade level, NAEP defines basic reading this way:

> Eighth-grade students performing at the Basic level should be able to locate information; identify statements of main idea, theme, or author's purpose; and make simple inferences from texts. They should be able to interpret the meaning of a word as it is used in the text. Students performing at this level should also be able to state judgments and give some support about content and presentation of content. (National Center for Education Statistics, 2009).

In 2009, three fourths of all U.S. eighth graders were at or above the basic level, and more than half of black students and three out of five Hispanic students were, too. But it's troubling again that so many eighth graders could not read on a basic level—especially given what we have already said about the considerable disadvantages of limited literacy.

Figure 1.1
Fourth Graders' Reading Achievement, as Measured by PIRLS (2011)

Country	Average Scale Score	Reading Achievement Distribution
³Hong Kong SAR	571 (2.3) ▲	
Russian Federation	568 (2.7) ▲	
Finland	568 (1.9) ▲	
²Singapore	567 (3.3) ▲	
†Northern Ireland	558 (2.4) ▲	
²United States	556 (1.5) ▲	
²Denmark	554 (1.7) ▲	
²Croatia	553 (1.9) ▲	
Chinese Taipei	553 (1.9) ▲	
Ireland	552 (2.3) ▲	
†England	552 (2.6) ▲	
²Canada	548 (1.6) ▲	
†Netherlands	546 (1.9) ▲	
Czech Republic	545 (2.2) ▲	
Sweden	542 (2.1) ▲	
Italy	541 (2.2) ▲	
Germany	541 (2.2) ▲	
³Israel	541 (2.7) ▲	
Portugal	541 (2.6) ▲	
Hungary	539 (2.9) ▲	
Slovak Republic	535 (2.8) ▲	
Bulgaria	532 (4.1) ▲	
New Zealand	531 (1.9) ▲	
Slovenia	530 (2.0) ▲	
Austria	529 (2.0) ▲	
¹²Lithuania	528 (2.0) ▲	
Australia	527 (2.2) ▲	
Poland	526 (2.1) ▲	
France	520 (2.6) ▲	
Spain	513 (2.3) ▲	
†Norway	507 (1.9) ▲	
²†Belgium (French)	506 (2.9) ▲	
Romania	502 (4.3) ▲	
PIRLS Scale Centerpoint	500	
¹Georgia	488 (3.1) ▼	
Malta	477 (1.4) ▼	
Trinidad and Tobago	471 (3.8) ▼	
²Azerbaijan	462 (3.3) ▼	
Iran, Islamic Rep. of	457 (2.8) ▼	
Colombia	448 (4.1) ▼	
United Arab Emirates	439 (2.2) ▼	
Saudi Arabia	430 (4.4) ▼	
Indonesia	428 (4.2) ▼	
²Qatar	425 (3.5) ▼	
ΨOman	491 (2.8) ▼	
✳Morocco	310 (3.9) ▼	

SOURCE: IEA's Progress International Reading Literacy Study – PIRLS 2011

▲ Country average significantly higher than the centerpoint of the PIRLS scale

▼ Country average significantly lower than the centerpoint of the PIRLS scale

Percentiles of Performance
5th 25th 75th 95th

95% Confidence Interval for Average (±2SE)

✳ Average achievement not reliably measured because the percentage of students with achievement too low for estimation exceeds 25%.
Ψ Reservations about reliability of average achievement because the percentage of students with achievement too low for estimation does not exceed 25% but exceeds 15%.
See Appendix C.2 for target population coverage notes 1, 2, and 3. See Appendix C5 for sampling guidelines and sampling participation notes † and ‡.
( ) Standard errors appear in parentheses. Because of rounding some results may appear inconsistent.

Source: Mullis, I. V. S., Martin, M. O., Kennedy, A. M., & Foy, P. (2007), PIRLS 2006 international report (p.37). Chestnut Hill, MA: TIMSS & PIRLS International Study Center, Boston College. Used by permission. © International Association for the Evaluation of Educational Achievement (IEA).

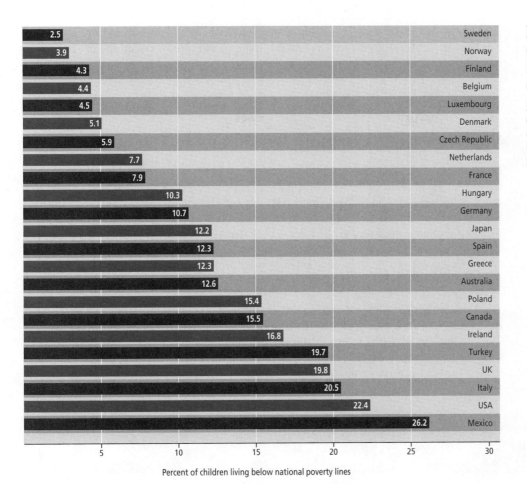

Figure 1.2
Children Living in
Poverty: An International
Comparison

Source: UNICEF Innocenti Research Centre.
(2000), *A League Table of Child Poverty in Rich
Nations, Innocenti Report Card No. I,* UNICEF
Innocenti Research Centre, Florence. Used by
permission.

Percent of children living below national poverty lines

- Differences in reading achievement are often related to socioeconomic status.
  That is not good news for American children, since about one in five of them
  lives in poverty. How does that compare with other countries? In the 23 wealthiest
  countries, the lowest incidence of child poverty was in Sweden, at 2.6 percent.
  The highest was in Mexico, at 26.2 percent. Slightly better than Mexico's rate of
  child poverty was that of the United States, at 22.4 percent (see Figure 1.2).

Poverty complicates children's learning in a host of ways that we will consider in Chapter 2.
It is not surprising that poor children—those from families who are eligible for free or
reduced cost lunches—tend to score well below other children in reading (see Table 1.1).

Table 1.1 Fourth Grade Reading Scores from the National Assessment
of Educational Progress, 2009

	PERCENT BELOW BASIC	PERCENT AT OR ABOVE BASIC	PERCENT PROFICIENT
All Fourth Graders	33	67	33
Black Fourth Graders	52	48	16
Hispanic Fourth Graders	51	49	17
English Language Learners	71	29	6
Children on National School Lunch Program	49	51	17
State with Highest Scores	20	80	47
State with Lowest Scores	49	51	18

Low family income does not necessarily mean students should perform poorly in reading. *Resilient students* are those who overcome difficult circumstances and learn to read in school. Poor children living in Asia are likely to be resilient—50 to 70 percent of them (PISA, 2009). But they are less so in the United States, where fewer than a third of children from poor family backgrounds tend to be resilient.

Struggling Reader

Why do some children have a really hard time learning to read?

Who Are the Struggling Readers?

If success in reading in the United States is spread unevenly, how many of our children have "reading disabilities"? A reading disability is said to be present when a child with normal intelligence who has had adequate instruction fails to learn to read. By this definition, experts have estimated that 10 to 20 percent of all school children have specific reading disabilities (Shaywitz, Escobar, Shaywitz, Fletcher, & Makuch, 1992). Some researchers suggest that the actual percentage of children with reading disabilities is much lower and that deficiencies can be overcome or prevented through appropriate reading-related experiences at home and proper instruction in kindergarten and first grade. (See the World of Reading box.)

Why are early reading experiences so important? The importance of a good beginning in reading—and the damage that can be done by a poor beginning—was underscored by Connie Juel (1988). Juel surveyed a group of first graders in a Texas public school, found the 20 percent who read least well, and carefully tracked the reading progress of 54 of these students for three years. At the end of the study, 86 percent of those children were

The World of Reading

How Many Children Have Specific Reading Disabilities?

A specific reading disability is a severe inability to read as well as one's intelligence and background would predict, in spite of having had normally effective teaching. There is no doubt that reading disabilities exist. Snowling (2000) followed one child with a severe reading disability from preschool to adulthood, and documented his difficulty reading texts and his primitive spelling strategies that remained with him as an adult.

But are most disabled readers constitutionally different from normally competent readers—that is, is there some abnormality in the ways their brains work that makes them disabled? Many people believe so. The United States has a huge industry devoted to the identification and treatment of learning disabilities, the largest number of which are specific reading disabilities. These disabilities have traditionally been treated as a categorically different set of problems from normal reading development. However, a growing body of evidence suggests that nearly all instances of specific reading disability, including dyslexia, may just be extreme cases of difficulty in normal reading development (Snow et al., 1998). Children with reading problems look much like children who can read; they just don't read as well (Stanovich & Siegel, 1994; Vellutino et al., 1996).

Going back to the definition of dyslexia as not learning to read in spite of otherwise effective reading instruction, we can ask if the problem really is the instruction children receive. Can teachers do better with poor readers than we are doing? When Frank Vellutino and his associates (1996) identified a large number of struggling first graders and tutored them intensively for a year using conventional best practices, only 3 percent of them continued to have difficulty learning to read, and only 1.5 percent had severe difficulties. Vellutino and associates concluded that the difficulties in learning to read may well be caused by deficits in certain cognitive abilities underlying the ability to learn to read, especially phonological abilities such as phoneme analysis, letter-to-sound decoding, name encoding and retrieval, and verbal memory. However, they found that "the number of children impaired by basic cognitive deficits represents a relatively small percentage of beginning readers compared with the substantially larger percentage of those children whose reading difficulties are caused by experiential and instructional deficits" (Vellutino & Scanlon, 2001, p. 317).

Vellutino and his colleagues (1996) concluded that most of the children who had been identified as possibly having specific reading disability did not suffer from abnormal brain function. Rather, they suffered from confusions, delays, poor starts, and the need for finely tuned and responsive instruction that was carefully tailored to their strengths and needs.

still in the bottom half of the class. Although reading problems had not been severe in first grade, they were serious by fourth grade. There was little reason to hope that these children would close the gap in later years. Why?

In a famous essay, Keith Stanovich (1986) showed that in learning to read, "The rich get richer and the poor get poorer." He meant that relatively small reading problems in the early years can discourage students from practicing their reading, so those small problems are compounded and grow into severe reading disabilities after three or four years. But children who start off relatively strong in reading get better and better.

Children learn to read by reading. But studies of reading habits show huge differences in the amount of reading children do. One study showed that the most prolific three or four readers in a fifth grade classroom read 100 times as much as the least prolific did (Anderson, Wilson, & Fielding, 1988).

Family and Community Involvement

Families make a difference in children's preparation to learn to read and write. On the average, children from poor families have more difficulty learning to be literate than children from middle-class homes do (Vernon-Feagans, Hammer, Miccio, & Manlove, 2001). But the exact reasons for this can be difficult to tease out. If a family is poor—and one fourth of America's children live in families that are poor—then poverty itself presents a complex set of stress factors (Ehrenreich, 2001). If you are poor, it is hard to raise a healthy and competent child. It is hard to buy and prepare nutritious food. It is hard to afford good-quality childcare. It is hard to find the time and energy between jobs to spend time with your child.

Nonetheless, researchers have identified family literacy practices related to children's success in learning to read and write. Many of these may be influenced by the school or by the school working in concert with community partners. Here is a set of factors that the National Research Council (Snow, Burns, & Griffin, 1998, p. 123) has identified:

Family Literacy

How would you persuade a skeptic that teachers should help families help their children learn to read?

1. *Value placed on literacy*: By reading themselves and encouraging their children to read, parents and other caregivers can demonstrate that they value reading.

2. *Press for achievement*: By expressing their expectations for achievement by their children, providing guidance in reading, and responding to the children's reading initiations and interests, families can create a press for achievement.

3. *Availability and instrumental use of reading materials*: Literacy experiences are more likely to occur in homes that contain children's books and other reading and writing materials.

4. *Reading with children*: Parents and other family members can read to preschoolers at bedtime and other times and can listen to schoolchildren's oral reading, providing assistance as needed.

Family literacy projects that encourage families to read to children and talk with them can have success (Vernon-Feagans et al., 2001). But helping families nurture their children's literacy is not a simple matter. Communication patterns within families are hard to change—even if we agreed that educators had any business trying to change them! A famous study showed that poor families offer children less verbal interaction than middle-class families do, and the shortage of interaction has a strong effect on the children's vocabulary size (Hart & Risley, 1995), which in turn shortchanges the store of meanings available to them as they try to learn to read and write.

GIVING ALL FAMILIES ACCESS TO READING MATERIALS   Here is another problem: It is known that children's preschool experiences with books and print also contribute to their success in learning to read once they arrive in school (Snow et al., 1998; Teale

& Sulzby, 1987). But low-income families have far less access to books than middle-class families do. Writing in the *New York Times*, David Bornstein notes:

> When we imagine people without books, we think of villagers in places like Afghanistan. But many families in the United States have no children's books at home. In some of the poorest areas of the country, it's hard to find books for sale. A study of low-income neighborhoods in Philadelphia, for example, found a ratio of one book for sale for every 300 children. Tens of millions of poor Americans can't afford to buy books at all. (Bornstein, 2011, unpaged)

Certainly children's services of public libraries can help, but poorer communities have fewer libraries with fewer books that are open fewer hours (Neuman & Celano, 2012).

Nearly all families in the United States have some contact with literacy materials, but many low-literacy families really do not seriously engage with print enough to provide experiences for children that teach them (Purcell-Gates, 1995). Even when low-income families visit libraries, the visits don't necessarily result in their finding materials to read (Neuman & Celano, 2010). Family literacy work is not always easy, but the title of Purcell-Gates' book about the illiterate mother and the semi-literate son—*The Cycle of Low Literacy*—underscores how important it is for educators to include families in their plans for promoting literacy.

Components of Reading Ability

What exactly are you teaching when you teach a child to read? Reading ability can be broken down into several different sets of concepts and skills. The most widely recognized ones are outlined below.

Concepts About Print

Imagine a child who had never watched someone read. If that child were in your kindergarten or first grade class, you would need to show her what a book is, how to hold it, what is print and what is a picture, the direction of the print across from left to right and down the page, that print contains letters and the identities of those letters, that letters combine into words and that words are groups of letters with a space on either end, that the same words are spoken each time someone reads the same page, and that those words add up to interesting information or a good story. Taken together, all of these facts are called *concepts about print*. Most children enter kindergarten with at least some concepts about print intact. But children vary widely in their exposure to print, so assessing and teaching concepts about print is part of the repertoire of every teacher of preschool, kindergarten, and first grade—and every teacher of special education in the primary grades.

Word Recognition and Phonics

Recognizing the words on the page is the next important reading skill. This skill has two parts. One is recognizing words instantly, as you would recognize the face of a friend. This is called *sight word recognition*, or recognizing words *at sight*. A word that has been seen many times, particularly if it refers to something interesting and its meaning is familiar, becomes a word a reader can recognize instantly. A good reader has many thousands of sight words in memory.

The other aspect of word recognition is puzzling out the identity of words readers can't yet recognize, and this is called *decoding*. When you read words like *glatz, charl, splane*, and *clorption*, you are decoding. A young reader uses decoding to figure out how to read the unfamiliar word *stripe* when he already knows how to read *stop* and *ripe*; or *dot* when he can read hardly any words at all, but knows the sounds represented by the consonants *D* and *T*, and the vowel *O* when it comes before a consonant. The sort of knowledge a reader applies when he decodes is called *phonics*. Phonics is knowledge of the relations between letters or groups of letters and speech sounds.

Phonics knowledge, in turn, has two parts. One is knowing the relationship between letters and clusters of letters called *graphemes* (a grapheme is a small unit of written language) and the speech sounds they represent. The other is awareness of those speech sounds, called *phonemes* (a phoneme is the smallest unit of speech sound). This latter sort of awareness is known as *phonological awareness* (which is the awareness of speech sounds in general, including syllables) and *phonemic awareness* (awareness of phonemes specifically).

Reading Fluency

Reading fluency has four aspects: recognizing words automatically and accurately, reading text efficiently (with appropriate speed), reading with meaningful inflection (the voice goes higher and lower, louder and softer), and grouping words meaningfully (for example, "Austin, [pause] the capital of Texas, [pause] is the home of the University of Texas."). Reading fluency is a combination of word recognition and comprehension. First, reading fluently *contributes to* comprehension because having the ability to read strings of words smoothly and accurately leaves the mind plenty of capacity to think about the meaning of the text (Perfetti, 1992; Pressley, 2000). Second, reading fluency *benefits from* comprehension because a reader can only read with good voice inflection and meaningful pauses if she understands what she is reading. Bear in mind that fluent reading can be silent as well as oral—we just can't hear the inflection and the word grouping when students are reading silently.

Like any other skill that we want to be able to perform automatically—be it tying a shoe, driving an automobile, sailing a boat, or hitting a tennis ball—reading fluency improves with practice. That is why thoughtful teachers provide children plenty of opportunities to read texts that are fairly easy for them, even as they sometimes assign more challenging texts, too.

Vocabulary

Vocabulary is the store of words and their meanings in memory. Having an adequate vocabulary helps reading in several ways. First, when you encounter words such as *epithalamion, ecclesiastical, primogeniture, dodecahedron,* or *unicameral,* you may struggle to decide what the letters are adding up to, only to discover you don't know the word they spell anyway. On the other hand, when you come across words like *muthuh, sista,* and *solja,* you can easily work through the unfamiliar street spellings because you do know the words they spell. Vocabulary helps us read by facilitating word recognition in just that way: You may more successfully puzzle through the spelling of a word you don't immediately recognize in written form if you already have the word in your vocabulary.

Vocabulary aids comprehension, too. Words are tokens of meaning. They are both labels for the facts and concepts we have learned and mental identifiers that we retain and will use to make sense of future experiences—whether in reading or in real life. It's not surprising that students' vocabulary size correlates positively with their reading comprehension scores. Monolingual English-speaking students vary widely in their vocabulary size, and for English language learners, limited vocabulary can be a debilitating problem.

Reading Comprehension

Reading comprehension is the act of understanding the meaning, of making sense of what is read. Comprehending what we read is the main point of reading, of course, but for decades, research has reported that comprehension has received less attention in the classroom than other aspects of reading, especially word recognition and phonics. That situation is changing, though.

When a student does it well, comprehension may look like a single competence, but there are many factors that contribute to it and many skills that comprise it.

One important aspect of comprehension is having *background knowledge*. It may seem odd to say that your capacity to understand something depends on how much you already know about it, but scholars find that is largely true. A model of comprehension known as *schema theory* (Pearson & Anderson, 1985) argues that to understand something, you need to interpret the new information using the knowledge you already had, and then sort the new information into your existing mental frameworks, or what is called your *prior knowledge*. Moreover, the better organized your prior knowledge is, the more likely you are to pay attention to aspects of the new information that will be helpful to know in the long run—and will help you comprehend still more new information (Alexander & Jetton, 2000). Background knowledge implies having labels or *vocabulary* for those things that are already known. We have mentioned vocabulary as a separate aspect of reading skill because it is often treated as such, but it is an important part of comprehension, too.

Visualizing or imaging—being able to picture what is suggested by the words in a text—is another aspect of comprehension. Not all text invites imaging to the same degree, but readers should be ready to come up with images in their mind when the words suggest them.

A competent reader can find main ideas or recognize what is most essential in a passage—the main claim or assertions, and also what details are used to support it—almost as if she were able to construct an outline of the text in her head. Going along with finding the main idea is *summarizing*. A competent reader can repeat back to you the essential points in a passage, with the less important information left out of the summary.

Making inferences is another aspect of comprehension, since a good reader can put together cues from the text with what he knows from experience to construct meaning, even when that meaning is not expressed explicitly.

Following the pattern of a text is also important in comprehension—whether the pattern is the plot of a story, the pattern of a poem, the structure of an argument, or the organization of an explanation. As students move up through the grades, they must be able to read intelligently in different genres that have different patterns (as well as other features such as specialized vocabulary, authorial voice, or ways of presenting truths). Stories usually introduce a setting in which characters encounter a problem, try different solutions, and experience an outcome with a consequence from which readers might derive some moral lesson. Most stories are not literally true, and they may range from highly fanciful (think *Harry Potter*) to highly realistic (think Walter Dean Myers's *Monster*, or Deborah Ellis's *The Breadwinner*). Their language can be full of imagery, dialogue, struggles between right and wrong, appeals to emotion, and evocations of suspense and relief. Texts from science are quite different, with specialized and exact vocabulary, structures of claim and support or explanation, and no protagonists and antagonists.

An aspect of comprehension that has recently gained attention is *reading comparatively across texts*. Adults read different, and often competing, texts that compare automobiles, insurance policies, vacation destinations, and political candidates. They look for insights on the same topic even when different texts don't share the same structure or address topics in the same way. They consider the author's point of view or perspective, possible biases, and credibility when they try to decide how to interpret statements and whether to accept them. Even students in the primary grades can get a multidimensional view of the Civil Rights era by reading a novel such as Rita Williams-Garcia's *One Crazy Summer*, then articles on the Civil Rights movement in *Cobblestone Magazine*, and also poems with civil rights themes in collections such as Arnold Adoff's.

Critical Reading

CCSS

The Common Core Standards (see page 21) are calling the attention of teachers—even primary school teachers—to techniques of literary criticism, ways of exploring the meanings of texts and ways texts have meaning. The approach that has been most popular since the 1980s has been *reader response criticism* (Bleich, 1975; Rosenblatt, 1978), which holds that the meaning of a text is actively created by the reader, with suggestions supplied by the print on the page. Teachers who follow this approach encourage students to talk about what a text means to them, and the teachers are not disturbed if different children respond somewhat differently to the same text. The Common Core Standards have called for renewed attention to an older kind of criticism (older in the sense that it was widely practiced before reader response approaches) variously known as *formalism* or *New Criticism*. Formalism focuses on the text and not the reader, and calls for close reading that carefully scrutinizes the structure and parts of the literary work: reading, rereading, and studying the text much as a biologist would examine a living organism—the parts, relationships among the parts, and their overall function in a meaningful work.

There are good reasons to support both approaches. Reader response teaching tends to be more engaging; in addition, listening to different responses to the same text mirrors what happens in society, where conservatives and liberals, black citizens and white citizens, or women and men often respond differently to the same event. Even though we respond differently, we need to understand and get along with each other, and classroom discussions that are run along the lines of reader response criticism can help develop interpersonal understanding. Formalism and its method of close reading, on the other hand, require readers to look carefully at genres, text structures, word meanings, connotations, allusions, and many other literary devices in order to understand how they work together to form a meaningful whole. Formalism and close reading require disciplined thought and hard work, and they develop students' investigative skills.

Phases of Reading Development

Using the word *development* to describe growth in reading ability implies that the learner doesn't simply wait passively to take in reading instruction from a teacher, but rather undergoes an interaction among growth, experience, and discovery that can be called *developmental learning*. Developmental learning proceeds according to these factors:

- Cognitive growth of learners, which opens up capacities for learning
- The provision of relevant models of skilled performance and challenges in learners' own performances from their surroundings
- Active discoveries initiated by the learners themselves
- Opportunities for learners to practice meaningful use of what they learn, and to work it into their ways of knowing and acting

Calling learning to read *developmental* suggests that all children go through roughly the same set of stages as they learn to read. It suggests that their maturation—simply getting older—plays a part, but that the stimulation, encouragement, modeling, and opportunities to practice reading and writing are important, too. Developmental learning follows fairly predictable pathways, although a learner's development along those pathways is usually more predictable in the early stages than in later ones.

Emergent Literacy

The earliest period or stage of learning to read and write has come to be called *emergent literacy*. In early childhood, before children enter formal instruction, they discover useful insights about literacy; these insights become the basis on which their later learning can be built, even the learning that is orchestrated by their teachers in school. In the emergent stage, learning about literacy involves:

Reading Aloud

- Learning about the nature of reading
- Learning what books are, what kinds of experiences come from them, and how they are put together
- Learning about language itself, that it comes in patterns like stories and poems, and that even though you cannot see it, it is real enough to be captured in books and revisited again and again
- Learning that language comes in units of words and even smaller units, and that the language one speaks while reading bears some kind of relationships to marks on a page.

In the field of literacy, as our awareness of emergent literacy has grown, teachers have promoted practices among families that help children's literacy to emerge. Head Start, the federally funded early childhood education program for disadvantaged children, now includes as part of its programming reading to children and other literacy activities that are embedded in children's daily play and learning activities. In some communities, parents are given a children's book when they leave the hospital with a newborn, to underscore the importance of reading to children and to make the point that it is never too early to begin reading to a child.

With their growing awareness of emergent literacy, teachers have developed ways to observe and assess children's early concepts of literacy. These include approaches such as Marie Clay's *Concepts about Print Test*, Elizabeth Sulzby's *Emergent Storybook Reading Inventory*, Darrell Morris's *Early Reading Screening Inventory*, and studies of invented spelling, as described by Richard Gentry or Temple, Nathan, and Temple (2013). Using these investigative approaches often yields amazing profiles of what children have discovered about literacy. However, they also give cause for concern when it turns out that important concepts about literacy have not yet emerged in one child or another, because we know that these children will need to have the concepts in place as they learn to read.

Learning to read in school without a fully developed foundation of emergent literacy concepts has been likened to trying to climb stairs when the first several steps are missing. Because teachers are aware of the importance of emergent literacy, they are now able to teach all children in a way that gives them another chance to develop emergent concepts about literacy. They can also provide finely tuned tutoring to children who need it so that more children can get off to the best possible start in learning to read and write.

Beginning Reading

In late kindergarten and first grade, most children enter the phase of beginning reading. Most prominent in this stage is their learning to read words, but children are also learning to understand what they read. The task of learning to read words from different combinations of letters on the page is so challenging that teachers often must remind children to "go back and read that line so it sounds like talk" or ask them, "Does that make sense?"

The stage of beginning reading comes after much prior learning. As we already noted, emergent readers must come to understand that print, and not pictures, talks (Clay, 1985) and that a reader is not free to say just any words when paging through a text but must come up with pronunciations of the words whose representations are printed there (Sulzby, 1985). They have a sense of the patterns of stories and poems, and they know how to follow them to make meaning.

With these understandings in place, children are able to concentrate on words and develop strategies for sounding them out, as well as develop sight

Reading for pleasure opens up a child's world and encourages imagination and inquiry.

vocabularies. They are ready, though they often need reminding, to find humor, suspense, and surprise in what they read—in other words, to make meaning from print. But their reading is still hesitant, and they still need much support from adults. They also need carefully crafted materials, with few words per page, predictable language patterns, and illustrations that help carry the meaning.

Building Fluency and Comprehension

Through late first and early second grade, most children have enough experience in reading words and following messages that their reading is becoming more and more fluent: more rapid and more accurate. For children who were read to often in early childhood, this period can be a joyful "catch up" moment: After a period of struggling to read texts that were far simpler and less meaningful than the stories they had long heard read to them, children are at last able to do for themselves what adults had to do for them. For children who are not so lucky as to have been read to, however, this period can be a hard trek through unfamiliar territory, as the fascinations of reading materialize only gradually. For the first type of child, teachers will find that their main task is to keep providing more books on the right levels to a hungry reader. For the second type of child, the teacher will have to celebrate gains but also gently and insistently push the child to read—and to read gradually more challenging texts.

If the teacher is successful, then all children will steadily amass sight words and increase both the quantity and speed of their reading. They will be preparing themselves for the next stage of reading, which is called *reading to learn and for pleasure*. Even so, wide differences will begin to open up here in the amount of reading children do and the size of their sight vocabularies.

Readers in this "fledgling" stage, as it is often called, are usually so preoccupied with getting the words right that they may forget about what the words are saying. However, they can, and should, be reminded to talk about the meaning of what they read. Teachers must make special efforts to make print meaningful through this stage.

Reading for Learning and Pleasure

By the beginning of third grade, and increasingly in fourth grade, something of a threshold is crossed, and the emphasis shifts from learning to read to reading to learn—and also reading for pleasure. By this time, children are expected to read and follow directions and to gain information from texts. In addition, they read chapter books and novels and have something to say about them in their response journals and in their book clubs, or wherever they discuss what they are reading.

Teach It! 55

The Writing Workshop

A period for reading and writing instruction is still provided every day, but more and more time is given to free reading and discussion, as well as to writing workshops. These activities are essential, because children must practice literacy to develop it. Nonetheless, there is still a place for teaching students how to comprehend, interpret, and compose. There is also still a need to make students aware of the structure of written words and the way our English vocabulary works. This is necessary because word knowledge is not gained only in the early years. The collection of words children encounter in text changes significantly at around fourth grade (from mostly words derived from Anglo-Saxon to words derived from Latin and Greek). At this point there are new features to be learned about words through the remainder of the elementary grades.

It is in fourth grade that problems in reading have traditionally become obvious because reading ability affects students' learning in other subjects. It is also because the unsuccessful struggles to learn to read well have led children to frustration and poor motivation. Indeed, children's self-esteem might have begun to suffer because they haven't succeeded in a skill that is highly valued in school (Stanovich, 1986). Although troubled readers can and certainly should be helped to overcome their difficulties, doing so is time consuming at this stage, especially since by this time there is much content to be learned throughout the school day. Because they understand how earlier experiences contribute to children's reading abilities, many teachers, and whole programs such as Reading Recovery, are placing their greatest emphasis on getting children off to a good start in reading, so that the problem of the "fourth grade slump" can be avoided wherever possible.

Mature Reading

After fifth grade and certainly by sixth grade, children who have made normal progress as readers have gradually shown other abilities that are characterized as mature reading. They read with an appreciation of the author's style, and they enjoy reading passages aloud to friends or try to imitate an author's style in their own writing. They read beyond the details of a work, and can summarize its main point argument or theme. They read with an awareness of the author's take on the subject, and may see a work as a metaphorical commentary on life. They can read several works on a theme and talk perceptively on the ways different authors' views affect the different presentations. They might practice critical literacy, argue back against the theme of a book, or take issues with its sexist or racist overtones. In any case, they are more analytical and more philosophical in what they look for in texts and in the ways they respond to them.

Mature readers are also more strategic. They can read for information, and they have strategies for previewing, questioning, marking, note taking, reviewing, and studying books they read for information.

As we noted at the outset of this section, one characteristic of developmental learning is that the earlier periods of development are more predictable and more commonly experienced than the later ones. That is clearly true with respect to mature reading. Some readers show evidence of mature reading by the time they enter fourth grade. Many more show it by seventh or eighth grade. But many others rarely do this kind of reading.

New Literacies

How is reading from the Internet different from reading from a book or a magazine?

The Recent History of Reading Instruction: How We Got Where We Are

The past twenty years have seen many changes to reading and writing instruction in the United States, and in most schools you will find teachers who have fascinating stories to tell of past movements and past practices. Your college library surely has methods books on the shelves written in earlier eras, with different assumptions, and different practices than what you will be learning now (although it is true that many good teaching practices have been in use for a long time). We offer the following as a way to keep track of what has gone before in the reading field.

Early Modern Descriptions of Reading

In 1908, Edmund Burke Huey (1908) chronicled the major approaches to teaching reading that were practiced in American schools in his time. He found an unreconciled difference between teachers who preferred to emphasize words as wholes and teachers who taught students the relationships between letters and sounds. As Huey noted, this distinction was already very old—perhaps 350 years old, according to one of his sources. Huey offered research—his own and that of others—that showed that the eye and brain take just as long to recognize a single letter as they do a whole word. This finding, building on a reaction to the heavy drill orientations of reading approaches in the late nineteenth century, encouraged a movement toward whole-word teaching approaches that lasted through the mid-1960s. Even then, the issue was not settled, and between Huey's time and ours, there has been an intense outpouring of research on the issue. Hundreds of conferences have been attended by thousands of educators, yet the tension between different approaches to teaching beginning reading remains.

Phonics Versus Whole-Word Reading

In the 1960s, Jeanne Chall (1967) reviewed the available research on the question of the best approaches to beginning reading. She found that in the decades leading up to the time when she was writing, most children in the United States were taught to read in basal reading programs, that is, in textbooks composed of short reading passages with graduated difficulty levels. For the most part, the basal reading programs, such as the popular Dick and Jane series, used whole-word approaches (what Chall called a "meaning emphasis") and did not teach phonics (what Chall called a "code emphasis"). According to the studies she reviewed, however, reading approaches that did use phonics showed better results than programs that did not. Following the appearance of Chall's influential book, publishers began to include phonics instruction in their basal reading programs.

But that did not settle the matter. Many teachers, such as New Zealander Sylvia Ashton-Warner (1963), continued to favor whole-word approaches and argued that their use emphasized meaning, whereas the phonics approaches could lead children to focus on the small parts of reading—the letters and sounds—without an adequate appreciation of what the letters were supposed to add up to. Indeed, some of the reading materials that came into use during the 1960s focused so much on letter-to-sound regularities that they left very little meaning to be pursued. "Linguistic readers" contained text like this: "A man had a tin pin. It's a pin for a cap. It's a cap for Dan." Advocates of meaning-centered reading instruction worried that if children mostly read text as pointless as this, they could easily become confused about the true purpose of reading: to construct meaning from print.

The Cognitive Revolution

The 1970s saw a revolution in the way scholars thought of language learning. The field of psycholinguistics was developing, largely under the influence of the ingenious linguist Noam Chomsky. The researchers whom Chomsky inspired began to find evidence that children learn language by exercising a built-in capacity for discovery. As long as they are in the company of people who talk to them and who model language, and as long as those around them honor children's own needs to communicate, children will learn to talk. Gradually, by stages, through an amazing exercise of finely tuned linguistic discovery processes, children learn language.

Almost immediately, theorists began to see ways to apply psycholinguistic theory to the acquisition of reading. Frank Smith wrote an influential book called *Psycholinguistics and Reading* (1973), in which he and others argued that children could learn to read in large part by discovery and encouragement. One of the contributors to that book, Kenneth Goodman (1967), had offered a conception of reading as "a psycholinguistic guessing game." Goodman's work, along with that of some imaginative Australians such as Don Holdaway (1979) and Andrea Butler and Jan Turbill (1985), gave rise to what came to be known as the *whole language movement*.

Whole Language

Whole language advocates embraced many child-centered approaches to teaching. The *writing process approach* popularized by Donald Graves (1982) and Lucy Calkins (1996) was taken up by whole language advocates and became part of the movement. So did the literature-based approaches of Dorothy Strickland (1991) and Nancie Atwell (1985). Whole language classrooms were (and are) bursting with children's creativity, as children have rich experiences that stimulate talk, as they read and listen to much good literature, and as they write out and act out their own ideas.

On the psychological front, the new field of cognitive psychology yielded studies of comprehension that greatly expanded our understanding of reading. A U.S. government grant to the University of Illinois created the Center for the Study of Reading, where Richard Anderson, David Pearson (1984), and others elaborated a theory of comprehension called *schema theory*, which stresses the reader's active role in making meaning. Schema theory was highly compatible with the work of both the psycholinguists inspired by Noam Chomsky and the constructivist theories of intellectual development inspired by Swiss psychologist Jean Piaget and others. The theory found ready acceptance in the 1970s and 1980s, and most reading experts still accept it today in some form or another as our guiding theory of how comprehension works. Like psycholinguistic research before it, schema theory seemed to lend support to the child-centered, discovery-oriented beliefs of the whole language movement.

Research-Based Emphasis

Still, the disagreements between the meaning-centered advocates and the code-centered advocates continued. In the late 1980s, the U.S. Department of Education commissioned another examination of beginning reading instruction. The resulting work was *Beginning to Read* (1990), by a psychologist, Marilyn Jaeger Adams. In it, Adams concluded that exposure to print and enthusiastic encouragement might work in some cases, but that they were not sufficient to teach all children to read. Like the evidence Jeanne Chall had reviewed twenty years before, the evidence Adams collected led her to conclude that reading approaches that explicitly and systematically taught children the code that links speech sounds to patterns of letters in words were more successful than those that did not. Adams urged teachers to give primacy to teaching children to decode and recognize words, even as they immersed the children in print and encouraged them to write.

Adams also highlighted another finding from research on reading: the importance of children's awareness of phonemes, the smallest sound units in spoken words. In a host of studies, phonemic awareness in first grade was found to make an important difference in whether children learned to read successfully. Adams urged teachers to emphasize phonemic awareness and letter-to-sound correspondences in their early reading instruction. She said in the conclusion to *Beginning to Read*,

> In summary, deep and thorough knowledge of letters, spelling patterns, and words, and of the phonological translations of all three, are of inescapable importance to both skillful reading and its acquisition. By extension, instruction designed to develop children's sensitivity to spellings and their relations to pronunciations should be of paramount importance in the development of reading skills. That is, of course, precisely what is intended of good phonics instruction. (Adams, 1990, p. 416)

Also in the late 1990s, a study of early reading difficulties was undertaken by the Committee on the Prevention of Reading Difficulties in Young Children, a group of reading experts assembled under the auspices of the National Science Foundation. The resulting report, *Preventing Reading Difficulties in Young Children* (Snow et al., 1998), recommended that teachers encourage students' growth in language and general knowledge, their exposure to and appreciation of literature, and their opportunities to write, while also providing instruction to boost phonemic awareness, knowledge of letter-to-sound relationships, fluency, vocabulary, and comprehension.

In 1997, Congress commissioned yet another group of experts to "assess the effectiveness of different approaches used to teach children to read" (National Reading Panel Web site, 2003). This was the National Reading Panel, organized by the National Institute of Child Health and Human Development (NICHD) at the National Institutes of Health. After reviewing what they considered to be evidence-based studies of reading over a two-year period, the National Reading Panel published their findings in *The Report of the National Reading Panel: Teaching Children to Read* (2000). In it, the panel made a number of recommendations, including a strong push for skills instruction, especially in the recognition of words and the skills that support word recognition: awareness of speech sounds and knowledge of phonics. (See the Web site of the National Reading Panel at <www.nationalreadingpanel.org>.)

No Child Left Behind

With the reauthorization of the Elementary and Secondary Education Act (U.S. Department of Education, 2001) called No Child Left Behind (signed into law on January 8, 2001), the administration of President George W. Bush insisted that every state develop learning standards in reading and test every child annually from third grade up. (Testing was phased in over a four-year period.) The act required that schools receiving federal funding use "evidence-based" instructional practices, and for its source of evidence, the Administration embraced the recommendations of the National Reading Panel, with special focus on five particular areas of focus: *phonological awareness, phonics, fluency, vocabulary,* and *comprehension.*

Armed with the No Child Left Behind legislation, the U.S. Department of Education was aggressive in its insistence that schools receiving federal funds use methods and materials that are backed by "SBRR," or "scientifically-based reading research." Democrats, Republicans, and a majority of the American people supported the emphasis on helping struggling readers, along with the use of state learning standards measured by end-of-year tests—although there was growing unease over the number of schools that were deemed "failures" under the NCLB initiative (see The World of Reading, below).

The World of Reading

Why Was *No Child Left Behind* Left Behind?

In the fall of 2011, President Obama rescinded the mandate that every child be reading on a proficient level by 2014 and invited states to put forward their own plans for documenting progress in teaching children to read. Why?

One answer is that the central goal of No Child Left Behind was not realistic. To have all U.S. children reading on a *proficient level* by 2014 meant that all children "... should be able to integrate and interpret texts and apply their understanding of the text to draw conclusions and make evaluations" according to the NAEP (2009). But there was little progress toward reaching that goal over the decade, in spite of all the attention placed on reading instruction. Only a third of our fourth graders across the nation had hit that target by 2009. Secretary of Education Arne Duncan observed that "[the No Child Left Behind law] created dozens of ways for schools to fail and very few ways to help them succeed" (quoted in Holland, 2011).

The heavy emphasis on reading itself may have been partly to blame. Under pressure to show progress on reading tests, the schools reduced the time they devoted to music, art, science, and social studies (arguably the subjects that build students' world knowledge and motivate them to read for information). For example, a national survey conducted for the

Center for Educational Policy found that after 2006, two thirds of the elementary schools reported cutting instructional time for social studies and science by 25 percent to 50 percent, for an average loss of 75 minutes per week compared to five years earlier (McMurrer, 2008).

It may also be that the exclusive emphasis on classroom instruction to improve reading scores was misplaced. The Economic Policy Institute argued that many of the causes of low reading achievement lie outside of the school: In the many poverty-stricken families, with absent and overworked parents and limited social services, attempts to address children's learning needs should focus on the well-being of children and their families, too:

Despite the impressive academic gains registered by some schools serving disadvantaged students, there is no evidence that school improvement strategies by *themselves* can close these gaps [in learning] in a substantial, consistent, and sustainable manner... [T]here is solid evidence that policies aimed directly at education-related social and economic disadvantages can improve school performance and student achievement. (*A Broader, Bolder Approach to Education.* Economic Policy Institute. <http://www.boldapproach.org/index.php?id=01>).

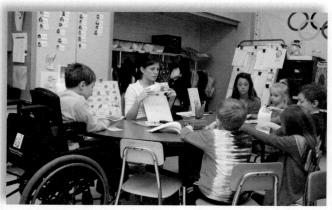

Education law in the United States requires that all students with special needs be educated in the "least restrictive environment."

CHANGES IN SPECIAL EDUCATION Until a couple of decades ago, the field of special education and the literacy field had little to do with each other. Special education and reading teachers were trained in different departments, where they learned different theories and practices; and in schools, special education teachers and reading teachers—even "remedial" reading teachers—worked separately. The separation has largely collapsed, for two reasons: First, in the latter part of the twentieth century, the framework for understanding reading and reading problems that guided both special educators and reading educators was given serious scrutiny, and now both fields have come to work from (mostly) the same theories of reading and learning. Second, special education law has evolved and now requires that children who are identified for special education services be "mainstreamed" into regular classrooms, where they may be taught by a classroom teacher and a special education teacher working together. Current special education laws have resulted in an approach known as *Response to Intervention,* or RTI, which calls for coordinated instruction for students with varying levels of need for attention, rather than a sharp distinction between children who are identified for special education services and everyone else.

RTI identifies reading teachers as contributors to special education because more than 80 percent of identified students have difficulties with literacy (Mesmer & Mesmer, 2008/2009). RTI is a process that permits an assessment of whether a scientific, research-based intervention results in an improvement in an identified child's academic performance. It is assumed that this continuing deficiency is not related to a visual, hearing, or motor disability, or intellectual disability, emotional disturbance, cultural factors, economic disadvantage, or limited English proficiency.

K–3 students are screened in accordance with Reading First literacy screening instruments and procedures to determine if they are at risk of not meeting prescribed benchmarks. If students do not meet benchmarks after scientifically valid interventions are applied, the RTI models provide for interventions in small groups to provide additional assistance. The children's progress is monitored using measures that are brief, but targeted at skills the children need to attain. If difficulties continue, individualized interventions are provided. If these are not effective, then each child's case is reviewed by a team of professionals to determine if he or she is eligible for special education. According to Mesmer and Mesmer (2008/2009), the RTI process is a useful alternative to a discrepancy model.

ENGLISH LANGUAGE LEARNERS The rights of students with limited English proficiency to be given appropriate education have been guaranteed by federal laws going back to the Civil Rights Act of 1964 and several decisions of the Supreme Court since then. These guarantees were extended to children of undocumented aliens in 1982 by the Supreme Court ruling on *Plyler v. Doe.* The numbers of school-age children who speak a language other than English at home has doubled to 20 percent since the 1980s, and about 6 percent of all U.S. students have limited English proficiency. These students are now found in many states, not just concentrated in just a few states as in the past.

LEARNING STANDARDS Since the nation's founding, the governance of education in the United States has been the responsibility of the states. In the 1990s, a decade after the founding of the United States Department of Education, the federal government was looking for a mechanism to exert enough influence over the states to lead a reform movement in education. An initiative called America 2000, launched in 1994 during the presidency of George H.W. Bush, introduced the idea of standards-based education. America 2000 called for states to set standards that defined "what all students should know and be able to do." The act set up a bipartisan federal panel to "certify State content standards and State student performance standards ... if such standards are comparable or higher in rigor and quality to the voluntary national content standards and voluntary national student performance standards." (See <http://www.ed.gov/legislation/GOALS2000/TheAct/sec211.html>.)

Within a decade, all states had set performance standards for children and had developed tests for those standards. But there was considerable variety from state to state in what children were expected to learn and what teachers were expected to teach.

Common Core Standards

CCSS

Common Core Standards: Overview

The National Governors Association Center for Best Practices (NGA Center) and Council of Chief State School Officers (CCSSO) set out to address the variety of learning standards found from state to state and came up with a common set of standards that students all over the United States should meet. They convened a panel of experts and in 2010 published the Common Core Standards for English Language Arts and Mathematics. Many corporations and foundations with an interest in education endorsed them, and as of this writing, the great majority of the states plus the District of Columbia have adopted them—so they apply to more than 80 percent of the students in the United States. Testing on the standards is scheduled to begin in 2014–2015.

The Common Core Standards define the knowledge and skills students should have within their K–12 education careers so that they will graduate high school able to succeed in entry-level, credit-bearing academic college courses and in workforce training programs. The standards:

- Are aligned with college and work expectations
- Are clear, understandable, and consistent
- Include rigorous content and application of knowledge through high-order skills
- Build upon strengths and lessons of current state standards
- Are informed by other top performing countries, so that all students are prepared to succeed in our global economy and society
- Are evidence-based*

In fact, the Common Core Standards are a serious departure from past practices in reading instruction. We can summarize the changes this way:

1. Children are pushed hard to read on or close to grade level, based on Lexile scores (Lexiles are measures of text difficulty).

2. Children are required to read a balance of narrative and informational text: 50 percent informational text at grade 4 and 65 percent at grade 8.

3. Students are expected to read about the same topic across several texts, often from different genres.

4. Students do close reading of texts and study the ways meanings are conveyed, and they make interpretations of texts and support their interpretations with reasons and evidence.

5. The standards are closely aligned to the skills that are tested on the National Assessment of Educational Progress, the PIRLS, and the PISA, the devices on which American students' reading performance is compared from year to year and from country to country.

6. Writing is used as a means of presenting claims and reasoned arguments.

7. Students are taught to use technology as tools for inquiry and research.

8. Since the Common Core Standards apply to English Language Arts (ELA) and mathematics, but not social studies and science, those latter subjects are being taught in integrated units with ELA and mathematics.

Multiple Roads to Balanced Literacy

The No Child Left Behind Act of 2001 established Reading First as a "high-quality evidence-based program for students" (ED.gov, 2004). Balanced literacy is widely viewed as an outgrowth of the National Reading Panel report of 2000, combining a literature-based focus on comprehension instruction with a strong explicit phonics component. Balanced literacy consists of five major elements (National Reading Panel, 2000):

- *Phonemic awareness:* teaching children "to focus on and manipulate phonemes in spoken syllables and words"
- *Phonics:* teaching children "letter-sound correspondences and their use in reading and spelling"
- *Fluency:* teaching children "to read orally with speed, accuracy, and proper expression" (*expression* referring to prosody, pitch, and intonation that indicates comprehension during oral reading)
- *Vocabulary:* helping children build knowledge of word meanings so that they can make sense of print
- *Comprehension:* teaching children the "active process that requires an intentional and thoughtful interaction between the reader and the text"

According to Strickland (2006), teachers can ensure maintaining balance in their reading programs by:

- Teaching reading skills with a focus on meaning, not as ends in themselves
- Providing daily instruction guided by the teacher and also independent work to enable students to internalize reading skills
- Helping students build knowledge as the result of a process, not by filling them up as empty receptacles
- Integrating print and electronic materials to reflect the modern multimedia world
- Interpreting standardized test scores in terms of informal assessment

There are several major approaches to reading instruction that provide these elements and also meet Strickland's criteria for a balanced literacy program. Some of these approaches incorporate the balanced literacy elements in their basic forms, and sometimes two or more approaches are combined to address all of them. We will present a basic overview of these major approaches next to place them in context with the elements of Reading First and with balanced literacy. In subsequent chapters, you will find more specific and detailed treatments about how to implement these approaches in the classroom.

Basal Reading Programs

Certainly the most frequently encountered approach to reading instruction is the basal reading program, quite likely the kind of reading program that your teachers used when you were in elementary school. Most basal reading programs address all five elements of Reading First, and they are stand-alone; that is, they provide all of the materials needed for a complete reading program. Even so, most classroom teachers will supplement a basal reading program with a classroom library of outstanding children's literature on a variety of levels and topics.

The typical basal reading program consists of reading textbooks sequenced by grade level for increasing difficulty. The difficulty of vocabulary is usually carefully controlled, as is the pace of introduction of new words. Basal reading programs contain narrative stories, expository text from science, social studies, and other areas of the curriculum, poetry, plays, riddles, jokes, song lyrics, and other types of text to read. There may be four or five small reading books at the kindergarten and first grade levels, two to four at the second grade level, often two at the third grade level, and one larger textbook at grade levels from four to eight.

Most modern basal reading programs are anthologies of original children's literature, often in complete form and with original illustrations. Vocabulary is not controlled in these programs. Some basal readers contain excerpts of longer pieces of children's literature. Often, selections of children's literature will not have all illustrations from the original work, or some illustrations may be partial renditions of the original. There may be simple text at the lowest levels that is designed for the teaching of reading skills. This text is usually not what we would characterize as authentic children's literature.

Lessons in basal reading programs are sometimes conducted with the entire class, although teachers who differentiate instruction according to children's needs may have two or more groups working on different levels and out of different books.

Basal reading programs also provide workbooks from which teachers typically teach such skills as phonemic awareness, phonics, comprehension, and vocabulary. They provide opportunities to practice writing, as well. These may be supplemented with large charts that can be used with easels or on word walls.

Basal reading programs also incorporate assessment tools that can be used to identify children's reading levels, their strengths, and their needs. These are frequently designed to be administered at regular intervals through the school year. Publishers of basal reading programs also often provide CD-ROMs or DVDs that can be used for listening centers in the classroom.

A teacher's manual always accompanies each reading textbook. This provides information about how to use the program lesson by lesson, how to use assessment measures, and other suggestions for strengthening the reading/writing program. The instructions in the manuals range from suggestions and recommendations from which teachers can choose to highly scripted programs in which every word the teacher should say while teaching the lesson is provided in the manual.

Basal reading programs can vary greatly in the way they are used depending on the philosophy of reading instruction being promoted. In some programs, it is assumed that children must master the sound system early. These are characterized as *part-whole* programs. In others, children are learning more holistic skills and whole words early in the program, along with the sound system. These are characterized as *whole-part-whole* programs.

Individualized Reading Instruction

In contrast to how structured and all inclusive a basal reading program is, an individualized reading program is at the other end of the continuum. There are no textbooks; instead, the children select their own children's literature to read. There is a need for a large variety of outstanding children's literature at different levels and on different topics to reflect the varying and changing interests of children throughout a school year.

Whole-class lessons are rarely seen in individualized reading programs. The main instructional interaction between teacher and child is the individual conference, which may occur every week or two. Teachers will occasionally form interest groups of children reading different books on the same topic. They may meet periodically to share their ideas about what they are reading. Teachers may also form interest groups around one story, and children reading at different levels can read the same basic story written at different levels.

Individualized reading programs require some extra effort to incorporate the five elements of Reading First, especially in the areas of phonemic awareness and phonics. For that reason, individualized reading programs are more often found in middle and upper grades than in the primary grades. Children are more independent readers at those levels, and there is not the problem of teaching word recognition skills without a textbook or workbook. Teachers who do implement an individualized reading program in the first grade will often also use a stand-alone word recognition program. A highly skilled and experienced teacher will be able to teach word recognition skills out of the context of the children's reading.

An individualized reading program can also be used in conjunction with a basal reading program. For example, a teacher may designate every Friday as an individualized reading day in which that approach is used instead of the regular basal program. A teacher who differentiates instruction may have one or two groups working in a basal reading program and another group (usually a more capable group of fluent readers) working in an individualized reading program.

Reader's Workshop

Teach It! 9

Guided Reading

Reader's Workshop is a more structured version of individualized reading that addresses the five elements of Reading First more routinely and transparently than individualized reading. Self-selection of authentic text in the form of children's literature and informational text is a parallel feature, but small-group lessons often resemble the basal reading approach (Atwell, 1998).

A typical reader's workshop time block might begin with a read-aloud in which the teacher, as an outstanding model of reading, shares different genres of children's literature for about ten minutes. There may be an interval of shared reading with the teacher in

Teach It!

Refer to the Teach It! appendix at the end of the book for further activities you can use to reinforce concepts discussed in this chapter.

Guided Reading and the Four Blocks

Guided reading is "a context in which the teacher supports each reader's development of effective strategies for processing novel texts at increasingly challenging levels of difficulty" (Fountas & Pinnell, 1996). The key elements of guided reading are:

- The teacher works with small groups.
- The children in each group are reading at about the same level.
- The teacher introduces stories and supports children's development of independent reading strategies.
- Each child reads the entire text.
- Independent, silent reading is the goal for each child.
- Over time, the teacher focuses on increasing the levels of text provided.
- The children are grouped and regrouped in accordance with outcomes observed and assessed by the teacher.
- Books are carefully leveled. That is, the difficulty levels of books available to the children are precisely determined so that they can progress in an orderly way.

Guided reading lessons are conducted in three essential stages. *Before the Reading* is a stage in which the teacher introduces a new and appropriate text, and the children converse with the teacher about the text, asking questions and building expectations. *During the Reading* is the stage in which the teacher observes problem-solving strategies used by children. The children read the entire text, or a unified part of it, to themselves silently (or softly in the case of younger readers) and ask for help when needed. In the *After the Reading* stage, the teacher involves the children

in responding to the story through such activities as writing, discussion, paired reading, and sharing personal responses. The children talk about the story, verify predictions they made before reading, and respond, usually through writing or perhaps drama (Fountas & Pinnell, 1996).

Guided reading is often combined with the structure of the Four Blocks approach (Cunningham, Hall, & Sigmon, 1999). Together, the four blocks address the five elements of Reading First and also combine many of the strengths of the basal reading program, individualized reading, and reader's workshop, while avoiding most of their limitations.

The four blocks are: guided reading, writing, self-selected reading, and working with words. Teachers can implement the multilevel aspect of the four block approach by teaching a lesson to the entire class, making the text accessible to all students with multiple readings involving read-aloud, shared reading, and paired reading in small flexible groups. They can add the writing and self-selected reading blocks of the approach as after-reading activities from the guided reading approach.

Although children in Reading First classrooms are often doing word study as a whole group, with all children working on the same skills, teachers may find it more useful to teach appropriate skills in smaller groups tailored to the needs of those particular children. Some children are more advanced and may have already mastered certain skills, while other children may lack the prior knowledge needed to achieve those skills. For example, some children will be ready to work with three-letter consonant blends (*str* and *spl*), while others will not yet have mastered two-letter consonant blends (*st* and *tr*).

As you can see, there are several roads to balanced literacy that also address the five major elements of Reading First: phonemic awareness, phonics, fluency, comprehension, and vocabulary.

Focus on Instruction

Assessment is a vital part of teaching reading and writing. Assessment allows teachers to determine how well a particular child is learning, how well an individual lesson succeeded, and how effective the whole program of instruction is. Assessment enables children to see for themselves how they are performing as they learn to read and write and what they can do to improve. It helps school administrators make decisions about the placement of individual children in special assistance and determine the design of a curriculum, as well as the in-service training needs of their faculty. Assessment also provides parents with feedback on their children's progress and identifies areas where they can provide support. It can even help parents and communities know how their schools are performing in comparison to other schools. With the advent of the No Child Left Behind legislation, assessment also has been used in an effort to determine which schools are performing satisfactorily in teaching children to read.

Assessment can take many forms, including testing. Although some formal and informal tests of reading and writing ability can be useful, some of the most informative kinds of assessments involve watching very carefully as children read and write under natural circumstances. The type of assessment that is used depends a great deal on what needs to be known and who needs to know it.

which the entire class reads together from a single text. This provides opportunities for work with fluency, word recognition skills, comprehension, and literary genres.

Guided reading (see Teach It!: Guided Reading and the Four Blocks) is a lesson stage that may occupy thirty minutes or more. While some children have a guided reading lesson on their level, other children are completing independent work, writing, reading independently, and working in learning centers. This is often followed by a mini-lesson that addresses a need of many of the children, perhaps to decode three-letter consonant blends or to make inferences. Children may then have a guided writing activity, again accompanied with mini-lessons for some children, such as how to use the comma in a series of nouns or how to use adjectives correctly. Time for independent reading is also provided during the school day, often in the form of silent sustained reading (SSR). For a designated interval, often from ten to twenty minutes, everyone in the classroom reads a book, magazine, material from the Internet, or whatever else they might choose, including the teacher.

Students, like adults, differ in interests, levels of reading ability, competence with the components of reading, and preferences in learning. As a new teacher, you will learn to make your instruction responsive to these differences and to accommodate ELLs by providing differentiated support through a multi-centered classroom organization and by developing flexible instructional routines and lessons. Orchestrating all of the variables that make classrooms exciting learning environments is challenging, but the rewards are clear!

 Guided Reading allows teachers to work with small groups of students to focus on specific literacy skills. Identify the strategies used by the teacher in the video to teach inferencing to this guided reading group of English language learners.

SIOP®
Sheltered
Instruction
Observation
Protocol®

What Is Differentiated Instruction?

The increasing diversity of students provides a visible reminder of how important it is that teachers provide appropriate, differentiated instruction so that all students can be engaged positively and productively each day they are in school. Students come with different background experiences and language, interests, and ways of engaging in learning activities. They have varied levels of knowledge of print and written language skill, different levels of content knowledge and vocabulary, and different home experiences and attitudes toward teachers and school. Creating classrooms where all students can learn means that both the classroom environment and the instructional program need to be designed to accommodate the range of interests and skills of students. Differentiation means taking into account all of these factors on which there are significant differences among the students and planning instruction so all students can be successful and enjoy their experiences.

It is important to start with students' strengths and help them develop the knowledge, skills, and strategies they need to become mature readers. The term *differentiated instruction* is used to represent these varied ways to tailor classroom experiences so all students can be productively learning. Carol Tomlinson (2000), who has worked extensively in differentiation, defines it well:

In the context of education we define differentiation "as a teacher's reacting responsively to a learner's needs." A teacher who is differentiating understands a student's needs to express humor, or work with a group, or have additional teaching on a particular skill, or delve more deeply into a particular topic, or have guided help with a reading passage—and the teacher responds actively and positively to that need. (p. 4)*

How can new teachers become this kind of responsive teacher and still meet the needs for student growth in determined areas of study? Knowing both students and curriculum is the key. Teachers begin the year by finding out as much as they can about the students under their care. Individual interviews with the children, interviews and informal conferences with parents or caregivers, and ongoing communication with them help teachers learn more about what the students are like in their out-of-school lives where they spend most of their time and energy.

Knowing the curriculum and what students need to be learning is the other starting point. Teachers need to become well versed in the content that is to be taught. They need to know the skills that students should be developing. With this understanding, the next step is to collect information about the students' levels of knowledge and skill with that content. The teacher's task is to plan and develop appropriate instructional activities that are also motivating and engaging to help students focus on what is important. This means that teachers need to know students well so they can build classrooms that reflect their needs, interests, and preferences in learning activities.

Differentiation involves providing appropriate *reading materials* to students so they can be successful readers. This is one of the most important starting points in differentiating instruction. Within one classroom the range of reading levels can be substantial. By some estimates, there is likely to be a range of two to four years in reading levels in the primary grades and four to eight years in the intermediate and upper grades. Because it is so important that students read materials that are at their instructional levels for guided reading and whole-class lessons, it is essential that teachers provide different texts to students—materials that are differentiated. Luckily, there are now many publishers in the United States who are producing materials on varied levels but with similar content. There is also a rich array of materials from which teachers and administrators can select so students can be placed with appropriate texts as they learn to read and as they learn content in the other academic areas.

Differentiation also involves knowing students well enough to *adjust strategy and skill instruction* to particular levels of need. Knowing and adjusting to reading levels is only the starting point. Students differ in their command of the components of good reading, too, and they need appropriate instruction. For example, some students will enter kindergarten knowing how to discriminate the important phonemes in English. They will benefit from some oral rhyming activities with poetry. Others will need to focus more attentively to develop discrimination of key sounds. For these students, some daily teacher-guided discrimination activities will be helpful.

Guided reading is widely used because it accommodates differences in students' reading development. Teachers can form groups of students with common reading skill development needs and monitor their engagement during reading. The format of a small guided reading group permits the teacher to address specific needs while permitting other students to work on other aspects of their reading development. This is an important aspect of differentiation: targeting students' literacy development needs.

Students also differ considerably in their *reading interests*. In the intermediate grades, particularly, students' interests span a wide range. From humor, comics, and manga to realistic fiction, biography, fantasy, sports, and informational books and magazines on particular topics, as well as a wide range of Web-based information, children's interests and preferences keep expanding. This is one of the reasons individualized reading is popular: Students can self-select the materials they want to read. Teachers need to be responsive to students' interests in their selection of books and materials for guided reading and whole-group modeling. They also need to insure that classroom libraries are developed with a range of books and magazines so all students find materials they want to read. With so many women as elementary classroom teachers, the inclusion of books in which boys, in particular, are interested creates a more inviting time for reading. Opportunities for students to engage in self-selected, silent, sustained reading as part of a basal or four-block instructional program respects these differences, too. Teachers can interview students, create periodic surveys of interests, provide book talks, and watch students' self-selection of materials as a guide.

Students also differ in the *support they need in learning*. Some children lack sufficient preparation or experiences needed for school activities. As a teacher prepares a group lesson on a topic, such as polar bears or fall holidays, it is likely that a few students may need more instructional attention "up front" prior to whole-group lessons so they can participate fully. This "jump-starting" of instruction is important for many. Other students need more time to practice new concepts and strategies. Providing a range of ways they can reinforce learning permits them to be successful. Giving students opportunities to draw or act out scenes from stories they are reading may be essential reinforcements for their learning. Some learn well when put in small groups to discuss and deepen their understanding of texts together. Others need time alone to reflect and write about their responses to texts. Some work well with partners in making content and strategies their own. English language learners, in particular, benefit from opportunities to work with a same-language partner so they can process new content in their own language and clarify any confusing content or vocabulary. It is valuable to provide students with a choice in the types of learning activities and settings that will help them be successful.

Accommodations for English language learners in the regular classroom can be made at many points. These students benefit when teachers become knowledgeable about their needs and find ways to support their learning with comprehensible and responsive classroom activities. A good lesson framework, used widely across the United States and internationally, that helps teachers be cognizant of learner needs is based on the Sheltered Instruction Observation Protocol (SIOP) that was developed by the Center for Applied Linguistics (Echevarria, Vogt, & Short, 2013). It includes guidance in developing both content and language objectives for lessons, activating students' background knowledge, providing appropriate language so directions and content are comprehensible to ELLs, and engaging students actively as learners. One section provides strategies that are most appropriate for ELLs. This model can serve as the foundation for professional development in schools with increasing numbers of ELLs.

---

*"Differentiated instruction" defined. *Leadership for Differentiating Schools and Classrooms,* Tomlinson, C. & Allan, S. D. (2000), page 4. Association for Supervision & Curriculum Development (January 1, 2000). ISBN-10: 0871205025. Used with permission.

Being a Professional Reading Teacher

Become Part of a Professional Community

Teaching is challenging work and can be exhausting, especially for new teachers. One of the best ways you can help yourself is by seeking out opportunities to become part of the multi-level professional community of educators.

Within the School

At the most immediate level is the community within the school. If you are fortunate, your school will have a reading/literacy coach or specialist who is available to help you get started, who can do demonstration lessons, and who can help you manage the curriculum expectations and assessments. Most schools provide some structured times for professional development in which the faculty meets regularly to discuss issues of common concern and to learn together. This may occur in grade-level or departmental teams. Ask if your school has a literacy team; if it does, this group of interested teachers can help you understand the school literacy context and expectations and also can provide significant support to new teachers. These teachers will often let you visit their classrooms to watch how they conduct parts of their instructional program—from doing guided reading to initiating inquiry units. New teachers also may have the option of working with a mentor teacher in a district-based induction program. Ask if such an option exists. If one doesn't, you might inquire about being assigned a personal mentor. This can be a helpful way to get to know the specific culture of the school and district and can prevent many frustrations. The school district or the larger county or service center might also have an optional set of good activities that can be used to increase the effectiveness of teachers. Ask about these resources, and watch for special programs that are advertised. Many new teachers feel too busy to add another commitment, but the rewards can outweigh the time demands.

Outside of School

Outside of school, teachers can seek out groups that meet regularly for discussions both of adult recreational books and of professional ones. Some teacher book clubs also read and discuss current children's books, which can help teachers become aware of new possibilities for students. With so many books published each year, it is difficult to keep up with the ones that might be appropriate for your students. You can attend book discussions hosted by bookstores and distributors with your teaching colleagues as well. These discussions can help to identify special books and upcoming events to link into the classroom. If teachers share their searches for books, magazines, and computer materials with each other, they can enjoy learning together as they find materials that are of interest to a wide variety of young people. Many school districts have Professional Development Centers where teachers in the district offer short courses and outside speakers provide seminars. If your school doesn't have a reading/literacy coach

or specialist, there may be one at the district level who is available to help you get started.

As you begin your journey of professional growth, share what you are doing with your students, who might not ordinarily think of teachers as learners, too. Children are intrigued when they see the professional journals and books that help their teachers evaluate their own teaching and that encourage them to expand their knowledge in new directions. Keep some of your professional materials in the classroom as a visible reminder that adults are readers and learners, too. Talk about your own reflection and questions.

Join a Writing Group

If you are going to inspire children to read, you must be a reader yourself. So it shouldn't surprise you to hear us make the same point about writing. If you haven't participated in an adult writing group, you may not know how completely satisfying it can be to put your heart and soul into creating something meaningful on paper and to have other people be moved by it. The experience comes as close to genuine communication with yourself and others as anything we humans can do. Many communities offer writing classes for adults who want to be motivated to write and to have opportunities to share what they write with others. If you attend one, you will quickly see that the point is not, as many believe, to see who has "true talent" as a writer. It is rather to help you find your voice as a writer. Finding your voice takes motivation, practice, and a little inspiration. Inspiration? The ancient Greeks believed in divine creatures called *muses* who blew ideas into people's heads (that is literally what "inspire" means). We advise our own writing students to assume that the Greeks were right. Think about it: If a divine creature were to blow an idea into your head, wouldn't you be more likely to do something with it if you were writing at the time, instead of watching television or listening to your iPod? So cultivate the habit of writing. Join a group if you can. You will quickly see what a marvelous activity writing really is, and you will motivate your students with your example. And, who knows? Like Regie Routman, Nancie Atwell, Will Hobbs, Paul Janezko, Cynthia DeFelice, Jim Burke, and countless other teachers who became writers, you may connect with a larger audience.

Professional Organizations

New teachers are also nurtured when they join professional organizations that hold conferences and publish journals and books designed to help teachers grow. For literacy teachers, that means becoming a member of the International Reading Association (IRA) <www.reading.org> and/or the National Council of Teachers of English (NCTE) <www.ncte.org>. These organizations have local and state groups that meet periodically to bring speakers to the area and sponsor special events; they also may offer grants to teachers who wish to attend a conference or develop some special student project. Both organizations have excellent journals that you can subscribe to either in print or online formats; *The Reading Teacher* (IRA) and *Language Arts* (NCTE) are both very useful sources of ideas and information. IRA and NCTE also jointly sponsor an important teacher support Web site, <readwritethink.org>, with its large collection of lesson plans that can be downloaded and easily used. These professional organizations also provide many opportunities for teachers to develop leadership skills by making presentations, being an officer, and working on advocacy when the need arises. Teachers enjoy their challenges most when they become part of the larger professional community. At a personal level, membership often results in new friends and a valuable support network. Local affiliates can be found by checking the Web sites of the national groups.

There are also two national professional organizations for teachers who are interested in the education of English language learners. Both also have state affiliates. They are Teachers of English to Speakers of Other Languages (TESOL) <www.tesol.org> and National Association for Bilingual Education (NABE) <www.nabe.org>. Participation with other teachers in the school or district can help to create a strong professional learning community.

Create a Professional Portfolio

Aristotle said "The unexamined life is not worth living," and with respect to teaching, influential educator John Goodlad (1984/2004) noted that what schools were most in need of was *mindful* teaching. Good teachers know what they are doing and why. Creating and maintaining a professional portfolio is a good way to organize your thinking about teaching—and also make yourself attractive to possible employers. Your university or college may already require teaching portfolios as part of your teacher preparation program. Indeed, many states now require them. If you have not been given specific guidelines for creating a portfolio, the following are components you should include so that you can build one on your own:

- *A résumé.* Also called a *curriculum vitae* ("the course of your life," in Latin), a résumé is an outline of your education and work experience. The career services office on your campus can help you prepare one if need be.

- *A statement of your philosophy about teaching.* A philosophy of teaching sets out your beliefs and values as a teacher. Few teachers have these ideas ready at hand—it takes reflection, and better yet, lengthy conversations with both your peers and experienced teachers to tease out a clear philosophy statement. Some helpful organizing topics are:
  a. *Goals as a teacher.* Remembering that our efforts are ultimately for the students, what are your goals for the children you will teach? What aspects of their competence as readers, learners, thinkers, and human beings do you aspire to develop? What image do you have in mind as an excellent teacher? What are your ideals for yourself as a teacher? What are you aspiring to be good at?
  b. *How you will achieve your goals.* What are your preferred approaches to teaching—referring to girls and boys, children from different social and cultural groups, students with different abilities or who have different language backgrounds? How do you intend to become the teacher your want to be? What will you do to prepare yourself, and what will you do to continue to renew and expand your competence as a teacher?
  c. *Why you value what you do.* Why are literacy and learning important to the students you will teach? Why is being or becoming a teacher of those things important to you? Why are they valuable to society?

- *Lesson plans.* It is advisable to include several lesson plans, carefully labeled. The plans should meet these criteria:
  a. *Showing sequential lesson plans* (at least two), demonstrating how you manage instruction over more than one day
  b. *Using informational text, narrative text, and poetry*
  c. *Employing technology*
  d. *Illustrating accommodations for students with disabilities and for English language learners*
- *Samples of students' work*
- *Photographs of classroom environments and projects you have developed*
- *A thematic unit that integrates reading instruction with social studies or science content*
- *A video or DVD of a lesson you are teaching*

Note two final cautions in preparing your portfolio. First, be sure that all examples presented are your own original work. If you use or adapt the work of someone else, be sure to give credit. Second, proofread everything carefully; you are presenting your best face in your portfolio, including your ability to write and spell in English.

For Review

Reading and writing are important parts of the school curriculum. They are tools that help students learn nearly everything else in the school day and continue to learn when they leave school. However, literacy is valuable as something far more than a school subject. Literacy leads to habits of language and mind that take readers beyond what they would find it natural to notice, think about, and communicate if they were not literate.

International comparisons show that U.S. students read fairly well, but the benefits of literacy are not shared equitably among students from different income groups or ethnic groups. When the National Assessment of Educational Progress has assessed reading ability, unacceptably high numbers of elementary age students have been found not to read with adequate comprehension. At the same time, studies show that few readers with disabilities have problems related to cognitive function. Ninety-seven percent or more, according to one study, could be remediated with appropriate instruction, although that instruction should be judiciously planned and intensively applied when necessary. These findings cast doubt on the still-continuing practice of treating so many children with "specific reading disabilities" as if there were something wrong with their brains.

The components of reading are interrelated, but reading can be viewed in terms of word recognition, fluency, vocabulary, comprehension, and critical literacy. Reading

develops normally through stages: emergent literacy, beginning reading, building fluency, reading to learn and for pleasure, and mature reading.

Teaching reading well requires that the teacher keep several things in mind. Effective reading instruction entails immersing children in real literature, teaching decoding skills and coaching children in their use, giving attention to comprehension and higher-order thinking skills, teaching learning strategies to children, giving frequent assessments, involving parents and caregivers in their children's learning, and respecting cultural differences.

Assessment of reading and writing ability is done for external and internal audiences. External audiences include parents, school administrators, and the general community—all of whom have a stake in knowing how well the literacy instruction program is working. External audiences usually want results from standardized tests. Assessment is also done for internal audiences, who are the children themselves and their teacher. Assessments for internal audiences typically include careful observations of children's reading and writing performance at real tasks, and are intended to shed light on what learners are doing well and what aspects of their literacy need improvement.

The history of research on reading instruction is nearly as old as the scientific study of psychology. But debates over instructional methods in literacy—such as the whole word versus phonics debate—have lasted for many generations. Arguments between advocates of holistic approaches and skills-based approaches have been heated in the past decade but appear to be easing with the emphasis on a balance of both. Research supports holistic instruction so that children see that literacy is meaningful; it also supports instruction in the alphabetic writing system—in phonics and the awareness of the sound system that underlies it—at least to those students who don't intuit the system. For the past two decades the federal government has pushed for research-based literacy instruction, with accountability monitored by means of standards and regular testing. The first wave of standards was passed by individual states, but recently a set of Common Core Standards is setting uniform expectations for reading and writing and mathematics in nearly all states.

For Your Journal

Go back to the Anticipation Guide that opened this chapter, and consider your answers to the questions posed. Divide a page of your journal with a vertical line. On the left side, write down one of your answers that you want to think about more. On the right side, write what you think about that topic now. Repeat the exercise with at least two more questions. Take your journal to class with you, and share your comments with your classmates.

Taking It to the World

1. Interview three primary grade teachers, and ask them how they have seen the emphases in reading instruction change in the past ten years. What aspects have stayed the same? What changes have they witnessed?

2. Many adults who have poorly developed reading skills don't perceive their limited literacy as a problem. Call the local chapter of Literacy Volunteers of America, and ask whether this has been their experience. Do many of the adults in the community who need help with literacy seek it? (A class might choose to appoint a committee to do this so as not to inundate the chapter with phone calls.)

3. The National Adult Literacy Survey noted that prisoners are more likely than the rest of the population to have reading problems. Have a member of your class interview the person in charge of education at a local or regional prison. To what extent are literacy issues related to the problems the inmates have faced?

New Literacies Connections

1. Visit the Web pages of the International Reading Association <www.reading.org> and the National Council of Teachers of English <www.ncte.org>. Can you tell what the emphases of these two organizations are?

2. The International Reading Association publishes an electronic journal called Reading On-Line. Log on and read an issue. What topics are of most interest to the readership at the moment?

MyEducationLab™

Go to Topic 9 (Organization and Management) in the MyEducationLab <www.myeducationlab.com> for your course, where you can:

- Find learning outcomes for Organization and Management along with the national standards that connect to these outcomes.

- Complete Assignments and Activities that can help you more deeply understand the chapter content.

- Apply and practice your understanding of the core teaching skills identified–in the chapter with the Building Teaching Skills and Dispositions learning units.

- Check your comprehension on the content covered in the chapter by going to the Study Plan in the Book Resources for your text. Here you will be able to take a chapter quiz, receive feedback on your answers, and then access Review, Practice, and Enrichment activities to enhance your understanding of chapter content.

The Social and Cultural Contexts for Teaching All Children to Read

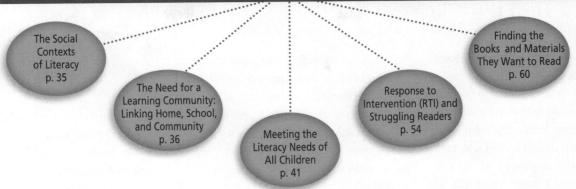

The Social and Cultural Contexts for Teaching All Children to Read

- The Social Contexts of Literacy p. 35
- The Need for a Learning Community: Linking Home, School, and Community p. 36
- Meeting the Literacy Needs of All Children p. 41
- Response to Intervention (RTI) and Struggling Readers p. 54
- Finding the Books and Materials They Want to Read p. 60

Anticipation Guide

The following statements will help you begin thinking about the topics covered in this chapter. Answer *true* or *false* in response to each statement. As you read and learn more about the topics mentioned in these statements, double-check your answers. See what interests you and prompts your curiosity toward more understanding.

_____ **1.** Reading and writing are both social and individual forms of communicating.

_____ **2.** Differences among students in classrooms have little effect on how teachers work with children.

_____ **3.** Cultural groups have distinct values regarding the importance of reading and writing.

_____ **4.** Almost all English language learners are found in large urban centers in the Southwest.

_____ **5.** African American Vernacular English is a dialect of English.

_____ **6.** Children's culture is reflected in their body language, the way they manage time, and the distance they maintain between themselves and others.

_____ **7.** A gifted child who is reading at grade level probably has a reading problem.

_____ **8.** Boys tend to have more reading problems than girls do.

_____ **9.** Children should be considered for special education only if they are two years behind their age level in expected achievement.

_____ **10.** Children with special needs benefit from being in general education classrooms for part of the school day.

A Classroom Story

Getting Parents and the Community Involved in the Classroom

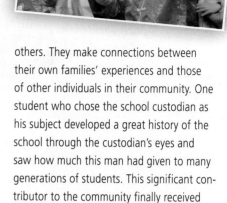

Marguerite has been teaching seventh grade for several years. Recently, many of her students have come from newly arrived immigrant families, especially from Asia and Eastern Europe. She wants to help these students understand American society and local community life, so she uses a resource unit on community biography from the state department of education. This unit integrates language arts and history as students study their own community members. She likes this project because it helps both her new students and the rest of the class understand how local communities, schools, religious groups, businesses, and government work together. As they do their projects and learn from each other, students develop pride in being part of their town.

Marguerite also uses this project to give her students a real purpose for developing their oral and written language skills. They use language by interviewing, collecting data, and writing biographies. Each student selects a special person in the community about whom he or she will write a biography. To complete the project, students need to develop questions to use in their interviews, conduct the interviews, and write up their findings. In addition, they conduct

research on the national and international events that occurred during this person's life, create a timeline of important events that correlate with the person's life, and collect pictures and other artifacts that pertain to the report. The results of their research will be presented on a three-part bulletin board that will be shown at the *Special Persons Fair*, which is open to the public. As she organizes the time frame for this unit, she works closely with the school librarian to locate resources that will help students gain more information about the local community, its history, and community leadership. The librarian introduced her to the collection of local newspapers on file and suggested that the public library also had a wealth of materials that students could use.

Confident because of her careful planning and well-organized resources, Marguerite quickly engages her students in the unit. The students benefit from her preparation and become very excited about what they learn about their own community during their research and interviews. In fact, throughout the unit students share what they are learning with each other. The enthusiasm and insights shared by students often spark new ideas and questions from

others. They make connections between their own families' experiences and those of other individuals in their community. One student who chose the school custodian as his subject developed a great history of the school through the custodian's eyes and saw how much this man had given to many generations of students. This significant contributor to the community finally received the special recognition he deserved.

The class shares their project results during *Special Persons Night* at school, to which they invite the subjects of their projects and other local community members. The large turnout of adults interested in the recognition of local community members lets students know the value of the project. The students learn a great deal about their own community: Both students and community members are proud of the students' accomplishments.

The activity creates a positive connection between the various parts of the community—old and new, those in leadership roles and many other (less noticed, but very important) contributors, and the students and teachers in the school.

We learn from those around us. We learn to act like them, to talk like them, to dress like them, to become part of a culture. Think of how you, as an infant and young child, learned to speak by following the models of those who nurtured you or how, as a teenager, you watched and then tried to talk and look just like your friends. The power of the social context is also very strong as people develop their literacy interests and behaviors. Children who come from families in which reading is a part of the fabric of their lives—in which family members keep books by their beds to read in quiet moments, where even bathrooms have piles of magazines, and where children are read to nightly—know that reading is important. They come to school with the expectation that they will become readers like the rest of their family members. Some students enter kindergarten facile with using computers and able to read and write. Other children, however, come to school without such extensive experiences and foundations for becoming literate. Yet, they want to learn and have also probably experienced the value of family members using cell phones to send text messages, observed relatives reading religious materials, noted environmental print, watched adults write and read, and played with computer games. Their experiences with literacy may be different, but all can provide strong motivation for learning to read and write.

In getting acquainted with our students, it is part of our job as teachers to find out about their literacy history as readers and writers. Students want to learn to read and write and to communicate well with others. We can make better connections to their expectations and experiences when we know about their lives and understand their personal purposes for literacy. The more we know about their literacy experiences, the more we can ensure that all students become part of a social network of children and adults who value literacy and who use it in many ways and for many purposes.

As teachers we also know the importance of the social nature of literacy beyond the home. Children compare themselves to those around them. Just ask students who are the best readers in their class—they know. Ask who should write the letter of thanks to the author who visited the school, and they will direct you to the best writer. Children in classrooms can easily fall into categories of participators and non-participators, achievers and non-achievers. Teachers need to know how to make the social dynamics of the classroom work positively for all students, so all can be engaged and succeed.

Twenty-first-century schools have fewer and fewer classrooms composed of children from one ethnic or cultural group who all speak English as their mother tongue and who are otherwise similar to each other. In fact, about 20 percent of the children in the United States have immigrant parents, and this percentage is increasing regularly (Suárez-Orozco, Suárez-Orozco, & Todorova, 2008). One in six students in American classrooms is African American, and soon one in five will be Hispanic, but still nine out of ten teachers are white. In most American schools, teachers are working with students whose ethnic backgrounds and possibly home languages are different from their own. As cultural and linguistic diversity are increasing, educators are finding ways to make schools and classrooms inviting learning communities where families and children learn from and with each other. This chapter highlights the research and best practices that emphasize the importance of reading and writing as social activities, not just as individual skills to be acquired.

Family Literacy

How were parents and community members involved in the schools you attended?

The Social Contexts of Literacy

Communities and families vary in their approaches and orientations to literacy, and many of these variations are grounded in historical and cultural circumstance. Not all Americans value the same forms of literacy in their lives. Research in mainstream American communities, as well as in varied cultural settings, has highlighted both the commonalities and the differences across families and among communities.

A classic study of variations in literacy was done by Heath (1983) and reported in her book *Ways with Words*. In this comparison of literacy in three different cultural groups in a mill town near Charlotte, North Carolina, Heath illustrates how the two working-class communities, Tracton and Roadville, provided their children with different cultural experiences related to reading and writing from those of the townspeople, whose use of literacy was more compatible with that of the schools. Roadville families' literacy was anchored in their fundamentalist church. They saw written works as creations that they themselves were unfit to question, and they discouraged their children from asking questions or telling stories. Tracton families were more playful and collaborative when it came to reading—it was not unusual to hear a mother standing on her front stoop reading aloud a line of a letter, and have neighbors up and down the block chime in with their ideas of what it meant. At school, children from Roadville seldom ventured ideas about texts. Their teacher saw them as dull and unimaginative. The children from Tracton eagerly helped each other read aloud, even though only one child had been called upon. Their teachers saw them as unruly and even prone to cheating. Heath was able to work with the teachers to help them better connect the children's home lives and their reading tasks in school, and everyone felt more successful as a result.

Since that early work of Heath, others have explored underlying values and styles associated with literacy. Delpit (1995) has provided insights about African American cultural variations in literacy. She argues that African American children are accustomed to a more direct form of teaching and discipline and that they need that kind of clarity for success. According to Delpit, the more indirect forms of teaching and discipline preferred by many middle-class teachers leave some students out. They often don't understand the cues that teachers provide about what is important and what the students' roles should be.

Research by Kelly (2000) with a group of Mexican American mothers revealed the high level of respect they accord teachers and schools. Even when they have had few opportunities for formal schooling themselves, they want their children to succeed. Their high regard for teachers, however, has a potential negative effect. They do not want to interfere with the teachers' role by helping their children learn to read before going to school. Because of this respect for teachers and their lack of a tradition of home literacy, their children often do not enter school with the same story reading and writing experiences that other children have. These families also thought that their children could learn English in school but that Spanish would remain the language used at home. This has both advantages and disadvantages. It poses a problem in giving English language learners enough opportunities to speak and use English to become proficient. It also means that the language of intimacy and familiarity is not English, so the school associations with English need to be very positive if students are going to learn it easily. Students who speak languages other than English can be encouraged to work and talk together so that they can practice English more regularly.

Because students are coming from increasingly diverse cultural traditions with varying literacy experiences, it is valuable to try to understand something of their family and cultural values, particularly those related to literacy and schooling. It is also important to find good ways to communicate with the parents and adjust to their needs (Gandara, 2010; Rueda, August, & Goldenberg, 2006). For example, some Hispanic parents feel intimidated when asked to come to school for parent conferences. They are unfamiliar with the traditions of U.S. schools and the customary relationships between teachers and families. In an attempt to honor the different experiences of the parents, one school district in California changed its format for parent nights. Instead of having each family come alone for conferencing, the schools have small-group conferencing. After the teachers lead a discussion of students' work and curriculum expectations, they answer questions from the parents. The teachers then make themselves available to individual families who wish to talk privately. This format has worked very well. The parents feel much more secure discussing issues of school learning in a group setting rather than alone with a teacher. Instead of creating high levels of anxiety among the parents, teachers' sensitivity led to a more comfortable and relaxed way to connect with parents in small groups.

The more teachers learn about the social contexts of their community, the better able they will be to respond appropriately to their students and to build new expectations and competence so that all students can attain the levels of literacy needed today. Despite the traditional values that many communities place on literacy, teachers who reach all their students successfully take time to learn about their students and expand their horizons to become versatile in their use of literacy in a wide variety of settings.

The Need for a Learning Community: Linking Home, School, and Community

Becoming aware of the relationship between community values and students' motivation and interests is a good starting place for understanding the setting in which one teaches. The cultural importance of literacy activities and the ways adults and children communicate affect how teachers can help their students most effectively.

New teachers should think of themselves as working in a community, not just in a school. Before entering the school and closing out the rest of the world, take time to become acquainted with the resources around you. For example, are there libraries you can link with to help provide the variety of reading materials you will want your students to have available to them? What resources are particularly relevant to the families you will be working with, such as community clubs, religious and ethnic centers, and local organizations and their leaders?

Your most powerful opportunities, however, come from within the school. As a teacher, you have a very important role for the parents and families of the children in your classroom. How you meet and relate to them is critical. Understanding the families' attitudes and values will help you work with the families as partners in developing children's literacy. You want to know them as well as possible to communicate effectively with them. Think of their needs and ways to build bridges between the school and their homes. What do they want to know? How can you support them in their efforts to help their children? Think of how you can involve them in the life of the school and the classroom. What is appropriate and beneficial for both you and them?

As a teacher, you will be part of a school community, too. The more you can participate as part of the professional team, sharing your own literacy and learning and growing with others in the building, the more successful you will be as a teacher. Do not wait until you have your classroom under control before you think about building your roles within this larger support team. Begin to envision yourself as a committed professional sharing with others.

Inside the Classroom

Along with the variation among communities in the way they express the values and functions of literacy, there is also great variation within schools in the way the value of literacy is expressed. A part of creating a community is designing an inviting and purposeful space in the classroom, one that maximizes the possibilities for establishing a real literacy community among students. Whether adjusting the physical environment or adapting the structure of reading and writing activities, each teacher can do a great deal to contribute to a school culture that stimulates literacy and honors students' contributions.

CREATE A LITERATE CULTURE   One of the first statements you make to students about what is important in school is what they observe in the classroom. Are desks grouped together? Are books and print materials displayed and easily accessible? Think about the classroom environment you want to create during your first year of teaching. What will the classroom look like? Remember, you will have a great deal to do in determining the kind of context you create for your students. Think of your classroom space as a visual and physical opportunity to invite your students to enjoy reading and writing. Think about some of the classrooms you have visited in recent years. How did the teachers make a clear statement that they valued reading and writing? Table 2.1 identifies things teachers can use in their classrooms to enhance the value of literacy.

One of the easiest and most important ways in which you can invite your students into literacy is by providing them with places where they can participate with others in literate activities. Every classroom with a library of appropriate books, magazines, and newspapers encourages the habit of reading. As you begin to create a library, determine the range of reading levels likely among the students, identify key themes and authors that children of this age enjoy, and begin building the collection. Many schools provide sets of books for each classroom. However, you will still want to evaluate the collection and make it as appealing as possible. It should contain material on a wide range of topics of interest to your students, and some of the collection should connect to the science, social studies, and special topics that the children will be studying. Ensure that there are books representing the various cultures from which students in the school come. All students deserve to find and see themselves in the books and magazines in their classrooms.

Another important step is to create an attractive place for literacy activities. If space is available, create both a reading corner and a writing corner. In the reading corner, house the classroom library and additional inviting reading materials in a space where students

Table 2.1 Visual Survey of a Literate Classroom

The classroom contains:

1. A special place for reading and writing—a reading corner, a writing corner, etc.
2. A classroom library of books students can use regularly
3. A collection of books students have written either individually or in groups (these could be big books, bound books added to the classroom library, etc.)
4. A rack with magazines and newspapers appropriate for the students
5. An author's chair and/or a reader's and writer's chair from which the students read to the rest of the class
6. Books and magazines the teacher is reading, both professional and personal
7. Examples on the walls or ledges of students' responses to materials they are reading—reviews of books, story maps of key points, sketches of interesting parts of stories, shared responses, etc.
8. Charts and other visuals that serve as strategy guides for students learning to read and write—reading strategies, fix-up strategies, steps in writing, word walls to guide spelling using key patterns, etc.
9. Visual "in process" charts of students' work—I-charts, matrices of learning, K-W-L charts, responses to questions for reflection, etc.
10. Illustrations of what students are studying and learning in content areas—science process journals and social studies artifacts
11. Books, magazines, and other materials that reflect cultures represented in your class or school
12. Examples of writing in different orthographies so that students can explore the varieties of written languages

---

Writing and Reading Connections

What kind of writing center would you like to create for students?

can browse through the books and curl up on the floor or in comfortable chairs to read. Some teachers find soft chairs, pillows, or even bathtubs in which children can relax and read. You can add small bins for paper so students can make notes about special ideas they find while reading and for stick-on notes so they can mark places for sharing with each other. Some teachers involve students in creating bookmarks so they can easily access their point of reading and have extra bookmarks available in the reading center.

The writing space needs a table and comfortable chairs. The space becomes more attractive when students can enjoy a range of writing tools and a supply of writing materials. Depending on the students' age, these will vary, but a selection of colored pencils and pens, some wooden ink blocks with special designs, and a variety of kinds of paper, some with designs, make writing more fun. Computers in this area can be used for writing and editing support by families and volunteers in early primary classes and by students as they become adept in using computers. In addition, dictionaries, thesauruses, and other writing aids should be displayed prominently for students' use. This area can house students' writing folders so that when they are ready to write, they can enter the process easily and, when finished, can refile their works in process.

ENSURE THE SHARING OF LITERACY A key to helping students become lifelong readers and writers is to develop the social nature of literacy by providing regular opportunities for children to engage with each other around literacy events. Too often, as students move up in the grades, opportunities to talk with others about what they are reading and writing disappear. Yet it is through sharing with others that students realize how central literacy can become in their own lives as part of their own enjoyment and learning. As you begin to plan for your literacy program, think carefully about including regular opportunities for students to engage with each other without the teacher dominating the discussion or exchange. Students need opportunities to work in paired reading and writing activities. They need to learn how to function as part of small cooperative literacy groups, knowing that they should be prepared with their own ideas to share and willing to listen and connect with what others say. They also need to have experiences in larger groups and whole-class discussions that build from their partner or small-group experiences.

Think–Pair–Share

For many students who are new to this country, talking in a whole-class setting is extremely difficult because they lack confidence in their command of English and of the culture of the school. Teachers can ease these students into the classroom academic life by using paired reading and talking as a first step before involving the students in larger group activities. As you think about all the literacy learning activities you will structure for your students, make sure students have frequent and regular opportunities to talk and share with their peers in non-threatening settings. Don't assume that students know what it is like to discuss a book or piece of text. You might need to spend a significant amount of time getting students familiar with "talk about text." One way to develop more book discussion is to begin a Great Books shared inquiry program. There is full training for teachers and group leaders in this program and materials that guide students' thinking about the rich stories and texts that are included at each grade level (Plecha, 1992; http://greatbooks.org). Many teachers now use some form of book club (Raphael & McMahon, 1994) or literature circle (Daniels, 2002) as a way of involving students in focused talk about what they are reading.

Another support for book talk is to help parents learn how to elicit reflection from their children. Some school districts have developed videotapes of the kinds of questions and follow-up comments that parents can use to help children talk about their reading. Others have prepared guides for parents to follow. One example is shown in Figure 2.1.

It is useful to help students share literacy with each other at all ages and grade levels. In this way, the shared, cultural aspects of reading and writing can become more alive for all

Literature Circles

Paired Reading

Figure 2.1 Tips for Reading with Your Child

TIPS FOR READING WITH YOUR CHILD

1. Find a relaxed time and setting.

2. Talk about the book as you read.
   * Look over the cover, title, author, and picture and predict what you think may happen and why you like the book.
   * As you read, share connections to your life.
      "Doesn't this seem like Aunt Dorothy?"
      "This picture reminds me of our trip!"
      "Oh, I remember feeling like this!"
   * Ask questions of your child. For example:
      "Do you know anyone like this?"
      "How would you feel?"
   * After reading, share your favorite parts. For example:
      "I really liked ..."
      "... was so funny!"

3. Reread favorite books.

4. Read many kinds of books—real world, poetry, folktales, humor, & fiction.

the students in the school. A very simple way to do this is for two different grades to become partners. Students are also joined into buddy pairs for reading and writing and meet regularly (e.g., weekly, every two weeks, monthly). The children begin to share their literate activities with children older and/or younger than they are. The older readers help the younger ones as they read from books they want to share; the older students might also help write responses to the reading—what the two like about the story, characters, or information. When the younger students write their own descriptions of a trip to the nature center, the older student buddies take dictation and help to create personal accounts of the experiences.

In some schools, the students who struggle with reading also get help from older students who are trained in some basic reading strategies. In this way, both groups of students gain, and the shared understanding of literacy develops naturally. One particular program, Tall Friends, pairs middle-grade, below-level readers with second graders who are also having trouble. The reading teacher works with the older students to develop some activities that will help the second graders focus on the phonic regularities of English by doing controlled word sorts and by learning to listen to and support students as they read orally from their instructional-level materials.

If a school does not have a vibrant, shared literacy culture, think about how to bring in some new focus to stimulate students' attention to reading and writing. There are many ways in which this can be done. One is to celebrate special days, from International Literacy Day, September 8, to Dr. Seuss's birthday, March 2. Some states have their own awards for good children's books. Illinois holds a contest each year to select students' favorite books as part of the Rebecca Caudill Awards Program. California's Young Reader Medal is similar. School participation in the selection of these books creates a new focus for the celebration of books. Other programs that recognize student writing can also help to add emphasis to school literacy. Inviting authors to visit the school and speak with different groups of students can make literacy and the process of writing and reading very real. Most states have some beloved and respected authors who are willing to visit schools, and bookstores will often help to bring authors to area schools.

Each of these examples highlights the importance of thinking of literacy as a community activity in the school. The more there is a climate of support for and interest in how students read and write, the more all students benefit. In addition, the more students talk with each other about their reading, the more they identify with books and reading.

START THE YEAR OUT RIGHT   Just as teachers can do much to create a warm, supportive literacy climate in the classroom, they can also help to model the importance and joy of literacy even before students start the year. Consider writing a letter to each of your new students before the year begins, introducing yourself and telling a little about your expectations for the fall. You can suggest that students bring with them an example of their own writing (if they are beyond the second grade) or a favorite book or poem. Some teachers ask students to bring pictures of themselves doing something they enjoy to put on a board for the first day. Each of these activities is an example of using literacy as a bridge to building relationships. Students love to receive mail, and some of the apprehension of starting a new year can be melted away with such simple, yet profound, gestures.

Teachers can also involve parents in events at the start of the year. By sending a letter home during the first week, introducing themselves, and describing what they will be doing in the classroom, teachers can build a bridge from school to home. Parents respond positively to a note from the teacher explaining what to expect for the fall. After an initial letter, the teacher might publish a weekly or monthly newsletter of the class events, with explanations of aspects of the reading and writing programs. Parents need to know how they can contribute. Knowing that they are important and are helping their children, most parents will become more involved in their children's developing literacy.

During the first week of school, literacy activities can also help the class to become better acquainted. Ask each student to bring a favorite book or magazine to share, give the students time to explain why they have selected the particular material, and listen carefully to them. This can be a good way to find out even more about the students' personal and home uses of literacy. For students for whom such selection and sharing might not be comfortable, conduct a book talk about several books and magazines in the classroom library and ask students to select the one they think they will like most. Having time to scan the materials gives each student an opportunity to share responses.

Getting to know the students quickly is important. Asking them to draw or write something about themselves is another way to elicit shared literacy activity. The bulletin board that can be created from this activity then becomes an invitation to read and learn about classmates. In one school, parents created the covers for the writing journals that the kindergarten and first-grade children were given the first week of school. Imagine the children's surprise when they realized that they would be holding a creation of their parents each time they wrote! Parents knew their children would be using their developmental spelling abilities as well as drawing to write messages each day when they spent time at the writing table.

Involving Parents in the School

It is impossible to discuss social contexts of literacy without focusing on parents, for they are the children's first and most important teachers. Teachers need to know as much as possible about the parents' cultural values and styles of communicating with their children so that the necessary adjustments to the school culture and style of each teacher can be made. Even the ability to talk about different ways of thinking, talking, reading, and writing can be useful to students, parents, and teachers. For example, you might suggest to a parent, "At school, we are trying to get the children to be independent in their reading by giving them time to figure out unfamiliar words for themselves. We ask them to look for three sources of information: visual, grammatical, and meaningful. Of course, you want them to read perfectly and fluently. Giving them the correct pronunciation of words helps this. However, right now we are trying to get the children to be more independent. If you could help reinforce our teaching strategy for the next few months, your child will feel more comfortable and, I think, reach the goal we both share." Accept that what the parents value and think is important, and then help them understand how they can assist the instructional program.

As already mentioned, relationships between parents and schools vary tremendously. In some communities, parents feel too intimidated to join the school culture. They want teachers to do their jobs and will support this as best they can. In other communities, parents are very involved in the schools, serving on curriculum committees, working on standards development, and visiting classrooms regularly. They might want to know a great deal about how reading is taught and might have a wealth of experience themselves guiding their own children's literacy development. When this is the case, home-school letters can be more specific with explanations of research and instructional priorities. Creating videotapes and having Parents' Nights and programs that explain how literacy develops can help to build good communication in these situations. Dealing with the variations in parent knowledge and expectations is a concern of the whole school and should be a shared decision of the faculty and administration. A key in all situations is being open to, and interested in, the parents' perspectives and concerns.

Family Literacy

What does this phrase mean: "Parents are a child's first teachers"?

Meeting the Literacy Needs of All Children

An Urban Classroom

Farah Al Jabar's fourth-grade class is located in a low-income area of a major urban center. Her thirty-six students represent, in about equal numbers, four major ethnic groups: African American, Asian, Hispanic, and Anglo. Almost half entered kindergarten speaking another language or dialect of English. Although all are at least minimally proficient in English now, many have gaps in their oral language vocabularies and in the background knowledge that corresponds to that of the middle-class children for whom the school curriculum and textbooks are typically designed. According to the results of informal reading inventories that she administered in the fall, many are reading below grade level, and a few are reading markedly below grade level.

Today, one group of ten children, all reading at grade level, is beginning to read a novel by Spinelli (1990a) entitled *Maniac Magee*, which was awarded the prestigious Newbery Award. It is not a particularly difficult story, but many vocabulary words are new to the children. In addition, some children lack background knowledge about substantive issues that underlie the story.

Farah ensured that she was incorporating the elements of the four-block guided reading model she applies in her classroom: guided reading, writing, working with words, and self-selected reading. Before the children read, she leads them through several brief anticipatory reading activities that prepare them to read the story with good understanding. First, she says, "Let's read the title of the book and look at the illustration on the cover," demonstrating and modeling how she makes predictions about text she will read. She asks, "What predictions can you make about this book?" One child tries to sound out the word "maniac," saying "m-m-maniac—What does it mean?" Another child quickly responds, "It's a word for a crazy person, somebody out of control." Another notices the shoes on the cover and asks, "Do those shoes belong to a boy or a girl?" Farah says, "Let's find out." She reads the two-page foreword of the book aloud to the children. She then explains, "The main character is Jeffrey Magee, but they call him 'Maniac Magee.' He's a boy about your age. Now what do you think the story might be about?"

Farah has already prepared the beginning of a semantic map to introduce the term *dump*, which the children will encounter early in the story. She asks, "What do you know about this word?" The children share the information they already have, and Farah records it in appropriate categories on the graphic organizer.

She then has the children close their books with their finger in place at the first page of the first chapter, and she asks them a question that will guide their silent reading of that page, beginning the guided reading part of her lesson where they will build knowledge through reading. She asks, "How does Jeffrey's life suddenly change?" They listen to the question, then open their books and begin reading silently. (Jeffrey is orphaned when his parents are killed in an automobile accident. He lives with an aunt and uncle for a short time and then runs away to live in a dump.)

As they read, Farah circulates around the group, motivating them by touching shoulders, smiling, and offering encouraging comments. Some children ask for assistance with words that are unfamiliar, even after the anticipatory reading activities. She quickly provides help so they can maintain their comprehension. This activity also provides an opportunity for her to briefly circulate around the classroom and supervise the work of other children who are working independently as they wait for their own small-group lessons.

As the children finish reading the page and begin to raise their hands to respond to the question, Farah returns to her seat. She repeats the question and calls on a child who says, "He went to live with his aunt and uncle—they weren't too cool." Another adds, "His mom and dad were killed in a car accident." Yet another says, "He ran away." Other children add new information and share other points of view. Finally, Farah asks one student to read aloud the sentence that provides evidence for the answer that all the students finally agreed on. She then asks another comprehension-level question about the same page, following this procedure through the three pages of this first chapter of the story.

In a consolidation activity at the end of the lesson, Farah asks, "How did the story begin?" A child responds, "Jeffrey's parents were killed, and he went to live with his uncle and his aunt." She asks, "What happened next?" The children continue to retell the story up to that point in their own words. Farah then says, "Write a short paragraph, and predict what you think will happen in the next chapter of the story. While I teach the other group, please read your library books." She moves on to work with another small group of children that is reading from an anthology.

Farah has exhibited many behaviors that tell us she is an outstanding teacher, some of which relate to her strong instructional program. She uses teaching strategies that support or scaffold comprehension and that help children build confidence. In reading aloud, she provided a model both of fluent reading and of thinking about what she read, as revealed in her follow-up question. Farah gave attention to working with words in analyzing

Story Maps

a crucial word in the story, *dump*, whose meaning was a key to understanding the circumstances in which Maniac Magee was living. She provided explicit guidance that scaffolded comprehension by asking higher-order questions before the children read. She provided an application and extension activity: writing a short paragraph to predict what might happen in the next chapter. And, finally, she provided time for self-selected reading.

Equally important are aspects of her approach that motivate the children, that indicate her high expectations and affection for them, and that demonstrate her deep understanding of the cultures from which they come. Choosing appropriate literature for the children is an important part of her planning. The main character of *Maniac Magee* is a boy who has very positive interactions with African American children in the story. She has also provided a large-print version of the book from LRS Large Print Publications (Spinelli, 1990b) for a partially sighted student in the group. Farah's next literature choice for this group is *By the Lake of Sleeping Children: The Secret Life of the Mexican Border* (Urrea, 1996), about life in a dump in Tijuana, Mexico, which parallels and connects with the setting of *Maniac Magee*. She takes much care to ensure that all children in her class see themselves in many different roles in the literature she provides for them. She directs the major part of her small discretionary budget each year to the purchase of sets of trade books to supplement her basal reading program.

Valuing Diversity or Coping with Differences?

We can view the diversity in Farah's classroom, and in most American classrooms, from at least two perspectives. On the one hand, teachers can consider that associating with people who are different enriches everyone. On the other hand, because diversity means that differences between children are greater than just the ordinary individual differences found among homogeneous groups of children, some teachers perceive it as a problem. Different languages can make it difficult to meet needs, group students efficiently for instruction, and provide materials that are appropriate for all children. Cultural differences arise, making teaching a complex and demanding act. These are legitimate concerns, but they should be viewed as challenges instead of as problems. Teachers who view it as a challenge consider diversity as an asset to be valued for the benefit of the children—one that enriches the learning of all—the students and the teacher.

CULTURAL DIVERSITY, BACKGROUND KNOWLEDGE, AND LITERACY The pervasive culture in U.S. schools, according to Gollnick and Chinn (2008), is essentially "based on the knowledge and perspective of the West (Northern and Western Europe)." Many believe that this culture is apparent in textbooks and curricula and in the cadre of teachers that staff most schools. It characterizes what teachers expect students to know when they come to school, and it serves as the basis for teachers' assessment of student outcomes. It often characterizes how teachers reinforce children's behavior, both positively and negatively; how they ask children questions and accept their responses; how they correct children; how they do, or do not, make the classroom safe for children; and how they use gestures and time. Clearly, schools cannot adopt the culture of each and every child, but they can accept the culture of every child, accommodate that culture, and use its presence and teachers' knowledge of it to help teach all children. According to Fitzgerald (1995), teachers must make reading instruction congruent with the background culture that children bring to their lessons.

Tasks that can be performed with assistance from others are considered to be in a student's zone of proximal development. Watch the video and reflect on the variety of supports the teacher provides during this interactive science lesson.

THE ZONE OF PROXIMAL DEVELOPMENT The work of Vygotsky (1978) provides another view of social constructivism that underlies children's cognitive development, with particular applications to the teaching of reading and language. The learning community includes culture, language, and important adults who guide children in their learning.

Vygotsky's concept of the zone of proximal development is especially important. According to his view, certain tasks can be performed by a student independently; some tasks cannot be performed at all, even with help; and some fall within the "zone," which can be performed with help from others. Those *others* in the classroom are teachers, paraprofessionals, and parent volunteers, or more capable student peers in cooperative learning group settings. Many implications for the effective classroom emerge from these concepts:

- Teachers need to design instruction that is at an appropriate level for each child—not so difficult that they fail, not so simple that there is no gain, but at a level where, with scaffolding (i.e., a support system), they can learn. A one-size-fits-all approach is not appropriate.
- Learning activities need to be done in meaningful contexts, not in isolation.
- Children need to construct their own meaning with the help of the teacher and other adults and peers in the role of facilitators.
- Children need to see relationships between what they are learning and the communities in which they live.

CULTURALLY RESPONSIVE CLASSROOM COMMUNICATION Children's language develops in a sociocultural context. How children use language in their homes and communities also has important effects on their use of language in classrooms, especially when they are learning to read and write. Although language arts and reading curricula often reflect a linear assumption about all literacy development in all of its forms, ethnographers remind teachers that they must view how parents use language in rearing their children, the range of types of language use in the home, and the amount of exposure that children experience with respect to the diversity of languages, speakers of languages, and ways of using language outside of their homes (Heath, 1986). Culturally responsive teachers apply their knowledge of the many cultures in their classroom to the way they respond to children, both verbally and nonverbally.

Verbal Communication Providing feedback to students is a vital teacher activity. When feedback is given across cultures, there is always potential for misunderstanding. Scarcella (1990) provides several categories of feedback behavior:

- *Interpreting student feedback* (how they indicate that they are paying attention). Most Americans nod their heads to indicate that they are listening. Asian students often nod to indicate that they are listening, but this does not necessarily indicate understanding.
- *Complimenting and criticizing* (how this is interpreted from both perspectives). Asian students might reject too many compliments as being insincere, whereas Hispanic students usually welcome praise.
- *Teacher correction of student errors* (how students view the way the teacher corrects errors). Students from some cultures want to be corrected and are concerned at a lack of correction. In other cultures, correction can be a humiliation. It is important for the teacher to consider how to treat this issue with each student in the classroom.
- *Student requests for clarification* (how, or if, students ask for help and how teachers interpret these requests). Teachers should carefully monitor the comprehension of their students, checking for understanding and watching for nonverbal behavior that might indicate a question that has not been expressed.
- *Spotlighting, or calling attention to a student's behavior in front of others.* Many children do not appreciate having attention called to them, especially from across the room. Teachers might be more effective if they walk over to students and softly give instructions, especially if student misbehavior is involved or even praise for older students. The teacher can avoid turning a small problem of inattention into a major problem of defiance.
- *Questioning and answering* (the purpose of questions). Asking questions is an important teacher instructional behavior. American teachers tend to ask many questions for the purpose of motivating critical thinking on the part of the students. But Heath (1983) has found that African American children are often confused by why teachers

ask questions when the teachers already know the answers. She recommends that these children be asked questions of the type they are asked at home, such as "What's that like?" or "What's happening?" To promote higher-order thinking, teachers often ask for opinions about what a character did in a story or how an author expressed an idea. Children from some cultures are uncomfortable in offering opinions; they can gain experience and confidence in acquiring this ability in small-group work before they express themselves in front of the entire class.

- *Pausing* (wait-time). Teachers tend to provide insufficient wait-time for students. They need to allow students time to think about their responses before going on to another student or accepting a response from students who always seem to know the correct answer before anyone else. According to Rowe (1974), teachers usually wait slightly more than one second. She found that when children were provided with at least three seconds of undisturbed wait-time, they responded more completely and correctly, the number of nonresponses decreased, and the number of volunteered responses increased.

Nonverbal Communication   Communication is often thought of only as a verbal process, but the important impact of nonverbal communication is considerable, especially when teachers work with children from many different cultures. For example, a frequent type of interaction between teacher and child is the teacher's need to correct the inappropriate behavior of a child. To show respect, an Anglo child usually looks in the teacher's eyes when being corrected. The same child shows defiance by looking at the floor instead of looking the teacher in the face. Conversely, a Hispanic child often shows respect to the teacher by looking at the floor, whereas defiance is shown by looking the teacher in the eyes. What message does the teacher send by saying to the Hispanic child, "Look me in the eye when I talk to you"? In this case, the teacher might be asking the student to demonstrate defiance. This is only one of many examples of the potential for cross-cultural misunderstandings between teacher and child, even when both are behaving appropriately for their own cultures.

Nonverbal communication is a form of paralanguage, which includes many aspects of behavior that teachers should understand. These behaviors are the clues that tell us someone is from another culture, and sometimes even what country they are from, although we might not be able to hear them speaking. You cannot be familiar with all culturally based nonverbal behaviors in your diverse classroom, but you can begin to reflect about the reactions of children to your nonverbal behaviors and about your own reactions to puzzling nonverbal behaviors of students. When student reactions to a teacher's behavior are counterintuitive, there is often a cultural explanation.

As children's experiences with life in the United States expand, they also begin to learn the appropriate nonverbal behaviors of the new language and culture they are assimilating. When they are successful, they are able to function comfortably in two cultures, making them bicultural. Teachers need to be sensitive to children as they go about the complicated task of becoming bicultural.

Linguistic Diversity: Today's Classroom Demographics

Who are the English language learners? Where are they? Everywhere! The 2010 census revealed a growing diversity in American classrooms in almost all parts of the country. Perhaps the most important aspect of this change is the number of children classified as English language learners, children who arrive in American classrooms with no English or insufficient English for learning to read and write in English. When teachers think of English language learners, they likely think of Hispanic children; indeed, Hispanics make up the largest population of English language learners. According to the 2010 U.S. census, the Hispanic population of the United States has risen from 12.5 percent to 16.3 percent of the total population (U.S. Census Bureau, 2011).

Data from the National Clearinghouse for English Language Acquisition and Language Instruction Educational Programs (NCELA, 2011) indicate that the most dramatic difference in the growth of Hispanic populations in the 2010 census was the continuing dissemination to smaller population centers. In 2008–2009, more than 10 percent of K–12 school populations were English language learners in Alaska, Oregon, California, Nevada, Arizona, Colorado, New Mexico, Texas, Illinois, Florida, and Puerto Rico. In Minnesota, Arkansas, Michigan, North and South Carolina, New York, Rhode Island, Massachusetts, Connecticut, Washington, Idaho, Utah, Kansas, Nebraska, and Oklahoma, the proportion ranged from 5 percent to 10 percent. The growth in numbers of English language learners in Colorado, Arkansas, Illinois, Kentucky, Mississippi, Georgia, and North and South Carolina was over 200 percent from 1997–1998 to 2008–2009. English language learners are not a monolithic population. Some are very proficient in speaking and understanding their mother tongue, and some are literate in that language. Some became literate in their home countries; others do so in programs of bilingual education here in the United States. As a result of living in refugee camps, some upper elementary and adolescent children arrive in this country with little or no school experience at all. Some English language learners are migrant children from rural areas without educational opportunities, and others were working and contributing to the family income. Some English language learners have limited proficiency even in their mother tongue, just as some native English speakers are limited in their English proficiency. As teachers consider the challenges today's students represent, they also must think in terms of possible solutions.

BILINGUAL EDUCATION Perhaps the most sweeping policy change to affect the education of English language learners in recent years was the 1974 *Lau v. Nichols* decision of the U.S. Supreme Court, which ruled that equal education did not result from providing exactly the same education to all children (J. Crawford, 1989; *Lau v. Nichols*, 1974). This decision required that school districts take positive steps to overcome the educational barriers experienced by students who did not speak English. Soon afterward, the Elementary and Secondary Education Act was amended with Title VII to make limited English proficient students eligible for federal funds and to permit their enrollment in bilingual education programs.

A 1981 court decision (*Casteñeda v. Pickard*, 1981) established three criteria for determining how programs of bilingual education were to be held accountable for meeting requirements of the Equal Education Opportunity Act of 1974. The criteria included the following:

- The program must be based on sound educational theory.
- The program must be effectively implemented with adequate resources for personnel, instructional materials, and space.
- Following a trial period, the program must be shown to be effective in overcoming language handicaps.

Although the *Lau v. Nichols* decision did not mandate bilingual education as a remedy, school districts found it to be one of the few ways to ensure that English language learners had equal access to education, that is, education in their mother tongue while they were learning English. The No Child Left Behind Act of 2001 replaced the earlier Elementary and Secondary Education Act (ESEA) Title VII, which formerly funded programs of instruction for bilingual children and was rescinded (García, 2005). The new law, Title III, continues to provide resources for what are called *English language learners*. Annual assessments of English-language proficiency are mandated, as well as requirements that these children meet state academic content and student achievement standards in English (Office of English Language Acquisition [OELA], 2004). The term *bilingual* does not appear in the new law, which now stresses skills in English only. There is no federal interest in the development of academic bilingual education programs for these children.

In late 2006, the Department of Education released regulations concerning English language learners (Federal Register, 2006) that allow school districts to delay the testing in reading of English language learners who have been in the United States for less than a year. Unfortunately, no evidence indicates that these children can learn English in one year, so the effect is minimal.

ENGLISH LANGUAGE LEARNERS AND LITERACY   Bilingual education, however, is a subject of much controversy. In recent years, initiatives in a number of states, including California, Arizona, and Massachusetts, have discouraged most bilingual education. They require instead a one-year period of immersion instruction in English as a second language, although the efficacy of this approach is not supported in the literature. In fact, abundant evidence indicates that children need two to five years of instruction in English as a second language before they are ready to learn to read in English (Thomas & Collier, 1997). An analysis of test scores from the 2002 California Stanford 9 test scores reported by the influential League of United Latin American Citizens (LULAC) (O'Leary, 2002) suggested that English language learners were not developing English fluency and that many were falling further behind in academic subjects. O'Leary reported that four years after the passage of California's Unz English Initiative, Proposition 227, more than a million limited-English immigrant students in second through eleventh grades in California still had not been mainstreamed in English-only classes, an indication of the failure of the policy. According to Slavin and Cheung (2004), bilingual programs don't harm the progress of English language learners in reading, and they usually improve it. Zehr (2008) concluded that there was no difference between bilingual education programs and immersion English programs in the reading achievement of English language learners at the fourth-grade level. In his own research, Jepsen (2009, 2010) found that by grades 3 to 5, there were no differences in the reading achievement of children in bilingual education programs and other programs (immersion). In a five-year study, Slavin, Madden, Calderón, Chamberlain, and Hennessy

Because of the changing demographic of the U.S. population, strategies for meeting the needs of non-English-speaking students have become a focal point of discussion in many communities.

(2010) found that children in traditional bilingual education learned to read well in Spanish and that they learned to read in English as well in transitional bilingual education as they did in structured English immersion

Goodman (1986) reminds us that bilingual children are not disadvantaged in some academic way. They are disadvantaged only if their linguistic strengths are not appreciated and if schools fail to build on their strengths. The International Reading Association (IRA) has recognized the efficacy of teaching children to read in the mother tongue while they learn to understand and speak English and before they begin learning to read in their second language, English. The IRA's resolution of support includes three major elements: (1) initial literacy instruction should be provided in the child's native language whenever possible; (2) although initial literacy instruction in a second language can be successful, there is a higher risk of reading problems than beginning with a child's first language; and (3) instructional decisions should support the professional judgment of the teachers and administrators who are responsible for teaching students whose first language is not English and who oppose any restrictive federal, state, or local initiatives (International Reading Association, 2001).

Dialects of English and Literacy

English language learners, whose mother tongue is not English and whose English proficiency is limited, are not the only children whose reading instruction is affected by linguistic factors. African American Vernacular English is a dialect of English that is spoken by many urban African American children in the United States. There are other dialects, including southern regional dialect, a mostly rural dialect of both Anglo and African American children.

AFRICAN AMERICAN VERNACULAR ENGLISH   Also known as *black dialect* and *ebonics*, African American Vernacular English is the dialect of the English language that is probably most frequently encountered in American classrooms. According to Labov (1970, 1972), African American Vernacular English is as logical and consistent as standard English, it can be reproduced, and it makes sense. It is merely different from standard English. A policy statement of the TESOL (Teachers of English to Speakers of Other Languages) (1997) board of directors stipulates that African American Vernacular English has been demonstrated in research to be a rule-governed linguistic system that has its own lexical, phonological, syntactic, and discourse patterns and that it therefore deserves pedagogical recognition. It is not a substandard dialect of English, and it is not poor English. It is a dialect that is widely understood and spoken among many inner-city African Americans.

There are many phonological and syntactical differences between African American Vernacular English and Standard American English (Rickford, 1999). Some of those identified by Johnson and Simons (1974) are presented in Table 2.2.

These characteristics of African American Vernacular English appear so consistently that they occasionally appear in the oral reading of children who superimpose their dialect over the words written on the page (Johnson & Simons, 1974). Teachers must consider whether there is a negative effect on reading comprehension or only on oral reading accuracy because both are possible, even in a single reading episode by an individual child.

ADDING STANDARD AMERICAN ENGLISH   Teachers demonstrate that they value the language of children when they accept the way the children communicate with each other and with members of their families and communities. In classrooms, however, teachers also need to help students add a second dialect of English: standard American English, a dialect that supports the children's continuing academic learning and offers access to higher education and desirable employment opportunities. The resulting bidialectical children resemble bilingual children in that they can readily switch back and forth between dialects according to the educational or social situation in which they find themselves. Part of the process of being bidialectical is knowing when and where to use each dialect.

Table 2.2   Some Differences Between Standard American English and African American Vernacular English

LINGUISTIC FEATURE	STANDARD AMERICAN ENGLISH	AFRICAN AMERICAN VERNACULAR ENGLISH
Initial and final sounds of /th/ (modified)	that, these	dat, dese
	both, breathe	bof, breave
Medial /v/ (modified)	seven	seben
Medial or final /r/, /l/ (deleted)	door	doe
	help	hep
Consonant clusters (deleted)	desk	des
	told	tol
Past tense marker	I talked to him.	I talk to him.
Copula deleted (the copula is a form of the verb "to be")	She is tall.	She tall.
Use of verb *be* (habitual)	Julie reads every day.	Julie be reading.
Subject-verb agreement	We were there.	We was there.
Double negative	Henry doesn't have a football.	Henry don't have no football.
Possessive (deleted)	The girl's dress	The girl dress
Question (reversal of subject and verb)	What is that?	What that is?

Source: Based on Johnson and Simons (1974).

In schools where an ESL program is already in place for English language learners, many ESL activities will be of value for children whose home and community language environment is African American Vernacular English. Teachers can use many intermediate and advanced ESL instructional strategies to add standard American English to the children's repertoire. The children will not require instruction at the basic stages of the natural approach for English language learners (described in Chapter 15), but participation in activities at the third stage of the natural approach will be helpful because they focus on communication, not on grammar. In addition, the activities described for "sheltered English" in Chapter 15 will support and enhance the children's development of background knowledge and vocabulary needed for effective reading comprehension. In schools where such a program is not in place because there are no English language learners, an oral language development program should be provided to help children acquire standard American English in much the same way that English language learners acquire English. This is not an ESL program, but rather a program of oral language development.

Rickford and Rickford (1995) suggest a very direct approach, beginning with an agreement among students that standard American English is appropriate for classroom interaction and writing. With that understanding, teachers should provide focused activities based on language needs that children demonstrate. Delpit (1990) suggests that these include dialect contrast activities in which students and teachers agree that learning standard American English is a goal; this would probably take place in the upper elementary grades and beyond. These dialect contrasts can be incorporated into dialogue journals, class logs, and student portfolios.

LITERACY ISSUES FOR AFRICAN AMERICAN CHILDREN The issue of mother tongue instruction has important implications for children who speak African American Vernacular English. If learning to read in Spanish while learning to speak English is the most effective program for Spanish-speaking children, then it could follow that speakers of African American Vernacular English should learn to read from materials written in that dialect while they are acquiring standard American English as a second dialect (Simpkins, Holt, & Simpkins, 1974). Indeed, some educators have advocated for this approach. There are, however, some significant barriers:

- There is not broad acceptance in the African American community for the use of African American Vernacular English as a language of instruction.
- Although some reading instructional materials have been written in African American Vernacular English through the years, they have not been broadly or systematically used.
- Limited research evidence at present supports the use of reading materials written in African American Vernacular English (Simpkins et al., 1974).
- There is a sense among some African Americans and others that the use of African American Vernacular English might be a tool for minimizing opportunities for success among African American children (Williams, 1991).

Given the highly controversial nature of the issue, there are several ways in which teachers can make effective and positive use of the presence of African American Vernacular English—and other dialects of English—in American classrooms:

- Value and acknowledge positively the communication efforts of children who use African American Vernacular English in the classroom.
- Avoid correcting pronunciation and syntactical structures from African American Vernacular English and other dialects of English used by children in their ordinary classroom discourse; such attempts betray a negative valuing of the way the children speak and, by implication, of the children themselves and of their family members and communities.

- Demonstrate valuing of the dialect by accepting it in the dictations of children in key vocabulary and language experience approach activities.
- In addition to using children's literature in which dialogue is in standard American English for read-aloud activities, incorporate children's literature that includes dialogue in African American Vernacular English and other dialects spoken by children in the classroom (Brooks, 2005, 2006; Sanacore, 2004).
- In activities that are designed to help children acquire standard American English, avoid references to the standard dialect as the "correct" or "better" way to speak.
- Use storytelling (Sanacore, 2004) and traditional cultural literary structures of the African American community, such as the praise song and the praise poem (Johnson-Coleman, 2001), and trickster tales, which are also a part of the Native American oral tradition. An Internet search at <www.google.com> will yield dozens of praise song, praise poem, and trickster tale resources.
- Ensure that phonological, morphological, lexical, and syntactical features of African American Vernacular English and other dialects of English are not used to penalize children in assessment activities, especially those that are not related to the purpose of the assessment (see Chapter 11).

Delpit (1990, 2008) offers suggestions for teachers to consider in educating children of color who are too often failed by our schools. She recommends that teachers do the following:

- Teach these children more, not less.
- Provide critical thinking experiences for them (also Sanacore, 2004).
- Challenge the racist view some individuals hold that these children are incompetent.
- Recognize and build on the children's strengths.
- Use metaphors, analogies, and experiences that are familiar to the children to connect them to school knowledge.
- Ensure that the children feel cared for, as in a family (also Sanacore, 2004).
- Identify the children's needs and meet them with a variety of strategies.
- Honor and respect the culture the children bring to school (also Ladson-Billings, 2009).
- Connect the children to their community, something that is greater than themselves (also Ladson-Billings, 2009).

Several best practices for teaching African American children are recommended by Edwards, McMillon, and Turner (2010):

- Provide texts to read that connect student interests and cultural contexts, especially for male students
- Use music to tell their stories, including hip-hop
- Increase the use of informational text
- Use narratives that touch on sensitive topics

Differentiating Instruction for At-Risk and Struggling Readers

Another aspect of diversity in American classrooms is a more generic category that incorporates children from all groups that are at risk of not learning to read. Through the years since the Coleman Report (Coleman et al., 1966), many terms have been used to describe students whose school achievement is below expectation, including *at-risk, disadvantaged, low-income,* and others. The constellation of factors often associated with at-risk students

Phonics and Phonological Awareness

Why do teachers need to take care that pronunciation differences among children are not penalized in assessment activities?

Struggling Reader

What are some of the factors associated with children who struggle learning to read?

includes the following: low income; inner city or rural; ethnic and/or language minority; non-English speaking; nontraditional family structure, including frequent absence of father; and high rate of school dropout.

Many students who exhibit the characteristics just listed have satisfactory or above-average achievement in school, and some students who exhibit none of the characteristics experience failure in school. But it is fair to say that these factors are strongly associated with low school achievement.

As a result of the Coleman Report (Coleman et al., 1966), a variety of federally funded efforts were initiated to alleviate the effects of these factors on low school achievement, especially in reading. These included Head Start, Title I and Title VII of the Elementary and Secondary Education Act (ESEA), and the Reading First and Early Reading First Programs. The most recent of these federally funded programs is the five-year Striving Readers Program, which sponsored eight research projects to determine the most effective ways of lowering the numbers of struggling middle and secondary readers.

The rapidly increasing influx of English language learners and other so-called disadvantaged students in U.S. schools provides a greater challenge than ever before to teachers whose charge is to promote the equitable access of all students to high-quality instruction in reading and writing. These students have generally been placed in compensatory or remedial programs, where they are expected to learn to read and write by acquiring isolated skills through interaction with incomplete fragments of language. Rarely do they emerge successfully from these programs into the mainstream; instead, frequently they leave the programs only when they leave school—all too often as early leavers or dropouts (A. N. Crawford, 1993).

Teach It!

Refer to the Teach It! appendix at the end of the book for further activities you can use to reinforce concepts discussed in this chapter.

Incorporating Authentic Children's Literature

The language-experience approach (LEA) to reading is a powerful tool for addressing culture and beginning reading that is based on the oral language of children. The approach centers on language as the vehicle for communicating thoughts and ideas. This Teach It! explores the approach with a lesson that incorporates authentic children's literature.

The first step is for the teacher to conduct a read-aloud of a piece of children's literature that is culturally appropriate—in this case, for a group of African American first graders—and that is also ideal as a stimulus for a language experience dictation. The book in this example is Patricia McKissack's *Ma Dear's Aprons* (1997), about a little boy living with his mother in a single-parent situation. In the story, David Earl's mother has a different apron for each day of the week, and David knows which day of the week it is by observing the apron his mother is wearing. Although there are seven days and seven aprons, the teacher might decide to read only up through the first three days and aprons. During the read-aloud, share the wonderful illustrations by Floyd Cooper, asking questions about the activities of the three days and the aprons that Ma Dear wears.

Then have the children dictate their brief version of the story. They might come up with something similar to the example seen in the figure. Accept the dictations of the children as stated, regardless of any cultural affectations.

In this collaborative chart story strategy, children negotiate with each other about what they want to dictate on the chart. Some children might

suggest changes that result in a dictation reflecting more Standard American English than the original version. The example shows two past tense verbs, "wash" and "iron," that were written as dictated by the children because no child suggested a change. The word "next" was pronounced as "nex"; the teacher should spell it correctly according to best practice in the language experience approach. The children should have many opportunities to read the text in a shared reading mode as the dictation is recorded and after the children's rendition of the story is completed.

On Monday, Ma Dear put on the blue apron.
She wash the clothes.

The next day she wore a yellow apron.
She iron the clothes on Tuesday.

David likes the green apron on Wednesday.
It had a treasure pocket.
There was candy in it.

COGNITIVE, AFFECTIVE, AND PSYCHOMOTOR FACTORS   Cultural and linguistic diversity are major factors for teachers to consider in planning reading instruction for children. But cognitive, affective, and psychomotor aspects of diversity also have an effect on reading.

The increasing diversity of our classrooms seems to bring with it an increase in the numbers of children who are struggling to read. Duffy-Hester (1999) examined several model reading programs for such children and found common guiding principles that should serve teachers well in working with troubled readers. Among these guiding principles are the following:

- Reading programs should be balanced, drawing on more than a single theoretical perspective. A one-size-fits-all approach to reading instruction inevitably seems to miss meeting the needs of some children. A balanced program touches on all of the learning modalities that diverse groups of children bring to the classroom.
- There should be a well-supported role for every element in a balanced reading program. Several currently popular direct instruction reading programs, for example, make heavy use of decodable text, fragments of unconnected text in which the students are to practice word recognition elements they have been studying. Yet little research supports the use of such text, whereas abundant research supports the use of connected text, especially in the promotion of reading comprehension (Allington, 1997).
- Word recognition, comprehension, and vocabulary development should be taught in the context of authentic reading and writing activities, not in isolation.
- Teacher read-aloud activities serve to build background knowledge and vocabulary, preparing children to understand their own reading of the text later.
- Authentic assessment provides valuable information that teachers can use to inform their instruction. Some assessment does not provide this type of information and takes up valuable time that children could use to read and write. We are reminded of a traditional dictum about assessment: "You don't fatten a pig by weighing it."
- Teachers should use their professional preparation to make instructional decisions about which reading programs they use.
- Staff development activities should provide time for reflection and opportunities to share experiences about best practices.
- The learner-centered goals and strategies that are most effective for troubled readers will serve other children well, too.

Other factors can affect the plight of troubled readers. Allington (2001) offers several research-based accommodations that relate to the organization of the school. Class size is an important factor, with research demonstrating that achievement is higher when classes are smaller, especially with children from low-income families (Achilles, 1999). Allington recommends a class size of twenty. Access to appropriate instructional materials is also important. In agreement with Duffy-Hester, he feels that programs should be designed to fit children; we should not force children to fit into programs. He recommends that no more than 20 to 30 percent of instructional time be devoted to single-source materials, that is, materials that all children in the classroom use in common. A third factor is that of honoring instructional time. No interruptions of the period for teaching reading should occur, not even public address announcements from the principal's office.

Allington then turns his attention to the question of access to intensive, expert instruction. He suggests that one-on-one tutoring is the most intensive type of instruction, but that real small-group instruction (four to seven students) is much more effective than traditional large-group or whole-class instruction. He further observes that pullout remedial reading programs, such as those underwritten by federal funds, frequently offer instruction in periods that are too short, but whose course is extended over too long a time span. He recommends offering a semester of very frequent and intensive support instead of a year of less intensive support. Finally, Allington suggests expanding instruction time for troubled readers. This can be accomplished by adding a second daily lesson, providing extended-day reading instruction through after-school programs, and offering summer school reading support to minimize summer reading loss.

INCLUSION IN GENERAL EDUCATION CLASSROOMS   Federal law calls for inclusion for many children identified for special education services; many are now placed in general education classrooms, although sometimes for only part of the school day. They are educated, to the maximum extent possible, in the same setting as their classmates without disabilities. This means that general education classroom teachers must address the needs of some children who have intellectual disabilities, or are physically disabled, or hearing impaired, emotionally disturbed, or from other special needs categories.

Under provisions of the law, students are identified as requiring assessment if they display any of the following specific conditions: intellectual disabilities; a hearing impairment, including deafness; a speech or language impairment; a visual impairment, including blindness; a serious emotional disturbance; an orthopedic impairment; autism; traumatic brain injury; a specific learning disability; deaf-blindness; or multiple disabilities. These children's needs must be assessed, and an Individual Education Plan (IEP) must be developed for each student (Individuals with Disabilities Education Act, 1997). The plan must include the following elements:

- Current levels of educational performance
- Annual goals and short-term objectives
- Need for special education and related services
- Explanation if the child cannot be mainstreamed in the general education classroom
- Description and schedule of special education services provided
- Description of transition services provided
- Assessment of student progress, including needed accommodations

The Individuals with Disabilities Education Improvement Act of 2004 (IDEA) is carefully aligned with provisions of NCLB (NEA, 2004). Special education teachers are required to be "highly qualified"; students with disabilities are required to be assessed annually in NCLB-required assessments, with some accommodations; and students must meet the same state standards as all other students, including English language learners, with some exceptions for students with severe cognitive disability. Needless to say, these provisions in the law are the subject of much discussion in all school districts as they attempt to meet these new requirements.

It is not only the physical needs of these students that should be addressed in inclusion efforts, but also the content of the curriculum. If students of color or girls need to see themselves in the literature they read, then so should students with disabilities. According to Landrum (2001), this benefits not only those students, but also students without disabilities, who need to learn about and accept differences. Landrum has developed a set of criteria for the evaluation of novels that feature characters with disabilities. Among her criteria are the following:

- *Plot:* Story events are realistic, not contrived; characters with disabilities are active participants.
- *Character development:* Characters with disabilities are presented as strong and independent, not passive and dependent; the focus is on what they can do, not on what they cannot do.
- *Tone:* The text avoids using such terms as *retarded, handicapped, and crippled.*

Struggling Reader

How is RTI different from previous federal efforts to assist struggling readers?

Response to Intervention (RTI) and Struggling Readers

For many years, it has been common practice to delay intervention in addressing struggling readers' problems until there was a two-year discrepancy between their measured and expected reading achievement. A child who shows signs of being a struggling reader in kindergarten, for example, would not receive any help until second grade. Vaughn and Fuchs (2003) describe this interval as "waiting to fail." Juel (1988) found that students who failed to learn to read before the end of the first grade tended to be unsuccessful in reading throughout the elementary grades, indicating that waiting for two years virtually ensures that the child will fail in reading.

Response to Intervention (RTI) is a set of regulations under the Individuals with Disabilities Education Improvement Act of 2004 (IDEIA) that provides new procedures for identifying and teaching children with learning disabilities. RTI constitutes a welcome change from the previous discrepancy model, permitting intervention based on identification of a struggling reader's needs as soon as a problem is recognized.

RTI programs generally consist of three components:

- Universal screening for the early identification of students at risk of struggling in reading
- Provision of tiers of instruction ranging from the regular classroom program to intensive intervention, sometimes in special education
- Continuous monitoring of student progress

RTI refers to recent changes in the application of special education laws, the Individuals with Disabilities Acts of 1997 and 2004 (IDEA, IDEIA). RTI refines IDEA with an assessment of the effectiveness of a scientific, research-based intervention in improving an identified child's academic performance, assuming that a continuing problem is not related to a visual, hearing, or motor disability, intellectual disability, emotional disturbance, cultural factors, economic disadvantage, or limited English proficiency.

Eight areas of low achievement are used as the basis for identifying specific learning disabilities, of which six are in the language arts: oral expression, listening comprehension, written expression, basic reading skill, reading fluency skills, and reading comprehension (International Reading Association, 2009).

K–3 students are screened in accordance with Reading First. Literacy screening instruments and procedures are used to determine if they are at risk of not meeting prescribed benchmarks. If students do not meet benchmarks after scientifically valid interventions are applied, the RTI models provide for interventions in small groups to provide needed assistance. The children's progress is monitored using measures that are targeted at skills the children need to attain. If progress is not noted, individualized interventions are provided. If these are not effective, then the child's case is reviewed by a team of professionals to determine if he or she is eligible for special education. According to Mesmer and Mesmer (2008/2009), the RTI process is a useful alternative to a discrepancy model.

An IQ measure is no longer used to assess the discrepancy between expected and actual learning outcomes. In any case, IQ tests are not useful with children whose English is limited (Gillet, Temple, Temple, & Crawford, 2012).

NO CHILD LEFT BEHIND (NCLB) AND READING FIRST   The interaction between IDEA and the successive effects of NCLB and Reading First created additional difficulties for the struggling reader. Despite assurances to the contrary, NCLB evolved as a one-size-fits-all approach to instruction. All children were typically provided instruction from the same materials using the same methodology and at the same level. RTI provides increased flexibility so that children receive appropriate reading instruction.

Characteristics of RTI: What It Is, What It Isn't

Educators in general and reading educators in particular have long suffered under highly prescriptive government mandates such as NCLB and Reading First. RTI provides considerable discretion to schools and school districts in designing their programs to meet the needs of students with reading difficulties.

RTI is not based on the earlier model that required a discrepancy between the student's IQ and his or her level of achievement (Johnston, 2010). Rather, it is designed to identify learning disabilities and ensure that identified students receive appropriate instruction. RTI permits the early identification of reading difficulties, resulting in early intervention instead of waiting for students to fail. It also reduces the over-identification of English language learners and other diverse groups of students. According to Fuchs and Fuchs (2009), the goal of RTI is not to prevent special education, but rather to identify those children who have disabilities and to avoid the negative consequences of children exiting school without academic competence.

The Multi-Tiered Structure of RTI

RTI programs are organized around a multi-tier system that is designed to prevent reading failure. It usually consists of three tiers, although this structure is not mandated by government regulation. Within this three-tier structure, Tier One is the general education or regular classroom instructional program, including the core curriculum. Tier Two provides additional intervention that is designed to address needs identified through assessment; it usually consists of small-group tutoring. Tier Three consists of intensive intervention that is often individualized or provided in small groups, sometimes by a special education teacher, sometimes by a reading specialist, and sometimes by a team (see Figure 2.2).

TIER ONE: GENERAL EDUCATION PROGRAM   Tier One consists of the general education program that is usually conducted by a well-trained classroom teacher in the regular classroom. According to Taylor (2008), effective reading instruction in grades K–5 includes phonemic awareness and phonics instruction, fluency instruction, vocabulary instruction, and comprehension instruction. Fuchs and Fuchs (2008) describe a benchmark assessment mode within Tier One. A part of the school population that may be at risk for reading failure is identified with a brief screening measure. A cut score for the measure is established, and children scoring below the cut score are identified as at risk. Some districts establish the cut score at about 20 percent of students, who will have further diagnosis. Tier One includes all students.

TIER TWO: SMALL GROUP INTERVENTION   The purpose of Tier Two is to meet the needs of students who have not made satisfactory progress with supplemental intervention through targeted support in Tier One. A common approach in Tier Two is to provide tutoring in small groups using an evidence-based approach. The focus is on accelerating reading growth, allowing students to catch up. Progress monitoring that shows growth leads to students being returned to the general program in Tier One (Fuchs & Fuchs, 2008). Most students are in Tier Two for a six- to eight-week period of progress monitoring to clarify the identification process.

TIER THREE: INTENSIVE INTERVENTION   Students who make unsatisfactory progress in Tier Two are referred to Tier Three, which involves intensive intervention services,

Figure 2.2 RTI Tiers

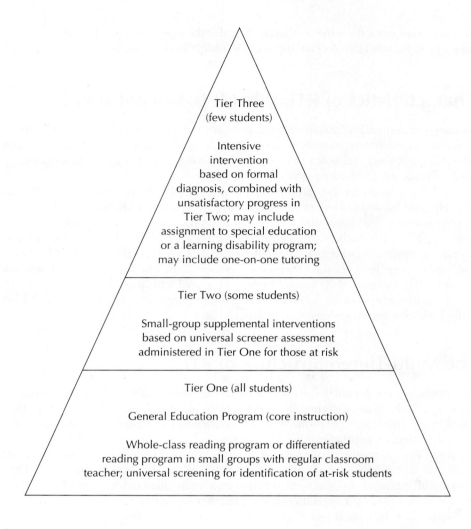

Tier Three
(few students)

Intensive
intervention
based on formal
diagnosis, combined with
unsatisfactory progress in
Tier Two; may include
assignment to special education
or a learning disability program;
may include one-on-one tutoring

Tier Two (some students)

Small-group supplemental interventions
based on universal screener assessment
administered in Tier One for those at risk

Tier One (all students)

General Education Program (core instruction)

Whole-class reading program or differentiated
reading program in small groups with regular classroom
teacher; universal screening for identification of at-risk students

often provided by special education resources. Longer individualized or small-group sessions are provided, including validated treatment protocols (Fuchs & Fuchs, 2008). Progress monitoring and diagnostic assessment continue in Tier Three, with the goal of returning successful students to Tier Two or Tier One. Many fewer students are in Tier Three programs than in Tiers One and Two.

The Role of Assessment in RTI

Assessment is a major part of RTI. It does not include a high-stakes assessment test to inform school districts about how they are doing in their literacy program, but it is instead designed to help teachers meet the needs of individual students at risk of failure in literacy. RTI assessment is conducted in several different modes at different stages and for different purposes, including screening, diagnostics, formative progress monitoring, benchmark progress monitoring, and summative outcome assessment (Wixson & Valencia, 2011). Major categories of assessment include curriculum-based assessment, diagnostic assessment, and progress monitoring.

CURRICULUM-BASED MEASUREMENT (CBM) OR BENCHMARK ASSESSMENT   CBM and benchmark assessment are often the terms used for the universal screening that takes place in the Tier One general education program. Assessments such as PALS or DIBELS are frequently used. In past approaches to assessment, only data for struggling students were collected and analyzed. In RTI, data are collected for all students in Tier One (Tileston, 2011).

DIAGNOSTIC ASSESSMENT   A very thorough diagnostic assessment is used with students who fail to reach the cut score in Tier One assessment. This diagnostic assessment is individualized according to the apparent needs of each student. According to Lipson, Chomsky-Higgins, and Kanfer (2011), it should include the following areas: phonological awareness, letter identification, sight vocabulary, fluency, decoding, vocabulary, comprehension, motivation, stamina, writing about reading, and text level, all of which can lead to effective differentiated instruction.

PROGRESS MONITORING   Progress monitoring is an important component of RTI (Moore & Whitfield, 2009). It includes regular and systematic assessment of the progress of students in all tiers.

Evidence-Based Literacy Programs

Many evidence-based literacy curriculum packages or validated treatment protocols are in common use as interventions to meet instructional needs in Tier Two and Tier Three RTI programs. The following are examples of programs frequently used: Peer-Assisted Literacy Strategies (PALS) Series; Read Naturally; and Reading Recovery. Evidence-based strategies also meet criteria for RTI. They are widely used strategies for specific purposes that have a strong research base, but they should not be used as scripted one-size-fits-all programs. As Johnston (2010) reminds us, an intervention effective for most children may not be effective for all.

Allington and Walmsley (1995, 2007) provide important principles that serve to strengthen programs of intervention for identified struggling readers:

- All staff, classroom teachers, special education teachers, and specialists are responsible for the education of all students, with emphasis on the reading expertise of the classroom teacher.
- All children should be provided with the same literacy experiences, materials, and expectations. Poor readers are too often placed in programs that limit access to literacy because their primary focus is on low-level skill development, oral reading, and word recognition—a fragmented program.
- All children should be educated with their peers, an approach characterized by inclusion, not segregation into special classes.
- The literacy curriculum for identified students and struggling readers should contain all of the elements that successful readers are experiencing in their lessons, including silent reading, reading full-length material, and reading for a variety of purposes, including pleasure. Joint planning between general education classroom teachers and those who provide instructional support outside the general education classroom is needed.
- Expert teachers provide high-quality reading instruction. These are usually general education classroom teachers with excellent preparation in the teaching of reading and writing.
- Instructional support programs for struggling readers should function as integrated wholes, rather than as a series of separately funded programs that address different issues: a single, unified instructional support program that involves all of the players in meeting children's literacy needs in an integration of remedial and, when needed, special education services.

Allington (2008) adds other important elements:

- Texts used must be matched to students' reading levels.
- Reading activity must be dramatically expanded—that is, actual reading, rather than studying about reading.
- Interventions must be coordinated with the curriculum in the classroom.
- Meaning and metacognition should be the focus of instruction.
- Needed expert teachers do not include paraprofessionals who use workbooks and low-level worksheets, a common intervention for struggling readers.

Members of the RTI Team and Their Roles

The successful implementation of RTI requires a collaborative team effort. It includes classroom teachers, reading specialists/coaches, special education teachers, school psychologists, building principals, district level administrators, and parents. There must be mutual respect among team members for the different kinds of expertise they bring to the RTI process. RTI provides a newly recognized important role for classroom teachers in that they frequently have more academic preparation and literacy teaching experience than other team members, even though they may not have had a great deal of practice with the processes of assessment and planning for students with reading disabilities.

Parents have a strong role in RTI when they are notified about their children's problems, as they must provide informed consent before any diagnostic assessment or intervention may take place (Fuchs & Mellard, 2007). Parents always have the right to request a comprehensive evaluation of their child.

RTI in Middle Schools

Gelzheiser, Scanlon, and Hallgren-Flynn (2010) describe several characteristics of RTI programs that are especially important for middle school students.

- Instruction that is responsive to their individual needs, as with other students at lower levels, is critical for middle school students, instead of providing the same packaged program to all.
- It is important to guide middle grade students toward independence in their own learning, as contrasted with strong teacher-controlled interaction in the earlier grades.
- Reading in the content areas of the curriculum is of great importance in RTI at the middle school level.
- Students at the middle school level should focus on coherence in the meanings of all words in order to strengthen their reading comprehension.
- Struggling students benefit from reading at a variety of reading levels for different purposes and from different genres.
- Motivation and attitudes toward reading are especially important at the middle school level, as many students have already given up.

English Language Learners and RTI

There is continuing concern about the overrepresentation of children from linguistic and ethnic minorities in special education classes (Hill, Carjuzaa, Aramburo, & Baca, 1993).

According to Damico (1991), referral to special education, and by extension to RTI Tier Three, should not be based on the following:

- Other factors that might explain the child's learning and language difficulties, such as the lack of opportunity to learn, cultural dissonance, and stressful life events, for example, among refugee children
- Language difficulties that affect the student at school, but not at home or in the community
- Ordinary needs of children to acquire English as a second language or the standard American English dialect
- Cross-cultural interference
- Bias in the assessment process, including data analysis that does not take into account the child's culture, language, and life experiences

The most problematic issue with respect to English language learners is their varying proficiency in English, which can range from speaking no English to being quite competent in their second language, even within the same classroom. Teachers and RTI team members should ask themselves if English language learners would have literacy problems if they were taught to read and write in their mother tongue, instead of English. If they would not, then their intervention should be a strong and formal ESL program. Klingner, Soltero-González, and Lesaux (2010) accordingly recommend that teachers should be knowledgeable about second language acquisition and also how to teach reading in English to children for whom English is their second language. Fisher, Frey, and Rothenberg (2011) emphasize that all teachers are teachers of language, providing instruction in all four domains: listening, speaking, reading, and writing. Scaffolding must accommodate the language levels of all students.

Many strategies can be used very effectively in teaching children with these needs. According to Gersten and Baker (2000), teachers should do the following:

- Build children's vocabulary and use it as a curricular anchor.
- Use visual representations to reinforce major concepts and vocabulary.
- Use the children's mother tongue as a support system.
- Adapt cognitive and language demands of instruction to the children by using sheltered English strategies.

Fisher, Frey, and Rothenberg (2011) additionally recommend that the multidisciplinary RTI team include expertise on children who are the English language learners. This will alleviate the problem of overrepresentation of English language learners within special education programs. Conversely, it can also address the problem of underrepresentation of these children when personnel who lack the needed language and cultural skills are not able to accurately assess their needs.

RTI and the Gifted

Teachers often conclude that gifted children do not have reading problems. Many or most learn to read at home if parents read to them, and the rest appear to learn to read quickly in kindergarten or the first grade. But we have found that teachers often make the following erroneous assumptions about gifted children:

- *Gifted children don't have reading problems.* The gifted child reading on grade level has a reading problem that should be diagnosed and addressed. Based on expectations, gifted children should be reading above grade level, usually several grades above their age-expected level. Although gifted children probably won't end up in Tier Three of RTI programs, they might appear in Tier Two.

- *Gifted children have mastered the basic skills of reading.* It isn't unusual to observe the fragmentation of basic skills among gifted children—they may have mastered most basic skills, but gaps may appear. They can be integrated into reading groups that are addressing identified areas of weakness at the time an appropriate lesson or lessons are offered, even though those groups are usually working below the levels of these otherwise more capable students.

- *All gifted children speak English well.* Often, gifted children can read in a language other than English, which means that their greatest need is to learn to understand and speak English.

Finding the Books and Materials They Want to Read

Diversity is important with respect not only to the learning characteristics of all students, but also to their need for appropriate texts to read and from which to learn to read.

The Print Environment of Students at Home

As might be expected, the print environment of the home and community is closely related to the factors of diversity described in this chapter. The newspapers, magazines, books, calendars, checkbooks, notes on the refrigerator door, Web site pages on the computer screen, and instructional manuals found in most middle-class homes may be absent from or less frequently encountered in the homes of children from low-income families. There might not be a tradition of reading and writing in the family, or perhaps a Bible or other religious book is the only representation of print in the home.

In a study they conducted, Halle, Kurtz-Costes, and Mahoney (1997) found that access to print was an important factor related to the reading achievement of African American children. In an international study of the relationships among reading achievement, home literacy environment, and school and public library availability of reading material in several countries, Elley (1992, 1996) reported that access to print was the most powerful factor associated with reading achievement, including the size of the school library. He found that frequent silent reading was the next most significant variable affecting reading achievement. McQuillan and Au (2001), consistent with earlier research, found that convenient access to reading material was associated with students reading more frequently. Voluntary and free reading was associated with increased levels of reading proficiency, supporting the need for easy access of students to things of interest to read.

Beyond the presence of text to read, the need for models who read in the home is also of great importance, especially when it is recognized that men and older boys are often less likely to read than are women and girls in the family.

Besides often being a factor in the low-income home, the absence of text also characterizes the low-income communities in which the homes are located. In a study of print resources in two low-income and two middle-income neighborhoods, Neuman and Celano (2001) surveyed the availability of reading materials for purchase, such as newspapers, magazines, and children's books; the quantity of signage; public places where reading took place, such as laundromats and bookstores; the availability of books in child care centers; and the quality of services and materials provided by school and public libraries. They found an overwhelming advantage of print resources in the middle-income neighborhoods, and they concluded that children in the low-income neighborhoods would have difficulty finding books of good quality, whereas those in the middle-income neighborhoods would have difficulty avoiding them.

In addition, the provision of a full-time or even part-time librarian is often related to the income levels of students in the schools. Neuman and Celano (2001) found that there were no trained school librarians in the low-income communities they studied, whereas the schools in the middle-income communities had well-trained and highly experienced school librarians. School libraries in the middle-income communities were also open more days and hours per week than those in the low-income communities. The same disparities were found in public libraries in the communities studied.

They concluded, as did Cunningham and Stanovich (1997), that the children who are most in need of a print-rich environment are the least likely to encounter it, resulting in a spiraling down of environmental opportunities for reading in the community, which in turn results in less motivation to read and still fewer opportunities to read. Allington (1983) adds that this situation is aggravated when these same children are enrolled in public schools in which low-level programs are provided to address their reading problems, resulting in their doing less reading of text than do children who read well. These programs involve major time commitments to studying about reading instead of time devoted to reading connected text.

Getting Books, Magazines, and Newspapers into Children's Hands

Given the diversity of children in our schools, especially children who are at risk of being troubled readers, teachers should take special pains to find books and other print materials that children will enjoy, books with characters and settings with which they can identify, books in which they can see themselves in positive roles, and materials that are of high interest and have visual appeal. A valuable resource of books and other sources of connected text that reflect cultures of diversity is found in Banks's *Teaching Strategies for Ethnic Studies* (2008). Banks categorizes many dozens of books in English for teachers and for children in the following groups: First Americans (American Indians, Native Hawaiians, and African Americans); European Americans (European ethnic groups and Jewish Americans); Hispanic Americans (Mexican Americans, Puerto Rican Americans, and Cuban Americans); and Asian Americans (Chinese Americans, Japanese Americans, Filipino Americans, and Indochinese Americans).

An abundance of books available in Spanish exist for children who want and need to read in that language (Schon, 2000, 2001, 2004; Schon & Berkin, 1996). Both children who did not have the opportunity to learn to read in their mother tongue and those who have acquired this ability in another school or country should be provided with opportunities to read more books in that language. It improves self-concept, offers evidence that the school and teacher value that language, and provides practice in reading that builds background knowledge and skills that transfer positively to reading in English later. Teachers should also be very careful about the use of so-called bilingual books that are written in two languages, usually with English and Spanish versions on facing pages. This practice ensures that children will acquire English in terms of Spanish, that is, a very ineffective translation approach. It is better for children to read a story in Spanish from one book and then read the same story in English from another book, as elaborated in later chapters. The children can use their background knowledge from the first experience to support their comprehension and learning of English in the second book.

Gifted children require a rich variety of books and other text materials to maintain their many and changing interests. They will often tackle books at a much higher level than the level at which they are reading because of their motivation and willingness to persist. Given good guidance, they can use the Internet very productively, too. Many sites are now available that are geared to younger children's reading abilities. Teacher sites like Thinkfinity (see <http://www.thinkfinity.org/home.aspx>) can also help teachers locate stimulating

When utilized properly, specially designed educational software or access to the Internet can offer a variety of opportunities for working with all children, regardless of their needs.

project ideas and resources for these students. This is less of a problem for children in the lower grades of a multigraded school because they will find reading resources for older children in the school library. But it can be a problem for the gifted sixth grader in a K–6 school, who needs access to a middle or secondary school library or an understanding teacher who is willing to check out books at the public library.

Finding materials that are high interest and low vocabulary enough for troubled readers, especially for boys, is a perennial problem for teachers. The teacher who is always conventional might have difficulty finding books that meet both criteria. A good resource for magazines is Magazines for Kids and Teens at <http://www.madisonpubliclibrary.org/kids/magazines>, which provides descriptions of the content and the reading and interest levels of dozens of magazines on a wide variety of topics, including some that publish students' own writing.

School budget problems are often a factor that affects the numbers of books, magazines, and newspapers available to children in the classroom. Some sources of text that teachers can exploit to augment those supplied by the school district are the following:

Making Individual Small Books

- School storage rooms, where surplus books are often hidden away
- Secondhand stores, public library book sales, yard sales, and swap meets, where teachers can often negotiate low prices with vendors "for the children"; returning to vendors at the end of the day and offering to buy all remaining books for a bulk price is often an effective way to maximize scarce teacher resources (many teachers spend their own money on books for children)
- Child-made books that result from collaborative chart stories, language experience approach activities, and other student writing activities
- Local public libraries that are usually available for walking field trips and that permit children to request library cards so they can check out their own books
- Commercial book clubs, which offer children's books at quantity discounts, usually with paper covers instead of hard covers. Depending on the number of books ordered by the children, many book clubs provide additional books for the teacher's classroom library.
- Newspapers that often sponsor programs to adopt a classroom and also often provide newspapers at no cost
- Support from parent groups, service clubs, and other community sources
- Reading Is Fundamental (RIF.org), which provides sets of books to schools at no cost

Finally, teachers should ensure that a wide variety of text is readily available for children to take home to read. Too many resources are so protected from loss or abuse that they are never used.

READERS WHO ARE BOYS   Much attention has been given to the roles of girls in literature for children in recent years—and with good effect. Whereas stories in basal readers and current literature anthologies tended to focus on boys in the most active roles in past years, there is now balance in the stories that the children read, not to mention representation of major cultural and linguistic groups as well. You might wonder why boys would be listed as a category of diversity among readers, but boys continue to have problems in reading that are out of proportion to their numbers in the population. Why do boys make up an almost overwhelming proportion of troubled readers? Among the many factors associated with this finding are the greater frequency of left dominance (left-handedness); lack of physical and emotional maturity compared to girls; greater frequency of attention deficit disorder; different cultural expectations for boys, including more physical activity and action; fewer positive reading models for boys; interest levels of books for boys; and female-dominated environment in schools, with teachers also favoring realistic fiction and character-related stories.

Teachers can take steps to ensure that boys do not continue to be overrepresented among the ranks of troubled readers:

- Provide more time in the initial stages of reading instruction for immature boys, especially those who exhibit signs of left dominance.
- Provide positive role models for boys: men and older boys who read.
- Provide books of interest to boys and nonfiction informational books about nature, history, biography, and sports.
- Provide magazines and newspapers that have more real-world interest and shorter texts.
- Permit more physical movement, for example, letting the children sprawl out on the floor when reading.
- Provide structured opportunities for children to discuss the text they are reading and writing about (Young & Brozo, 2001).
- Recognize the importance of archetypes of masculinity in picture books and story books for boys (Zambo, 2007).

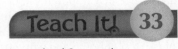

Instructional Conversations

In addition, boys will enjoy recent offerings in the immensely popular *Captain Underpants* series (Pilkey, 2000): *Captain Underpants and the Invasion of the Incredibly Naughty Cafeteria Ladies from Outer Space*, *Captain Underpants and the Wrath of the Wicked Wedgie Woman*, and *Captain Underpants and the Attack of the Talking Toilets*. Teachers who understand and appreciate the sense of humor of nine-year-old boys will recognize the appeal of these titles and the opportunities for stimulating those boys' creative writing instincts. A search on "books for boys" on <http://www.Amazon.com> or <http://www.Google.com> will yield dozens of additional books that appeal to boys of various ages.

In a study by Farris, Werderich, Nelson, and Fuhler (2009), they concluded that the following types of books appeal to boys:

- Easy to read books with enticing covers
- Realistic fiction and fantasy books that are part of a series and by a favorite author
- Informational books that have short illustrated passages
- Novels and non-fiction books that are graphic

For Review

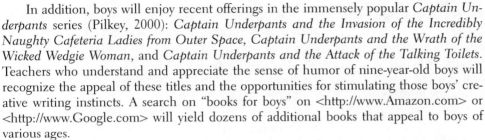

This chapter considered the social and cultural contexts of literacy for children in grades K–8. Different social and cultural groups have views of literacy that reflect their own realities and needs, which might vary from the mainstream view. It is important to acknowledge the validity of the various views of literacy as instruction is planned for children from these social and cultural groups.

Teachers can often create their own cultures of literacy within their classrooms by the way they value those points of view and by their organization of the physical environment of the classroom and selection of instructional materials and trade books for their students. A shared literacy environment creates the most effective tone for extending literacy to all. To involve parents and extended families in our shared literacy community, teachers must begin early in the school year with communications that welcome families to the classroom and request their support for classroom efforts.

Because of the diversity that is found in U.S. schools today, it is the rare classroom in which the children all come from a single cultural, ethnic, or linguistic group. A typical classroom now has children from several cultures and ethnic groups. Most have some children who speak another language at home, usually Spanish. Almost all classrooms will have mainstreamed children with special needs for at least part of the school day. This diversity can be viewed as a problem, but a more healthy viewpoint is to appreciate the richness of the diversity and use it as an asset in teaching. Response to Intervention (RTI) places new demands on classroom teachers and the expertise they bring to literacy. Their new role in assessing students and providing instruction for those who struggle with reading extends all the way from Tier One through Tier Three of RTI, including special education.

This diversity also provides many challenges for teachers. They must be aware of cultural differences far beyond holidays and foods. Aspects of nonverbal communication are particularly important in determining how teachers relate to their students and their families. Teachers will encounter children who speak another language or dialect of English at home and who might not be able to communicate effectively in standard American English in the classroom. Recent demographic trends indicate that teachers who had not yet encountered these children in their classrooms earlier will find them there now.

It is clear that many children struggle to learn to read in our classrooms. Some of them are at risk of failure because of environmental factors, such as living in low-income, inner city, or rural areas and coming from ethnic or linguistic minority groups. It is sometimes tempting to address the needs of these children with one-size-fits-all approaches to literacy instruction, but their strengths and needs vary greatly, and so should the programs that are provided to teach them to read and write. Some children struggle with reading because of cognitive, affective, and psychomotor factors. Teachers must be sensitive to children with needs for accommodations that are new to them and also must be flexible to the need to work closely with colleagues from special education so that these children can have a school experience that is as similar to that of most students as possible. RTI is a multi-tiered approach to assessment, diagnosis, and instruction that addresses the literacy needs of all children as soon as they enter school. When needs appear, no matter the grade level, the needs are addressed immediately, leaving behind the former policy that required a gap of two years between children's expected and actual achievement before interventions would begin.

Finally, it is necessary to find print materials that are interesting and culturally appropriate for children to read. Children need to see themselves in what they read. They need large numbers of books and other sources of text at many levels, including both narrative (story) and expository (informational) texts.

For Your Journal

1. Now that you have read Chapter 2, return to the Anticipation Guide at the beginning of the chapter. What differences are there in how you would answer the open-ended questions now?

2. The true-false questions in the Anticipation Guide addressed many myths about the demographics of children in our schools and about children's learning. After you read and found answers to the questions, which one(s) surprised you the most? Why?

Taking It to the World

Now that you have considered the implications of classroom diversity, think about your classmates when you were in the third grade. In terms of diversity, how does the student population of the classroom to which you are assigned now compare to that of your own third-grade classroom? Make a list of positive outcomes that the children of today exhibit as a result of the increased classroom diversity they experience.

New Literacies Connections

1. Family Connect offers connections to book and electronic initiatives for literacy access, including assistive devices and low-vision aides for individuals with vision impairments. Visit their Web site at <http://www.familyconnect.org/parentsite.asp?SectionID=72&TopicID=347&DocumentID=3820> and explore at least two of the listed resources. What is the primary focus of each resource, and how might each help you as a teacher?

2. Visit the "Guys Read" Web site <www.guysread.com>, a Web site that focuses on supporting boys' reading. How does this Web site help to encourage guys to explore connections to feelings through reading? Identify three books recommended by other guys as appropriate for early readers.

MyEducationLab™

Go to Topics 10 (Struggling Readers) in the MyEducationLab <www.myeducationlab.com> for your course, where you can:

- Find learning outcomes for Struggling Readers along with the national standards that connect to these outcomes.
- Complete Assignments and Activities that can help you more deeply understand the chapter content.
- Apply and practice your understanding of the core teaching skills identified in the chapter with the Building Teaching Skills and Dispositions learning units.

- Check your comprehension on the content covered in the chapter by going to the Study Plan in the Book Resources for your text. Here you will be able to take a chapter quiz, receive feedback on your answers, and then access Review, Practice, and Enrichment activities to enhance your understanding of chapter content.

What Reading Teachers Need to Know About Language

What Reading Teachers Need to Know About Language

The Sounds of Language p. 69

Vocabulary: Words and Their Meanings p. 76

Syntax: Ordering and Inflecting Classes of Words p. 78

Anticipation Guide

The following statements will help you begin thinking about the topics covered in this chapter. Answer *true* or *false* in response to each statement. As you read and learn more about the topics mentioned in the statements, double-check your answers. See what interests you and prompts your curiosity toward more understanding.

_____ **1.** You study French to learn about the French language and Spanish to learn about the Spanish language. The study of languages in general is known as *linguistics*.

_____ **2.** Chinese has an ideographic writing system; written characters relate to ideas. English has a syllabic writing system; written characters relate to spoken syllables. And Japanese has an alphabetic writing system; alphabetic letters relate to small sound units called *phonemes*.

_____ **3.** Over the centuries, the pronunciation of English sometimes has changed more than the writing system. Many English words are spelled the way they used to be pronounced.

_____ **4.** Morphemes can only be purchased with a prescription from licensed pharmacies.

_____ **5.** Onsets and rimes are the smallest particles of phonemes.

_____ **6.** The words *elect* and *college* are related to each other. Both come from a Latin word meaning "to choose."

_____ **7.** Vocabulary words face two ways: they are a record of what you have learned in the past, and they enable you to learn more in the future.

_____ **8.** The emphasis on close reading that comes with the Common Core Standards will require that teachers think more carefully about grammar—about the ordering and inflection of words.

_____ **9.** A relative pronoun can refer to blood relatives, but not relatives by marriage.

_____ **10.** A proper noun is the correct choice of noun to use in formal situations, dressed in your best clothes.

A Classroom Story

Teachers Use Linguistics

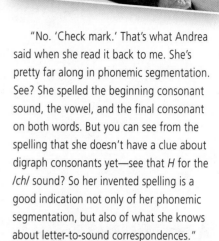

Janet Reardon feels lucky to have been assigned to this second grade class for her observation period. She will be student teaching next fall, and she has filled a notebook with ideas she can use. Her cooperating teacher is Alan Parsons. It is exciting to watch him interact with children, and he is also generous with his time and advice, especially when Janet asks him about topics she has been studying at the university in her literacy class.

Last Friday she asked him how he assessed phonemic awareness.

"Yes, I do use the Yopp-Singer phonemic awareness test from time to time. You should try it out yourself. But the truth is, I can tell a lot about how a child is coming along in phonemic awareness by looking at her invented spelling."

"How?"

"For instance, when a child strings a lot of letters in a line without any obvious connection to sounds, I don't expect the child to have a concept of word or much in the way of phonemic awareness. But if a child writes down a few letters for a word—what is called 'early phonemic' spelling—you can be pretty sure that she has started to be aware of phonemes."

"How do you know? What does the spelling tell you?"

"Well, for a kid to invent spellings, she has to be able to break a word down into its phonemes, and then match each one of those phonemes with a letter. But there's more."

"There always is."

"You'll get used to it. When she uses 'letter name spelling' when she writes, we know she's further along in phonemic segmentation. What's more, you can get an idea of what she knows about letter-to-sound correspondences from her early spelling. Look at this spelling: *HAK MIK*."

"Hack Mick"?

"No. 'Check mark.' That's what Andrea said when she read it back to me. She's pretty far along in phonemic segmentation. See? She spelled the beginning consonant sound, the vowel, and the final consonant on both words. But you can see from the spelling that she doesn't have a clue about digraph consonants yet—see that *H* for the /ch/ sound? So her invented spelling is a good indication not only of her phonemic segmentation, but also of what she knows about letter-to-sound correspondences."

"Amazing."

"Totally. Go back and tell your classmates to pay attention to linguistics. Especially to phonology."

"What's that?"

"That's for you to find out. Have a great weekend."

"Reading is talk written down," teachers say, and in many ways the statement is true. In order to read, children and young people need to know the language that print represents. And in order to teach reading well, you need to understand children's talk—children's language. The study of language, as distinct from the study of any particular language such as Japanese or Spanish, is known as *linguistics*. In this chapter we will pay attention to those parts of language that matter the most in learning to read and write. The key ways that reading and writing depend on oral language are:

- **Phonology,** or the **sounds of language,** how some (but not all) of them affect the meanings of words
- **Morphology** or **word structure,** the ways words are made
- **Vocabulary,** the ways that words convey meaning
- **Syntax,** the ordering and inflection of words in sentences
- **Text structure,** the way texts are organized
- **Varieties of language,** including dialects and different kinds of discourse.

| Love | Wealth | Virtue | Lucky | Beautiful |

Figure 3.1
Chinese Ideographs

The Sounds of Language

You often hear reading experts talk about "letter-to-sound relationships," but do you really think about what those sounds are? If the language is Chinese, the "sounds" are not sounds at all, but ideas. The same written character is rendered into different words, depending on the dialect of Chinese that one speaks. Hence, the Chinese writing system is called *ideographic*, for "ideas written down" (see Figure 3.1).

If the language we spoke were Japanese, the written characters would mostly represent spoken syllables. Each character that represented a consonant would represent a vowel, too. Each consonant and vowel combination (such as *ka, ki, ke, ko,* and *ku*) gets a different graphic character. Hence, the Japanese writing system is syllabic (although Japanese does use some ideographic characters, called *kanji*, for content words–see Figure 3.2.)

The English language represents sounds at one level smaller than a syllable. Our alphabet letters represent *phonemes*, vowel or consonant sounds. For example, each of the three sounds that make up the word *cat*: /k/, /æ/, and /t/ is a phoneme.

If the English language used ideographs instead of letters of the alphabet, we would need to learn *a million* characters for all the words, according to the Global Language Monitor <http://www.languagemonitor.com>. If English used a syllabary instead of an alphabet, we would still need to learn around 2,700 characters to represent all of our syllables (Barker, 2006). Since the English language uses an alphabet, we can get by with 26 characters—or 52, if you count upper case and lower case letters. That's a big advantage in simplicity. But there is a price to pay.

Reading ideographs, matching graphic images with ideas, is easily done. Small children recognize the logos of their favorite soft drinks and fast foods, and soon after learn the Arabic numerals (and those are ideographs, too: *1, 2,* and *3* are called "one," "two," and "three" in English, but "moja," "mbili," and "tatu" in Kiswahili). Matching characters with syllables is harder, but still not very difficult. Middle school students who struggle to read words spelled alphabetically can be fairly easily taught to read words transcribed by their syllables (Gleitman & Rozin, 1973). But reading alphabetic writing—matching a string of characters with their corresponding speech sounds at the level of phonemes—is the most challenging of all. Many children struggle to break out phonemes in spoken words, and this difficulty causes problems in reading written words (Snow et al., 1998). That's why the economy of having the few graphic symbols in an alphabetic writing system comes at the price of having to focus on smaller bits of sound in language. Teachers can help children

sa	shi	su	se	so
さ	し	す	せ	そ
ta	chi	tsu	te	to
た	ち	つ	て	と
na	ni	nu	ne	no
な	に	ぬ	ね	の

Figure 3.2
Japanese Hiragana,
Syllabic Characters

cope with these difficulties if they become aware of the sounds of English (the topic of the next section) and also of the English spelling system (which is dealt with in Chapter 10).

Phonics and Phonological Awareness

How do we make the two kinds of phonemes: vowels and consonants?

Phonology: The Sounds of English

Since English has an *alphabetic writing system*, words are written by making matches between small speech sounds or *phonemes* and alphabet letters. Let's take a closer look at how we make the two kinds of phonemes: vowels and consonants.

HOW ENGLISH VOWELS ARE MADE Vowel sounds are produced when you vibrate your vocal cords and breathe across them. But what makes the difference between one vowel sound and another? That is, what are you doing when you produce the sound of *"EEEE"* as opposed to *"AHHH"*? The answer lies in how and where you hold your tongue in your mouth while you breathe past your vibrating vocal cords. The sound of *"EEEE"* is made with the tongue high in the front of the mouth, while the sound of *"AHHH"* is made with the tongue low in the back of the mouth. But there is more.

Vowels: Long and Short, or Tense and Lax? Teachers use the terms "long" and "short" to mean the sounds represented by the letter *I* in *kite* (a "long" vowel sound) and the letter *I* in *kit* (a "short" vowel sound). But it doesn't take you any longer to say *kite* than it does to say *kit*. So "long" and "short" doesn't capture the difference between the two kinds of vowel sounds.

What does? Say *feet* and *fit* aloud, and stretch out the vowels as you pronounce them. Notice what happens in your mouth when you say each. Poke your finger firmly into the muscle under your jaw and say them again. This time you should feel your tongue muscle tense up when you say the vowel in *feet* and relax when you say the vowel in *fit*. Because of the tensing and relaxing of the tongue muscle when you make the sound of *ee* and *ih*, linguists call these vowels *tense* for the "long" vowel sound and *lax* for the "short" vowel sound.

Now we have some confusion, because the long and short versions of the same vowel letter, like the letter *I* in *kite* and *kit* and the letter *A* in *mat* and *mate*, sound very different from each other. The short vowel sounds are all lax vowels, as linguists call them. But as *sounds* they are matched with long vowel sounds that don't sound like them. There are historical reasons for this. Essentially, between the fourteenth and sixteenth centuries the pronunciations of English vowels changed, but their spellings didn't (see Temple, Nathan, and Temple, 2013 for further discussion). And as we shall see in Chapter 10, the mismatch between vowel sounds and vowel spellings cause problems for beginning readers and writers.

Diphthongs and Monopthongs Listen to the vowels in *he* and *soil*. *He* contains a single vowel sound and *soil* contains a double vowel sound. The technical term for a single vowel sound is a *monopthong* (a term we almost never hear) and the term for a double vowel sound (two closely pronounced vowel sounds) is a *diphthong*. The vowel sounds in *out* and *soil* are diphthongs. And that is a term you do hear more often. Diphthongs and monopthongs can confuse young writers and English language learners because our spelling acknowledges some diphthongs but not others. The diphthong in *boil* is spelled with two letters. But the vowel in *so* is a diphthong, too (*so-eww*) although it is spelled with only one letter. The same is true with the long sound of A (which is spelled with one letter although the actual sound is *ay-ee*), and the long sound of I (pronounced *ah-ee*).

HOW ENGLISH CONSONANTS ARE MADE We know that vowels are produced when you vibrate your vocal cords while you are breathing out. Consonants are made when you interrupt that flow of breath in some way. There are many ways to interrupt it. If you completely stop it momentarily, you produce what are called *stop consonants*, such as the sounds represented by *p*, *b*, *d*, *t*, *k*, and *g*. If you buzz the breath slightly, you produce the *fricative* consonants represented by the letters *s*, *z*, *th*, *f*, and *v*. If you stop the air flow and then hiss it, you get *affricate consonants*, such as the sounds represented by the letters *ch* and *j*. And if you direct the airflow out through the nose, you get *nasal consonants*, such as the sounds represented by the letters *m*, *n*, and *ng*.

Which consonant sounds you produce depend on two more things: where in the mouth you produce the interruption and whether the vocal cords are vibrating when you make the interruption. Let's illustrate. If you stop the airflow through your mouth with the back of the tongue raised against the top of the mouth toward the rear, you get the sound of /g/ or /k/. If your vocal cords are vibrating while you do it, you get the sound of /g/. If they are not vibrating, you get the sound of /k/. Similarly, /b/ and /p/ are made by closing the lips. The sound of /b/ is *voiced* (that is, the vocal cords vibrate the whole time it is made), and the sound of /p/ is unvoiced (the vocal cords don't start vibrating until about 40 thousandths of a second after you start producing the sound).

Teachers of primary grades should be aware of the ways speech sounds are made, because as children begin to experiment with spelling, you will see they listen very carefully to speech sounds and their similarities, even when they can't talk about what they are hearing. For example, young children often spell the sound represented by *TH* with the letter *V*. It helps to know that the name of the letter *V* is a "buzzed" (fricative) and voiced sound that's made in the front of the mouth, just as the sound /th/ in *then* is. (The only difference is that the sound of /v/ is made with the upper teeth on the lower lip, and the /th/ sound in *then* is made with the tongue on the fleshy ridge behind the upper front teeth.) And since children expect a single phoneme to be spelled with a single letter, *V* is a natural choice for the sound of /th/, which is spelled with two letters. (More on this later.)

Consonant Blends and Consonant Digraphs   *Consonant blends* are two or more consonants pronounced one right after the other, like the first two letters in *slip*, the first three phonemes in *split*, or the last two phonemes in *help*. In these words each of the consonants can be heard distinctly if you pronounce the word slowly.

Consonant digraphs are single consonant sounds that are spelled with two letters. The beginning consonant sounds in *then*, *chip*, and *shirt* are consonant digraphs. (The word *digraph* comes from two Greek words meaning "double writing"). To repeat, the difference between blends and digraphs is that in consonant blends, each of two or more consonant phonemes can be heard distinctly, but in digraphs, two consonant letters spell a single phoneme.

Why do we have digraph consonants in English? They came about because the Roman alphabet was originally developed to represent the sounds of Latin, and was borrowed to write English. But English had some sounds that did not occur in Latin, so the Roman alphabet had no letters to stand for the English sounds of /sh/, /ch/, or /th/. To signal when those sounds were meant by writers, early scribes came up with the convention of writing an H after certain Roman letters: *SH*, *CH*, and *TH*. The spelling of *WH*, though, is a strange exception. The sound represented by *WH* is really a consonant blend and not a digraph. You really may hear two consonant sounds /hw/. *HW* is the way that sound was originally spelled, until scribes in the twelfth and thirteenth centuries reversed the order of the letters, to make them look like *CH*, *SH*, and *TH*.

The Challenges of Phonological Awareness   When children realize that words they speak are made up of small bits of sound called *phonemes*, we say they have *phonemic awareness*. Children usually show phonemic awareness in late kindergarten and early first grade (Goswami, 2000). Some children have trouble with phonemic awareness even into first and second grade, and if they do, it may be hard for them to learn to read. Why is phonemic awareness challenging for children? It is probably because words really cannot be spoken so slowly that each of their phonemes can be heard distinctly.

You may think it's obvious that the phonemes exist in words, but you know that fact from indirect evidence. You know it because you can substitute a /b/ phoneme for the /k/ in *cat* and get *bat*, and you can substitute an /n/ phoneme for the /t/ in *cat* and get *can*. Once you began to read, you saw that letters tended to be matched with phonemes in words such as *CAT*, and that reinforced the idea that phonemes can be heard separately.

CCSS

- Foundational Skills 1: Phonological Awareness

The World of Reading

Bring on the Linguists!

Scholars in the field of linguistics have contributed much to our knowledge of reading and writing. For instance, Professor Catherine Snow of the Harvard Graduate School of Education has authored many important works on children's language development in home and school settings. She chaired the National Reading Council that produced the influential work, *Preventing Reading Difficulties in Young Children* (Snow et al., 1998).

Charles Read, who trained in linguistics at the Massachusetts Institute of Technology, is often credited with bringing to light the fascinating practice of invented spelling in children (Read, 1975).

But Read had a great deal of help from another linguist and educator, the late Carol Chomsky (1971). Carol Chomsky's husband, Noam Chomsky, is the most influential linguist of the past century, and he, too, has contributed to our thinking about children's word recognition and comprehension—especially the idea that there are processes occurring "beneath the surface" of children's understanding of written language.

Michael Halliday, a linguist from Scotland, charted his son's use of functions of language, and contributed a very useful menu of ways to help children develop their ability to communicate, and later to read.

Teach It! 12

Phonemic Segmentation with Elkonin Boxes

But young learners without that experience in reading are often challenged by the task of separating or *segmenting* phonemes in words.

Note that we are not saying children cannot hear the phonemes. Of course they can. Most English-speaking three-year-olds can correctly "show you the cat" and "show you the bat." It's the task of saying slowly the three sounds in CAT that young children find difficult.

Developmental Milestones
in Phonological Awareness

Stages of Literacy Development	Developmental Milestones in Phonological Awareness
At the end of kindergarten:	• At the syllable level: Most children can distinguish single-syllable words from words with two syllables when they hear them. • At the onset and rime level (*p + at = pat; l + ight = light*—see below): Most children can match a target word with a rhyming word. • At the phoneme level: Most children can pick out words that begin with the same sound as a target word and can tell you the odd word out—the one that does not begin with the same sound as the others.
Two months into first grade:	• Given two letters on cards, most children can combine them and pronounce the word they spell (*in, on, at, it, up*) • Given a three-phoneme word, most children can say the word that is left when the beginning consonant is deleted: *bat/at, sit/it, cup/up.*
By the end of first grade:	• Most children can pronounce two-phoneme words slowly and separate the phonemes: /t/ - /oo/; /b/ - /y/. • Given longer words, most children can leave off the first consonant and pronounce what is left: *b—utterfly.* • Given three isolated phonemes, most children can combine them to make a word: /s/ /æ/ /t/ = *sat.*

Source: After Hall, S. and Moats, C. from *Straight talk about reading: How parents can make a difference in the early years.* (1999). Chicago: Contemporary Books.

DEVELOPMENTAL MILESTONES IN PHONOLOGICAL AWARENESS Most preschool children can't show you that they know words are made up of phonemes, but most second graders can. How does that awareness develop? Hall and Moats (1999) present the pathway taken by normally developing children in kindergarten and first grade (see the "Developmental Milestones in Phonological Awareness" box).

Syllables, Onsets, and Rimes

Syllables are rhythmic pulses in words. The word *final* has two of them, *fi* and *nal*, while *awareness* has three: *a* + *ware* + *ness*. In the word *awareness*, you can see that a vowel can stand alone as a syllable, but consonants cannot (at least not in English). Some languages such as Spanish, Japanese, and Kiswahili have relatively few syllables. In Spanish, roughly 50 different syllables can be combined to make most of the words in the language. The words of the English language, though, are made up of a couple of thousand different syllables (Barker, 2006). Few teachers of English would bother to have students learn groups of syllables, as teachers of Spanish, Portuguese, and Kiswahili regularly do.

English syllables can be open or closed. An *open syllable* ends in a vowel, and a *closed syllable* ends in a consonant. All three syllables in *banana* are open syllables, and both syllables in *problem* are closed syllables. When these words are divided at the end of a line of print, the hyphen goes after the vowel in words with open syllables like *final (fi-nal)* and *recess (re-cess)*, and after the consonant in words with closed syllables like *picnic (pic-nic)* and *knapsack (knap-sack)*. The vowel in an open syllable often has its "long" sound, and the vowel in a closed syllable usually has its "short" sound. Compare *capable* and *captain*; *meter* and *metric*; and *human* and *humble*.

Syllables can be broken into smaller units called *onsets* and *rimes* (Trieman, 1985). The *onset* is the initial consonant sound of a syllable, if there is one, and the *rime* is the vowel plus any consonant sound that comes after it. For example, in *cat*, the sound represented by C is the onset and the sound represented by AT is the rime. But the word *at* has only a rime, AT. Children who have experience playing with onsets and rimes—which is what we do when we recite nursery rhymes—have been shown to have an easier time learning to read words (Bradley & Bryant, 1985).

Morphology: How English Words Are Built

The study of the ways words are built is called *morphology*. In English, words are built in several ways. They can stand alone, like *cat*. They can be made up of two or more separate words, like *firehouse*. They can have prefixes and suffixes added to them, like *unforgettable*. And they can be built out of ancient parts, like *biology* and *biography*.

COMPOUND WORDS When two or more root words are combined, as in *houseboat* and *lawnmower*, they make compound words. Dictionary writers have three different ways of writing compound words:

> *Houseboat*: Words that are frequently spoken together are joined without a space. Those words are made plural by adding *-s* at the end of the last word: *houseboats*.
>
> *Mother-in-law*: Other compound words are joined with hyphens. When these words are made plural, the *-s* is added to the more important word: *mothers-in-law*.
>
> *Boa constrictor*: Some words are often said together, but are written separately.

PREFIXES AND SUFFIXES All of us are aware that we can add an *-s* or an *-ed* or an *-ing* onto a root word in English word to change its meaning. We can also add *re-*, *un-*, *non-*, and *dis-* to the beginning of a word to change its meaning, too. Those meaning-changing units that are added before the root word are called *prefixes*, and those added after the root word are called *suffixes*. The general name for both of them is *affixes*. Some suffixes mark the person, number, and tense of a verb, like she *fishes*/they *fish*; and we *fished* but you are

 Syllables can be broken into smaller units called onsets and rimes. What strategies has the teacher in this video chosen to help develop her students' ability to use onsets and rimes as they write?

Word Hunts

Analytic Phonics Lesson

CCSS
• Foundational Skills 2: Phonics and Word Recognition

Word Sorting

Making and Breaking Words

Morphemes and Reading

Being aware of morphemes helps a person read. Even third graders use word parts to recognize words—especially in words like *hilly* and *helpful*, where the original word part is easily visible, or "transparent" (Carlisle & Stone, 2005). To read words that are typically encountered from the fourth grade on, it is more useful to be aware of the morphemes that make up words than to try to match letters with individual sounds (Reichle & Perfetti, 2003). Being aware of morphemes makes it possible to identify as many as 60 percent of unknown words that are encountered in the middle grades and above (Nagy et al., 1989). So, for example, a reader who knows that *inter* means "between" and *planetary* refers to "planets" can figure out that *interplanetary* means "between planets." Children beyond the early elementary years who are aware of morphemes in words register better comprehension (Carlisle, 2000).

The strident emphasis on phonics—letter-to-sound correspondences—that the No Child Left Behind legislation ushered in might distract teachers from the realization that there are other important things to know about words, especially beyond the primary grades. Some of those things include the parts that make up words and where those words came from.

---

fishing. Others mark the plural form of nouns, like one *cat* and two *cats*. Such additions are called *grammatical inflections*. Besides grammatical inflections there are prefixes and suffixes that can change the meanings of words, like *unkind, retie, underestimate,* and *likeable*. Table 3.1 shows some prefixes and suffixes that are found in children's vocabularies.

WORDS FROM ANCIENT PARTS Both prefixes and suffixes have less obvious forms that attach to parts of words that are not as easily recognized as root words. For example, *gradual* and *annual* appear to share the suffix *-al*, which has the meaning "in the manner of." But what do *annu-* and *grad-* mean? Both are ancient root words that came from Latin. *Annus* meant "year," and *gradus* meant "step." So in modern English, *annual* means "year by year," and *gradual* means "step by step." Ancient root words like these are called *historical morphemes*. There are many ancient prefixes and root words contained in thousands of English words. Most come from Latin and Greek. They are usually found in the vocabularies of children above third grade. Learning them can expand children's vocabularies, and will help children read and spell more words.

Table 3.2 lists some common historical morphemes. More will be found in Chapter 6.

Table 3.1 Prefixes and Suffixes

PREFIX	MEANING	EXAMPLES
sub-	under	submarine, subway, substandard
dis-	not	distrust, disrespect, distasteful
mis-	not	misunderstand, misguided, mislead
inter-	between or among	interstate, international, intercity
pre-	before	preschool, pretest, preview
SUFFIX	**MEANING**	**EXAMPLES**
-er	more than	taller, shorter, quicker
-ful	containing	hopeful, wishful, bountiful
-ly	in the manner of	beautifully, miserly, shortly
-ness	state of being	goodness, highness, badness
-less	without	painless, toothless, penniless

Table 3.2 Prefixes and Word Roots from Latin

PREFIX	MEANING	EXAMPLES
com, con, col, cor	together	collect, contract, correct
e-	out of	elect, eject, emigrate
ab	from, away from, by	abstract, abrupt
ad—, al—, ac—	to, toward	admit, accord, ally
ROOT WORD	**MEANING**	**EXAMPLES**
-lect, -lege	choose	elect, collect, college
-ject, -jac	throw	inject, reject, eject, adjective
-rupt	break	interrupt, abrupt, disrupt, erupt
grad-	step	graduate, gradual, grade

ETYMOLOGIES: WORD ORIGINS In many dictionaries, you will find listings for words that look like this:

give. (giv). Vt gave, giv'en, giv'ing. [OE giefan]

CCSS

• Language Standard 5: Vocabulary Acquisition and Use

What do these notations mean? The part in parentheses is the pronunciation; **vt** means that the word is a transitive verb—that is, a verb that takes an object to complete the meaning. *Gave, given,* and *giving* are the past, past participle (the form used in compound verbs like *have given* or *had given*), and present participle (the form used in compound verbs like *is giving* and *were giving*). The part in brackets means that the word came down to us from an earlier word—in this case from Old English (OE). Words in English are derived from many sources. Nonetheless, it is possible to map out a rough lineage for a great many of the words you use in English. When you trace the origins of words or look at their histories, you are dealing with their *etymologies.*

The English language traces its origin to Anglo-Saxon. In the fifth and sixth centuries C.E., Germanic peoples from northern Germany and the Netherlands invaded England and pushed the indigenous Celts north into Scotland and west to Wales and Ireland. They brought their Germanic language with them, and it came to be called Anglo-Saxon (Anglo comes from Angles, the name of one of the Germanic tribes, and Saxon from another of those tribes). In the eighth and ninth centuries, Vikings raided from Scandinavia, and Old English became a mixture of Germanic, Norse, Danish, and Dutch words.

In 1066, the Normans from France conquered England and brought with them not only an early version of the French language but also Latin, which became widely used in the church, the government, and other places of higher culture—to the exclusion of English, which remained the language spoken around the hearth, on the farm, and in the market. Hundreds of words from Latin and Greek (Greek was read in the monasteries), as well as French, were absorbed into English in this period.

In 1476, William Caxton brought the first printing press to England and began printing books in English, giving an enormous boost to the language. The language he wrote, Middle English, had a sort of dual structure, consisting of Anglo-Saxon words and Latinate words. You can see this duality in the English words for food. The animal you call a *pig* (an Anglo-Saxon word) on the farm is called *pork* when it reaches the dining room table. *Pork* is a French word, from Latin. The *cow* (Anglo-Saxon) in the pasture became *beef* (French and Latin) in the dining room. *Sheep* on the farm (Anglo-Saxon word) became *mutton* (French and Latin) in the dining room. This all came about because English was spoken on the farm by workers, but French was spoken in the dining rooms of the ruling class. To this day, our language has a core of words that came through Old English from Anglo-Saxon. These are very often the common, basic items in our vocabulary: the words

As children explore words on their own, they begin to find meaning in the words and to learn how to use words for different purposes.

children learn first, the words you use when you are being most direct. But there is another body of words, from Latin and Greek, that are more specialized, more scientific, and more limited to educated usage. Thus, you find the Anglo-Saxon words *cat* and *dog* and the corresponding Latin words *feline* and *canine*; you also find the Anglo-Saxon word *feel*, the related Latin word *sensitive*, and the related Greek word *sympathy*. Today the English language can be described as having an Anglo-Saxon base and a superimposed Latin vocabulary. About a third of our words are Anglo-Saxon and most of the rest are from Latin (and through Latin, from Greek). There are also many loan words from Spanish, modern French, German, and other languages.

CCSS

• Language Standard 4: Vocabulary Acquisition and Use

Vocabulary: Words and Their Meanings

Vocabulary is knowledge of words and their meanings. The more words children have in their spoken vocabularies, the easier it will be for them to learn to read. This is true for three reasons:

- *Having a word in the spoken vocabulary makes it possible to recognize that word in print.* Having the word in their vocabulary allows children to confirm more quickly if they have deciphered a printed word correctly. It is frustrating for beginning readers to struggle to decipher a word from its letters, only to realize that they don't know the word anyway. Having the word in their vocabulary allows children to use meaning-based strategies for word identification strategies, such as, "Think of a word that begins like this one, that would make sense in this sentence."
- *Having more words in the spoken vocabulary boosts children's language awareness.* The more children are aware of language, the better able they are to read words—to be aware of their parts and their sounds (Wong-Fillmore & Snow, 2000).
- *Having words in the spoken vocabulary boosts reading comprehension.* Words are tokens for concepts. They are units of meaning. The size of children's vocabulary is a measure of their knowledge of the world. It is also a measure of their potential for understanding new information. Let's elaborate on these issues now.

Levels of Vocabulary Knowledge

What do we mean by *knowing* vocabulary? Beck et al. (2002) suggest a continuum of word knowledge that looks like this:

- No knowledge
- General sense, such as knowing *mendacious* has a negative connotation
- Narrow, context-bound knowledge, such as knowing that a *frustrated* person is unhappy because she can't have what she wants, but not knowing that a good defensive player can *frustrate* the other team's efforts to score a touchdown.
- Having knowledge of a word, but not being able to recall it readily enough to use it in appropriate situations
- Rich, decontextualized knowledge of a word's meaning, its relationship to other words, and its extension to metaphorical uses, such as understanding what someone is doing when they are *devouring* a book (p. 10).

Knowing vocabulary well means not just understanding what words in a book mean, then, but knowing words in a range of contexts, in associations with other words, and in connection with one's experience—to have words as one's own.

Exploring Children's Vocabulary

The job of teaching vocabulary seems truly immense. Nagy (1985) estimates that by ninth grade, students have to cope with a total written vocabulary of 88,500 words (Nagy & Anderson, 1984). Were we to try to teach all those words, the prospect of teaching children nearly 10,000 words a year would be daunting indeed. But Beck et al. (2002) have found a useful way to break down those numbers.

- *Tier One Words.* There are many thousands of words already in children's spoken vocabulary that we won't usually have to teach. Beck et al. call these words *Tier One* words, and they include examples such as *mother, clock,* and *jump.*

- *Tier Three Words.* Then there are many more thousands of words that are so highly specialized that they are almost never used outside of the disciplines in which they are encountered. These *Tier Three* words—like *monozygotic, tetrahedron,* and *bicameral*—are best learned in the science, social studies, and other classes where they are tied to the content under study.

- *Tier Two Words.* That leaves the *Tier Two* words—the words with wide utility that most children don't have in their spoken vocabularies, such as *dismayed, paradoxical, absurd,* and *wary.* Beck et al. (2002) estimate that there may be about 7,000 Tier Two words, and even if we teach children half of them—or about 400 words a year—we will have gone a long way toward growing children's vocabularies and equalizing children's access to learning.

In Chapter 6 of this book we will describe ways of teaching Tier Two vocabulary, the general-purpose words many children do not know. In Chapters 7 and 13 we will share ways of teaching Tier Three words, content-specific words.

 Words with multiple meanings can be confusing for students to learn and challenging for teachers to teach. What methods is the teacher in the video using to help her students learn multiple word meanings?

POLYSEMY, IDIOMS, AND COLLOCATION   *Polysemy* means "having multiple meanings." (Speaking of etymologies, *poly-* comes from a Greek word meaning "many" and *sem-* comes from another Greek word meaning "signal" or "meaning.") Many Tier One words are polysemous. For example, *can* can mean "to be able to" or "a metal container"; in slang, it can mean a toilet. The *can can* is a dance. *Tree* can refer to a large plant, or to the act of frightening an animal into climbing one. A *telephone tree* is a network of people who call others, and a *tree diagram* is a graphic organizer that shows taxonomic relationships. Oddly, more Tier One words are polysemous than the words on the upper tiers; and by the time you get to Tier Three, the words have very limited meanings: *monozygotic, polygamous,* and *chiaroscuro* have one meaning each.

Collocation refers to words that naturally occur together (*col-* means "together" and *loc-* means "place." Both morphemes are from Latin). In English we say *dine out* and not *dine away.* We say *eat in,* not *dine in*; *best friends,* not *superior friends*; *fast food,* not *quick food*; *commit a crime,* not *perform a crime.* These collocations do not often translate from one language to another: in English we say *think of . . .* but the same expression in Spanish is *think on.* Native speakers have little trouble with collocation, but English language learners often do.

Idioms are words or phrases that have a meaning that is not predictable from the literal definition. Many idioms are formed by adding prepositions (see page 86 below) to verbs. Note the different meanings of these examples: *fall in, fall out, fall to, fall away; run in, run into, run out of, run away, run over, run off* (two meanings), *run about; tell on, tell off; buy in, buy out, buy off, buy up; pay up, pay down, pay out,* and so on. Many idioms have stories connected to them: *To kick the bucket* ("to die") refers to kicking the bucket from under a hanging victim; *three sheets to the wind* is a sailor's term for a drunken person.

A sheet is the line (what sailors call ropes) that controls the tension on a sail. If one sheet gets loose in the wind, a boat is a little out of control, and if *three* sheets are loose in the wind, the boat is under no one's control.

Denotations and connotations refer to the literal and figurative meanings of words. The *denotation* is the precise definition. The denotation of *dog* is a member of the canine family, often domesticated. The *connotation* is what the word suggests. Oddly, though many of us love our dogs, the denotation of the word *dog* is negative: *Dog* can refer to something that doesn't work very well, or to a person who is treacherous. The denotation of a *bear* is a carnivorous or omnivorous mammal from the *ursidae* family; but the connotation is that what it names is very difficult, as in "That exam was a bear," or "The month of April saw a bear market."

Tier One and sometimes Tier Two words often have connotations, but Tier Three words are all denotations. That exam may have been a *bear*, but not an *ursida*; that treacherous guy you thought was your friend may have been a *dirty dog*, but not a *contaminated canine*.

Syntax: Ordering and Inflecting Classes of Words

Syntax, a more precise word for grammar, refers to the set of rules that order words of different types and their inflections meaningfully in sentences. Syntax can be thought of as a kind of code that enables speakers and writers to encode meaning, and hearers and readers to decode meaning. There are many reasons why teachers of literacy need extensive knowledge of syntax. First, and most important, readers rely on their knowledge of syntax to make sense when they listen, speak, read, and write. Second, many young writers struggle to produce sentences in Standard English. Third, English language learners are in particular need of someone who can answer their questions about English syntax. Fourth, the Common Core Standards, which have been adopted by 45 states and the District of Columbia, call for students to read and write in Standard English, and also to be able to do close readings of texts. Close reading often requires an explicit understanding of syntax. The Common Core Standards have criteria for spoken language that students must meet, and those standards relate to syntax.

Syntax occurs on two levels. At the conscious level, we think of syntax as the common set of rules taught in school, such as "A verb must agree with its subject in person and number." But conscious syntactical knowledge is only a fraction of what you know that enables you to produce and understand sentences. Consider, for example, the following sentences:

- *I would go bike riding if I weren't tired.* (But I won't go bike riding because I am tired.)
- *I will go bike riding if I'm not tired.* (I don't know yet if I will go bike riding.)
- *I go bike riding if I'm not tired.* (When I'm not tired, I usually go bike riding.)
- *I'm going bike riding, and I'm not tired.* (I expected to be tired, but I'm not.)
- *I did go bike riding, and I'm not tired.* (Somebody said I would be tired if I went bike riding, but I went anyway, and, guess what? I'm not tired.)

If you have ever taught English as a second language, you have surely found that although the differences in the meanings of these sentences were obvious to you, it was difficult to tell non-native speakers how to produce sentences that convey those shades of meaning. That phenomenon happens because on a deep level you know the "rules" of syntax (because there really are rules that explain how each of the above sentences is made), but you cannot explain what you know. Linguists call this *tacit knowledge*—we

Table 3.3 Subjects and Predicates in Simple Sentences

SUBJECT	PREDICATE
The girl	scored the goal.
The fans	were very happy.
The game	was a triumph.

have it, but it's not conscious. The lion's share of our knowledge of syntax is tacit. But if you are going to help children read, write, and speak Standard English, you will have to make a hefty amount of that knowledge conscious. The following sections will remind you of things you already know about the English language, on some level. But we are betting that some of the explanations, at least, will be new to you.

Kinds of Sentences, and Their Parts

To begin at the beginning, sentences have subjects and predicates. The *subject* of a sentence is the noun phrase that is the agent or doer of the action in the sentence. The *predicate* is the verb (the action word) and any noun, adjective, adverb, or prepositional phrase that follows it. Table 3.3 shows some examples of subjects and predicates. All of these examples are *simple sentences*—sentences with one subject and one predicate.

A simple sentence can have a compound subject and also a compound predicate:

The players and the cheerleaders trained in the sun and performed in the rain.

The players and the cheerleaders is the compound subject and *trained in the sun and performed in the rain* is the compound predicate.

SENTENCE TYPES AND PATTERNS   Sentences come in four types and four patterns. The **types** of sentences are declarative, interrogative, imperative, and exclamatory. The first type of sentence, **declarative sentences**, state something straight out.

Juan was a gymnast.
Alicia was impressed by his moves.

are both declarative sentences. (It doesn't make a sentence any less declarative to have the verb in the passive voice.)
Interrogative sentences ask a question.

Was Juan a gymnast?
Was Alicia impressed by his moves?

are both interrogative sentences. Note that interrogative sentences usually place an auxiliary (or "helping") verb, such as *was*, *were*, *does*, or *did*, at the beginning of the sentence. Note, too, that interrogative sentences may add an auxiliary verb if they didn't already have one:

Juan was a gymnast. Was Juan a gymnast?
Juan fell. Did Juan fall?

Sentences can also be made interrogative by adding a **tag question** to the declarative form:

Juan was a gymnast, <u>wasn't he</u>?
Juan fell, <u>didn't he</u>?

An **imperative sentence** gives a command.

> *Watch out!*
> *Don't smoke in here.*

are both imperative sentences. Classifying sentences as imperative can get fuzzy when degrees of politeness are involved. For example, a guard in a museum would say, "Don't smoke in here," but a person who is obligated to treat another with respect might say, "Sorry, this is a no smoking area," or "Would you mind waiting until you are outside before lighting that?" The forms of those two sentences are declarative and interrogative, respectively, even though the intent of both is imperative.

An **exclamatory sentence** shows excitement. It is almost always punctuated with an exclamation point.

> *We won!*
> *Today is a snow day!*

are both exclamatory sentences.

The **patterns** of sentences are simple, compound, complex, and compound-complex.

A **compound sentence** has two or more independent clauses. An *independent clause*, also called a *main clause* because it expresses a main idea, is a group of words that could stand on their own as a sentence.

> *The players practiced but the cheerleaders goofed off.*

Take out *but* and both of the clauses would make sense by themselves. These clauses carry equal weights of meaning.

A **complex sentence** is made up of an independent clause and one or more *dependent clauses*. Since an independent clause expresses the main idea in a sentence, a dependent clause comes along to help explain or clarify that main idea.

> *Women who drive trucks are road warriors, too.*

The independent clause here is *Women . . . are road warriors, too.* The dependent clause is *. . . who drive trucks . . . .* The independent clause makes a point about women, and the dependent clause tells which women we are making a point about.

Relative clauses are one kind of dependent clause. Relative clauses can be restrictive or unrestrictive. **Restrictive clauses** add information that is limited to a subset of the subject of the sentence. **Unrestrictive clauses** share information that applies to the whole group. Compare these two sentences:

> *Women who always say what they want get their way.*
> *Women, who always say what they want, get their way.*

In the first sentence the clause *who always say what they want* is restrictive, because it says we are talking only about those women who say what they want—not about all women. In the second sentence the clause is unrestrictive, because it purports to tell us something about all women. Unrestrictive clauses are set off from the rest of the sentence by commas in writing and by very brief pauses in speech. But these commas and minuscule pauses signal a *huge* difference in the meaning of the two sentences.

Compound-complex sentences, as the name implies, are sentences made up of at least two main clauses and at least one dependent clause.

> *We wanted to watch television because we were exhausted but they wanted to play football because they'd just woken up.*

That is a compound-complex sentence because it has two main clauses—We *wanted to watch television* and *they wanted to play football*, and because it also has dependent clauses—*because we were exhausted* and *because they'd just woken up.*

PARTS OF SPEECH   Let's start with nouns. **Nouns** are names. Historically, that's what the word *noun* means, and it is related to *nominate* ("to put someone's name forward"), *nominal* ("in name only"), and *nomenclature* ("about the naming of things"). **Proper nouns** begin with capital letters, and they name particular people, places, or things. We can say "I like to swim in the *ocean*" (here *ocean* is a common noun), but "Once I swam in the Atlantic *Ocean* (and now *Ocean*, and also *Atlantic*, are proper nouns); or "I want a *drink*" but "I want a *Diet Pepsi*."

Nouns can be **concrete**, things you can touch, throw, or dip your finger into, like *flower*, *football* and *milk*; or **abstract**, general things like *happiness* or *luck*. The difference matters in the way we construct sentences: You can say *I have a football* but not **I have a happiness*. (In linguistics, we conventionally put an asterisk [*] before an ungrammatical sentence.)

We have count nouns and mass nouns, too. **Count nouns** name things that can be counted, like *one duck, two ducks*. **Mass nouns** name things that can't be counted but have to be measured, like *money* and *milk*. You don't say **one money, *two moneys*. You have to say *some money*, or *much money*. That's why we say *money* and *milk* are not count nouns, but mass nouns. As for count nouns, you say *many ducks* but not **much ducks*, because *ducks*, like *bucks*, *trucks*, and *clucks* (but not *luck* or *muck*), are count nouns. Standard English would have you say *Ten items or fewer* because *items* is a count noun—but tell that to your local supermarket!

Most nouns come in **singular** (for one) and **plural** (for more than one) forms, like *pigeon* and *pigeons*. Abstract nouns only come in the singular form, though: *She has good luck*, but not **They have good lucks*. (The same is true of mass nouns: We say *He has ten dollars*, but not **He has ten moneys*).

Plurals normally add *-s* to a singular noun, as in *dog* and *dogs*. Note, though, that the *-s* or *-es* ending has three pronunciations:

dog/dogs (the sound is "zzz")

fish/fishes (the sound is "izzz")

duck/ducks (the sound is "sss")

Some plurals are irregular. *Child/children, woman/women, man/men, ox/oxen, mouse/mice, goose/geese, foot/feet, tooth/teeth* all came from Old English, where words commonly changed internally to make plurals. Some plurals change internally but still add *-s*: *wife/wives, dwarf/dwarves, shelf/shelves* (and note that the plural of *roof [roofs]* experiences the same internal sound change as *wife/wives* and *knife/knives*, but the *F* spelling doesn't change to *V*). Some nouns don't change at all from singular to plural: *deer/deer, fish/fish, trout/trout, bison/bison*.

Words from Latin often have irregular plurals, too. Latin nouns came in different genders and each made its plural differently (see Table 3.4).

Most *proper names* form plurals just as common nouns do: by adding *-s*. Brad and Angelina can be referred to together as the *Pitts*, and more than one Kennedy are *Kennedys*. (Note that the spelling rule, "Change the Y to I and add *-es*" does not apply to proper nouns.) When a proper noun ends in *s, z, ch*, or *sh*, we add *-es* to form the plural. More than one Jones are *Joneses*, the many members of the Bush family are *Bushes*, our friend Chris Hatch and his wife are the *Hatches*, and Miriam Martinez and her husband are the *Martinezes*. None of these plurals needs an apostrophe (which will be news to many mailbox painters in America!).

Note that many other languages don't behave this way. Both French and Spanish pluralize the article (the word corresponding to *the* in English), but not the proper noun (*Los Calderón, Les Sarkozy*). English language learners may be confused by that difference.

There are some rare cases where an apostrophe is used with plurals. The plurals of numbers and letters need apostrophes: *1's, 2's, 3's; A's, B's, C's; M.D.'s* and *Ph.D.'s*. But that's about all. American writing, even in some pretty expensive signs, is rife with inappropriate apostrophes in plurals.

Possessives of nouns are generally straightforward: Add *-'s*. Adding possessives to proper names works the same as with common nouns, with a few exceptions. Proper names ending with an *S* may take an apostrophe only, or take *-'s*: *Charles' book* and *Charles's book* are both acceptable, according Strunk and White's *Elements of Style* (1979)—just be consistent about it.

Table 3.4 Plurals of Nouns from Latin

GENDER	SINGULAR	PLURAL
Feminine	larva	larvae
	antenna	antennae
	alumna	alumnae
Masculine	nucleus	nuclei
	focus	foci
	syllabus	syllabi
	alumnus	alumni
	fungus	fungi
Neuter	datum (rare)	data
	opus	opera
	medium	media
	millennium	millennia
	memorandum	memoranda
Others	index	indices
	axis	axes
	thesis	theses

Count nouns in English are preceded by **articles**: *a football* or *the football*. Articles don't mean much, except they let us know if we have heard the word before in this conversation. If you say, "I bought **a** football" using the **indefinite article**, your friend might say, "Oh, that's nice." But if you say, "I bought *the* football," using the **definite article**, your friend will say, "Which one?" or "What football?" because by using the definite article you implied that you had already mentioned a football.

The use of articles is not the same in all languages. Some, like Chinese, don't use them at all. Others use them differently from the way English does. For example, in English we say "Love conquers all," but in Spanish they say *El amor lo vence todo*, or "*The love conquers all.*"

It is not unusual for a child who is a native speaker of another language to have trouble with definite and indefinite articles in English.

Pronouns stand for nouns and avoid a lot of tedious repetition. There are many kinds of pronouns, as you can see in Table 3.5. English language learners may need to learn these English pronouns. To native speakers they may be second nature, although in many dialects they may be used in non-standard ways, such as *Me and my brother went fishing, Get your hands off them shoes,* and even *This here is mine; that there is yourn* (although you have to go pretty far out of town to hear that). A problem pronouns cause for comprehension is one of reference, when it is not clear who is meant when a text says *this, that,* or *it.* Consider this passage, for an example of unclear pronoun reference:

> *Alicia was only four feet tall. She had a fierce dog and a wry sense of humor. Her father was a noted politician. This made her feel a little out of place sometimes.*

What made her feel out of place—all of those factors or just one? The use of the pronoun *this* doesn't say, and because it doesn't, the meaning of the passage is unclear.

Verbs are words that name actions. Verbs come in different **tenses**, too. A verb tense refers to the time that the action takes place. Note the verb tenses in Table 3.6. In grammatical terminology, *perfect* means that something is completed, so the present perfect means that as of the present, an action has been completed; the past perfect means that in the past an action had already been completed, and so on. *Progressive* means that an action is going on. The present progressive tense means that an action is going on in the present; the past progressive tense (also called the *imperfect* tense) means that an action was going on in the past, and so on.

Table 3.5 Varieties of Pronouns

PERSONAL PRONOUNS		
Subjective	*I [he, she, it] did it.*	can be subjects of sentences
Possessive	*This is my [your, her, his] book*	indicate ownership
Objective	*He saw me [you, her, him, us]*	receive actions or follow prepositions
Reflexive	*I cut myself; You cut yourself, etc.*	the action is done to oneself
Intensive	*I like it myself; You like it yourself, etc.*	emphasize the subject
DEMONSTRATIVE PRONOUNS		
As determiners	*I want those [this, them, these]*	stand for something that is indicated
	These shoes, or That book.	point to a certain thing
INDEFINITE PRONOUNS		
	I want some. I don't have any.	point to a category of unspecified things
RELATIVE PRONOUNS		
	She wants a dog that hunts. This is the germ which caused the illness.	introduce dependent words or clauses
INTERROGATIVE PRONOUNS		
As pronouns	*Who moved my book? Where is the fire? What caused the smoke?*	stand for an unknown person, place, or thing
As determiners	*What book? Which fire?*	point to an unknown thing
NEGATIVE PRONOUNS		
	Nobody knows the trouble I've seen. This is no one's business. We're going nowhere, but nothing can stop us.	stand for an unknown person, place, or thing

The forms of verbs vary with their **person** and **number**. Their number can be singular or plural, and they may occur in the first, second, or third person (see Table 3.7).

People have moods. So do verbs: the indicative mood, the conditional mood, and the subjunctive mood. The **conditional mood** is used in a main or independent clause of a sentence to suggest that an action depends on something else:

I *would run* if I weren't so tired.
I *would have run* if I hadn't been so tired.

The **subjunctive mood** is used with verbs in the dependent clause of a sentence (see page 80 above) to refer to something that is uncertain, contrary to fact, hypothetical, hoped for, or doubtful:

Table 3.6 Verb Tenses

VERB TENSE	EXAMPLE
Simple present	*Juan skates*
Simple past	*Juan skated*
Simple future	*Juan will skate*
Present perfect	*Juan has skated*
Past perfect	*Juan had skated*
Future perfect	*Juan will have skated*
Present progressive	*Juan is skating*
Past progressive	*Juan was skating*
Future progressive	*Juan will be skating*

Table 3.7   Person and Number of Verbs in the Present Tense

	SINGULAR	PLURAL
First person	I run	We run
Second person	You run	You (all) run
Third person	She runs	They run

> *If I <u>were</u> you, I wouldn't touch that wire.*
> *We insist that our money <u>be</u> refunded.*

Often the subjunctive mood sounds archaic, though. When Jack's Giant roared,

> *Fee, fie, foe, fum! I smell the blood of an Englishman!*
> *<u>Be</u> he alive or <u>be</u> he dead, I'll grind his bones to make my bread!*

we knew he was an *old* giant, who lived a long time ago.

The **indicative mood** is the straightforward one we most often use. It is used to make factual statements and to ask questions:

> *You didn't touch that wire.*
> *Did he refund our money?*

There are four classes of verbs: transitive active, transitive passive, intransitive linking, and intransitive complete.

Transitive verbs take objects. **Objects** are receivers of the action named by the verb. Objects can be **direct**—the person or thing that something happens to—or **indirect**—the person or thing who is the beneficiary of the action. Note these sentences:

> *Sheila collects DVD's* (*DVD's* is a direct object), and
> *Sheila gave Herbert a DVD* (*Herbert* is an indirect object and *DVD's* is a direct object).

In the preceding sentences, the verbs are **transitive active**, because the sentences are framed in the **active voice**. Sentences in the active voice take the form **subject** (the agent or doer of the action) + **verb** + **object** (the receiver of the action). When sentences are framed in the **passive voice**, the verbs are **transitive passive**. Here are some examples:

> *DVD's are collected by Sheila* (which sounds pretty stupid, but is technically correct) and
> *Herbert was given a DVD by Sheila* (which sounds more reasonable).

When a sentence is framed in the passive voice, the grammatical subject of the sentence functions either as a direct or an indirect object. In the sentence, *DVD's are collected by Sheila, DVD's* is the grammatical subject but *DVD's* are still the items given, the receivers of the action. In the second sentence, *Herbert was given a DVD by Sheila, Herbert* is the grammatical subject, but he is the beneficiary of the action, and not the one who did the giving.

Discerning the difference between sentences in the active voice and those in the passive voice can be challenging for young readers and English language learners. These readers often expect the grammatical subject of the sentence to be the agent of the action and not the object or the beneficiary of it.

Passive sentences cause another kind of problem, in that they don't have to mention who is actually behind the action. Politicians famously exclaim, "Mistakes were made!" and the passive construction allows them to slip by without saying who made them. (But try that with your mother!)

Intransitive linking verbs resemble equals signs in arithmetic. In

Juan <u>is</u> a gymnast
Juan <u>seems</u> happy
Alicia <u>became</u> ill

the verbs *is*, *seems*, and *became* are all linking verbs because they link the subjects of those sentences with either the things they are or their states. The verbs are considered intransitive because in grammatical terms, transitive verbs take objects and intransitive verbs don't.

Intransitive complete verbs don't link anything, and they don't take objects, either. They are complete unto themselves.

Sheila coughed.
Juan sneezed.
The car exploded.

Main verbs, auxiliary verbs, participles, gerunds, and infinitives are all verb forms. In the sentences *DVD's are collected by Sheila*, and *Herbert was given a DVD by Sheila*, the transitive passive verbs took the forms *are collected* and *was given*. *Collected* and *given* were the **main verbs**, and *are* and *was* are **auxiliary verbs**, or **helping verbs**.

The main verb in a passive sentence has the form of a **participle**. Many past participles end in *-ed* and resemble the past tense, but several do not. We say *The food was cooked*, and *He has <u>cooked</u> the food*. But we also say *The medicine was <u>taken</u>* and *She has <u>taken</u> the medicine*—and the underlined forms are all participles. Participles can function as adjectives, too. You can say *The eggs were fried*, and here the sentence is cast in the passive voice using a transitive passive verb consisting of an auxiliary verb and the participial form of the main verb. You can also say *She likes fried eggs*, and now the participle *fried* functions as an adjective modifying *eggs*. For still more variety, participles come not just in past forms (*fried* in the last sentence is a **past participle**) but also in present forms. In *The sun is baking us*, the verb *baking* is a **present participle** serving as part of a present progressive tense (see above). In the sentence *We stood in the baking sun*, now the present participle *baking* is serving as an adjective.

We can twist verbs into another function called **gerunds**. A gerund is a verb ending in *-ing* that functions grammatically as a noun:

I like <u>baking</u>.
<u>Making</u> mistakes cost Sheila her job.

The **infinitive** form of a verb—*to* + the verb—functions in much the same way a gerund does:

I like <u>to bake</u>.
<u>To err</u> is human; <u>to forgive</u> is divine.

Modal verbs are a special class of auxiliary verbs, and they indicate fine shades of meaning, including the likelihood of something occurring, someone's ability to perform an action, permission to do something, or obligation to do something (Palmer, 2001). Here are some examples:

Ahab <u>might</u> return soon. (likelihood)
Ahab <u>can</u> return as soon as he finds the money for a ticket. (ability)
Ahab <u>may</u> return here any time he likes. (permission)
Ahab <u>must</u> return at once! (obligation)

The differences between these modal verbs is sometimes ambiguous. For instance, not all speakers use *may* and *can* with contrasted meaning, so we hear *Can Rodney come over?* when the question is, does Rodney have permission, not the ability, to come over. Similarly, *Rodney may come over* can be interpreted to mean either that it's possible but not certain that Rodney will come over, or that he has permission to do so. Being sensitive to these seemingly minor grammatical features makes a big difference in comprehending the meanings of the sentences. (And there's yet another reason for close reading!)

Adjectives say something about nouns and **adverbs** say something about verbs, adjectives, or other adverbs. The adjective *black* in *She drives a black Porsche* tells us something about the Porsche; and the adverb *recklessly* in *She drives recklessly* tells us something about the way she drives it. Words that mean roughly the same thing have adjectival and adverbial forms, like *a slow car* (adjective) and *a car that goes slowly* (adverb). As in these examples, adverbs are often made by adding *-ly* onto an adjective. People don't always observe the distinction between adjectives and adverbs in speech—we often say *Go slow*. But in writing, and in formal speech, we will prefer *Go slowly*. Children should be aware of the difference, even if they don't always observe it.

Adverbs tell us more about adjectives in sentences like *Shirley is very funny* (where *funny* is an adjective telling us how Shirley is, and *very* is an adverb telling us how funny); or *Shirley drives completely carelessly* (where *carelessly* is an adverb telling us how Shirley drives, and *completely* is another adverb telling us just how carelessly).

Conjunctions are words that join things—other words, phrases (a group of words), or clauses (a group of words with a subject and a predicate—see above). They come in three varieties: **Coordinating conjunctions** join words, phrases, and clauses that are of equal importance grammatically: *I like tea and coffee; I like tea and I like coffee; I don't like tea but I like coffee; I drink coffee in the morning and after lunch.* **Correlative conjunctions** come in pairs: *I like both tea and coffee; I like neither tea nor coffee; I like not only tea but also coffee.* **Subordinating conjunctions** join dependent clauses to another word or main clause: *I like her because she is nice; She's very wise although she's young; He has been unhappy since he lost his bicycle.*

Prepositions are words that show relationships between other words. In these sentences, the prepositions are underlined:

> She was almost hit *by* a car.
> That is *beside* the point.
> The duchess swept *into* the room.
> The Frisbee flew *across* the lawn.
> Let me tell you the story *about* a man named Charlie.

Prepositions come in phrases, consisting of a preposition followed by a noun (or something like it) plus that noun's modifiers. Prepositional phrases function much like modifiers.

> We escaped *by quickly hiding in the smelly sewer*.

In the above sentence, *by quickly hiding* is a prepositional phrase (*hiding* seems like a verb but in that form it is a gerund, and it functions grammatically like a noun). *In the smelly sewer* is a prepositional phrase, too.

Syntax and Reading

Syntax is important in literacy. First, and most obviously, syntax is needed to make meaning from text. In many examples in the previous section, a reader needs to understand the syntax to derive the right meaning of a sentence. Syntax matters in word recognition, too. Often, teachers will ask a reader who struggles over an unknown word, "What would make sense here?" And if the child is reading the sentence, "The mother hoped the jar would contain money, but it d_____," the word *but* will help the reader figure out that the next word should say *didn't*. The conjunction *but* tells the reader to expect those words to convey a meaning counter to the beginning phrase. Syntax matters, too, in writing Standard English, and, of course, in gaining acceptable scores on tests of knowledge of the English language arts. Finally, students who are English language learners must learn the syntax of English, and they will often be relying on their teachers to clarify problems. The challenge is that most knowledge of syntax is the *tacit knowledge* of native speakers, including teachers. Teachers must work extra hard to understand on a conscious level the syntactic concepts they use on a working, tacit level.

Text Structure

The materials children read come in structures that have loose "rules" similar to the rules of syntax we reviewed in the previous section. As students have experiences reading different types of texts, they learn those rules—normally on a tacit or unconscious level. Having the rules in their minds helps readers follow along with the text—just as knowing the order of a religious service or of a football game helps someone follow or take part in the proceedings.

The structures of stories—called *story grammars*—are the most commonly taught text structures. But informational texts have structures, too: cause-and-effect, question-and-answer, problem-and-solution, taxonomy, chronology, general exposition, and arguments-and-reasons.

STORY GRAMMAR   The most thoroughly studied of the structures of discourse (*discourse* roughly means "a body of talk") is story grammar. Consider the story "The Frowning Princess" in Figure 3.3.

Story Maps

Figure 3.3
The Frowning Princess

The Frowning Princess

In a faraway time and a distant place, there lived a king and his daughter. She frowned. From morning to night, she frowned and frowned and frowned. Even if you saw her in her sleep, she would still be frowning.

The royal advisor worried. "This is terrible, your majesty. A frowning princess is like a cloudy day," he said. "The people will think there is something wrong with your kingdom if the princess doesn't stop frowning."

"I pay you well, so I guess you are right," said the king. "We must find a way to make my daughter stop frowning."

The king and the royal advisor told the princess every joke they knew. But kings and royal advisors are not funny people, and after they had told both of their jokes, the princess was still frowning.

They brought a dozen monkeys and three trained hyenas to the palace. Nobody got any sleep for days. The princess frowned even harder.

Then it happened that a chambermaid put her head between her legs to clean under the princess' bed. Seeing the princess from this odd position, the chambermaid discovered something. "The princess is smiling," she thought. She told the princess to stand on her head and look into the mirror. When the princess saw her reflection, she tried to turn her upside-down frown right-side up. So, of course, she smiled.

Now the princess smiles all the day long. The king, his advisor, and the people are happy. It may be that the princess is still trying to frown, but I won't tell if you won't.

Table 3.8 Story Grammar Applied

ELEMENTS OF STORY GRAMMAR	EXAMPLES
The **setting**, a place and time	"In a faraway time and a distant place . . ."
There are **characters**	". . . a king and his daughter . . ."
An **initiating event**—something that creates a problem to be solved, and sets further events in motion.	"She frowned. From morning to night, the princess frowned and frowned and frowned."
There is one or more **episodes** that contain . . .	
An **attempt** to solve the problem	"The king and the royal advisor told the princess every joke they knew."
Which has an **outcome**	". . . the princess was still frowning."
Possibly another **attempt**	"They brought a dozen monkeys and three trained hyenas to the palace."
Which has an **outcome**	"Nobody got any sleep for days. The princess frowned even harder."
Possibly another **attempt**	"A chambermaid put her head between her legs to clean under the princess' bed. Seeing the princess from this odd position, the chambermaid discovered something. 'The princess is smiling,' she thought. She told the princess to stand on her head and look into the mirror."
Which has an **outcome**	"When the princess saw her reflection, she tried to turn her upside-down frown right-side up. So, of course, she smiled."
There is a **resolution**	"Now the princess smiles all the day long."
There is a **consequence**	"The king, his advisor, and the people are happy."

Source: Based on Stein, N. & Glenn, C. An analysis of story comprehension in elementary school children. In R. O. Freedle (Ed.), *New directions in discourse processing* (pp. 53–120). Norwood, NJ: Ablex Publishing Corporation. 2009.

Stories such as this one have a set of identifiable elements, or slots, into which the particulars of the story are placed. These slots are almost always organized in a particular order. (The terms *identifiable elements* and *particular order* are signs that one is talking about grammar or syntax.) For example, a story consists of a setting, one or more episodes, and a consequence. An analysis of the story "The Frowning Princess" using this story grammar model is found in Table 3.8.

Children as young as kindergarten age have a sense of story grammar, and they appear to use it to comprehend stories (Stein & Glenn, 1979). Teaching children story grammars improves their comprehension (Olson & Gee, 1988). Such instruction has been found to be especially helpful for children with learning disabilities (Gersten, 1998).

CCSS

• Informational Text 4: Craft and Structure

STRUCTURES OF INFORMATIONAL TEXTS The Common Core Standards have mandated that a large portion of students' reading be done in informational text. Accordingly, the varieties of informational texts used in schools have proliferated greatly. The following are some frequently used structures.

Question and Answer Many popular books for young readers pose questions about outlandish topics, and then provide answers. Melvin Berger's True or False books (2008, 2009, 2010) are good examples. Books for older readers pose larger questions and develop longer answers.

Problem and Solution Some texts pose a problem, engage readers in thinking about how it might be solved, and then explain solutions.

Taxonomy A taxonomy is an organizing chart. Some texts explain the varieties of members of a category that are related to each other. Melvin Berger's *Chomp!* (1999) does that for sharks; *Snap!* (2002) does it for crocodiles and alligators.

Chronology A chronology is an unfolding of a series of events through time. Janis Herbert's *American Revolution for Kids* (2002) lays out a series of chapters that are each somewhat self-contained stories about a part of the Revolution, arranged in chronological order. The two dozen books in Franklin Watts Publishers' *Wicked History* series provide the chronology of events in the lives of characters who were deliberately chosen not only for their importance, but also for their fascination for young readers, especially boys: Vlad the Impaler, Catherine the Great, Hitler, Genghis Khan, and others.

Comparison and Contrast Many texts are arranged to make comparisons. Steve Jenkins' *What Do You Do With a Tail Like This?* (2008) teaches zoology to young readers by discussing living creatures (monkeys, scorpions, elephants, and more) one at a time and comparing and contrasting them by that feature (tails, eyes, claws).

General Exposition A widely used structure for informational texts is similar to the chapter you are reading now. It sets out a main topic, subdivides it into smaller topics, and provides details for those smaller topics.

Arguments and Reasons Arguments are everywhere—in political campaigns, on newspapers' editorial pages, in advertisements, and, increasingly, in texts for children. Argumentative text typically states a claim of something the reader should believe or do or both. Then it lists reasons that support the claim, along with evidence that supports each reason. All of those things are marshaled toward a conclusion by the use of logic. Jen Green's *Why Should I Save Water?* (2005a), and *Why Should I Recycle?* (2005b) are good examples of argumentative works for young readers.

Variations in Language Use

DIALECTS AND THE GRAPHOLECT Members of different geographic, social, and cultural groups use language in unique ways. Some of the uniqueness is captured in dialects that the groups use. *Dialects* are variations of a language that are noticeable, but not so profound as to make for different languages. *Geographic dialects* are reflected in the differences in the word pronunciations, word choice, and conversational styles of speakers from Hibbing, Minnesota; Goliad, Texas; or Ocracoke, North Carolina. *Social dialects* are reflected in the speech of people from different social classes. *Ethnic dialects* are reflected in the speech of people from different racial groups. Of course, all these dialects overlap, as would be found in the speech of a professional African American family from the southern Appalachian Mountains.

Differences among dialects present greater problems to some children learning to read than to others, because books are produced in the dialect chosen by the publishers and that dialect inevitably resembles the ways of talking of certain groups of people, and not others. That has been true as long as we have had writing. For example, in 1476, when William Caxton printed the first books in English for the masses, he wrote down the local way of speaking, the dialect of Wessex—and even that dialect was badly distorted by his assistants, who came from the continent and struggled with English. So reading texts from Caxton's press was a stretch for many people in England. In contemporary America, written language differs to some extent from *everyone's* speech—in the choice of words and the structure of sentences and the patterns in which information is presented. The dialect in which printing is done has been called the *grapholect*—literally, the dialect of writing. But if there is such a thing as a grapholect, it is closer to urban educated, white, middle-class speech than to any other spoken dialect. It should not be surprising that some African American educators and children's advocates proposed teaching African American children in *Ebonics*, as if the speech of African Americans were a different language. And they are right to insist that there is not a hard-and-fast difference between a dialect and a language: Sixty years ago, the Yiddish linguist Max Weinreich quipped that "A language is a dialect with an army and navy" (quoted in Joseph, 2004). Or we might say a language is a dialect with a body of literature.

New Zealand educator Marie Clay stood near two children playing when someone else's mother called her child. The two children looked up, and one said, "Her b'ain't a

Language and Diversity

What are three ways in which language use differs in social situations?

DIFFERENTIATED INSTRUCTION

SIOP®
Sheltered
Instruction
Observation
Protocol®

The Language of School

English language learners and other students who need extra support in the classroom can be helped to learn the content of the curriculum if the right kind of scaffolding is supplied. Sheltered instruction requires that the teacher carefully think through the demands that the language of the lesson, the content of the lesson, and the learning tasks the lesson will place on the student. Then the teacher takes steps to make all three accessible. As California teacher and professor MaryEllen Vogt writes,

> For ELL's [English Language Learners] to become successful in learning content, they need to learn not only English grammar and vocabulary, but also "the language of school." . . . What we have learned from these students is that they need assistance with all three knowledge bases: knowledge of English, knowledge of the content topic, and knowledge of how tasks are to be completed. Together, these are the key components of academic literacy. (Vogt, 2000, pp. 335, 336)

Vogt goes on to recommend the following:

- Make the objectives of the lesson—for both the language to be used and the content to be learned—very explicit, including writing it on the board.

- Engage the students in active and meaningful activities (not just seatwork), and use various means to communicate information: graphic organizers, examples, analogies, repetitions. Communication between teacher and student and among students is frequent.

- Relate the lessons to the students' prior experiences and background knowledge.

- Choose key vocabulary for the lesson and introduce it in advance, highlight it during the lesson, and review it at the lesson's end and periodically thereafter.

- Word lessons carefully and speak clearly and distinctly.

- Explain how tasks are to be carried out, then give examples of the kinds of responses that are expected, and explain why.

- Scaffold writing assignments with graphic organizers and other outlining aids; scaffold reading assignments with study guides, written questions, and outlines for note taking.

- Encourage higher-order thinking by means of many techniques.

- Use group work, including paired work.

callin' we. Us ain't belong a she." The children went on playing. Clay observed that the speaker used a non-standard form of every word in the sentence—yet the sentence was completely understandable to the children, and to Clay, too. If language is a code, it's not a strict code like a string of symbols that has to be typed into a computer in a particular format or the machine won't recognize it. We can express ourselves in many different ways and still be understood.

We must be careful with dialects, first, because no one would want to extinguish the beautiful variety of expression that exists in dialects. Second, linguists assure us that no dialect is superior to another in expressing meanings (Labov, 1973; Wardaugh, 2010). Third, one's speech is tied up with one's culture, friends, family, and self—and rejecting a dialect is tantamount to rejecting a person.

Yet even before the Common Core standards called for the teaching of Standard English, child advocates and educators from many quarters were calling on the schools to provide every student with access to Standard English not only because Standard English is the language of print and the mainstream media, but also because being able to speak and understand Standard English when situations call for it gives people opportunities they might not have otherwise. The recommended approach for teachers is to address the matter directly. Explain that Standard English is in the curriculum to be taught because there are advantages in knowing how to use it.

REGISTERS   Another way in which speakers use language differently is the many social registers all people employ when talking to people they hold in different degrees of intimacy and respect. Even a kindergarten child uses different forms of address when she is talking to another child, her mother, or her teacher. In English, different degrees of intimacy and formality are signaled by the amount of indirection that is used. Compare the following sentences:

"Hey, open the window!"

"Please open the window."

"Would you mind opening the window?"

"Don't you think we need some fresh air in here?"

Other languages signal these differences with grammatical forms. Spanish has the familiar form of the pronoun *tu*, used with close friends and family members, and the formal *usted*, used with adults. Romanian has *tu*, which is familiar, but also *dumneavoastra*, which is more formal and distant, and *dumneatá*, which, as one Romanian explained, is "so polite that it's insulting." Linguists use the term *registers* to refer to the ranges of speech speakers have for expressing themselves in different social situations:

- A *ceremonial register*, used in religious functions and formal affairs such as school graduations
- A *professional register*, used in giving an explanation at school, such as discussing a lesson in science or language arts
- A *polite register*, used in informal situations with people the speaker does not know well
- A *casual register*, used when telling a story or sharing jokes with close friends.

In teaching, you may need to point out these different registers to students because there are appropriate and inappropriate times to use each register. A person may be considered rude, uncouth, pompous, or insulting if she or he uses the wrong register in any situation. In addition, when it comes to close reading, being aware of both dialects and registers adds one more layer of meaning for students.

For Review

If reading is making sense of talk written down, then teachers need more than a passing acquaintance with linguistics, the study of language, in order to teach reading well.

In this chapter we explored the main areas of language knowledge, including the sound system of language or *phonology*, the collection of words to be learned or *vocabulary*, the ways words are formed or *morphology*, the ordering and inflecting of classes of words or *syntax*, and the social use of language, including *dialects* and *registers*.

English uses an alphabetic writing system, so the letters of the alphabet relate to individual speech sounds. But morphemes or meaningful word roots and affixes are also important both in the structure of words and in the act of reading them.

"Knowing" a word happens on several levels, and there are also different "tiers" of words to be known. Having the ability to negotiate those tiers can help reduce the burden of teaching and learning the 90,000 different words that are typically used in elementary through high school.

Most of what we know about syntax is *tacit* knowledge— we can use it but we can't talk about what we know. But teachers are called on to explain the syntax of Standard English to all students on some level, especially to English language learners.

Teachers need to be aware of the varieties of registers and dialects of language. Dialects and registers are a great part of the richness of language, but we need to make sure all children have control of the grapholect, the "dialect" of written language.

For Your Journal

1. Review the answers to the anticipation guide on the first page of this chapter. What answers would you give to those questions now that you have read this chapter?

2. If you still need proof that you have tacit knowledge of English grammar, that is, knowledge that enables you to talk and listen but of which you are largely unaware, try this exercise. Explain what is wrong with this sentence: *Ignacio is playing with a red big ball.* State the rule that you would use in writing the sentence correctly.

3. Families from different social backgrounds think of literacy in strikingly different ways. How did you use literacy in your family when you were growing up? What materials did the people around you read? Did they share or discuss them with each other? If so, how? Was there bedtime reading? If so, what was it like?

Taking It to the World

Interview a guidance counselor at a middle or high school or a counseling psychologist who treats adults. Interview a foreman or manager at a business or manufacturing plant. With regard to their clients or the people they supervise, to what extent do these professionals find that people's problems are related to their difficulties in using language for different purposes—for self-awareness, for getting along with others, for giving and receiving directions clearly? Do these people believe that schools have a role in teaching communication for different purposes?

New Literacies Connections

The Internet has many excellent sites with information on language.

Professors Lily Fillmore and Catherine Snow have an excellent summary of language concepts for the teacher available online at <http://www.cal.org/ericcll/teachers/teachers.pdf>. The work is entitled *What teachers need to know about language,* and it was originally published in August, 2000, by the U.S. Department of Education's Office of Educational Research and Improvement. This 50-page monograph is written in a question-and-answer format with chapters on oral and written language, and language and diversity. It's an excellent summary of essential knowledge about language by two distinguished scholars.

There are several sites on the Internet that provide rich examples of how sounds are made, including diagrams of the mouth, recordings of sounds, and even spectrographic displays of sound waves produced with sound.

1. Professor George Dillon at the University of Washington has a wonderful site <http://faculty.washington.edu/dillon/PhonResources/> that provides information about speech sounds and also links to numerous other sites that provide detailed information and tutorials.

2. Visit the "Vocal Vowels" exhibit at the San Francisco Museum of Science's online Exploratorium <www.exploratorium.edu/exhibits/vocal_vowels> to see how a duck call can be made to produce human vowel sounds by modifying the production chamber.

3. Noted linguist Peter Ladefoged provides a comprehensive site devoted to speech sounds at <http://hctv.humnet.ucla.edu/departments/linguistics/VowelsandConsonants>.

MyEducationLab™

Go to Topics 2, 4, and 5 (Phonemic Awareness/ Phonics, Vocabulary, and Comprehension) in the MyEducationLab <www.myeducationlab.com> for your course, where you can:

- Find learning outcomes for Phonemic Awareness/ Phonics, Vocabulary, and Comprehension along with the national standards that connect to these outcomes.
- Complete Assignments and Activities that can help you more deeply understand the chapter content.
- Apply and practice your understanding of the core teaching skills identified in the chapter with the Building Teaching Skills and Dispositions learning units.
- Apply and practice your understanding of the core teaching skills identified in the chapter with the Building Teaching Skills and Dispositions learning units.

- Check your comprehension on the content covered in the chapter by going to the Study Plan in the Book Resources for your text. Here you will be able to take a chapter quiz, receive feedback on your answers, and then access Review, Practice, and Enrichment activities to enhance your understanding of chapter content.
- Visit A+RISE. A+RISE® Standards2Strategy™ is an innovative and interactive online resource that offers new teachers in grades K-12 just in time, research-based instructional strategies that meet the linguistic needs of ELLs as they learn content, differentiate instruction for all grades and abilities, and are aligned to Common Core Elementary Language Arts standards English language proficiency standards in WIDA, Texas, California, and Florida.

Emergent Literacy

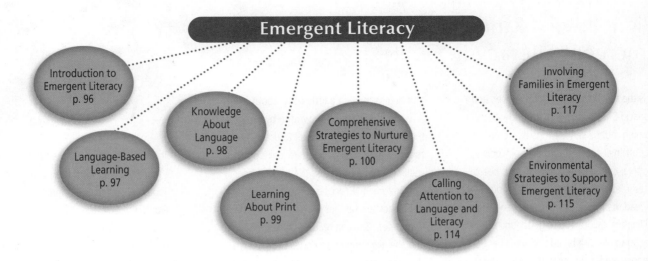

Emergent Literacy

- Introduction to Emergent Literacy p. 96
- Language-Based Learning p. 97
- Knowledge About Language p. 98
- Learning About Print p. 99
- Comprehensive Strategies to Nurture Emergent Literacy p. 100
- Calling Attention to Language and Literacy p. 114
- Environmental Strategies to Support Emergent Literacy p. 115
- Involving Families in Emergent Literacy p. 117

Anticipation Guide

The following statements will help you begin thinking about the topics covered in this chapter. Answer *true* or *false* in response to each statement. As you read and learn more about the topics mentioned in these statements, double-check your answers. See what interests you and what prompts your curiosity toward more understanding.

_____ **1.** When you get right down to it, learning to read is "natural."

_____ **2.** The ability to tap out individual phonemes in words is normally developed by the end of kindergarten.

_____ **3.** Concepts about print, such as the arrangement of print on the page or the fact that people read the print and not the pictures, are learned by some children without their having to be taught them, but others need instruction.

_____ **4.** Children don't need to be aware of the features of language to learn to talk, but they do need some language awareness in order to learn to read and write.

_____ **5.** All children know what words are and that their language is composed of them. We don't need to teach them that.

_____ **6.** We can teach children a lot about reading and writing through passive means, such as labeling items in the classroom.

_____ **7.** Dialogic reading is a means of teaching children about both printed and spoken language.

_____ **8.** Reading aloud to children is a waste of valuable instructional time. If it is to be done at all, it should be left up to parents.

_____ **9.** Teaching reading is such a complicated undertaking that parents should be discouraged from taking any part in it.

_____ **10.** Parents read to their children much more than they used to. This is true of people from all income groups.

A Classroom Story

Vignette of a Kindergarten Classroom: Emergent Literacy in Context

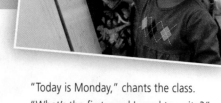

It is the second Monday in November, and Ignacio Diaz's kindergartners know the morning routine very well. As they enter, they take off their coats, stuff their lunch boxes into their cubbies, and check the job board to see who will give the weather report, who will lead the Pledge of Allegiance, and who will line the children up to go to lunch. Then they go to the task board and see what their rotations are for the language block. Their names are pasted in quadrants with symbols, indicating who will go to the independent study center, who will work with the teacher in the reading circle, who will write, and who will have reading time. Charmaigne enters the room and hands her teacher a book baggie, a plastic bag that holds a book and a group of games and activity sheets.

"Mama said she liked the drawing I did of Toad. Or maybe it was Frog. . . . How do you tell them apart again?" she says. "And she said to tell you we finally figured out how to do the alphabet game."

Ignacio laughs and puts the book baggie into a bin to be repacked for another child to take home.

As children come in from various buses, Charmaigne wanders to the library corner

and begins reading a little book about frogs. It is one of her favorites, written by Henry, the boy who taught them all to draw cartoons. Henry's penciled letters make dubious spellings that flow across the page in pencil, but Charmaigne focuses on the neat black letters her teacher has written with a felt-tipped pen. She can read some of the words, and she likes finding the ones she knows. Henry's drawings always make clear what is going on in his books, so when Charmaigne wants to, she can hold the book up and tell the story aloud as if she were reading it, even though she does not yet know many of the words.

The class is all here, and Charmaigne's turn has come to lead the Pledge of Allegiance. She knows what a flag is, but the word *flag* is taped underneath it anyway. It begins with *F*, just like the title of Henry's book, *Frogs*. Now Mr. Diaz calls the children to the rug in front of the chart stand.

"Who knows what today is?" he asks.

"Monday," says Henry.

"Right," says Ignacio. "And I'm going to write 'Today is Monday' right here on the chart. Let's say that sentence: 'Today is Monday.'"

"Today is Monday," chants the class.

"What's the first word I need to write?"

"Today," Charmaigne offers.

"Good. I'm going to start writing up here," and he points to the upper left hand corner of the sheet. "What's the first sound we hear in 'Today'?" Some children, including Charmaigne, chant the *tuh* sound, over and over. After a moment's hesitation, other children join them.

"Aw, you're champions. Now, what letter will we use to spell the *tuh* sound?"

With the children and Mr. Diaz taking turns offering up sounds and naming letters to spell them with, the morning news is written on the chart. It covers four lines. Ignacio is careful to show the children that he begins writing over on the left side, then writes across to the right, then returns to the left but down one line, and continues writing to the right again.

The children read the sentences through three times as Ignacio points to every word with his "Harry Potter wand," the stick he uses for pointing to words.

Introduction to Emergent Literacy

If they grow up in a community where others read and write, children learn a great deal about those things years before they meet their first teacher. They learn by their own efforts, and they employ an amazing capacity to look closely at language, tease out its patterns, and work their way toward competent use through a succession of more and more sophisticated stages, or layers of strategies. Certainly children depend on adults to "put literacy in their way"—surround them with print, read to them, and set up opportunities for them to try out their own versions of reading and writing. These opportunities are a hidden advantage for children who have them, and allow those children to start right into reading instruction with understanding and enthusiasm. But while some children get thousands of hours of early experiences with literacy at home, other children get few. So teachers of children in preschool and in the early school grades have a lot of work to do to prepare all children to make a good start in learning to read and write. We call this whole enterprise *emergent literacy*. It's a mix of what children first discover for themselves and what adults help them learn about literacy.

Emergent literacy means:

- a period in children's experience between the time when they first notice print and wonder what people are doing when they work with it, and the time when they can read words; and also

- the early informal and formal teaching that children receive in preschool and early kindergarten at the hands of careful teachers who make sure that all children understand what reading and writing are and what they are for, so they can benefit fully from reading instruction.

Because print represents spoken language, children must understand the language that comes from print, and know a good deal about that language and about the features of the print that represent that language. Learning language, learning about language, learning about print, and learning how print and language go together in reading and writing are the aspects of emergent literacy that will be explored in this chapter.

Language-Based Learning

Native speakers have acquired a working knowledge of the English language by the time they enter kindergarten. On average, they have vocabularies of around 2,000 root words (*run* is a root word, but *runs*, *running*, and *ran* are derived words), although children with limited language exposure may have half that (Biemiller, 2009). They can speak and understand most kinds of simple sentences and follow many stories and explanations. Remember, too, that between one child in every seven and one in every five speaks another language at home, and these children will need help learning the English language.

Understanding and being able to use language is not enough. When children learn to read, they have to be conscious of language, too. Because print represents spoken language, emergent readers need to be aware that their language is real—it is not just noise that accompanies thoughts and actions, but something that can be written down in sentences. They must know that sentences are made up of words, and they must be aware that spoken words consist of syllables and the smaller units called *phonemes*.

They also need to be learning about print—which side of a book is up, that the print is what talks, that it's arrayed on the page from top to bottom and left to right, and some other things as well.

LANGUAGE COMPETENCE   If you learned English as your first language, you may not be aware of the different aspects of your competence. Most of your knowledge of English will be *tacit*—that is, knowledge you can use, but normally you are not conscious of it. Helping children acquire a language, especially if they are not native speakers, will require that you make more of your knowledge of language conscious. Being competent in a language has many parts: words, sounds, rules of syntax, and social conventions (polite and less polite ways of saying things).

VOCABULARY   Children in the emergent literacy phase (preschool through early first grade, usually) should know words for common concepts and actions, as well as common adjectives. They should understand nuances of words, the slight

Short periods of dedicated instruction can help struggling readers improve their reading skills.

CCSS

• Language Standards 1 and 2: Conventions of Standard English; Language Standards 4, 5, and 6: Vocabulary

• Speaking and Listening 4: Presentation of Ideas

CCSS

• Speaking and Listening 6: Presentation of Ideas

• Language Standards 1: Conventions of Standard English

CCSS

• Speaking and Listening 1: Comprehension and Collaboration

Language Experience or Group Dictated Story

differences in synonyms for the same action (*run, jog, dash*), and be able to think of opposites of adjectives and verbs. They also should be able to think of things in terms of categories (*A duck is a kind of bird*).

SYNTAX   Syntax, or the rules of grammar, has two parts. One is the ordering of words in sentences. The other is the inflectional endings that indicate the number indicated by a noun and whether it is in the possessive form, and the person, number, and tense of verbs.

Children in the emergent literacy stage should be encouraged to speak in complete sentences with Standard English inflections on verbs and nouns. Some dialects of English, such as Black English, do not use inflectional English in the ways Standard English does. But because written English uses conventional inflections, children need to know them.

SOCIAL USES OF LANGUAGE   Social uses of language are not strictly related to literacy, but because certain kinds of social behavior are necessary if children are going to take part in the discussions that will help them comprehend texts and express themselves orally and in speech, children will need to learn the conventions of turn-taking and keeping comments focused on the topic. The Common Core Standards include productive participation in discussions in the English Language Arts goals.

Knowledge About Language

Being able to use a language, technically called having *competence* in a language, is different from knowing *about* a language, or what is technically called *metalinguistic awareness* (*meta-* is a Greek affix meaning "about"). You have a lot of metalinguistic awareness of a language you have studied, because much foreign language instruction is typically a study about a language. When languages are acquired in early childhood from being around others, however, we don't typically learn much *about* them. What is to be known about language that is relevant to literacy? The most important aspects are the concept of word and phonological awareness.

THE CONCEPT OF WORD   The concept of word (Morris, 2005) is knowing that a frantically uttered expression such as "MamacomequickYvonneseatingmycandy" is actually made up of the words "Mama, come quick. Yvonne's eating my candy." This is not an easy feat. Even adults can have trouble separating the speech stream into word units. The corresponding aspect of the concept of word that applies to print is knowing that in print, words are indicated by clusters of letters separated by spaces.

Not being aware of words in speech puts children at a disadvantage when they are learning to read. Instead of focusing on each word in their minds as they say it, children who do not have the concept of word might scan their eyes across a whole line of text, or they might look at only a single letter, or they might confuse written words with spoken syllables. A child who doesn't have the concept of word and isn't looking at the correct word unit is not likely to have learned to recognize new written words from the activity. But the child who has the concept of word, who looks at the written words at the instant each is sung or read, will likely have made matches between some of the written versions of the words and the spoken versions. That child should be able to recognize some of those words in the future.

PHONOLOGICAL AWARENESS   Beyond the level of words, there are other levels of speech of which emergent readers must be aware. These are syllables, onsets and rimes, and phonemes. *Syllables* are the pulses of language. They are the "beats" we hear in *elbow* (two syllables), *love* (one syllable), and *popsicle* (three syllables). As was discussed in Chapter 3, onsets and rimes are the next largest parts of syllables: The *onset* is the beginning consonant sound (if the syllable has one) and the *rime* is the vowel sound plus any consonant sound that follows. In *cat*, the onset is /c/ and the rime is /at/. In *step*, the onset is /st/ and the rime is /ep/. As the smallest speech sounds in language, *phonemes* roughly correspond to individual letters. *Dig* has three phonemes: /d/, /I/, and /g/. *Clam* has four phonemes: /k/, /l/, /æ/, and /m/. (Note that we conventionally represent phonemes with slashes on either side.)

In terms of phonological awareness, there is a range of tasks that children are recommended to perform:

- Clapping out syllables in spoken words (*ba/na/na*)
- Producing rhymes for single-syllable words (*bit—kit; bat—cat*)
- Segmenting single-syllable words into phonemes (*bit = b/ih/t*)
- Breaking off a phoneme from a single-syllable word (*sat → at*)
- Adding a phoneme to a single-syllable word (*b + at = bat*)
- Substituting phonemes in single-syllable words to make new words (*sit → sat; sit → bit; sit → sick*)

A good deal of research (e.g., Adams, 1990; Snow et al., 1998) has shown that children who are aware that words can be broken into phonemes and can manipulate phonemes will have an easier time matching letters and sounds when they begin to read than children who are not familiar with phonemes. We also know that even short periods of instruction on working with phonemes can improve children's word reading (Blachman, 2008).

Learning About Print

Now let's look at the print side of things. As we said, children's emergent literacy is partly knowing about language and partly knowing about print. Print awareness includes having an understanding of the following:

- *Concepts about print:* the set of ideas about what print is and how it works
- *The alphabetic nature of writing:* the idea that, in languages such as English, German, Spanish, and Kiswahili (but not Japanese or Chinese), writing works by using units of letters to represent language at the level of phonemes
- *Alphabet knowledge:* the ability to recognize and produce many letters of the alphabet
- *Orthographic concepts:* an understanding of the rules that relate letters to sounds.

CONCEPTS ABOUT PRINT New Zealander Marie Clay (1975) offered this account some years ago of a novice teacher giving a reading lesson to a group of beginning readers:

> *Suppose the teacher has placed an attractive picture on the wall and has asked her children for a story, which she will record under it. They offer the text, "Mother is cooking," which the teacher alters slightly to introduce some features she wishes to teach. She writes: Mother said, "I am baking."*
>
> *If she says, "Now look at our story," 30% of the new entrant group [children who are just beginning reading instruction] will attend to the picture. If she says, "Look at the words and find some that you know," between 50 and 90% will be looking for letters. If she says, "Can you see Mother?" most will agree that they can, but some see her in the picture, some can locate M, and others will locate the word Mother.*
>
> *Perhaps the children read in unison, "Mother is ..." and the teacher tries to sort this out. Pointing to said, she asks, "Does this say is?" Half agree that it does because it has s in it. "What letter does it start with?" Now the teacher is really in trouble. She assumes that the children will know that a word is built out of letters, but 50% of the children still confuse the verbal labels word and letter after six months of instruction. She also assumes that the children know that the left-hand letter following a space is the "start" of a word. Often they do not. (pp. 3–4)*

As this example shows, there are many concepts about print that children must have in place so that in a reading lesson, they can orient themselves properly to a book and direct their attention appropriately. These concepts include knowing the layout of books;

CCSS
- Foundational Skills 2: Phonological Awareness

Phonics and Phonological Awareness

Why must emergent readers be aware of syllables, onsets and rimes, and phonemes?

CCSS
- Foundational Skills 1: Print Concepts

Teach It! 6

Big Book Lesson

Phonics and Phonological Awareness

Phonics is the system by which letters and clusters of letters represent speech sounds.

Teach It! 13

Working with Names to Teach the Alphabet

Teach It! 20

Analytic Phonics Lesson

knowing what the print and the pictures do; knowing how print is laid out on the page; knowing the terms used in reading instruction, such as "the beginning of the sentence," "the end of the sentence," "the first word," and "the top of the page"; knowing what a word is; knowing what a letter is and that uppercase and lowercase letters are different versions of the same thing; and knowing at least some marks of punctuation.

ALPHABET KNOWLEDGE Alphabet knowledge is an important part of a child's emergent literacy. Some children learn to recognize most letters of the alphabet before they enter kindergarten, and all are expected to recognize and produce all 26 letters by the beginning of first grade. Knowing the letters does two things for a child: it gives us an idea of how much exposure to print a child has had and it helps that child learn to read (Walsh, Price, & Gillingham, 1988).

LETTER-TO-SOUND CORRESPONDENCE: LEARNING PHONICS A child realizes that language is real and comes in units of words, syllables, and phonemes. The child can now produce not just letter-like forms, but also many actual letters. The child has learned to orient himself or herself to books. The child realizes that ours is an alphabetic writing system that works not by showing pictures of things, not by representing syllables, but by matching letters with phonemes. Now what?

Now comes the process of discovering the system by which writing spells words, and letters and clusters of letters represent sounds or groups of sounds. This kind of knowledge is called *phonics*. It is also called *orthographic knowledge* and *letter-to-sound relationships*. The patterns that relate letters to sounds are complex. They come in layers that are peeled back, essentially in stages, by the child who is encouraged to be an active explorer of written language.

Many of the learning outcomes that have been described up to now are displayed in chart form in the table, "Developmental Milestones: Emergent Literacy."

Nurturing Emergent Literacy

Moving children along toward literacy—and giving thoughtful extra boosts to those children with gaps in their awareness of reading and writing—is the teacher's task in the phase of emergent literacy. Teachers use four kinds of strategies here:

- *Comprehensive strategies.* These strategies develop many skills at once, and include reading aloud, shared reading, and shared writing.
- *Strategies to develop specific skills.* Some skills should be taught directly, like alphabet knowledge, hearing sounds in words, phonics, and strategies for comprehension.
- *Strategies calling attention to language and literacy.* Teachers who support emergent literacy model clear language, point out key points about language print, and think aloud as they read and write.
- *Environmental strategies.* Young children's literacy is supported in passive ways, too, by having a classroom environment and classroom routines that support reading and writing. A literacy-rich classroom environment includes learning centers that encourage drawing and early writing, literacy-centered play, a reading corner, a classroom library, listening centers, charts and posters, and technology that allows children to guide themselves through a reading experience.

Comprehensive Strategies to Nurture Emergent Literacy

Comprehensive strategies develop several aspects of emergent literacy at once. They include interactive reading aloud, Shared Reading, Sharing the Pen Writing, and Guided Reading.

Developmental Milestones
Emergent Literacy

Stages of Literacy Development	Developmental Milestones	Teaching Strategies
Exploring Print (Beginning Kindergarten)	• May tap out syllables in most words, but not phonemes • Holds a book the right way up and can point to the front. • May know that print "talks" and not pictures. • May recognize some letters and may be able to write a few of them. • Writing shows no relation between letters and sounds. P2X = "little." • After memorizing a short text, cannot voice-point to the words accurately. • When listening to stories, some will respond to parts of them with movements and chants; others will follow the plot with displays of expectation, suspense, and relief. • Can make up a story while paging through a familiar picture book. • May draw pictures and tell you about the scene he or she is describing. • May write captions to pictures or other compositions, using invented symbols and random letters.	• Read-alouds—teachers read daily to children, thinking aloud and emphasizing plot structure (who the characters are, what the problem is, what they do to solve the problem, what happens, how things are at the end). The same story is reread several times and children are later invited to pretend-read it themselves. • Sing-alongs and rhyming games. • Morning message: The teacher asks children to take turns helping introduce and write up the day, date, month, and weather, as well as the day's activities. Rebus symbols are used for weather and names of activities. • Assignment charts: Children's names printed on tagboard are divided among slots in a pocket chart according to their tasks and center assignments for the day. • Shared reading—the teacher carefully points at large print while pronouncing words. The teacher carefully names aspects of reading—"letters," "words," "direction," "top of the page," "bottom of the page," and calls attention to individual letters and words that are repeated. • Teaching the alphabet. • Incorporating print in play activities—post office, grocery store, etc. • Writing Workshop: Children have opportunities to communicate with pencils and colored pencils; encouragement to write captions; opportunities to share what they have drawn and written.
Becoming Familiar with Print (Late Kindergarten) Logographic Reading	• Can begin to tap out phonemes. • Can provide rhyming words. • Still can't confidently voice-point at word units. • Knows way around books. • Can write own name. • Uses invented spelling to write words or phrases as captions to pictures. • Invented spelling begins to represent sounds in words, but only a few: LL = "little." • May recognize most letters and associate upper- and lowercase letters. • Sometimes writes letters and lines of print backwards, unless shown where to start writing. • Less pretend reading—the child often refuses to read, because she knows she doesn't know the words; or reads only the few words she knows.	• Read-alouds—teachers continue to read two or three times daily to children, thinking aloud and inviting the children's comments and predictions. At least one book per day is reread several times and children are invited to pretend-read it themselves. • Children are invited to reenact stories using drama, puppets, or flannel boards. • Sing-alongs and rhyming games. • Morning message: The teacher asks children to take turns helping introduce the day, date, month, and weather, as well as the day's activities. Rebus symbols are used for weather and names of activities. • Assignment charts: Children's names printed on tagboard are divided among slots in a pocket chart according to their tasks and center assignments for the day. • Alphabet teaching activities. • Shared reading, with the children reading lines after the teacher. • Sharing the pen writing. • Writing Workshop: Children have opportunities to communicate with pencils and colored pencils; encouragement to write captions; opportunities to share what they have drawn and written.

Stages of Literacy Development	Developmental Milestones	Teaching Strategies
Beginning Finger-Point Reading (Beginning First Grade) **Early Alphabetic Reading**	• Can tap out phonemes. Many can combine phonemes to make new words: *s + top = stop*. • Many children can voice-point at word units. • Those who can voice-point are learning some words from encounters with print. • Writes with invented spelling, and includes letters for most sounds that are heard. A few high frequency words are spelled conventionally. • LDL = "little." • Still makes active responses to stories, like chanting and moving. Is increasingly following the plot and other patterns, too, as demonstrated by predictions and comments.	• Read-alouds—teacher continues to read two times daily to children, thinking aloud and inviting the children's comments and predictions. The teacher emphasizes parts of the book: the title, the author, the illustrator. • Children are invited to reenact stories using drama, puppets, or flannel boards. • Sing-alongs and rhyming games. • Morning message uses longer sentences and introduces new words. • Charts for tasks and center assignments are still used. • Shared reading, with the children reading lines after the teacher. The teacher calls attention to the title, the author, and the illustrator and introduces other terminology as needed, such as "first word," "bottom of the page," etc. The teacher teaches lessons on letter sounds and word recognition. • Sharing the pen writing teaches letter-to-sound correspondences and conventions of capitalization and punctuation. • Language Experience Approach. • Guided Reading: In small groups, children are led to finger-point read simple texts. • Word study activities (see Chapter 5). • Writing Workshop: Children have opportunities to communicate with pencils and colored pencils; encouragement to write captions; opportunities to share what they have drawn and written
Finger-Point Reading (Mid First Grade) **Alphabetic Reading**	• Can more easily tap out phonemes, and can combine phonemes to make new words: *s + top = stop*. • Can more easily produce rhyming words, in games like "Ding, dong, dell…" • Is able to finger-point read simple predictable books with strong picture support. • Continues to acquire sight words from reading activities. • Is able to sound out predictably spelled words, letter by letter. • May write messages of two or three lines. Invented spellings are mixed with more conventionally spelled words. • LEDL or LETL still spell "little." • Is able to take highly predictable books home to read aloud.	• Read-alouds—teacher continues to read two times daily to children, thinking aloud and inviting the children's comments and predictions. The teacher emphasizes parts of the book: the title, the author, the illustrator. • Children are invited to reenact stories using drama, puppets, or flannel boards. • Sing-alongs and rhyming games. • Morning message uses longer sentences and introduces new words. • Charts for tasks and center assignments are still used. • Shared reading, with the children reading lines after the teacher. The teacher calls attention to the title, the author, and the illustrator and introduces other terminology as needed, such as "first word," "bottom of the page," etc. The teacher teaches lessons on letter sounds and word recognition. • Sharing the pen writing teaches letter-to-sound correspondences and conventions of capitalization and punctuation. • Taking dictation; using the Language Experience Approach. • Guided Reading: In small groups, children are led to finger-point read simple texts. • Word study activities (see Chapter 5). • Writing Workshop: Children have opportunities to communicate with pencils and colored pencils; encouragement to write captions; opportunities to share what they have drawn and written. • Focused lessons are offered on both the conventions of writing and strategies for composing (see Chapter 10).

READING ALOUD Reading aloud is one of the most useful, active things adults can do to nurture children's literacy growth. Many of the abilities that are considered essential to literacy can be developed as children listen to a book read aloud by a family member or teacher. Among the main benefits of being read to are the following:

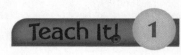

Teach It! 1

Reading Aloud

- *It expands their vocabulary.* As Stanovich (1992) has pointed out, there are words that are more commonly encountered in books—even children's books—than in conversation or from watching television. Listening to books being read aloud helps children learn a literate vocabulary.

- *It develops their ability to comprehend written language.* Research on reading comprehension tells us that it involves component skills that include perceiving main ideas and supporting details, making inferences, venturing predictions and confirming them, and visualizing in the mind's eye what the words suggest. Children have the opportunity to develop all of these abilities from listening to a book being read aloud and discussing it.

- *It encourages enthusiasm for literacy as they participate in the reader's excitement.* When children first learn to talk, parents slow down and exaggerate their speech and their gestures as if to say, "This is how language works. This is how we show excitement and interest. This is the way we soothe each other." Similarly, when adults read books aloud with expression, they have the opportunity to show children how written language conveys the full range of emotions. This not only will make literacy appealing to children, but also will show them how to derive meaning from and associate emotions with the language of print.

- *It makes them aware of the structure of stories and of other kinds of texts.* Skilled readers learn to find questions and pursue answers according to the structure of whatever text they are reading. A story shows characters in settings and the problems they have and how those problems are solved. Expository writing frames questions about topics and goes about answering those questions. By reading texts aloud and commenting on them, a careful teacher can help students to become aware of the recurring structures of different texts and use them to guide their comprehension.

CCSS

Helping Young Readers Comprehend Narrative and Informational Text

The Common Core Standards ask children as young as kindergartners and first and second graders to notice and navigate literary structures and content. They are expected to ask about and explain details in a text, identify genres of texts, follow plot lines and retell stories, identify narrators, describe events from different characters' points of view, perceive messages and themes, explain how the authors' word choices contribute shades of meaning to the text, and compare and contrast different versions of the same story. They should be able to recognize the roles of authors and illustrators, and discuss the meaning that is provided by text and pictures, respectively. (See the Common Core Reading—Literature Standards for Kindergarten, grade 1, and grade 2 <http://www.corestandards.org/ELA-Literacy/CCRA/R>.)

The children who are being asked to meet the standards listed above are the same ones who may just be learning the alphabet and the layout of books, or struggling mightily to pronounce individual words or to read whole sentences without making mistakes. They may well be too busy trying to decipher the printed page to think about themes, characters' points of view, authors' word choices, and the like. But while they are learning to process print, they can learn the skills and concepts from the standards if teachers concentrate on them as they read texts aloud and discuss them with children.

Teach It!

Refer to the Teach It! appendix at the end of the book for further activities you can use to reinforce concepts discussed in this chapter.

Suggestions for Reading Aloud

We suggest following these steps whenever you are reading aloud to students:

1. **Decide on Your Objectives for This Reading-Aloud Session.** As we noted on page 103, the Common Core Standards require that even young students be able to pay attention to and explain details, identify genres of texts, follow plots and retell stories, perceive morals and themes, understand the effect of word choices, compare versions of the same story, understand the roles of author and illustrator, explain the contribution of words and pictures to the meaning of a text, and more. Think about which combination of these skills you plan to develop through this read-aloud session.

2. **Prepare to Read the Text.** Read the text through yourself before you read it to students. Decide how you want to read it—with humor, with drama, with questions to whet curiosity? If there are voices to bring to life, decide how you want to make each one sound. If you decide to stop reading to ask for predictions or discussion, decide where the stopping places should be. If there are any words or ideas that will be unfamiliar to the students, make a note to pronounce them carefully and explain them to the students. If there are details of the plot, or word choices, or characters' experiences to be emphasized, find the places they occur and plan how you will ask about them.

   Practice reading the text through more times until you can read it smoothly, with expression.

3. **Arrange Space and Behavior.** Before you begin the read-aloud session, make sure the students are seated where they can see and hear you. Remind the students, if you need to, of the behavior you expect of good listeners: hands to themselves, eyes on the teacher, and ears for the story.

4. **Help the Students Set Purposes for Reading.** Tell the students the title of the text and the author's name. Say a little bit about the author if you know—where she or he grew up, and ask about other works the author has written that the students may know. Tell the students what the text is about, and what you think is especially interesting about the text. Explain the skills or concepts you want them to focus on.

5. **Read the Text with Expression.** Read a little slowly—remember that listeners need time to think about and understand what you are reading. Vary the volume—the loudness—and the pitch of your voice. Sound like you are enjoying it!

6. **Follow Up the Reading.** Ask the students what they liked about the text. What did it make them think of? Why?

7. **Reread the Text.** Read the text a second time through. Pause for comments. If there are any chants given in the book, ask students to repeat them. If there are interesting issues raised, take time to discuss them. If there are interesting facts presented, take time to review and understand them. If there are interesting questions raised, talk about ways to keep investigating them. If you have planned to teach particular skills and concepts, the second reading is the place you can take more time to go over them.

8. **Extend the Experience.** Taking ideas from the text and exploring them through drama, song, drawing, discussion, field trips, videos, or further readings are all recommended ways to boost students' sense of the value of encounters with literature, and to help them remember the concepts and language and other features of the text.

Reading aloud two or three times each day should be a regular feature of every classroom from preschool through the primary grades and on through the elementary grades. Even when children are learning to read, it is not until fourth grade that many children's reading ability approaches the speed and fluency with which teachers can read to them. Many children's reading rate will take much longer to develop. Therefore, the teacher's reading aloud is a necessary source of language, of stories, and of information for children. Please see the Teach It Box for detailed guidance on reading aloud to children.

INTERACTIVE READING ALOUD   Interactive reading aloud invites participation by children. Teachers do three main things when they read aloud interactively.

CCSS

• Speaking and Listening 1: Comprehension and Collaboration

1. *Use questions and prompts to guide children's attention as they listen.* As they introduce the story, they raise questions and ask children to listen for answers. If they are reading a story, they may ask about the main character, the problem, what the character will do to solve the problem, and what will happen as a result.

If they are reading an informational book, they will ask students what they already know about the topic, and then ask children to listen to see what else they can find out. As they read the story, they will ask the children what they are learning, then ask predictions about what they will find out next.

2. ***Think aloud, and point to important parts of the text.*** They may call attention to what the picture is showing and what the text is saying. They may talk about words or parts of words such as plural markers or past tense endings.

3. ***Invite comments and discussion after reading.*** They may ask children to choose their favorite part of a story, or the most interesting thing they learned about a topic, and to say why they chose it. They may ask children to retell what they heard, and ask other children to help fill in details.

CCSS

• Speaking and Listening 1: Comprehension and Collaboration

MORE RESPONSE OPTIONS FOR YOUNGER CHILDREN   The meanings of books can loom larger in children's imaginations when they are provided with opportunities to respond to the books in various ways. Although children of all ages can talk about what they read (Morrow & Gambrell, 2004), younger children find it most natural to respond to books with their whole bodies: by getting up and moving around, by chanting chants, by acting out parts, and by drawing key scenes. English language learners have more opportunities to participate if meaningful responses to stories are encouraged through drama, music, and art rather than through discussion only.

Use Chants   A very engaging form of response to a story is to repeat a key phrase or chant every time it occurs in a book. English language learners profit from repeating shorter chants, which become nuggets of remembered language that are useful models of grammar and good for pronunciation practice. (See page 111 for a list of good sources for chants.)

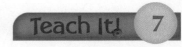

Making Individual Small Books

Use Drama   Many children's books have clear patterns of actions that are easy for children to act out. Some books, such as Michael Rosen's *We're Going on a Bear Hunt* (2003) and Frances Temple's *Tiger Soup* (1992), are already scripted for children to act out. Both have chants and movements that the children will enjoy. *The Three Billy Goats Gruff* is not scripted as a play, but it has simple, repeated actions and chants that are easy for children to practice and perform. The whole story can be rehearsed and staged in a single class period. Single scenes of longer stories can be acted out, too, if time is short.

Acting involves interpretation. You can encourage children to interpret stories imaginatively as they rehearse the dramatizations: "How does the little goat feel when he sees the troll? How might he look at that point? What would his voice sound like?" Props help children get into character. In *The Three Billy Goats Gruff*, horns made of construction paper bring the goats to life, and a robe and a club add to the troll's fierceness.

Use Art   Drawing is a favorite way for children to respond to a story. The drawings may be extended by asking the children to leave space at the bottom of their papers and think of one line they want to dictate to the teacher. The children can rehearse reading these lines and then take them home to read to family members.

DIALOGIC READING   When working with individual children, one approach called *dialogic reading* helps put the child in the active role as a storyteller and not just as a listener. Dialogic reading has shown gains in children's language acquisition and growth in concepts about print (Whitehurst & Lonigan, 2001).

Dialogic reading is intended to be used by parents, teachers, and volunteer tutors, for example, college students working in special literacy programs such as America Reads or Jumpstart. In some communities, training in dialogic reading is available through family literacy programs offered by public libraries. The training is supported by twenty-minute videotapes (Whitehurst, 1994). Adult readers are taught to read interactively with the child. Two acronyms, PEER and CROWD, are used to remind the adult readers of the steps.

PEER is a mnemonic for a strategy used to nurture language development with younger children as they read a book together with an adult. The letters stand for:

Prompt the child to name objects in the book and talk about the story.

Evaluate the child's responses and offer praise for adequate responses and alternatives for inadequate ones.

Expand on the child's statements with additional words.

Repeat—ask the child to repeat the adult's utterances.

For more advanced children, a more detailed form of dialogic reading called CROWD is used. The acronym CROWD identifies five kinds of questions adults ask:

Completion prompts. Ask the child to supply a word or phrase that has been omitted. (For example, "I see a yellow duck looking at ___.")

Recall prompts. Here the child is asked about things that occurred earlier in the book. ("Do you remember some animals that Brown Bear saw?")

Open-ended prompts. Here the child is asked to respond to the story in his own words. ("Now it's your turn: You say what is happening on this page.")

Wh- prompts. The adult asks what, where, who, and why questions. ("What is that yellow creature called? Who do you think Brown Bear will see next?")

Distancing prompts. Here the child is asked to relate the content of the book to life experiences. ("Do you remember when we saw a yellow duck like that one swimming in the lake? Was it as big as this one?")

SHARED READING   Shared Reading (Booth and Schwartz, 2004; Holdaway, 1979) is a strategy for guiding the students' attention through the reading process. It requires a "big book"—a book large enough so that all can easily read the print; an easel to place the book on, so the teacher's hands are free for pointing; and a pointing stick.

Seat a group of up to ten children close enough to you so that they can see the text, and also feel a sense of community. With the book on the easel, use your pointer stick (a ruler or something more exotic, like a Harry Potter wand) to point to each word as you read

DIFFERENTIATED INSTRUCTION

SIOP®
Sheltered
Instruction
Observation
Protocol*

Emergent Readers

Emergent literacy faces in two directions. In one direction, it focuses on the concepts about reading, writing, and written language that children have acquired at home. The teacher can build on them and make a bridge that connects what children are figuring out for themselves with the formal reading curriculum. In another direction, emergent literacy helps us realize the concepts and abilities that some children have not developed yet—concepts and skills they will need to be successful in learning to read and write. These children will need to:

• Be read to, to boost their vocabulary and their familiarity with books.

• Explore print, as in giving dictations and having someone read them back.

• Learn the letters of the alphabet.

These are critical experiences, but fortunately it is not such a long list. One way to make sure children get these experiences is to recruit and supervise volunteers. The U.S. Department of Education provides funding for college students to be paid from work-study funds to serve as tutors. Many colleges and high schools have service learning classes in which students are required to perform some kind of community service. Student volunteers can offer effective help to young readers who need it. The key to the success of such efforts is the teacher's supervision. Tutoring is far more effective when a teacher assesses the children in advance to see exactly what they need, and orients and supervises the tutors to make sure they provide the right help (Morris, 2005).

it. But read the words smoothly and fluently, keeping in mind that you are modeling fluent reading.

Big books are large versions of children's books with print and illustrations that can be read by a group of children. While teachers sometimes make big books themselves, many publishers are producing big book versions of simply written picture books, especially those with highly patterned texts that are especially good for emergent and beginning readers.

Big books can be used to show children the layout of books and also to practice reading and rereading text. In a typical lesson with emergent readers, the teacher reads the book twice.

Using big books is a valuable way to introduce students to reading and to help them become familiar with all the elements in books.

On the First Reading

- Put the big book on an easel, and call the children's attention to the cover. Point to the title, and have the students read it aloud with you. Ask the students to say what they think the book will be about, given the title, and invite their ideas and predictions.

- Point to the cover illustration, and invite the students to say what they see. When they think of the title and consider the picture, what do they think will happen in the story?

- Open to the title page, and point to the author's name. Make sure the children understand that this is the person who wrote the book. Do the same with the name of the illustrator. Do the children know any other books by either one of them?

- Now turn to the first page of text and read it aloud, pointing to the words as you go. Read several more pages this way, pausing to discuss a picture or to comment on an action.

- Ask the children to make predictions, even predictions about what will happen on the other side of a page. Sometimes rhyming books have a phrase on one page that ends in a word that is matched with a phrase on the next page ending in a rhyming word. You might pause at the page turn and ask the children what will come next. For example, on one page of John Langstaff's *A Hunting We Will Go* (1991), from an English folk song, are the words:

> *A hunting we will go*
> *A hunting we will go*
> *We'll catch a fox*

Before turning the page, pause and ask the children to predict what comes next. The text continues:

> *And put him in a box*
> *And then we'll let him go.*

On the Second Reading

Now get the children to help you read the book.

- Go back to the beginning of the book, and invite the children to read it again with you. Using a stylus or something similar, choral-read a page with the children.

- Still pointing to the words, echo-read the next page with the children.

- Silently point to the words in a repeated phrase, and invite the children to read them.

- Finally, invite individual children to come up and read a line of text as you point to the words.

On a Third Reading

Now you may teach a lesson with the text—using the following activities.

- Mask a word with your hand or with a piece of tag board, and ask students to guess it from context, or from context with only the first letter showing, or the first two letters, and so on.

- Write four or five sentences from the text on strips of paper, and have students arrange them in order in a pocket chart.

- Cut apart a sentence and have a student or students arrange the words in order in a pocket chart.

- Pass out word cards and have students match them to words in the text, or with words that begin with the same letter, or that rhyme with them, or that contain the same syllable.

- Pass out cards with lowercase letters on them and have students match them with uppercase letters in the text, and vice versa.

- Point to capital letters at the beginnings of sentences and explain why they are there.

- Point out the function of punctuation.

- Ask students to point to words that show how something looked, or how someone felt, or what someone did, etc.

You may have a discussion of the book. Ask the students about favorite parts of the text. You may put questions to them—open-ended questions that connect to the students' backgrounds, and experiences, and even to other books they have read.

Following the reading with the group, leave the big book available for children to read individually and to each other.

Teach It! 11

Shared Reading

GUIDED READING   The Guided Reading strategy, developed by Irene Fountas and Gay Su Pinnell (2001), is done with small groups, usually between four and seven children. They are grouped by their reading level, and the lesson is carried out with a book that is moderately challenging—that is, one in which children can read about nine words out of ten without help. Ideally, the children are seated at a crescent-shaped table with the teacher inside the arc, so he is close to each child.

The lesson begins by previewing the book, both to arouse interest and also to pre-teach a few key words the children might need. You may do a picture walk through the text to support the children's understanding. Introduce the book in a way that connects with and builds on the children's prior knowledge. "Hmm . . ." you might say, "This looks like a story that could be about a friendship; see, it says (pointing to the text) *Lost and Found* by Oliver Jeffers (2005) and if we look at the picture, the boy and the penguin are hugging. What do you think it's about?"

After children have the opportunity to talk with you and one another, you may then shift to looking at some key vocabulary words from the text that you have prepared in advance on word cards. Remember, too many words can overwhelm children, so just do a few, perhaps only two. As you show the words, pronounce them and discuss their meanings. This is an opportunity for word study to begin, but don't focus yet. Rather, the next step is to read the story.

Read aloud the first page or two, and thinking aloud about the characters and their situation. Ask questions to engage the students. Once you decide the students know enough to continue reading on the own, invite the children to "whisper-read" to text—reading just loudly enough for you to hear and monitor their reading, but not enough to bother their neighbors.

As the children read, younger children—kindergartners and first graders—are invited to point to each word as they read. (They will be asked to stop pointing once their reading becomes less halting.) Listen for children having problems, lean in and offer encouragement, correct reading problems, and invite children to reread a line.

Following the reading, the children are invited to have a discussion about what they read, in order to make sure they see that getting the meaning is the purpose of reading.

Later, you may go back and teach a lesson, from the text. The lessons are similar to those we saw under Shared Reading (see page 106 above).

Finally, the books may be set out for the children to reread with a buddy, to practice reading for fluency.

SHARED WRITING   In Shared Writing (Tompkins, 2000), the teacher and the children produce a text together. The text can be inspired in many ways:

- A counting text based on a theme: "One hungry lion, two scared gazelles," etc.
- A story, perhaps based on a children's book, such as *Frog and Toad* or *Corduroy*.
- Seasons or months
- Special things about each student

Depending on the children's needs and the teacher's objectives, the teacher can carefully emphasize the spelling, the way the words are arranged on the page, the punctuation, or the choice of words ("Let's use words that make the readers see what we mean!").

A sample lesson in shared writing might go as is shown in the "Teach It! Box.

Teach It! 52

Shared Writing

WRITING WORKSHOP   Beginning in kindergarten, many teachers conduct writing workshops three or four days per week. For emergent readers and writers, teachers begin by reminding children of the topics they want to write about. Children who are reluctant to begin writing immediately might draw a picture of their topic. The teacher reminds the students to leave space at the bottom of the drawing for their writing. The children then have a period of ten to fifteen minutes for writing and drawing at their seats. Those who have drawn pictures write captions underneath their drawings. Then, one at a time, they

Teach It!

Refer to the Teach It! appendix at the end of the book for further activities you can use to reinforce concepts discussed in this chapter.

Sample Writing Lesson

After discussing an exciting event with his students, a teacher gathers kindergartners around an easel and invites them to help write about the event. First they agree on a short sentence they want to write:

A fireman came to school.

They practice saying the sentence several times so that everyone is aware of the words. The teacher then tells the students that they will write the first word and asks, "Who can tell us what letter we need to write?"

A child suggests the letter *A*, and the teacher accepts it, writes it slowly on the easel, and then says, "We wrote *A*. Now what's the next word we want to write?"

After someone says, "*Fireman*," the teacher says, "Right. It's *fireman*. That's a new word, so I'm going to leave space between the word *A* and the first letter of this new word."

The teacher puts his finger after the *A* to identify the space and says, "What is the first sound we hear in *fireman*?"

When the students identify the first sound, the teacher asks, "What letter are we going to use to write the *fuh* sound in *fireman*?"

The teacher pauses for responses and then says, "Right. It's *F*. Who can come up and write the letter *F* for me?"

This process continues as the group works through the entire sentence. When they are finished, the teacher might end up with

A FIRMN CAM TO SKOL.

The teacher concludes by saying, "This could say *A fireman came to school*. Later on, I will show you another way to write it."

The teacher recognizes that these kindergarten children—most of whom are prephonemic or early phonemic spellers—will not be ready to focus on the silent letters in *fireman* and *came* or on the uncommon spelling of *sch* in *school*. Later, when the children can produce letter name spellings, the teacher will show them where silent letters and other conventional spellings would be added to these words to show the students the next challenges they will need to master. But for now, matching letters with phonemes is a sufficient challenge for these children. Shared writing lessons can be conducted almost daily with a class. In the meantime, children should be encouraged to use writing every chance they get.

take the page to the teacher and read it aloud to her or him. The teacher writes the words correctly above the child's words and might take this opportunity to show the children how letters represent sounds. During sharing time, children share their works with the rest of the class.

The writing workshop should have a period of time set aside for focused lessons that show students how to handle particular aspects of writing.

Teaching Specific Skills

In addition to the comprehensive teaching strategies described in the preceding pages, teachers need to teach specific skills, too. Often, skills can be taught as part of a comprehensive teaching strategy, such as shared reading, guided reading, or writers' workshop. What matters is that the skills be taught systematically, according to a curriculum of concepts and skills that children need at each grade level. Here we describe skills instruction to develop phonological awareness, to teach the alphabet, and to teach phonics.

TEACHING PHONOLOGICAL AWARENESS   Children who are aware of the sound constituents of words have an advantage when it comes to learning to read words because they will be aware of the units of words that are matched with letters. The National Reading Panel (2000) recommends that teachers teach phonological awareness from kindergarten through grade 2. This teaching may occupy a short part of each day—six or seven minutes—to yield the 20 hours-a-year of phonological training that the NRP recommends. Activities to boost phonological awareness can take place at several levels.

LISTENING FOR SPECIAL WORDS   From Mary Hohman (2002) comes the suggestion of using "Magic Words." Say a word like *hotdog*, and tell the children that you are about to tell a story that will have the word *hotdog* in it—and that they should clap their hands when they hear the word. Start telling the story. For instance, you could say, "Last summer I went down to the park. I was really hungry, so I walked up to the food counter and ordered a—hamburger. The waitress said 'We don't have hamburgers. I'll have to make you a hotdog.'"

Make up several stories with the word *hotdog*. Then ask the children to choose a new magic word, and then you make up a story that has that word in it. The children can take turns making up stories of their own with "magic words" in them, and tell these stories to others.

Next, you can raise the level of challenge of the magic word game by asking children to listen for two words together. If those words are *ironing board*, for instance, you might say, "My father was ironing his shirt. He was ironing it on the table, but the table got too hot. He was ironing it on the floor, but the floor was too dirty. 'Daddy,' I said. 'I know. Why don't you try ironing on the ironing board that's in the closet?'"

You can also have children listen for one word repeated two times, such as "Short short."

> *"There was a girl named Short. But Short wasn't short. Short was tall. Her friend Gladys was short. One day Gladys asked Short, 'If you were short, Short, your name would match you better.'"* (Temple & MaKinster, 2005)

CLAP OUT WORDS   You can make clapping games that range from the simple to the elaborate. Clapping their hands to the words you pronounce is an easy game. Clapping in a sequence adds more challenge: hands together, hands on knees, hands on chest, hands on sides of thighs. Have children clap to the words as you say these words with emphasis:

> *"When—I—go—to—Lu's—big—house*
> *I—like—to—play—with—Lu's—pet–mouse."*

SONGS, CHANTS, AND POEMS   Songs and chants are a natural way to get children to pay attention to rhymes—and also to memorize words, phrases, and sentences that will aid language development. Songs, chants, and poems are also a lot of fun to learn and repeat.

A song like this one invites hand claps and close attention to the rhymes:

Miss Mary Mack
Dressed in black
Silver buckles
Up and down her back

The lyrics are available in book form. Tutors and new teachers are advised to seek out collections of songs, especially those with tapes. The following are good bets:

Beall, Pamela Conn, Nipp, Susan Hagen, & Klein, Nancy Spence. (2002). *Wee Sing 25th Anniversary Celebration*. New York: Price Stern Sloan.

Cole, Joanna. (1990). *Miss Mary Mack*. New York: Morrow.

Delacre, Lulu. (2004). *Arrorro Mi Nino: Latino Lullabies and Gentle Games*. New York: Lee and Low.

Graham, Carolyn. (2004). *Let's Chant, Let's Sing*. New York: Oxford University Press.

Jenkins, Ella. (1997). *Ella Jenkins Songbook for Children*. New York: Music Sales Corp.

Milnes, Gerard. (1999). *Granny, Will Your Dog Bite?* Little Rock, AR: August House.

Orozco, Jose-Luis. (1994). *De Colores and Other Latin American Folk Songs for Children*. New York: Dutton.

_____. (1997). *Diez Deditos and Other Play Rhymes and Action Songs from Latin America*. New York: Puffin.

_____. (2002). *Fiestas: A Year of Latin American Songs of Celebration*. New York: Dutton.

Silberg, Jackie, Schiller, Pam, & Wright, Debbie. (2002). *The Complete Book of Rhymes, Songs, Poems, Fingerplays*. Lewisville, NC: Gryphon House.

Swasos, Elizabeth, & Cepeda, Joe. (2002). *Hey You! C'Mere! A Poetry Slam*. New York: Arthur Levine.

All of these are valuable additions to a teacher's personal collection. Also, experienced teachers know many other songs that you can learn from them. Songs for transitions, songs that introduce tasks, songs to celebrate special people—all of these are essential for a teacher's repertoire. When you find a teacher who knows these songs, write them down! And also, bring along a device for recording sound so you can capture the tunes.

At the Syllable Level

- Children can clap along to the syllables in their names—"Bet-ty," "Ta-kee-sha," "Da-vid."
- Children can raise their hands when the teacher says a word with one syllable, two syllables, or three syllables.
- When the teacher says "One syllable!" a child must say a one-syllable word; when the teacher says, "Two syllables!" and calls on a child, that child says a word with two syllables; and so on.

At the Onset and Rime Level

- Children are asked to supply rhymes to complete couplets such as the following:

Ding, dong, dell
Kitty's in the _____ (well)
Ding, dong, dasement

Figure 4.1
Elkonin Boxes

Source: Elkonin, D. B. "Personality psychology and the preschool age child." In the collection *The personality development of the preschool age child.* Moscow, 1965.

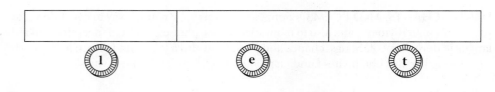

Kitty's in the _____ (basement)
Ding, dong, dimming pool
Kitty's in the _____ (swimming pool)

- When the teacher says a target word, such as *boy*, the children raise their hands when they hear a word that rhymes with it as the teacher reads from a list of words such as "*tea, tock, tack, toy.*"
- When the teacher says a word such as *bat* and then pronounces the sound /k/, the children say a new word that begins with the sound /k/ and rhymes with *bat*: *cat*.

At the Phoneme Level

There are three kinds of tasks that are generally used to increase children's awareness of phonemes: One is **phoneme segmentation**. *Segment* means to break something into small parts. Phoneme segmentation tasks have children take spoken words and break them into their individual sounds.

- A spoken exercise goes like this: "If I say *dog* /d/ /o/ /g/, you say *cat, ball,* and *foot* the same way."
- The children place letter markers into boxes as they pronounce each letter sound. Then they say the word that is formed by the sounds (Elkonin, 1965) (See Figure 4.1.)
- Once children begin to learn letter sounds, they can practice pushing tokens marked with letters. For example, given a card marked with three boxes, and the three letter chips, *l, e,* and *t*, the child places each letter into the box, pronouncing its sound at the same time: *ull, ehhh, tuh* and then saying the whole word *let*.

A second way children become aware of phonemes is to combine phonemes into words. For example:

- The teacher asks, "What word do I get if I add the sounds of *ih* and *tuh*? or *suh* and *ay*? or *cuh, uh,* and *puh*?

A third way that children become aware of phonemes is to delete a phoneme from a word and say the word that is left over. For instance:

- The teacher asks, "What word to I get if I take off the sound *suh* from *slot*? Or if I take off the sound *duh* from *find*?

Games that work with phonemes can be playful, of course. For example, the children can sing a song that substitutes the vowel sounds:

I like to eat, eat, eat, apples and bananas
I like to eat, eat, eat, apples and bananas.
I like to oot, oot, oot, ooples and bonoonoos
I like to oot, oot, oot, ooples and bonoonoos
I like to oat, oat, oat, oples and bononos
I like to oat, oat, oat, oples and bononos.

Teaching the Alphabet

"Whole-part-whole" is the mantra of many seasoned teachers. It means *begin by showing students how larger chunks of language are used meaningfully. Then call their attention to the parts. Then have them use the parts in the context of the whole.* That suggestion can be applied to teaching the alphabet. Children pay closer attention to the letters of the alphabet after they have come to notice writing as a holistic display; and they learn the letters as they use them when they are trying to write and read messages.

WORKING WITH NAMES   Cunningham and Allington (2003) suggest that teachers call children's attention to the alphabet by focusing on their names. A teacher writes each child's name on a piece of tagboard and puts all of the names in a box. Each day the teacher draws out a name, and calls that child forward and interviews him or her—asking about favorite pastimes, pets, games, and so on. Then the teacher puts the child's name on the bulletin board and explains that this word is a name. The teacher can point to the letters, reading left to right, and have the children count the letters. Now the teacher can call attention to the letter that begins the name. If the name is *Nancy*, the teacher can ask if the children can spot a small letter that looks like the big letter that begins the name *Nancy*. The teacher can ask if other children have Nancy's letter N in their name (each child has her name taped to her desk, of course). Each day another child's name is drawn from the box, that child is interviewed, and the teacher calls the children's attention to the letters in this new name. As this activity is carried on day after day, the children are naming more and more of the letters of the alphabet, including the other letters that make up each name, both upper- and lowercase.

ALPHABET BINGO   Another way to help children recognize letters of the alphabet is to pass out cards with the letters of the alphabet written on them where the numbers would be written on a Bingo card, as in Figure 4.2.

Figure 4.2
Alphabet Bingo

The order of the letters may be scrambled. All upper- or lowercase letters may be used in the beginning, and then a mixture of the two is used as children are able. The children are given cardboard chips just the size of the cells. As a letter is called out, each child places a chip over that letter. The child may call BINGO! when she has a row of chips arranged up or down, side to side, or diagonally.

JUMPING LETTERS   From Patricia Cunningham's energetic teaching (Cunningham & Allington, 2003) comes an idea that associates letters with sounds in children's minds. The teacher (or the teacher and the class) thinks of a movement or action that can be paired with each letter of the alphabet. Then the children shout the letters and make the movements: JUMP! for J, LEAP! for L, SING! for S, and so on. The class may go out on the playground to practice these first, to give them an air of excitement, and later the letters may be acted out a little less exuberantly in the classroom. It can be great fun to call out the letter and ask children to perform the action, or demonstrate the action and have children shout the letter.

LETTERS ON THE WEB   There are many fine programs on the Internet that help children learn the alphabet. As you know, such sites can come and go quickly, but as of this writing, the following were good bets.

- "Alphabet Action" from Learning Planet.com shows the letters in order on the page. When the child clicks on a letter, he hears the name of the letter pronounced, and a picture of a word that begins with the letter.
- "Mrs. Alphabet," at <www.mrsalphabet.com>, offers songs and chants for every letter of the alphabet, and many other activities.
- "Haunted Alphabet" from Kaboose.com presents a spooky picture with letters of the alphabet hidden in it. A child clicks on a letter and it is magically transported up to its place in the alphabet. If she clicks on a shape that is not a letter, she hears screechy laughter (which some children will find to be more fun!).

Entering "Alphabet" in a search engine will turn up dozens of activities that can be accessed at no charge, including interactive games children can play on the computer and downloadable worksheets that can be duplicated for the class.

TEACHING PHONICS   Instruction in phonics, or letter-to-sound correspondences, should begin in kindergarten. Phonics instruction can be a natural part of the comprehensive strategies of guided reading and shared writing, in which the teacher calls attention to the spellings of words, has children predict the letters that spell them, and guides children in reading and spelling words that share the same spelling rimes—(the rime, remember, is the vowel and consonant element that follows the onset: in *bat*, *b*- is the onset and -*at* is the rime).

Calling Attention to Language and Literacy

Teachers of the early grades are primarily teachers of language. They use language carefully, which means they speak clearly and articulately, and they use interesting vocabulary. They think aloud about words and sentences, calling attention to interesting synonyms and antonyms, to inflectional endings, and to other aspects of language that the curriculum calls out, or that are shown to be necessary by their observations of the children.

PREPARING YOURSELF TO BE A LANGUAGE MODEL   To be an enthusiastic and knowledgeable model of language takes more than knowledge of skills; it takes learning a lot about language yourself. If you are still in school, it would be a good idea to take a course in *linguistics for teachers* (such courses are normally part of the preparation of teachers of English to speakers of other languages, or TESOL teachers). Some recommended reading you can do are your own is:

Adger, Carolyn Temple, Snow, Catherine, & Christian, Donna. (2002). *What Teachers Need to Know About Language (Language in Education) Language in Education: Theory and Practice*. McHenry, IL: Delta Systems.

Moats, Louisa Cook. (2012). *Speech to Print: Essentials for Teachers*. Baltimore, MD: Brookes.

Sacks, David. (2004). *Letter Perfect: The Marvelous History of Our Alphabet from A to Z*. New York: Broadway.

Temple, Charles, Nathan, Ruth, & Temple, Codruta. (2013). *The Beginnings of Writing* (4th Ed.). Boston: Allyn and Bacon.

And, of course, you should read lots and lots of books for pleasure, both children's books and adult books, fiction, nonfiction, and poetry.

A TOUR GUIDE TO WRITTEN LANGUAGE As models and guides, teachers are tour guides to the details of written language as well as spoken language. With early emergent readers, as teachers read big books or dictated text, they point to each word (to demonstrate the concept of word), they run their hand under lines of print (to indicate the direction in which we read), they point to uppercase and lowercase letters, and they indicate punctuation and what it calls on readers to do.

They point to titles on the covers of books, and the names of authors and illustrators. They lead discussions of pictures and texts and point out when they indicate the same or different things.

COGNITIVE APPRENTICESHIPS The idea of cognitive apprenticeships means that children in school can be considered as understudies or apprentices of skilled language users, readers, and writers—their teachers (Collins, Brown, & Newman, 1987). In an art studio or on a job in the skilled trades, people learning a craft work for many years under the direction of people who are more skilled than they are. The skilled master craftspeople or journeymen teach as much by example as they do directly. They learn to slow down their procedures and "think aloud" as they work, so the apprentice can have the richest exposure to skilled practice. In a classroom, a teacher models her own practices in language use, her own thought processes as she reads, and her own decisions as she writes. The idea of cognitive apprenticeships is not so much a teaching strategy as a mindset that a generous and effective teacher can adopt, in order to maximize opportunities to teach children about language and literacy.

CCSS

• Foundational Skills 1: Print Concepts

• Language Standards 1 and 2: Conventions of Standard English

Environmental Strategies to Support Emergent Literacy

To promote literacy, reading and writing are made part of the classroom environment. The classroom itself should demonstrate both the importance of literacy and the way literacy works while also providing many opportunities for children to observe and use written language. There are many ways in which classrooms can be arranged passively to immerse children in print.

LABELS Label objects around the classroom with written letters that are readable from far off. Every several days, take time to "read the room" with the children together (Fountas & Pinnell, 1996) as you or a student points to the labels with a pointer or ruler. Remind students to listen for the first sounds in the words, such as in *door* and point out that the first letter in *door* is D.

LITERACY PLAY Make props readily available to support children's dramatic play. Some of these props might include

Taking time to "read the room" labels provides an opportunity for children to observe and use written language.

reading and writing. For example, the doctor's office has an eye chart and a pad for the doctor to write prescriptions. Shelves in a grocery store center might have labels (fruit, soup, bread) where the grocer would stock the items, along with pads handy for the customers to use for writing grocery lists.

CLASSROOM LIBRARY   Create a classroom library in a corner of the room. It should have a carpet and comfortable chairs (such as beanbag chairs) for creating an inviting reading environment. Include a space for displaying books so that children can see their covers, and change the books on display every few days to catch the children's attention. Books should accommodate a range of tastes, from informational books with bright illustrations to simple patterned books. On a regular basis, read a book or part of a book aloud and then place it on display in the library corner to entice children to look it over. The classroom library should include books written by individual classroom authors and books written or dictated by the whole class—perhaps books of favorite jokes and riddles, books about animals, and books about the seasons.

CHARTS AND POSTERS   Display on the walls around the classroom posters of children's books and pictures of authors. You can solicit these directly from children's book publishers. Children know authors such as Rosemary Wells, Dr. Seuss, Arnold Lobel, Cynthia Rylant, and Alma Flor Ada, and they get excited when the teacher announces that the class has a new book by one of these or other authors they know and like. You can also display charts of interesting things, such as volcanoes and maps of the town or neighborhood with the children's street names labeled. You could also include autobiographical posters with each child's name and something special that each child has dictated. Children love to see their own works posted.

CLASSROOM POST OFFICE   Include in your classroom a post office where children can mail letters. Each child could have a mailbox (constructed from three-inch cardboard tubes) for receiving mail. Have children write each other letters at least once a week; the teacher should also make a point of writing something to put in each child's box every few days.

WRITING CENTER   Create a writing center with paper, markers, and pencils. Include magazines as sources of pictures that can be cut out and glued to attach them as illustrations for children's compositions.

DISPLAYING PRINT   Even as you invite children to write inventively, including mockwriting, or read to them and show them print, you also need to show them individual letters and demonstrate how the letters are formed. There are many ways of doing this:

- Alphabet letter cards can be posted around the room, with pictures of objects that feature that letter.
- Games for matching letters, coloring letters, and tracing letters can be laid out for children to play with at center time.
- Magnetic letters and link letters (cardboard letters with edges cut like jigsaw puzzle pieces) can be placed in centers, so children can arrange them to match words printed on tagboard, including their classmates' names. (Note that for beginners, letters all of the same color are preferable to letters of mixed colors.)
- Children can practice writing letters at their desks as the teacher writes a model. They can use large-ruled paper for this or individual slates and chalk. Later, they can practice writing letters with a grease pencil on a transparency film overlaid on sample words with large letters.
- Alphabet strips can be taped to children's desks. A strip of tagboard with the letters of the alphabet carefully printed in lowercase can be attached to each child's desk in front of the pencil tray. Such strips are available commercially, or they can be produced by the teacher or by an aide.
- The teacher can teach children the alphabet song, pointing to the letter cards on the wall as the children sing the song slowly.

- Children's names can be written on cards and taped to their desks, with the first letter of the first name written in a bright color. Then the children can practice saying, "A is for Ana, B is for Bart," and so on.
- Sandpaper letters on cards can be used in centers for children to trace with their fingers.
- Letter cards can be sent home so that parents can play letter recognition games with the children.
- Alphabet books can be made. Prepare a blank book for the class and print a letter on the top of each page, A to Z. The children think of objects that begin with the sound of that letter and take turns drawing pictures of those objects on the appropriate page.

Your Portfolio

What happens in children's lives before they go to school is a very important determiner of their success in reading years later. Consider writing an advice column for a parent newsletter in which you make recommendations about what they can do at home to support reading for their younger children. It can be a publication suitable for inclusion in your portfolio.

Teaching Resources

CLASSROOM-PRODUCED BOOKS   Classroom-produced books provide a useful and enjoyable way to showcase children's authorship and to share their works with each other. Single-author books typically are written or dictated by a child (if written, they have corrected text pasted or written in by the teacher or parent volunteer) and, of course, they are illustrated by the child-author. Composite books are collections that all of the children in a class contribute to. The range of such books is very broad, but for emergent readers, the following are recommended. These can be written by the children themselves (with corrections written in darker ink) or simply dictated. Remember that because the books are intended to be read repeatedly by children, the text should be spelled correctly.

ALPHABET BOOKS   Every child is assigned a letter and writes a word that begins with that letter and draws a picture of it.

COUNTING BOOKS   A group of children are assigned numbers 1 through 10. They draw pictures of 1, 2, 3 (and so on) of something and then write the name of the things (e.g., birds, pennies, cars) next to or under each drawing.

RIDDLE BOOKS   Children contribute individual riddles. The riddle is written on one side of the page and the answer on the other.

JOKE BOOKS   The jokes of five- and six-year-old children are funny, if only for their lack of obvious humor. Individual children can contribute jokes to a whole class book.

CONCEPT BOOKS   Concept books focus on one or a few specific topics, such as kinds of animals, sports, famous people, things to be thankful for, or images we associate with each season. Ideas for topics are limitless.

Involving Families in Emergent Literacy

The day a child leaves home to enter kindergarten is a poignant one for families. Many parents feel the shock of having well-meaning strangers take over much of their child's upbringing; but for parents who feel "different" from the school because of

Family Literacy

How can teachers help parents celebrate their children's entering kindergarten, and form lasting partnerships with parents?

language, culture, or income, the feeling of estrangement can be particularly pronounced. Kindergarten and first grade are especially important times for teachers to reach out and invite parents to take part in their children's education.

Keeping parents involved in their children's education is important for the children, too. Parental involvement in school is linked to everything from children's academic achievement to good behavior (they will be less likely to be disruptive); and it even reduces the risk that they will use drugs later on (National Center for Educational Statistics, 1999, 2002). Of course, parents help children's literacy learning at home, too; and the amount of time parents devote at home to reading to their children, telling them stories, and teaching them songs is clearly related to the gains children make in literacy. Likewise, a child's level of reading ability in English is related to the mother's reading ability in English.

But there is good news here, too. Over the last twenty years there have been big gains in the amount of support families give their children in reading—with the biggest increase by far in the poorest families. These increases in parent involvement are the result of enormous efforts by the schools, the public libraries, and even social services—often working together.

For emergent readers, families can be involved in their children's literacy instruction in two ways: in the school and at home.

In the Classroom

First, it is desirable for parents to come into the classroom and take part in activities. They can help move instruction forward by reading to children, taking dictation, and helping publish and bind books. They can also tell stories, especially family stories; and they can demonstrate family traditions and crafts. In this latter way, they can make their families' lives part of the curriculum.

At Home

Family literacy initiatives can also be reinforced at home by sending home to parents materials and ideas for helping develop their children's literacy. Two good examples of home-directed family literacy initiatives are home books and book baggies.

HOME BOOKS   Simple books with very short and predictable texts can be written and sent home for children to read aloud to their parents. Eight-page home books can be made from one sheet of paper, printed on both sides, and assembled with the two double pages stapled one inside the other. Pictures are added to remind the children of what the text says. A sample text for a home book is shown in Figure 4.3.

Figure 4.3
A Typical Home Book

Where is my dog?	In the yard?
No.	In the closet?
No.	In the kitchen?
No!	He is under my bed!

The teacher reads the book through twice with the children before they take it home so that they will be able to read it on their own. Instructions go home with the book for parents to read the book with their children and to read it many times, if possible. Home books can go home once a week. They provide useful practice in reading and help children to acquire concepts about print and even sight words.

BOOK BAGGIES   A book baggie consists of a simple paperback book in a bag with an accompanying activity sheet (such as instructions to draw a favorite character, a word hunt, or an alphabet matching game) and perhaps a recording of the book on tape. Parents are encouraged to read the book with the child and take time to do the accompanying activity. Children should be told how to take care of the book bags when they go home. A book bag may spend several days at a time with each child and then be repacked with a new activity sheet and passed along to a different child.

 Children who struggle with reading often benefit from participating in a family literacy program. Explore family literacy programs in this video and learn about the benefits to children, families, schools, and communities.

Help with Family Literacy

A parent who was a regular volunteer in a Head Start classroom worried aloud because her child was going into kindergarten the next fall.

"But you can still volunteer in the kindergarten," the teacher pointed out. "They will be happy to have you."

"Me? Suppose they hand me one of those school books to read?" the troubled mother said.

Like this mother, there are parents who do not volunteer to help in school and do not read to their children because they cannot read well themselves. For those parents, the agencies that used to provide adult literacy services are now offering family literacy programs, in which parents who are English learners are taught basic English and parents who need help with reading are taught to read to their children. These programs can be quite successful, since the imperative of helping the children can serve as a motivation for parents to improve their own literacy skills, and the stories they practice to read to their children can be appropriate fare for developing their own reading fluency. For information on programs that offer literacy services to parents, contact the following organizations:

- ProLiteracy (Formerly known as Literacy Volunteers of America) at
- The Barbara Bush Literacy Foundation at <www.barbarabushfoundation.com>
- The National Center for Family Literacy at <www.famlit.org>

For Review

Emergent literacy refers to the period from early childhood through kindergarten and even into first grade, in which children learn about language and print and about reading and writing. In recent years, scholars have come to recognize the role of the child's own discoveries in learning to read and write, and research in literacy has identified aspects of literacy that teachers can help children to develop.

Children's literacy begins to emerge at home, well before they enter school. Once they enter kindergarten and first grade, their literacy develops through a combination of children-driven discoveries and experiences orchestrated by a teacher. A successful teacher of reading and writing in the early years must be part careful observer of what children have discovered and are discovering for themselves, and part bridge builder—carefully constructing experiences that will lead children from where they are to their destination as successful readers and writers. The teacher must be part instructor, too: directly teaching key aspects of language and print that children will need so they may learn to read and write.

Even though all but a few children learn to comprehend and speak their first language by the time they enter school, they must continue to develop and elaborate their language competence—vocabulary, syntax, and awareness of sounds in language. They must learn about the features of print and how print works. Marie Clay has provided a set of concepts about print that children must honor in their reading. She has also described a set of graphic principles that children try to master in their writing even before they can form recognizable letters. The English writing system is alphabetic—letters of the alphabet represent words by their smallest sounds, called phonemes. This concept, too, must be discovered or otherwise understood by children. Once children recognize the alphabetic principle, they are ready to figure out how letters represent sounds, or phonics.

Teaching for emergent literacy includes instruction in language, particularly in paying attention to the words, syllables, onsets and rimes, and phonemes. Younger children should be taught concepts of print including layout of books and the recognition and production of the alphabet. They should be read to extensively, especially because they need to be learning the vocabulary that comes from books, and concepts and skills of comprehension and knowledge of literature and informational texts. The Common Core Standards include a host of such skills and concepts that children should learn by participating in read-aloud sessions, at the same time they are learning to read print.

Parents are children's first teachers, and careful teachers include parents in the school's efforts to help children's literacy emerge.

For Your Journal

1. Take a moment to review your answers to the questions in the Anticipation Guide that opened this chapter. Has your thinking changed? If so, write about the changes in your journal.

2. Some teachers and literacy experts expect children to learn much of what they need to know about literacy from their own discoveries: from being surrounded by books and charts, being read to, and having chances to read and write on their own level. Others rely less on discovery and plan to teach virtually all the skills of reading. If you could think of these teachers as being placed along a continuum, where along this continuum would you place yourself?

Taking It to the World

1. What are your first memories of reading and writing? Can you remember not being able to read and write? Were you curious about these activities? What things did you do to teach yourself about them?

2. Visit a preschool—a Head Start program, if possible. Ask the teachers what they do to support children's early literacy. How and when are reading and writing used during the day? How have their approaches to supporting children's early literacy changed over the last ten years?

3. To learn about efforts to involve parents in supporting children's literacy, interview an elementary school teacher or administrator. How are parents' ideas and volunteer efforts brought into the classroom? What things are sent home to help parents help their children? What special efforts are being made toward increasing family literacy?

4. Continuing with the interview in item 3, how are English learners being supported as they learn to read and write? How is the school working with their parents?

5. Speak with a kindergarten or first-grade teacher about how he or she assesses students' concepts about print and what types of screenings are used to assess students' reading skills.

6. Visit the Jumpstart Web site <www.jstart.org/about/> to determine whether there is a Jumpstart program near your community. What are some possible ways in which you might be able to volunteer some time?

New Literacies Connections

1. Visit the literacy homepage of the North Central Regional Educational Laboratory at <www.ncrel.org/litweb> and do a search for "emergent literacy." Examine the numerous articles and connections to useful information and materials.

2. The National Right to Read Foundation <www.nrrf.org> provides thorough information and support on phonics instruction. The site also raises a number of concerns about issues such as emergent literacy and invented spelling. Visit the "Topical Essays" page to read the critiques of these and other topics.

3. The Center for Research in Early Reading Achievement is a federally funded consortium of five universities. Its Web site <www.ciera.org> might be the single best site on emergent literacy, with research reports, book reviews, news of conferences, and links to other sites.

4. Investigate the "Read to Me" program run by the Idaho State Library <www.lili.org/read/readtome/index.htm>. What programs do they offer to promote family literacy?

MyEducationLab™

Go to Topic 1 (Emergent Literacy) in the MyEducationLab <www.myeducationlab.com> for your course, where you can:

- Find learning outcomes for Emergent Literacy along with the national standards that connect to these outcomes.

- Complete Assignments and Activities that can help you more deeply understand the chapter content.

- Apply and practice your understanding of the core teaching skills identified in the chapter with the Building Teaching Skills and Dispositions learning units.

- Check your comprehension on the content covered in the chapter by going to the Study Plan in the Book Resources for your text. Here you will be able to take a chapter quiz, receive feedback on your answers, and then access Review, Practice, and Enrichment activities to enhance your understanding of chapter content.

Phonics and Word Knowledge

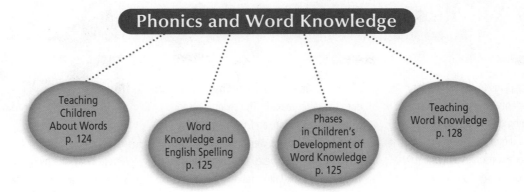

Phonics and Word Knowledge

- Teaching Children About Words p. 124
- Word Knowledge and English Spelling p. 125
- Phases in Children's Development of Word Knowledge p. 125
- Teaching Word Knowledge p. 128

Anticipation Guide

The following statements will help you begin thinking about the topics covered in this chapter. Answer *true* or *false* in response to each statement. As you read and learn more about the topics mentioned in these statements, double-check your answers. See what interests you and what prompts your curiosity toward more understanding.

_____ **1.** Teaching children to read words in Japanese may be easier than teaching them to read in English.

_____ **2.** *Sight words* are words that are not decoded, but that are recognized instantly.

_____ **3.** As they learn to read words, children most naturally learn first to read letters, then syllables, then whole words.

_____ **4.** *Phonics* is an umbrella term for a variety of explicit, implicit, and systematic ways to show children how the print-to-speech/speech-to-print system works.

_____ **5.** Decoding requires the skill of transforming written words into spoken words. Spelling requires exactly the same thing.

_____ **6.** If you pronounce any English word slowly enough, you can distinctly hear each one of its constituent sounds, its phonemes.

_____ **7.** A consonant digraph is a single sound—one in which two separate consonant sounds cannot be heard—even though it is spelled with two consonant letters.

_____ **8.** Knowing where a word came from makes little difference in reading that word.

_____ **9.** Word walls are groups of words, usually arranged in columns, written on chart paper and hung on the wall.

_____ **10.** The English spelling system is so irregular that looking for patterns in it is a complete waste of time.

Literacy Activities in a First-Grade Classroom

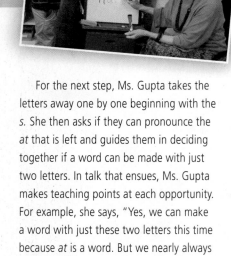

Maria Gupta plans to show her first-grade students how words are constructed by building them from consonants and vowels. On a digital overhead projector she lays out cut out consonants in one row and vowels in another. She has chosen the letters the children can recognize and name. The children are ready to study ways those letters can combine and spell words.

Poised to begin, she calls the children's attention to the screen. "Class," she says, "here is a way I think you'll find interesting to learn how words are made. Watch me make a word and take that word apart, and make another word!" Ms. Gupta moves the consonant *s* from the row of consonants. She thinks out loud as she does this, and she continues to think aloud as she moves through the modeled lesson.

"Okay, I'm moving the *s*. What sound does this letter make?" The children respond with the *sssss* sound, and she asks for the name of this letter as well. "Correct. I'm putting it down here where I'm going to build a word. But, I think I need more letters to make a word. Now I'm getting a vowel; I'm going to try *a*, hmm . . . okay, we have *sa*. I'm going to think of a word that begins with *sa*; you try, too, and I'll get another letter. I'm going to try *t* because I may have thought of a word spelled *s a t*." She moves the letter *t* beside *s* and *a*, and asks the class if they know this word. Many of the children respond correctly, but not all of them. Ms. Gupta says, "Yes! It's the word *sat*. Let's say all three sounds. We can hear them and then put them together to make *sat*. *Sat* is a word!" Ms. Gupta says, "Its nice to learn to make words."

For the next step, Ms. Gupta takes the letters away one by one beginning with the *s*. She then asks if they can pronounce the *at* that is left and guides them in deciding together if a word can be made with just two letters. In talk that ensues, Ms. Gupta makes teaching points at each opportunity. For example, she says, "Yes, we can make a word with just these two letters this time because *at* is a word. But we nearly always need more letters to make a real word in English because we don't have many two-letter words!" Ms. Gupta repeats word building in the same way with other consonants and vowels.

Teaching Children About Words

This chapter is about what children need to know in order to read words, and how we can teach them word knowledge. It assumes that the children have reached the point at which:

- They know most of the letters of the alphabet.
- They realize that spoken words can be broken down into smaller units of sound.
- They are curious about the ways that print represents spoken words.

Now they are ready to learn about the English system of spelling, so they will be able to read the words they encounter daily in print, and write the words they want more or less correctly. Fully learning how English words are read and spelled will take some time—years, in fact. Most children can learn the basic letter-to-sound correspondences by the end of first grade, but knowing what to do when you add inflectional endings to words, sorting out homophones and homographs, spelling prefixes and suffixes, and then dealing with morphemes from Latin and Greek sources—well, all of that will take most of the elementary school years.

Word Knowledge and English Spelling

The relations between letters and sounds in English are understandable, but they are certainly not simple. In languages matched with spelling systems with *shallow orthographies*, where one letter spells one and only one sound, word recognition and spelling are simple matters. But over the centuries English has developed a *deep orthography*. The spellings of many of our words don't have very much to do with their sounds, but rather with their histories and their relations to other words. In English, we begin by teaching children which letters make which sounds, but we cannot stop there. We need to teach them layers and layers of word knowledge beyond simple phonics.

Phonics and Phonological Awareness

How would you describe the relation between word recognition and phonics?

Phases in Children's Development of Word Knowledge

Over the years as students learn to read and spell words, there are two kinds of developments taking place. One is children's growing awareness of the structure of words. Another is that the words learners encounter at higher grade levels are getting more sophisticated.

Let's look now at phases of word recognition and the kind of instruction that can help children at each phase. Bear in mind that the ages assigned to each phase are approximate, and many children will be found ahead of or behind these estimates.

WORDS AS WHOLES: THE LOGOGRAPHIC PHASE   When children are just beginning to notice words around them, they tend to recognize familiar words as whole displays. These children, usually preschoolers and kindergartners, may recognize the word *look* by associating the two O's with eyes. They may identify the same word with different but related names, calling a Crest toothpaste label at one time "Crest" and at another time "toothpaste" (Harste, Woodward, & Burke, 1984). They are not yet reading the letters in the words, but are trying to find any identifiable feature that will help them remember the words, almost as if the words were faces. Frith (1985) and Goswami (2000) called readers in this phase *logographic readers*, which is just a Greek way of saying they are reading words as whole displays.

Children in the *words as wholes* or *logographic phase* of word reading often give no response at all when faced with words they do not know. They do not yet have a strategy for sounding out words. Marsh et al. (1981) called this phase of word recognition *"glance and guess"* because children look at a word and call it by the few names of words they know, or say nothing at all. They have no means yet to begin to recognize words by associating sounds with their letters.

Teaching logographic word readers focuses first on having the children amass many words that they can read (Cunningham & Stanovich, 1998; Juel, 1988; Lehr, Osborn, & Hiebert, 2006). To help the children acquire sight words, the teacher may use the strategies of labeling objects around the classroom (the clock, the door, the shelf), doing shared reading (see pages 106–108), or using the language experience approach (see pages 130–131). The teacher begins to call children's attention to letters, starting with the consonant sounds that begin words. But the main emphasis is on having children accumulate several dozen sight words—words they can recognize easily—not only to help them begin to read, but to give them the wholes (words stored in memory) from which they can learn the parts (letters and their relations to sounds).

Teach It!   19

Word Wall Activities

LETTER-BY-LETTER READING: THE ALPHABETIC PHASE   More advanced children—usually in mid-kindergarten—begin to read words by their letters, but not yet by very many letters. The reader who is early in the letter-by-letter or *alphabetic phase* might read the first consonant of a word and call it by the name of another word she or he knows that begins with that sound. A word such as *ball* might appear to children like this: **bxxx.** The child might correctly read the word, especially if she is helped by the context (as in "The girl tossed the b____."), but when she sees it alone she might readily confuse *ball* with *bat*, *bark*, or *beep* (Morris, 2006).

Shared Writing

Word Sorting

CCSS

• Foundational Skills 3: Phonics and Word Recognition (Note that the Common Core Standards are quite explicit on the lessons about letter-to-sound relationships children should learn at each grade level.)

Making and Breaking Words

Watch the boy in this video play a matching game to practice onsets and rimes. How will automaticity with this skill benefit him now and in the future?

As they advance into first grade, most children begin to read more and more of the letters in words. When they attempt to read a word, rather than calling out the name of another word that begins the same way, a child might sound out every letter, even if it means pronouncing something that doesn't make sense. A child might say, "We went to the fire sta-ty-on" instead of "fire station." With practice, students produce fewer nonsense word readings and read words more accurately.

Children are acquiring a growing body of *sight words*, which they can read accurately and quickly without having to decode them. This rapid word identification occurs after a period of sounding out the words, or phonological recoding, as linguists call it. Ehri (1991) suggests that the earlier practice of reading words alphabetically—figuring them out letter by letter—lays down pathways to the memory that makes it easier for children to recognize the words when they see them later. She explains,

> When readers practice reading specific words by phonologically recoding the words, they form access routes for those words into memory. The access routes are built using knowledge of grapheme-phoneme correspondences that connect letters in spellings to phonemes in the pronunciation of words. The letters are processed as visual symbols for the phonemes, and the sequence of letters is retained as an alphabetic, phonological representation of the word. The first time an unfamiliar word is seen, it is read by phonological recoding. This initiates an access route into memory. Subsequent readings of the word strengthen the access route until the connections between letters and phonemes are fully formed and the spelling is represented in memory. (p. 402)*

Frith (1985) and Goswami (2000) called readers in the early part of this phase *transitional alphabetic readers*. Those in the later end of the phase they called *alphabetic readers*. In both cases, the important point is that the readers are looking at the relations between individual letters and individual sounds.

Teaching letter-by-letter or alphabetic readers focuses first on teaching children the common letter-to-sound matches—beginning with consonant sounds and then moving on to long and short vowel sounds, and consonant digraphs and consonant clusters. Teachers often use shared writing (see page 135), sound boards, word sorts, and word walls (see pages 132–139) for this purpose.

CHUNKING: THE ORTHOGRAPHIC PHASE   By late first grade and on to the middle of second grade, most children are looking beyond matching one letter to one sound, and are focusing on vowel and consonant combinations, such as *-at*, *-ock*, *-ake*, and *-ight*. Children are visually separating words into *onsets* and *rimes* as Trieman (1985) calls them. (We also call them *phonogram patterns*.) They can read by analogy; that is, if they can read *bake* and *take*, they can also read *rake* and *stake*. To clarify, *onsets* and *rimes* refers to the beginning element and what follows in spoken syllables, while *phonogram patterns* refer to the written form of the latter part of syllables. So the spoken word *cat* has the onset [k] followed by the rime [æt]. And the rime [æt] corresponds to the phonogram pattern *-at*.

Reading by chunking means not only that children can read letters in clusters, but also that they begin to recognize that some groups of letters such as *bite* have a long vowel sound and some such as *bit* have a short vowel sound, depending on the ways the vowels are marked (in this case, by the presence of a silent E).

Frith (1985) and Goswami (2000) call this phase of word reading *orthographic* (which is a Greek way of saying "writing by the rules") because the children are looking beyond individual letter-to-sound relations to rules that connect larger units of word parts and spelling. (The *orthographic phase* was the last of Frith and Goswami's phases of word recognition. But we have added two more. Read on!)

Teaching readers at the chunking or orthographic phase focuses on the common rimes or phonogram patterns. Teachers use word sorts (see pages 136–139), word walls (see page 134), word wheels (see page 139), and making and breaking words (see pages 133–134) for this purpose.

*Ehri, L. C. (1991). Development of the ability to read words. In R. Barr, M. Kamil, P. B. Mosenthal, & P. D. Pearson (Eds.), *Handbook of reading research* (Vol. 2). New York, NY: Longman.

The World of Reading

Synthetic Phonics and Spelling

Synthetic phonics was described by Jeanne Chall in her book *Learning to Read: The Great Debate* (1967), which, along with Rudolf Flesch's book, *Why Johnny Can't Read* (1956), is often cited as part of the great debate over reading and spelling instruction. This debate has raged for years and continues today.

For years, the "look-say" method of learning words dominated the teaching of reading in the United States. The best known look-say reading series was the Dick and Jane series. These texts helped millions of children learn to read by repeating words in stories until children learned them as sight or known words. However, although these children demonstrated good comprehension and vocabulary in first grade, they were not as accurate in word recognition as the children taught with a phonics approach. Some children picked up enough knowledge to become good readers and spellers for life, but many did not.

Some teachers of the look-say approach included a phonics component, teaching parts of words (letter/sound relationships) after the children knew them on sight. However, some teachers included no phonics component in their instruction. Fewer still taught phonics that connected children with the English-language spelling patterns, let alone with their teaching of reading or writing. Spelling was a subject unto itself. Historically, spelling instruction has gone through several notable shifts. From the 1920s to the 1960s, spelling was a process of rote memorization. Learning to spell depended on word memorization and weekly tests prescribed by the spelling book. It was not grounded linguistically and had nothing to do with language learning. In the 1960s and 1970s, spelling was seen as a language-based process that involves abstracting, or learning, regular sound/spelling patterns. Beginning in the late 1970s and continuing today, spelling has been seen more as a developmental process, one in which there are definable patterns of learning, and spelling is taught based on those developmental patterns (Henderson, 1986; Temple, Nathan, & Temple, 2013; Templeton & Morris, 2000).

None of these approaches was totally wrong. In fact, the memorization and abstraction approaches laid the groundwork for the developmental recommendations in this book. The period of linguistic abstraction showed that spelling was a language process (including memory) that is involved in all learning. We now know better how to implement synthetic phonics in language-centered and developmentally appropriate ways that make sense to children. We know that spelling instruction supports orthographic knowledge and that spelling and word recognition are important to reading comprehension (Perfetti, 1985; Stanovich & Cunningham, 1993). Thus attention to spelling instruction should not be left to be done on an as-needed basis (Templeton & Morris, 2000, p. 537). Spelling and phonics should be viewed as a means of studying and seeing words as tools that serve reading, writing, and vocabulary development (Templeton, 1991). Research continues to seek greater understanding of how children learn to spell and read and how we can improve all children's literacy instruction.

MEANINGFUL WORD PARTS: THE MORPHOLOGICAL PHASE From first grade up, normally advancing readers enter a phase of word recognition that could be called the phase of reading by *meaningful word parts*. Because those meaningful word parts go by the technical name *morphemes*, we choose to call this the *morphological phase* of word recognition. In truth, it is not strictly a phase, because children can still be learning phonogram patterns (the focus of the preceding orthographic phase) even as they begin to attend to morphemes in words. Also, because some morphemes are encountered earlier than others and some morphemes are more obvious than others, the morphological phase of word recognition stretches over many years. There are three main kinds of issues at play in the morphological phase.

One issue is presented by *compound words* like *fireman* and *birdhouse*. Compound words are made up of two (or more, but usually two) morphemes, each of which could also stand alone as a meaningful word. Readers from late first grade and second grade are recognizing the "small words within the big words," as many teachers put it. Compound words are usually not challenging to understand, but because they add to the length of words, they may make the words daunting to young readers.

Another issue in the morphological phase is recognizing *grammatical morphemes*, such as plural markers and verb tense endings: the difference between *bird* and *birds*, and *want* and *wanted*. These grammatical markers, which are also called *inflectional morphemes*, always are attached at the ends of words. They do not change the meaning of words, but rather refine the meaning, as in telling if there is more than one of something, or if an action is happening in the present or already happened in the past.

A third issue is that words can have *derivational morphemes,* too. These are *prefixes* and *suffixes* such as the *un-* in *unkind,* the *-ful* in *helpful,* the *non-* in *nonsense* and also the *-ness* in *happiness.* These morphemes can never stand alone, but they can change either the meaning (as in *kind → unkind*) or the part of speech (as in *happy → happiness*) of the words to which they are attached.

If this no longer strictly sounds to you like phonics, you're right. As word knowledge advances, many more considerations go into reading and writing words than just letter and sound relations.

Teaching readers at the morphological phase, the phase of meaningful word parts, should include explicitly teaching them about those word parts. Teachers continue to use word sorts, word walls, and making and breaking words and other word-building games. Children also should be encouraged to read a great deal. They need to see many words— thousands of words—used meaningfully in interesting text, and also have their attention called to the structures of words.

WORD HISTORIES AND FAMILIES: THE DERIVATIONAL PHASE From about fourth grade up, students who read with at least average proficiency can recognize that words like *telegraph, telephone, biology,* and *biography* contain word parts that they recognize. They may notice that *telegraph* and *graphic* (as in graphic novel) have something to do with each other, which in fact they do: both have the word part *-graph,* from a Greek word meaning "to write." They may notice a shared part in *telephone, telescope* and *telepathy: tele-,* it turns out, comes from another Greek word meaning "at a distance." Proficient readers may be aware that *sanity* is related to *sane, grave* (as in, "a grave look") is related to *gravity, sign* is related to *signal,* and *sympathy* is related to *pathetic.* We call this phase *reading for word histories and families,* or the *derivational phase.* We say *derivational* because, as you can see, words like we just saw were derived from the same older sources. Word reading at this phase is still further away from a matter of letters and sounds. It combines word recognition and vocabulary knowledge.

Teaching readers at the phase of word histories and families again includes explicit teaching about word families and word histories. Teachers need to make an interesting subject out of the study of words. Students should have ready access to dictionaries with word histories or etymologies. They can be assigned projects in which they research word origins and see how the histories of words relate to their spellings and connect them to other words. Students need to be encouraged to read prolifically, and to talk about interesting words at the same time they discuss other aspects of texts.

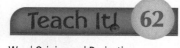

Word Origins and Derivations

Teaching Word Knowledge

In the sections that follow, we make suggestions for teaching word recognition. Before we begin, note that children at different phases in their development of word recognition need different kinds of instruction. When it comes to teaching word recognition, one size does not fit all. In word recognition, as in other aspects of reading instruction, children need differentiated instruction.

Teaching the Whole Word or Logographic Reader (K–Grade 1)

Modified Reading Recovery Lesson

Children at the logographic phase of word recognition are emergent readers. They are just beginning to recognize words as wholes, so we encourage that. As children learn to recognize several dozen words as wholes, they will pay more attention to the letters that make up those words.

WHOLE-PART-WHOLE TEACHING   Begin word study at all levels by paying attention to words in the context of meaningful sentences before you focus attention on individual words and their parts. The few minutes of extra time that are required to pay attention to the context may well keep some children from becoming confused and will make it more likely that children will apply what they learn from the word study sessions when they are reading words in connected text. Several models of whole-part-whole teaching follow here: shared reading, the language-experience approach, and guided reading.

Reading Words in Context   Children who are getting familiar with words need structured opportunities to focus their attention on the written word at just the instant they hear the spoken word, so they can build a connection in their memories. There are two tried-and-true teaching methods that accomplish this. One is the *shared reading method* (Booth and Schwartz, 2004; Holdaway, 1979). The other is the Language Experience Approach, which is presented in the Differentiated Instruction Box on pages 130–131.

Making and Using Word Banks

Using either the shared reading method or the language-experience approach, you can extend the children's word learning by using *word banks* (see below).

Word Banks   Once a student has demonstrated she has learned to recognize a word that is separated from other words, write that word on a piece of thick paper or tag board and give it to her to put into her *word bank*, a personalized collection of words in a container such as a zipper-close plastic bag or an index card box. Students should practice reading the words in their word banks every day or every other day. They can

- Read the words to partners or to parent volunteers.
- Group the words into categories, such as things, actions, animals, etc.
- Group all the words that begin with the same letters.
- Do "word hunts": look for the same words in children's books.

Try to find time to review each child's word bank every week or ten days. If there are words the child cannot read correctly, take them out of the word bank and put them in a special envelope inside or beside it. The child can practice reading those words later, and if they are read correctly, the words can go back into the bank.

A teacher using a pocket chart in class.

SIOP®
Sheltered
Instruction
Observation
Protocol*

The Language-Experience Approach for English Language Learners and Struggling Readers

The Language Experience Approach, or LEA (Crawford et al., 1995; Stauffer, 1975), works for people of all ages who are learning to read and need additional support. The LEA is unique in that it uses the student's oral language to teach written language, that is, to teach reading. There are several cumulative steps to take when teaching with the LEA and many variations of it. The following is a step-by-step process we recommend. Use it with a small group or in working with one child.

First Lesson

In the first twenty- to thirty-minute lesson, complete these three steps.

Step 1: Discussion. Talk with students about their experiences (e.g., their favorite foods or birthday parties). Respond positively, be curious about their stories, and value their input. Let the children know that you will write down some things from their stories that they can all read together. In later LEA lessons, the discussion topics could be about science or current events.

Step 2: Dictation. Ask the children what to write, select some of their responses, and write them on large chart paper, an overhead, or a computer screen. Be sure everyone can see your writing. Make teaching points about where to begin writing as you think appropriate. Read each sentence and ask children to read it back to you.

Step 3: Reading the Text. Now it's time for the children to read their text. But first read it to them again and guide them to watch the words as you run your finger or pointer under them. Then have the children read along with you, and finally they read on their own.

To extend the lesson, give the children copies of the text and have them practice in pairs or alone. Emphasize that this is just practice; give the children time and support to engage deeply in reading their own language.

In this initial two-day cycle of LEA, the first lesson consists of motivation and discussion, dictation and reading, and shared reading, as just described. On the following day, there are several additional steps.

Second Lesson

Step 1: Reading the Text. Read the text again and prompt careful watching of the words as you point to them. Then have the children read with you. Practice this as much as needed. When reading sounds somewhat fluent, have the children take turns reading on their own. Include everyone. Every child can read even if it is only a word or two with your support.

Step 2: Reassembling the Text. Before step 2, make copies of the sentences on sentence strips in the order they appear on the original text. Begin the lesson by having the children look at the whole text and then have them look for the first sentence. As

children point out each sentence, put them in a sentence strip holder or adjustable pocket chart one at a time and practice reading them together. Each time, read the sentence and then read the entire text. Again, children can take turns reading individually as they are able. You can also ask children to point at the sentence that tells [fill in blank].

This two-day cycle is repeated once or twice every week with a new theme for each set of lessons. Children will not learn all the words at first, but keep developing new charts for them to maintain interest. Be sure to keep copies available so children can practice. When you notice that children have learned a number of words, you can add a third lesson on sight vocabulary and move on to a three-day LEA cycle.

Third Lesson

Step 1: Reassembling the Words into Sentences. Before step 1, cut each sentence strip made for the second lesson into individual words. Place the words in the pocket chart or even on the chalk rail. Place them in a random order and support the children in reassembling the words into sentences. Have the original story nearby so they can refer to it as needed. Build independence by asking children, "If you don't know a word, can you find it in our story? Now read the sentence. Can you read the word?" As sentences are reassembled, guide the reading of the whole text from time to time. Finally, you can implement other word activities. Here are a few ideas:

- Give word cards from the sentences to the children, and ask them to find the words in the text.
- Say, "Here is the word _____. Find the same word in the text."
- Make a large chart paper copy of one of the texts with some words left out. Tell the children that some words are missing and ask if they can identify them. Read with the children, pausing when you come to a missing word. Support them in "guessing the missing word" and write it in.
- Guide the children to write and keep a personal file collection of the words they learn. Begin with a few words and encourage building the collections and game playing with the word cards.

For further support of word recognition, you might color code sentence strips and word cards. Or various colors might be marked on the back of cards. Word cards are inevitably mixed up as children work with them at their desks or tables. They are easily sorted back into word groups of original sentences according to the colors on the reverse side.

Several weeks or even months after the third lesson activities, children will likely show signs of recognizing using letter-sound correspondences in words. This is a signal to add a fourth day to the cycle, one for word analysis using the context of words the children now recognize at sight.

Fourth Lesson

Step 1: Word Recognition Study. The children read the story, they find words that have the same beginning, and you support their learning to associate letters and sounds using words they already know. Guide the children to draw conclusions, that is, to make phonic generalizations out of their observations of letters and corresponding sounds. Continue to use the written language, the words, sentences, and whole texts that have evolved from the children's oral language dictations. This makes powerful use of their background knowledge and helps them to extend their knowledge of sounds and letters in known words to new words. You can also bring out old LEA charts from time to time for review lessons and practice.

Repeated readings develop fluency and automaticity (when children recognize words automatically). As word recognition becomes easier, they are able to focus attention on comprehension (Samuels & Farstrup, 2006).

Morning Message   As a technique for getting students to understand written language and focus on words, morning message (Kawakami-Arakaki, Oshiro, & Farran, 1989) gets high marks. Use chart paper or a pocket chart, and write the words in handwriting large enough for all of the children gathered in front of you to see. A typical morning message says

> *Today is Wednesday, October 17th.*
> *The weather is snowy.*
> *We have art today.*
> *Surprise! Today is Janisha's birthday!*

Ask the students what words you should write. If a child says "Today," ask which letter it should begin with. If she volunteers "T," ask if it will be an uppercase or a lowercase T. A child can come forward and write some of the letters for you. The other children can "air write" (make gestures of writing in the air) while one child writes on the chart.

Write some of the words that are often repeated on separate pieces of thick paper. Either tape them to the bottom of the chart or arrange them in a lower pocket of the pocket chart. Invite children to come forward, find the proper word, and either tape it onto the chart (the tape is already placed on the back of the word) or insert it where it should go in the pocket chart. Have the child read the sentence aloud before inserting the word in the sentence, then read the sentence with the word in place.

Next, have all of the children practice reading the lines of print as you follow along beneath the words with the pointer. First, they read the lines aloud as you point, then they choral-read the text, then they echo-read, and then different groups of children are invited to read.

Finally, ask individual children to come forward and point to any words they can read alone (that is, in isolation). Bracket each word with your hands as the child reads it. If he or she is successful, write the word on a small piece of thick paper and present it to the child. That word then goes into the child's word bank for later practice.

Labeling the Room   Each child's name should be printed in big letters on her or his desk. The important items around the classroom should be labeled, too—the blackboard, the clock, the door, the window, the books, science center, the sink—with cards bearing letters 3 inches high so they can be read from anywhere in the room. In time, children can write or trace the labels you prepare. Take time every other day to "read the room": first as a whole class, then in small groups taking turns to read the signs together. Every few weeks, change some signs around (so that the label "sink" is over the door, for instance) and ask who notices anything wrong. Ask the children to move the words to the correct locations.

Words that are used as labels can be put in students' word banks, too, if the students can read them correctly.

Teaching the Letter-by-Letter or Alphabetic Reader (Grade 1)

CCSS

• Foundational Skills 3: Phonics and Word Recognition

As alphabetic readers, children are beginning readers who have learned several dozen words and are paying attention to the letters in words and associating them with sounds. The goal of our instruction with these children should be to help them notice more and more letters as well as the sounds with which they are associated. It will also help to call students' attention to sounds in words.

PICTURE SORTS   Make sets of 1 × 2-inch cards with pictures on them, depicting objects that begin with different sounds. For example, *sun, sundial, sail, sand, soda; can, candy, cat, cart, calendar; dog, dart, dish, diaper, diamond; goat, girl, gorilla, guitar, gun.* Place one member of each group side by side on the table. Scramble the rest of the pictures, and then ask a child to name the picture aloud and then place the picture cards one at a time in a column below the appropriate picture. Once children become proficient at this, substitute a card with a letter as the guide card at the top of the column.

Picture cards can be downloaded for free at:

- <www.kellyskindergarten.com/picturecards/picturecards.htm>
- <http://pals.virginia.edu/pdfs/activities/beginning-sounds/picture_sorts.pdf>

Commercially prepared picture sort cards are available from these companies:

- Teaching Resource Center
- ReallyGoodStuff.Com <www.reallygoodstuff.com>

PLASTIC LETTERS   Gather two to five students in front of you. Using sets of plastic letters (some are sold in toy stores with magnetic backs to stick to refrigerators), make a word like *band.* Say the word aloud, and then take the letter *s.* Exaggerate the sound of /s/, and tell the students to watch what happens when you substitute the *s* for the *b.* You get *sand.* Demonstrate this several times, and let some of the children make the same substitution. Then hold up the letter *h* and ask who can tell what word we will have when we substitute the letter *h* for the *s* in *sand.* Then follow with *l.* Pairs of children can follow up by playing this game themselves. On other days, you can introduce other phonogram patterns and other beginning consonants.

SOUND BOARDS   A *sound board* (Blachman & Tangle, 2008) is a device for showing students how words are constructed. Sound boards are about the size of a notebook, and are worked with by one child at a time. It is useful to have a dozen sound boards in a classroom or enough for the entire class. They can be used initially for up to six for a group working with the teacher, and another half dozen to have children using in learning centers.

To construct a sound board, cut a piece measuring 11 × 14 inches from a sheet of poster board; then tape three strips of a different color from the board 1-1/2 inches deep across the long side of the board. Now make grapheme cards (cards with letters and letter units) 1 × 3 inches long. Turning them long side up, write letters exactly the same size on the top half only of each card (the bottom half of the card will disappear into the pocket). Prepare cards with consonant letters on them (written with a broad tip marker in black ink) and other cards with vowel letters and vowel teams (written in red ink).

Single consonant cards should include: **b, c, d, f, g, h, j, k, l, m, n, p, qu, r, s, t, v, w,** and **z.** Digraph consonant cards (a digraph is two letters that spell a single sound) should include **ch, th, sh, wh, ck,** and **ph.**

Vowel cards should contain *a, e, i, o,* and *u.* Vowel team cards should contain **ai, ay, ey, ee, ea, ie, oo, ou, ow, oi, oy, au, aw,** and **ew.** Vowel-plus-consonant cards should contain **ar, er, ir, ur,** and also **al** (as in **walk, calm,** and **bald**) (after Blachman, 2000).

The top pocket is for storing learned consonants and the middle pocket is for learned vowels. The bottom pocket is for making words. A manila envelope is attached to the back of the sound board for storing grapheme cards.

To use the sound board, put a consonant such as *s* in the bottom pocket. Pronounce its sound. Then put a vowel letter *a* to the right of it and pronounce its sound. Then put a consonant letter *t* to the right of the vowel and pronounce it. Say all three sounds and then pronounce the word *sat*. Now ask the student to repeat the activity, using the same three letters. Take away the letter *s* and ask him to sound the other two letters out and pronounce the word *at*. Then pick up a new consonant letter card such as *p* and pronounce its sound. Put the *p* to the left of *a* and *t* and ask the student to pronounce all three sounds and say the word *pat*.

Sound boards can be used in many ways. To work with beginning consonants and phonogram patterns, you prepare two to four phonogram patterns such as *-ip*, *-ap*, *-ick*, and *-ack*, and a set of cards for consonants (such as *l*, *t*, and *s*) and consonant digraphs (such as *ch*, *sh*, or *th*). Children make many words by changing the consonant or consonant digraph before a single phonogram.

PUSH IT SAY IT   From Johnston, Invernizzi, and Juel's Book Buddies program (1998) comes the *Push It Say It* technique. Here you prepare word cards as follows. One set of cards should be consonants (such as *s*, *b*, *c*, *t*, *m*), and the other should be phonogram patterns (such as *-at*, *-it*, *-op*). To carry out the activity, first demonstrate it to a student, as follows:

1. Put a consonant card and a phonogram card separately on the table in front of the student. Drawing out the consonant sound ("ssssss"), push the consonant card forward.

2. Then, drawing out the sound of the phonogram ("aaaaaat"), push the phonogram card forward.

3. Now pronounce the resulting word (*sat*).

Next, provide the student a consonant card and a phonogram card and ask her to repeat what you did.

MAKING AND BREAKING WORDS   Iverson and Tunmer (1993) developed a procedure for "making and breaking words." The procedure is carried out with a set of plastic letters and a magnetic board (available in most toy stores). The procedure can be done one on one, or on an overhead projector (digital or traditional) for the whole class.

The teacher asks the student to move the letters around to construct new words that have similar spellings and sound patterns. For instance, the teacher arranges letters to make the word *and*. The teacher announces that the letters spell *and* then asks the student what the word says. If the student seems uncertain, the teacher forms the word again, using different letters, says its name, and asks him to name the word.

As a next step, the teacher scrambles the letters and asks the student to make *and*. Again, if assembling scrambled letters proves difficult, the teacher spreads the letters apart, in the proper order, at the bottom of the magnetic board and asks the student to make the word *and* with them in the middle of the board. When the student has made the word, the teacher asks him to name the word. If the student responds correctly, the teacher scrambles the letters and asks him to make the word again and to name the word afterward. The teacher repeats the procedure until the student is able to assemble the letters and name *and*.

As a next step, the teacher puts the letter *s* in front of *and*, then announces what he has just done. The teacher takes a finger and moves the *s* away and then back and says, "Do you see? If I put *s* in front of *and*, it says *sand*." The teacher asks the student to read the word *sand*, and the student runs a finger under it. Now the teacher removes the *s* and points out that with the *s* removed, the word is now *and*. With the *s* pushed aside, the teacher asks the student to make *sand*. If the student correctly makes the word, the teacher asks him to name the word he has made. Next, the teacher instructs the student to make *and*. As a next step, the whole procedure is repeated, making *hand* and *band*. Now the teacher can make *sand*, then *band*, then *hand*, and *and*, asking the student to name each word as it is made. When the student can do so successfully, the teacher scrambles the letters on the board, and puts the letters *s*, *b*, and *h* to one side. Now the teacher challenges the student to make *and*. If the student can do so, he is now challenged to make *hand*, *sand*, and *band*. The student is asked to read each word after it is made.

Word Wall Activities

WORD WALLS   Word walls (Cunningham, 1995; Cunningham, Hall, & Sigmon, 2007) can provide strong support in children's learning and teachers' systematic instruction. Word walls consist of words that children are learning arranged alphabetically on the walls of the classroom in ways that allow the words to be easily seen and accessed. Word walls should be interactive, made and used by both the teacher and the children. Much good instruction can spring from various kinds of words on walls, including serving children's self-assessment needs. Here is a brief description of two types of word walls and how they be might be used (see also Bear et al., 2007; McGee & Richgels, 2003; Pinnell & Fountas, 1998):

- A *picture-word wall*: Post the words from favorite books, inquiry units of study, and words and pictures with the letters of the alphabet. It is nearly always best if words are put on the wall during the teaching process.
- A *literature-based picture-word wall*: This example can be applied with young children and older children. Picture having read *Lilly's Purple Plastic Purse* (Henkes, 1996) or *Lilly's Big Day* (Henkes, 2006). You introduce the word wall by showing an enlarged picture or colorful sketch of Lilly on the wall with Lilly's name under it. Next, you ask for suggestions about other words children want to add from the book. You write their words in full view, leaving space for the pictures that will come. The children are asked to remember their favorite word. Next, they are asked to draw a picture that depicts or explains their word and write the word and explanation. The teacher talks the children through some examples of what they might write.

As children's development progresses, word walls change from picture-word walls to word-only walls. Word hunts and word sorts expand the word study. Books are reread to keep a focus on meaningful reading and reading for enjoyment. Imagine the word walls on science and other inquiry work you can have with middle and upper grades.

SIGHT WORDS   Sight words are learned primarily through sheer exposure. Repeated readings are key. Children should reread their favorite books while they also select challenging books from several the teacher recommends. Importantly, sight word knowledge helps children progress in reading to the point that reading is easy and joyful. When they have enough sight words in their memory, students are able to read with less effort and can concentrate more on meaning and reading comprehension.

Sight word walls contain high-frequency words that are posted as the children encounter them in their reading and in lessons. The teacher should engage children in doing sight word walls regularly (Cunningham et al., 2007). When word walls are used daily in the course of reading, writing, and spelling, they are embedded in authentic literacy practice. This is how you can create and use a sight word wall:

- Add words gradually (about five per week).
- Make words highly accessible by putting them where all students can see them, writing them in large print with big black letters, and using colors for words that are often confused, such as *for*, *from*, *that*, *they*, and *this*.
- Select only the words children encounter most frequently in their reading and the words they use most frequently in their writing. Do not overwhelm them or yourself with too many words. Nothing succeeds like success!
- Practice the words by saying, spelling, and writing them ("do the wall").

WORD WALL CHANTS   From Joe Fuhrmann come the following suggestions for word wall chants. As the children and the teacher review the words on the word wall, they use different and engaging ways to spell out the letters and then read the word. Some of the chants can be done with the children at their seats.

- *"The chicken"*: Flapping your arms up and down as you say each letter
- *"The movie star"*: Blowing kisses, like a starlet on awards night as each letter is said
- *"The opera singer"*: Singing each letter, and finally the word, in an operatic voice
- *"The volcano"*: Saying each letter louder and louder, until you shout the word
- *"The nose"*: Holding your nose as you say the letters and the word

Other chants can be done standing up and moving around.

- *"Dribble and shoot"*: Dribbling each letter and shooting the word
- *"Mexican Hat Dance"*: Chanting letters as each foot goes forward
- *"Pumping iron"*: Pretending to hoist a heavy weight as you say each letter; then pretending to put the bar back on the frame as you say the word with an exhausted voice
- *"Frog jump"*: Beginning standing up, crouching a little lower as you say each letter, then leaping as you say the word

SHARED WRITING   Shared writing is a way for the teacher to demonstrate how spoken words are broken into their sounds and spelled with letters, and also to engage children's participation in writing. After sharing a poem or discussing an event that is exciting to the children, the teacher gathers students around an easel and invites them to help him write about what they just heard. First, children agree on a short sentence they want to write, for example, "A firefighter came to school." The children practice saying the sentence several times so that everyone is aware of the words. Then the teacher says, "Now we're going to write the first word, 'A.' Who can tell us what letter we need to write?" A child suggests the letter A. The teacher accepts it and writes it slowly on the easel. Then he says, "We wrote A. Now what's the next word we want to write? Right. It's 'firefighter.' That's a new word, so I'm going to leave space between the word A and the first letter of this new word. [He puts his finger after the A to demonstrate the space.] What is the first sound we hear in 'firefighter'? Right: it's 'fuh.' What letter are we going to use to write the 'fuh' sound in 'firefighter'? Right: It's F. Who can come up and write the letter F for me?" A child comes up and writes the letter. The teacher proceeds in this way, having the children supply the letters they can, and adding the sounds himself that the children do not hear. If a child makes an error in writing, the teacher puts a piece of wide correction tape over the error and helps the children write the correct letter.

Conduct shared writing lessons with the class almost daily when children are in the alphabetic phase of writing. In the meantime, encourage the children to use writing every chance they get.

GUIDED READING   As you saw in Chapter 4, guided reading is done with a small group of children or as few as two children to support children's progress in reading development, including fluency, comprehension, and word knowledge. The texts used in guided reading gradually become more and more challenging (Fountas & Pinnell, 1996). Even when you want to use guided reading to emphasize word study, it is important to create a meaningful context for the words. Thus, you begin the lesson with a focus on meaning before proceeding to word study. Detailed steps for Guided Reading are presented in Chapter 4, pages 108–109.

Guided Reading and the Four Blocks Approach

Teaching the Reader at the "Chunking" Phase: The Orthographic Reader (Grades 2 to 3)

Children in the "chunking" or orthographic phase of word reading are beginning to pay attention to spelling patterns, or what linguists call *onsets* and *rimes*. At the beginning of this period, children are ready to understand that if they can read *hit* and they know the sound represented by the letter *s*, they can also read *sit*. Toward the end of this period, they must learn how to cope with two-syllable words, homophones, and other challenges English orthography poses to the reader. Teaching activities at the orthographic phase work extensively with patterns of spelling.

WORD SORTS   Word sorting activities include sorting words by spelling or phonogram patterns—for example, words that are spelled like *rock*. Word sorts also may focus on the concepts that words represent—for example, sort all the weather-associated words in one row (*rain, snow, . . .*), and sort all the cooking-associated words in another row (*stove, bowl, . . .*). Word sorting by affixes and words provides sound practice and the kind of hands-on activity that older children appreciate.

Sorting instruction encourages children to see words as objects that they manipulate and own by organizing and classifying them. Jerry Zutell (1999, p. 105) notes, "Organizing objects, events, and experiences into categories and classes is a fundamental way we make sense of the world around us. The act of sorting makes words concrete objects of study."

The first time children do word sorts, it is good to begin with a small-group demonstration. After children have had a lively experience with a text—whether by reading a big book, reading back a dictated story, or reading a trade book—the teacher calls their attention to a small group of individual words. These words are chosen because they share patterns that can be generalized to other words. By *generalized*, we mean that once children have noticed a pattern in one word, they can apply that pattern to help them read other words. For example, the words *sit* and *cub* can be chosen for children who are early orthographic readers, because they introduce patterns that other words share (see below). These words are written on cards of thick paper or tag board. If they will be used in front of a small group of children, use 3 × 5-inch cards.

Now the teacher writes on new cards several words that share the same phonogram patterns as *sit* and *cub*. For example, he writes *fit, bit,* and *kit*; and *tub, rub,* and *sub*.

The teacher then puts the two original cards on the table or in the top pocket of a pocket chart, side by side. He reads both words several times, pointing to each word, to make sure that all of the children can read them. Next, the teacher scrambles the remaining cards. Then, he draws one of the remaining cards—let's say it is *rub*—and holds it up for the children.

"Where does it go?" he asks. "Should I put it in the columns with *sit* or with *cub*?" Note that he doesn't read the word he drew yet.

The children say it goes in the column under *cub*. Then the teacher says, "Let's read down the column. *Cub* and *rrrrrrr*—. . ."

The children say "*Rub!*" The teacher congratulates them, and then he stresses the point that once they could read *cub*, and they saw that the new word began with *r*, they could read it: "*rub*."

Now he invites children to come up one at a time to choose words from the scrambled set and place them under the guide words, *sit* or *cub*. Later the teacher can add another group of words to the sets: *dad, sad, mad,* and *had*.

After the children demonstrate that they understand how the activity works, they may practice in pairs. Once the procedures for word sorts have been taught to the class, pairs or trios of students can play word sort games with groups of words that have been prepared in advance. The procedures for the game work the same as in the group lesson just described.

- Prepare groups of words on 1 × 2-inch cards, about the size of a business card.
- Create four to five examples of each spelling pattern.
- Make sure that each student can read at least one word from each group. These words should be used as the guide words. They should be placed at the top of the

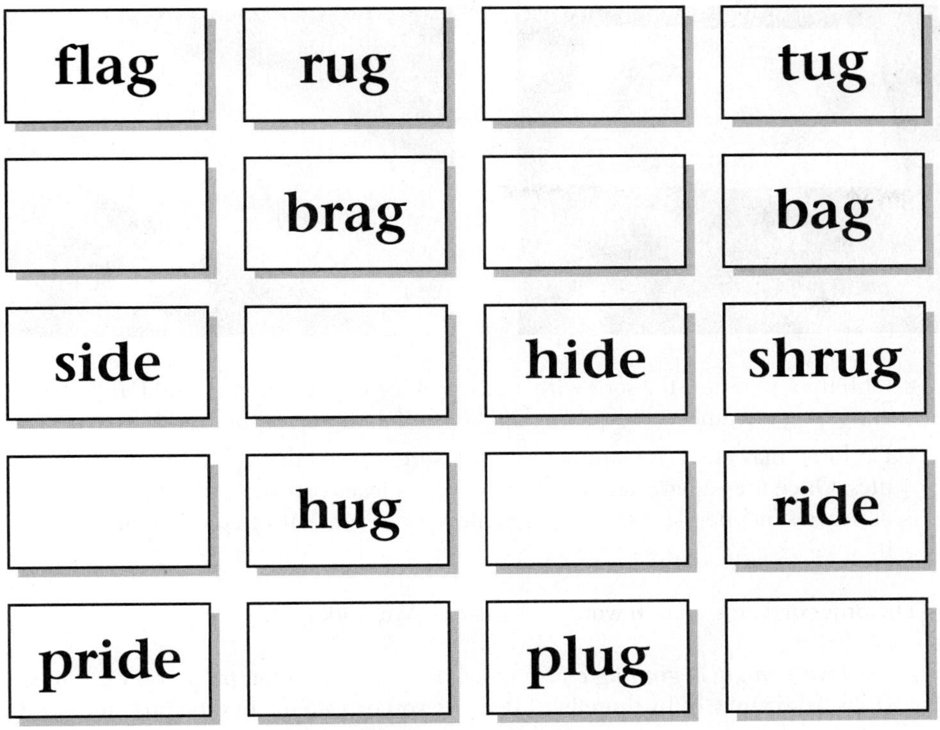

Figure 5.1
The Memory Game

flag	rug		tug
	brag		bag
side		hide	shrug
	hug		ride
pride		plug	

column, and during the word sorting game, the other words should be placed one at a time underneath them.

- Leave the other cards face up and scrambled.
- Have children take turns choosing a card from the scrambled pile, placing it in the column beneath the guide word, and reading down the column of words.

A memory game can now be used to give children more practice with the patterns. Once the students have sorted the words into their respective columns, they can put the cards face down on the table in front of them, arranged in rows (see Figure 5.1). Taking turns, one student turns over two cards. If they match (that is, if they share the same phonogram pattern), that student gets to keep those cards. They continue playing in turns until all of the cards are paired with other cards and taken off the table.

Further practice with the patterns can be provided with board games. Groups of cards arranged into patterns make good board games. In the "Race Track" game, a board with fifteen to twenty blank spaces is drawn up. Sets of word cards that share spelling patterns are shuffled and dealt to two to four players. One player rolls one die and moves her marker piece (similar to marker pieces in a Monopoly game) the number of spaces showing on the die. If she is the first to land on a space, she may put down one card on the space. The next player who lands on that same space must put down a word with the same spelling pattern or forfeit a turn. The game continues until all cards are exhausted. Note: It can add a welcome element of chance if you add some wild cards to the stack: "give two cards to the person to your right," etc. (see Figure 5.2).

After children become accurate with word sorts, they can extend their expertise by seeing how quickly they can sort, using speed sorts. This activity supports fluency and healthy competition in a game-like task. (Sixth to eighth graders really like them.) Like so many developmentally appropriate activities, speed sorts build intrinsic motivation and provide that all-important sense of satisfaction!

A speed sort is done as follows:

- Use a timer of some type. Egg timers really help and are quiet!
- Children sort as fast and as accurately as they can.

Figure 5.2
Board Game for Word
Sorts

 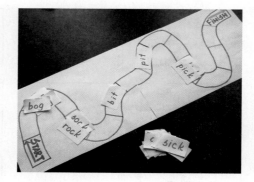

- Children self-assess the sorts with a rubric alone or with another child. If they encounter any uncertainty, they skip the word and later get help with it.
- Children may chart the number of words sorted correctly in a set number of minutes. Once the activity has been taught well, a teacher-made charting sheet aids children's independent charting. Learners thrive on healthy competition with themselves.

The order of words used in word sorts matters. We work in this order:

- ***Start with single beginning consonants.*** For demonstration purposes, we can begin with **m** and **s**. Why those two? Because you can stretch out the pronunciation of the sounds (try stretching out the sound of *t*, if you don't believe us!), and also the two sounds are nicely contrasted. Then you can add **l** and **n** because those, too, can be stretched out. Later, you can add **b, d, f, h, p,** and **t**. Those letters usually represent a single sound each. Choose the most different letters to introduce together. Avoid grouping **b** and **d** because they look similar; and also avoid **d** and **t** because they sound similar. Beginning consonants are introduced with picture sorts, and later you can substitute letters on cards for the pictures.
- ***Then introduce short vowel phonogram patterns.*** Use words with these short vowel patterns:
  -an, -ad, -ap, -at
  -ed, -et
  -it, -ip, -id
  -ot, -ob, -op
  -up, -ub
  -ill, -ell
  -ack, -eck, -ick, -ock
  -ank, -ink, -ump
- ***Now make groups of words with the same short vowel, in different spelling patterns:***
  For example, *cap, bad, sack, stab,* and *sank* as a group contrasted with *jump, pup, cut, stub, rut,* and *duck.*
- ***Introduce r-controlled vowels:***
  -ar, ur, -ir, -or
- ***Introduce words with -all.***
- ***Introduce consonant blends at the beginning of words:***
  dr-, tr-, cl-, pl-, st-
- ***Introduce long vowel patterns:***
  -ate, -ake, -ail, -ame, -ain, -ay
  -eat, -eal
  -ice, -ide
  -ool
- ***Introduce patterns with -ook and -ull; and wa-.***

- *Then two-syllable words*, such as *mother, table, kitten,* and *happy.*
- *Then compound words*, such as *into, cowboy, steamboat,* and *football.*
- *Then words with inflectional endings*, such as *-er, -est, -ing,* and *-ed.*

WORD HUNTS Word hunts help children make connections between spelling the words and reading them. This is important because some children do not automatically apply what they learn in word study activities when they are trying to read words in texts. Word hunts also incorporate children's literature, poetry, or other whole texts. The Teach It! box shows a sample lesson that uses a word hunt based on a poem.

WORD WHEELS On a piece of thick paper or tag board, write a phonogram pattern like *-an, -it,* or *-ock.* Leave space to the left of the pattern. Then cut out a round piece of the same material, and write consonant letters such as *f, s, h,* and *p* (for *-it*) facing outward around the edges of the circle. Attach the circle to the slip of paper with the phonogram pattern using a brad, as shown in Figure 5.3. Children can rotate the circle until a beginning consonant lines up with the phonogram pattern, and then pronounce the resulting word.

FLIP CARDS Instead of a circle with consonants as in the word wheels, cut out a set of short cards (1 inch × 1 inch), write consonant letters on them, and staple them to a longer card (1 inch × 3 inches) with a phonogram pattern written on it, as shown in Figure 5.4. Children can fold back the short cards to pair up different beginning consonants with the phonogram pattern and then read the resulting word.

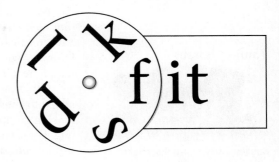

Figure 5.3
A Word Wheel

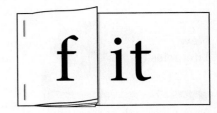

Figure 5.4
Flip Cards

Teach It!

Refer to the Teach It! appendix at the end of the book for further activities you can use to reinforce concepts discussed in this chapter.

Word Hunts

In the fifth week of school, student teacher Breanna demonstrates a word hunt for her children. She works with eight to ten children at a time. Breanna reads the poem "Books, Books" by Ritsa Tassopoulos (Personal communication, April 10, 2002) to the children from a large chart and then says, "Now, let's read it together."

Books, Books
Books, books fun to read
Books, books just what I need
Books, books fill my head
Books, books in my bed
Books, books morning noon and night
Books, books make me feel just right. *

The children follow along well. After reading, the children reread together in partner groups. Breanna says, "What do you notice about some of these words?"

Children talk. They share their observations and volunteer to read rhyming words (times and rhymes).

Breanna says, "Now I'm going on a word hunt. I want to find two words that don't rhyme."

Thinking out loud about rhyming and non-rhyming words and how they sound and look, she lists two words—*head* and *need*—in separate columns. Breanna organizes the group into pairs and asks them to work together. She says, "Copy these two words onto your papers and make them look like this (pointing to the columns). Find rhyming words to match the top word in each column. The words can be new ones you think of, words from our word walls, and words in this poem. Get ready to talk about what you've found. This is just practice. No one has to get everything right; it's just practice. Don't worry, we'll have fun talking about what makes words rhyme."

*Ritsa Tassopoulos. Used with permission.

Word Sorting with Two-Syllable Words

Learners in grades 2 through 4 must learn what happens when syllables meet. This is more of a challenge for spelling than for reading, but readers must be aware of the problems raised by the vowel marking systems of English. For example, the spelling pattern of *bat* is fairly easy to learn. But when *bat* adds the grammatical ending *-ed* or *-ing*, the consonant must be doubled. If it were not doubled, the E or the I would have the effect of marking the vowel in *bat* long, giving it the pronunciation *baited* or *baiting*. Conversely, the final two consonants in *sing* are enough to insulate the vowel from the lengthening effect of *-ing*, so nothing needs be added to its final consonants. And here is an oddity: Because the *x* in *ax* is made up of two sounds, it insulates the vowel from the lengthening effect of any following vowel, so we write *axes* and *axing*. But words that contain a long vowel already do not need to double the final consonant: *dream, dreaming; cool, cooled*.

Children can be taught when and when not to double consonants if endings are added to single-syllable words. To teach children to sort for two-syllable words, begin by making groups of words that double the final consonants before adding the ending *-er* or *-ing*. For example, the guide words might be *batted* and *dreaming*. The "scrabbled" words can be *call, steal, sit, start, run,* and *cut*. Children place each word under a guide word depending on whether the word doubles the final consonant when the ending is added.

Family Literacy

Suggest a lesson plan that might encourage support from families.

FAMILY AND COMMUNITY   Home support by families or caregivers can be built from nearly any lesson that is taught at school. For example, easy word sorts can go home for five- to seven-minute practice sessions; word sort games can be especially fun when played with a loved one. Simple turn-taking and charting progress or keeping score (with little ones winning!) create a game. With take-home sorts, include for the adults one page of simple and limited suggestions for conversations about words. Ask for a "read around the house" adventure. Adults help children read any and every word they find in the kitchen, bathroom, or elsewhere. Groups of parents, caregivers, and children who play together or attend community functions will benefit from getting together to support their children in literacy play. Some thoughtful adult structure and guidance can help regular play groups move into literacy games and activities.

New Literacies

Do an online search for a good word recognition program.

NEW LITERACIES   For home and school technology materials, look into word recognition software programs. A good program that is very popular with young children is *Wiggle Works* from Scholastic Publishing and the Center for Applied Special Technology. *Wiggle Works* focuses on emergent, early, and fluent language development using reading, writing, speaking, and listening. It contains a variety of creative activities that entertain while also building skills. Additional programs can be found online at Superkids.com <www .superkids.com>, where teachers and parents can check out various programs and read reviews of their efficacy. For an up-close look at how two second-grade teachers have used technology in their classrooms, visit <http://buckman.pps.k12.or.us/room100/room100.html>.

Word knowledge instruction with older students focuses more on structural analysis and understanding word derivations.

Teaching the "Meaningful Word Parts" or Morphological Reader (Grades 3 and 4)

Children in the "meaningful word parts" or morphological phase of word reading are coping with compound words, grammatical endings, and prefixes and suffixes. There are places for explicit teaching—explanations of how words work—extended exploration of words, and also copious reading for students to learn what they need at this phase.

STRUCTURAL ANALYSIS   Structural analysis is the activity of examining the parts of a word to help arrive at the meaning of the whole word. This procedure works when (1) the word is a compound word, or is made up of root words and prefixes and suffixes, and (2) the students understand the meanings of those affixes.

As we pointed out in Chapter 3, English words are built from other words. *Compound words* are built three different ways. Knowing whether to write two words together, like *motorboat*, to join them with a hyphen, like *mother-in-law*, or to write them separately, like *fire truck*, is a challenge for spelling rather than for reading. But readers can find long words like *grandmother* or *grasshopper* to be daunting, so teachers often give the advice, "Find a little word that you know inside that big word," and we hold our thumb over part of the word to focus their attention on the other part of the word.

Make 3 × 5-inch cards with these words on them: *foot, ball, basket, ball, rain, coat, lawn, mower, mother, in, law, ninety, six, ice, cream, desk, top, all,* and *right*. Also, make five hyphens ("–") on cards. Place these in the bottom rows of a pocket chart. Have the students help you assemble words to make compound words. Which ones are joined together without spaces? Which ones are joined with hyphens? Which ones are written separately? For more movement in the classroom, write the words and the hyphens on tablets. Pronounce the words aloud and have teams decide if the students holding the words should stand shoulder to shoulder, have a hyphen between them, or stand apart.

To work with *prefixes and suffixes*, make 3 × 5-inch cards with these prefixes and suffixes on them: *dis-, inter-, re-, un-, under-, -able, -al, -ant*. Place these on the bottom row of a pocket chart. Make another set of cards with these root words: *trust, do, act, depend, believe, stand, nation,* and *consider*. Place these word cards on the next-to-bottom row. Then have the students help you combine root words, prefixes, and suffixes into words that you place on the upper rows of the pocket chart. (As an alternative, you can write the prefixes, suffixes, and root words on small pieces of acetate and have the students build words on the overhead projector.) For follow-up, make a word wall of words with prefixes and another word wall of words with suffixes.

WORD JOURNALS   A useful way to have students record and recall words from word-sorting and word-building exercises is to have them keep a word journal. A word journal is a medium-size spiral notebook, with sections labeled according to the groupings of words it contains. These groupings might contain all the categories into which words have been sorted during word-sorting activities. To record compound words, have the students divide a page with two vertical lines to make three columns. In the left-hand column, they can write compound words that have the parts written together; in the central column, words joined with hyphens; and in the right-hand column, words written separately. For words with prefixes and suffixes, students set aside half a page each for words with *un-, re-, inter-,* and *dis-, -ant, -ful,* and *-able*. They add words to those pages from time to time as they come across them from their reading. The teacher reminds the class to share aloud some of their new entries. These also can be added to the word wall.

Teaching the Reader of "Word Histories and Families" or the Derivational Reader (Grade 4 and Up)

At the phase of derivational reading, the challenges of reading words have to do with:

CCSS
• Language Standard 4: Vocabulary

- Understanding how words are built from historical spare parts from languages that are no longer spoken
- Thinking of relationships between words that have common ancestors
- Reading words whose spellings honor their histories rather than their present-day pronunciation

We use the term *derivational* for this phase because the most common challenge is reading words derived from other words.

Connect Two

WORKING WITH WORDS WITH PARTS FROM ANCIENT SOURCES   Most of the words in the English language are made up of ancient parts from Latin and Greek, for example, *fortunate, masculine, ignition, sensitive, symphony,* and *microscope*. As you can see from the examples, those words are considered more mature vocabulary items, so children don't read very many of them before fourth grade, unless they are precocious readers. From that point on, however, readers encounter more and more of them, and it is very useful for students to recognize their parts, know their range of meanings, and be able to figure out at least roughly how the words should be pronounced as well as what they mean.

STRUCTURAL ANALYSIS WITH LATIN AND GREEK PARTS   Make 3 × 5-inch index cards of the Latin and Greek prefixes in Table 5.1. Display them in a pocket chart for the students. Explain that they came from two languages, Latin and Ancient Greek, that are no longer spoken, but that contribute to most of the words in the English dictionary. Then discuss their meanings.

Then make 3 × 5-inch index cards of the word roots in Table 5.2. Display them in a pocket chart for the students, and discuss their meanings, too.

Have the students help you join prefixes and stems to make words. Discuss what you think the words mean. Then check the meanings in a dictionary to be sure. (Note: Some possible words are *collect, college, elect, object, dejected, eject, reject, conjecture, abrupt, erupt, disrupt, corrupt, revolve, evolve, devolve, contain, detain, retain, attain, contort, distort, retort, torture*.)

Make smaller sets of word cards and have pairs build words with them. Make a word wall on which to display sets of these words. Have students record them in their word journals.

WORD REPORTS   Assign students to teams that will research words that share common roots. Give each team a historical root word, such as *grad-, -meter, bio-, -graph, -tele-,* or *miss-*. Have them look through dictionaries and find all of the words that contain their word root. They may prepare a chart of their findings and present their work to the class.

FAMILY AND COMMUNITY   As we stated earlier, the importance of family or caregiver involvement in children's word learning does not decrease with the child's age. An easy and interesting mall walk creates a discovery game for older students. It involves giving the child a list of Greek root words: *aero* (means "air"), *bio* (means "life"), *geo* (means "earth"), *log, logy,* or *logue* (means "word" or the study of something), *meter* (means "measuring"), *phone* (means "sound"), *therm* (means "heat"), *photo* (means "light"), *hydro* (means "water"),

Table 5.1	Prefixes, Suffixes, and Root Words of Latin Origin
PREFIX OR SUFFIX	**MEANING**
con-, com-, col-, cor-	together
ab-	from, away from, by
ad-, al-, ac-, at-	to, toward
de-	down from, off
dis-	lack of, not
e-	out, out of
re-	back, or again
-ure	state of
pre-	before

Table 5.2	Roots of Latin Origin
ROOT	**MEANING**
-lect, -lege	choose
-ject, -jac	throw
-rupt	break
-tort-	twist
grad-	step
-volt, -volve	turn, roll
-tain	have, hold
-dict	say or tell
-mit or -miss	send

and so on. The child and adult(s) identify words in the mall signs that have a Greek root and do a structural analysis of the word. For example, a father spots "log" in a word on a store sign, the child reads "logo," and the father and child read the sign: "T-Shirt Logos in One Hour." Many word games are created once adults and older children begin to play them. For example, consider the derived, polysyllabic, and plural words seen on driving trips. Work in the community might well be part of the literacy activities of the middle and upper elementary student. Volunteer work provides many opportunities for literacy and its authentic use.

A teacher models the use of context clues in this video. How does she teach her student to use context clues to determine the meaning of unknown science vocabulary words?

Helping Students Read Words in Context

When teaching children to learn and recognize words, it is very important to help them connect the words they've studied with similar words they come across in reading various texts. You can help children of all ages become more keenly aware of this in many ways.

Effective teachers know that demonstration and modeling provide a good beginning.

In conducting such demonstrations, you model your thinking out loud to show the children that this is the kind of thinking they should also do. Imagine yourself reading a text on a large chart or in a big book in view of the children. The conversation goes something like this.

Teacher: Humm. . . . I'm not sure about this word (silently draw your finger under the word *motorcar*), but it looks like one I know because we did a word sort with *motorboat* in it. And this story is about driving to the store. What do you think, children?

A few children respond that they see *c-a-r* and almost immediately some respond in unison saying, "car!"

Teacher: Nice observation! I like the way you watch carefully and connect words you know with new words. And you are thinking about what is going on in the story. Good thinking, you used the context!

Once children have been taught through teacher modeling, remind and support them by teacher talk to connect known words to unknown words using everything they already know to learn more and more words. Watch carefully and seize opportunities to affirm children's accomplishments in acquiring word knowledge in their reading.

Word learning strategies discussed in this chapter such as word hunts can also be adapted and expanded. Rather than hunting for the same studied words in books, children hunt for words that are similar to those in a list of known words given to them by their teacher or that they write on their own.

Also, as noted earlier in this chapter, word walls built from social studies, science, or literature units provide words that are similar to studied words. Call children's attention to comparing and contrasting such words to their studied word walls and invite them to find similarities.

A powerful teaching tool for any instruction is your classroom talk and use of language (Johnston, 2004). Often, rather than directly telling students something, asking them questions provides strong motivation. Consider a seventh-grade teacher observing a student puzzling over the word *periscope* in a book about submarines. Because in this class they study Greek and Latin roots, the teacher initiates the following conversation.

Teacher: Is there a word you know that looks like this one?

Student: It looks a little like *telescope*.

Teacher: Yes. We've had that one. Do you know any other words that are similar to this one (pointing to periscope)?

Student: Well, we also had *microscope* in science the other day.

Teacher: Hmm. . . . what's this book about?

Student: Submarines. Is it periscope?

Teacher: How did you know?

Student: I remembered the scope part. And the "up periscope" I saw in a movie.

Teacher: Great thinking!

Here you saw the teacher guide the student to use multiple cues to get the unknown word. As so often is the case, use of multiple cues supports children's literate thinking. Importantly, this teacher's talk attributed competence to the student. This is a wonderful way of building independence and students' awareness that they are in charge of their word learning.

For English Language Learners

The Challenges of English Phonics

English phonics presents special problems to English language learners. Several key differences are listed below.

- In most languages that use alphabets, vowels have one sound only. Different vowel sounds are represented by different letters. Having long and short vowel sounds represented by the same letter, as in English, is contrary to the expectations of speakers of most other languages. Be sure to explain that in English, vowel letters can stand for different sounds, but that there are clues to indicate which sound a letter makes in different environments.

- Speakers of other languages may be puzzled by our labels "long" and "short" for vowels. Actually, the vowels the labels refer to are not long and short at all but *tense* and *lax*, as linguists call them. Some languages really do have long and short vowels: the same vowel sound can be made for a longer time or for a briefer time. Long vowels (long in duration, that is) are often spelled with two vowels in languages that have them, like Saab in Swedish. These matters may cause confusion for speakers of other languages.

- Speaking of tense and lax vowels, the English language often signals differences between many vowel sounds with the tensing and laxing of the tongue when the sounds are made, such as in *bet* and *bait*. Other languages, particularly Spanish, do not make that distinction. Spanish speakers may thus find the vowel sound in *bait* difficult to distinguish from the vowel sound in *bet*. English also makes a distinction between consonant sounds that are voiced and unvoiced—that is, the vocal cords vibrate the whole time the first consonant in *bat* is made, but the vibration is delayed a bit when the first consonant in *pat* is made. Chinese speakers do not make this distinction, and may have difficulty telling these sounds apart.

- All languages have their own sets of allowable and not allowable sound combinations. Causing difficulty for English speakers are Kiswahili words that allow [ny] and [ng] at the beginning of a word, as in *nyama ya ngombe* ("meat of a cow," or "beef") and words in the Mende language of West Africa that begin with [gb], as in *gbarbartee*, ("turmoil"). In English we find all of the above sound combinations, but only in the middle of a word where two syllables come together, as in *Tanya* and *longbow*, and *tugboat*. In the Spanish language, the consonant combinations [st], [sk], and [sp] cannot begin words, which is why Spanish speakers tend to say "es-school" and "es-sports." Speakers of Spanish will have trouble pronouncing many word-initial consonant blends.

- Students who attended school before coming to the United States may have studied English, but with strikingly different pronunciation from what is spoken here. In East Africa, for instance, what sounds like "way" can be the English word *way*, *were*, or *where*. Be sure to call attention to the American pronunciation of such words.

For Review

Throughout the elementary grades, children need systematic, frequent, and flexible opportunities to learn words. They must have word knowledge instruction that is grounded in reading as a sense-making and meaningful activity. Many word-learning activities may be used successfully from grades 1 to 8 in exclusive practice time periods of about ten to fifteen minutes. About thirty minutes of word work in context and in exclusive teaching and practice usually works for most children. Use a whole-part-whole approach in highly contextualized word instruction, especially in exclusive word study. That is, always return to word, sentence, and whole text meaning. It

is recommended that you teach children the relationships between letters and sounds, beginning with individual letters and individual sounds and soon moving to groups of letters that spell parts of syllables, that is, onsets and rimes.

This chapter focused on word knowledge, what it contributes to the reading process, and why it is important. It highlighted phonics and how to handle teaching word recognition, how much phonics to teach and for how long, and how to conduct word and phonics assessments. Ongoing assessment, an inseparable part of instruction, was emphasized. English language learners and struggling readers were given specific attention.

For Your Journal

Imagine a grade level you want to teach or are teaching. Make a list of what you need to know about teaching

words. Jot down any related concerns or frustrations you have at this point or anticipate having later.

Taking It to the World

The debate about whole-word versus phonics instruction as ways of teaching children to read has never been as simple as people often make it sound. Virtually all teachers read to children, invite children to write, and give them opportunities to explore meaningful print; and virtually all teachers point out letter-to-sound relationships to children. But there are differences in the emphasis that teachers put on these activities.

Either alone or with a partner, interview two or three first-grade and two or three second-grade teachers about their approaches to teaching reading. What things do the teachers at the same grade level have in common? What aspects of teaching are approached differently?

Ask them also to what extent their reading approaches are left up to their own decisions and to what extent their approaches are guided by reading coaches at the school level or district level.

New Literacies Connections

1. Visit Freereading.net for free lesson plans for teaching word study: <www.freereading.net/index.php?title=Word-Form_Recognition_Activities>.

2. Read Ron Cramer's suggestions for using the Language Experience Approach here: <www.literacyconnections.com/Cramer.html>.

MyEducationLab™

Go to Topic 2 (Phonemic Awareness/Phonics) in the MyEducationLab <www.myeducationlab.com> for your course, where you can:

- Find learning outcomes for Phonemic Awareness/ Phonics along with the national standards that connect to these outcomes.

- Complete Assignments and Activities that can help you more deeply understand the chapter content.
- Apply and practice your understanding of the core teaching skills identified in the chapter with the Building Teaching Skills and Dispositions learning units.

Helping Readers Build Fluency and Vocabulary

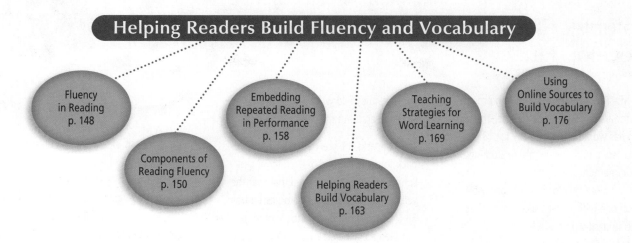

Helping Readers Build Fluency and Vocabulary

- Fluency in Reading p. 148
- Components of Reading Fluency p. 150
- Embedding Repeated Reading in Performance p. 158
- Helping Readers Build Vocabulary p. 163
- Teaching Strategies for Word Learning p. 169
- Using Online Sources to Build Vocabulary p. 176

Anticipation Guide

The following questions will help you begin thinking about the topics covered in this chapter. Answer *true* or *false* in response to each statement. As you read and learn more about the topics in these statements, double-check your answers. See what interests you and what prompts your curiosity toward more understanding.

_____ **1.** Fluency and vocabulary are both considered key areas of reading ability by the U.S. government.

_____ **2.** Reading fluently consists entirely of reading quickly.

_____ **3.** Children who read fluently tend to understand what they read.

_____ **4.** Teachers should never model fluent reading for children, for fear of discouraging them.

_____ **5.** An average reading rate for a third grader is about 30 words per minute.

_____ **6.** Vocabulary is knowledge of words and word meanings.

_____ **7.** All children enter school with very nearly the same number of words in their vocabularies.

_____ **8.** Having a word for something in your vocabulary makes it more likely that you will notice it.

_____ **9.** Vocabulary knowledge is one of the best predictors of reading comprehension.

_____ **10.** Research suggests that while it helps to teach vocabulary, we don't need to teach all of the words children need to know.

A Classroom Story

Volunteer Tutors Help Children Develop Fluency

Katie Flowers directs a tutoring project for a small liberal arts college. The program has worked continuously for 13 years, and is very popular with college students. Nearly one hundred of them volunteer each term to go out to a local school and work one on one with a first-, second-, or third-grade student who has been recommended by a teacher for extra help.

At the beginning of each semester, the students are given a couple of hours of training. Then they go out to a local school two times each week, both before and after school. Each time the students go out, they follow a lesson plan with five parts. The lesson plan was borrowed from Darrell Morris's *Howard Street Tutoring Manual* (2005)*:

1. Read an easy book to develop fluency.
2. Read a harder book to help the children learn new words.
3. Do a word study task—phonics or vocabulary.

4. Have the child write something.
5. Read aloud to the child.

Katie asks the teachers to fill out feedback forms at the end of each term. Last spring, one teacher reported that over the year a third-grade student progressed from 58 to 153 words per minute. Another teacher reported a big increase in a child's Lexile score on a commercial reading test. These and other comments from teachers attest to the success of the students' tutoring, but they also reveal something else. The teachers' comments nearly all emphasize the aspects of reading that are stressed under the federal No Child Left Behind legislation: phonemic awareness, phonics, word recognition, fluency, vocabulary, and comprehension. Over the past twenty years, these aspects of reading have always been stressed in the tutoring program, just as all of them have been emphasized in Morris's Howard Street model. But Katie realizes she should adjust

the emphasis of the tutoring on some of these aspects, at least to make sure the tutoring "stays on the same page" with where the teachers are now placing their emphases.

Two areas that call for more attention are fluency and vocabulary. Katie sets about making sure her first training session this fall will show her student-tutors how to do repeated reading, readers' theater, and choral reading. She thinks to herself that the tutors and their young charges will need to work in groups some of the time in order to do these fluency activities—and that will bring some welcome variety to the tutoring sessions. She also plans to show the tutors how to lead Word Conversations, and also how to use semantic maps, semantic feature analysis, and some other vocabulary building activities.

*Darrell Morris' lesson plan. *Howard Street Tutoring Manual*, 2nd ed. (2006). Used by permission.

 The teacher in this video discusses the importance of reading fluency and shares strategies to foster children's fluency. What strategies have you learned to support reading fluency?

Both reading fluency and vocabulary are important areas of children's reading ability. As we will demonstrate in this chapter, if children are to read well, they must read fluently—with appropriate rate, automatic word recognition, and meaningful phrasing. Reading fluency can be taught, and it should be. Vocabulary, which can be thought of as a growing storehouse of tokens of meaning, is also critically important for students of all ages to develop. Students must learn tens of thousands of words during their school years, and most of them will be learned through reading. There is much that teachers can do to help students learn words and their meanings.

Part I: Fluency in Reading

CCSS

• Foundational Skills 4: Fluency

"Dance like nobody's watching, . . . sing like nobody's listening." That advice from Mark Twain is true whether we are dancing, singing, swinging at a baseball, or reading. Conscious attention to the act itself takes concentration away from the purpose of the activity, and it makes our performance stiff, self-conscious, and unsuccessful. With regard to reading, it has been demonstrated that those who are lacking in reading fluency have diminished comprehension—the more they're thinking about pronouncing the words, the less they're thinking about the meaning (Foorman & Mehta, 2002; Perfetti, 1985; Samuels & Farstrup, 2006).

Thus reading fluency has two parts to it: effortless efficiency at word recognition and the ability to render the text expressively so that it sounds like it makes sense. Here is the National Reading Panel's (2000) definition of reading fluency:

Fluency is the ability to read a text accurately and quickly. When fluent readers read silently, they recognize words automatically. They group words quickly in ways that help them gain meaning from what they read. Fluent readers read aloud effortlessly and with expression. Their reading sounds natural, as if they are speaking. (p. 22)

Fluency is not just word recognition. Children can score well on word recognition tests without being able to read smoothly, accurately, and with expression in connected text. Fluency is not just comprehension. Children can demonstrate comprehension skills without performing the rapid acts of understanding that characterize fluency—although we do know that unless children read fluently, their comprehension is likely to be impaired (Pinnell et al., 1995).

Between the component skills of word recognition, vocabulary, and comprehension skills on the one hand, and the ultimate goal of successful reading on the other, reading fluency stands in the middle—serving as the driving force that orchestrates those skills and puts them to work in reading text, so that with experience over time, learners will acquire the large vocabularies, the versatility with sentence and text structures, and the background knowledge they need to become successful readers. Jay Samuels and Alan Farstrup (2006) compare learning to read fluently with learning to drive a car. Fluent reading, like fluent driving, requires the orchestration of many tasks at once. A beginning driver can only focus on one task at a time, but a fluent driver can change lanes, obey signals, watch for traffic, and choose which route to take, all while carrying on a conversation or listening to a talk show on the radio.

Drivers learn to drive with some training and a great deal of practice. Readers need practice, too. But most young readers don't get enough of that practice. One careful study of fifth graders' reading showed just how scant that practice can be (see Table 6.1).

Table 6.1	Differences in Amounts of Independent Reading by Fifth Graders	
PERCENTILE RANK	**MINUTES OF BOOK READING PER DAY**	**WORDS READ IN BOOKS PER YEAR**
98	65.0	4,358,000
90	21.1	1,823,000
80	14.2	1,146,000
70	9.6	622,000
60	6.5	432,000
50	4.6	282,000
40	3.2	200,000
30	1.3	106,000
20	0.7	21,000
10	0.1	8,000
2	0.0	0

Source: R. C. Anderson, P. T. Wilson, and L. G. Fielding, in *Reading Research Quarterly, 23*, 285–303 (1988). Reproduced with permission of Wiley Inc.

According to this study, the average fifth grader reads less than five minutes a day. That prompted one of the researchers to observe, "If you walk into a typical elementary school today, you would have to say that you were among non-readers" (Wilson, 1992). The good news is that 14 minutes of reading per day amounts to a million words read in a year, so efforts to increase children's time spent reading need not change children's lives dramatically to have some results. But such efforts will not soon close the gap between good readers and poor readers. In one year, the top six readers read as much as the bottom six readers would read in 54 years, and the top three readers read as much as the bottom three readers would read in two centuries.

On the positive side, we know that some of children's favorite moments in reading instruction come as they listen to the teacher reading aloud to them fluently and with animated expression, and also when they themselves perform fluent reading aloud brilliantly in front of their classmates (Ivey & Broaddus, 2002). As a second grader who participated in a study of oral reading exclaimed to Martinez, Roser, and Strecker (1999), "I never thought I could be a star, but I was the best reader today."

Fluent reading was itself elevated to star status among the five main emphases in "scientifically-based reading instruction," the approaches that are sanctioned under the federal *No Child Left Behind* Act in 2003. That means that reading programs that hope to receive government funding need to show that reading fluency is a priority. It also means that reading experts consider an emphasis on reading fluency to be a best practice in reading instruction.

Under the Common Core Standards, reading fluency is included in the Foundational Skills for Reading, where the fourth standard in each of grades kindergarten through 5 is the expectation that students will "Read with sufficient accuracy and fluency to support comprehension" <http://www.corestandards.org>.

CCSS

• Foundational Skills 4: Fluency

Components of Reading Fluency

Fluent reading consists of four integrated features, according to Rasinski (2003). One is *accurate word recognition*. A fluent reader does not stumble over words, but recognizes most of them automatically. A second feature of fluent reading is a *reasonable rate of reading*. This does not necessarily mean that faster is better, though, because there are two more features of fluent reading that keep a reader from reading too hastily. The third feature is *meaningful grouping of words*. A fluent reader would read the sentence, "The girl, bursting with pride, stepped forward to take the prize" with pauses where the commas are—otherwise, the meaning of the sentence would change. The last feature is *expressive reading*—putting correct emphasis and emotion into the reading, so that it "sounds like talk," as many teachers say.

Rasinski, Reutzel, Chard, and Linan-Thompson (2011) recommend that teaching reading fluency include these six emphases:

1. *Model fluent reading.* Teachers should demonstrate both fluent and disfluent reading and discuss the differences, so that children will know what sort of performance they are aiming for.

2. *Provide explicit instruction.* Teachers should demonstrate, discuss, and provide practice in each of the four features of fluent reading described just above.

3. *Offer opportunities to read.* As we saw above in Table 6.1, children vary tremendously in the amount of reading they do. A goal of teaching should be to give children plentiful opportunities to read, both within and outside of the classroom.

4. *Supply appropriate texts.* Appropriate texts will be accessible to young readers—materials that they can read with and without help, depending on the task. They should include a range of genres, with a balance between fiction and

informational books. And they should include series books, or at least books by the same author.

5. *Guide students' reading.* Teachers should help students choose books and set goals for their reading. At regular intervals they should engage them in conversations about what they are reading. They should praise students for the aspects of fluency they are practicing, and offer them guidance on the practices they need to learn.

6. *Monitor students' reading.* Whether students are reading silently or orally in class, teachers should monitor them to make sure they are staying on task. Monitoring reading means making sure not only that children are participating in reading tasks, but also that those tasks require sustained, meaningful reading of texts.

Modeling Fluent Oral Reading

As a five-year-old, one of the author's daughters loved to pretend-read books. Once she picked up Bill Martin's *Brown Bear, Brown Bear, What Do You See?*" and read, "Wuh, wuh, wuh once . . . thuh, thuh, thuh, there . . . wuh, wuh, wuh, was . . . a buu, buh, buh, bear . . ."

"Annabrooke," I said. "What in the world are you doing?"

She beamed and said proudly, "I'm reading like a first grader!"

The anecdote should make us pause to ask, do our students know what fluent reading sounds like? Many students may not, if most of the reading they hear around them is the word-by-word struggles of other neophyte readers.

Teachers should be careful to provide models of fluent reading for their students. We mean this in two senses. First, teachers should actually demonstrate the concept of fluent versus disfluent reading. Second, teachers should frequently read aloud to students and entice them with examples of rich language read well. (Please see the Teach It! Box for suggestions.)

Teach It!

Refer to the Teach It! appendix at the end of the book for further activities you can use to reinforce concepts discussed in this chapter.

Demonstrating Fluent Reading

To show students what fluent reading looks like and sounds like, begin by reading a passage to the students in two ways. First, read it haltingly and uncertainly, in a voice that suggests you are concerned with slashing your way through the words and getting a disagreeable experience over with. In other words, read disfluently. Then read the passage again, but this time with your voice full of expression and interest, with pauses and emphases. Show that you are enjoying the message of the text and not simply struggling to pronounce the words. That is to say, read fluently. Then ask the students which reading they preferred and why. In the discussion that follows, call attention to the qualities of fluent reading:

- The reader is thinking about the message and not just about pronouncing the words.

- The reader varies her voice between loud and soft, and between faster and slower.

- The reader groups words meaningfully.

- The reader may show emotion—enjoyment, surprise, and excitement— as she reads.

Later, read aloud to the students again, reading as fluently as you can and "thinking aloud" as you read. That is, pause to explain to the students a decision you just made—such as where to pause, what words to group together, or how to read a character's voice—in order to read fluently.

Read Aloud with Expression

When you read aloud to children, you are pointing out for them what is important and interesting in books. You convey enthusiasm and paint events with importance using your voice. Your voice is a marvelous instrument, capable of communicating joy, drama, humor, excitement, and importance. If you do not have very much experience reading to children, or even if you do, it is worth taking the time to become a charming and charismatic reader.

QUALITIES OF VOICE   Have you ever watched a golf coach demonstrate the proper way to drive a ball? The coach will slow down and exaggerate the swing to give the learner time to watch the grip of the hands, the planting of the feet, the rotation of the hips, and the swing of the arms. Reading aloud to children is like that: You slow down and exaggerate the swings of the voice from fast to slow to high to low; you add pauses to create suspense; you read the action as if you were seeing it and the dialogue as if you were hearing it. Listen to a recording of a professional actor reading a children's book. Note the way the actor gives life to characters, creates suspense, moves the story quickly along in spots, and slows it down for dramatic effect in other places. All of these are techniques that you can imitate, and they will add power to your reading aloud.

When you read aloud to students, you can point out what is important and interesting in books, and convey enthusiasm, joy, drama, humor, and excitement.

BRING CHARACTERS TO LIFE   When books have more than one character in them, it helps animate the reading if you read each character's lines in a different voice. Younger characters might get higher voices; older characters lower ones; and wiser characters slower, more thoughtful voices. As a rule of thumb, try to portray personality styles—clever, lazy, humorous, haughty—in the different voices, rather than the character's ethnicity or region of origin—since doing the latter may be offensive to some.

CHOOSE TEXTS FOR READING ALOUD   Your school librarian, or the local children's librarian, will have good recommendations for read-alouds. There are printed sources you can rely on for suggestions as well. The International Reading Association annually sponsors the Children's Choices Project, in which teachers across North America ask children to select the books they enjoy most from each year's new publications. *The Reading Teacher* publishes the results. The American Library Association's monthly journal *Bookbird* publishes reviews of books with curricular tie-ins. And the *Hungry Mind Review* publishes suggestions of books that are especially provocative and interesting for young people.

Read books from parallel cultures often. American children are truly fortunate to have books available that reflect the lives of all of our children, from nearly every cultural group and nation. As Rudine Simms Bishop (1999) reminds us, books from parallel cultures can serve as *windows and mirrors*: as *windows* into other cultures that are different from the readers' own, and as *mirrors* of the readers' own culture, to give those readers reflections of their own experience. The best books each year about African American children's experience compete for the Coretta Scott King Award. And the best books about Latino children's experience compete for the Américas Award.

Don't overlook informational books—especially books about science and social studies topics—when choosing books to read aloud. Children enjoy hearing about the real world, too. Informational books for young people are written with as much skill and artistry as fictional works, but listening to them and understanding them exercises different kinds of concentration and comprehension (Pearson & Duke, 2002). The National Science Teachers Association's journal *Science and Children* recommends good titles for children in their field. The National Council for the Social Studies' journal, *Social Studies and the Young Learner,* recommends good books for young readers as well as topics from the social sciences. Finally, articles from the excellent specialized journals on scientific, geographical, and historical topics, such as *Ranger Rick, National Geographic World,* and *Cobblestone,* can make excellent read-alouds as well. Remember, a key to a good read-aloud is that you, the teacher, have surveyed the text, planned how to read it orally, and determined where to put emphasis.

Teach It! 26

Fluency Oriented Oral Reading

ENGAGE THE STUDENTS AS YOU READ   When you read a text aloud to your students you should take steps to call attention to your fluent reading. Make sure to point out to students how you:

- Match the emotional qualities of the passages—serious, humorous, exciting, urgent—with your tone of voice.
- Stress the important words in the passages.
- Honor the punctuation—pausing at commas, stopping at periods, and raising your voice at the ends of sentences with question marks.
- Read the dialogues as if people were actually talking.

Your reading will be more successful if you take steps to engage the students as you read. These steps include previewing the text, pausing to raise suspense before important parts of the text, asking for predictions, inviting the students to read repeated parts of the text with you, and rereading the text to invite the students to read more of it with you.

EXTEND THE MEANING OF THE TEXT   After reading a text aloud to the students, you may further engage them with the meaning of the text during follow-up activities. These include dramatizing the students' favorite parts (see pages 201–202), posing reader response questions (see pages 185–186), having the students do a free-write, or having them do a "Sketch-to-stretch" activity (see page 200) or fill out a four-way response chart (see below).

FOUR-WAY RESPONSE CHART   To make a four-way response chart, the students each take a sheet of paper and divide it into four panels. In one panel they write an important quote (younger readers write just a few words) they remember from the text. In another panel they draw a picture of an important character or scene. In a third panel they write about or draw what the text reminded them of or made them think about. In the last panel they write what they liked about the text (adapted from Preece, 2000).

Supporting Children's Reading for Fluency

There are at least three general approaches to supporting children's reading for fluency:

- Sustained silent reading
- Directed activities, such as repeated reading
- Artistic means, such as readers' theater and choral reading with voice choirs

THE ROCKY ROAD OF SUSTAINED SILENT READING   In the 1960s the practice of Uninterrupted Sustained Silent Reading or USSR was introduced to boost the quantity of children's reading. Later (perhaps because of the collapse of the Soviet Union?) the practice was renamed Drop Everything and Read, but the idea was the same: to declare a period of about 20 minutes each day in which everyone in the building—teachers, principal, custodians included—would read for pleasure. There was to be no instruction, no testing, and for the most part little supervision of children's reading during these intervals.

In a report published in 2000, however, the National Reading Panel (2000) concluded that there was not enough reliable evidence that supported the benefits of sustained silent reading to justify a recommendation that the practice be used in schools. The Panel did not find evidence that the practice was *not* beneficial, either; but their finding persuaded many policy makers to discourage the use of sustained silent reading, at least during the school day. Independent reading was still assigned after school.

What was wrong with sustained silent reading? Some critics (e.g., Kuhn & Stahl, 2003) worried that many students would not stay on task during sustained silent reading time without monitoring by the teacher, and since the teacher was supposed to read, too, that monitoring would not be available. Others worried that, left to their own devices, students would choose material that was too easy to increase their fluency by much (Shanahan, 2002). As Reutzel et al. (2008, p. 38) put it, "[T]he traditional implementation of SSR (Sustained Silent Reading) has been criticized for the lack of teachers' teaching, monitoring, interacting with, and holding students accountable for their time spent reading."

Still, logic (and math) are on the side of sustained silent reading, if it can be done in such a way as to appease the criticisms just mentioned. Given the amount of time children spend reading outside of school (see Table 6.1 on page 149), just 15 minutes of sustained silent reading per day *triples* the average fifth grader's accomplishment. It amounts to *20 times* the reading done by the least avid five readers, and *150 times* that of the two or three least avid readers. That's a lot of bang for 15 minutes of instructional time.

In recent years the practice of sustained silent reading has been redesigned to include monitoring by the teacher and an emphasis on comprehension, and these new practices are showing beneficial results.

SCAFFOLDED SILENT READING (SCSR)   Reutzel et al. (2008) added several enhancements to Sustained Silent Reading in a method called *Scaffolded Silent Reading*. In daily lessons, teachers begin with a mini-lesson in which they demonstrate an aspect of fluent reading. First, the teacher models fluent reading, and then discusses the demonstration, making points about such features as expressive reading, self-correction when she misread a word, meaningful word grouping, or an appropriate reading rate. Then the students read for 15 minutes from a self-selected text on their particular independent reading level (a text at an *independent reading level* is one in which the student reads more than 95 percent of the words correctly). Although the readings are self-selected, students must read selections from each of a range of genres of literature: folktales, fables, adventure, science fiction, sports, mystery, biography, historical fiction, autobiography, poetry, and fantasy. Students also are assigned 15 minutes of out-of-school reading each day, which is certified by their parents. The teacher has a five-minute weekly conference with each student in which she monitors the student's fluency and comprehension, and has the student set goals for completing the book. In a study of third graders in four low-income schools, ScSR proved to be as effective in boosting fluency and comprehension as a method that featured repeated oral reading.

REPEATED READING   In this method, a child practices reading the same moderately challenging passage repeatedly up to four times until she or he can read it at a predetermined level of speed and accuracy. To carry out repeated reading, select passages of between 50 and 500 words, depending on the reading rates of the children. The passages should come from different sources, but they should be running text and not poetry or lists. Informational text should be mixed in with fiction. Find a text written at each student's *instructional level*—that is, the student should be able to read the text with 90 to 95 percent accuracy—making one error for each 10 or 15 words. It is important that the text be somewhat challenging, so the student has room to improve. But if the text seems a little too difficult for the student, offer support, such as *echo reading* (you read a line and the child reads a line).

Sit next to the student in a quiet place, and listen as the student practices reading the text repeatedly. Keep a copy of the text yourself on which you can mark the student's reading errors. Errors are words that are omitted, or for which other words are substituted, or that are mispronounced. If the student does not say a word, wait two seconds and say the word yourself, and count that as an error. Time the student's reading for exactly 60 seconds, then stop the student, count the total number of words read, and subtract the errors from the total. The child should practice reading the text several times—preferably until she reaches the criterion score for her grade level (see Table 6.2).

Table 6.2   Average Reading Rates

GRADE LEVEL	TARGET NUMBER OF CWPM
Second half of first grade	60 CWPM
Second grade	90 CWPM
Third grade	100 CWPM
Fourth grade	110 CWPM
Fifth grade	120 CWPM
Sixth grade or higher	140 CWPM

Source: Rasinski, 2003.

CWPM means "correct words per minute," that is, the total number of words read, minus the words read incorrectly.

Once the child has reached the criterion score, assign her another text of equivalent or greater difficulty to practice reading. From time to time, ask the child to read a passage she has not prepared, and measure the reading rate for an independent comparison.

Keep a record of the child's efforts on a log such as the one in Figure 6.1.

GUIDED REPEATED ORAL READING (GROR)   This type of small-group lesson is a step beyond repeated reading. The lesson begins with the teacher modeling fluent reading and then discussing what she or he did that made the reading fluent. Then the students are given a section of text written at their independent reading level and asked to read and reread it three to five times. The students may pair up and buddy read (each partner reads a sentence or a paragraph, and the other partner helps with difficult places). Using a fluency phone, made by parent volunteers from PVC pipe (see Figure 6.2), can motivate repeated reading. The student reads the text into the telephone, as if she or he were a new reporter calling in an important story.

The teacher monitors the students' reading and discusses the meaning of the passage with them afterwards.

Figure 6.1 A Chart for Recording Repeated Readings

Child's Name:				
Name of Passage	Dates Read	Date Ended	CWPM	Comparison Text Rate

Instructions: Record the name of a new text the student is working on, and enter the dates that he or she reads the text. In a separate row, you may enter the date of each day the student reads the same text, and enter the CWPM ("Correct Words Per Minute") attained that day. When the child reaches the criterion score, enter the date of that achievement. Occasionally (at least every two weeks) have the child read a text of similar difficulty that he or she has *not* prepared. Enter the name and date in the first two columns, and enter the fluency score (in CWPM) in the right-hand column.

Figure 6.2
A Fluency Phone

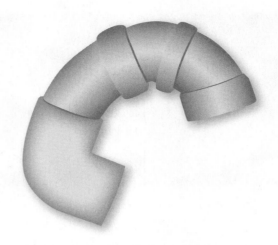

Teach It! 27

Paired Reading

Family Literacy

How can you demonstrate most attractively a strategy to promote reading fluency so that parents will want to do it with their children at home?

Practicing Fluency With and Without the Teacher's Guidance

The method of repeated reading requires that the teacher set aside the time to listen to individual students reading. Rasinski (2003) recommends setting aside time each day for repeated reading instruction. If that recommendation is followed, the teacher of a moderate-size class might reach each child for a few minutes each week. What should the students do when they are not with the teacher? Four suggestions are *paired reading, buddy reading, Radio Reading,* and *Fluency Oriented Reading Instruction* or FOOR.

PAIRED READING   In paired reading (Topping, 1987), a fluent reader is matched up with a less fluent reader. The "more fluent reader" in this method might be a parent volunteer, a tutor from the local university, or even an older student.

The two readers work together on a passage that is chosen at the less fluent reader's instructional reading level. The more fluent reader begins by reading the passage aloud to the less fluent reader. Next, the two read the passage through several times in unison. Then the less fluent reader takes over the reading, while the more fluent reader monitors the partner's reading. The more fluent reader corrects the other's errors by saying the word correctly, and by having the partner reread the sentence in which the misread word occurred. The fluent reader might say, "Read that sentence again and make it sound like you're talking to me."

Labbo and Teale (1990) suggest having a less fluent reader from an older class pair up with a younger reader who needs support and carry out the paired reading procedure. Research shows that the activity can be beneficial to both students.

BUDDY READING   Buddy reading is another way for students to practice reading for fluency without the teacher's devoting time to individual students. At its simplest, two students take turns reading paragraphs of the same text to each other. A more elaborated version begins with the teacher reading from a big book or a projected text while running his hand under the words and using a fluent delivery. Then pairs of students take turns reading passages from the text (Koskinen & Blum, 1986). How are the pairs formed? In one approach, the teacher divides the students into four groups of readers, from the most fluent (group 4) to the least fluent (group 1). Students from group 4 are paired with students from group 2, and students from group 3 are paired with students from group 1. Some teachers find that students spend more time on task if they are allowed to choose their own partners.

Family Literacy

The paired reading procedure and other related methods can be carried out by parents with their own children. During a parents' night at your school, you can give parents an orientation in the method of paired reading. Begin by pointing out the importance of reading fluency. Show the parents the statistics on children's book reading (see page 149). Parents will be surprised to learn how even 10 or 15 minutes a day of support for their child's reading can greatly increase the amount of reading the child might otherwise do. Point out the benefits that can be gained from this: as many as a million words read, with accompanying boosts in vocabulary and understanding.

Show parents how to carry out the steps of the paired reading procedure. Remind them to keep an encouraging tone as they work with their child.

Send home passages for the parent to read with the child that you have found to be on the child's instructional level. Send notes of encouragement to the parents who carry out the procedure, and recognize them at school.

Some parents might be interested in offering to support students' reading fluency by using these methods with other students in the community—or they might be persuaded to come to school and volunteer to read with children in the classroom.

In paired reading a fluent reader is matched up with a less fluent reader.

RADIO READING   Any successful strategy to promote reading fluency requires repeatedly practicing reading the same text. A motivator for repeated reading is performance. The strategy of radio reading (Nichols, Rupley, & Rasinski, 2009) combines both. The teacher prepares chunks of text at appropriate levels for each student (that is, slightly challenging) and invites the students to reread it repeatedly in preparation for a group performance in which they will read their text aloud as if they were radio announcers. The scripts may be part of the same news show, with each student taking a different part. Only the teacher and each student have copies of the text, so the other students must listen for comprehension.

FLUENCY ORIENTED ORAL READING (FOOR)   This strategy combines group instruction with paired study. FOOR (Kuhn, 2004) proceeds in a three-day cycle. The teacher assembles a group of students who are on roughly the same instructional reading level. Copies of the text are provided for the students and the teacher.

Day 1: The teacher fluently reads a passage aloud to the students. The teacher may "think aloud," and call attention to the way he reads the words in groups, and how he provides emphasis with his voice to important words (see pages 152–153 for discussions of fluent reading). The teacher may discuss the meaning and invite comments. Then teacher and students echo read the text. They take turns echo reading the entire text.

Day 2: The students pair up and take turns reading the text—each one reading a sentence or a paragraph.

Day 3: The students come back together in the original group with the teacher. Now they choral read the text—that is, they all read the text as if with one voice. The students may take turns reading parts of the text in dramatic fashion, following the ideas of readers' theater (see pages 158–160 below).

Would students rather practice fluent reading with a computer or with an adult? What is the best balance to keep them motivated?

New Literacies

The National Reading Panel (2000) recommends two kinds of activity to help students learn to read fluently: modeling fluent reading and guided repeated reading, with monitoring and feedback offered to the student. Guided repeated reading ordinarily takes one-on-one attention from a competent adult. But computer-based programs have been able to provide much of this support. Typical computer-based programs offer students text passages to read from fiction, poetry, and informational genres, with the passages organized at different difficulty levels. Devices are usually built in to test students' word-reading accuracy and reading rate. Students can read passages repeatedly and test themselves to see scores improve.

Embedding Repeated Reading in Performance

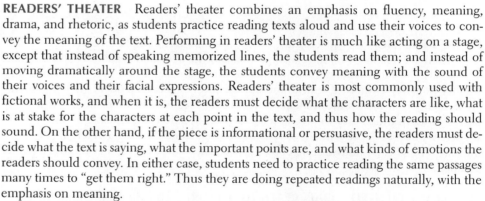

Language education is about more than skill development. Teachers want to cultivate children's appreciation for language and broaden the variety of literature that children can enjoy. So it is recommended that teachers use literary performance as another approach to teaching children to read fluently. Two such activities are readers' theater and choral performance.

Readers' Theater

READERS' THEATER   Readers' theater combines an emphasis on fluency, meaning, drama, and rhetoric, as students practice reading texts aloud and use their voices to convey the meaning of the text. Performing in readers' theater is much like acting on a stage, except that instead of speaking memorized lines, the students read them; and instead of moving dramatically around the stage, the students convey meaning with the sound of their voices and their facial expressions. Readers' theater is most commonly used with fictional works, and when it is, the readers must decide what the characters are like, what is at stake for the characters at each point in the text, and thus how the reading should sound. On the other hand, if the piece is informational or persuasive, the readers must decide what the text is saying, what the important points are, and what kinds of emotions the readers should convey. In either case, students need to practice reading the same passages many times to "get them right." Thus they are doing repeated readings naturally, with the emphasis on meaning.

As they prepare to read a fictional text with readers' theater, players should discuss the setting of the text, who the characters are and what they are like. Then they should read portions of the text several times in order to read the lines fluently and with the expression that is called for. It helps if the teacher offers coaching, asking the students:

- "What is your character feeling right now? How do you sound when you feel that way? Should your voice be loud or soft? Fast or slow?"
- "What might your character think about what the other character is saying? How will your character sound, then?"
- "What is going on at this point in the story? How is your character reacting to it?"
- "How is your character changing as the story proceeds?"

As they prepare to read an informational or argumentative text, readers decide what the message of the text is and how they feel about it. Then they decide what points to read with greater emphasis, where to put pauses for suspense, what parts should be said quietly, what parts loudly, and what parts to hammer home. They think about how the beginning and the end of their piece should sound. The teacher's side coaching helps the students make these decisions.

Both the teacher and the other students can offer comments and suggestions after each practice reading.

Selecting Texts for Readers' Theater Fictional texts for readers' theater can be found in picture books and chapter books, and in the many commercial sets of readers' theater scripts now available. Some of these even have different levels of reading for particular parts so differentiation can occur within the same production. The best choices are those that contain a good deal of dialogue. For example, *White Dynamite and the Curly Kid* by Bill Martin, Jr., and John Archambault is written entirely in dialogue. Frances Temple's *Tiger Soup* contains a readers' theater script in the dust jacket. Chris Raschka's *Yo! Yes?* is a simple dialogue between two little boys with a multicultural theme. When using longer books, choose dialogues taken from pivotal scenes in the plot. *Roll of Thunder, Hear My Cry* by Mildred Taylor contains many scenes in which confrontations between people of different races is thoughtfully handled. Kate DiCamillo's *Because of Winn Dixie* contains many poignant encounters between characters. Informational or argumentative texts should be interesting and powerful. News stories of historical events make good texts for readers' theater. So do speeches, such as Martin Luther King, Jr.'s "I Have a Dream" speech.

To get the class ready for a readers' theater activity, do the following:

1. Make a photocopy of the text you plan to use for readers' theater.
2. Read through the text and mark the parts that should be read by different readers. Create a code for different readers, such as a capital letter to represent the name of each different character, and a capital N followed by a number for narrator number 1, 2, 3, and so on.
3. Put brackets [ ] around the parts that will be read by each reader, and write in a letter over each section to indicate who should read it (Carrick, 2006).
4. Strike through any parts that do not need to be read. Often "He said," "she replied" and the like can be eliminated without affecting the meaning.
5. The text can be duplicated and distributed with the marks just described—but it will be easier for students to read if you type it out with each character's name by his or her part.

Scripted texts for readers' theater are available in which roles are identified for readers of different levels of fluency.

Book containing readers' theater scripts include the following:

Braun, W., & Braun, C. (1995). *Readers' theater: Scripted rhymes and rhythms.* Calgary, Alberta: Braun and Braun Educational Enterprises.

Coleman, M., Farley, J., & Holliday, S. (2001). *Readers theater level 1.* Columbus, OH: McGraw-Hill. (grade levels 2–5)

Crawford, S. A., &. Sanders, N. I. (1999). *15 irresistible mini-plays for teaching math.* New York: Scholastic.

Farley, J., & Sishton, J. (2001) *Readers theater level 2.* Columbus, OH: McGraw-Hill. (grade levels 3–7)

Glassock, S. (1995). *10 American history plays for the classroom.* New York: Scholastic.

Glassock, S. (2001). *10 Easy-to-read American history plays that reach all readers.* New York: Scholastic.

Hoberman, M. A. (2001). *You read to me, I'll read to you.* Boston: Little, Brown.

Haven, K. (1996). *Great moments in science.* Englewood, CO: Teacher Ideas Press.

Pugliano-Martin. C. (2000). *25 just-right plays for emergent readers.* New York: Scholastic.

Pugliano-Martin, C. (1999). *25 Spanish plays for emergent readers*. New York: Scholastic.

Worthy, J. (2005). *Readers theater for building fluency*. New York: Scholastic. (grade levels 3–6)

Web sites with scripts for readers' theater that are available for free include:

Blau, L. *Monthly scripts readers' theater language arts ideas.* <www.lisablau.com/freescripts.html>

Lansky, B. *Classroom theatre.* <www.fictionteachers.com/classroomtheatre/theatre.html>

Shepard, A. *Readers theater (Readers' theater: Free scripts).* <www.araonshep.com/rt.rte.html>

When you assign roles in readers' theater, you can give all the students roughly equal chances to participate. There can be several narrators. Students can read the lines for more than one character (although if they do, they should read the same characters' lines consistently—and they might develop different voices for different characters). The same script can be read by more than one group, and the "readings" (as in interpretations) can be compared later. Another way to involve more students is to choose different scenes from a longer work, and assign each scene to a smaller group of students.

CHORAL READING IN VOICE CHOIRS   Choral reading is another performance-oriented way of practicing reading for fluency. As in readers' theater, because students are reading and rereading to get just the right sounds to convey meanings and emotions, the practice of repeated reading is embedded in a meaning-driven activity. Choral reading can be done with poetry, speeches, or other texts. When they are choral reading poetry, readers should practice over and over again to get the sounds right. What are the possible variations of sound? Texts may be read:

- By the whole chorus, by individuals, by pairs, or by two alternating sections
- In loud or soft voices
- Rapidly or slowly
- Melodiously, angrily, giggling, or seriously

Voices in Unison   When children chorally read a poem in unison, you can add an emphasis on meaning to the practice of reading for fluency by discussing the circumstances or the context in which it might be said. For example, the following poem, "The Grand Old Duke of York," has a martial rhythm, so you can invite the children to imagine they are a platoon of soldiers marching along a road. From a single vantage point, they are very quiet when they are heard from a distance, then louder as they approach, then very loud when they are right in front of the person, then quieter until they are very quiet. Have them practice reading the poem in unison, going from very quiet to VERY LOUD to very quiet again.

The Grand Old Duke of York (Traditional)

The Grand Old Duke of York
> *He had ten thousand men.*
He always marched them up the hill
> *Then he marched them down again.*
And when they were up they were up.
> *And when they were down they were down.*
And when they were only halfway up
> *They were neither up nor down.*

Poems in Two Parts   Reading poems in two parts, or *antiphonally*, allows a sort of call-and-response or dialogue pattern. It is more challenging for two groups of children to read different lines of the same poem while keeping the rhythm intact, and the challenge leads naturally to many repeated readings as the children work to perfect their reading. The repeated reading is desirable, of course, because the practice builds fluency.

"Come Play Catch?" by Bucksnort Trout can be read either by two individual children or by two groups. One group takes the words on the left and the other takes the words on the right. The children should practice reading the poem until they can keep up the rhythm perfectly.

Come Play Catch?

Hey, Cousin Kenny, can you come play catch?
>   *Can you catch come, come? Can you come play catch?*
Whatcha say, Cousin Kenny, can you come play catch?
>   *Can you come catch, come play catch—huh?*
Hey, Aunt Jody, can you come jump rope?
>   *Can you rope jump, jump? Can you come jump rope?*
Whatcha say, Aunt Jody, can you come jump rope?
>   *Can you rope jump, come jump rope—huh?*
Hey, Uncle Harry, can you come hopscotch?
>   *Can you scotch hop, hop? Can you come hop scotch?*
Whatcha say, Uncle Harry, can you come hop scotch?
>   *Can you scotch hop, come hop scotch—huh?*
Hey, gorilla, will you put me down?
>   *Will you down, put, put? Pretty please, down, down?*
Whatcha say, gorilla, will you put me down?
>   *Will you down put, put me down—huh?*

To add an emphasis on meaning, the teacher can provide a context and roles for the speakers of the two parts. The following traditional poem, "It's Time to Go to Bed," can be read with the left-hand lines spoken by a patient mother to a grumpy child, whose lines are on the right. Then the children can be asked to read the poem several more times, with the mother growing increasingly impatient and the child growing increasingly stubborn. Of course, many other scenarios are possible.

It's Time To Go To Bed

It's time to go to bed.
>   *What time is it?*
It's time to go to bed.
>   *What time is it?*
It's time to go to bed.
>   *I don't want to go to bed.*
You have to go to bed.
>   *What time is it?*
You've got to go to bed.
>   *I don't want to go to bed.*
You must go to bed.
>   *I don't want to go to bed.*
>   *I'm not sleepy.*
>   *I'm not sleepy.*
It's time to get up.
>   *What time is it?*
It's time to get up.
>   *What time is it?*
It's time to get up.
>   *I don't want to get up.*

> You have to get up.
>> I don't want to get up.
> You've got to get up.
>> I don't want to get up.
> You must get up.
>> I don't want to get up.
>> I don't want to get up.
>> I'm sleepy.
>> I'm sleepy.
>>> *(Preece, 2009)*

Poems in Rounds Rounds are songs and poems that are sung or read with the same lines read by different people beginning at different times so the words overlap each other. Reading poems in rounds adds another layer of challenge that requires still more practice—and, as we have said, practice means repeated reading, which leads to fluency. The country poem, "Can you dig that crazy music?" whose author is anonymous, can be said as a round, with up to three parts. When they are performing the poem, have each group begin reading right after the group before it completes the first line. Have each group read the poem through two times fully, going straight without a pause from the last line on the first reading to the first line on the second reading. The second time through, the first group repeats the last line while the second group reads it, and then the first and second group repeat the last line as the third group reads it. It helps if someone claps to keep time.

> *"Can you dig that crazy music?"*
> *Can you dig it, Can you dig it, Can you dig it, Can you dig it?*
> *Can you dig that crazy music?*
> *Can you dig it, Can you dig it, Can you dig it, Can you dig it?*
> *Oh, look. Here's a chicken come struttin' down the road.*
> *Now, now. There's another on a barbed wire fence.*
> *Maaaaaa-ma!   Maaaaaa-ma!*
> *Get that son-of-a-gun off my porch!*

Family Literacy

Look at the Reading Is Fundamental Web site, and describe how families can use it to support children's literacy development.

Encouraging Out-of-School Reading

Children need to read to become readers, and there is nothing quite so motivating as having their own book in their hand to take into a corner and read. Commercial book clubs like Scholastic (http://teacher.scholastic.com/clubs/) distribute catalogues periodically to classrooms (Scholastic's come every month) and children can choose to purchase books at below-retail prices. Some companies also hold book fairs in schools; they make attractive displays of books that children can purchase.

Reading Is Fundamental <www.rif.org/about/programs/default.mspx> is a well-established program that gives new books for free to children and families, especially in lower-income communities, including migrant workers' camps. RIF also sponsors community-based literacy activities.

Public libraries conduct many activities to interest children and their families in reading. The children's librarians often hold special events after school and on weekends and during the summer to get children in the habit of using the library. The American Library Association is a valuable ally of reading teachers. Their Association for Library Services to Children <www.ala.org/ala/alsc/alsc.htm> links 4,000 children's librarians around the country. Their Web site gives a window onto their activities to promote reading among children.

For out of school reading children should be matched to books written at their independent reading level—that is, books in which they can read almost all of the words without help.

Some community-minded organizations have put their resources behind the goal of encouraging children to read. Notable among these is Pizza Hut, whose Book It! program rewards millions of children across the United States who meet their reading goals with personal pan-sized pizzas and other prizes (see their Web site at <www.bookitprogram.com/>.

Differentiating Instruction: English Language Learners

Measures of reading fluency count the number of words read in a period of time and subtract from that number a reader's errors in word reading. Fluency scores may be reported as words read correctly per minute (CWPM) or the reading may be characterized qualitatively on a rubric such as Rasinski and Zutell's *Multidimensional Fluency Index* (Rasinski, 2003). When fluency assessment is conducted with native speakers, we assume we are testing children's speed and accuracy at reading words, whether the children read words as wholes or decode them. We are also indirectly assessing their understanding of the materials, since being able to follow the syntax of the sentences, the structure of the text, and the meaning of the ideas contribute to the rate and accuracy of reading.

Be aware, though, that English language learners may score poorly on reading fluency measures, but not for the same reasons that native speakers do. English language learners' poorer performance on both rate and accuracy can be caused by difficulties in rapidly pronouncing words in an unfamiliar language (Ockey, 2010). The good news is that such readers may comprehend words that they mispronounce.

The methods in this chapter that provide practice in fluent reading may be challenging for English language learners. The practice of repeated oral reading can be helpful for English language learners, but teachers should take extra care to avoid making it embarrassing. English language learners may read faster silently than they do orally, so practices like Scaffolded Silent Reading are recommended for them (see page 154).

Part II: Helping Readers Build Vocabulary

Knowing vocabulary is essential to comprehending what one reads (Blachowicz, Fisher, Ogle, & Watts-Taffe, 2006; Davis, 1944). For nearly a century, research has stressed the relationship between vocabulary knowledge and text understanding (Baumann, Kame'enui, & Ash, 2003; Blachowicz & Fisher, 2000; National Reading Panel, 2000; Whipple, 1925). In this section we will outline what research tells us about vocabulary and how it can be taught and learned. The following sections describe the major components of good vocabulary instruction.

CCSS

• Language Standard 3: Vocabulary Acquisition and Use

What Is Vocabulary?

Vocabulary is knowledge of words and word meanings (Lehr, Osborn, & Hiebert, 2006). This is not as simple as it sounds. That definition implies that vocabulary has two parts: the word and the meaning that the word stands for. Since a word is a sign for a concept, a student may or may not have the concept that an unknown word labels. For example, children may not know the word *interrogate*, but they do know what it is to have someone question them in order to find out if they did something wrong! On the other hand, many children will lack both the label and the concept behind the word *ennui*, because few of them will knows what it is for a person to be sated over a long period of time to the point where nothing is capable of exciting that person.

In addition to consisting of words and their meanings, vocabulary also varies between being either receptive or productive. *Receptive vocabulary* refers to the words students can understand when they hear or see them, and *productive vocabulary* refers to the words they can use themselves. And, of course, words can also be received and produced in speech or in print.

An individual's receptive vocabulary is usually larger than his or her productive vocabulary, either in speech or in print; that is, most people can understand more words than they feel confident enough to use. And most students' spoken vocabulary is larger than the number of words they can recognize or use in print, at least until after fourth grade, when the gap is largely closed (Loban, 1976). That means that for teachers of the primary grades, "vocabulary" is as much an issue of helping students recognize the printed form of words they already understand in speech as it is of expanding children's knowledge of unfamiliar words and their meanings. For teachers of older students, the issues of "vocabulary" are particularly about helping students learn challenging content words that they know neither in speech nor in print (Lehr, Osborn, & Hiebert, 2006). It is also the time when students need to learn how words are formed and modified by affixes and bases. The changes in word usage over time and the multiple meanings related to individual vocabulary terms are also parts of what exploration of vocabulary entails.

Besides consisting of signs and the concepts they represent, being receptive or productive, and occurring in speech or in print, words vary in some other ways, too. Many words have multiple meanings—like *bank, root, staff, vessel, glass, row,* and *star.* Some words have completely multiple meanings—like the bank of a river and a savings bank (although the meanings were originally much closer). And some words have much closer multiple meanings, like a *glass* window and a drinking *glass.*

Words have denotations and connotations, too. *Denotations* are the literal meanings of the words, and *connotations* are the associations we have for those words. So the word *tyrant* has the denotation of someone who governs with little regard for the governed, and the connotation of a terrible, brutish person.

Words differ in their degree of *formality* and *informality,* as well as their *propriety* and *impropriety.* Informal and formal words with roughly the same meaning are "Hi" and "Greetings," and "automobile" and "ride." Propriety adds a different dimension and refers to words that are not allowed to be used on the school grounds, or for which our grandmothers sometimes threatened to wash our mouths out with soap.

What Does the Research Say About Vocabulary?

Over the last decade there have been several excellent reviews of the research on vocabulary. Together, they make clear how important attention to vocabulary is and the contribution good vocabulary makes to reading comprehension.

Perhaps most importantly, vocabulary knowledge is one of the best predictors of reading comprehension (Davis, 1944, 1968). Why this is so may relate to the fact that vocabulary knowledge can be used as a measure of general verbal ability that underlies learning (Terman, 1916). It is also true that the ability to make inferences is a critical component both in reading comprehension and in learning the meaning of new words (Sternberg & Powell, 1983). Both explanations have strong support in the research literature. In addition, text meanings are conveyed by the words authors choose; to understand these meanings requires knowledge of the words.

We also know that there are great differences in students' vocabularies. One factor contributing to these differences is related to economic conditions in the home. Hart and Risley's (1995) long-term study of vocabulary development in children during the first years of life revealed significant differences that were strongly related to parental income and welfare status. Children in economically disadvantaged households were exposed to significantly fewer words and to less oral engagement. These conditions affected the children's breadth of vocabulary use as well as their rate of vocabulary growth during these formative years. Hart and Risley found that when these economically disadvantaged children enter school, they possess only about half the vocabulary of their more advantaged peers and thus they begin their school careers at a disadvantage.

Another factor contributing to the size of students' vocabularies is the amount of reading they do. Keith Stanovich (1992) demonstrated that children who were avid readers had much larger vocabularies than children who did not read so much, even when the children had the same levels of general intelligence. Perhaps a big reason for this is that written language is a far richer source of vocabulary than either speech or television. As Figure 6.3 demonstrates, even a children's book has a richer vocabulary than a prime-time adult television show, even more sophisticated vocabulary than the conversation of college-educated adults. The best way to get a bigger vocabulary is to read.

Research studies have also demonstrated that vocabulary knowledge is a critical factor in the school success of English language learners (Carlo, August, & Snow, 2005; Folse, 2001; Nation, 2001). Knowledge of English vocabulary is one of the strongest correlates associated with the discrepancy between the reading performance of native English speakers and English language learners. This correlation remains despite the fact that many English language learners possess a large vocabulary in their native language (Garcia, 1991; Goldenberg, Rezaei, & Fletcher, 2005; Verhoeven, 1990).

The impact of readers' vocabularies is most clear in the comprehension of academic content. While most students, including those who are disadvantaged and English language learners, do well with conversational English, it is when they engage in more academic topics that the differences emerge. Cummins (1980) describes these differences as basic interpersonal communication (BIC) and cognitive academic-language proficiency (CALP). For learners to be successful in school, they need to become increasingly competent with academic language. This is clearly an ongoing process. Teachers need to be sensitive to the fact that the more dense materials are with content-specific terminology, the more support students will need in making sense of the materials. Stories and literature are much less dependent on specific terms used by authors than are the informational texts used in science, social studies, and mathematics.

The CCSS contain many places where vocabulary is highlighted. The standards differentiate two types of academic vocabulary: general academic terms and domain-specific ones. The first category includes terms that have applicability across several disciplines,

Figure 6.3 On the "Richness" of Vocabulary from Different Sources

	Rank of Median Word	Rare Words Per 1,000
I. Printed Texts		
Abstracts of scientific articles	4,389	128.0
Newspapers	1,690	68.3
Popular magazines	1,399	65.7
Adult books	1,058	52.7
Comic books	867	53.5
Children's books	627	30.9
Preschool books	578	16.3
II. Transcripts of Television Shows		
Popular prime-time adult shows	490	22.7
Popular children's shows	543	20.2
Cartoon shows	598	30.8
III. Adult Speech		
Expert witness testimony	1,008	28.4
College graduates, friends, spouses	496	17.3

The "rank of median word" refers to how common or rare the word is. For instance, "the" is common and has a low score. "Antidisestablishmentarianism" is a rare word and has a high score.

Source: Hayes and Ahrens (1988).

like the words *summarize*, *structure*, and *environment*. Within the group of general academic terms there is a subset of "school-specific" words and phrases that describe processes learners need to employ (*compare/contrast*, *underline*, *diagram*, *find supporting evidence*, etc.) These academic terms and their specialized meanings often pose the greatest challenges for English learners. (Graves, 2006; Marzano, 2004). The other category of academic terms and phrases are domain-specific, which means they are part of a particular content or topic: *artery*, *blood vessel*, and *vertebrae* are examples of words that relate specifically to the study of biology. In their recent analysis of the academic vocabulary in fourth- and fifth-grade science and mathematics texts, Scott and her colleagues (2011) report that expert teachers identified over 4,035 conceptually new terms in the science textbooks and 2,848 terms in the math books that students needed to know in order to understand the content. These high levels of academic terms indicate the real challenges students confront in comprehending the content materials they are asked to use.

While the demands for vocabulary learning are high, research studies also indicate attention to vocabulary development is valuable for all students (Graves & Silvermann, 2010). Good instruction makes a difference. In their summary of the instructional research, Blachowicz, Fisher, Ogle, and Watts-Taffe (2006) explain that good vocabulary instruction:

- Takes place in a language and word-rich environment that fosters the word consciousness, motivation, and ownership that support incidental word learning.
- Includes intentional teaching of selected words, which provides multiple sources of information and opportunities for repeated exposure, use, and practice.
- Includes the teaching of generative elements of words and word-learning strategies in ways that give students control over their own strategic behaviors.

How Do We Teach Vocabulary?

CCSS

- Language Standards 4, 5, and 6: Vocabulary Acquisition and Use

- Standards 4, 5, and 6 of the Common Core Standards Language Standards, K–5 address vocabulary development, the subject of the second half of this chapter.

Efforts to teach vocabulary can be organized around these principles:

1. Motivate students to be open to learning words by promoting a respect for language.
2. Create a language-rich environment in which students can learn words through general acquisition.
3. Teach specific words (during language arts and during specific content study).
4. Teach students strategies for learning new words.
5. Use assessment to monitor students' vocabulary learning.

Promoting Respect for Language

Having a word in our vocabulary means we can notice something. Each word is a flashlight that illuminates another corner of our experience (Patterson, 1984). In psychological research, it was demonstrated years ago that we most readily recognize what we have a name for (Brown, 1958). This point was made in a classroom setting by Mary Cowhey (2006):

> *During my first year teaching, I estimate I lost twenty to thirty minutes of instructional time each day dealing with post-recess conflicts, long tearful renditions of who did what to whom, fraught with passionate contradictions and denials . . . The following summer I took a workshop in Second Step, a "violence prevention curriculum." . . . I was surprised when some students really couldn't identify emotions such as disgusted, scared, and angry in photos of children. Before I began teaching Second Step lessons, I observed a couple of boys "joking" with some other children. They didn't notice when one of the other children became upset, and continued "joking" even when the other child began to cry. When I*

intervened, the jokers said "We were just having fun." I asked if they thought Patrick, who was crying, was still having fun. They said yes. (p. 40)

As Mary Cowhey's example makes clear, having a word in one's vocabulary means that one understands the word and can connect it to experience. Indeed, she goes on to say that her lessons about emotions

. . . explicitly teach children to read facial expressions, body language, and tone of voice to name the emotion being expressed, to recognize cause and effect, and to realize that two people can have very different feelings about the same situation. (Cowhey, 2006, p. 40)

But without the word, there is nothing to anchor the experience in consciousness, and nothing to enable one to communicate about it to others.

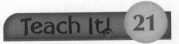

Teach It! 1

Reading Aloud

Creating a Language-Rich Environment

A cornerstone of classrooms rich in language is teachers reading aloud to students from a variety of books just beyond the students' own reading levels. Most of the vocabulary students will want and need to learn can be introduced naturally through the oral reading or "read-alouds" by the teacher. Teachers at every grade level can entice students into developing interest in words and language as they read aloud. Pausing over interesting terms and phrases, thinking aloud and elaborating on words, exploring the images created by text passages, and savoring particular words are all ways teachers can help students develop interest in words and build their vocabularies. Teachers can also ask students to listen for interesting, beautiful, and curious uses of language and then take time after an oral reading to discuss what students noted. It is useful to write these words and phrases on the board so all students, particularly English language learners, have the advantage of both hearing and seeing the terms.

In the intermediate and middle grades, students also take great pleasure in word play and jokes. Reading humorous pieces and challenging students with riddles and jokes can connect with students' developing explorations of the richness and complexity of language. (For example, Nothing succeeds like success/no—recess; I've heard of trade schools, and I'd like to; What's black and white and red/read all over?—(newspaper). Teachers often have bulletin boards devoted to multiple-meaning words or confusing phrases.

The classroom also is enriched when teachers make available a collection of books that explore and play with language. Students enjoy reading books like *Bullfrog Pops!: Adventures in Verbs and Direct Objects* (Walton, 2011); *Miss Alaneus* (Frasier, 2007); and *Baloney* (Scieszka, 2005). In addition, books with puzzles and word games, rhymes and riddles, and magazines that introduce varied topics in inviting formats encourage language exploration. Critical to these classroom collections on language is a good set of dictionaries—all students should have their own and the classroom should contain more adult and larger dictionaries for reference. Making available and teaching students how to use both dictionaries and classroom thesauruses provides them with independent tools for expanding their language. In classrooms with English language learners, some bilingual dictionaries are also important. The whole class can enjoy exploring how different words are expressed in each language and can learn a great deal when the different forms of the words are displayed in the classroom.

Some Web sites also include frames for you to create your own games and crossword puzzles with words children need to review from your instructional program. FunBrain is one: <www.funbrain.com/words.html>. Vocabulary University is good for upper elementary and middle grades: <www.vocabulary.com/>. The PBS television series *Between the Lions* has put many word games online at <http://pbskids.org/lions/games/>. "Surfing the Net With Kids" keeps you up to date with new recommended links for word games: <www.surfnetkids.com/games/Word_Games/>.

Play with words is an important component in children's vocabulary development. Don't overlook it!

Teach It! 21

"Word Conversations" for Primary Grades

The middle school literacy coordinator in this video demonstrates strategies to support students' acquisition of content-specific vocabulary. Identify the multitude of methods that she uses to support the students' vocabulary development in addition to their comprehension and fluency.

General Vocabulary Development and Content-Specific Terms

Connect Two

Semantic Feature Analysis

At the primary level, teachers informally expand students' vocabularies through their oral language use and their reading to students. By the time students are in the intermediate grades, teachers become more specific in their attention to vocabulary learning. Both in literature and in other content areas, specific terms are needed to insure comprehension of text materials. By attending to these terms, teachers can also build the vocabulary knowledge students will need for school success. The less students are stimulated at home with rich oral language contexts, the more important it is that teachers focus on and reinforce vocabulary development.

Teachers are often unsure about what words they should teach directly. Yet there are good sources of help in making those decisions. Most basal reading programs now include a vocabulary strand and highlight some key words that are essential to the selections. Focusing students' attention on a small set of words prior to reading a literature selection will help them notice these words as they read. The terms can then be discussed after the reading, and students can practice using them in their own speaking and writing. The same is true in most science, social studies, and other content area curricula. Textbooks often identify key terms that are basic to the content. Teachers can highlight these and ask students to Rate Your Knowledge (Blachowicz, 1987) Look at the example shown in Figure 6.4 for a Rate Your Knowledge chart that was used as a pre-reading activity.

If we had to teach all of the words children need to learn, we couldn't do it. Nagy and Anderson (1985) put the number of words in "printed school English" at 88,500! And that was just through ninth grade! There is no way to teach 10,000 words a year. Most of these words will have to be learned from experience, especially from reading. But teaching helps, too.

Beck and her colleagues have come up with a way of approaching the seemingly enormous task of teaching vocabulary (Beck, McKeown, & Kucan, 2002). As we saw in Chapter 3, they identified three "tiers" of words. The first tier includes common, everyday words that most of us know. The second tier of words are those that we encounter frequently in school and in reading and that are used in a variety of situations; knowing these words provides a foundation for many kinds of learning. In the CCSS usage, these are general academic terms and are worth teaching in language arts and reading. The third tier of words includes the specialized vocabulary terms connected to particular content, identified as domain-specific in the CCSS. They have specific meanings that need to be developed. These terms are only taught as they are needed for specific content understanding.

Figure 6.4 Rate Your Knowledge Chart

These are words we are going to be using during this unit. Mark how familiar you are with them as we begin. Those that are not so familiar are words to put in your learning journal so you can build your understanding of them during our study.

Key Words	New to Me	Have Seen	Know Well
mummy			
pyramid			
scribe			
artisan			
pharaoh			

Another useful guide for content words is the one developed by Marzano (2005). He and his colleagues collected all of the academic terms needed for students to be successful with state and national standards and then sorted them by school levels. The Academic Vocabulary List includes key words for 11 subject areas, including science, mathematics, language arts, history, social studies, the arts, and health. These words are then organized according to four levels: level 1 = grades K–2; level 2 = grades 3–5; level 3 = grades 6–8; and level 4 = grades 9–12. These lists provide a good reference for teachers who want to assess and then develop their students' vocabularies for academic reading and learning.

A final important source for words is the students themselves. Some researchers have demonstrated that involving students in selecting the words to be studied is a productive strategy (Fisher, Blachowicz, & Smith, 1991; Haggard, 1982). Students are able to self-select important terms that are similar to and equally valuable to those the teachers select. And, when students self-select terms, their involvement has the added benefit of motivating them to learn the terms more deeply.

Teaching Strategies for Word Learning

Students need to develop independent strategies for dealing with the new words they will meet both in school and in other areas of their lives. The goal is that when they encounter unknown words, students can examine the context for general clues, look at the structure and morphology of the word itself (the internal context) for clues, or consult a reference, if needed. They will also determine if the word is one they want to add to their general vocabulary. If it is, then they will employ a strategy to help them retain the word—by creating a word card, making a personal association and practicing it, or using some other memory device.

Teachers can do a great deal to help students become active language learners. For students to maximize their opportunities to expand their vocabularies, they need to be actively engaged in their own learning. They need to be helped to develop some awareness of how they can learn new words and to explore strategies for attending to words and rehearsing them. It is important that teachers not give the false impression that word learning is the same as memorizing definitions for terms on a list the teacher supplies. Teachers do a big disservice when they pass on this traditional and ineffective approach to word learning. Rather, teachers need to guide students to understand that word learning is an ongoing and cumulative process. We start with a kernel of meaning for a new term and then keep expanding our understanding of how that term is used in varied situations. Each time learners encounter the term in print or in oral language, they can check out their own understanding against the new input and then modify their association network for the term.

A graphic format that helps students understand the ways an understanding of new terms is built is the Concept of Definition Map (see Figure 6.5) that highlights the relations among words and their meanings (Schwartz & Raphael, 1985).

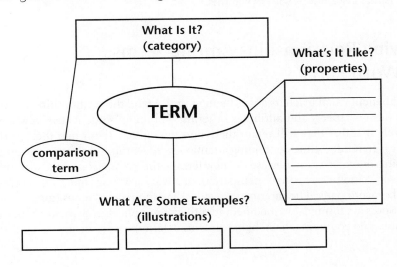

Figure 6.5 Concept of Definition Map

Source: Schwartz & Raphael in "Concept of Definition: A Key to Improving Students' Vocabulary," *The Reading Teacher 30*(2), 1985. Reproduced with permission of Wiley Inc.

Figure 6.6 A Semantic
Feature Analysis

	Bear live young	Have gills	Cold-blooded	Have milk
SHARKS				
DOLPHINS				

The new term is listed in the center of the Concept of Definition Map. Above the term, the student indicates the larger class of word to which the new one is related. Then the student elaborates the description of the term with more categorical and semantic information related to the word's definition, along with examples and nonexamples. Some variations of the map also ask students to draw an example of the term. By building this kind of association web around the new term, students can develop a better concept of what word learning entails.

Semantic feature analysis is another activity that helps illustrate semantic relationships among words. Semantic feature analysis provides a graphic display that focuses on the features that distinguish words in a particular category from one another, such as various types of vehicles or human relatives. The teacher creates the matrix either as a model or with students during a unit of study. (See Figure 6.6 for an illustration.)

The students then determine which features each of the terms possesses and finally are able to compare and contrast similar terms. In their research to determine the effectiveness of various approaches to vocabulary learning, Bos and Anders (1989, 1990) compared the effectiveness of three semantic relatedness techniques (mapping, semantic feature analysis, and semantic/syntactic feature analysis) to definition study with students of various ages and abilities. They concluded that all three of the interactive techniques were more effective than that traditional approach to having students write and study definitions.

More recently, an added component has been included in word learning—having students create visual diagrams or pictures of the targeted terms. Marzano (2005) includes in his six-step process for helping students learn new academic terms the component "Students create a nonlinguistic representation of the new term." After the teacher provides a description of each term to be learned, students first write their own explanation of the term, and then represent the term in a graphic organizer, picture, pictograph, or cartoon form. In this way English language learners and students with nonverbal strengths can build personal associations with new terms.

Showing Relationships Among Terms and Word Parts

Word Origins and Derivations

Students benefit when teachers guide them to understand the relationships among words and the various aspects and attributes of terms. The more students use new terms, the more likely it is that they will retain them and incorporate them into their working vocabularies. To reinforce the continuing attention word learning requires, you can give students points or credit when they use the new terms either in oral class discussion or in their written work. Another important component of a word learning strategy is for students to identify key word parts. The intermediate grades are the years to focus students' attention on how words are formed and modified. Identifying morphemes, particularly derivational morphemes and common affixes, helps students determine word meanings. Activities that

DIFFERENTIATED INSTRUCTION

SIOP®
Sheltered
Instruction
Observation
Protocol*

English Language Learners

In a case study focused on using visual enhancements with English language learners and other reluctant readers (Ogle, 2000), struggling, less-than-enthusiastic science students became much more eager learners when their teacher developed a vocabulary card deck for them. Each week there were eight terms to be learned for which students were given 4 × 6-inch note cards. On one side, the students wrote the term and a description based on information from the teacher. On the other side, the students drew what they thought represented that term. During the week, students were given five minutes at the beginning of each science class to test their friends on the word cards. They would show the pictures to another student, who would have to guess what term was being illustrated. The increased motivation and learning were apparent. Students who had barely contributed to class became eager to see if their drawings would elicit the accurate connection for the class terms. José turned out to be a fairly gifted artist, and soon other boys were calling on him to help them more creatively illustrate terms. He also provided suggestions for depicting some of the more abstract concepts. A nearly invisible student became a central resource to the class with his artistic talent, and in the process, the teacher also learned that he had more to contribute about science than she had expected. While he hesitated to speak in class, he didn't hesitate to illustrate ideas. (See Figure 6.7 for an example of a student's word cards.)

involve students in brainstorming and creating word splashes of related terms focus attention on related terms and how meanings can be deduced from partial knowledge (e.g., *disrupt* = *dis* (apart) + *rupt* (break up). Then students can connect the morpheme -*rupt* to other words they may know like *interrupt* and *corrupt*. Students can take the prefix *dis-* and brainstorm other words with the same prefix—or even the prefix used as a standalone slang word, "Don't 'dis' me."

A more advanced activity for students in sixth grade and up is to take word parts of historical morphemes (such as -*rupt*, -*graph*, and *tele*-) and historical affixes (such as *con-*, *sym-*, and *a-*) and link them together using a connected word web (see Figure 6.8). Students draw circles around the historical morphemes and connect them with lines to the same historical morphemes in other words. Then they do the same with historical affixes. Finally, they try to infer the meaning of unknown words if they know what the historical morpheme and affix mean; and they try to infer the meaning of the historical morpheme

Figure 6.7 José's Word Cards

Figure 6.8 A Connected Word Web

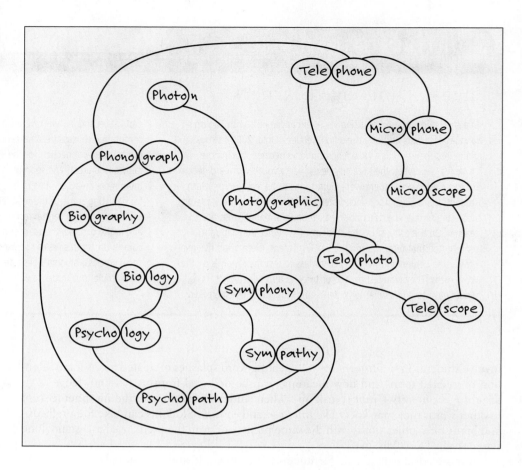

and affix if they know what some of the words mean. Make sure you have a good dictionary with etymologies (word histories) handy to check their answers.

Introducing and Focusing Attention on New Vocabulary

WORD CONVERSATIONS FOR K–1 When young readers (kindergarten and first grade) are learning new words, Beck and colleagues (2002) suggest that teachers conduct a rich discussion of words that includes these six steps:

1. Contextualize words, one at a time, within a story. For example, with kindergartners, the teacher could use Don Freeman's perennially popular *Corduroy* (1978) as a pretext for introducing the words *insistent, reluctant*, and *drowsy*. The teacher says, "In the story, Lisa was reluctant to leave the department store without Corduroy [her new teddy bear]."

2. Ask the children to repeat the word so as to make a phonological representation of it.

3. Then explain the meaning of the word in a child-friendly way: "*Reluctant* means you are not sure you want to do something."

4. Now provide examples of the word in other contexts: "I am reluctant to go swimming in the early summer when the water is cold."

5. Next, ask children to provide their own examples: "What is something you would be reluctant to do?"

Charting Students' Word Learning

Teachers have struggled with how to evaluate students' vocabulary knowledge since word learning is not a one-step process. Words are learned gradually over time as more and more associations with terms are experienced. Yet it is also important for teachers to find out how much of the vocabulary needed to comprehend particular texts is known by students before the texts or materials are used. If students lack a significant number of key terms, then more pre-reading and concept building needs to be done. Teachers also need to determine what strategies students possess so they can figure out new terms in context as they read. If students can use context effectively and know how to identify combining forms and affixes, they have good tools to help them as they read.

However, teachers also need to know how supportive the texts are in helping students access new terms. Supportive texts will provide meanings for important terms through restatement, illustrations, and examples. The terms may be identified in bold type or in italics. Some texts define terms in the margins. Other texts or text sections may not provide these scaffolds and key terms may remain opaque and students will require outside support for the vocabulary to become meaningful.

Before asking students to read a text or begin a unit of study, teachers can easily identify students' familiarity with key terms. Several informal activities provide good starting points. Using a Rate Your Knowledge chart of the terms, students can indicate their levels of familiarity with them before reading. As students are completing the activity, teachers can move around the classroom, making an informal assessment of how the students are responding. Teachers can also ask students to "Connect 2–3 of the Terms" and write a sentence using the terms as an initial assessment. The students who struggle to create interesting and accurate sentences can be noted and more vocabulary work can be provided. An alternative activity is to have students sort new terms into concept groups and then to label the groups. Each of these informal activities provides a way for teachers to get an initial assessment of students' familiarity with key terms and concepts needed for learning.

These same activities can be used at the completion of the study, also. Changes in levels of knowledge of terms, ability to write using the terms accurately, and ability to cluster similar terms by concept are what is expected from focused learning. Both students and teachers can compare beginning and ending knowledge levels and evaluate growth together.

If the study permitted focus on particular combining forms or affixes, the same kind of pre–post assessments can be given. Creating an activity in which students are asked to divide several key content words into their parts (prefix, base, suffix) and provide meanings for each is a quick way to determine how comfortable students are in using word parts. Any unfamiliar word part can then be included on a study list—with students searching for other similar words, with groups creating lists of families of terms, etc. At the conclusion of the unit, students can be asked to create a list of related terms, define some unknown terms with the familiar parts, or engage in using the word parts in some creative way.

By focusing assessment on specific terms that are used in the stories, informational texts, or general unit concepts, teachers and students can take the word-learning journey together. Specific targeted words and word-learning tools are valuable to monitor, and the concreteness of the gains motivates students to continue their learning.

6. Finally, ask the children to repeat the word they have been talking about, so as to reinforce its phonological representation.

Word conversations are not as easy as they look. Teachers need to do the following:

- Choose books carefully to provide a meaningful context for introducing the vocabulary.
- Think carefully about the words, and formulate child-friendly explanations of the word meanings.
- Plan questions to relate the words to the children's experience.
- Remind the children of the words they are studying, giving them several opportunities to pronounce the words. (See Beck et al., 2002, for further discussion of this approach.)

Activities to teach vocabulary should relate words to a meaningful context, to other words, and to the students' own experiences. The following activities satisfy these requirements by making connections (to self, personal stories, and other books); collaborating with peers (interpersonal dynamics through all the language arts); exploring meaning

Figure 6.9
Vocab-O-Gram

Before we read the Japanese folktale, see what you can predict about how these terms will be used. Put each term in the box with which you think it is connected. Words: bitterly cold, weaving, reed hats, empty cupboards, New Year's Day, kind old man, stone statues, fortunate, Jizo, guardian god of children, old woman, hungry, no coal, sack of food, thank you, village, gift.

Characters	Setting	Problem
Feeling/Tone	Solution	Other Words

Teach It! 61

Cumulative Semantic Map

(asking questions; making statements; interpreting; using higher-level thinking such as application, synthesis, and evaluation); and participating as an active reader (summarizing, predicting, confirming, and clarifying).

VOCAB-O-GRAM   Terms that are important to a piece of fiction can be highlighted for students through the use of a vocab-o-gram. The terms are listed and the students are asked to sort them according to the story elements of plot, setting (time and location), characters, conflict, and resolution. Words that just don't seem to be clearly identified with the elements can be placed in the mystery category (see Figure 6.9).

SEMANTIC WEB   A semantic web is a way to organize information graphically according to categories. There are several ways to use semantic webs. The most open-ended way is to draw a circle on a page and write a topic word in it. Then, together with the students, the teacher thinks of aspects of the topic and comes up with examples or aspects of that subtopic.

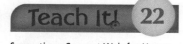

Teach It! 22

Semantic or Concept Web for Upper Grades

One approach to semantic webs is the character web, in which the name of a character is written in the circle in the middle of the display. Then words that describe the character are written as satellites around the character's name. Examples that illustrate each attribute are written as satellites around the descriptive words. Figure 6.10 depicts a semantic web on dolphins.

Figure 6.10 A Semantic Web

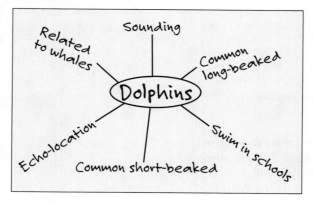

WEBBED QUESTIONS   Schwartz and Rafael (1985) suggest guiding the students' responses to a semantic web and having them offer answers to three questions asked about the target word, as shown in Figure 6.11:

What is it?
What is it like?
What are some examples of it?

CONCEPT OF DEFINITION MAP   This beginning web can then be turned into the more formal Concept of Definition Map in the upper grades. (See Figure 6.5 for an example of a Concept of Definition Map.) In creating the map, students extend their

Figure 6.11 Webbed Questions

Dolphins

- What are they like?
  - Care for young
  - Related to whales
  - Eat krill
  - Some are vegetarians
- What are they?
  - Blow holes
  - Breathe air
  - Ocean animals
  - Mammals
  - Small ones
  - Of many kinds
  - Large ones
  - Also called porpoises
  - Smart!
  - Used by the US Navy for spying
- Not to be confused with Mahi Mahi!
- What are some examples of them?
  - Atlantic spotted
  - Bottle-nosed
  - Short-beaked
  - Common dolphin

attention to new terms by asking themselves to describe the term and find examples of it. Some teachers have added a section for students to illustrate the term and/or use it in a sentence. In both basic semantic webbing and in creating maps, students learn to think of words as related to larger concepts. They also begin to look for associations and attributes for the terms being learned.

CONCEPT LADDERS Concept ladders (Gillet & Temple, 2003) provide yet another way for children to organize their thinking and to categorize, thus supporting comprehension. The concept ladder shown in Figure 6.12 would be useful in a study on volcanoes and earthquakes. It also helps students think of new terms as having important attributes that distinguish them from other similar terms.

 The Frayer Model is used in this video, in a middle school math class, to support students' ability to learn content vocabulary. Why is the Frayer Model a successful tool to learn new vocabulary in math and in other content area classes?

Figure 6.12 A Concept Ladder

What kind of thing is this?	What is it a part of?	What causes it?
What are the kinds of it?	What are its parts?	What does it cause?

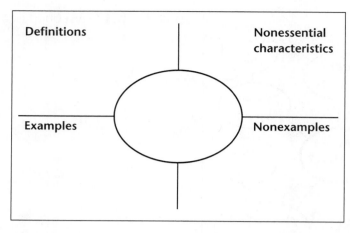

Figure 6.13 The Frayer Model

THE FRAYER MODEL   Another graphic organizer for laying out words for a concept in relation to other words is the Frayer Model (Buhel, 2001). The Frayer Model directs students to think of essential and nonessential characteristics of a concept as well as examples and nonexamples of it. The model is best used to name a common concept that has many characteristics and examples. That way, the students are able to consider a larger number of words in context (see Figure 6.13).

Teachers can do a great deal to build students' interest in words and language by having newspapers, magazines, and books from other languages in the classroom and referring to them periodically. Listening to music from other countries and cultures is another way to develop sensitivity to languages and vocabulary different from our own. Because so many of our academic terms come from Latin and Greek origins, it is often interesting to compare forms of the words we use with those in Spanish and other languages of the students in the classroom. For example, during the political elections in the fall or during school elections, it would be interesting to put the terms on the board and ask students to supply the equivalent terms in their home languages. What would *election, candidate, voting, campaigning,* and *party* look like in Spanish, French, Farsi? Asking the question and taking time to compare languages is another way to expand students' flexibility with words and the ever-expanding corpus of words in English.

Using Online Sources to Build Vocabulary

Teachers can stimulate students' interest in words by using the online resources on vocabulary Web sites. Some have a new word each day that can be shared; others are great for providing word histories and noting new words that come into our language. There are a number of dictionaries, so terms can be looked up and the definitions and references compared. One of the easy ways to help students explore language is to introduce them to the resources now available on the Web. These tools are particularly useful for English language learners because they can use the online resources to look up words that they don't know in English and get helpful hints on what other sites are useful. There are several fun sources for words listed below.

General vocabulary and interesting information about words:

<www.eduplace.com/kids/hmsv/>

<www.wordsmith.org>

<www.vocabulary.com>

<www.funbrain.com/whichwords/index.html>

Spanish-English dictionaries available at:

<www.yourdictionary.com>

<www.my-spanish-dictionary.com>

<http://education.yahoo.com/references/dict_en_es/>

Students explore new vocabulary online.

DIFFERENTIATED INSTRUCTION

SIOP®
Sheltered
Instruction
Observation
Protocol'

Creating Acrostics

Getting to know your students is made interesting and enjoyable by asking each student to create an acrostic poem of their name. Each letter in the student's name is written in vertically down the left side of the piece of paper. The students select descriptive words that begin with the letters of their name and then use these terms to create the poem. For example, Diedra created her poem in the following way:

Daring

Interested

Explorer

Doing

Rambunctious

Activities

It is very easy to identify some of the things that Diedra may be interested in doing, given the window on her personality and interests she opens. Each student's poem is distinctive; even those who are shy generally reveal that aspect of their selves, too. Teachers can use this activity as a way to build awareness among a class of the value of selecting words carefully. Involving students in several steps makes it more likely that they will find good terms. Start by brainstorming lots of words that begin with each letter of a person's name. Then give students thesauruses and have them search for additional words that may be even more illustrative of what they want to say about themselves. Model this with your own name if they seem unsure of how to proceed. The dictionary can also be helpful in leading students to just the right words. These resources make it more likely that they will find just the right terms to describe themselves. Finally, before the poems are completed, have students check their acrostics with a partner for a final review. The final poems can be read orally, posted in the room, and combined with lists of students' favorite music, books, and activities. It certainly is a good way to focus students' attention on the value of words and the connotations and nuances each word we use contains.

For Review

Traditionally, reading instruction focused on word recognition and comprehension. Now we realize that reading fluency needs our attention and so does vocabulary. These two aspects are included in the five Building Blocks for Literacy that are identified for special attention by the National Institute for Literacy.

Reading fluency is not just reading rate. In fact, sometimes children read *too* fast. Reading fluency includes easy and natural rate, appropriate to the material, along with intonation and proper phrasing. Fluency can be learned, and that means that attention to teaching children to read particular texts fluently will carry over to their reading of other texts. Reading fluency aids comprehension: the more naturally and fluently a child reads, the more attention that child will have left over to think about the text.

Approaches to teaching reading for fluency include:

- Model fluent reading.
- Provide explicit instruction.
- Offer opportunities to read.
- Supply appropriate texts.
- Guide students' reading.
- Monitor students' reading.

In this chapter we showed techniques such as repeated reading, and also approaches embedded in performance, such as choral reading of poetry and readers' theater.

Vocabulary, too, is getting more attention in reading instruction than in the past. Vocabulary is a big divider: some children have at least twice as many words in their vocabulary as others, and the vocabulary size affects their understanding, not only of text, but of the world around them. Words are labels for concepts, and the more concepts we have, the more easily we can notice things and think about our experiences. There is a vast vocabulary to learn, so teachers must prioritize. One way is to focus on useful words that children don't yet know (as opposed to words they are learning anyway, or words that are included in disciplinary study). Several suggestions for teaching vocabulary were provided in this chapter, including encouraging respect for words, teaching relationships between them, and teaching their parts. Also, children can be helped to recognize words in context. A key to vocabulary development is creating classrooms alive with talk and curiosity about vocabulary. Teachers who encourage children's explorations with words and provide tools for them to use give children a good start.

For Your Journal

Fluent reading means reading with expression and not just reading quickly. Fluent reading is a skill that many adults need to work on, especially if we are going to be models for children.

Find a well-known children's book with rich language. J.R.R. Tolkien's *The Hobbit* is a good choice. Or Kate Di-Camillo's *Because of Winn-Dixie*. Practice reading passages of it aloud. Then go to the library and check out the audio book versions of the books. Listen carefully to the professional readers.

Choose one reader and listen for two minutes. Then write in your journal: What makes this person's reading so interesting to listen to? How many of the qualities of reading fluency that were described in this chapter are present in the readings? How does the reader group words? How does the reader use intonation—make his or her voice rise or fall at certain points? How does the reader bring characters to life?

Finally, try reading the text yourself the way the professional reader did it. Try tape recording your reading, and analyze it the same way you did the professional reader's. Afterward, decide what aspects of good oral reading you do well. Decide what aspects you want to work on. Write these things in your journal. And be sure to practice.

Taking It to the World

How much does vocabulary matter to people? Sit down with two or three classmates and make a list of as many ways as you can that vocabulary matters in people's lives. It might help get the conversation going to recall the self-help books published for adults that promise them more successful careers if only they will master a larger vocabulary or the vocabulary items on the SAT test.

Think also of times—in films or in the discourse of our politicians—when having a larger vocabulary is held up as a sign of snobbery.

After making a list of both kinds of situations, try to reach a conclusion. What are the advantages of having a large vocabulary? What caveats should be kept in mind about using the right words at the right time? How will you use these conclusions in your teaching?

New Literacies Connections

1. Many software packages are now available that purport to help build children's reading fluency. Consider the aspects of reading fluency we have explored in this chapter—automatic word recognition, reading rate, and expressive reading. Then look up "reading fluency software" on a search engine. Review the descriptions of three or four programs. How many of the above-mentioned aspects of reading fluency are built into them?

2. Go to the SuperKids! Web site at <http://www.superkids.com/aweb/pages/reviews/vocab/> and look up several of the vocabulary-building software programs that are reviewed there. To what extent are the five principles of vocabulary (see page 166) taken into account in these programs?

MyEducationLab™

Go to Topics 3 and 4 (Fluency and Vocabulary) in the MyEducationLab <www.myeducationlab.com> for your course, where you can:

- Find learning outcomes for Fluency and Vocabulary along with the national standards that connect to these outcomes.
- Complete Assignments and Activities that can help you more deeply understand the chapter content.
- Apply and practice your understanding of the core teaching skills identified in the chapter with the Building Teaching Skills and Dispositions learning units.
- Check your comprehension on the content covered in the chapter by going to the Study Plan in the Book Resources for your text. Here you will be able to take a chapter quiz, receive feedback on your answers, and then access Review, Practice, and Enrichment activities to enhance your understanding of chapter content.

- Visit A+RISE. A+RISE® Standards2Strategy™ is an innovative and interactive online resource that offers new teachers in grades K-12 just in time, research-based instructional strategies that meet the linguistic needs of ELLs as they learn content, differentiate instruction for all grades and abilities, and are aligned to Common Core Elementary Language Arts standards English language proficiency standards in WIDA, Texas, California, and Florida.

Reading Comprehension, Part I: Making Sense of Literature

Making Sense
of Literature
p. 182

Understanding
Reading
Comprehension
p. 183

Teaching for
Comprehension
p. 191

Assessing
Comprehension
p. 207

Anticipation Guide

The following statements will stimulate your thinking about the topics of this chapter. Answer *true* or *false* in response to each statement. As you read and learn more about the topics in these statements, double-check your answers. See what interests you and what prompts your curiosity toward more understanding.

____ **1.** Comprehension, or understanding what you read, is entirely a process of memorizing the details of the author's message.

____ **2.** Comprehension is the aspect of reading that has traditionally gotten the most attention in classrooms.

____ **3.** Comprehension relies on what a reader already knows about the topic of the text. The more you already know, the more you are likely to understand from the reading.

____ **4.** Good readers constantly monitor their understanding, to be sure they are making sense of the text.

____ **5.** Teaching a student to read with comprehension is not at all like teaching athletic skills or skill in art.

____ **6.** Good comprehension lessons have three parts: consolidation, building knowledge, and anticipation, in that order.

____ **7.** Following the structure of the text helps the reader make sense of what is written.

____ **8.** Teaching comprehension is complete once the reader understands the meaning of a text.

____ **9.** Literary aspects like plot, characterization, literal and figurative language, and the characters' point of view may concern teachers of literature, but not teachers of reading.

____ **10.** The Common Core Standards treat reading comprehension as a single skill: comprehension is comprehension, regardless of the type or topic of the text.

Reading for Comprehension in a Fourth-Grade Classroom

The students in Hank da Silva's fourth grade at North Street Elementary School can predict the day's events in broad outline, but not completely. They know that after the morning class meeting, they will talk about their topics in social studies. They have been reading about the settlement of the Great Plains in their social studies text. At the same time, they have been reading Patricia McLachlan's *Sarah, Plain and Tall* and Laura Ingalls Wilder's *The Little House on the Prairie*. Mr. da Silva reads to them from *Letters from a Woman Homesteader*, a work of nonfiction told in the form of letters home from a feisty single woman in the 1880s. He has also bookmarked and assigned three Internet sites where students will find information about the settlement of the Great Plains by European Americans.

The class has written dual-entry diaries every day about their readings. They have also created a Venn diagram comparing what skills people have to have if they move to a new place now compared to what skills people needed in the days of the homesteaders. Figure 7.1 shows what the class has come up with.

This morning, Mr. da Silva is conducting a discussion of a couple of pages of the social studies book. He begins by pointing out that sometimes textbooks do not make their meanings very clear.

"Take right here, for instance," he points out. "The text says, 'Westward expansion gave the new country a constant sense of excitement, of new possibilities.' What do you suppose the author means by that sentence? Let's start with 'Westward expansion.' What do you suppose he means by *expansion*? If the author were here, what do you think he would say about that?"

After lunch, Mr. da Silva has reading workshop. According to the rotation chart on the wall, some students read independently. Today those students are doing something special: They are writing self-assessments about their reading comprehension, which they will later give to Mr. da Silva. A group of six students who are reading Phyllis Reynolds Naylor's *Shiloh* meet with Mr. da Silva for a literature circle; each of the six students is conducting a part of the discussion, according to a role she or he has been assigned. Mr. da Silva takes part in the discussion, but he also is taking occasional notes. He writes about how the discussion is going. He writes a note to remind himself to have the students ask more questions of each other in the literature circle rather than just reporting on what they think. He also makes a note that four of the students do not seem to make the connection between the boy's asking the shopkeeper for stale bread to feed the dog he has hidden away and the food that people in the community begin leaving for his father, a mail carrier. In other words, they are not making inferences. In the course of the next week, Mr. da Silva will make a point of reading with each one of these students to see what they know about reading comprehension. He will also teach a mini-lesson on making inferences during reading workshop tomorrow.

Making Sense of Literature

The goal of reading instruction is for all students to read with comprehension—understanding what they read. Comprehension in reading is also a sort of thermometer measuring the intellectual life of a classroom. True, teaching children to read with understanding is partly a matter of teaching them a special set of reading skills. But it is also a matter of exposing students to literature—both fiction and nonfiction—cultivating their knowledge about a range of subjects, stimulating their habits of inquiry, helping them make connections between ideas, and inspiring in them a broad range of interests. Researchers tell us that reading comprehension has too often been left to chance, as if understanding would happen if only children could read the words. Surveys of reading instruction in elementary schools, from thirty-five years ago (Durkin, 1978–1979) and more recently (Pressley, 1999), have found that word recognition instruction is common

Figure 7.1

What You Need to Live in a New Place

Skills You Needed in the 1880s

Both Times

Skills You Need Now

Breaking the land
Plowing the land
Growing crops
Taking care of animals
Keeping yourself well
Making a house
Making clothes
Cooking food
Storing food

Doing things for yourself

Reading and writing
Working a computer
Driving a car
Keeping house
Shopping
Keeping your children safe from crime
Cooking
Making your money last

enough, but it is rarer to find teachers trying to develop their students' comprehension. Reading comprehension is heavily stressed in state standards for literacy, and especially so in the Common Core Standards.

In this chapter, we talk about ways to help students understand narrative texts. Chapter 8 is devoted to teaching readers to understand and learn from informational text. First, we set out some ideas about reading comprehension.

Understanding Reading Comprehension

Reading comprehension has two sides to it. On one side we focus on what the reader already knows about the topic of the text, and on his or her strategies to make sense of the text. Because this side of comprehension focuses on the reader's efforts to construct knowledge, we call this the *constructivist side*. The other side of comprehension is the *textual side*. The focus here is on the ways texts convey meaning, including the nuances of vocabulary, the plot or other text structures, the author's point of view, references to other texts, and other literary devices.

Constructing Meaning: How the Reader Makes Sense of the Text

A reader is a sense-maker, one who works to construct meaning from a text. Many reading specialists' favorite explanation of how meaning construction works is schema theory, articulated many years ago by Richard Anderson and David Pearson (1984).

SCHEMA THEORY Schema theory (Anderson & Pearson, 1984) holds that readers understand what they read by finding clues in the text that lead them to summon up frameworks of stored knowledge from their memories. These frameworks of prior knowledge

 Schema theory refers to the prior knowledge that a person possesses about a topic, and it helps readers to make sense of what they are reading. How does the fifth-grade teacher in the video activate her students' schemas in order to support their comprehension of the text?

have been called *schemas*. Once readers have a schema in mind, they use it to make sense of the other details. There is a complementary relationship between readers' schemas and the details on the page. Noting the details tells them which schemas to evoke, and evoking the schemas helps them to make sense of the details. Consider the following example:

> *Shawn's footsteps slowed as he approached the door to Belinda's apartment. Two children were ahead of him, already knocking on the door. They were dressed in the proper clothing. But Shawn had on his old jeans. Shawn was also embarrassed because he was empty-handed. His mother had been at work when he got home from school, and he hadn't any money of his own.*
>
> *The door swung open, and there was Belinda in a nice dress and a party hat.*
> *"Hi," she said. "Come on in."*
> *"Hi," he said as he sidled into the apartment, his hands behind his back. Inside, the table was set for the celebration and piled high with the things other children had brought. Shawn avoided the table and slid into a corner.*
>
> *Just then, Belinda's mother shouted from the kitchen, "Get ready to sing, everybody. Here it comes!" She marched ceremoniously in from the kitchen holding forth her beautiful creation, her face brightened by the nine tiny flames.*

If you spent your childhood in the United States, you surely realized that the passage tells of a birthday party. Once you worked that out, you summoned a cognitive scheme that led you to feel Shawn's embarrassment because he hadn't worn party clothes or brought what each of the other guests had piled on the table—a birthday present. You also knew what song would be sung ("Happy birthday to you . . ."), and what it was the mother proudly carried in from the kitchen (a birthday cake with nine candles). How much of what you understood about the passage was actually supplied by the text? And how much information did you yourself supply?

The World of Reading

Reader Response in Action

Diane Barone (1992) reports on a second- and third-grade class in which the teacher was having her students record their reactions to each chapter of Roald Dahl's *Danny the Champion of the World* (1998) in a kind of response journal called a *dual-entry diary* (see pages 196–197). An early chapter in the book describes the cozy days enjoyed by Dahl's protagonist, living in a gypsy wagon with his father. After reading this chapter, a student in the class wrote that he was expecting the woman to come into the story at any time. The teacher was puzzled, because the only woman who had been mentioned in the book was the boy's late mother, who had died before he was born. But in entry after entry, her student registered his worry that the woman might come into the story on the very next page. As it turned out, this young reader had lived a cozy existence for some time alone with *his* own father—until the father found a female companion. For the little boy, the woman really did come along, and the boy no longer had an exclusive claim to his father's attention.

The boy created a poem out of *Danny the Champion of the World* that was about the almost-too-good-to-be-true bliss of a boy's living alone with his father and his feeling of dread at its loss. The boy's concerns had led him to write responses that seemed bizarre at first. Yet it serves as a good example of how stories can evoke different responses from different people, children included. Teachers need to be aware of this critical piece of information.

As the boy's reading of *Danny the Champion of the World* suggests, there can be striking variations in the interpretations or poems created by different readers. That is why David Bleich (1970) urges teachers to think of literature discussion groups as interpretive communities. *Interpretive communities* are places where readers share their responses to works of literature so that communities of understanding can be formed. The sharing of individual responses not only contributes to a larger understanding of a work, but also promotes students' awareness of each other's thinking. Becoming aware of others' thinking is of particular value when the students come from different social and cultural backgrounds.

It takes special approaches on the teacher's part to set up an interpretive community. Merely asking students to answer literal questions will not do it. Teachers need to create a risk-free environment and to conduct—or let students conduct—discussions that invite personal responses to questions such as, "What did you notice in the text? What did it make you think of? How did it make you feel?"

Schema theory is a powerful way of understanding comprehension. It shows us that students' prior knowledge, or their *schemas*—like the knowledge you just brought to the birthday party scenario—is very important to their reading comprehension. It also shows us that understanding is real activity. Readers do not passively absorb meaning from the page; they construct meaning by trying to make sense of details according to the schemas they already possess in their memories.

READER RESPONSE THEORY   Reader response theory is an explanation of what happens when individual readers make meaning from literary texts (Bleich, 1978; Iser, 1978; Rosenblatt, 1978) (see the World of Reading box). As formulated by Louise Rosenblatt, reader response theory suggests that three considerations are involved whenever a fictional text is read meaningfully: the *reader*, the *text*, and the *poem*.

The Reader   The reader brings her background knowledge to the reading. That knowledge includes the meanings she holds for words; her likes, dislikes, fascinations, and fears; her experience with works of a certain style or genre or works by a certain author; and her experiences in the world with certain people, places, and things.

The Text   The text consists of the words put on the page by the author, along with the images, if any, provided by an illustrator. It includes the design and layout of the book—or, if it is an electronic text, it can add audio, links, and other aspects of the presentation to our list of features. The text is, in short, all of the things put in front of the reader or audience to respond to.

Authors, illustrators, and designers of books and other media have a full range of artistry at their disposal in creating a text. Writers select words for their exact meanings, but also for their figurative associations and connotations, as well as their appeal to the senses. Authors create settings and characters, and they roll out events in patterns and plots, depicted from a particular perspective, narrated in a certain style and tone, all working together to drive home a theme. Illustrations may duplicate what the text says, they may show just a few aspects of what is written, or they may create irony by suggesting something very different from or even contradictory to the text.

The Poem   The *poem* is the word used for the meaning of a text that each reader constructs. Readers have knowledge of things in the world, and much of it varies from place to place, culture to culture, and age group to age group. Readers have knowledge of literature in general and some genres and authors in particular. They also have drives, concerns, and preferences. They bring all of this with them when they read a text. But there are always things they don't bring, since readers have gaps, too. They may lack relevant world knowledge, or understand little of the dynamics of literature, or have limited vocabulary. What they bring and what they do not bring to a reading will dispose them to attend to certain aspects of the text, ignore other aspects, and even supply still other aspects of their own. The particular mix of what is in the text and what the reader brings to the text is unique to each reader. And that is what is called the *poem*. (Rosenblatt is using the historical sense of the word *poem*, meaning a "created thing," not necessarily something that rhymes!)

The poem is what comes to mind when you think back on a book you have read. It is not just the author's exact words. It is not just your memories from your own life and your knowledge of word meanings and literary devices that you called to mind as you read. It is a construct that is made of both.

But here is a question: Where should we say the meaning of a particular text resides? Does a text "mean" whatever any reader thinks it means? Or does each text have a particular meaning? Scholars disagree on the answer, and tend to take positions along a spectrum between one position that affords a reader a lot of freedom to make her own meaning and the opposite position that insists there is a fixed meaning to every text that every reader should "get." The way you teach will be influenced by the position you take. If you believe in the reader's freedom to make meaning, you will ask open-ended questions and encourage alternative interpretations of a text. But if you believe a text has a fixed meaning, you

Schema Theory and Background Knowledge

Schema theory and reader response criticism both stress the importance to comprehension of what a reader already knows. But learners who come to our schools from other cultures and other parts of the world may either lack relevant background knowledge, or—what may be even more confusing—have different associations for the same referents. A wedding is a happy occasion, right? Not in some parts of India, where a bride may be bartered away by her parents into a miserable subservient role in a family of strangers. Going out to a restaurant is a pleasure, not so? Not in Morocco, where going out to a restaurant brings scorn on a family because it is assumed that the wife is too lazy to cook. Be careful to look for places in texts where culture-based background knowledge may be essential to readers' understanding, and explain that knowledge as you need to.

will encourage your students to arrive at that meaning, and you will discourage alternative interpretations.

A middle ground is to make sure the students understand the devices texts use to convey or afford meanings. Educating readers about the workings of literature will give them relevant tools to make sense of literary texts.

Textual Factors in Comprehension

Complementing the constructivist side of comprehending fiction, the other side of the issue of comprehension is what the reader should know about the ways literary texts are constructed.

LITERARY TEXTS COME IN *GENRES*   Knowing whether a text is a folktale, a fantasy, or a work of realistic fiction shapes a reader's expectations for what is likely to happen in the work—or at least it should. Readers should be aware of genres of literature and be able to explain their features and the way awareness of the genres influences what they expect to happen in a story.

CCSS
• Literature 5: Craft and Structure

LITERARY TEXTS HAVE SETTINGS, CHARACTERS, PLOTS, AND THEMES   It organizes children's expectations when they recognize that stories introduce characters in a setting. The characters have problems they try to solve and goals that they attempt to achieve over a series of events called a *plot*. The Common Core Standards express the expectation that children will recognize these elements and be able to talk about them as they discuss stories.

CCSS
• Literature 1: Key Ideas and Details

LITERARY TEXTS USE LANGUAGE IN UNIQUE WAYS   Literary texts differ from informational texts in striking ways. Literary texts use language that appeals to the senses far more than informational texts. A children's book or poem regularly uses words that suggest sights, sounds, and feelings. Poetry uses words that have sensory qualities—words may be chosen because their sounds reinforce the message being conveyed. Literary writing has distinctive tones: It may be comical, somber, suspenseful, or lyrical, and the choice of words and length and rhythm of sentences all contribute to the tone. Literary language can be both literal (saying things directly) or figurative (saying things by association). It often uses comparisons—similes and metaphors. Finally, although literary texts may tell truths—as in lessons about the human experience—their details do not reliably relate directly to reality. From reading the *Harry Potter* books you can learn truths about destiny, the conflict between good and evil, and the power and limitations of friendship, but you can't use the books as a roadmap that will lead you to an actual Hogwarts School.

Acts of Comprehension

What are key strategies and skills that children and other readers use to comprehend text? Researchers have agreed on several. This list, derived from Pressley and Afflerbach (1995), captures the issue nicely. Comprehending a passage well involves the following:

Engaging prior knowledge

Knowing vocabulary

Visualizing details and events

Following the patterns of texts

Asking questions and pursuing answers

Making inferences

Monitoring comprehension

Noting main ideas from supporting details

Summarizing and rehearsing main ideas

ENGAGING PRIOR KNOWLEDGE   When they begin to read, good readers focus on the topic of the text, decide what they already know about it, and make predictions about what they are likely to learn. As they read, they go back and forth between what they knew about the topic and what they are finding out. When they are finished reading, they might reexamine what they knew or thought they knew and take note of how their knowledge has changed on account of the reading they have done. Not all readers do this fully developed version of engaging prior knowledge and checking new information against it, but readers should at least sense the topic of the reading and be reminded of what they already know about it.

Families can support children's development of comprehension by keeping up their contributions to children's background knowledge and supporting children's voluntary reading. Teachers can remind parents of the importance of taking their children to the library and museums and of putting informative children's magazines on their children's gift lists. *Ranger Rick* <www.nwf.org/rangerrick/index.html>, the nature magazine, features enticing photographs of animals in the wild and articles on wildlife that fascinate children ages seven and up. *Cobblestone* magazine <www.cobblestonepub.com> features interesting articles on historical topics that appeal to children ages nine and up. *National Geographic World* <www.nationalgeographic.com> features highly illustrated articles on everything from undersea exploration to mountain climbing, and *Sports Illustrated for Kids* <www.sikids.com> follows teams and players and talks about the basics of the sports.

For general reading, including stories to read, *Cricket* magazine <www.cricketmag .com> for children ages eight and up and *Ladybug* for slightly younger children feature work that makes good reading by well-known and aspiring children's authors. *Highlights for Children* <www.highlights.com> also features stories and interesting informational articles, as well as riddles and games.

VISUALIZING DETAILS AND EVENTS   In creating works of fiction, authors take pains to describe events so the reader can visualize them and be drawn into the scene, or in Langer's term, "step into the envisionment." Here is the beginning of Frances Temple's (1996) *The Beduins' Gazelle*:

> *Halima sat with her chin resting on her knees, close enough to touch her kinspeople, yet with her mind far away. The singsong of the storyteller's voice lulled her. The lanterns threw a soft glow on the dark wall of the tent, on the red and brown embroidered cushions, on the familiar faces of the listening women and children. Halima played with her bangles, her mind drifting with the story.* (p. 1)

The author's appeals to sights, sounds, and touch lead a competent reader to create an image of the scene in a Bedouin's tent in North Africa, where the events of the novel will soon unfold.

Family Literacy

How can families support children's development of comprehension?

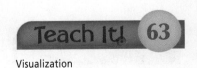

Visualization

For English Language Learners

New Literacies

How is the structure of a Web site different from the structure of an article?

KNOWING VOCABULARY   Knowing the words in a text is an issue both in word recognition and in comprehension. As an aspect of comprehension, vocabulary items can be considered building blocks of understanding. It is possible to understand a text without knowing all the words, by making inferences from the context surrounding the unknown word. But making such inferences ties up concentration that might otherwise be used to comprehend the larger meaning of the text. Whether by making important information unavailable or by distracting attention, a shortage of vocabulary makes comprehension harder. A good reader has a vocabulary available that is nearly equal to the vocabulary she or he encounters in reading.

FOLLOWING THE PATTERNS OF TEXTS   Texts come to us in genres, which are a combination of purpose and pattern. The narrative or story genre, for instance, has the purpose of relating fictional events in an entertaining or edifying way that usually evokes an emotional response. Stories follow structures or patterns called *story grammars*. A story usually introduces a main character and other characters in a setting and engages that character in an initiating event that leads the character to set a goal; then there might follow a series of episodes in which the character makes attempts to reach the goal. Each attempt has an outcome, and then follows a consequence, the state of affairs at the end of the story (Stein & Glenn, 1979). As we discussed in Chapter 3, research and experience have shown that even by the time they are in first grade, listeners and readers use their knowledge of story grammar both to understand and to produce their own stories.

Of course, texts have other kinds of structures, too. Patterns such as lists, taxonomies (hierarchical lists), descriptions, comparisons, and cause-and-effect and problem-and-solution explanations guide readers' understanding. Persuasive essays use the structure of claims, reasons for the claims, and evidence to support the reasons.

Text on the Internet has a sort of concatenated structure; that is, items are linked to other items, as in a chain or a web. Readers can click on a term within an entry and be taken at once to a new entry that explains the term. While reading the new entry, readers might be invited to click on another term within that entry and be taken to a new entry explaining that term. So an entry on mammals might allow readers to click and go to an explanatory entry about elephants. There they might be invited to click and go to another entry or even a whole new Web site on Tanzania because that country is home to many elephants. The challenge to the reader, of course, is to keep in mind the topic of the original search and the questions that guided that search.

Reading by the pattern can help to guide the reader's understanding below the surface events toward the deeper logical structure of the text. Readers who know how to follow the patterns of text when they read learn to raise questions and search for answers according to the way the text reveals its contents. When they are reading a story, readers can identify the problem that the character has and try to anticipate the solution to the problem. When they are reading a problem-and-solution explanation, readers can identify the problem and look for solutions.

Teach It! 40

Story Maps

Teach It! 31

Directed Reading-Teaching Activity

ASKING QUESTIONS AND PURSUING ANSWERS   As they come up with ideas related to the topic of the text, good readers make predictions about what they will find out.

For English Language Learners

Text Patterns Differ by Culture

The stories most often read in the United States and Canada have predictable plot structures: A character has a problem, and the whole story is a series of attempts to solve the problem and reach a resolution. Such patterns are less common in the books children read in Argentina, or even France—where the goal of the writer is to be wildly imaginative—and predictability is considered a failing. North American children's literature often features realistic fiction—stories about children who might have once lived, even though they were invented by authors. But realistic fiction for children—like literature of any kind for children, for that matter—is rare in most of the world. Books that are popular with children in North America are rarely didactic; that is, they don't overtly teach moral lessons, and if there are lessons to be learned, it is left to the reader to infer them. Stories for children in most of the world, though, far more often do teach moral lessons, and these lessons are stated explicitly, so there is little room for children to make inferences. To comprehend the books they are presented in American schools requires that readers from other cultures come to know the rules of the game those books are playing. Otherwise, our books may be as baffling to English language learners as a game of rugby is to an American football player or a game of cricket to a baseball player.

Then they monitor what they are learning from the text to see whether those predictions are being confirmed. When good readers read a story, they can follow the outlines of the plot to generate predictions and experience satisfaction or surprise as those predictions are confirmed or refuted by what happens. In fact, authors count on readers' acts of prediction to evoke emotional experiences of suspense, surprise, and completion as patterns of events raise expectations and sometimes thwart and sometimes satisfy them.

MAKING INFERENCES   When readers have to work out for themselves information that is not directly supplied by the text, they are making inferences. Fiction writers often leave gaps in the text (Iser, 1974) that must be filled in by the reader's inferences, and readers experience the activity as engagement. Even young readers make inferences. For example, kindergarten children enjoy listening to Harry Allard and James Marshall's ever-popular picture book *Miss Nelson Is Missing* (1977), about a too-sweet school teacher who is replaced by a very mean substitute teacher. Most young children, but not all, can infer the substitute teacher's identity from the next-to-the-last page of the book. There, the illustration shows (but the text does not mention) an ugly black dress hanging in the sweet teacher's closet underneath a box with the word WIG written in upside-down letters.

Struggling Reader

How can we help struggling readers read with comprehension?

MONITORING COMPREHENSION   Good readers are aware when a text is making sense, and they realize when it does not. Perhaps they misread a word, or they assumed the text was going to say something that it does not. Then the breakdown in their comprehension leads them to go back and make a "repair." They reread the misinterpreted word or reconsider where the argument is going so that they again have the feeling they are understanding the text. Comprehension monitoring, then, assumes that readers think on two planes: They think about what the text means, and they are also aware of their own understanding or lack of it.

In the case of fictional or poetic texts in which there is figurative language or symbols, or irony to be navigated, the reader has more interpreting to do.

NOTING MAIN IDEAS AND SUPPORTING DETAILS   Readers who are aware of the argument of the text can distinguish main ideas from small details. Consider, for example, a child reading this passage from *Charlotte's Web*:

> *On foggy mornings, Charlotte's web was truly a thing of beauty. This morning each strand was decorated with dozens of tiny beads of water. The web glistened in the light and made*

a pattern of loveliness and mystery, like a delicate veil. Even Lurvy, who wasn't particularly interested in beauty, noticed the web when he came with the pig's breakfast. He noted how clearly it showed up and he noted how big and carefully built it was. And then he took another look and saw something that made him set his pail down. There in the center of the web, neatly woven in block letters, was a message. It said:

    SOME PIG!

Lurvy felt weak. He brushed his hand across his eyes and stared harder at Charlotte's web.
(White, 1952/1980, p. 77)

There are many details in this passage about the way the spider's web looked. But a reader who gets the main idea will focus on the fact that the spider has written words, they describe her friend Wilbur the pig, and they have been noticed with great surprise by Lurvy, the farmhand. The child who has been following the plot of the story will realize that Charlotte's writing is a possible solution to the main problem of the book because it is meant to impress Wilbur's human owners so they will spare the little pig's life.

Readers who distinguish main ideas do so by following the argument of the text. They understand the problems the text is setting out to solve, and they are aware when information is significant as answers to questions or solutions to problems posed by the text: Such information is a main idea.

SUMMARIZING AND REHEARSING MAIN IDEAS Once they identify main ideas, good readers might slow down, reread the passage that contained them, and rehearse the ideas so that they will remember them later (Pressley & Afflerbach, 1995). Following the reading, the readers might retell the main ideas to themselves, or they might reread important passages aloud to a friend. Good readers might reread the key passages in the text to make sure the main ideas were stated the way they remembered them. In this way, good readers hope to store the main ideas in memory and learn from the reading.

Scaffolding: From Strategies to Skills

Once you are aware of the component abilities that make for reading comprehension, you can deliberately and overtly teach readers to use those strategies until they become internalized, that is, until they become skills (Duffy & Roehler, 1989).

Skilled and struggling readers use the same processes to read with comprehension that we just described. But struggling readers might need more support to make sure they use all of these strategies and orchestrate them into fluent reading with comprehension. Kame'enui (1998) recommends that teachers of struggling readers employ these steps:

Story Maps

1. **Make strategies explicit.** Through modeling, think-alouds, and regular reminding, show students how to carry out each of the comprehension strategies described in the previous sections.

2. **Supply scaffolding.** Scaffolding is temporary support for students as they learn to do a task or apply a skill. Scaffolding may be used for a short time and then withdrawn when students can function independently. An example of scaffolding is a story map, in which students are asked to identify the character, setting, problem, and solution in a story they are reading (see Figure 7.4 on page 205).

3. **Connect ideas.** Remind students of ideas they find in a text they have seen on a field trip or in a lesson in another subject. Struggling readers might be so preoccupied by the act of making sense of what they read that they do not think about the larger ideas. They need the teacher to point out to them the relatedness of ideas.

4. **Provide background knowledge.** Struggling readers might not have the background knowledge they need to make sense of what they read. A story about an early twentieth-century immigrant's journey from Europe to America will make little sense to a student who does not realize that Europe is a continent that lies

thousands of miles across the ocean from America or that until not long ago, travel from Europe was so difficult and expensive that people who made the trip could not go back.

5. *Review skills and ideas often.* Struggling readers need to be reminded of both the skills they have learned and the ideas they have gained. And they need to apply these abilities and ideas in new settings.

Teaching for Comprehension

Teaching for comprehension and response is not just a matter of teaching skills. Although it is important to develop children's reading strategies and to support these strategies until they become skills, it is also essential to develop children's familiarity with literature as well as their knowledge and interests. In the pages that follow we present several methods and strategies for teaching reading comprehension and response to text.

Organizing Instruction for Comprehension and Response: The ABC Model

Children should have many opportunities to read for meaning and for pleasure in personally chosen books that are not used for instruction by the teacher (Block & Pressley, 2001). Children should also have lessons in which the teacher guides them through aspects of comprehension so that they will internalize those aspects and practice them when they are reading independently. Teaching comprehension successfully requires that teachers engage students' thinking and invite students to keep their minds appropriately active throughout the reading process. The ABC model offers instructional choices for guiding comprehension—for activities to be used before reading (in the *a*nticipation phase), during reading (in the phase of *b*uilding knowledge), and after reading (in the phase of *c*onsolidation) after Vaughn and Estes (1986) and Steele and Meredith (1997). The ABC model is flexible. Within its three parts or phases, the teacher can make many choices. So, eventually, can the students, because they need to internalize the pattern of thinking captured by this model and use it when they read independently.

STRATEGIES FOR THE ANTICIPATION PHASE   Before they read, students should think about the topic, then recall their prior knowledge about it. If they don't have very much prior knowledge about the subject or if their thoughts about it are disorganized, the teacher might want to spend some time telling the students more about the topic and organizing their thinking about it. Readers should wonder how their present knowledge about the topic might relate to the text they are about to read. If they are to read an informational text, what do they still want to know about the topic that they might learn from this text? If it is a fictional text, what other works do they know by this author or in this genre? What does their prior knowledge lead them to expect from this reading? This preliminary phase of the lesson is what we call the *anticipation phase*.

Teaching goals in the anticipation phase are to prepare the students to read with comprehension. We want them to do the following:

- Connect the topic (or the genre, or the author) of the text they are about to read with their prior knowledge.
- Raise questions about the text they are about to read and set purposes for reading.
- Know the vocabulary they will need to make sense of the text.

Several teaching approaches can be used to achieve these goals.

How does the think/pair/share activity encourage anticipatory reading?

Focusing Questions   Questions that make a connection between what the students already know and what the reading will cover are valuable ways to prepare for a reading. In keeping with the goal of encouraging principled knowledge, it is advisable to steer questions toward the main ideas of the passage.

For example, a group of fifth graders are reading Pam Conrad's *Pedro's Journal* (1992), a fictional account of Columbus's historic voyage. Before the students begin reading the first chapter, the teacher asks, "If you were about to sail three ships across the Atlantic Ocean in 1492, at a time when nobody knew for sure what was on the other side of the ocean, what three pieces of advice would you give yourself?"

The students might discuss the question as a whole group, or using the think/pair/share procedure (see below). Doing so activates thoughts and ideas that will help them make sense of and appreciate what they will encounter as they read the book.

Think/Pair/Share   Focusing questions can be still more effective when a mechanism has been provided for all students to consider and answer them. Think/pair/share (Kagan, 1997) is a cooperative learning activity in which the teacher puts an open-ended question to the class, preferably by writing it on the board. Children are given two minutes to respond to the question individually. (Often they are asked to do this in writing.) Next, each child turns to a partner, and they share their answers with each other. Finally, the teacher calls on two or three pairs to share their answers with the class. Then the class begins reading the text. In a think/pair/share activity, every student—even in a class of 30 or more students—is motivated to think about the topic and to discuss it with someone else.

Anticipation Guide   Anticipation guides are used with fiction or with informational text. In using an anticipation guide (Vaughn & Estes, 1986), the teacher prepares a set of questions with short answers (usually true/false answers) that tap important aspects of the topic of the text. The questions are distributed to children on a worksheet, and the children are asked, individually or in pairs, to answer the questions as best they can before reading the assigned text. After reading the text, they return to the questions at the end of the class to see how their thinking has changed. Figure 7.2 provides an example of an anticipation guide.

Paired Brainstorming   When factual information will be shared, older students can be asked to make personal lists of the facts they know or think they know about the topic of the reading (Vacca & Vacca, 1986). After two minutes, they turn to a classmate and combine their lists. The teacher can make a master list of the class's ideas and post them on the board or on a piece of newsprint so that the students can compare them with the ideas they have after they have read the text.

Figure 7.2
Anticipation Guide for *Pedro's Journal*

Instructions: Before reading *Pedro's Journal*, answer these questions *true* or *false* on the left-hand side. After reading the book, enter new answers on the right-hand side.

Answer Before   *Answer After*

_____   1. Columbus was well liked by his crew.   _____

_____   2. Columbus prepared his ships to sail in front of the wind.   _____

_____   3. Columbus's captains were very loyal to him.   _____

_____   4. The first people Columbus met lived in a city.   _____

_____   5. Columbus was very respectful of the people he met.   _____

_____   6. Columbus seemed very interested in finding gold.   _____

Terms in Advance   A teacher may display a set of key terms that will be found in a reading and ask students to ponder their meanings as well as the relationships between the terms. The students are asked to predict how this particular set of terms might be used in the passage they are about to read. For example, if they are going to read *Miss Nelson Is Missing*, the terms might be as follows:

kind teacher	*mean substitute*	*police inspector*	*return*
misbehave	*make faces*	*homework*	*disguise*

STRATEGIES FOR THE BUILDING KNOWLEDGE PHASE   Once students have had their expectations raised for what they are about to read, they are ready for activities that will help them construct meaning from the text or build their knowledge. As they read, students need to compare their expectations with what they are learning from the text. They should be able to revise their expectations or generate new ones as the text reveals more information, raises more questions, or plants more clues. They also need to think about what they are reading and be able to identify the main points. They will need to reflect on what the text means to them personally and fill in any blanks in the text—that is, to make inferences about what the text says. Finally, they should be able to question the text, to argue with it. We call this phase of the lesson *building knowledge*. Several strategies for helping students to build knowledge are described next.

In the video, an expert shares research-based strategies that are recommended by the National Reading Panel to support students' reading comprehension. Which strategies do you personally find useful when reading difficult texts?

Think-Alouds   A think-aloud is an activity in which a skilled reader reads aloud a passage of text and talks through her cognitive processes as she makes sense of the text. Think-alouds are patterned after coaching in sports, or the teaching of a craft. When a basketball coach teaches dribbling and shooting, she gathers the players around and then shows them how she dribbles and shoots. Then she guides and corrects them as they practice doing the same thing. When a potter shows apprentices how to throw down the clay at the center of the wheel, poke her thumbs into the whirling mass and pull up the sides, she does that many times in front of the students. Then she guides and critiques their practice. The same technique of offering demonstrations and then guiding students' practice can be used in teaching reading with comprehension, too, as a teacher reads a page out loud to a group of students and then verbalizes what is going through his mind, phrase by phrase. Think-alouds work best when the teacher is well prepared. Since the purpose of a think-aloud is to describe processes that are carried out automatically and unconsciously, it is not easy to find words for these processes. It is advisable to (1) choose in advance the passages to use for think-alouds, (2) determine the comprehension processes that the children still need to understand, and (3) practice in advance how you will explain those processes.

Readers' Workshop   A readers' workshop combines a think-aloud with guided practice. The teacher typically begins with a brief demonstration of a skill in comprehension or other type of skill. The demonstration is followed by a discussion of the skill, with the goal of making the students able to verbalize the strategy that the teacher has used; for example, finding a main idea and the details that support it, making judgments about a character from the details that are provided, or deciding on the meaning of a phrase of figurative language. The teacher then asks individual students or pairs of students to read a passage or section of text aloud, using the newly taught skill. The students may read for self-selected books, and older students may keep a journal of their responses as they read. The teacher monitors their reading, and, as the students present to the others what they have read and how they responded, the teacher discusses with the students their success in using the skill.

Guided Reading   The guided reading procedure (Fountas & Pinnell, 1999) provides an excellent opportunity to teach comprehension. Guided reading proceeds in three steps.

1. ***Prepare the children to read with understanding.*** Begin with some of the following preliminary activities.

Teach It!   9

Guided Reading

A teacher using Guided Reading support as students read.

"Word Conversations" for Primary Grades

Know-Want to Know-Learn (K-W-L)

Save the Last Word for Me

- *Preview the text.* Show them the cover illustration, the title, and some of the pictures inside. "Think aloud" and speculate on what the text might be about. You may discuss the author and the kinds of books she or he writes.
- *Introduce the genre.* Whether the book is a folktale, a biography, a tall tale, or a work of realistic fiction, you may expect different things to happen in the text.
- *Go over vocabulary.* Tell the students that they will meet some interesting words in this text. Name them one at a time. If the schedule allows, do a *word conversation* to introduce each word.
- *Teach other skills.* Depending on your objectives for this lesson, teach a brief focused lesson on the skills you want the students to practice. For example, if you want the students to pay attention to the plot of the story, you can prepare them to fill out a *story map* (see pages 205–206), such as the one found in Figure 7.4 on page 205. Show the whole group how to fill out a story map, and later have them fill out a story map themselves after they have read the story.
- *Read the story to them.* If the story is challenging for some of the students, you may choose to read it aloud to them first. If you have a big book version of the text available, they can read along with you.
- *Begin a K-W-L* (Know-Want to Know-Learn—see pages 236–242), a *DRA* (Directed Reading Activity—see pages 195–196), or a *DRTA* (Directed Reading-Thinking Activity—see page 196). Comprehension strategies that ask children to discuss what they know and what they think they will find out can be introduced now.

2. *The students read the text.* The students may read the text on their own or in pairs. A number of useful strategies for having them read with a purpose are found in the section called "Building Knowledge" later in this chapter.
   - *If you are conducting a DRA, a DRTA, or a K-W-L,* they read to an assigned stopping place and have questions to guide their search for information.
   - They may *buddy read,* that is, take turns reading paragraphs or pages.
   - They may use the *Paired Reading/Paired Summarizing* technique (Crawford et al., 2005). That is, one student reads a paragraph aloud and summarizes it. The other student asks questions about the passage that both answer. Then they change roles with the next paragraph, and so on.
   - They may read with *text coding* (Crawford et al., 2005). That is, the teacher helps students think of a set of four to six questions or issues they wish to track as they read the text. For example, if they are reading a passage about acid rain, they may be asked to look for passages that say where it occurs (W), others that say what its sources are (S), others that describe the chemical reactions that make it happen (CR), others that talk about the damage it does (D), and still others that talk about possible preventions of the problem (P). As they read, the students pencil in the letter indicating which kind of information they have found.

3. *The group reviews what they have learned.* After the students have read the text, the teacher brings them back together to discuss the text and to consolidate what they have learned.
   - *Discussions can use many of the formats described in this chapter.* These methods include Sketch-to-Stretch, shared inquiry, dual-entry diaries, Save the Last Word for Me, and dramatization.
   - *Revisiting the skills you introduced.* Assuming you began the lesson with certain skills in mind—understanding characterization, following the plot, getting the main idea, and so on—you will revisit those skills now. Have the students or pairs of students explain how they read and what they discovered, and make sure everyone understands and can carry out the practice you introduced.

Questioning the Author   The Questioning-the-Author technique, designed by Isabel Beck and her colleagues (Beck et al., 1997), rests on the realization that readers sometimes fail to understand what they read, not because they are incompetent, but because the authors haven't made their meaning sufficiently clear. When students listen to their peers reading their works aloud in a writing workshop, they don't hesitate to say, "I don't know what you mean right there. Help me understand." Yet when young readers come across unclear passages in a published text, they often assume that the problem is theirs for not understanding, rather than the author's for not writing clearly. This focused reading technique encourages students to question what they don't understand in a text.

To prepare to conduct the Questioning-the-Author procedure, choose a portion of texts that will support an engaged discussion of 20 to 30 minutes. Read through the text in advance and identify the major concepts that the students should glean from the text. Plan frequent stopping points in the text to devote attention to the important ideas and inferences in the passage. Write some probing questions to be asked at each stopping point to motivate discussion.

Conducting the Questioning-the-Author lesson then proceeds in two stages:

Stage 1. Preparing the Students' Attitudes. Begin the discussion by reminding students that comprehension often breaks down because authors don't tell readers everything they need to know. Things may be unclear. Ideas may have been omitted or hinted at but not stated. A good way to comprehend is to think of questions you would ask the author if she or he were present and imagine what the answers might be. Because the author is not present in the classroom, the class will attempt to answer for the author.

Stage 2. Raising Questions About the Text. Now have the students read a small portion of the text. At a preselected stopping point, pose a question or query about what the students have just read. Early in the text, initiating queries might be:

- What is the author trying to say here?
- What is the author's message?
- What is the author talking about?

Later in the text, follow-up queries might include:

- So what does the author mean right here?
- Did the author explain that clearly?
- Does that make sense with what the author told us before?
- How does that connect with what the author has told us here?
- But does the author tell us why?
- Why do you think the author tells us that now? (from Beck et al., 1997)

As you ask these questions, ask several students to contribute ideas. Prod the students to clarify their thoughts, to elaborate on their ideas, to debate each other's ideas, and to reach a consensus opinion.

The Directed Reading Activity   In the Directed Reading Activity, a teacher poses a question to the students before they read a section of the story, and asks them to read the section to find the answer. The teacher's questions are meant to guide the students' attention to the important part of the story. An early question might ask about the setting. Another might ask about the main characters and the problem they face. Another might ask about the characters' attempts to solve the problem. And another might ask about the outcome of those attempts and their consequences—how things turn out for the characters in the end.

Questions can address more subtle features of the text, too, as asking students to identify the way the author lets you know what kind of person a character is, or to explain how an author foreshadows something that will happen later, or to infer what a character's motives are or how one character feels about another.

In a single day's reading, the teacher usually breaks the text into about five sections, and will choose the stopping points in advance. More stops may break up the flow of the story, but fewer stops may not direct the students' attention to all of the important places in the story.

Once students gain skills at identifying characters, their main problems, and their efforts to solve them, they may be ready to move on to the Directed Reading-Thinking Activity (see below). Many teachers continue to use the Directed Reading Activity, however, in order to help students develop key aspects of comprehension.

Directed Reading-Thinking Activity

The Directed Reading-Thinking Activity The Directed Reading-Thinking Activity (Stauffer, 1975), or DRTA, uses the dynamic of prediction and confirmation to create interest and excitement around a reading assignment, provided the text is a work of fiction with something of a predictable structure. The DRTA is normally done with a group of six to ten students; this size is large enough to yield a range of predictions but small enough for everyone to participate. It is advisable that the students be roughly matched for reading ability, because all students must wait for the slowest one to finish reading each section.

The DRTA can be used by itself, or it can follow one of the activities we introduced in the anticipation phase. Some teachers precede the DRTA with the terms-in-advance procedure or with the anticipation guide.

The teacher prepares for a DRTA by choosing four or five stopping places in the text, yielding more or less same-sized chunks of text. The stops should be placed right at points of suspense, places where the reader has been given some information and is wondering what is going to happen next (in other words, where the commercial break would be placed in a television thriller). One of these is normally right after the title. The Teach It! box demonstrates the DRTA process.

In a DRTA, the questions are worded in an open-ended way. The teacher asks, "What do you think will happen? Why do you think so?" More specific questions from the teacher would take some of the initiative for making predictions away from the children, and the point here is for children to learn to ask their own questions about what they are reading.

There are a number of ways to scaffold a DRTA to make it more accessible to students. One is to read the text aloud instead of having the students read it. This variation of the method goes by a different name: the directed listening-thinking activity. Another is to think aloud yourself. If the predictions are slow in coming or seem to be going too wide of the mark, the teacher can offer a choice. For *Miss Nelson Is Missing*, the teacher might say, "I'm wondering if Miss Nelson has gone away to teach in another school where the kids are better behaved, or if she'll come back to her same class. Which one do you all think will happen?" Finally, in third grade and above, instead of a teacher-directed activity, a DRTA can be done by individual students or pairs of students.

STRATEGIES FOR THE CONSOLIDATION PHASE By the time they enter the consolidation phase, the students have gone through the text and have begun to comprehend it. They need to go further, though, and apply the meaning in order to convert it into useable knowledge. They need to summarize it and be able to interpret and debate the meaning while applying it to new situations and creating new examples of it.

Students need to practice higher-order thinking with the issues from the text. After they read, students should be able to think back over the material and summarize the main ideas. They should compare what they found out with what they thought about the subject when they first approached the reading. If the ideas are not transparent, students should be able to interpret them. If the text is evocative in some way, students might be able to make personal responses to the ideas, such as applying them to the way they normally think or to the realities of their own lives. Students should also be able to test out the ideas—using them to solve problems or think up other solutions to the problems posed in the text.

Dual-Entry Diary

Dual-Entry Diary The dual-entry diary (Berthoff, 1981) is a kind of journal students use to record responses to readings. To make a dual-entry diary, the students draw a vertical

Teach It!

Refer to the Teach It! appendix at the end of the book for further activities you can use to reinforce concepts discussed in this chapter.

Conducting a DRTA

The directed reading-thinking activity is a sound strategy for helping students build knowledge as it helps create interest and excitement around a reading assignment. Following are the steps in a DRTA:

1. Tell the students that you are about to read a story together, using the method of prediction. The activity should be enjoyable, but it is necessary that they follow your instructions closely. You will tell them to make predictions about what they are going to read. Then you will have them read short passages of the text and stop. It is very important that they stop reading where you tell them to and not read ahead until asked.

2. Tell the students the genre of the story: realistic fiction, tall tale, folktale, etc. After naming the genre, ask them what kinds of characters they expect to meet. Ask what kinds of events they expect to happen.

3. Read the title, and show the students the accompanying picture, if there is one. Ask them what they think will happen. Remind them that it will not be possible to know for sure, but ask them to stretch their imaginations and take a guess. Press for the most specific answers you can get. Write some of these on the board. (Remember to leave room to write three more rounds of comments.)

4. Before the students read on, ask them to consider the predictions they have heard and silently choose the one they think is most likely to happen. Then ask them to keep their predictions in mind as they read to the next stopping place.

5. Now they should read (silently) to the stopping place and turn their books over when they have finished.

6. At the stopping place, review several of the predictions and ask the class whether the predictions are seeming to be borne out by the text or contradicted. Ask for proof from the text: Which predictions are coming true? What evidence do the students find in the text that makes them think so? You can put check marks on the board next to the predictions that are coming true, minuses next to those that are not, and question marks beside those that are uncertain. Ask the students how things look now in the story.

7. After some discussion, ask the students to make more predictions, choose the most likely ones, and read ahead as in step 4.

8. When the students have reached the end of the story, review the predictions, and ask the students what it was that made them guess what turned out to be the correct predictions. What was it about the characters, the plot, or the genre of the story that helped to guide their predictions?

CCSS

Common Core Standards for Discussing Literature

The Common Core Standards treat students' ability to participate in a discussion of literature as a language skill rather than an aspect of their reading comprehension (CCSS Speaking and Listening: Comprehension and Collaboration, Standards 1, 2, and 3), which means that a single lesson will have objectives for developing students' comprehension of a text and other objectives for helping them learn to discuss ideas from the text. The teaching strategies that follow in this section are useful for developing students' ability to participate in discussions of literature.

line down the middle of a blank sheet of paper. On the left-hand side, they write a passage or draw an image from the text that affected them strongly. Perhaps it reminded them of something from their own experience. Perhaps it puzzled them. Perhaps they disagreed with it. Perhaps it made them aware of the author's style or technique.

On the right-hand side of the page, they write a comment about that passage: What was it about the quote or image that made them choose it? What did it make them think of? What question did they have about it?

There are a number of ways in which these journals may be treated next. Students can exchange them and comment on each other's quotes. The teacher can take them up (a few each day) and comment on them. Or the children can bring them to a discussion group in which they are reading a common book and offer their comments to the discussion.

Save the Last Word for Me   Save the Last Word for Me (Short, Harste, & Burke, 1996) provides a framework for a small-group or whole-class discussion of a text. The procedure is especially good for encouraging children to take the lead in discussing their reading. The steps of the strategy are as follows:

1. After being assigned a reading to do independently, students are given note cards and asked to find three or four quotations they consider particularly interesting or worthy of comment.
2. The students write the quotations they have found on the note cards.
3. On the other sides of the cards, the students write comments about their chosen quotations. That is, they say what the quotations made them think of, what is surprising about the quotations, and why they chose them.
4. The students bring their quotation cards to discussion groups. The teacher calls on someone to read a card aloud.
5. After reading the quotation on his or her card, the student invites other students to comment on that quotation. (The teacher might need to help keep comments on the subject of the quotation.) The teacher also may comment on the quotation.
6. Once others have had their say about the quotation, the student who chose it reads his or her comments aloud. Then there can be no further discussion. The student who chose it gets to have the last word.
7. That student can now call on another student to share his or her quotation and begin the process all over again. Not all students will be able to share their quotations if the whole class takes part in the activity, so the teacher will need to keep track of who shared quotes and make sure other children get chances to share their quotes the next time.

The students in the video are engaged in literature circles. What strategies does the teacher use to prepare her students to successfully engage in their literature circles?

CCSS

• Literature 1 and 2: Key Ideas and Details

Literature Circles   *Literature circles* (Short & Kauffman, 1995), *grand conversations* (Eeds & Wells, 1989), and *book clubs* (Raphael et al., 1995) are all terms for literary discussions in which students' curiosity about the text is allowed to play a directing role.

Students in such discussions typically have read the same work; that work might be a short text they have already read or heard, or it might be a longer work that is discussed while students are still in the middle of it. The choice of texts for literature circles is critical because not all works are equally successful in evoking interested responses. Those that do often have a core mystery, elements that invite more than one interpretation, and a clear connection to issues that matter to the students.

These discussion groups may at first be conducted with the whole class at once until students have grown familiar and comfortable with the procedure. Then they may be conducted in smaller groups of four or five students meeting simultaneously. Literature circles are conducted several times a week. Early in the year, they might last no more than 20 minutes, but as students gain experience and confidence

Literature circles can result in fascinating discussions.

talking about literature, they might run for up to 40 minutes, not counting the time it takes to read the text. Everyone is free to offer comments and questions in literature circles, and students are reminded that they are free to address their comments and questions to other students and not always to the teacher.

The role of the teacher in a literature circle is mainly to be a spirited participant; however, Martinez (in Temple et al., 2013) points to four additional roles teachers play:

1. *The teacher is a model.* The teacher might venture her or his own questions or responses to get a discussion going. The teacher is careful to speak as one seeking

Common Core Standards and Vocabulary for Literary Discussions

As part of the comprehension of literature, the Common Core Standards include having vocabulary to discuss characters and their feelings and motives, settings, and actions (CCSS, Comprehending Literature: Key Ideas and Details, Standards 2 and 3). Students should also have control of literary terms, so that they can talk about an author's craft (CCSS, Comprehending Literature: Craft and Structure, Standard 5). Teachers should be careful to model and also explicitly teach the words students will need in order to discuss stories from the inside out (as if the characters were real people and the events actually happened) and from the outside in (as if they were writers and were interested in the way the author created the work).

insights and not as a lecturer. The teacher's statements might begin, "I wonder about . . ."

2. ***The teacher helps students learn new roles in a literature circle.*** Although all students know how to have conversations, they might need reminding of ways to participate in conversations in a classroom. These include rules such as the following:
    - Sit in a circle so that everyone can see each other.
    - Only one person speaks at a time.
    - Listen to each other.
    - Stay on the topic.

3. ***The teacher moves the conversation forward.*** Without dominating the discussion, the teacher might invite other students to comment on something one student has said. The teacher might ask a student to clarify an idea. Or the teacher might pose an interesting open-ended question that she or he has thought about in advance. (Such interpretive questions are discussed in the section on shared inquiry later.)

4. ***The teacher supports literary learning.*** Lecturing about literature is not an adequate substitute for having students think and talk about it; nonetheless, it helps if teachers supply students with concepts and terms they can use to give form to ideas they are trying to express or insights they are struggling to grasp. A student might notice that there is a point in a story where tension is highest because the main question in the story is about to be answered. The teacher tells the student that this is a *climax*. Researchers have noted that students' discussions go deeper when they have literary terms available to them (Hickman, 1979, 1981).

When conducting cooperative learning activities, the teacher might need to assign students particular roles to play in a group. Over time, when individual students learn to play the many roles of encourager, timekeeper, facilitator, recorder, and summarizer, they eventually learn all of the aspects of a good participant in a group because a good participant may practice most of these roles at once.

Literature circles often function better when students have particular roles to play. Also, by performing designated roles, students may exercise the many tasks that are carried out by an effective reader and discussant of literature. Table 7.1 outlines roles that students may play in a literary discussion (Daniels, 1994, 2001).

Five suggestions make the use of these roles more successful:

1. Teach the roles to the whole class, one at a time. The teacher might read or tell a story, then introduce one of the roles—for example, the connector. The teacher might then call attention to a connection between something in the text and something in real life. Then the teacher will invite several students to do likewise. Over several days, many of the roles can be introduced in this way before students use them in an extended discussion.

Table 7.1   Roles in a Literary Discussion Group

- *Quotation finder:* This student's job is to pick a few special sections of the text that the group would like to hear read aloud.
- *Investigator:* This student's job is to provide background information on any topic related to the text.
- *Travel tracer:* When characters move from place to place in a text, this student's job is to keep track of their movements.
- *Connector:* This student's job is to find connections between the text and the world outside.
- *Question asker:* This student's job is to write down (in advance of the discussion) questions for the group to talk about—questions he or she would like to discuss with the others.
- *Word finder:* This student's job is to find interesting, puzzling, important, or new words to bring to the group's attention and discuss.
- *Checker:* This student's job is to help people in the group do their work well by staying on the topic, taking turns, participating happily, and working within time limits.
- *Character interpreter:* This student's job is to think carefully about the characters and to discuss what they are like with the other students.
- *Illustrator:* This student's job is to draw pictures of important characters, settings, or actions so that the other students may discuss the pictures.
- *Recorder:* This student's job is to take brief notes on the main points raised in the discussion.
- *Reporter:* This student's job is to report on the group's discussion to the teacher or to the whole class.

2. Encourage students to ask questions from their roles rather than to say what they know. For example, the character interpreter might invite the other students to construct a character map or a character web about a character and venture his or her own ideas only after the other students have shared their own.

3. Choose only the most useful roles for a particular discussion. Sometimes four or five roles are sufficient.

4. Rotate students through the roles. Each student should play many roles over the course of several discussions. The accumulated experience of playing many of these roles adds dimensions to each student's awareness of literature.

5. Be careful not to stress the roles more than the rich discussion of the literary work. Having students carry out the roles is a means to the end of sharing their insights about a work. Once the conversation is under way, the teacher should feel free to suspend the roles and let the conversation proceed.

Sketch-to-Stretch   An ingenious device for having students of all ages respond together to a literary work is Sketch-to-Stretch, from Short et al. (1996). After the students have read and thought about a poem or a story, they are invited to draw pictures that symbolize what they believe are the main ideas or central themes of the piece. One student shows his or her drawing to a group of students, and they interpret the picture, saying what they think it means and how its images relate to the literary work. After the other students have had their say, the student who drew the picture is invited to give his or her own interpretation of the picture.

Shared Inquiry Discussion   The Great Books Foundation developed the shared inquiry method to accompany their literature discussion program (see Plecha, 1992), which has been conducted in thousands of schools and libraries for more than 30 years. Shared inquiry is a procedure by which the teacher leads a deep discussion into a work of literature. It is best done with a group of eight to ten students, to maximize participation but allow for a diversity of ideas. The procedure follows these steps:

1. Before the discussion takes place, choose a work or part of a work that encourages discussion. Such a work should lend itself to more than one interpretation

(not all works do this well) and raise interesting issues. Folktales often meet these criteria surprisingly well.

2. Make sure that all of the students have read the material carefully. (The Great Books Foundation insists that students read material twice before discussing it. But in our experience, a reading using some of the comprehension methods just described can make the students very aware of the contents of the reading selection.)

3. Prepare four or five discussion questions. These should be what the Great Books Foundation calls *interpretive questions*, and they have three criteria:
   a. They are real questions, the sort you might ask a friend after watching a provocative film.
   b. They have more than one defensible answer. (This criterion guarantees a debate. If it is not met, the discussion won't be a discussion but a "read my mind" exercise.)
   c. They must lead the discussion into the text. (A question such as, "Why was the giant's wife kinder to Jack than his own mother was?" leads the children to talk about what is in the text first, even though they might then comment on what they know from experience. A question such as, "Have you ever done anything as brave as Jack?" leads the discussion away from the text and out into 25 different directions.)

4. Write the first question on the board, and ask the students to think about the question and then briefly write down their answers. (If the children are so young that writing answers is laborious, allow plenty of time before calling on anyone. This allows them time to think about their answers.) As you invite students to answer, be sure to ask reluctant speakers to read what they wrote as well. Encourage debate between students, pointing out differences in what they say and asking them and other students to expand on the differences. Press children to support their ideas with references to the text or to restate ideas more clearly. However, avoid correcting a child or in any way suggesting that any one answer is right or wrong. Finally, do not offer your own answer to the question. Keep a seating chart of the students' names with a brief record of what each one has contributed. When the discussion of a question seems to have run its course, read aloud your summaries of the students' comments and then ask whether anyone has anything to add.

5. Once the discussion gets going, follow the children's lead and continue to discuss the issues and questions they raise.

Even when they don't use the whole approach, many teachers use aspects of the shared inquiry procedure in conducting book discussions. For example, they might ask students to write down ideas to bring to a discussion, or they might take notes during the discussion, or they take care to draw out the students' ideas and not dominate the discussion themselves.

Drama in Response to Stories   James Moffett (1976), a brilliant teacher of the language arts, pointed out many years ago that forms of literature differ in the degree to which they move closer to or further away from actual events. An essay about human nature is *abstract* (the word comes from two Latin morphemes that mean "drawn away from"), far removed from actual events. A story is more concrete, getting closer to events. Still, by putting events into story form, an author summarizes them, compresses actions, and leaves out much of what might really have happened. Drama, however, is live action: It is nearly as close to the real events as we can get because it plays the events out in real time for us so that we can see, hear, and feel them as they unfold. Here is Moffett's shorthand way of stating these points:

- Drama shows what is happening.
- A story tells what happened.
- An essay tells what happens.

What can students learn by acting out a story? What does it mean to "unpack" the meaning of a story?

Dramatizing a story, or a part of a story, can be a very effective way for children to unpack its meaning. Dramatization should be done after the children have read or heard a story and have had a chance to air their first thoughts about it. The Teach It! box on page 203 demonstrates a procedure for dramatizing a story.

The teaching approaches that we have considered up to now encourage discussions of stories or enactments of them. It is also useful to lead students in activities that teach them particular aspects of stories.

Teaching Key Aspects of Comprehension

The teaching strategies that were presented in the previous sections are lively and natural ways to invite students to think about and comprehend what they read. But there are times when teachers need to work on individual aspects of comprehension. The Common Core Standards name several of them. The CCSS expect students in the elementary grades to be able to:

1. Recognize main ideas and understand how details support them.
2. Perceive the theme of a work, and be able to summarize the work.
3. Identify, describe, and compare characters, settings, and main events in stories, along with the details by which they are developed.
4. Have a robust understanding of the language used in literature, including literal and figurative language, and metaphors and similes.
5. Recognize different genres of literature, and be able to follow their structures to arrive at or construct the meanings of literary works.
6. Understand the point of view from which a story is told, and the points of view of different characters within a story, and the difference in the point of view of the characters or the narrator and the reader.
7. Recognize, in an illustrated text, the relative contributions the written words and the illustrations make to the meaning.
8. Compare and contrast different versions of the same story, or different works by the same author or illustrator.

Individual aspects of comprehension can be developed in any of three ways, or a combination thereof:

- Developing the skill in the context of a more global activity
- A game or other exercise that practices that skill
- A graphic organizer

Common to all three is that the skill should be clearly demonstrated, expressly named, and discussed so that students are conscious of it, and given guided practice. If the latter two approaches are used, the skill should soon be practiced in a holistic reading and discussion activity, and not left as an isolated piece of learning.

ATTENTION TO ASPECTS OF COMPREHENSION IN CONTEXT Many of the aspects of comprehension just listed can be developed using the teaching strategies described earlier in this chapter, so long as conscious attention is paid to the aspect you want to develop.

Teach It!

Refer to the Teach It! appendix at the end of the book for further activities you can use to reinforce concepts discussed in this chapter.

Dramatizing a Story

Dramatizing a story allows children to take a closer look at a story by getting a real feel for the action. The procedure for dramatizing a story is adapted from the works of Spolin (1986) and Heathcote (Wagner, 1999).

Immerse students in the story. You need to make sure the students get the story on a literal level—that they know what happened. This might mean reading the story to them or asking them to reread the part you are going to dramatize.

Warm them up to do drama. There are many warm-up activities that work well to prepare students to act with more expression:

1. **Stretches:** Have the students stand in a circle. Now tell them to stretch their arms as high as they can as they spread their feet apart and make very wide faces. Now tell them to shrink up into tiny balls. Then stretch out big again. Have them do the same with their faces: Lion face! (expansive expression). Prune face! (shrunken expression).

2. **Mirrors:** Have students stand opposite each other. One is the person, and the other is the person reflected in the mirror. Have the person move (slowly) as the other mirrors the person's movements. Then switch roles.

3. **Portraits:** Have students get into groups of four or five. Have them think of something to depict that uses all of them as parts. For example, to depict a skier, children can act as poles, skis, and the person.

4. **Superactions:** This activity is more complex. Explain to the students that when we do things with other people, we often act on two levels: what we are doing and what we mean by what we are doing. For example, when we pass somebody we know in the hallway, having just seen the person a short time before, we might nod and say, "Hi." But when we see a friend in the hallway who has just come back to school after a long illness, we might say "HI!" with more exuberance. In both cases, the action is the same: to greet the friend. But the *superaction* is different. In the first case, it is just to show the person that we know he or she is there; in the second case, it is to show that we are surprised and delighted to see the person. Now practice dramatizing superactions by setting up brief situations, such as a waiter taking a customer's order. Write superactions on small pieces of paper, and give one privately to each actor. Have different pairs of students act out the same scene, with the same actions but with different superactions,

leaving time for the other students to guess what they thought the superaction was and say why they thought so.

Choose critical moments. It can be particularly useful to dramatize just a few choice scenes from a story, especially the turning points when the most is at stake. In "Jack and the Beanstalk," such a scene might be when Jack first approaches the Giant's castle, knocks on the door, and is greeted by the Giant's wife.

Segment the situation. Now assign students to take each of these roles. Invite other students to join them as they think about the situation from each character's point of view. What must be on Jack's mind when he approaches the huge door? What do the door and the walls of the castle look like? How large are they in proportion to Jack? What does Jack hear around the place? What does he smell? How does the place make him feel? What makes him pound his fist on the door? What is at stake for him? What are his choices? What will he do if he *doesn't* knock on the door? Why does he decide to do it?

Do the same for the Giant's wife. How does the knocking sound to her—thunderous or puny? What does she think when she sees the small but plucky boy at her door? What thoughts go through her mind, knowing what she knows about her husband? What are her feelings as she looks down at Jack?

Ask the actors to focus their minds on a few of these considerations as they prepare to act out the scene.

Dramatize the scene. Use minimal props and minimal costumes to help students think their way into their roles. Ask the other students to watch carefully and see what the actors make them think of.

Side coach. As the director, don't be passive, but take opportunities to make suggestions from the sidelines that will help children act more expressively. You might ask, "Jack, do you feel scared now or brave? How can you show us how you're feeling?"

Invite reflection. Ask the other students what they saw. What did they think was on the characters' minds? It is worthwhile to invite several groups of students to dramatize the same scene and have the class discuss the aspects of the situation that each performance brings to light.

CCSS

Common Core Standards and Aspects of Comprehending Literature

Many teachers consider it a successful class if all of the students are engaged in a story and are eager to talk about it. The Common Core Standards remind us that there are different levels of quality to students' talk. Students should be able to talk about characters, setting, plots, themes, and genres. They should be able to talk about the main ideas and details of story, and also about the craft that produced it and its structure (CCSS Comprehending Literature: Key Ideas and Details, Standards 1–3; Craft and Structure, Standards 4–6).

Take for example, the skill of perceiving the theme of a work and being able to summarize the work. The teacher can demonstrate and explain that skill and provide guided practice in using it, in the context of the following strategies that were presented earlier in this chapter: Readers' Workshop, Guided Reading, and the Directed Reading Activity. The teacher can also use Think-Alouds to demonstrate the skill.

GAMES AND OTHER FOCUSED ACTIVITIES TO TEACH ASPECTS OF COMPREHENSION The dynamics of a game played with a group can motivate students to use a skill. Here are several games devised to teach comprehension skills.

Stories and Themes In order to teach students to find themes to stories, prepare a set of very short stories that clearly illustrate themes. Or, use a selection from Aesop's Fables with the ending proverbs removed (see <www.storyit.com/Classics/Stories/aesop.htm> or <www.aesops-fables.org.uk/>). Write out a set of theme statements for the stories, or collect the morals from the fables. (For the purpose of this exercise, theme statements and morals to fables are close enough to be used interchangeably.) Divide the class in half. Project a short story or fable, and have a person from Team A read it aloud. Then project the list of theme statements or morals. After conferring with each other, Team B members must select the appropriate theme statement or moral. Be sure to take a minute to discuss why the theme statement or moral fits the story. Then have a member from Team B read aloud the next story, and ask Team A to choose the most suitable theme statement or moral.

- *Stories and Summaries.* Use the same game structure as Stories and Themes. Have one team read aloud a short story. Have the other team choose the most appropriate summary from a set that you have prepared ahead of time. After each turn, discuss what made that an appropriate choice of a summary.

- *Characters and Descriptions.* Using the same game structure as above, prepare a set of sentences that name actions that a character does. Prepare a set of adjectives that describe personalities. Team A reads the list of actions. Team B must choose from the list the adjective that best describes the character who performed those actions.

- *Main ideas and supporting details.* Before reading a book aloud to the class, choose two or three main ideas from the book. Write each of these ideas on a strip of tagboard. Find two or three sentences from the book that provide supporting details to each main idea and write those, too, on tagboard. After reading the story, explain what a main idea is and what supporting details are, by using examples (other than the ones you have prepared on tagboard). Then have the class form two groups; mix up the supporting details and distribute them to the two groups. Hold up a main idea, and invite the children to come forward and hold up the supporting details cards they think fit with it underneath. Do the same for the other ideas until all cards have been used.

Graphic Organizers Several graphic organizers have been developed that help develop specific skills of comprehension.

- *The Language Chart.* Created by Hoffman and Roser (1995), a Language Chart guides students to compare several different stories, works by the same author, or works illustrated by the same artist. At the same time, it leads to thinking about themes, characters, and plots. To use a Language Chart, you might choose three or more books with features in common and construct a language chart as a means of comparing them. The language chart lists titles of books in one column (the X axis) and lists questions about themes, characters, plots, or styles in one row. After each book has been read, the teacher or a student leads a discussion about each question, and then uses the students' answers to fill in the box at the intersection of the book title and question, as shown in Figure 7.3.

Figure 7.3 A Language Chart

Books by William Steig	What Was the Problem?	What Was the Solution?	How Were Things Different at the End?
Sylvester and the Magic Pebble	Sylvester got turned into a rock.	His parents found the magic pebble and wished him back to his old self.	Sylvester was happy to be normal.
Caleb and Kate	Caleb got turned into a dog.	Kate said the magic words and changed him back.	Caleb and Kate were glad to be together.
The Amazing Bone	Pearl was going to be killed by a wolf.	The bone said a charm and shrank the fox.	Pearl was glad to be home with her family.

- **Story maps.** The *plot* of a story is a way in which authors organize places, people, actions, and consequences to make all of those things meaningful for the reader. The elements of a plot are as follows:
  - **The setting:** the time and place the story happened
  - **The main characters:** the persons the story is about
  - **The problem:** the challenge the main character faces, which it is his or her goal to solve
  - **The attempts:** the effort or series of efforts the character makes to solve the problem, along with their outcomes
  - **The solution:** the attempt that finally pays off in solving the problem or the event that otherwise puts an end to the action
  - **The consequence:** how things are for the characters at the end, including what the events of the story meant for them

  You can help students use the plot consciously in understanding a story by using a *story map*, a chart that invites them to identify the keys parts of a story (see Figure 7.4). The process builds their responsiveness to the structures of story plots. For students younger than second grade, it might be preferable to use a simpler

Figure 7.4 A Story Map

Setting	Characters	Problem	Attempts	Solution	Conclusion
In . . .	there was	who wanted	so she . . . , but . . . And she . . . but . . .	Finally, she . . . and . . .	In the end . . .

Figure 7.5
A Character Cluster

version of a story map consisting of only the setting, the characters, the problem, and the solution.

- *Character clusters.* A way to link attributes, including descriptions, actions, and feelings, to a person so that a character is created is the *character cluster,* which is a a semantic web with the character's name written in the middle, main features of the character written as satellites around the character's name, and examples of those features written as satellites around the features. Figure 7.5 contains an example of a character cluster.

- *Character maps.* When characters in stories interact with other characters (which is most of the time), students need some way of keeping track of them and their relationships with each other. *Character maps* are graphic organizers that guide students' thinking about relationships between characters. In a character map, you write the names of two or more characters in their respective circles. The circles should be spaced widely apart on the page. Then draw arrows between the characters. Along the arrow that points from Character A to Character B, write about how Character A feels about Character B. Along the arrow that points from Character B to Character A, write about how Character B feels about Character A. An example of a character map for two characters in Mildred Taylor's *Roll of Thunder, Hear My Cry* (1997) is found in Figure 7.6.

Figure 7.6 A Character Map for *Roll of Thunder, Hear My Cry*

Feels loyal to him but doesn't really trust him

> —— —— —— —— ——>

Cassie

<—— —— —— —— ——<

T.J.

Hangs out with her and her brothers sometimes; wants to prove himself better than them; but he will betray them if it's to his advantage

Assessing Comprehension

We have seen in this chapter that reading comprehension is a complex activity that includes readers'

- Prior knowledge and their willingness to use it to generate questions about what they are reading.
- Willingness to seek answers to questions and construct meaning.
- Ability to follow the pattern or structure of the text.
- Metacognition—thinking about their understanding and rereading to repair their understanding when it fails.
- Making mental images of what is described in the text.
- Perceiving main ideas and how details support those main ideas.
- Making inferences—merging textual clues and background knowledge.
- Connecting the meaning to other texts and to issues outside of the text.

There is no simple way to measure all that. The most thorough approaches to the assessment of comprehension are observations of the reader's attempts to comprehend. In addition, you may wish to use a more quickly administered device, recognizing that such a device will yield an incomplete picture of a reader's comprehension.

Approaches to assessing comprehension include the following:

- *Observational assessments*: You observe and assess students' comprehension behaviors as students demonstrate them in real reading tasks.
- *Self-assessments*: You ask students to observe and critique their own use of comprehension strategies. Self-assessments have the advantage of teaching students to be mindful of reading strategies and to be deliberate about their use when they read.
- *Quantitative assessments*: Periodically, you might gather data that allow you to compare students' performance against some standard, such as grade-level expectations.

Observational Assessments

One kind of observational assessment is simply to keep a folder for each student into which you place observations that you write down every few days. The observations consist of whatever strikes you as being worthy of note: for instance, a student can provide background knowledge on a topic or cannot; a student makes predictions that honor the plot of a story or offers random predictions; a student makes a straightforward inference or fails to; a student states a main idea or says something else when asked to.

A more systematic way of making observational assessments is to keep a checklist of reading behaviors—in this case, comprehension behaviors. Schedule an eight- to ten-minute period every other week to read with each child, individually or in a group of no more than four, and record observations on a checklist such as the one shown in Figure 7.7.

Using Informal Reading Inventories

Teachers and students also need to know how well students are reading in comparison with their grade-level group. Teachers and grade-level teams can focus attention on aspects of teaching that need improving, but only if they have evidence that tells them where the strengths of their instructional program are as well as the areas in which they need improvement.

Figure 7.7 Observing Comprehension

Student's name: _____ Date: _____

Material read: _____ Level: _____

1. Before reading

a) The reader appeared to be familiar with the topic (or the author or the genre) of the text before reading.

No prior knowledge shown	Some prior knowledge shown	Much prior knowledge shown

b) The reader raised questions about the content of the text before reading.

Did not produce questions, even when prompted	Asked some (vague) questions when prompted	Volunteered intelligent questions

c) The reader was able to make predictions about what was coming in the text.

Did not produce predictions, even when prompted	Made imprecise or illogical predictions	Consistently made logical predictions

2. During reading

a) The reader read aloud with animation that honored the meaning of the text.

Read without meaningful inflections and word groupings	Sometimes showed meaningful inflections and word groupings	Consistently showed meaningful inflections and word groupings

b) The reader knew the vocabulary in the text.

Did not appear to understand many key words, and made little effort to learn what they mean	Did not appear to understand some key words, and made occasional effort to learn what they mean	Knew most key words, and often used context to approach the meanings of unknown words

c) The reader continued to ask questions and make predictions.

Did not produce predictions, even when prompted	Made imprecise or illogical predictions	Consistently made logical predictions

(Continued)

d) The reader found answers to questions or confirmed predictions.

Found answers to some questions, but mostly when the answer closely matched the question	Rarely found answers to questions, even when prompted	Actively pursued answers to questions, often without prompting

e) The reader was able to make inferences.

Rarely made inferences even with supportive questions	Made more obvious inferences	Consistently made inferences, and picked up on subtle nuances

f) The reader monitored comprehension.

Frequently misread words in the text without self-correcting	Occasionally misread text and made some self-corrections	Rarely misread text and reliably self-corrected

g) The reader perceived main ideas or claims and the details that support them.

When asked, did not distinguish between more and less important statements	Did restate some main ideas when asked	Consistently restated main ideas, and could provide support for them from the text

3. After reading

a) The reader could retell or summarize the text.

The retelling had major gaps	The retelling was fairly complete	The retelling was complete, and the reader summarized the main points

b) The reader identified themes in texts.

Did not offer thematic statements when asked (for example, to choose a title for a chapter)	Sometimes, but inexactly, could answer questions about "the main thing you learned" from the text	Consistently made appropriate statements about the main meaning or theme of a text

Several kinds of assessment devices are available. For the purpose of getting a close look at readers' strengths and areas of need, probably the most informative are informal reading inventories. Informal reading inventories must be administered one at a time, so they are time consuming. But the fact that they yield both quantitative results (in terms of reading levels) and detailed portraits of most areas of students' reading abilities makes them worth the investment of time.

Informal reading inventories (IRIs) are thoroughly discussed in Gillet, Temple, Crawford, and Temple's *Understanding Reading Problems* (2012).

Although teachers can make their own IRIs, most teachers prefer to use commercially available ones. Here are some recommended informal reading inventories:

Temple, C., Crawford, A., & Gillet, J. (2008). *Developmental literacy inventory: Emergent reading through high school.* Boston: Allyn and Bacon.

Lauren, L., & Caldwell, J. (2010). *Qualitative reading inventory-5.* New York: Pearson Education.

Silvaroli, N., & Wheelock, W. (2003). *Classroom reading inventory.* New York: McGraw-Hill.

For more information on IRIs, see Chapters 10 and 12. Other procedures for assessing reading comprehension, including the Cloze procedure and the Lexiles Framework, are discussed in Chapter 10.

For Review

Reading comprehension is using the knowledge we already have to understand the new information we find in the text. It is an active process in which we quest after new knowledge and make meaning in the process. Responding to literature, too, is an active process in which we bring our own expectations and associations to the words the author has strung along the pages of the text.

The advent of the Common Core Standards has reminded us that fully comprehending fiction requires some specialized knowledge of aspects of literature, including characters, settings, plots, and themes, as well as the knowledge of literary concepts and terms for discussing those characteristics.

Comprehension has several components: knowing the vocabulary of a text and being able to follow the text's structure, visualizing it, making predictions about it, summarizing its meaning, getting the main ideas in it, making inferences within it, interpreting it, arguing with it, and monitoring one's comprehension of it.

To encourage students to carry out that activity, there are teaching techniques we can use before, during, and after the reading or during the phases of a lesson we have called *anticipation, building knowledge,* and *consolidation.* In the anticipation phase, we remind students to think of what they already know about a topic, raise questions about what they are about to read, and otherwise prepare for reading. In the building knowledge phase, we guide students in using strategies to set expectations and meet them and to clarify meanings. In the consolidation stage, we have a host of methods for having students think back over what they have gained from the reading, respond to it, interpret it, critique it, apply it, and debate it.

For Your Journal

1. Return to your answers to the anticipation guide that opened this chapter. Look at the items for which your answers remained the same. In your journal, explain how you came to know the answers. Look at the items to which your answers changed, and explain how your thinking has changed.

2. This chapter explained how reading comprehension of fiction and response to literature work. Chapter 8 focuses on teaching students to comprehend and learn from informational text. What do you think the main differences are between teaching students to

comprehend and respond to fiction and teaching them to do this for informational text?

3. Recall the vignette of Hank da Silva's classroom that began this chapter. He used a combination of strategies for teaching students to read with comprehension.

Think of a class you have taught or might teach. Describe the combination you might choose from the reading comprehension strategies you have seen in this chapter. How would you make them work together?

Taking It to the World

1. When they observed skilled teachers teaching reading comprehension, Michael Pressley and his colleagues (1996) found that they usually taught their students to do the following:
   - Make predictions of what was to come in the text based on their prior knowledge
   - Generate questions about issues in the text
   - Seek clarification about confusing parts
   - Form mental images of what they read
   - Relate what they already knew to what they are reading in the text
   - Make summaries of what they have read

   Alone or with a group of your fellow students, observe three reading lessons in a primary grade school. Do these six activities capture what the teachers are doing by way of helping the children read with comprehension? Do they do other things as well, such as

encouraging students to make inferences or debate about what they read?

2. Go to a school, and practice a shared inquiry lesson (see pages 200–201). Make sure you use a text that has a core of mystery to it (many folktales work fine), and prepare your questions carefully according to the criteria given on those pages. Before you put the questions to the children, though, write out your own best answers to your questions. How do the students' answers compare to yours? Are you surprised? If so, what surprises you and why?

3. Using the same text as in your shared inquiry lesson, try the dramatic activities described on page 203 with your classmates. Then try the activity out in an elementary school. What different insights about the text come to light when you dramatize it rather than discuss it?

MyEducationLab™

Go to Topic 5 (Comprehension) in the MyEducationLab <www.myeducationlab.com> for your course, where you can:

- Find learning outcomes for Comprehension along with the national standards that connect to these outcomes.
- Complete Assignments and Activities that can help you more deeply understand the chapter content.
- Apply and practice your understanding of the core teaching skills identified in the chapter with the Building Teaching Skills and Dispositions learning units.
- Check your comprehension on the content covered in the chapter by going to the Study Plan in

the Book Resources for your text. Here you will be able to take a chapter quiz, receive feedback on your answers, and then access Review, Practice, and Enrichment activities to enhance your understanding of chapter content.

- Visit A+RISE. A+RISE® Standards2Strategy™ is an innovative and interactive online resource that offers new teachers in grades K-12 just in time, research-based instructional strategies that meet the linguistic needs of ELLs as they learn content, differentiate instruction for all grades and abilities, and are aligned to Common Core Elementary Language Arts standards English language proficiency standards in WIDA, Texas, California, and Florida.

Reading Comprehension, Part II: Understanding and Learning with Informational Texts

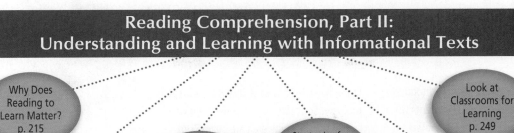

Anticipation Guide

The following statements will help you begin thinking about the topics of this chapter. Answer *true* or *false* in response to each statement. As you read and learn more about the topics in these statements, double-check your answers. See what interests you and prompts your curiosity toward more understanding.

_____ **1.** There has been a big shift from fiction reading to informational reading by adult readers in the United States.

_____ **2.** Primary children get too confused with the different formats of nonfiction texts. Instruction in using nonfiction should wait for third grade and above.

_____ **3.** Teachers in the United States have changed their teaching practices to show students how to comprehend informational material.

_____ **4.** One of the best ways to show students how to read informational text with comprehension is to read an informational text yourself and discuss it with your students.

_____ **5.** Having prior knowledge helps students to comprehend, but one kind of prior knowledge is about as useful as another.

_____ **6.** Students who have had an extensive introduction to a topic are likely to be more motivated to learn about it than are those with only superficial knowledge.

_____ **7.** Just as stories have a "grammar" that readers can follow to understand the story, informational texts have recognizable structures.

_____ **8.** Reading strategies for informational texts are the same as those for fiction.

_____ **9.** Informational texts have so many different structures that there is little point in teaching students the parts of an informational text.

_____ **10.** When it comes to teaching vocabulary, teachers should stress only the words the authors of the text prioritize.

A Classroom Story

Reading to Learn in a Primary Classroom

Teacher Debbie Gurvitz likes to introduce her first- and second-grade students to informational reading through integrated units of study. In the spring, she develops an expanded science unit that involves a real problem-based inquiry. It serves as a way of expanding students' reading skills in nonfiction and of teaching some science standards. Recently, Ms. Gurvitz focused the unit on pond life and the relationship between the quality of the water for animals and the human community. To introduce the unit, she invited a naturalist from the local nature preserve to speak to the students. When the naturalist showed the students some of the animals from the pond, they became fascinated with the mutant frog he included. "Wow, that's weird!" "That doesn't look like the frog I have at home. Who did that to it?" "What happened?" The children's questions came naturally and quickly. Garth, one of the first graders, expressed the feelings of the whole group when he said, "Ms. Gurvitz, we really have a problem!"

Ms. Gurvitz took her lead from the children and helped them to focus their study of the natural environment on the frog problem. They began by framing the problem—exploring what facts and information they already knew and identifying the questions they had. On a large piece of chart paper they made a list of what they knew about frogs. She helped them write questions for research; these also filled a sheet of chart paper and were hung on the wall. As a result of these discussions, she divided the class into smaller groups that searched for information to help solve the problem. In this case, it was a very real problem. Scientists do not understand why so many frogs in the area are being born with strange-looking body parts. This created an authentic study full of the kinds of ambiguities that are found in most scientific research.

Ms. Gurvitz was careful to make sure she could locate the kinds of reading texts the children could read. She wanted some that would be at an independent level for all the children and some that would be good instructional-level texts for her guided reading groups. After collecting the books, she leveled them to ensure that she could accommodate the whole class with appropriate materials.

In considering the language arts and reading objectives she wanted to address, Ms. Gurvitz focused instruction on helping students find answers to questions they posed. She wanted them to learn to use the table of contents and the index in books to locate the information they needed. She knew this would be a good opportunity for them to learn to make decisions about what sections of a text they would read and to gain control over information searching as contrasted with fictional reading. She also wanted the children to learn to make notes about what information they were collecting so that those notes could guide their reporting. To do this, she made copies of the Amazing Fact Sheet (see Figure 8.1) and put them in a shoe box on the inquiry table so students could take one whenever they wanted to save some interesting or important information.

As she introduced this way of making notes, Ms. Gurvitz used one child as a model. Side by side at the overhead transparency, she and Andrew made a note card of the information he wanted to remember.

"Andrew, what do you want to write?" Ms. Gurvitz asked.

"It says that frogs lay lots of eggs in water," Andrew replied.

Ms. Gurvitz encouraged him, "So, can you write that on your Amazing Fact Sheet?" As Andrew began to write on a transparency, the other children watched. When he tried to write "water," he hesitated.

"What is giving you trouble with that word?" Ms. Gurvitz asked. "Can you find it written somewhere?"

With that nudge, Andrew turned to the book again and located the word; without any further help, he finished his writing. Ms. Gurvitz reminded him to list the book title, the author, and the page that contained the fact on his note. Finished, he then signed the note on the Reporter line.

Ms. Gurvitz praised his efforts: "Good work, Andrew."

She concluded the mini-lesson by reminding the children that when they found interesting information, they should write that on an Amazing Fact Sheet and put it in the Amazing Facts Box on the counter. Each morning, Andrew and other children read their cards during the morning share time and used them to build their knowledge.

Figure 8.1 Amazing Fact Sheet

```
┌─────────────────────────────────────────────────────────────────┐
│                       AMAZING FACT SHEET                          │
│  An amazing fact about frogs is that                              │
│                                                                   │
│  _____      │
│                                                                   │
│  _____      │
│                                                                   │
│  Found in (provide the source of your information)                │
│                                                                   │
│  _____      │
│                                                                   │
│  Written by _____  p. _____    │
│                                                                   │
│  Reporter _____  │
└─────────────────────────────────────────────────────────────────┘
```

Figure 8.1 Amazing Fact Sheet

To be human is to be a learner. Young children are full of questions, so many that parents and teachers are sometimes amazed by the depth and breadth of children's curiosity. As we grow, we continue to be curious about the world around us and ask questions. To find answers to these questions, we read informational materials—from textbooks like this one to Web sites, newspapers and magazines, cookbooks, travel guides, biographies, and self-help and diet books. To be successful learners in school, we, like all students, must learn to read and study about concepts that society considers important. These are generally elaborated on in textbooks and other reference materials, including a wide range of sources on the Internet. Therefore, it is important in our role as teachers to prioritize helping young readers develop the joy in and ability to read a wide range of materials. Children need guidance so they can become confident and flexible readers empowered by the variety of strategies they have developed to navigate the wide range of materials and formats in the informational materials they encounter daily. They also need to learn to study new material and find strategies that will help them retain that material.

Why Does Reading to Learn Matter?

Our purpose in much of the reading we do is *to learn*. Schools require students to use textbooks and a wide variety of other resource materials throughout the grades. Unfortunately, too often we just assume that students will develop good strategies for using informational materials and knowing how to prioritize what they need to remember. Most schools also spend little time teaching students how to use text materials effectively for answering their own questions and for creating reports. Yet this kind of reading becomes increasingly important as students progress through the grades. In fact, one of the major motivations behind the development of the CCSS was the nearly 200-point Lexile gap that was identified between the level of difficulty of most high school texts and those required of college freshmen and students moving into the workforce. Because learning materials beyond high school are more challenging than those students are currently prepared to comprehend, the CCSS have moved up the text difficulty range for each grade level from K–12. (See CCSS Appendix A, p. 8.) For example, current eleventh–twelfth-grade texts are in the 1070–1220 range, but the new levels increase the expectation for these students to read texts between the 1215 and 1355 levels. Lexile measures don't equate with grade levels, but a comparison of current texts and the new "stretch" levels means students need to be reading more challenging texts from primary grades on.

While much of school learning still depends heavily on textbooks, they won't be used well unless teachers show students how to use these and other resources effectively. Most middle and secondary school teachers also expect students to engage in independent research and to write informational essays and reports. With the expanded expectations within the CCSS, now elementary students are also being asked to write at least four short research papers a year. To develop the skills needed to be successful learners, all students need to be engaged in reading and enjoying informational texts from the primary grades onward throughout the grades.

What we read outside of school also underscores the importance of knowing how to read and use informational materials. Recent research studies on the reading habits of adults reflect the shift away from fiction to informational reading and digital texts (CCSS, 2010; Harris Interactive, 2011; Smith, 2000). We read newspapers and magazines to find out about the world around us and our favorite activities. We browse the Web to gain in-depth information and alternative points of view. We read biographies to learn more about how humans engage with issues and thrive in this world. We read self-help books and health and fitness magazines and blogs because we want to improve our health and lifestyle. We read spiritual and religious books to reflect on our beliefs and deepen our quality of living.

As a society, we read a preponderance of *informational and digital texts*. We want to know as much as possible—about ourselves as well as the rest of the world. Publishers recognize this shift in interests and are publishing more and more informational texts, in both printed and electronic formats. The wide range of magazines being published reflects the diversity of reader interests. Just check a magazine stand for the hundreds of specific topics that are available to address particular interests and tastes of readers. The best-seller lists generally have one section for fiction, another for nonfiction, and often a third for digital materials. One of the real transformations in the last decade has been the explosion of materials available for us to read on an enormous range of topics on the Web as well as in more traditional publishing venues. This explosion, luckily, is also true for the availability of informational materials for students. It is now quite easy for teachers to compile a set of short, informational books on a single topic that is within the range of reading abilities of the students and that includes a variety of formats and genre.

Common Core State Standards

CCSS

• Informational Texts 10: Range of Reading

The new CCSS make the inclusion of informational text reading clearly an important part of the responsibility of elementary teachers from kindergarten forward. In fact, the standards include two sets of standards, one for literary reading and the other for informational reading. In addition, the standards connect the development of reading ability with social studies, science, and technical subjects. This is a dramatic shift from the focus on fiction reading that has dominated reading instruction in the past. In the Anchor Standards for Reading, Standard 10 states that students: *Read and comprehend complex literary and informational texts independently and proficiently.*

Within the Informational Text Standards for K–5, the standards for first and second grade are shown below, and each subsequent grade has a similar, appropriate expectation.

CCSS

Comprehending Informational Text

Grade 1: Standard 10. With prompting and support, read informational texts appropriately complex for grade 1.

Grade 2: Standard 10. By the end of year, read and comprehend informational texts, including history/social studies, science, and technical texts, in the grades 2–3 text complexity band proficiently, with scaffolding as needed at the high end of the band.

Knowledge Standards and High-Stakes Assessment

The current focus on knowledge standards (science, math, and social studies) and measuring what students learn each year puts pressure on teachers to cover more content. This means that students are asked to read more and remember what they are taught. In this climate of rising expectations, students who have read widely possess the background knowledge that enables them to remember new material and deepen their knowledge schemata. Instead of diminishing, the demands on learners as readers are increasing.

Another implication of the current accountability climate for teachers is that the assessments of students' reading abilities are now balanced between reading for literary purposes and reading to learn. These assessments reflect the fact that for students to be successful as readers throughout schooling and life, they need to read for a variety of purposes from a variety of materials. Reading fiction for pleasure is only one of many forms reading takes. More important for school success across the curriculum is the ability to read informational texts and learn from them (Ogle & Blachowicz, 2001).

Standardized tests, state performance assessments, and the current international tests (Donahue et al., 2001; Organization for Economic Cooperation & Development, 2010) all incorporate a variety of materials and purposes. Reading for information is as important as reading for literary purposes. Like many current state assessments, the framework for the National Assessment of Educational Progress (NAEP) has an equal proportion of literary and informational items at fourth grade and 55 percent informational items at eighth grade (National Assessment Governing Board, 2008). The CCSS assessments being developed by the two national consortia, PARCC (Partnership for Assessment of Readiness for College and Careers) and Smarter Balanced (the Smarter Balanced Assessment Consortium), also give equal priority to fiction and informational reading.

Instructional Priorities

Clearly, elementary teachers need to conceptualize their reading instruction so that it introduces children to a broad range of quality reading materials; for most teachers this means putting more emphasis on informational reading than was their own experience as students. It also means guiding children to attend to the content of what they read, to think of the important ideas and the supporting details in a single text, and then to compare and contrast the information in several texts. Teachers can build these habits in students in a variety of ways.

1. Read aloud to students regularly from interesting, high-quality informational books and articles. Develop a collection of high-quality informational books, magazines, and articles that can be expanded each year. As you build your collection, school and community librarians are good resources to consult in selecting outstanding books. Also helpful are the annual lists of recommended trade books compiled by the National Science Teachers Association and the National Council of Social Studies. More extensive recommendations are available from the School Library Association and in resource books and chapters (Knoell, 2010; Temple, Martinez, & Yokota, 2014).

2. Include some author studies that focus on writers of informational materials—and there are many. Think of the interests primary grade children

The layout of a book or magazine can either encourage or impede the understanding of the content. What would the design of a textbook need to look like to be attractive to middle school students?

develop exploring the books of Donald Crows, Lois Elbert, Gail Gibbons, and Seymour Simon; intermediate level readers love books by Jim Arnosky, Ruth Heller, Jim Murphy, and Joanna Cole; and middle grade readers find intriguing the content of authors like Mark Aronson, Russell Freedman, and Walter Dean Myers.

3. Whenever possible, read from more than one author on the same topic. When you find magazine articles connected to some of the books you use, copy or print them out and put them inside the texts. Put sticky notes containing the titles of similar books inside books you read. Then when you read orally, share from at least two or three (include poetry, too) and "think aloud" about style, focus, and the information they contain.

4. Help students develop engaged reading by modeling and thinking aloud as you read from short, well-written informational texts. As you read aloud, show the text on a visualizer so students can follow along as you read. Highlight key terms, underline new ideas, write questions in the margins, and engage students in responding to the author's ideas. With such engaging experiences with short mentor or model texts, students can easily be led into reading a variety of other materials alone, with partners, or in small groups.

5. With the adoption of the CCSS, there is an increased interest in developing integrated curriculum units. In fact, that is what is suggested in the PARCC guides to curriculum. When elementary and middle reading programs are constructed in units with broad themes (some focused on content in social studies and science), students can experience a range of texts on the same topic or theme and deepen their understanding of the variety of ways authors express ideas and convey information. With longer units, teachers can introduce several genres, develop strategies for students' reading and thinking, and differentiate the instructional support students need. This type of content-based unit structure has been implemented in many schools and districts already (Guthrie & Ozgungor, 2002; Ogle, 2011; Pearson, Cervetti, & Tilson, 2008), and examples of units teachers have designed for the CCSS are also available (see <www .commoncorecurriculum.org>). Many publishers have supported this focus of instruction by making collections of materials on a single topic or theme available, and others have created short, highly visual informational books for young readers at a range of reading levels. By integrating instruction, teachers can develop both literacy and content and also improve learning in both areas (Pearson et al., 2008).

Through thoughtful planning, teachers can provide a broad range of instruction in reading strategies and purposes, and make students comfortable negotiating a variety of text types. Because purpose has such a powerful effect on individual reading habits (Duke, Caughlan, Juzwik, & Martin, 2012), it is important to provide opportunities for many purposes, from learning new information to performing tasks to recreating experiences and representing them in new ways. Teachers can prioritize the importance of reading to learn by instructing students in how to locate and synthesize information in textbooks as well as the reference materials that are used heavily in schools. This kind of reading ability often determines whether students will be successful throughout their schooling.

Informational reading does not develop automatically, and it deserves concerted attention by teachers. In an electronic environment where we have access to a world of information, students must learn to use this new source of informational materials as they engage in inquiry and report writing (Biancarosa, 2012). Reading across texts, comparing authors and ideas, and evaluating materials are important priorities. Students' abilities to read, write, and think critically are necessary, especially with the range of unedited ideas available on the Internet. Today's elementary and middle school classrooms can be alive with the kinds of experiences that help students develop these skills.

Understanding Comprehension in Informational Texts

Learning from reading is an active, ongoing process that can be described by what we do before, during, and after engagement with a text. Just as we do with reading literature, we follow the simple ABCs of reading to learn. We begin by anticipating what we want and need to learn. Then, we build knowledge as we read and engage with authors. Finally, we consolidate the ideas with what we previously knew, sometimes modifying those ideas and sometimes expanding on them. This ongoing process is also a recursive one. That is, with each new set of ideas we read, we rethink what we knew, ask new questions and set new purposes, and build on the ideas that are freshly ours. Some essential aspects that undergird active reading to learn include the following:

- Assessing schemata or prior knowledge
- Assuming a metacognitive orientation
- Setting one's own purposes and asking questions
- Actively seeking information and making notes so that it can be retained for connecting and organizing ideas
- Forming interpretations of what is read
- Consolidating new information and ideas
- Analyzing and evaluating the sources and adequacy of information
- Creating a synthesis and representation of the learning that can be shared
- Reaching conclusions about and finding applications of what has been learned

Reading is a complex process, and orchestrating these various facets of comprehension takes guidance and much practice. Students deserve to have teachers who are able to explore and explain how to orchestrate the comprehension processes. One powerful way teachers do this is by modeling thoughtful engagement with some challenging texts in each unit. In the language of the CCSS this is providing guidance in "close reading." For primary children, one can guide students in a two-level picture and story walk through the text, noting how the illustrator communicates ideas and how the subsequent pictures connect with earlier ones. For example, in the book *Redwoods* by Jason Chin (2009) the illustrations show a boy learning about the redwoods by reading a book as he moves from the subway into the forest. The teacher notes the use of the books and guides, "I wonder why the boy is always reading?" Later she comments, "Now he is reading a different book on how to climb big trees. It seems the boy is learning everything from what he reads; let's see if that's what the author is trying to do here."

Following this picture walk the teacher begins reading the book, thinking aloud and asking children what they notice:

"What is the big idea on this page?"

"Why do the redwoods grow so tall?"

"I was surprised by the way the author used the phrase 'well suited' to refer to what the trees get from the environment."

"What questions does the page raise in your minds?"

"What words does the author use that help us create images of the trees in their environment?"

"How does the author demonstrate the phrase 'big round masses along its trunk'?"

"The author helps us understand the meaning of 'epiphytes' with this picture."

"What do you think the author wants us to think will happen next? Why?"

After participating in this type of shared reading of the text, teachers can write some of the major questions that can guide students' thinking on the board and ask students to share their own thinking with a partner or by writing ideas and questions on sticky notes as they read. In the intermediate and upper grades teachers need to continue to provide modeling of the thinking involved in reading more complex and demanding texts. Readers need to focus on the ideas developed by authors (key ideas, details, and examples) and the structure and techniques used by writers, and they also need to think critically about how these ideas and points of view compare and contrast with those of others.

As students develop their own control over reading to learn, all aspects of the comprehension process need attention. It is useful to model the ways readers orchestrate these skills, and these modeled lessons need to be complemented by lessons focused on helping students deal with individual strategies: finding main ideas; connecting these ideas with details; recognizing how vocabulary is introduced and developed; identifying techniques authors use to construct their texts; summarizing texts; and then comparing and contrasting different texts for ideas and point of view. The way teachers introduce learning tasks to students and provide them with instructional tools to use as they learn will determine to a great degree students' success at becoming strong at comprehension. By planning carefully across each year, beginning with initial assessment of what students already know and can do and then structuring good teaching and guided practice activities that build on this knowledge will lead both teachers and students to success.

The Importance of Background Knowledge

Reading is always an active, constructive process during which students need to activate what they know to make sense of text. Readers comprehend by having the details in the material they are reading lead them to evoke relevant knowledge schemata. Then they use these schemata to give meaning to the details and, ideally, to understand the meaning of the whole passage. There are at least four kinds of background knowledge that readers need in order to comprehend well. The first is knowledge of the vocabulary. The second is knowledge of text structure. The third and fourth deal with content knowledge, both topical and principled.

VOCABULARY   One of the most important tools in understanding content is having a grasp of how the key terms are used in a specific content. Vocabulary represents the knowledge of words and their meanings. In reading, the issue of vocabulary knowledge ranges between word recognition and comprehension. In word recognition, children may labor to recognize a word in print, but once they recognize it, they may or may not know the spoken word and its meaning. Obviously, a reader must know the meanings of most of the words in a text to be able to read it successfully. When reading informational texts, the demands of learning the academic terms can be enormous. One author likened content textbooks to dictionaries with elaborated definitions of terms (Newkirk, 2012). Given this reality, it is important that students learn strategies to identify important terms, know how words are formed, and understand how to use context to determine meaning (Blachowicz, Fisher, Ogle, & Watts-Taffe, 2013; Nagy & Townsend, 2011).

KNOWLEDGE OF TEXT STRUCTURE   The structure of a text is a little like the grammar of a sentence. Because you understand the grammar of a sentence such as "The man bit the dog," you know who was bitten and who did the biting. In the same fashion, if you understand the structures of stories, you know how to follow a plot. If you can understand the structure of explanations, you know how to find the questions and get the answers to them. If you understand the structure of persuasive writing, you know how to spot the claim and weigh the support for it (Duke et al., 2012; Goldman & Rakestraw, 2000). The more you know about the way informational articles and texts are generally organized, the more you will be able to predict and read actively. This knowledge of structure also helps you retain what you read, because you can organize the ideas into major categories for memory.

TOPICAL CONTENT KNOWLEDGE The term *topical content knowledge* represents a fairly shallow level of knowledge, consisting of little more than some passing familiarity with the subject of the reading. For example, assume that while reading, a little girl is faced with a scientific passage about ducks. If she has seen a Donald Duck cartoon (and realizes that the character of Donald is based loosely on a real duck), she will have some topical knowledge about ducks. She will realize ducks have beaks, two wings, and two webbed feet and that they make quacking sounds. This amount of knowledge will not help much when reading a scientific text about ducks, but at least it will help her picture what is being talked about.

PRINCIPLED CONTENT KNOWLEDGE In contrast to topical content knowledge, principled content knowledge entails a deeper kind of understanding. It consists of familiarity with the topic as well as an understanding of its parts, its causes and effects, and other issues related to it (Gelman & Greeno, 1989). For example, readers who have learned about geese and know something about the lives of migratory aquatic birds will have principled knowledge with which to understand a scientific passage about ducks. Readers with principled knowledge are better prepared to understand challenging passages than readers who have only topical knowledge. Their curiosity is likely to be deeper, and their expectations will conform more closely to the unfolding presentation of information in the text. The reader with topical knowledge, by contrast, might recognize isolated parts of the information in the text, but will be less prepared to make sense of the flow of information or the more important ideas in the text.

The Teacher's Role in Guiding Instruction

The choices teachers make in determining instructional focus and the kind of guidance they provide greatly influence the way students think as they read and make a difference in the kinds of knowledge students gain about the subject matter in the curriculum. Too often, content reading becomes frustrating for both students and teachers. To prevent this, teachers need to take care to focus instructional time on the most important aspects of comprehension development. As we already noted, a key is to ensure that students have an understanding of how the content or text they are reading is organized. This framework provides a structure within which students can distinguish key ideas from those of lesser importance. During instruction, teachers have several important tasks. These include modeling and guiding engagement with text, teaching skills and strategies, eliciting students' own interests and motivation, and providing adequate time for students to explore ideas and concepts in depth.

DEVELOPING PRINCIPLED KNOWLEDGE The kinds of knowledge students gain about the subject matter in the curriculum are very important. In reading to learn, the content-specific information needs attention, something that is not a priority when reading fiction. A key to comprehending a text is having the ability to link ideas presented within and across sentences to create a sense of a whole text. Teachers influence students' knowledge formation in two important ways: by the questions they ask and by the depth of study they encourage with their students.

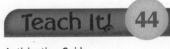

Teach It! 44

Anticipation Guide

The Questions Teachers Ask The ideas to which you call children's attention by means of your questions or comments influence the course of the children's thinking about what they read and study. You can direct students' attention toward important ideas or trivial ones. When reading a story, it makes a difference whether you dwell on minor details or ask questions that call attention to the deep structural elements of the story: the character's problem, goal, conflicts, and solutions to problems or the author's message or theme in the story. When reading informational text, it matters whether you call attention to minor details or to important ideas such as chronological development, cause and effect, or hierarchical relationships between ideas.

The Depth to Which Teachers Lead Children to Study a Topic You can encourage children to gain deeper knowledge about topics by staying with subjects for more than brief periods. You also can enhance children's understanding by looking at topics through many different disciplines. For example, look at a historical phenomenon such as immigration through fictional works in addition to the social studies text. By seeing phenomena through the eyes of fictional participants, students have more possibility of connecting with, visualizing, and interpreting the concept. Lengthy discussions, especially those that make connections between the subject of study and the children's own experience, also make it more likely that children will form deep, principled knowledge about a subject (Allington & Johnston, 2002).

SKILLS AND STRATEGIES In addition to some background knowledge with which to understand text, readers need skills and strategies. *Skills* are processes that readers use habitually. *Strategies* are the processes by which they use their skills under conscious control. Teachers need to know what skills and strategies students possess and consciously develop a strong repertoire of both in all students.

When children first learn to read, they may be taught to perform comprehension activities consciously as reading strategies. For example, when they come across a word they do not know, the teacher might urge them to read to the end of the line to get a sense of the meaning of the sentence, and then go back and guess the unknown word. This strategy is known as the *reading ahead/reread activity*. Later on—possibly much later on and after continued support from the teacher—when the readers habitually use the context to figure out unknown words, the behavior has become a skill.

When students are working with difficult material, however, or when they want to be especially careful in their reading, skilled readers often employ some reading strategies consciously (Pressley & Afflerbach, 1995). For example, even when their reading skills are adequate for comprehending a section in a social studies text, readers might consciously choose to apply the strategy of summarizing and rehearsing main ideas to remember them for a discussion the next day.

INTEREST AND MOTIVATION Performing acts of comprehension takes some effort, and exerting effort takes will. No wonder children are more likely to take the trouble to do what they need to do to understand what they read when the topic is interesting to them. This fact, although not always honored in school curriculum offerings, has been recognized for the better part of a century (Beane, 2002; Dewey, 1913; Guthrie & Davis, 2003). But readers may be interested in a topic in different ways, and these differences have consequences. In the opening vignette, as Ms. Gurvitz began her unit on the pond, she had a naturalist speak with the children and show them samples of the frogs that were deformed. This piqued their interest. Readers might be interested in a topic because it has been presented in an engaging way—with exciting illustrations or dramatic writing and explanation points. Or they might be interested because they have some reason to find out more about a topic and they want to know more about the line of inquiry the text is following. For example, because you want to know how to help your present or future students read with comprehension, you might find this text of particular interest. You likely don't need movie poster-like illustrations to draw you into the ideas presented here. If you pick up the Sunday magazine in your newspaper, however, it might take an interesting picture with a curiosity-provoking caption to get you interested in reading about something that is new to you.

These individual *motivations* for learning correspond to the kinds of prior knowledge readers have about a topic. Readers who have principled knowledge about a topic tend to be interested in adding to and deepening that knowledge, whereas readers with shallower, topical knowledge might not be motivated automatically to learn more about something through reading. Research has shown (Alexander, 1998) that readers with these different kinds of background knowledge notice different things in a text. Readers with only topical knowledge might focus on flashy or exotic details to the exclusion of main ideas and arguments, whereas those with principled knowledge might do just the opposite.

THE "MATTHEW EFFECT": ASPECTS OF COMPREHENSION ARE INTERRE-LATED What we have just considered as separate aspects of comprehension—prior knowledge, strategies and skills, and interest—are in fact interrelated. Although it is true, as Duffy and Roehler (1989) and others have shown, that children can profit from being taught to carry out comprehension strategies, it is also true that reading comprehension develops as a conglomerate of achievements (Alexander et al., 1994). For example, engaging prior knowledge can be helped along by teaching; however, for this teaching to be successful, children must have some prior knowledge of the topic to call on. Moreover, children are more likely to have deep enough interests in the topic to use the strategies of applying prior knowledge, making predictions, arguing with the text, or finding main ideas, unless their prior knowledge is deep and principled. To carry this point further, if their prior knowledge about a topic is deep and principled, then their interest in the topic will also extend below the surface to main ideas and structures of argument.

The process is cyclic and is an example of what researcher Keith Stanovich (1986) called the "Matthew effect" in reading, a term derived from a passage in the gospel of Matthew about the rich getting richer and the poor, poorer. The more you know the easier it is to learn more; the more quickly you develop early literacy skills the faster your reading accelerates as you can read more. When young readers have deep and principled knowledge, they will have deep interest; if they have deep interest, they will use thoroughgoing strategies of comprehension; and if they use thoroughgoing strategies, they will gain more principled knowledge (see Figure 8.2). The cycle works the other way, too. A reader might lack deep knowledge, not habitually use thoroughgoing reading strategies, or have only superficial interest in the topics being read. These factors may interact to prevent satisfactory comprehension. The best teaching for comprehension, then, includes attention to all these aspects:

The Matthew Effect is a biblical reference that means "the rich get richer and the poor get poorer." Watch this video to understand how the Matthew Effect relates to students' reading abilities.

- Creating a learning environment in which students can become immersed in a topic over time and explore it deeply
- Guiding students' attention to the way the texts they read are organized
- Helping students develop principled knowledge by encouraging them to consider ideas deeply, and pointing them toward the main ideas and the underlying structures and issues

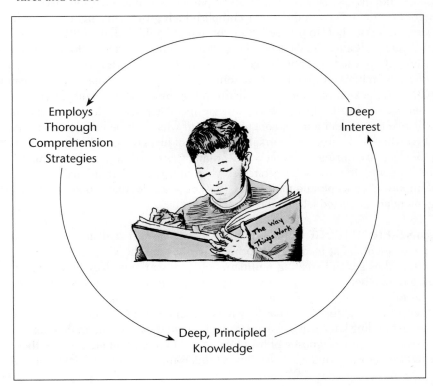

Figure 8.2 The Matthew Effect in Reading Comprehension

- Teaching thoroughgoing, powerful strategies for comprehending and remembering and then supporting and reinforcing these strategies until they become habituated into skills

- Engaging children in deep discussions of what they read and getting them to think about, write about, and respond to what they read so they will understand issues deeply and extend their curiosity to other meaningful topics in their world

- Focusing their attention on the vocabulary of the topic or area so they develop a more precise way of thinking and differentiating ideas

- Encouraging students' questions and taking their inquiry seriously, weaving their deep-seated interests into the very fabric of the school day

Student Engagement

Although the teacher's role in developing a thoughtful class is critical, students play equally important roles as learners. Right from the beginning of the school year, teachers need to take time to observe how students approach learning. How involved and aware are students of what learning entails? They need to be active—and interactive—if they are going to be successful learners. People learn best when they do so strategically. That means taking charge of their own reading with a clear purpose. Just as in reading fiction, students need to be actively engaged while reading and learning from nonfiction and other content materials. Because content material is usually dense with ideas to be learned, the following strategies are especially important.

Think-Pair-Share

ANTICIPATING   Students need to anticipate—to ask what they want to learn from the reading. They do this by first assessing what they know, what the task demands are, and what needs to be accomplished. For young students, this initial orientation is modeled in the K-W-L framework discussed later in this chapter. As students begin their engagement with a new topic, watch them and discuss with them how they begin. Do they skim through the material and activate what they know and make connections with the text? Do they look closely at diagrams or pictures and think about their meaning?

Once students have assessed their starting point in learning, they then need to develop a plan for how to proceed in order to accomplish their goals. This includes knowing that there are options for how to proceed. Students too often think that all they can do is read and then reread. Rather, they need to know they can use a variety of tools to guide their acquisition of knowledge. They are going to want to make notes when they encounter new information that is important or use some form of marginal notation if they can keep the materials. Stick-on notes serve wonderful purposes in helping students keep track of what they want to learn. These notes can be grouped later to chunk information in a way that will give the student a more coherent sense of what is to be learned. Some students learn best when they can create a graphic network of ideas or draw diagrams of what they learn. Being active during the process of learning is essential. It takes little time to check whether students are using active strategies when they read informational material that is full of important concepts and main ideas. (Several strategies that support students' active engagement are discussed later in the chapter.)

Reciprocal Teaching

BUILDING KNOWLEDGE   Students build knowledge as they deal with the ideas they are reading about. That means monitoring what they are thinking and learning, asking questions as they go, and creating summaries of ideas for themselves. Some students like to think aloud, others make notes in the margin or on sheets of paper, some prefer drawing key ideas to represent the text's main ideas, and some like to share with another person what they are getting out of a text as they read. Teachers need to model each of these approaches to building knowledge. Asking students to put stick-on notes in their text material as they read is an easy diagnostic of how they attend to important elements of these texts. Students also enjoy hearing what classmates think is most important from what they have read, so group sharing at the end of a reading period can be very productive. Teachers also can create large bulletin board displays or butcher paper matrices on which students can post what they think is most important and interesting in what they read. These then can serve as ongoing records of students' growing knowledge. As teachers expand the options for engaged reading and help students practice these strategies frequently, they will become better equipped to make decisions about which strategies work best for them in particular situations.

CONSOLIDATING WHAT THEY LEARN   As students continue to build their knowledge and understanding as a result of reading, they also consolidate what they are learning. That means going back and thinking again about how the ideas fit together and what they mean. Students can create a new graphic representation of what they have learned. They might write an outline and then elaborate on it in a summary, or they might want to talk to someone about the ideas they have gained. If students are using a textbook or a guide from a teacher, they can return to the questions or talk about the main objectives. If students are going to retain important ideas, they need to do something actively with them—by summarizing or extending what the authors have presented.

Most elementary students need sustained teacher guidance and support to develop the habit of rehearsing what they are learning. Several graphic organizers discussed later in this chapter can help students to organize their thinking and provide good visual reviews of content. If they transform the ideas they are learning into a new form, students have a greater chance of remembering them. Simply asking the question "What did that mean to me?" helps students to stay active metacognitively. Strategies for working together to read, question, and reflect can be used with even the youngest students, who can learn to work in pairs and ask each other what they have learned (Pressley, 2002).

Finally, good readers engage in evaluation of both the materials they read and their accomplishments. If the text seems unclear or lacking in information, they might decide to read other sources of information to clarify ideas or to confirm accuracy and currency. Good readers also assess the achievement of their own purposes. Returning to their questions or categories that were unclear, good readers make sure they understand and have met their own purposes. They know that learning takes effort. Those who are not confident learners often feel disadvantaged when there are intense content expectations. You can help them to realize that they can learn new material, but it is a process that takes time and active involvement on their part. It is essential to give insecure learners and second-language learners models of process learning and time to rehearse and clarify ideas. They need to understand that reading a text once is never enough if the material is new and important. Studies of effective fourth-grade teachers (Allington & Johnston, 2002) revealed that they often help students to engage in rehearsing the same materials many times as a tool to their learning. Regularly modeling and reinforcing a process of anticipating, building knowledge, and consolidating learning will create active, confident readers (Pressley et al., 1998).

Teach It! 45

Graphic Organizers

The Nature of Informational Texts

Reading to learn is linked generally to reading informational materials, not pieces of fiction or poetry. Successful reading for the sake of learning requires readers to develop specific strategies to use magazines, trade books, newspapers, primary documents, and Internet sites. For example, readers of informational texts will notice that they don't have to start on the first page and read to the end of the material. Rather, by using the table of contents and index, they can find a pertinent section without reading the whole text. Or they might be able to skip parts that are less essential to their purposes. The first thing they might observe about informational material is that it is organized differently from fiction both internally and externally.

Developing Familiarity with External Features of Informational Texts

One of the first things we notice when we pick up nonfiction or informational materials is that they generally have a format different from fiction, with many external aids to help readers negotiate them. These aids include the following:

Table of contents

Chapters

Headings and subheadings

Illustrations (e.g., maps, graphs, diagrams, pictures, cartoons)

Captions

Index

Vocabulary noted in italics or other graphic ways

Glossary of terms

References

In surveying the features of books, we note that in addition to a table of contents, these books generally include a glossary and an index. The chapter titles are worth some attention because they are often key indicators of how the author has organized the information. Within each chapter, there is likely to be a further breakdown of information with headings and subheadings designed to guide our reading to important content or main ideas. Many books and articles also highlight key vocabulary with italic or boldface type or in marginal notes that provide explanations of the terms. A well-organized informational piece includes several of these external features that help us locate the part of the text we want to read when we have particular questions we want answered. In addition, because timely, accurate information is important, readers need to be aware of both the copyright date and the author's qualifications.

Books for very young readers are just now becoming more complete, so looking for chapter divisions is important before books are selected for primary students. Check to see whether the pages are numbered because it is hard to locate and return to information without some pagination. As you help children use informational books, be sure you have high-quality books available for them. Sometimes the color photographs are stunning, but the rest of the important book features are inadequate or missing. Some books now display graphics in a wide variety of places on the pages and often on a two-page spread. The captions are often placed variously, too. Sometimes the captions are beneath the picture; at other times, they are beside or even above the illustrated material. Only by carefully studying the individual pages and mapping the positions of text, graphics, and captions can their relationships be determined. It is important to share with the children that process of exploration and what readers must learn about the text layout. Without support from teachers, young readers can overlook much of the richness of these new informational texts. When you introduce a new informational text or textbook, it is useful to do a picture and visual walk through the text. Each new text deserves attention because there are so many different formats and organization is highlighted in so many ways.

FOCUS STUDENTS' ATTENTION ON FEATURES The increased focus on informational text reading means that students need to develop their abilities to use the features of informational texts that help them build their understanding. The CCSS standards for informational reading elaborate on the development of these skills and place much of the focus for this instruction in the primary grades. See Standards 5 and 6 for first and second grades below.

Write Informational Book Reports A good way to reinforce the special nature of informational books is to have first- and second-grade students complete nonfiction book

Knowing Features of Informational Text

First grade, Information Reading Standard 5.   Know and use various text features (e.g., captions, bold print, subheadings, glossaries, indexes, electronic menus, icons) to locate key facts or information in a text efficiently.

6. Name the author and illustrator of a text and define the role of each in presenting the ideas or information in a text.

Second grade, Information Reading Standard 5.   Distinguish between information provided by pictures or other illustrations and information provided by the words in a text.

6. Identify the main purpose of a text, including what the author wants to answer, explain, or to be comfortable with the features that help them navigate these materials.

reports using the checklist shown in Figure 8.3 that is part of a four-sided "booklet" a team of primary teachers created. By having a checklist of features, children develop a habit of using these features regularly. In addition, the book report asks students to tell what they liked, what they learned, and what would make the book better, and then to draw a picture that reflects the main idea of the book (adapted from D. Gurvitz).

Preview Informational Texts   Intermediate-grade teachers also can have children preview expository texts they are using both as textbooks and as other resource materials. Students have fun when teachers prepare scavenger hunts that can be completed by using text features like the Table of Contents, index, and glossary. For example, a partner scavenger hunt based on the book *Hurricane* (Haselhurst, 2006) included the following:

1. Which chapter gives information on how to prepare for a hurricane?
2. Where is information that clarifies the differences between hurricanes and tropical cyclones?
3. On which pages are there maps of hurricane paths?
4. Where is the term *debris* defined?
5. How is the book organized to help keep your interest and help you learn?

Figure 8.3 Nonfiction Book Checklist

Title _____	
Author _____	
Nonfiction Book Checklist	Something I liked about this book:
_____ 1. Table of contents	
_____ 2. Index	
_____ 3. Photographs	
_____ 4. Realistic, accurate illustrations	
_____ 5. Maps	
_____ 6. Diagrams	
_____ 7. Captions—bold lettering	Something I learned from this book:
_____ 8. Glossary—words and definitions	
_____ 9. Page numbers	
_____ 10. Other	

At the beginning of the year, it is always good to refresh students' use of all the ways information is available. Reading aloud to students from magazines and books and consciously thinking aloud provides further opportunity to focus their attention on illustrations, captions, and other presentations of information. Viewing a transparency of the first one or two pages in a chapter or article with the class lets you talk with the students about what they do when they navigate a page of informational text. In fact, informational texts are similar to the computer programs with which many students spend a great deal of leisure time. Students can have fun exploring the similarities and differences in materials presented in these two formats. After such a comparison, encourage students to add diagrams and other visuals or links from their textbooks to other sources. They can become active in making materials more accessible. Rather than feeling overwhelmed by texts, students need to develop confidence in using texts and in going beyond single texts when these are not clear. (See Being a Professional Reading Teacher.)

Predict Tables of Contents   Intermediate-grade students should begin to anticipate how informative expository material is organized. By third grade, most students should be able to predict what might be in the table of contents of an animal book (e.g., description, habitat, food, family). Before studying regions of the earth in fourth grade, some students should be able to identify possible topics that will reoccur with each region studied (e.g., plants, animals, geography, human life). Fifth graders need to know that biographies have some common topics that are used to organize information (e.g., early life, education, hardships, accomplishments). One way to assess students' awareness of these expert ways of organizing content information and then using it to prepare for reading and learning is to have them create a possible table of contents alone or with a partner. In this way, teachers can help students to think more deeply and to begin to develop principled knowledge (see the Teach It! box).

Create Chapter Graphic Organizers   At the middle-grade level, some teachers have students identify and use the external structure of chapters in textbooks and magazines to make notes. They skim through the chapter and create a graphic organizer or map of the chapter with the title in the center and each of the main headings on one spoke of their spider map (see Figure 8.4). This graphic organizer is then used while students read to help them understand how the information is related. This mapping of the text can also

Being a Professional Reading Teacher

Collecting Books for Reading Aloud

Teachers model good reading for their students. One way you can prepare for your role is to build a collection of texts that you can read to your students. You probably remember some special books that teachers read to you. You may also remember teachers who read aloud to you from the newspaper or current magazines. Begin collecting informational materials you can share with your students. Find good biographies and autobiographies that you can use to entice students into reading about real people and events. (For example, Barack Obama has written a very accessible autobiography, *Dreams from My Father: A Story of Race and Inheritance*.) Locate books about special holidays like the Mexican Day of the Dead, the Muslim religious month of Ramadan, and the American holidays

of Halloween and Fourth of July. With increasingly diverse student populations in our schools, all students can learn about important traditions. These make good read-aloud texts.

If you read magazines like *National Geographic* and *Smithsonian*, start making a file of good articles that you can read to students to entice them into expanding their own interests. As you visit schools, talk with teachers about the magazines they bring in to share with their students and start making a list of resources that can deepen what you can bring to your future students. Reading aloud to students from informational texts is an important part of building students' familiarity with these resources and expanding their interests.

Using the Table of Contents to Predict

There are many ways to help students become familiar with the structure and organization of informational materials. One of the easiest is to predict what content a book might contain and then check the table of contents to see how the authors have organized the text. For example, before beginning an oral reading of a book on polar bears, a first-grade teacher asked her students what they thought they might learn as they listened to her read this interesting book. One eager boy blurted out, "How they fish for their food!" Soon other children volunteered their ideas: why they are white, how they take care of their babies, and more. The teacher praised the children for their ideas and then turned to the table of contents of the book. She ran her finger down the list of chapters or sections and said, "Um, yes, the book begins with 'An Arctic Home'—that must tell about where they live. 'A Fight for Food'—that must tell us about how they

get their food." In this way she modeled for the students the way they could begin to think like experts—and build the foundation for principled knowledge of polar bears.

With older students, skimming through the headings of an article or chapter can provide an overview of the author's organization. When these reader aids do not indicate the text structure, students can do a quick read and use stick-on notes to label the text parts as they occur. Then students can create a graphic organizer to guide their reading of the material. Many teachers have found that having students learn to create graphic organizers of informational texts (articles, chapters, or books) provides a good road map for reading materials that might seem so dense that readers are in danger of getting lost in details.

be used as an interactive guide for reading. The students can brainstorm what they know about each section before reading; write those ideas on the map; highlight the areas that are least familiar and that will require slower reading, note making, and possible rereading; and then make notes on their map of new information as they read. This active engagement helps students to focus and retain information as they read.

Jigsaw Text Sections   Another strategy teachers employ to help students utilize the external structure of articles and chapters is to have a chapter read in cooperative fashion using a type of "jigsaw" cooperative learning strategy. The class first previews the text and identifies the major sections, which the teacher writes on the board. Then the class is

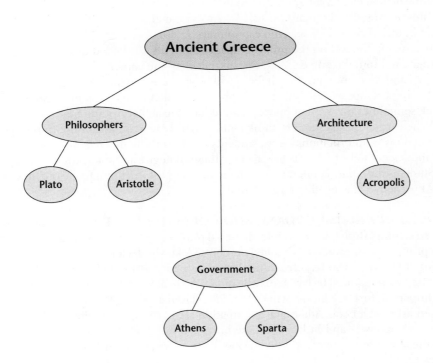

Figure 8.4 A Chapter Graphic Organizer

divided into teams, with one team assigned to each major section. Each team of students reads and creates a visual report of the key ideas of their one section of the text. Because many of the informational chapters and articles have such a heavy load of information, asking students to learn just one section from reading makes it manageable. Each group then reports on their section. Serving as "teachers" for the rest of the class both enhances the students' engagement in reading and creates a shared environment for learning.

Metacognitive Graphic Organizers

USE VISUAL AND GRAPHIC INFORMATION   Information presented visually in pictures, diagrams, and graphics is also critical in many informational texts. Graphic books are also becoming more and more available on content topics. You can also think of an informational book you have recently read or a children's book such as *Face to Face with Manatees* (Skerry, 2010) or *The Manatee Scientists* (Lourie, 2011) with their amazing photographs, informational sidebars, maps, drawings, and journal features. Today, good informational books, textbooks, and magazines use more pictures and visuals to enhance engagement and help readers understand the concepts than ever before. Much of the information, in fact, is presented in the pictures, graphs, diagrams, maps, cartoons, and their captions. This visual information is often essential to understanding the content. Teachers need to help students read this information and integrate it into the rest of the narrative textual content.

There are several ways to guide students' use of these texts to learn. First, assess how students attend to pages of busy text. Informally ask students individually to describe how they read a two-page spread in a book or magazine. As they share, make notes of their approaches. Where do they start? Do they read the visually presented information? When do they read it? Do they integrate the visuals and the running text? Do they read captions on graphs and pictures? Are they aware of how they approach reading when the materials are presented in a variety of formats? Do they integrate these different sources in notes they make or in summaries they create?

Questions such as these can help you to assess students' engagement with text materials. From this assessment, you can develop your instructional focus. A good starting point is modeling how to approach busy text by doing think-alouds such as the following with groups of students. Make a transparency of one or two pages of text. Using an overhead projector, demonstrate how you survey the page, noting the different layout of information and graphics and raising questions that are stimulated by the text. Start by looking at the title of the chapter or section and note the way the sections are marked—with boldface print or words in capital letters, for example. Then, focus on the visuals, such as pictures, diagrams, or notes in the margins. Ask, "Why did the author/s use this cartoon? What is its role in this section? Let's see, the caption says . . . Oh, yes, I bet it is an example of . . ." By covering up the text on the projected pages, students can be led to survey the graphic information. From this survey, students can reflect on the content they think is being emphasized and what questions they believe will be answered on the next page or two. In this way, the importance of using the visually presented material may become clearer to them. In fact, sometimes this kind of preview can reduce the actual reading time considerably.

When teachers take time to think aloud about how to approach the mixed types of presentations in informational texts, students begin to think metacognitively about their own approaches to texts. Adults use many of these strategies automatically when appropriate. Students, by contrast, often need to hear another person's thinking before they understand how active they need to be as readers.

UNDERSTANDING THE ORGANIZATION OF INTERNET SITES.   Internet Web sites have an external structure just as informational print texts do. The organization is different from print, but has some of the same elements. A key to deciding if a Web site is worth reading is knowing who has created it. This information is located on the initial page of each site and is required by law. It may be under the heading, "About Us" or "Home." This is an important first step in surveying a Web site. It is like looking for the author, illustrator, and publisher of a book. Additional information about the site can often be found in the section on Sponsors and in links that are provided. Just as students may find it useful to draw the layout of a page of a printed textbook, they also can learn a great deal about Web

Comprehending Non-Textual Information

According to CCSS Information Standard 7, students should be able to:

Third Grade: Use information gained from illustrations (e.g., maps, photographs) and the words in a text to demonstrate understanding of the text (e.g., where, when, why, and how key events occur).

Fourth Grade: Interpret information presented visually, orally, or quantitatively (e.g., in charts, graphs, diagrams, time lines, animations, or interactive elements on Web pages) and explain how the information contributes to an understanding of the text in which it appears.

Fifth Grade: Draw on information from multiple print or digital sources, demonstrating the ability to locate an answer to a question quickly or to solve a problem efficiently.

site layout by sketching the various sections on two or three Web pages and then comparing them. See Figure 8.5 for a general frame for this evaluation.

Evaluating Sites Web sites are often selected by teachers or through adult supervision. However, it is also good to teach students how to identify good Web sites themselves. A step that precedes going to the Web site itself often comes as students use a search engine (AolKIDS, Yahooligans, Awesome Library, etc.) to locate possible sources online. The URLs tell a great deal about the site authors and can help in the selection of a good Web site. Sites that are government- or university-sponsored are generally more reliable than those that come with a ".com" address. Teachers can help students in site selection by writing a sample set of URLs on the board as students begin the study of a particular topic where they will use online sources. For example, as students in one class began researching information about the building of the Statue of Liberty, their teacher wrote the following URLs on the board and asked which ones they thought would provide the best, most reliable information:

1. <www.nps.gov/Elis> (National Parks Service)
2. <www.nyctrip.com> (travel company with tours to the site)
3. <www.statueofliberty.org> (private organization supporting the statue)
4. <www.wikipedia.org>
5. <www.NYDN.com> (*New York Daily News*, with stories written by subscribers)

In the discussion that followed, students thought about the impact of site sponsors and promoters on the information presented; these insights helped the class become more critically aware of how to look for information. The teacher followed up this initial part of the search for sites by showing students how they could also cross-check information by using encyclopedias that are online or checking print sources and textbooks that are edited before being made public.

Once a few Web sites are selected, students need to learn to navigate the sites themselves. The organization of Web pages varies considerably, and the best formats keep evolving. Some have key categories and options listed in ways that make them easy to use; others can be cluttered and take several steps to navigate. Taking the time to walk through Web site

Home	About Us	Connect	How to ...	Programs

Figure 8.5 Analyzing Internet Sites

structure using an LCD projector and to "think aloud" about how to scan the various parts of the visual layout can be very helpful to young users. Research by Leu and others (2007) indicates that all too often, students don't explore Web sites in enough depth to make the most of the resources that are available. Knowing how material is organized and which categories are the most general are important keys to using Webs sites. So, too, is interpreting the visually presented information. Students can use some of the same methods for looking at Web pages that they use for scanning and interpreting pictures and visuals in texts.

Developing Understanding of Internal Organization

Another key to reading and learning from materials written to inform is becoming familiar with the way the writer has organized the ideas. As readers of narrative stories, we have learned—often first by listening to stories our parents read to us—that fiction has a predictable pattern. We read to find out who the characters are, what problem they encounter, and how they go about resolving it. Then we savor their victory at the end. No similar single pattern characterizes informational texts; however, there are clearly discernable structures that it is important to help students identify. Even very young children are often quite able to recognize and use some of these patterns (Langer, 2011). The most common ways of organizing ideas in informational texts include the following:

Description (main ideas and details)
Compare/contrast
Problem/solution
Cause/effect
Sequence of events

These varying patterns can make predicting and organizing ideas more difficult for novice readers; therefore, it is all the more important that teachers provide guidance so students can learn to identify these internal structures. As they do, their ability to write informational pieces and reports more effectively also will improve. Here again, graphic organizers can help students recognize the underlying organization of texts. Figure 8.6 shows some simple models.

CCSS
• Literature and Informational Texts 5: Craft and Structure

COMPARE TEXTS One way to introduce internal patterns of texts is by collecting several books on the same topic and guiding students to compare their internal structures. By introducing the reading of the book in this way, you engage the students to think in terms of the big picture about what an author is trying to accomplish in a text. An easy way to create varieties of texts is to download articles from online encyclopedias and Internet articles and compare their organization. This can be a starting place for contrasting and comparing longer articles and books (see the Being a Professional Reading Teacher box). By comparing and contrasting two to three texts on the same topic, you can help students understand how point of view and perspective influence writing. This is also one of the expectations of the CCSS informational reading standards. See the box with Craft and Structure, Standard 6.

CCSS
• Literature and Informational Texts 6: Craft and Structure (Point of View)

WRITE TEXTS A good way to help students apply their knowledge of text organization is to have them write their own books using the structure of one they have studied. For example, during a unit on insects, third-grade students used Brown's (1949) *The Important Book* as a model for their writing. Each student wrote about his or her chosen insect and used the book structure as a guide. They took the text's predictable pattern,

> *The important thing about _____ is that _____. They have _____, _____, and _____, but the important thing about _____ is _____,*

and wrote about insects. One child had studied bees and wrote, "The important thing about a bee is that it stings. It is true that a bee has two pairs of wings and collects honey,

Figure 8.6 Graphic Organizer Models

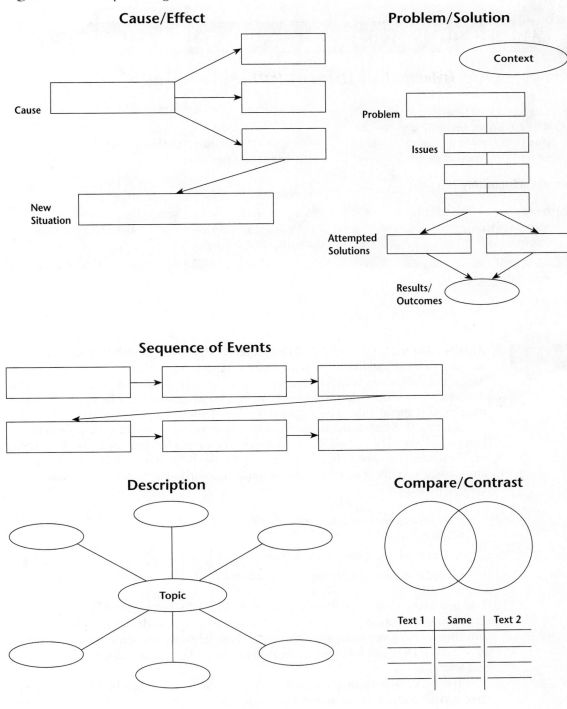

Cause/Effect

Cause

New Situation

Problem/Solution

Context

Problem

Issues

Attempted Solutions

Results/ Outcomes

Sequence of Events

Description

Topic

Compare/Contrast

Text 1	Same	Text 2

but the important thing about a bee is that it STINGS!" Each child used this same pattern to write about his or her insect and the teacher then collected the pieces into a class book, *Important Insects*. This experience helped students focus their attention on simple, predictable text structures. Later, the teacher introduced other, more standard structures used by authors of informational books they were reading. With this concrete experience in writing, the students were more attuned to organization and the structure of ideas.

Being a Professional Reading Teacher

Develop Interest in Informational Reading

As children develop their abilities to process information through reading, expository text becomes a very important source. What are the major differences between processing expository text and processing narrative text? What strategies are most effective?

Reading Comprehension in Expository Text

- Why is background knowledge such an important factor when students are reading informational text? How can we tap that knowledge before and during reading?

- How are vocabulary and text structure factors in understanding expository text?

- Name some effective strategies for reading informational text. Compare and contrast them with strategies for reading narrative text.

Text Features

What text features do authors of expository text use? How can they be useful to students reading this textbook? How would the appearance of this textbook change without them?

Connect Two

ATTEND TO VOCABULARY AND CONTENT-SPECIFIC TERMINOLOGY A key to learning content material is to give attention to vocabulary that conveys key concepts. Again, the differences between reading for one's own purposes and reading to learn are dramatic. When one reads for oneself, unfamiliar vocabulary can be ignored. In fact, good readers attend only to information that they know is helpful in comprehending. As a result, they skip unfamiliar terms. In reading to learn, however, this practice can hinder comprehension. The unfamiliar terms are often exactly what the reader needs to attend to. Therefore, you need to help students develop the habit of attending to key terms that are content carriers. There are three important components to vocabulary learning in content materials:

- Words the authors prioritize (e.g., with boldface, italics, marginal definitions, or illustrations)
- Teacher-highlighted key new terms
- Students' own monitoring of what words are new and need to be learned

The first place to start in attending to vocabulary is by noting what the authors have already indicated as important. Without teacher guidance, students often overlook these aids. Because authors often assist readers by highlighting these terms, helping students to preview material to find these indicated words can be a great support to later reading and learning.

Teachers can help students note key words, too, by creating a list of key terms and then giving students some activities to focus their attention on these terms. One easy way to do this is to ask students to connect two (or three) of the terms and create new sentences using them. Even if the students do not know much about the words, they can have fun anticipating what they mean. Working with partners to create new sentences gives children a chance to use the words orally, too, thus increasing their awareness of the words both visually and orally. A more sophisticated activity is to ask students to chunk new words into categories and then label the groups and justify them to the class. The children now are attuned to these words and will definitely notice them as they read. (See the Differentiated Instruction box for ideas to use with English language learners.)

DIFFERENTIATED INSTRUCTION

Reading Comprehension: Understanding and Learning with Informational Texts

Many students who speak languages other than English in their homes do very well with conversational English, and teachers may be unaware of the need to provide specific instruction when it comes to the academic vocabulary necessary for content area reading and learning. Yet this is an area deserving particular attention. Research studies have highlighted the fact that there is a great difference between conversational English and academic English competence. Teachers can do a lot to help English language learners be successful in this area of academic learning by focusing on vocabulary development.

Begin by assessing students' depth of understanding of key academic terms. For example, if the unit in social studies is about the westward movement of European pioneers across the continent, then terms like *pioneer, covered wagon, wagon train, trails, obstacles,* and *hardships* will probably be needed. These are terms that students would not encounter in normal conversational contexts. They are academic terms needed for this particular unit of study. In a similar way, as a unit in science on light is initiated, teachers highlight terms that will be used and check to see if academic terms like *opaque, translucent, transparent, reflection,* and *refraction* are familiar to students.

Because these are words not used in regular conversational English, they need to be highlighted and taught specifically.

It is often helpful to English language learners to make a list of key terms and then compare them with the same terms in their home language. Because there are many Latin-based cognates used in English, this can make the learning task much easier. For example, the science terms can be listed on one side and the Spanish terms on the other.

Opaque	opaco/a
Reflection	reflexión
Refraction	refracción
Translucent	translúcido/a
Transparent	transparente

English language learners will be much more successful if teachers focus on key academic terms and provide them with extended opportunities to practice these words and phrases. It is in academic English that these English language learners deserve our help.

In addition to noting key words from the subject matter, teachers can be alert to important words from the text that are not content specific. Words from academic discourse that are not limited to a single subject area, but are also not much used in everyday speech are sometimes called *Tier Two words* (Beck, McKeown, & Kucan, 2002; Kucan, 2012). For example, *cotyledon* is a word that is specific to biology or botany; and *differentiate* is a word that is used in many contexts, but not normally in speech. Tier Two words are helpful for students to know because they are often encountered in their reading.

The Web site *WordSift* (<www.wordsift.com>) will let you paste in a passage of text and have it scanned to distinguish the easier words from the more challenging words—many of them Tier Two words. The program highlights the words; then, if you click on one, it will display a semantic map with words related to the target word. It will also show photographs of the words.

Students need to follow their initial search for terms with some active ways of retaining them. You can model this process by keeping a list of key terms on the board or on a word wall. This list can include both the words you introduced and ones the students identify as important. Then students can find more examples of these words being used in other places in their reading and listening and build a more elaborate meaning for the words. Asking students to draw their own images of the terms also helps to lock new words and meanings in place.

Elaborating associations with new words through drawings and personal examples will help students to retain the words. Concept maps for the terms can also be used (see Figure 8.7). In this way, students learn that terms have meanings, associated examples, and attributes. Specific terms are critical in content learning. Marzano (2004) has provided an excellent summary of the key academic terms students need to know and use to

New Literacies

How can your use of specific vocabulary help students develop their interest in precise language?

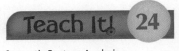

Teach It! 24

Semantic Feature Analysis

Teach It! 21

"Word Conversations" for Primary Grades

Figure 8.7 Concept of Definition Map

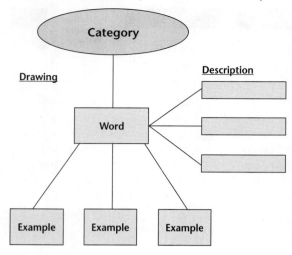

meet the content standards in each of eleven academic areas. Some school districts are now identifying key terms that students should know and be able to use for each grade level. This is one way they are highlighting the importance of specific academic language in learning.

With the importance of vocabulary in informational materials, students need to develop their own metacognitive control over what words are new to them, and they need to develop ways to retain those particular terms and their meanings. Individual vocabulary notebooks and word cards are good tools for students to use to rehearse and practice these words. Making new vocabulary a part of the oral talk of the classroom is an essential component in this process. Some teachers employ a reward system to encourage usage, such as giving students points when they hear and note a new word being used by a fellow student. This highlights oral as well as written vocabulary recognition and provides an internal incentive as well.

Strategies for Active Reading of Informational Text

As students become familiar with the structure of informational text, they must develop ways to engage actively with the authors of those texts and think about the content. There are some basic strategies worth practicing to the extent that students can use them on their own. These strategies have been developed independently, but often work well when used together. Here are few basic guidelines worth remembering:

1. Build the habit of students underlining (their own books) or putting sticky notes on important ideas and information. This habit can also be extended by making notes or graphic outlines of important information. It is the practice of reading with a pencil and paper at one's side.

2. Model and reinforce the importance of previewing informational material carefully and then rereading. There is an overwhelming amount of information in a good text and one reading is not sufficient.

3. Develop in students the habit of using all the visual information available as they read—making the connections the authors and illustrators provide for readers.

Prereading Preparation

Until students are able to take control of their learning by finding their own questions and level of knowledge, it is unlikely that they will retain much of what is studied. Therefore, the time spent activating personal and class interest is important.

 The K-W-L strategy supports students' ability to connect their prior knowledge to their new learning. How is the K-W-L used in this video to support students' learning about coral reefs?

K-W-L Students become much more engaged in reading when they and their interests are the starting point for new inquiry and learning. *K-W-L* (Ogle, 1986, 1991) is a group process in which the teacher models and guides active engagement with informational texts. It uses the knowledge and information students bring to help each other build a better starting place for learning and for sharing the results of their reading. The adept teacher weaves together what some class members know (either topical or principled knowledge) and stimulates questions for all to pursue as they read to learn. The process also helps students who lack confidence in both reading and writing because the teacher is the first one to write on the board (see Figure 8.8). This permits children to see the written forms of

Figure 8.8 K-W-L Guide

1. K – What We Know	W – What We Want to Learn	L – What We Learned and Still Need to Know

2. Categories of Information We Expect to Use:

A.   E.

B.   F.

C.   G.

D.   H.

3. Where We Will Find Information:

1.

2.

3.

4.

Source: K-W-L Guide, D. Ogle (1986), from "K-W-L: A Teaching Model That Develops Active Reading of Expository Text," in *The Reading Teacher, 36*(6), 564–570. Reproduced with permission of Wiley Inc.

K-W-L charts provide a good strategy for motivating students' interest in new topics.

Teach It! 43

Paired Brainstorming

key terms they will encounter later in the text. It also models what the students will write on their own guide sheets (see Figure 8.8) or in their learning logs.

What We Know   The teacher and students begin the process of reading and learning by brainstorming together what they know (the **K** in K-W-L) about the topic. The teacher guides students to probe their knowledge statements and find conflicting or partial statements of what they know. For example, as a group brainstorms what they know about the desert, one student says, "Nothing much lives there." Another volunteers, "That's not true! I know lots of insects live there. I just read a book about tarantulas." The teacher can encourage more student engagement by continuing the thinking: "Does anyone else know something about what lives in the dry, barren lands of the desert? Can anyone frame a question that may help us find out more?"

Another student chimes in, "We'd better find out what animals can survive there with little water or food." The teacher writes on the blackboard, overhead, or computer what the students ask as their own questions and what they volunteer they think they know, writing down their ideas just as the students say them (see Figure 8.9). The teacher does not correct or evaluate, but encourages and stimulates students to think broadly about what they bring to the study. Through this brainstorming process, some questions or uncertainties generally surface.

The teacher's role is to help students activate their knowledge and develop interest in the topic. Some basic rules are established at the beginning:

- All ideas are acceptable.
- Say what first comes into your mind. These ideas will be checked and edited or revised later.
- Listen to each other, but do not judge the quality of ideas.
- The goal is to get as many different ideas out as possible in the time allotted.

As ideas are voiced and written down, they might seem random and unconnected. At this point, you need to make a decision. If the group is engaged and ready to think a little more deeply, ask the students to think of ways in which the experts organize information on this topic. This move to a deeper level of thinking (to principled knowledge) can begin by first focusing on categories of information about which the children already have some intuitive knowledge. You can initiate reflection: "Look at what we listed in the 'Know' column. Are any of these items connected? For example, I see three items about animals that live on the desert. I also see some plants. Can you find other items that go together in a category? What are the basic categories of information we are likely to need to use?" In this case, the categories might be those shown in Figure 8.10.

The teacher might also begin simply by asking students to step back and think about the topic generally: "If you were going to write a table of contents on this topic, the desert, what would you include?" The ideas that students volunteer can be listed at the bottom of the "Know" column.

WHAT WE KNOW

Lots of snakes

Sand and windy

Cactus

Road Runners

Tarantulas

Hot weather

No water

No rain

Gila monster

Lizards

Bats

Phoenix

Sun City

Oil under the ground

Utah and Arizona

Figure 8.9   What We Know About Deserts

What We Want to Know   With a variety of ideas being shared, the teacher can easily ask what the students want (the **W** in K-W-L) to know. Again, it is the students'

Figure 8.10 Categories of Information

Categories of Information:

A. animals   C. location   E. physical features

B. climate   D. plants

responsibility to think of real questions as you write down what they say. These questions form the second column on the worksheet or blackboard. If students are not familiar with the process of generating their own questions, you might need to model some questioning at the beginning. You might be able to extend comments made by class members into questions.

For example, if the class is beginning a unit on the desert region and someone has listed cactus as a plant in the desert, you can extend this by suggesting, "I wonder whether there are any uses people make of cactus in the desert?"

You can write this in the "We Want to Know" column and continue to guide students to find questions, suggesting, "Is there anything else we might want to learn about the animals that live on the desert? Do we have to be careful of any of them? If we were hiking, should we watch out?"

This process puts the students right in the center of any new study. Rather than beginning with a text and previewing it, the students and the teacher become active listeners and recorders. This group-focusing effort helps students think about the range of ideas that they and others already have on the topic. It should also help them make new connections and become intrigued by what they don't know. Listening to each other can stimulate new vocabulary and associations; the writing done by the teacher often helps more reluctant readers begin to make associations between oral language and the written forms of words they will encounter as they read.

Once the students have discussed the topic, they are more ready to begin their own reading. It might be useful to have students write down on their own worksheets or learning logs the pieces of information they individually think they know and the questions they want to know more about. In this way, both the group and the individual are respected. You could have students work in pairs to do both the writing and reading because this is more stimulating and supportive of some children who lack confidence in writing and taking risks.

What We Learned   You can diagnose from this discussion what texts will be most useful to the students. It might be that what you thought would be adequate turns out to be inappropriate. Rather than reading the planned text, the class can collect other materials and even write some of their own materials as needed. This is where the Internet can come in handy as a resource. Look up a few sites and bookmark them for the class. If the text or texts in the classroom and school library are appropriate, students can read and make notes on their own about what they learn (the **L** in K-W-L)—both answers to their questions and unexpected information they think is interesting and/or important. Many teachers create large bulletin boards with sections for the "What We Know," "What We Want to Learn," and "What We Learned" sections of the K-W-L project. Students can keep adding information and questions to the class chart as they study. Small index cards work well for this kind of class activity. You can also make photocopies of material or graphics that students find and want to have shared.

K-W-L+   After years of working with students in content areas, teachers know that even with motivation and engagement, students will not remember much of the new information the first time they encounter it. Therefore, the "plus" in **K-W-L+** (Carr & Ogle, 1987) extends this learning process by asking students to do more reorganizing of what they have learned by making a semantic map or graphic organizer of the key information (see Figure 8.11). Students select the major categories and list facts under those categories, thus rethinking what they are learning.

Figure 8.11 K-W-L+
Semantic Map

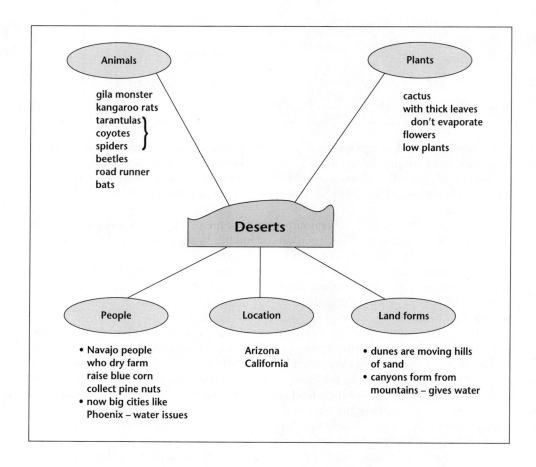

Finally, they write what they have learned in an essay, summary, or more personal form (see the example in Figure 8.12). The cognitive activity needed to use ideas they have been learning in a new written format deepens memory and provides an additional opportunity to consolidate their learning. Engaging actively in this variety of learning gives the students a sense of how they can become active learners on their own, even when the teacher is not present. Reorganizing and rehearsing new knowledge and connecting it with what was previously known establishes for students the effort needed in learning and reinforces their personal self-esteem because they possess a productive process for school tasks (see the Assessment box). This whole process prepares students for the expectations contained in the CCSS that call for "integration of knowledge and ideas" (Standards 7–9).

CCSS

Synthesizing Information from Several Sources

Reading Standards 7–9, Integration of Knowledge and Ideas

7. Integrate and evaluate content presented in diverse media and formats, including visually and quantitatively, as well as in words.
8. Delineate and evaluate the argument and specific claims in a text, including the validity of the reasoning as well as the relevance and sufficiency of the evidence.
9. Analyze how two or more texts address similar themes or topics in order to build knowledge or to compare the approaches of the authors.

I-CHART   Using multiple sources of information is an important way to help students find texts that meet their own levels of knowledge and interest, discover answers to their own questions, and compare and contrast authors' points of view. It encourages the critical thinking so needed in the world today. Yet many students have a difficult time using

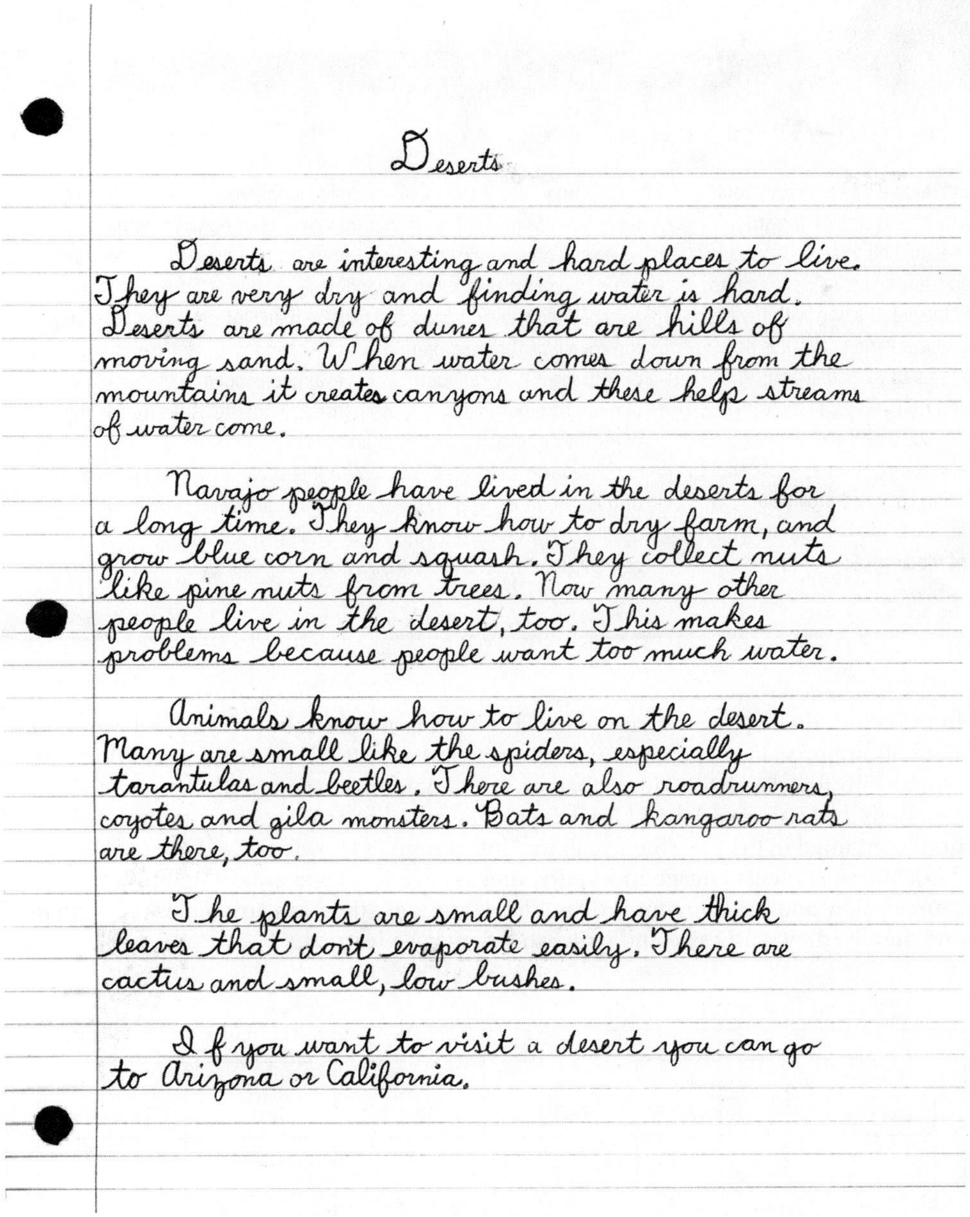

Figure 8.12 K-W-L+ Essay

Deserts

Deserts are interesting and hard places to live. They are very dry and finding water is hard. Deserts are made of dunes that are hills of moving sand. When water comes down from the mountains it creates canyons and these help streams of water come.

Navajo people have lived in the deserts for a long time. They know how to dry farm, and grow blue corn and squash. They collect nuts like pine nuts from trees. Now many other people live in the desert, too. This makes problems because people want too much water.

Animals know how to live on the desert. Many are small like the spiders, especially tarantulas and beetles. There are also roadrunners, coyotes and gila monsters. Bats and kangaroo rats are there, too.

The plants are small and have thick leaves that don't evaporate easily. There are cactus and small, low bushes.

If you want to visit a desert you can go to Arizona or California.

more than one source effectively. Hoffman (1992) has developed a very useful tool in the *I-Chart* (see Figure 8.13), which helps students take important questions, select three to four sources of information they want to use to explore those questions, and then come to their own conclusion about the questions they framed initially.

Once students have used the K-W-L process to activate their knowledge and interest, they select some key questions for more in-depth research that they can do together. The class or small groups can decide on the questions they want to concentrate on and write these on the chart. Then the best sources of information to answer the questions are selected, usually with teacher help and guidance, and they are also listed across the top of the chart. This simple framework establishes that multiple sources are needed when seeking answers to questions.

The practice of summarizing the information and answering their own questions scaffolds the process of inquiry well. Using the I-Chart establishes a simple framework for a systematic search for information. The chart also includes a column for interesting

Involving Students in Self-Assessment

As children move into the intermediate and middle grades, they should be involved in monitoring their own growth as readers. Having students maintain Reading Logs helps them become more self-conscious about their reading habits, preferences, and strategies. Asking them to keep a record of all the books and articles they read along with their responses to the pieces is an easy starting place. Periodically, it is helpful to ask all students to record their responses to particular texts. In this way you can compare how students respond and what focus they reflect. Asking students to share their responses with each other is a good way to stimulate a discussion of the various ways readers attend to and construct meaning from texts. Reading Logs can provide an on-going record of engagement and help teachers know if students need to be encouraged to expand their range of readings. Some students tend to stay in one genre or with very easy books.

Another way learning can be made visible to students is to have them keep samples of texts that they have marked with marginal notes or sticky notes during the four quarters of the school year. They can return to earlier text notations and analyze changes. If students are engaged with several units and reading many informational texts over the course of the year, there should be changes in depth and range of responses they can look for. For example, students can track the number of times they make comparisons across texts, as well as the times they question authors' inferences, ask questions of a text, and visualize ideas presented. The K-W-L sheets can be a good component of this kind of activity, too. Students can evaluate the quality of their questions, the extent to which they fulfill their desires to learn new content, and the graphic organizers and summaries they create.

information, that is, pieces that do not fit the basic questions but still are relevant to the students' inquiry. This often becomes an important way to take notes on ideas that can be shared with the class later—ideas that are full of potential for more reading.

Both the KWL+ and the I-Chart are frameworks that prepare students for the expectations contained in the CCSS that call for "integration of knowledge and ideas" (Standards 7–9). When students engage in inquiry, they read and integrate information from varied sources, they analyze different text structures and note the ways authors use of evidence, and, finally, they synthesize and write what they have learned.

Figure 8.13 I-Chart

Questions	What We Know	Text 1	Text 2	Text 3	Summary
1.					
2.					
3.					
Interesting new info./ New questions					

Reading Strategies

K-W-L and the I-Chart are frameworks through which teachers can engage students personally and cooperatively in thinking about their relationship to a content area to be studied and in setting a course for learning. The frameworks do not show students how to actually engage with the text as they read it, however. That is where good instruction can help students as they work with interesting texts. Several ways teachers can guide students in reading carefully and with good comprehension follow. In addition, it is good to visit the CCSS standards as you consider how you can help students develop text comprehension. The "key ideas and details" is the first section of the CCSS. See the CCSS box below.

CCSS

Close Reading of Informational Text

Anchor Reading Standards 1–3, Key Ideas and Details

1. Read closely to determine what the text says explicitly and to make logical inferences from it; cite specific textual evidence when writing or speaking to support conclusions drawn from the text.
2. Determine central ideas or themes of a text and analyze their development; summarize the key supporting details and ideas.
3. Analyze how and why individuals, events, and ideas develop and interact over the course of a text.

SHARED AND CLOSE READING   Primary students need many opportunities to be guided by their teachers in thinking as they read texts with many ideas and combined types of information. The teacher-guided practice of shared reading was developed for use with big books; however, it also works well when teachers use the large-size news magazines (*Time for Kids*) that can be put on easels. The teacher draws students' attention to the text features, the visuals, and information about the authors. Then, depending on the reading abilities of the students, the teacher either reads most of the text or involves students in reading small sections. The first read is followed by second and third reads, with students taking over more of the reading as well as the rereading of important portions. This practice permits teachers to model key comprehension strategies and then listen as students copy the same moves.

When a large text isn't available, teachers can develop close reading by using the same news magazines or articles from children's magazines. By showing the text on a visualizer, the teacher can guide students in reading for key ideas and arguments, along with locating supporting information and examples in the text. Instructions to find important ideas and either underline them or have the teacher mark them can focus students on careful reading. Ask students questions like:

"What did you think was most important in this paragraph?"

"What information does the author give to explain ?"

"Can you draw lines to connect the ideas/examples that fit together?"

"What questions do we need to ask?"

Developing the habit of close reading comes with these teacher-led group activities, followed by gradually releasing the responsibility to students, putting charts of ways to question texts and monitor comprehension on the walls, and then having students read with partners, implementing their own careful reading together. As students realize how much there is to think about and connect, they appreciate the time it takes to reflect on the texts and share their ideas and questions with one another. This practice also helps students gain comfort with the more academic vocabulary they encounter throughout most informational materials.

PAIRED READING/PAIRED SUMMARIZING   Paired reading/paired summarizing is another classroom reading activity that supports students' engagement with short texts. In paired reading/paired summarizing, students join a partner and they read a text together; then, they divide the text into chunks of one or two paragraphs. The first student reads a chunk aloud as the other student reads along silently. Then, the first student summarizes what the passage said. The second student then asks questions about the passage to probe its meaning. Both students attempt to answer the questions. The students exchange roles for the next passage. As in the implementation of most routines, students will play their roles more effectively if the teacher first demonstrates what is meant by making an effective summary and by asking good questions and gives students a chance to respond to some examples.

RECIPROCAL TEACHING   One of the most researched strategies for engaged reading of informational text for intermediate and middle students is *reciprocal teaching*. Developed by Palincsar and Brown (1986) to help less able readers handle the demands of expository texts, reciprocal teaching includes four different strategies that students learn to use. You first model each of the strategies and then turn the teacher's role over to the students. The students apply what they are learning by becoming teachers for their classmates and guiding the continued reading of small portions of text. The four basic strategies are as follows:

1. Summarize what has just been read.
2. Think of two or three good questions about the passage.
3. Clarify any ideas or information that was not clear.
4. Predict what you think will be in the next part of the text.

In conducting a reciprocal teaching exercise, decide in advance how large the chunks of text will be that the students will read before you engage them in thinking about that portion. The text units should be short enough that the students can discuss each in five to seven minutes. Tell the students you will be the first discussion leader and that the students should pay attention to how you conduct the discussion, not just focus on answering the questions.

Model reading a short section of text and creating a summary of the main ideas. Depending on the group and the amount of time needed to teach each of the four strategies, you might spend several sessions on a single strategy, or you might model more than one at a time until all four strategies become part of the readers' response to each paragraph or segment. Students learn to ask good questions about the text through this process. They also learn to identify problems that hinder comprehension—vocabulary items that are unfamiliar, for example, or references that are confusing, or other unclear aspects—and ask questions to clarify these problems posed by the text. Finally, they learn to make predictions about where the text is leading. Students then assume the teacher role for each segment of text so that during a class period, many students have had the opportunity to lead their fellow students in considering the meaning of a common text. You can create a visible chart of the four strategies to help students understand the process. This becomes a guide for students when they lead the discussions.

This form of guided and shared reading has been effective in helping less able readers make sense of dense text material. The combination of good interactive strategies with group-oriented teaching and a shared learning approach helps students maintain interest in and focus on the material they are studying. The Teach It! box provides an example of how one teacher used reciprocal teaching in his classroom.

It is not easy to generate increased interest or to give students a sense of power when dealing with difficult and dense reading material. Both reciprocal teaching and the teaching strategy—Questioning the Author—(see pages 273–274 in Chapter 9 for a detailed discussion) give teachers and students supportive alternatives to round robin reading, a still overused way to have students read content texts.

METACOGNITIVE GRAPHIC ORGANIZER   Although several variations that are helpful for intermediate and middle grade students have emerged in recent years (Radcliffe,

Reciprocal Teaching

George Mead and five of his fifth-grade students are reading a short informative text on crocodiles and alligators. Mr. Mead is still modeling the reciprocal teaching process with these troubled readers because they have had only a few experiences with the process. He has decided in advance that this text is best read in units of paragraphs. These students are very unconfident about their abilities as readers and the text is dense.

Mr. Mead announces that he will be the discussion leader for the first paragraph. He advises students not only to pay attention to the paragraph and participate in the discussion, but also to observe carefully how he conducts the discussion. They know that each of them will play the role of the discussion leader when the next paragraphs are read. Mr. Mead has prepared a chart that lists the steps that are taken after each paragraph is read. He refers the students to the chart to help them follow the procedure he is using as he leads the discussion. Mr. Mead asks everyone to read the first paragraph silently. When they are finished, he gives a verbal summary of the paragraph and looks around at the students to ask if they would summarize the passage in the same way or if they have something to add. Next, Mr. Mead formulates a question. He takes care with the question because as well as eliciting their ideas, he is demonstrating the art of questioning for the students. He asks, "What are the easiest ways to tell the differences between alligators and crocodiles?" He draws out the students' ideas on this question and affirms their suggestions. When Matt volunteers that the shape of the mouths might be easier to notice than either how their teeth fit together or whether the animal has sensory pits, especially if one was coming at you, he gets a nod.

Next, Mr. Mead attempts to clarify parts of the paragraph that are unclear to the students. He notes that the word *crocodilian* is used for the whole group of reptiles that includes crocodiles, alligators, and caimans. He asks whether someone can clarify when to use *crocodilian* and when to use *crocodile*. As the students try to differentiate the uses of the terms orally, Mr. Mead knows that they are becoming more familiar with these words in both their reading and their speaking. To help them as they clarify, he writes the words on the chalkboard as one student explains that *crocodilian* should be above the other three words, *crocodile, caiman,* and *alligator,* because they are all examples of this group of reptiles. Then Mr. Mead goes on to make a prediction, suggesting that the text will probably tell how these different reptiles survive. Finally, he assigns the next section of the text.

After that paragraph is read, Mr. Mead takes another turn as discussion director to make sure the students fully understand how to carry out the steps in conducting a discussion before it becomes their turn. Mr. Mead often refers to the chart as he conducts each step in the discussion. He knows that if the students do not clearly understand how to conduct the procedure, he will have to intervene later, which will undermine the students' autonomy and confidence. Before the third passage is read, Mr. Mead points to the student on his left and asks her to lead the next discussion. After that student has had her turn, the role of discussion leader passes to the student on her left, and so on.

Caverly, Hand, & Franke, 2008), the key to the metacognitive graphic organizer strategy is that students create their own graphic organizer as they preview a chapter of text and use this visual as a guide for their reading. The term *metacognition* refers to the process in which learners are self-aware of their own learning needs and can monitor and adjust to the demands of the text. Students place the title of the chapter or article in the center of a sheet of paper and then add the major headings from the chapter as they survey the material. After doing this, they return to the text and look at the visual information in charts, diagrams, and the like. They put key ideas from these visuals on the graphic where appropriate under the headings. They can add sub-heads if necessary to make the flow of the text clear. Once the author's structure and visuals are clearly framed, students return and do the metacognitive check by asking themselves and marking which sections are familiar (✓), which are unknown or unfamiliar (?), and which seem interesting (+). Sections that seem most necessary for the course, if that is the purpose of reading, can be highlighted with an asterisk (*). In this way, readers create a personal guide for reading and study. Then, while reading, students can make additional notes on the outline or on sticky notes.

When they have finished reading, students review the graphic and the notes they made and decide whether to revise the graphic, add to it, or write some extended notes to rehearse the important ideas. The final step of note-making is designed to encourage student reflection and learning. What an individual student does depends on how much detail needs to be absorbed to achieve the learning goal. It might be that the actual organization of the text is different from what the student initially drew and requires creating a revised text graphic. Or it might be that there are many new ideas, and the student needs to write a summary explaining the meaning of the ideas. Students monitoring their own learning can adjust this final stage of learning to their own needs to retain the content.

Personal graphic guides are very helpful to many students. They combine attention to the text with attention to the learner at the same time. In longer chapters, they help students maintain their focus on how all the ideas and sections fit together. They also provide a great tool for review and rehearsal later.

Questioning

Before we close this section on learning, it is valuable to address the role of questioning for both teachers and students. Asking and answering questions are major parts of the life of schools. Each of the active strategies described here requires both teachers and students to become good at asking important and thoughtful questions. Questioning is an important active thinking activity that learners use while reading and trying to make sense of text. It is a central part of comprehension for students and teachers. Therefore, it is valuable to spend time both in analyzing the questions you ask and in developing students' sensitivity to what constitutes good questions and good questioning. A starting place is to discuss with students what role questioning plays in learning and what they think good questions are. Direct the discussion to include the realization that some questions ask for very specific and direct information (e.g., "What was the pharaoh's role in religion?"), some for more abstract interpretations or conjectures (e.g., "What effect did the caste system have on how people treated each other?" or "What similar situation have we had in our country?"), and some are very personal (e.g., "What do you think or how do you feel?").

You also need to record yourself during class discussions and to analyze periodically how you use questioning. Traditionally, and continuing into today, many teachers have used questions to find out how well students have comprehended what they read. The teacher asks the student a question, the student answers, and the teacher gives some evaluative feedback. Researchers refer to this form of school dialogue as *I-R-E* (initiation, response, evaluation) and conclude that the process helps teachers test students more than it aids student comprehension (Mehan, 1979). To encourage students to ask good questions and engage in metacognitive self-monitoring, you need to model good thinking when sharing ideas out loud and questioning students.

You can use questioning to model the process of thinking before and during reading. Begin a lesson or introduce a story by asking students what they already know about a topic. This kind of questioning activates students' own thinking. Most teachers use questions to help students connect ideas, consolidate what they have read, and reflect on ideas. However, you can ask much more thoughtful and reflective questions by first considering how you want to focus students' reflections about what they have read. Think about how you can involve students in reflecting together to deepen their responses to questions you or the texts pose.

Many educators focus on the nature of the process of constructing meaning and argue that questions should ask students: "What do you predict will happen?" "What else could have been done?" and "What does this remind you of?" They argue that the reader–text interaction should be the focus of attention and that questions should derive from those interactions. Do readers connect and respond personally to what they read? Can they establish a purpose and fulfill their own purpose? This focus leads to another range of questions about text construction or engagement. Some students never seem to connect text to their own lives or to the reality around them. Thinking of this dimension of questioning can be helpful in planning for activities so that students see school learning as part of their own world (see the World of Reading box).

As we take time to consider the role of questioning in learning, we need ways to categorize and analyze the nature of our questions. There are some commonly used frameworks that can be used to help us in this activity. The most widely used is probably one developed by Benjamin Bloom and his colleagues in the 1950s. Bloom's taxonomy was not initially created for use by teachers, but was developed as a taxonomy of educational objectives to measure school goals and assessment. However, teachers saw its value and have used it as a tool to help them reflect on their classroom questioning patterns. The taxonomy has seven levels of questions: memory, translation, interpretation, application, analysis, synthesis, and evaluation.

In research studies of classroom talk, it is not uncommon to see analyses of the levels of teacher questions. In some descriptions of reading comprehension and reading assessment, Bloom's seven levels have been chunked into three or four levels. For example, one common way of describing reading is by thinking of literal, interpretive, applied, and critical levels of comprehension to define kinds of questions in relation to text.

Raphael (1986) has helped students to think about sources of information for questions they are to answer by creating four categories:

- **Right there:** Questions that can be answered directly from the text
- **Think and search:** Questions that require more than one piece of information from the text
- **Author and you:** Questions that go beyond the text
- **On your own:** Questions that rely on the reader

The whole strategy is called *Question-Answer-Relationships* and provides very practical definitions that make it easy for students to become more involved in both planning their strategies for responding and becoming aware metacognitively of the range of responses they need to be able to make to the text.

Taxonomies provide a helpful language to think about questioning and the kinds of thinking we want to help stimulate in students. Some teachers keep the levels of questions in their teacher manuals or put them on the bulletin boards so that both they and students are more aware of the need to go beyond the literal or memory level. Other teachers do not like to use taxonomies to evaluate comprehension. Rather than conceiving of them as a hierarchy, these teachers see taxonomies as an array of options that are available to use as appropriate.

Because the process of asking and answering questions is a critical part of teaching and evaluation, some focused attention to questions is necessary. By considering the nature of the questions they ask and the questions in the materials they give students, teachers can make the questions as valuable as possible. Modeling and attending to questioning provides the context for students to become more aware of their own questioning and encourages them to develop questioning skills that are useful to their own learning. Two strategies to use while students are reading that help them apply their knowledge of good questions are ReQuest and paired reading/paired summarizing (which was discussed earlier).

REQUEST PROCEDURE   The ReQuest procedure (Manzo, 1969) is best suited for use with informational texts. In this procedure, two students read through a text, stop after each paragraph, and take turns asking each other questions about it, which the other student must try to answer. It helps if the teacher serves as a partner when the technique is first introduced. Because one goal for teaching comprehension is to develop principled knowledge of the topic, the teacher's questions serve as valuable models of ways to inquire about the important ideas in a text.

For an example of the ReQuest procedure in action, assume you have assigned the students in the class to pairs. Amalia and David are reading a text together. After they both read the first paragraph silently, Amalia asks David three good questions about that paragraph. She asks questions about main ideas. She asks questions that probe beneath the surface. She asks what importance some item in this paragraph might come to have later in the text. David answers those questions as well as he can. After David has finished answering Amalia's questions, they both read the next paragraph. Now it is David's turn to ask Amalia questions about the new paragraph, and Amalia has to answer them. When both students

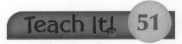

Teach It! 51

ReQuest Procedure

have brought to light the information in that paragraph, they read the next one, and Amalia gets the first turn at asking David several good questions about that paragraph, and so on.

The ReQuest procedure can be used well with a whole class, too. One way to do this is for the class to read one or two paragraphs from the text. Then, the students pause and close their books, and take turns asking the teacher all the questions that come to mind. Following that, they read a new paragraph and the roles are reversed: The teacher asks the students several good questions, taking care to model not just factual questions, but also those that probe concepts and implications. After several such exchanges, the teacher might shift the activity to ask students to predict what the rest of the assignment will be about and state why they think so (Vacca & Vacca, 1996). Another variation for a whole-class use of the ReQuest procedure is to assign students to teams of three and have them take turns asking and answering questions.

Engaging in Research

Taking notes while reading can help the reader identify the details of information content and organize them for understanding.

An important part of study reading is learning to conduct research and write reports. This skill has often been left for the middle grades, where teachers demonstrate a semiformal approach to research. However, the new CCSS include research as an ongoing part of the task of informational reading, with the expectation that students will engage in several short research projects each year. In kindergarten and the primary grades, the focus is on shared research and writing projects; by the intermediate grades, students should be able to identify their own interests and conduct research on their own and then share it with others in written and oral forms. It is clear that when primary-grade teachers engage students in informational reading and research, the process can be scaffolded so that by the time students reach the middle grades, they are already confident in the skills that permit them to conduct good research. Think back to the activities that have been described already. Research requires the following:

- *Asking good, researchable questions.* Learning to narrow one's topic is a basic skill that needs to be developed. When children use K-W-L and I-Charts, they become experienced in finding good questions.

- *Locating good sources of information.* Integrated units that are framed around students' questions develop their abilities to find the materials they need and to locate within the texts the sections that will answer their questions.

- *Making notes of important ideas.* Children who get in the habit of writing Amazing Fact Sheets have already learned how to make good notes. The use of graphic organizers and journals also helps students build good note-making skills.

- *Critically evaluating information.* Students who have regularly read several texts on the same topic know the importance of evaluating the sources of information they use and cross-checking them for accuracy and currency. They learn to check the authors of Web sites for their expertise and biases. They also know that textbooks and encyclopedias are good, reliable backup sources for their use.

- *Organizing information.* When students learn to chunk ideas as part of the K-W-L process, when they cluster new vocabulary, and when they learn to look for and use internal text organization in their reading and writing, they develop skills in organizing ideas into interesting and coherent texts. The more writing they do throughout the elementary grades, the more confident they become in creating interesting and meaningful texts.

- *Presenting information visually and graphically.* Students who have studied how authors and illustrators present visual information and weave it together with the connected texts are more able to create their own. The computer tools and digital cameras that schools possess make this task an exciting one for young students.

Look back over the different strategies that help to engage students actively as learners across the content areas. All of these taken together prepare students to be active, thoughtful learners. With this foundation, doing research and writing reports and even creating a more formal research paper are not difficult.

As we think of learning new material and conducting research, writing becomes an essential part of the ongoing literacy curriculum. When children write regularly, they develop their skills and fluency as writers. Regular writing, just like regular reading in a variety of genres for a variety of audiences and purposes, creates confident and capable learners. The more students can engage in their own inquiry on topics and questions of their choosing, the more they will want to write and share what they learn. The more they write, the more comfortable they will become with informational texts and the more able they will be to consider alternative ways authors can present information to connect with their readers. These experiences also prepare them for the focus of most of the writing they will be asked to do throughout their schooling: reports, summaries, and expository and persuasive essays.

Look at Classrooms for Learning

As teachers take seriously the importance of helping children use informational materials confidently, the greatest challenges are finding the time and structuring the learning experiences properly. Two general approaches are often used. The first is to think of teaching reading as finding a balance between the reading of fictional literature (for literary purposes) and the reading of informational material (to learn). The second approach is to create integrated units of instruction and combine standards and strategies for both literacy and content learning. If your school has basal readers, check to see that there is a balance of literary fiction and nonfiction and informational selections. Many of the newer basal reading programs include more varied selections, as publishers are recognizing that students need to become familiar with these texts. You also need to provide experiences in integrated content units so students learn the value of using a range of informational resources in their learning.

Involving English Language Learners

Integrated content units provide an open framework in which teachers can involve students at all levels of language competence in classroom learning experiences. Because the unit model provides for a range of materials and activities, students with little English can participate using resources in their own language and can begin their learning in their first language. Helping English language learners to create vocabulary lists with words in both English and their first language makes their participation in the general classroom activities more possible.

Teachers and other students can often gain from the English language learners' knowledge about the topics of study. Often, their experiences have been rich in the content of focus. For example, students from South America might have personal experiences with some varieties of frogs we consider exotic and might have a sense of their value that is different from the sense of urban dwellers in North America. Children from North Africa can contribute much to the study of civilizations that have derived from ancient Egypt or of studies of deserts. All children bring with them their experiences, language, and folktales and stories that can enrich any unit of study. Think of the potential resources represented by diversity in the classroom, and seek out what your students and their families can bring to each other.

Language and Diversity

How could such a class chart be used to stimulate interest in word histories?

New Literacies

What particular benefits come from using online resources for second language learners?

During the development of the units, English language learners also can participate in ways that go beyond verbal learning. They can take major roles in creating the visual displays and the graphic representations of the topics, as in the development of the murals of the frog issue. If some dramatic presentation of content is part of the unit, these students can build their English skills by memorizing parts and participating in group presentations.

Using Computer Resources

Units of instruction provide an ideal place to introduce the use of computer resources. A number of excellent Web sites exist that can be resources to learning. With the help of the instructional media or technical support team in a school, specific and appropriate Web resources can be bookmarked for a class and students can participate in learning from these resources. Many also contain great visual content, so students with limited English proficiency can learn in easy ways.

The computer also makes the development of reports easier for all. Digital cameras make it possible to dress up reports (e.g., by importing pictures of direct explorations during science units) and clip art and free photographs on the Web help students create impressive reports. By the middle grades, many teachers help students create podcasts and movie trailers as part of their research reporting. The ease with which corrections can be made on the computer gives students more freedom to compose their own reports and not fear misspelled words or poor handwriting. Students take great pride in producing reports with great graphics and high-quality print that reflect their best work. Knowing that their work can be turned into high-quality products serves as an incentive to many students. For primary students, the support of parent helpers or older-grade aides in the classroom can make the computer accessible and not consume all of the teacher's time.

Planning Instruction: A Reflection

Teachers can build a strong reading to learn curriculum in both of these ways—by creating a balance between fiction and informational material in the reading block of the day or by integrating reading to learn instruction with content units. Our experience has been that for new teachers, it is easier not to do all the instruction through integrated blocks initially, but to first be sure there are resources for the range of reading and learning needs of students in your class. It is critical to pay attention to what students bring with them in terms of their skills and strategies for reading informational texts and to provide instruction so they can develop increasingly sophisticated knowledge of how to read to learn using a variety of materials and for a variety of purposes. Reading to learn from science content is different from reading to learn from social studies materials. Both are different from reading that is taught as if a selection of text were sufficient just to be read and enjoyed.

For Review

Students are eager to learn about the world around them. Teachers can do much to provide the scaffolds so they can do so successfully. This chapter began with an explanation of why teaching students to use informational texts is so important. Then the ABC model of active reading was applied to reading for information. Four kinds of background knowledge were identified: vocabulary, text structure, and content knowledge, both topical and principled.

Many children have little experience with informational materials. Therefore, specific features were explained that you need to introduce to students. These include external features such as chapter headings and subheadings, captions, illustrations, the glossary and index, and even the table of contents. The internal structures of informational texts are also important for students to identify so they can determine what information is important and worth retaining. The use of graphic organizers, having students jigsaw the reading of sections of texts, and having them write using the pattern of the authors, were suggested as ways to highlight text organization.

This chapter introduced two frameworks and several instructional strategies that help students become aware of and utilize these features and become active questioners and thinkers. K-W-L and I-Charts help frame students' inquiry. Reciprocal teaching, close reading, metacognitive graphic organizers, and ways to develop good questioning through paired reading/paired summarizing and ReQuest help students build their knowledge as they engage actively with text ideas.

Finally, the chapter concluded by highlighting the importance of helping students develop their abilities to engage in research and establishing a rich classroom environment where students' inquiry can be nurtured with print and technological resources.

For Your Journal

Keep a record of all the reading you do for one or two days. Note the material you read, the time you spent, and how you engaged yourself in the materials, including what you thought and felt as you read. Try to remember your school experiences, and write about what kinds of materials you were taught to read. What tips did you learn for reading and comprehending informational material?

Taking It to the World

1. Most children are curious about the world around them. Yet sometimes teachers get very busy meeting all the curricular demands and overlook students' interests as a natural connection point to content. Visit a school library or a public library and become familiar with some of the excellent magazines available for young readers. Sit down and talk with some children about which of the magazines they enjoy most. Then, see whether the library has a service that permits you to search the magazines by topic so you can use articles in the future as you develop your own teaching units and extend readings on key topics in the curriculum.

2. Try out your skills in eliciting from students what they know about a topic and helping them articulate good questions to extend their knowledge. The K-W-L process is an easy way to start. Ask a teacher to allow you to teach a lesson with a small group of students around some topic of current interest, such as an item in the news or some community event. Have two or three short texts with you so you can read to the students to help them answer their questions after the first two steps in the K-W-L are complete. Keep a copy of the chart you create so you can reflect on the students' knowledge and interests after the session.

New Literacies Connections

Visit the National Geographic Kids Web site <www.nationalgeographic.com/kids/>, and investigate what it has to offer young children. How does it utilize graphics to enhance the information? Is the layout organized in a way that is easy to follow? What options are available to help students search for more information about specific topics?

MyEducationLab™

Go to Topic 5 (Comprehension) in the MyEducationLab <www.myeducationlab.com> for your course, where you can:

- Find learning outcomes for Comprehension along with the national standards that connect to these outcomes.

Critical Thinking and Critical Literacy

What Do Critical
Thinkers Do?
p. 255

Critical Thinking
and "The New
Literacies"
p. 256

Thinking Critically
About Texts
p. 257

Critical Thinking:
From Understanding
to Teaching Practice
and Back
p. 266

Anticipation Guide

The following statements will help you begin thinking about the topics of
this chapter. Answer *true* or *false* in response to each statement. As you read and
learn more about the topics in these statements, double-check your answers.
See what interests you and what prompts your curiosity toward more understanding.

_____ **1.** Even primary grade children can think
deeply about texts if they are asked good
questions.

_____ **2.** Critical thinking is the process of reasoning
and reflecting in order to decide what to
believe or what to do.

_____ **3.** Critical literacy is concerned with the social
or political purpose of messages and the
contexts in which they are understood.

_____ **4.** The structures of stories are usually very
different one from another, to keep them
from being boring.

_____ **5.** To find ways stories influence readers, don't
look at just one story, but at many—the
effects of stories accumulate.

_____ **6.** Engaging students in deep discussions of
stories and essays is an excellent way to meet
many of the Common Core Standards.

_____ **7.** A *Socratic Seminar* is a form of debate only
practiced by the Cincinnatus Society of Ohio.

_____ **8.** Good arguments usually consist of claims,
reasons, and evidence.

_____ **9.** It is not good to teach children to be skeptical
of some things they read. It will make them
bitter people if done too early.

_____ **10.** Fortunately, all arguments students read
before they reach high school will be logically
formed and honest.

A Classroom Story

Suppose *Beauty* Had Been Ugly?

Midge Burns' combined class of second and third graders has just finished listening to her read Marianna Mayer's version of *Beauty and the Beast*.

"I'm wondering about something," says Mrs. Burns. Second grader Connie smiles. It is April of the year, and Connie knows Mrs. Burns always begins an interesting discussion with those words.

"Suppose Beauty had been ugly. Do you think the Beast should have married her?"

"That would be sort of no fair if he wouldn't," says Abigail, looking unsure.

"What do you mean?" asks Mrs. Burns.

"I mean, the Beast shouldn't expect Beauty to love *him* if he's not willing to love *her*. . . I mean. . ."

"They're both ugly, so they should get along," says Daniel.

"I think there's a something like a moral to the story," says Michael.

"And what's that?" asks Mrs. Burns.

"I think it's saying 'Don't judge the book by the outside. . .'"

"Don't judge the book by its cover," offers Phillip.

"That's right," says Connie. "They called her Beauty, but that just meant she was kind and gentle and she looked out for other people. 'Cause you don't marry people just 'cause they look good."

"Then let me ask you something else," continues Midge Burns. "Suppose Beauty had been a boy in this story, and the Beast had been a girl." (A whoop goes up from the children.)

"That would be a problem," says Laurinda.

"Why is that?" asks Mrs. Burns.

"I saw it on TV that the girls asked boys to the prom. I don't think that's right. Besides, suppose the woman in the story was older than the man?" Laurinda clearly looks troubled.

"Why do we care?" demands Michael. "We don't know how old Beauty or the Beast is. The story doesn't say. But you should be free to marry whoever you want."

"My Mom says it's not OK for a girl to ask a boy to marry her. That's what my Mom says. I'm not sure if that's true," says Harriet.

"It doesn't matter," repeats Michael. "But I'll tell you what bothers me. In these stories, the guy marries this woman he doesn't even know."

"That's true. And I wish the woman would say, 'How can I marry you? I don't even know you. I don't even know what your *attitude* is,'" says Connie.

"I know," says Harriet. "In these stories, the people are marrying complete strangers. They don't even know if they change their underwear. . ."

CCSS

Common Core Standards and Good Discussion

The children in this vignette exercised many of the skills called for in the Common Core Standards. They asked and answered good questions, they discussed the theme of the story, they drew on evidence for the story to support their own interpretations, they thought deeply about the motivations of characters in the story, and they (vehemently!) distinguished their own take on the events from the apparent perspective of the author. In the process, they addressed Reading Standards for Literature, Standards 1, 2, 3, and 6; and Speaking and Listening, Standards 1 and 2. Not bad for one discussion! In subsequent lessons, they can do still more. They can compare Mayer's retelling of "Beauty and the Beast" with the Disney film. They can also compare it to the Russian version, "The Snot-Nosed Goat" (from the Afanas'ev collection of Russian Fairy Tales) and to the Appalachian version, "A Bunch of Laurel Blooms for a Present" (from Marie Campbell's *Tales of the Cloud Walking Country*).

What Do Critical Thinkers Do?

In this example Midge Burns is inviting her students to practice critical thinking. We know that she's encouraging critical thinking because of several things she does:

- *Her questions take a critical attitude.* Not only do the questions flow from the assumption that students are capable of coming up with their own responses, but they also imply that the meanings suggested by the text can be scrutinized and challenged, and possibly rejected in favor of better ideas.

- *Her way of conducting the discussion shares the responsibility for making meaning.* The teacher spreads responsibility for making meaning by expecting the students to provide ideas. And while she sometimes says things to help students express themselves more clearly, she doesn't position herself as the authority on the meaning.

- *She treats the meaning-making as a social activity.* She encourages students to interact with each other, sometimes to build on each other's ideas and other times to critique them, but at all times to work toward more sophisticated thinking.

- *She has thought hard about the text herself.* She has examined the text for the issues it raises that might be important to the students and the attitudes and assumptions it conveys. Even though she doesn't plan to share her own insights, she has constructed a general idea of ways the discussion might go.

The students are thinking critically, too. We can see that because they:

- *Offer insights and not just recycled facts.* They are aiming to think through what the text might mean, and what they can do with the meaning.

- *They behave as if they feel free to question and to doubt.* They don't passively accept the suggestions made by the text.

- *They follow the ramifications of ideas.* They "try ideas on for size" in real life, and they make connections to other things they have read and heard.

- *They offer support for their assertions.* They advance ideas, and support their ideas with evidence.

- *They listen carefully to each other and build on each other's ideas.* They don't just passively agree, though; they are willing to question each other's assertions, and venture alternatives.

Defining Critical Thinking

Philosophers usually define *critical thinking* as a process of reasoning and reflecting that is done in order to decide what to believe or what course of action to take. Critical thinking is usually done in response to something—a problem in real experience, something we read, or an argument we hear (Fisher, 2001). But a philosopher's definition can miss a lot of what children and teachers do when they think critically in classrooms. Young critical thinkers like those in Midge Burns' class do several things well.

- They read or watch or listen as if the meaning of the text were the starting point in their pursuit of greater awareness and not the end point. They ask not only "What does the text mean?" but also "What can I *do* with the meaning?"

- They make meaning by constructing interpretations of what they hear and read and supporting those interpretations with evidence from the text.

- They use reading and discussions of reading as opportunities to know what their classmates think, even joining their ideas with those of others to create more sophisticated insights.

Teach It! 39

Value Line

- They look below the surface of texts, and use their knowledge of literary structures and genres as they construct meaning and venture interpretations.
- They hold texts up to scrutiny, sometimes questioning their messages and the purposes of those behind the messages.

Defining Critical Literacy

When readers examine the social, political, and cultural purposes and values that the texts they read reflect, they have *critical literacy*. Critical readers may ask who is behind the text and why the argument is being made. They may ask whose voices are missing from the text. They may "talk back" to the text, and construct different readings of it. When they ask these kinds of questions, they are becoming "text critics" (Freebody & Luke 1990). Critical readers learn that texts are powerful as tools to influence readers. That is why teachers like Midge Burns help students examine the unstated value messages behind texts.

New Literacies

What do you consider "new" in the literacies in your life?

Critical Thinking and "The New Literacies"

Until recently, television and radio stations in America were required by the Federal Communications Commission (FCC) to address at least two sides of every controversial issue they raised. But in 1987, the "Fairness Doctrine" was abandoned, and since then commentators with unapologetically partisan agendas have been allowed to say almost anything they want on the air, however groundless, and even call it "news." Similarly, material that was put in print and shared with the public came mostly through mainstream media that screened the material for fairness and accuracy. But with the rapid growth of the Internet as a source of information, material can now reach the public without any filtering. Books, magazines, and newspapers are mostly still accountable for what they publish, and they are screened for accuracy before they are released to the public. But texts on the Internet are mostly unedited and, while they may look "authoritative," they are often filled with strongly biased and misleading information. This state of affairs requires that students learn to apply their own filters. As Leu and his associates (2010) explain,

> *Whereas critical evaluation is important when reading offline information, it is perhaps more important online, where anyone can publish anything; knowing the stance and bias of an author become paramount to comprehension and learning. Determining this in online contexts requires new comprehension skills and strategies. For example, knowing which links take you to information about who created the information at a site (and actually choosing to follow these links) becomes important. So too, is knowing how to check the reliability of information with other information at other sites. Students do not always possess these skills. In one study (Leu et al., 2007), 47 out of 53 higher performing online readers in 7th grade believed a site designed to be a hoax was reliable (Save the Endangered Pacific Northwest Tree Octopus: <http://zapatopi.net/treeoctopus/>), despite that most students indicated in an interview that they did not believe everything they read online. Moreover, when told the site was a hoax, a number of students insisted it provided accurate and reliable information.* (p. 4)

Defining New Literacies

Leu and his colleagues have taken the lead in arguing that teaching students to read must involve teaching them the "new literacies" of online reading. In the twenty-first century, the dominance of the Internet, of ebooks, iPads, and other devices as information sources and as communications facilitators makes their argument strong. These literacies are not static; in fact, it seems that there are new forms of Internet literacies emerging regularly. That is why Leu chooses to call them "literacies" and not "literacy." Some options like Twitter, YouTube, and Ning stimulate more student-to-student exchanges and help students create their own visual and verbal messages. There is a nearly overwhelming amount of information available on the Internet; it is important that students learn to navigate the Web and use it for many different purposes. Schools bear responsibility to provide guidance for students, particularly since students from less affluent families still may lack regular access at home to the Internet.

In describing the necessary functions teachers can help students develop for online literacy, Leu (2010) includes five essentials:

1. Identifying important questions
2. Locating information online
3. Analyzing information (sources and content)
4. Synthesizing information
5. Communicating information

Leu and colleagues (Coiro & Dobler, 2007; Leu, 2009) explain that while those skills just listed are similar to the literacy skills required to read print on paper effectively, literacy functions work differently when the information is online. In fact, some students who do very well comprehending online materials have been very poor at comprehending in traditional text tasks. The reverse is also true.

It is important that teachers help students learn to think deeply and comprehend whether they are reading printed text on paper or viewing text online. Online literacy is more interactive and more engaging for many students. The strong use of visual information may support comprehension in distinct ways. Clearly, the new literacies that have come with new technology warrant the attention of those of us who are concerned with children and young people's literacy.

CCSS

Common Core Standards and New Literacies

The Common Core Standards call for students to be able to interpret information from digital sources (Comprehending Informational Text, Standard 7), and they require that students be able to distinguish between the author's point of view and their own (Comprehending Informational Text, Standard 6) although the standards don't point out the need for extra care in judging the reliability of Internet-based texts.

Thinking Critically About Texts

Even preschool children encounter persuasive messages. Saturday morning television shows abound with advertisements to make children want to buy things. Children shower arguments on each other, sometimes primitive, sometimes not. Although some adults might wish to hold off on discussing persuasive messages with children—especially dishonest messages—more and more teachers are deciding that children should learn to understand and—if necessary—to protect themselves from such messages in the elementary grades. In the rest of this chapter, we will first take a broad view of how texts work—beginning with narratives, then going on to informational and persuasive texts, and finally considering what happens when students read several texts on the same topic,

Good teachers press students not just to understand, but to think deeply about material that is presented to them.

CCSS

• Literature 1, 2, and 3: Key Ideas and Details

sometimes even texts from different genres. Then we will present teaching strategies for guiding students' reading and thinking about different kinds of texts for different purposes. Some of the strategies may encourage critical thinking; others may encourage critical literacy. In this chapter, as in real classrooms, we will often mix the two.

Looking Closely at the Structure of Literature

Even the most familiar story such as "Cinderella," "Beauty and the Beast," or "Jack and the Beanstalk" may be influencing young readers' and listeners' attitudes and beliefs in subtle way. Here, we will pay attention to two kinds of influence fictional texts have on readers. The first point is that fictional texts often relate symbolically to people and actions in the real world. A single text, or more likely, a collection of texts, may have the effect of conveying certain attitudes toward groups of people, certain actions, or certain values. The second point is that the structure of a particular text may lead the reader toward a certain attitude about characters and events, and these same attitudes may carry over into readers' beliefs about the real world.

THE WEB OF NARRATIVE AND "THE WAY IT IS."   Anthropologists sometimes look at the many stories or other texts that are circulated in a society and note that they constitute a common story, a sort of web of narrative. This may be called the *mythos*: whether it is a story or a series of stories, or even a series of advertisements or a string of video games, the collection of texts become familiar and understandable because they say the same things again and again. The *mythos* may consciously or unconsciously relate to a kind of logic of "the way things are." Anthropologists may call this unspoken understanding of the social order the *logos*, a tacit understanding of "how things are" and "how things work." For example, traditional fairy tales spin a narrative web that portrays males as active heroes who go on quests, and females as passive creatures who wait to be rescued and become prizes to be won by the bold masculine heroes. Male heroes often strive aggressively or violently against those who are cast as foes. Females use extreme kindness and self-denial to achieve—not their goals, because in traditional stories females are often punished if they have goals—but to have things turn out well.

Although they are "just stories," through much repetition the web of narrative normalizes a certain understanding of "the way things are." In traditional stories told in European and American culture, "the way things are" is that only aggressive males and self-denying females have things turn out well. The winners, usually males, are solitary figures who triumph over others, and have no sympathy for those who stand in their way.

Of course, the *mythos*—that is, traditional Western stories taken as a whole— teaches a *logos* that may be far out of touch with society as it is today. For instance, can you imagine having a class of boys and girls—or teaching in a school faculty of men and women—who behaved that way? This is a big reason children need to think critically about stories.

DRAMATIC ROLES   Looking more closely at the structure of individual narratives shows how a story shapes readers' reactions to it. From experience hearing and reading stories and watching media, readers construct what has been called a *story grammar* (Mandler & Johnson, 1977; Stein & Glenn, 1979): a set of rules that help them make sense of who is doing what and the meaning of the characters' actions.

One version of a story grammar assigns roles to characters (Souriau, 1955; Temple, Martinez, & Yokota, 2014). A character in a story may be the hero or the protagonist,

Character Clusters and Character Maps

For English Language Learners

the person whose needs give rise to the actions in the story and with whom readers most strongly sympathize. Another character may serve as a rival, a person against whom the hero competes to get what he wants. Yet another character may be the helper, who supports the hero. Readers sense who is playing what role, and their loyalties are directed accordingly: They cheer the hero (and may forgive his aggression), they spurn the rival (and may give him little sympathy), and they appreciate the efforts of the helper (but don't give her much consideration beyond what she does for the hero).

Authors don't often tell readers who is playing what role; readers make those judgments for themselves. But once readers do assign characters to roles, their affections may be strongly shaped: Once we decide that Jack is the hero of "Jack and the Beanstalk," we cheer him through his adventures, and we may forgive his thievery, and even murder. Once we cast the giant as the rival, we don't much sympathize with him, even as he is robbed and killed. And once we think of the giant's wife as a helper, we don't give her another thought once she has helped Jack for the last time.

CCSS

Common Core Standards and Characters' Perspectives

CCSS Standard 6 for Reading Literature asks that students understand the effect of characters' points of view on the way events are portrayed. Dramatic roles (see above) are a sturdy device for helping students retell a story from different characters' perspectives. It can be fascinating to put another character in the protagonist's role and ask what she or he wants (and why), who opposes her, and who helps, and why.

CHARACTERS AS STAND-INS FOR OTHER PEOPLE   Characters in stories have special meanings for us in our own lives. For example, we can say the story of "Cinderella" is about what happens when a deserving but overshadowed young person like Cinderella competes for recognition against overprivileged people like Cinderella's haughty stepsisters. Kate DiCamillo's *Because of Winn-Dixie* is about what happens when a troubled child (Opal), who is searching for community, reaches out to the people around her, who are also suffering and lonely, but powerless in their isolation.

Cinderella and Opal are like many other people we know. We speak of "Cinderella" sports teams, who have these same attributes of being deserving but overlooked until

The World of Reading

The Hero Cycle

Stories abound of people who start out underappreciated, and then are challenged to do something that requires strength and courage and that benefits other people, and finally they reach some triumphant state by the end of the story. *Holes, Hoot!, Because of Winn-Dixie, Harry Potter*, and *The Lord of the Rings* follow this pattern. Joseph Campbell wrote a famous description of this kind of plot in his book, *The Hero With a Thousand Faces* (2008). The plots of many hero stories are so similar, wrote Campbell, that they are telling the same story: the *monomyth*, or *hero cycle*.

Campbell's monomyth begins with an unlikely **hero** (not yet recognized as such) who resides **at home**, neglected and underappreciated by those around.

The hero hears a **call to adventure**. Sometimes it literally is a call, as when the hero is sent on a quest to find something that will eliminate a threat and restore order at home. (Think of *The Hobbit* or *The Lord of the Rings* trilogy.) Sometimes the quest is more figurative—the hero must survive an ordeal and develop his own strength (as in *Hatchet*) or restore his family's reputation (as in *Holes*), or bring harmony to a community (as in *Because of Winn-Dixie*).

The hero must cross a **threshold** into a special place where the full range of her or his powers may be at play, a place that Campbell calls the **land of adventure**. The threshold may be impossible to cross—in myths and folktales, it will take magical aid for the passage to be possible. The hero may face and pass **tests** in order to gain (sometimes magical) assistance from a **helper** in order to cross this threshold. In "Jack and the Beanstalk" something of a joke is made of these tests, but they are enough to win magical aid for Jack in the form of beans from the helper, the strange little man that Jack meets on his way to market. Crossing the threshold into the land of adventure is serious business, though. In "Jack," had it not been for those magical beans, no other-worldly beanstalk would have bridged the distance between earth and the sky, just as few people idly make their way into Narnia, or Never-Neverland, or Oz, or Hogwarts.

Once the hero has made it over into the land of adventure, he or she goes through a death-like experience. Campbell likens this to descending into **the belly of the whale**, recalling the story of Jonah from the Old Testament. Here a person's childlike self dies away so the adult can be born. When the young protagonist of the hero story emerges from the belly of the whale, he or she has adult-like powers. In "Jack and the Beanstalk" perhaps the Belly of the Whale is the copper cooking pot where he hides from the giant. The Belly of the Whale in "Hansel and Gretel" may be the witch's house.

The hero must prove himself or herself against a stern father figure. Is the young person capable of being taken seriously as a hero? Only the ultimate test against the supreme authority figure will decide the question. Campbell called this competition with the authority figure **father atonement**.

At the height of the journey, the hero seeks a prize, a magic potion, a key that will have some benefit to those who are waiting back on earth. The hero must win it or steal it, in a move that Campbell calls **the elixir theft**. In older stories and those derived from them, the elixir, which means "medicine," is often an actual item—the Holy Grail, the Golden Fleece, the magic hen and magic harp, the Firebird; or the sorcerer's stone, or the Ring. In modern stories it may be something more abstract, like harmony and engagement among the people of Naomi, Florida, in *Because of Winn-Dixie*.

Following the theft of the elixir, the hero often has to make a dramatic escape or **flight** from the father figure, back across the threshold from the land of adventure into the real world, where the hero once again finds himself or herself **at home**. But, of course, when the hero is at home at the end of the story, unlike the beginning—when the hero was all unrecognized potential, the hero is now a fully developed human being, with all of her or his talents expressed to their fullest.

What value does knowledge of the monomyth have to those of us who want to discuss literature with children? The monomyth provides a ready means of comparing stories, of making text-to-text comparisons. It provides a way to compare current TV and video heroes to those from literature. It also helps us question the basic assumptions of how the stories unfold: Why is the character a male in most classical tales? Do individuals have to take these journeys alone?

one day they burst into glory. And many a youngest child, feeling that other siblings get all the breaks, has identified with Cinderella. Opal in *Because of Winn-Dixie* reminds us of Maniac Magee (in Louis Sachar's book by that name) because Maniac, too, is a kid who lacks a normal support group and who ultimately creates community. In real life they both remind us a little bit of other peacemakers, like Mother Teresa and Martin Luther King, Jr. But they also remind us of some children in dysfunctional families, who must do more than their fair share to make things right for the others in their surroundings.

The dynamics of identifying characters with other characters works like this: We look at characters in stories horizontally and vertically. We look horizontally at the relationships between characters, and once we see who occupies the slots in those relationships, we look vertically at categories of people like that. The horizontal dimension is akin to the grammar of a sentence, and the vertical dimension is akin to the parts of speech.

This brings us back to the question of how stories have meaning for us. We can ask of "Cinderella": When do we feel overlooked and underappreciated? What do we do at those times to find relief? Especially if we don't have fairy godmothers? And doubly especially if we don't want to wait for a prince to come calling? We recognize the problem presented in these stories and see if we find part of ourselves in those problems. Then we critique the solutions offered by the stories. If we don't buy the story's solution, then we can decide upon a better one.

Thinking Critically About Texts Other Than Stories

Even preschool children encounter messages that try to persuade them of things. Saturday morning television shows abound with advertisements to make children want to buy things. Other children make arguments, sometimes primitive, sometimes not. Although some might wish to hold off on protecting children from persuasive messages—especially dishonest messages—more and more teachers are deciding that children should begin to deal with such messages in the elementary grades. In this section we will discuss two approaches to understanding messages that may be out to persuade readers and listeners. One is to look at arguments, and the other is to subject messages to systematic doubt.

EXAMINING ARGUMENTS When faced with a message that seeks to persuade us or even inform us, students can learn to look closely at the ways in which the

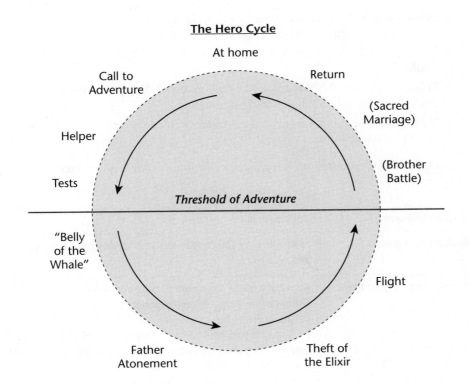

Figure 9.1
The Hero Cycle

Source: After Joseph Campbell, *The Hero With a Thousand Faces.* Novato, California; New World Library, 2008, p. 210. Used by permission.

arguments are made. Teachers can help younger students approach arguments in a simple way. Let's assume students are given a piece of persuasive writing such as the following.

> *Dogs make better pets than cats. There are two good reasons. First, dogs are good companions. Second, they guard your house and keep you safe.*
>
> *Dogs make good companions because dogs are friendly animals. The ancestors of dogs hunted in groups, so they had to learn to get along with others. The ancestors of cats hunted alone, though, so they never had to learn to get along with others.*
>
> *Dogs protect your house because they want to protect the place they live. They are friendly to people and other dogs they know, but they want to keep strangers away—at least until they know them. Cats won't protect your house. They mind their own business when people come around.*
>
> *Wouldn't you rather have a cuddly dog than a snobby cat?*

Students ask these questions:

- *What are you saying?* What claim or suggestion is the message making?
- *What are your reasons for saying it?* What reasons does the message give about why we should accept that claim or suggestion?
- *What evidence do you have?* What evidence does the message give that would make us believe each reason?

With regard to the example, we can answer the questions as in Figure 9.2. A good argument will make clear claims, with clear reasons, and ample evidence to support each reason.

WHAT IF THE TEXT DOESN'T PERSUADE FAIRLY?   Many texts don't argue fairly, of course. To understand how misleading arguments work, more tools are needed. Students can be led to ask four questions such as these to look below the surface of misleading arguments:

- *What's missing?* A statement may seem perfectly OK with its claims and reasons and evidence—until we realize what it has left unsaid.
- *Is this for real?* Are there "facts" in the text that we might have reason to doubt?
- *What's in the words?* What loaded words are used? "Loaded" words are terms that pass judgments without making arguments.
- *Who cares?* Texts often argue as if all readers wanted a state of affairs that we don't necessarily value.

For an example of these questions being asked of the topic of dogs and cats, see Figure 9.3.

Figure 9.2
Looking at Arguments

What are you saying?	Dogs make better pets than cats.
What are your reasons for saying it?	First, dogs are good companions. Second, they guard your house and keep you safe.
What evidence do you have?	Dogs make good companions because dogs are friendly animals. The ancestors of dogs hunted in groups, so they had to learn to get along with others . . . Dogs protect your house because they want to protect the place they live. They are friendly to people and other dogs they know, but they want to keep strangers away . . .

What's missing?	The argument about dogs and cats doesn't mention that dogs are more costly to keep and are sometimes aggressive toward innocent people.
Is this for real?	What proof, beyond simply saying so, does the text offer that dogs have always been gregarious and cats have always been solitary?
What's in the words?	Using the word "snobby" to describe cats is unfair because it goes beyond the evidence. The text hasn't proved that cats believe themselves too good to spend time with others, as the word "snobby" suggests.
Who cares?	The text assumes that everyone wants a companionable pet. But many readers may prefer their pets to be more independent and to require less frequent attention.

Figure 9.3
A Further Look at Arguments

WHAT IF AN ARGUMENT DOESN'T LOOK LIKE AN ARGUMENT? Many of the messages children see in a day are intended to persuade them. But few of them take the form of well-formed arguments, with claims, reasons, and evidence (see Figure 9.4).

There are four "scans" (based on Alan Luke and Peter Freebody's [1999] "Four Resources Model" of reading) that we can give such texts to figure out what they are and how they work, what they mean, what we will do with them, and what they're doing and why they're doing it.

1. **What kind of text is this? How does it work?** On the first scan, we try to determine what kind of text we are looking at. Is it a story, a piece of information, an advertisement, or something else? We should be alert to texts that pretend to be one thing, but turn out to be something else: entertainment that is selling something, etc.

   Once we know what it is, we can also ask how it works. Each type or genre of text has its own code, its own set of rules. A story has a plot (characters, setting, problems, solutions, and consequence). A persuasive essay has logic (claim, reasons, and evidence). An informative piece has its structure of presentation (cause and effect, steps in a procedure, chronology, taxonomy, comparison and contrast). An advertisement has its rhetorical strategy (an ideal situation that can be attained by Joe or Jane Average if she or he will only consume a certain product). Once we are aware of those rules, we can use them to decipher its meaning.

2. **What does this text mean?** Texts can have meanings on many levels. Once we identify the meaningful parts of a text, we can ask what associations those parts bring to mind. We can ask how those parts work together to create meaning. And we can generate one or more readings for the text.

3. **What can I do with this text?** Once we have arrived at some meanings of the text, we can choose what to do with it. There are many ways to read a text. We

**Stay ahead of the pack
On a Bronwyn bike**

Figure 9.4
Persuading Without an Argument

can read to be entertained. We can read to be informed. We can read to be persuaded, or to have our views reinforced. If we decide to be critical, we can ask what effects the text is trying to have on its readers. In some cases, readers decide to take direct action—they may write letters to advertisers, they may speak for change at a school or community meeting, or they may create a civic project to bring about change.

4. ***What is the text trying to do, and why?*** Once we adopt a critical stance to the text, we can ask what the text is trying to do to us. We can ask about the motives of those who wrote it. We can decide whose views and interests are advanced by the text, and whose views and interests are left out.

Asking about the simple advertisement that began this section, we might see responses like those in Figure 9.5.

READING ONLINE WEB SITES   The set of questions Luke and Freebody (see above) developed are excellent to use when reading Web sites. In addition, when using Web resources, a preliminary step needs to include asking the question of who sponsors a site and what their authority and purpose is. Too many students approach Web information in the same way they approach printed texts: If it is there, it must be true. Even when Leu et al. (2007) informed students about the inaccuracies in a site, they continued to respond that "if it is there, it must be right"—a real call for our action in giving more attention to critical literacy.

These questions about site sponsorship also are connected to the purposes for which one seeks information. If I want to get a range of ideas for how to clear my garage of

New Literacies

What questions can encourage students to check multiple sources for their information?

Figure 9.5

Four Ways of Looking at a Questionable Text

1. What kind of text *is* this? How does it work?	This thing looks like an advertisement. Advertisements work by showing an idealized person who looks like a mirror image of the reader. Since the person in the image is exaggeratedly happier and more successful than the reader, the reader wants to know how he or she can be like that idealized person. Then the reader notices that the idealized person is using the product being advertised, and is led to conclude that by using the product he or she too will be as happy and successful as the person in the image. Bingo!
2. What does this text mean?	Associations? The boy on the bicycle in front is smaller than the others. He looks like he is in competition with them, and he is winning. They look frustrated, which confirms this interpretation. Since the lead boy's bicycle is shown more clearly and colorfully than the other clunkers, the advertisement suggests that the bicycle is the key to the boy's success and happiness. The caption confirms this. Thus the meaning of the whole advertisement seems to be that if you buy this bicycle, you will stay in front of the other boys who are your competition. But maybe the boy on the lead bicycle is trying to escape from the boys behind him. That's another possible reading of the advertisement. Either way, discerning readers may decide that the text is setting up an unhappy division between the boy in front and the boys behind him. Hmm. A more expensive bicycle may help you get ahead of your friends. But it may also keep you from having friends.
3. What can I do with this text?	Readers might be persuaded by the advertisement, and hound their parents to buy them a Bronwyn bike. Or they may choose to question the advertisement, and reject its message.
4. What is the text trying to do and why?	The text is trying to persuade readers to buy a Bronwyn bicycle. Surely the people who paid for the advertisement want to sell bicycles. Whose voices are left out? People who worry about consumerism being pushed onto children. Also, people who would like information about products, and not just imagery.

Common Core Standards: What If the Informational Books Are Biased?

The Common Core Standards require that by fourth grade, half the texts that students read be informational, and that proportion increases to 55 percent by eighth grade. Students as early as grade 2 should be able to identify the purpose of a text (Comprehension of Informational Text, Standard #6).

That standard is not as simple as it may seem. Many adults have been appalled by the trend to politicize science in recent years. In the area of climate change, sophisticated campaigns have been launched to counter the consensus finding of climate scientists that human beings cause global warming and that global warming threatens life on the planet. Children wishing to read up on global warming might come across Holly Fretwell's *The Sky's Not Falling: Why It's OK to Chill About Global Warming*. They would have to do a little research to find that according to the *Los Angeles Times* (Simon, 2007), the publisher of *The Sky's Not Falling* (who also published *Help! There Are Liberals Under My Bed!* and other such titles for children) expressly solicited manuscripts that would argue that humans are not causing the planet to heat up. (The winner of the bid turned out to be an economist who works for a think tank that fights environmental protection laws.) The book was commissioned as a rebuttal to a children's book version of Vice President Al Gore's Academy Award–winning documentary *An Inconvenient Truth*. Laurie David and Cambria Gordon's *The Down-to-Earth Guide to Global Warming* (2007) presented Vice President Gore's summary of scientific consensus on the subject.

Whether children's books are commissioned by big business or by the political left or right to interpret the world for children with a particular slant, it is likely that as more informational books come into schools, more politically motivated discourse will come along with them. Identifying the purpose of many of these texts will not always be easy. Teachers and children will need to develop their critical literacy so that they can be clear on who is saying what, and why.

spiders, I may try some sites that are from government health offices and some that are individuals or from blogs. Then the authorship may be varied. If I want to learn more about the relationship between Ponce de Leon and Christopher Columbus, I am going to want only reliable sources, not speculation or opinions. Then the URLs I use should be ".edu," or a reliable student-oriented search engine like "Ask." The democratization of the World Wide Web means that even elementary students need to learn to think critically about what they are seeing and reading online. Before asking "What does this text mean?" it is helpful to ask "Who is sponsoring this site and why?" Beginning with this question makes students better and more productive learners. They can decide if they will read further, and can more easily respond to the question, "What is the text doing and why?"

Online formats are becoming more varied all the time. It is good to help students identify the variety of forms of online communication they will encounter. Some elementary classrooms use discussion formats so students can share their own ideas with other students in distant locations; some connect students to adults for book discussions (e-bookchats). These are good ways to help students develop their persuasive abilities. Asking questions of the sources of these communications and knowing whose voices are being expressed is foundational. The more students use online exchanges, the more they become aware of how differently we can respond to the same issues and texts; it can whet their appetite to listen more actively for varied perspectives and interpretations.

Texts That Take Different Approaches to the Same Topic

Different texts may take different approaches to the same topic without expressly arguing with other texts. For example, a health textbook warns preteens not to get hooked on consumerism, particularly when it comes to clothing and cosmetics. An article in a magazine that is largely sponsored by the clothing and cosmetics industry shows preteen girls how to buy just the right products in order look glamorous. For younger readers, a book chapter may emphasize a live-and-let-live approach to all living things, including bees and spiders. Another book chapter may warn of the dangers of spider bites and bee stings.

With fictional works, different stories may show the same issue in very different lights. Many of the books of Roald Dahl, such as *Matilda*, *The Witches*, and *George's Amazing Medicine* show adults as oppressive despots, and they delight in the child protagonist's triumphing over them. Other works, such as Vera Williams' *A Chair for My Mother* or Kate DiCamillo's *Because of Winn Dixie*, show adults as so preoccupied with their own problems that they are largely helpless, and the child protagonist makes generous and heroic efforts that bring comfort to the adults as she grows in her awareness of adults' emotions and motives. Such different works don't explicitly argue with each other. Nonetheless, children may be confused by their differing messages if teachers don't help them make sense of the differences.

Critical Thinking: From Understanding to Teaching Practice and Back

CCSS

• Informational Text 8: Integration of Knowledge and Ideas

Now that we have surveyed some ways of thinking through how texts do their work, it is clear that readers have a choice: They can read texts actively or passively. They can take control of the understandings they derive from the experience of reading them, or they can allow the text to have the effect on them that the author intended, almost without realizing it. Teachers can make the difference in the ways students approach texts. In the following sections we will share techniques for helping students read while engaging their critical faculties. The chart in Figure 9.6 will relate teaching strategies to the descriptions of critical thinking and how texts work that we have just described.

Figure 9.6
Matching Strategies to Purposes in Critical Literacy

A View of Critical Thinking and How Texts Work	Corresponding Strategies for Teaching
Establishing *purposes* and identifying *authorship* and *credibility*.	Developing purpose-setting questions and plans. Checking site sponsorship.
Responding and Articulating a Position in Relation to the Text	The Discussion Web Debates Value Line
Looking Closely at the Structure of Texts Structure of folk and fairy tales 　　*Mythos* and *logos* 　　The Hero Cycle Informational and persuasive structures Propaganda techniques Visual and graphic components	Graphic overview of text structure Analysis of text arguments and evidence Evaluating a Web page Creative Dialogue Reading for structured opposites Matrix of story comparisons
Thinking Critically about Literature and Informational Texts 　　Examining Arguments 　　What If the Text Doesn't Persuade Fairly? 　　What If an Argument Doesn't Look Like an Argument?	Analyzing propaganda tools Anticipation/Reaction Guide Questioning the Author Socratic Seminar

General Strategies to Encourage Discussion and Debate

In this section are several teaching strategies that encourage discussions to lead students into critical thinking and critical literacy.

THE DISCUSSION WEB   The discussion web is a cooperative learning activity that involves all students in deep discussions of readings. The discussion web proceeds with the following steps:

1. The teacher prepares a thoughtful binary question—a question that can be answered "yes" or "no" with support. For example, in discussing "Jack and the Beanstalk," a binary discussion question might be "Was Jack right to steal from the giant?" For Louis Sachar's book *Holes*, the question might be "Did Stanley succeed in the end because of his personal qualities, such as being strong and good, or was it because the luck of his family finally changed?"

2. The teacher asks pairs of students to prepare a discussion web chart that looks like the one in Figure 9.7. Those pairs of students take four or five minutes to think up and list three reasons each that support both sides of the argument.

Good teachers encourage students to develop and express original interpretations.

Figure 9.7
Discussion Web

**Was it wrong for Jack
to steal from the giant?**

1. In pairs, list 3 or 4 reasons to support a "yes" answer to that question, and 3 or 4 reasons to support a "no" answer. Write those reasons in the spaces provided.

YES!　　　　　　　　　　　　　　　　　　NO!

_____　　　　　_____

_____　　　　　_____

_____　　　　　_____

_____　　　　　_____

_____　　　　　_____

_____　　　　　_____

_____　　　　　_____

2. Now, each pair joins another pair. First, share all of your reasons to support a "yes" and a "no" answer. Then, discuss the question to reach an answer you can agree on. Write it in the space provided.

Conclusion:

_____

_____

_____

_____

_____

_____

3. Next, each pair of students joins another pair. They review the answers they had on both sides of the issue and add to each other's list. Then they argue the issue through until they reach a conclusion, that is, a position they agree on, with a list of reasons that support it.

4. At the conclusion of the lesson, the teacher calls on several groups of four to give brief reports of their position and the reasons that support it. The teacher can invite groups to debate each other if they took different sides of the argument.

 Students in this video engage in a debate that is scaffolded by reading their social studies textbook. As you watch, focus on how the teacher incorporates the students' prior knowledge of personal and historical events in order to prepare them to participate in the debate.

DEBATES   With students in third grade and up, it is often useful to follow the discussion web activity with a debate. The purpose of the debate is not to declare winners and losers, but to help the students practice making claims and defending them with reasons, even when others defend different claims. Working with claims, reasons, and arguments and debating ideas without attacking people—these are key elements in critical thinking.

To have a debate, you need a binary question (that has a yes/no answer). Since the discussion web we saw above also uses binary questions, you can follow the discussion web with a debate. Here are the steps:

1. Think of a question you think will truly divide the students' opinions, and put the question on the board for all to see. If you are not sure the question will divide the students roughly equally, ask for a show of hands on each side of the issue before going forward.

2. Give students an opportunity to think about the question and discuss it freely.

3. Ask students to divide up: Those who believe one answer to the question is right should go stand along the wall on one side of the room, and those who think the other answer is right should stand along the wall on the other side. Those who are truly undecided (that is, after thinking about it, they believe that both sides are partially right or neither side is right) should stand along the middle wall.

4. Explain or review the two ground rules:
   a. Don't be rude to each other. (You might have to explain and demonstrate what this means.)
   b. If you hear an argument that makes you want to change your mind, walk to the other side (or to the middle). Here is a hint to the teacher: As the debate proceeds, you can model the behavior of changing sides with a pantomime, by looking thoughtful for a moment after someone offers a good argument and moving to that student's side.

5. Give the students on each side three or four minutes to put their heads together and decide why they are on that side. Ask them to come up with a sentence that states their position. Then ask them to appoint someone to say that sentence.

6. Begin the debate by asking one person from each side (including the undecided group) to state that group's position.

7. Invite anyone on any team to say things (counterarguments or rebuttals) in response to what the other team has said or give more reasons in support of their own side.

8. Monitor the activity to make sure the tone stays away from negative attacks. Ask for clarification. Offer an idea or two as necessary from the devil's advocate position. Change sides. Encourage the students to change sides if they are persuaded to.

9. When the debate has proceeded for ten or fifteen minutes, ask each side to summarize what they have said.

10. You may follow the debate with a writing activity: Ask each student to write down what he or she believes about the issue and why.

(See Chapter 8 for suggestions of ways to structure this writing activity.)

VALUE LINE   A cooperative learning activity that is an extension of the debate procedure is the value line (Kagan, 1994). The value line is well suited for questions that have more than two good answers, and students might have a range of answers along a continuum. Here are the steps:

1. Pose a question to the students on which answers may vary along a continuum. For example, after reading Beverly Cleary's *Ramona and Her Father*, you might ask the children, "Do you think Ramona's parents really understand her?"

2. Give the students three minutes to consider the question alone and write down their answers.

3. Now stand on one side of the room and announce that you represent one pole, or extreme position, on the argument. You might say, "Yes, I think Ramona's parents understand her perfectly, 100 percent of the time." Invite a student to stand at the other end of the room to represent the other pole of the argument. The student might say, "No, I don't think Ramona's parents understand her. Not at all. Never."

4. Now invite the students to line up between the two of you in places along the imaginary value line between the two poles of the argument. Each stands at a point in the line that reflects his or her position on the question. Remind the students to compare their views with those of the students immediately around them to make sure they are all standing in the right spots. After hearing others' answers, some students might elect to move one way or another along the value line.

5. Students may continue to discuss their responses with peers on either side of them.

6. Identify three or four clusters of students who seem to represent different views on the question. Invite them to prepare a statement of their position and to share it with the whole group.

7. As an option, the formed line may be folded in the middle so that students with more divergent views may debate their responses with their peer on the opposite side.

8. You might want to follow this exercise with a writing opportunity in which students write down what they think about the issue and why. In this way, the value line serves as a rehearsal for writing an argumentative or persuasive essay.

CCSS

Common Core Standards and the Structure of Arguments

CCSS Standards 2, 5, and 8 for Reading Informational Text require that students follow the structure of arguments (main ideas plus support, plus the logic of proof). The first writing standard asks that students as young as first graders be able to state an opinion and support it with reasons. The Discussion Web, Debates, the Value Line, and similar strategies are excellent ways to help students understand arguments and to prepare them for writing argumentative essays.

Strategies That Unpack the Structures of Narratives

FOLLOWING DRAMATIC ROLES   As French drama critic Etienne Souriau (1955) pointed out many years ago, a large part of the way we understand characters in stories is by the symbolic roles they play in the plot. That is because, whether we are watching sports or reading fiction, it is normal for us to cheer the hero, boo the rival, and have a warm place in our hearts for the trusty helper. Authors of stories wittingly or unwittingly use these propensities to shape the reader's reactions to characters: assigning one the role of protagonist or main character, another the role of helper, and another the role of rival or enemy.

Making children aware of the roles characters play in stories can help them interpret the stories and, eventually, to better understand how stories work. Following are common roles that occur in stories:

- The *hero* is the person whose desires and needs drive the story forward. In "Jack and the Beanstalk," to use that story as an example, the hero is Jack.
- The *goal* is the hero's main need or desire. In "Jack and the Beanstalk," Jack's goal seems to be to get money or to get some independence and not be thought of as a dolt.
- The *rival* is the person who stands between the hero and her or his goal. The rival in "Jack and the Beanstalk" is certainly the giant.
- The *helper* is a person or persons in a story who helps the hero achieve his or her goal. In "Jack and the Beanstalk," there are a couple of candidates for the helper: the mysterious old man who sells him the beans and the giant's own wife.

The teacher can use dramatic roles in several ways to think about stories. One way is to have students nominate candidates for each of the roles and discuss their choices in small groups or as a class. These discussions can become lively, because not all role assignments are obvious. Is the helper in "Jack and the Beanstalk" the mysterious old man or the giant's wife? If it is the giant's wife (and the giant is the rival), why should she help the person who is striving against her husband? Is Jack's goal to obey his mother, to get money, to satisfy his curiosity, or to prove himself? Or is it all of these things? Discussing these issues takes students deep into the story.

Another way of using dramatic roles is to help students take different perspectives on a story. The teacher does this by asking students to take a character who seems to be playing one role and ask how the story would be changed if we imagined that character playing a different role. For example, in "Jack and the Beanstalk," suppose the giant's wife were the hero; that is, suppose we saw things from her perspective. What is her goal? Who is her rival? Exploring these questions can lead to some very interesting discussions of stories; it also exercises the comprehension strategies of inferring and interpreting.

EXPLORING THE HERO CYCLE   Many myths, religious legends, and folktales from the Western tradition follow the Hero Cycle or Monomyth structure we described on pages 260–261. Many contemporary heroic tales also closely follow the pattern: *The Hobbit, The Lord of the Rings, The Dark Is Rising, Harry Potter, The Prydain Trilogy, The Golden Compass* (maybe), and many others. The original *Star Wars* film was expressly written to fit the pattern of the Hero Cycle. The Canadian critic Northrop Frye argued that all (Western) literature shares a common genealogy, and that contemporary stories reflect themes and structures from older ones. To the extent that is true, it can be an interesting exercise to compare stories children are reading to the Hero Cycle.

We suggest that you introduce the Hero Cycle by having the students read and discuss several relatively short stories that follow the pattern fairly closely. One might be "Jack and the Beanstalk." Others might be novels such as *Because of Winn-Dixie, Maniac Magee,* and *Holes.*

After reading and discussing each story, construct a Language Chart (Roser, Hoffman, & Farest, 1992) graphic organizer like the one shown in Figure 9.8. Use it to record summaries of the discussions of each story. Discuss the patterns that the stories have in common, too. These questions can help organize a discussion of the pattern:

1. What were all of these heroes like at the beginning of their stories? What did they think of themselves then? How did others think of them?
2. What were these heroes like at the end of their stories? In what ways did they change?
3. What qualities did the heroes show in order to meet their challenges successfully? Why were *they* the ones who had those qualities?
4. What did the heroes win? Why were these things important?

5. Why do you suppose older people told younger people stories like these, generation after generation after generation?

6. How might these patterns play out in your own lives? How will *you* be a hero? What talents and qualities will you develop that are uniquely yours to help you succeed? What challenges might you face to prove your worth? What might you achieve that will be worthwhile to others?

Once the students have a clear sense of the Hero Cycle pattern, you can discuss other works that fit it more indirectly, or don't fit it at all. For an example of the latter, it is striking to examine African American tales like "Wiley and the Hairy Man," "The Tailypo," and "Barney McCabe," as well as Afro-Caribbean tales like the "Anansi" stories, which differ from the pattern in that the characters are no better off at the end than they were in the beginning.

Contemporary realistic stories tend not to pit their characters against such daunting challenges as do the folktales, nor do they win such exaggerated rewards. Nonetheless, the characters face important social and psychological challenges, and they achieve rewards that matter in their lives. Psychological critics such as Bruno Bettelheim (1975) and Maria Von Franz (1996) argue that these amount to the same thing, since the challenges and rewards of the folk and fairy tales were symbolic of the social and psychological challenges that are named as such in contemporary literature.

Students can discuss contemporary works they have read in terms of a shortened version of the hero cycle, as shown in Figure 9.8.

BEHAVIOR AND REWARDS. People who worry about violence in the media point to the number of violent acts that not only go unpunished but also win for the perpetrators what they wanted. Critics correctly worry that this is a formula for influencing viewers:

> *"The characters commit X deed, and get what they want.*
> *Therefore, young viewer, you should commit X deed to get what you want."*

But there is a more subtle formula at work in literature that children read, especially the traditional literature, where different types of characters get different results for different kinds of actions.

In stories like "Cinderella" or "Beauty and the Beast," for example, it is clear that men get different rewards than women do for the same actions. Consider the chart in Figure 9.9.

You get the idea. The "yes-yes-yes's" are all successful: They're the males who go after what they want. So are the "No-no-yes's": They're the females who don't go after what they want. The ones who fail, and who are often horribly punished, are the "No-yes-no's": The females who go after what they want. That's a no-no in Western folktales.

Figure 9.8 A Shorter Version of the *Hero Cycle*

	"Jack and the Beanstalk"	*Maniac Magee*	*Holes*	*Because of Winn-Dixie*
Character in the beginning				
Challenge				
Great struggle				
Achievement				
Character at the end				

Figure 9.9
What They Wanted and
What They Got

	Male?	Actively sought what they wanted?	Got what they wanted?
Beauty	No	No	Yes
Beauty's sisters	No	Yes	No
Beast	Yes	Yes	Yes
Cinderella	No	No	Yes
Cinderella's sisters	No	Yes	No
Cinderella's prince	Yes	Yes	Yes
Sleeping Beauty	No	No	Yes
Sleeping Beauty's prince	Yes	Yes	Yes
Snow White	No	No	Yes
Snow White's stepmother	No	Yes	No
Snow White's prince	Yes	Yes	Yes

Constructing a chart like this with students can be a helpful exercise—but only if there is plenty of time for the students to question whether these patterns make sense in their own lives.

READING FOR STRUCTURED OPPOSITES   A useful way of interpreting stories is to look for their contrasts, ask what things are similarly contrasted in other stories, and then find parallel contrasts and tensions in our own lives (Levi-Strauss, 1970). A method for doing that is called *reading for structured opposites*. A folktale works very well for introducing this method and could be taught like this:

1. Ask the students to think of the two characters in the story they are reading who are most unlike each other or most opposed to each other. For example, if the story is "Jack and the Beanstalk," the two characters might be Jack and the giant.

2. Write the names of those two characters at the heads of two columns (see Figure 9.10). Ask the students to come up with contrasting descriptive words about these two characters. That is, ask for a word that describes one character; then ask for an opposite word that describes the other character.

To take "Jack and the Beanstalk" as our example, those might be Jack and the giant, obviously. Let's begin with them. What words would we use to describe each of them? Each of these columns—a bundle of features with a name at the top—can be called a *category*. We will do more with the categories in a moment.

Figure 9.10
Looking at Relations
Between Characters
Horizontally

Jack	The Giant
Young	Old
Poor	Rich
Small	Huge
"Plucky"	Dull
Seems weak	Seems strong
"On his way up"	"Over the hill"

Others Like Jack	Jack	The Giant	Others Like the Giant
David	Young	Old	Goliath
Marty (in *Shiloh*)	Poor	Rich	Judd Travers (in *Shiloh*)
Peter Pan	Small	Huge	Captain Hook
Robin Hood	"Plucky"	Dull	Sheriff of Nottingham
	Seems weak	Seems strong	
	"On his way up"	"Over the hill"	

Figure 9.11
Looking at Relations Between Characters Horizontally and Vertically

The dynamics between these characters can be called a *relationship*. In this case, it's a relationship of rivalry—Jack wants what the giant has, and the giant wants to keep what he has and eliminate Jack as a threat (eat him, if possible).

Now who else do we know who could occupy the same *category* with Jack, or occupy the other category with the giant—paradigms which are partially defined by their relationship with the other—in this case, the rivalry of the young, poor, underprivileged one who is on his way up, and the older, bigger, richer one who is desperately clinging to his or her privilege? We will nominate a few and write them in the outer columns to the left of Jack and to the right of the giant (see Figure 9.11).

Wow. It now seems that Jack and the giant are actually more than mere characters in a story. They are bundles of features with names attached—characters who remind us of other characters. Who are other candidates who share these paradigms, and occupy the same categories with each other? (See Figure 9.12.)

There. You may have noticed that in exploring the contrasted characters and their characteristics in this story—in both their categories and their relationships—we have explored text-to-text relationships and text-to-life relationships.

QUESTIONING THE AUTHOR In the Questioning the Author teaching strategy, also called QtA (Beck, McKeown, & Kucan, 2002), the teacher does three things.

First, the teacher reminds students that authors are people like themselves, with their own ideas, experiences, foibles, and prejudices. When authors communicate with audiences, they sometimes tell readers exactly what they need to know; but often, they take too much for granted and leave out needed explanations. Or they may slant their message to suit their own beliefs, without inviting the reader to disagree. In classrooms where students write and share their works with each other, students are not surprised when their peers make points that aren't clear, or state positions with which they disagree. They find it natural to question their peer-authors at those times. The teacher tries to evoke that same confidence in questioning an author when students are faced with the work not of a peer, but by a published author.

Figure 9.12 Comparing This Story to Others

Others Like Jack in Real Life	Others Like Jack in the Arts	Jack	The Giant	Others Like the Giant in the Arts	Others Like the Giant in Real Life
Serfs	David	Young	Old	Goliath	Nobles
Slaves	Marty	Poor	Rich	Judd Travers	Owners
People	Peter Pan	Small	Huge	Captain Hook	Tyrants
Workers	Robin Hood	"Plucky"	Dull	Sheriff of Nottingham	Sweatshop managers
Children		Seems weak	Seems strong		Bullies
		"On his way up"	"Over the hill"		

The second step is to ask the students to have an imaginary dialogue with the author, and ask about things that are not clearly stated, points where more information is needed, or claims with which they disagree. Here are some basic questions students might ask:

- What is the author trying to say here?
- How can we restate this idea, in words we all can understand?
- Why is the author telling us this now?
- What does the author want us to believe? Why?
- What is the author's point of view?
- How might someone with a different point of view have explained this point?

The third step, which is usually combined with the second, is to invite the students to provide the answers they might expect an author to supply to their questions. A group of students is usually able to do this, because their collective ideas may be smarter than their individual ideas.

Teach It!

Refer to the Teach It! appendix at the end of the book for further activities you can use to reinforce concepts discussed in this chapter.

Socratic Seminar

With students in late elementary and middle school, nearly any topic to be interpreted or explored from different points of view can be used in the Socratic Seminar. The purpose of the Socratic Seminar is to empower students to conduct discussions on their own. The teacher provides a structure that usually leads to successful discussions, but after modeling the process by leading the first few discussions, the students are the ones who ask the questions and conduct the discussion. A Socratic Seminar is not a debate. The ideas offered do not compete with each other. Rather, they often build on each other to reach a mutually constructed and deeper understanding of an issue. Asking good questions and developing ideas in concert with others is good practice in active learning and critical thinking. Taking responsibility for preparing the questions and conducting the discussion intensifies the experience for the students.

Socratic Seminars are done with the whole class. If the group is larger than twelve (and it usually is), a fishbowl arrangement is used. That is, between eight and twelve students sit in a circle conducting the discussion, and the other students array themselves around that group, close enough to hear the discussion.

The Socratic Seminar requires no particular resources other than a text or a topic that students can discuss. It helps if the seating is treated flexibly; that is, either the chairs are moved into a circle, or students sit so they can face each other in a circle. The seminar itself usually takes 40 minutes. Twenty minutes or more will be needed to introduce the idea, and then students will need time to prepare for the seminar.

To conduct the Socratic Seminar, the teacher first immerses students in an interesting topic. The topic can come from literature, social studies, art, science, or any topic about which there are layers of understanding, different interpretations, or diverse implications. One of the easiest ways to introduce the Socratic Seminar is to discuss a piece of literature that the whole class has read. A seminar is also productive midway through a unit of study in which students have acquired a significant amount of information on a topic or theme.

The teacher prepares the students to formulate questions for discussion. The Socratic Seminar requires that everyone discuss good questions. Eventually, students may formulate the questions, but for the first couple of sessions, the teacher may prepare them and use his or her questions to model for the students the kinds of questions that are preferred. A suggested approach to formulating questions worthy of deep discussion is Grant Wiggins' and Jay McTighe's (2005) concept of essential questions. Essential questions usually:

Lead into the heart of a topic and its controversies

Invite many answers from different perspectives

Invite rethinking of old knowledge in a new light

Lead to discovery and "uncoverage" vs. "coverage"

Encourage deeper interest in the subject; students keep on questioning

Are framed in a provocative and enticing style.

In practical terms, you may use the following set of suggestions:

A Socratic Seminar is a time to have a good discussion. To have a good discussion, you bring up things you are curious about, things you think are important. To have an even better discussion, you ask your classmates questions—but real questions—questions you don't know the answer to. Those can serve as guidelines. To prepare for a Socratic Seminar, you should plan some real questions—that ask about things you are interested in, that you think are important. And the questions should be real in the sense that you don't already know the answers ("Read my mind" questions are not allowed!).

Often these questions point in either of two directions, as we see in Figure 9.13.

The teacher explains the ground rules for the seminar. One set of suggestions are these:

Be prepared to participate

Don't raise hands—just find a good time to speak and jump right in

Invite others in the circle into the discussion

Refer to the texts or other resources that have been studied

Make comments that are appropriate, respectful, and focused

Listen to and build on one another's comments

Be sure it's OK with others before you introduce a new question

Ground rules are introduced at the beginning of a seminar. It is best if the group is reminded of them often. If a student does an excellent job of adhering to a ground rule, the teacher may point that out, since positive reinforcements will make students feel more responsible than criticisms will.

Participating students (between eight and twelve of them) sit in a circle. The other students gather around what is called the "fishbowl" (so called because their discussion will be observed by the others—see the next section for instructions).

The teacher may invite a student to ask a question and have the other students respond. The other students share their thoughts about the question, and also refer both to each other's answers and to the material being discussed.

When the responses to a question seem to have run their course, another student may raise a new question, or an aspect of an old one. It is considered polite for that student to ask if anyone had more to say about the previous question first, and to wait for any more responses before raising a new question.

After the teacher gives the signal (usually after five minutes), students who are observing from outside the group may "tap into" the group. That is, one student at a time approaches a student in the circle, and taps that student gently on the elbow. Then the new student takes that student's place in the discussion group. The new student should respond first to what the group has been talking about before introducing a new question. From time to time the teacher can invite a student to sum up the positions that have been heard, and ask if there are more ideas.

Following the Socratic Seminar, students are asked to evaluate their participation. They can be asked to write responses to questions such as:

What did you learn from this seminar?

How did you feel about this seminar?

How would you evaluate your own participation in this seminar?

What can you do to improve your participation in the next seminar?

The teacher "debriefs" the discussion by reviewing the ideas and arguments that came to light. Or she may ask each student to write a journal entry or a personal essay, writing down what he believes about the issue and why.

For future Socratic Seminars, students can be asked to bring "Entry Sheets" on which they have written at least three questions for the others to answer, as well as their own thoughts on those questions. Another device for structuring the seminar would be to pass out small pieces of paper to each student, have them write their name and their class period on it, and ask them to write a short entry each time they offer a question or a response to one. These can be given to the teacher at the end of the class period to keep track of the students' participation.

Questions That Focus *In* (on the article or topic)	Questions That Focus *Out* (to the world outside the text or topic of study)
1. If the question is about a story, you can ask about: A character's motives. ("Why did she agree to do that?") The relationships between characters ("Do you think he is a good influence on her?") What is going to happen (if we haven't finished reading it yet). Why the author wrote the story. ("What did this author want us to see or to understand?") What the action had to do with the setting. ("Can you picture this story happening anywhere else? Why not?") Why the author used certain words, or a certain style of writing. ("Why do you think the author said it that way?") Something the author has done particularly well. ("What do you think is the best feature of this story?") 2. If it is an informational topic or work of nonfiction, you might ask: What are we learning from this that we didn't know before? Is this argument convincing? What other points of view have we learned about? Is there more to be said about this topic?	1. If the question is about a story, you can ask about: Whether the characters made good choices. ("Would you have done what he did? What is another way to solve that problem?") Whether the behavior pictured in this story should serve as a model for us in real life. ("Is that the way boys should really behave with girls? Suppose she was your sister?") The consequences of the actions. ("What do you suppose happened to each one of those characters after the story was over?") About connections to other stories and to real life. ("What other stories does this remind us of? Who or what does this remind us of in real life?") 2. If it is an informational topic or work of nonfiction, you might ask: Do we think this is true? How do we know? What is the most important idea? If we believe what this text says, what should we do?

Figure 9.13 Questions About Stories

Figure 9.14
Structuring an
Argumentative Essay

I think . . .	
because . . .	
Evidence for that is . . .	
Also because . . .	
Evidence for that is . . .	

Discussion Web

Reading to Follow Arguments

Students from fourth grade and up are ready to look at the ways persuasive texts and media make arguments. When they are given guidance, they can become quite expert at asking about evidence for perspectives they read and view.

PRODUCING ARGUMENTS   One good way to prepare students for this kind of thinking is to have them produce arguments of their own—and a lively way to do that is to:

- Engage students in issues.
- Ask each student to take a position on the issues.
- Have students debate with others from their position.
- Ask students to write about their position.

A graphic organizer such as the one in Figure 9.14 may be used to help students from their brief position essay.

ANALYZING ARGUMENTS IN TEXTS   After the students can confidently write out their own arguments according to this structure, they are ready to outline the arguments of others. Note that it is best to begin with short, simple, and clearly structured arguments such as the essay on dogs and cats found on page 262 above. Teachers may write their own sample essays to give students practice, making sure those essays (1) state a claim clearly, and (2) offer two or three reasons for the claim, (3) with each reason being immediately supported by evidence. It is advisable to use the words *reason* and *evidence* right in the essays, to help students identify them.

Then the students take notes about the essay in a graphic organizer such as the one in Figure 9.15.

Once the arguments are laid out this way, the teacher and students can discuss whether the reasons logically support the claim, and whether the evidence really supports the reasons.

Some students may be ready to move beyond tracking the simple form of arguments, and pay attention to one or more of these:

- missing information (MI)
- loaded words (LW)
- faulty assumptions about what the world needs (FA)

The students can locate and mark places where these problems occur, underlining the offending phrases and putting the corresponding letters in the margins near the problem phrases.

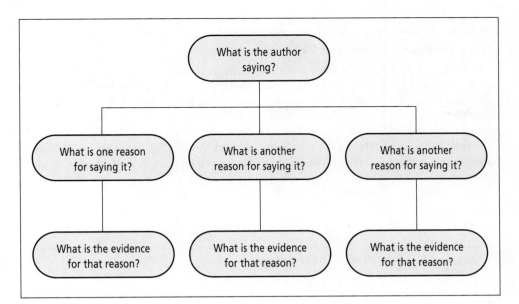

Figure 9.15
A Graphic Organizer for Arguments

WORDS AND THEIR CONNOTATIONS   For an exercise on loaded words—words that carry judgments that have not been justified—teachers sometimes use an exercise like the following. Students are shown a chart with rows of words divided into three columns. In the middle column goes the most neutral word. In the left-hand column goes a negative word—a word with negative connotations—and in the right-hand column goes a positive word—a word with positive connotations (connotations are the other things a word means beyond its literal meaning, especially the value judgments a word conveys). The students may fill in the blanks in a chart like the one in Figure 9.16, and later create charts of their own.

LOOKING AT ARGUMENTS THAT DON'T SAY THEY ARE ARGUMENTS   Not all of the messages that seek to persuade people state their claims clearly or offer reasons supported by evidence about why we should accept those claims. So it can be valuable for students to learn how to do a little detective work before they let themselves be persuaded by something they read, see, or hear. The graphic organizer in Figure 9.17 is adapted from Luke and Freebody's "Four Resources Model of Reading" (Luke & Freebody, 1999) that was discussed on pages 263–264. Teachers may practice asking the question about a simple text first—even a text as simple as a stop sign. Then the class can move on to another kind of text, such as an advertisement.

Teach It! 24

Semantic Feature Analysis

Figure 9.16
Words and Their Connotations

Negative	Neutral	Positive
Shack	House	Palace
Cowardly	Cautious	Prudent
Sluggish	Slow	Guarded
Oversized	Large	
Fat		
		Confident
	Casual	

Common Core Standards and Word Connotations

Standard 4 of the Common Core Standards both for Reading Literature and Informational Text asks students to understand literal and figurative language, and also to understand vocabulary from the different academic disciplines. Although the standards don't acknowledge it, under figurative language, the choices of words often have value associations (*patriots* are good people, *terrorists* are bad people, but in some contexts the words could apply to the same person). We can use the term *nominal assumptions* for those occasions where we choose a word with a value attached to it, but without defending the value judgment. Teachers who promote critical literacy will have to go beyond the Common Core Standards in this instance.

Figure 9.17
Looking Critically at Messages

1. What *is* this?	Decide what kind of message this is.	
	Then decide how we should read it.	
2. What does it mean?	Now, list some of the words or images in the message that caught your eye—What do they make you think of?	
	Next, say what you think the whole message means.	
3. What is it for?	Decide what you can do with this text.	
	Say what you think others may do with it.	
4. Who is behind the message?	Explain what you think the text is trying to do.	
	Say who you think might want the text to do that, and why.	
	Then say whose point of view you think is left out.	

Strategies That Compare Multiple Texts with Common Themes

What? So What? Now What?

COMPARING TEXTS Primary as well as upper grade teachers introduce students to the value of reading multiple texts and thinking of how texts function when they create thematic and inquiry units. These units usually begin by posing some question for exploration like, "How should we treat the insects in our environment? Should we use insecticides and try to kill them or are there some that are useful to us?" or "How important is it to share with others what we have?" Teachers collect an array of materials that are accessible to students (at their reading levels and that capture their levels of interest and knowledge). These materials represent a range of genres and formats so students can compare and contrast how authors present ideas and information.

Know-Want to Know-Learn (K-W-L)

USING INFORMATIONAL TEXTS Many classes begin their inquiries with a group K-W-L with the teacher creating a chart of what the students think they already know about the topic. During the discussion that ensues, the teacher also helps students generate questions that will guide their initial inquiries. Once the students have embarked on their reading, viewing, and searching for information, the teacher can bring them back together to formulate key questions that can then be put on the class Inquiry Chart (Hoffman, 1992). The teacher also selects some of the best texts for students' use in this class activity. Small groups of students can take turns examining the texts and recording what they learn from the authors. The groups can either record their information and ideas on 8 × 11-inch record sheets or put what they learn on sticky notes to be included on a large class I-Chart.

As students read from different sources of information, their awareness of how authors have to select and leave out information grows. The ways authors explain ideas and provide visual information also vary considerably. Students attend to these characteristics and teachers can guide them to make comparisons about which texts are most useful and which could use revision to be more "considerate" to them as readers. See an example of an I-Chart that the teacher used as students completed their unit in Figure 9.18. As part of the culmination of this unit, groups of students wrote their own books and took time to consider the structure, ways they would present information, and the themes they wanted to communicate. The children developed a deeper understanding of the relationship between texts and readers throughout this process.

Children are often amazed by the amount of partial information and misinformation contained in some of the documents. As one group of second graders exclaimed, "These two books are confusing—one says there aren't brown recluse spiders in the middle part of the country; the other says they can be found everywhere in dark, damp areas. One makes spiders sound like they are really helpful; the other tells about a woman who almost died when a brown recluse bit her while she was rocking in her chair and shows an ugly picture of an arm of someone bitten."

Story Maps

READING MULTIPLE VERSIONS OF THE SAME STORY Another way to help young students understand how texts function in social contexts is to read and examine several texts written by different authors using the same basic story. One of the easiest to use is the Cinderella tale. Almost any library will have several versions of this tale that can be explored. Teachers can read some tales to students and have them chart the similarities and differences in the tales, their structure, their characters, the challenges faced, the ways the problems are solved, and the underlying message the author seems to want readers to accept. For example, after reading the classic French version of Cinderella, students who read *The Rough-faced Girl* (American Indian tale) and *Mufaro's Beautiful Daughters* (West African tale) can discuss the different challenges the girls face and ways they are able to overcome their hardships. The pictures or drawings are also worth examining critically to see how the context and characters are represented. Children may want to create their own illustrations or locate others online or in other books. Figure 9.19 shows an example of how one first-grade teacher helped her students think deeply about different versions of the folktale *Stone Soup*. This activity led students to analyze the major story elements and then compare the ways the authors developed the basic story theme in a variety of settings.

Figure 9.18 Inquiry Chart

Topic:	Guiding Question 1	Guiding Question 2	Guiding Question 3	Guiding Question 4	Other Interesting Facts and Figures	New Questions
WHAT WE KNOW						
Source 1						
Source 2						
Source 3						
Summary						

Source: Inquiry Chart, J. Hoffman (1992), "Critically Reading/Thinking across the Curriculum: Using I-Charts to Support Learning," in *Language Arts, 69*(2), 121–127, © National Council of Teachers of English. Reprinted with permission.

Figure 9.19 *Stone Soup*: A Single Story from Multiple Perspectives

Title	*Stone Soup* M. Brown, 1947	*Stone Soup*, T. Ross, 1987	*Nail Soup*, Zemach, 1964	*Group Soup*, B. Brenner, 1992	*Stone Soup*, Muth, 2003
Characters					
Setting Genre					
Problem					
Resolution					
Theme or Lesson Learned					

For Review

This chapter has focused on critical thinking and critical literacy. It is difficult to say exactly at what age children can read (or listen, or view) deeply. Vivian Vasquez (2004) has demonstrated how it is possible to encourage even preschool children to look deeply into the messages they are subjected to, and to challenge some of them. When children are working with ideas they are deeply immersed in, including stories, they are capable of sophisticated thought. This chapter described some of the kinds of thinking that texts evoke. It began by examining what is meant by critical literacy and why that is so important in the twenty-first century. It argued that students need to read carefully to understand the structure of texts, to connect with the texts, and to ask questions about authors' purposes and the cultural significance of their underlying values. Then it proceeded to some ways of analyzing the structures of stories for the ways they guide readers' responses, including structured opposites and what were called "categories and relationships." Further on in the section that described conceptions of reading, we looked at the logic of argumentative texts and then at ways of examining texts that weren't clearly argumentative, but still seemed to have persuasive intentions.

The second half of the chapter set out methods for guiding students' reading through different kinds of texts. First presented were strategies for helping students develop an understanding of how similar texts can be structured very differently and communicate different messages, eliciting students' responses to texts; then techniques for examining and weighing arguments were provided, and finally suggestions for looking at all kinds of messages that seek to influence readers.

For Your Journal

1 Take a moment to review your answers to the questions on the Anticipation Guide that opened this chapter. Has your thinking changed? If so, write about the changes in your journal.

2 Read the story "The Ugly Duckling" by Hans Christian Andersen. There is a version online at <www.ivyjoy.com/fables/duckling.html>. Does this story have an uplifting message for everyone? Think through this story using the four scans of Luke and Freebody described on pages 263–264. Write down your conclusions and share them later with your class.

Taking It to the World

Watch an hour of mainstream children's television one Saturday morning. Pick any one of the frameworks of analysis presented earlier in this chapter, such as "The Web of Narrative and 'The Way It Is.'" Write up your insights using a Dual Entry Diary format.

This Is What a Dual Entry Diary Looks Like	
In this column indicate the section from the show that made you pause.	In this column, write your comment on it: What was striking about it?

New Literacies Connections

Explore the University of Connecticut's Web site on the New Literacies at this address: <www.newliteracies.uconn.edu/team.html>. Read a research article or two and be prepared to summarize it for your classmates.

MyEducationLab™

Go to Topic 7 (Reading and Writing in the Content Areas) in the MyEducationLab <www.myeducationlab.com> for your course, where you can:

- Find learning outcomes for Reading and Writing in the Content Areas along with the national standards that connect to these outcomes.

- Complete Assignments and Activities that can help you more deeply understand the chapter content.

- Apply and practice your understanding of the core teaching skills identified in the chapter with the Building Teaching Skills and Dispositions learning units.

- Check your comprehension on the content covered in the chapter by going to the Study Plan in the Book Resources for your text. Here you will be able to take a chapter quiz, receive feedback on your answers, and then access Review, Practice, and Enrichment activities to enhance your understanding of chapter content.

- Visit A+RISE. A+RISE® Standards2Strategy™ is an innovative and interactive online resource that offers new teachers in grades K-12 just in time, research-based instructional strategies that meet the linguistic needs of ELLs as they learn content, differentiate instruction for all grades and abilities, and are aligned to Common Core Elementary Language Arts standards English language proficiency standards in WIDA, Texas, California, and Florida.

Teaching Children to Spell and Write

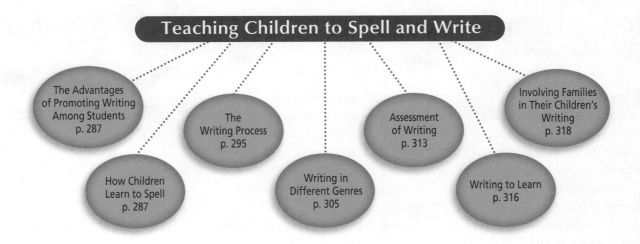

Teaching Children to Spell and Write

- The Advantages of Promoting Writing Among Students p. 287
- How Children Learn to Spell p. 287
- The Writing Process p. 295
- Writing in Different Genres p. 305
- Assessment of Writing p. 313
- Writing to Learn p. 316
- Involving Families in Their Children's Writing p. 318

Anticipation Guide

The following statements will stimulate your thinking about the topics of this chapter. Answer *true* or *false* in response to each statement. As you read and learn more about the topics in these statements, double-check your answers. See what interests you and prompts your curiosity toward more understanding.

_____ **1.** Being a poor speller can make a student a disfluent writer.

_____ **2.** When we speak of a writing process, we mean a process by which many successful adult writers as well as schoolchildren produce written compositions.

_____ **3.** The goal of writing instruction is to teach children to write everything once and write it correctly.

_____ **4.** Children can help each other learn to write.

_____ **5.** It is generally better for teachers to assign writing topics than to let children choose their own.

_____ **6.** Children need different levels of support as they learn to write. Some children flourish in the open atmosphere of the writing workshop, but others need more explicit guidance.

_____ **7.** It is important for teachers to write in front of children and demonstrate writing as a studio craft.

_____ **8.** The difference between editing and revising is that editing is done only by professional writers.

_____ **9.** There is no such thing as different levels of support teachers give to writers at different ages. Writing is a sink-or-swim affair.

_____ **10.** Learn first, then write about what you know. Writing about what you haven't learned yet is a waste of time.

A Classroom Story

The Writing Process in a Third-Grade Classroom

At West Street School in Geneva, New York, Anne Bergstrom is trying a new approach to her third graders' study of African geography. The school's experience has corroborated what the National Assessment of Educational Progress has found: Not only do elementary students need to know more geography, but they also need to know how to think with geographical information. So this spring, because their student teacher from last fall, Sarah Barry, is studying in Dakar, the capital of Senegal, Ms. Bergstrom has arranged to conduct an inquiry lesson on Senegal via the Internet.

In the fall, the students located Senegal on a map and discussed its tropical climate and its history as a slave state and as a colony of France. They researched and read material about Senegal from the National Geographic Web site. They also did their best to make sense of the U.S. State Department's Web-based information. In December, the students thought of questions they wanted Sarah to investigate, wrote them on a piece of chart paper as part of a K-W-L chart (see Figure 10.1), and sent them to Sarah in an e-mail.

Sarah wrote the students an e-mail from Senegal and asked them how they wanted her to find answers to their questions: "Who do you want me to talk to? What do you want me to ask?" The students took turns writing e-mails to Sarah on the classroom computer. But Sarah realized that there are fascinating things about Senegal that the students did not know to ask about. So she sent them occasional transmissions that she called "mysteries," intriguing photographs with questions attached. The students took turns writing to Sarah about the mystery; they sent guesses or questions they wanted to ask her. In a way, Sarah became an extension of the class, their remote-control anthropologist.

In the spring, Ms. Bergstrom had the students prepare write-ups of what they had learned. The students used the writing workshop to focus on their topics, write a first draft, revise their drafts, edit them, and prepare them for publication. Later, the class collaborated on a joint composition: the script for a class play about aspects of life in the West African country of Senegal, which they performed for an audience of the whole school.

Figure 10.1
The First Questions We Have

The First Questions We Have

1. Do they go swimming?
2. What is the population?
3. Do they know about King's fight for freedom?
4. How do they talk?
5. What do they eat?
6. How hot does it get?
7. What are their houses made of?
8. What do they do in their spare time?
9. Was it a slave trading place?
10. What do they celebrate?
11. What games do they play?
12. What kinds of animals do they have?
13. What are their religions?
14. How do people treat each other?
15. What kind of jewelry do they wear?
16. Does anyone have piercings or tattoos?
17. Do they trade? What do they trade with other countries?
18. Does everyone have a job?
19. Are there homeless people?
20. How do they dispose of trash?
21. Do they brush their teeth, and if so, with what?

The Advantages of Promoting Writing Among Students

Even preschool and kindergarten children are eager to write—that is, if we accept making communicative marks on paper as "writing." As we saw in previous chapters, writing down ideas word by word and sound by sound helps young learners take a close look at the language they speak and the system of print that represents it. But emphasizing writing has other advantages, too:

- Writing makes students more observant, both of their own inner experiences and of the outside world.
- Being writers makes students closer readers of other writers. Young writers are sensitive to language and style, and can feel like "workers in the same vineyard" as Dav Pilkey, Kate DiCamillo, Steve Jenkins, and other admired authors.
- Writing makes students more reflective as they record an idea, examine that idea in print, and maybe come up with a further idea.
- Writing builds community. As students work hard to capture and communicate their thoughts and experiences and as they listen to their classmates' efforts to do the same, students reveal themselves to each other and come to better understand each other.
- Applied to literature and to other subjects in the curriculum, writing responses and other kinds of inquiry also serve as a powerful learning tool.

In this chapter we will present many ways teachers can help children learn to write. We begin by talking about spelling—how it is learned and how it is taught. Then we will look at different levels of instruction and support for children's composing. We will explore the well-known "writing process," a set of activities through which writers often create works. We will look in more detail at many ways of teaching and supporting writing in different genres, too—narrative, poetry, journals, and the nonfiction genres of persuasion, description, and explanation. Finally, we will present ways of teaching students to use writing in order to learn in the disciplines.

How Children Learn to Spell

Children can and should be taught to spell correctly. But in the beginning, children do not need to be able to spell in order to communicate on paper. Many teachers of preschool and kindergarten encourage their students to organize and communicate their ideas by making scribbles and drawing on paper. Over time, children gradually add both learned and invented spellings to their graphic productions.

One of the most fascinating discoveries of the past century in the literacy field has been about children's ability to recognize the ways in which letters represent sounds in print and their inclination to experiment with their own spellings. The discovery of invented spelling followed naturally from what was learned about the ways children learn spoken language: Children see people around them communicating in some medium (in this case, print); decide to try out their own versions of that communication; organize their versions according to rules or patterns that are logical, though incorrect by adult standards; and gradually, bit by bit or phase by phase, modify their strategies so that they grow closer and closer to the versions they hear and see adults using.

Sure enough, children appear to go through phases as they experiment with invented spellings for words (Bear et al., 2007; Gentry, 1989; Schlagal, 1989; Temple et al., 2013). Progress through the phases depends on three things: children's own developing concepts of how the English spelling system works (what we call their word knowledge), the levels

Table 10.1   Comparing Descriptions of Spelling Development

	All Children Read	Gentry; Schlagal	Schlagal, 1989[1]; Bear et al., *Words Their Way*[2]; Ganske, *Word Journeys*[3]
Mid kindergarten	Prephonemic	Precommunicative	Emergent
End of kindergarten	Early Phonemic	Early phonetic	
Mid first grade	Letter Name	Phonetic	Letter Name
End of second grade	Orthographic	Transitional	Within-Word Pattern
Late second grade through fourth grade and beyond	Morphological		Syllable Juncture
Early fourth grade through adulthood	Derivational		Derivational Constancy

[1]Schlagal, R. C. (1989). Constancy and change in spelling development. *Reading Psychology, 10*, 3, 207–232. Reprinted by permission of the publisher (Taylor & Francis Ltd, <http://www.tandf.co.uk/journals>).
[2]Bear, D., Invernizzi, M., Templeton, S., & Johnston, F. (2007). *Words their way*. Columbus, OH: Pearson.
[3]Ganske, K. (2000). *Word journeys*. New York, NY: Guilford. Used by permission.

Figure 10.2
Prephonemic Spelling

Source: Temple, C., Nathan, R., Burris, N., & Temple, F. (1993). *The beginnings of writing* (3rd ed.). Boston, MA: Allyn & Bacon.

Figure 10.3 Early Invented Spelling

Source: Temple, C., Nathan, R., Burris, N., & Temple, F. (1993). *The beginnings of writing* (3rd ed.). Boston, MA: Allyn & Bacon.

of challenge that system presents to them as they move through the grades, and, of course, what and how they are taught. How do we describe children's spelling development? Different writers label the phases differently. The labels we will use here are from Temple, Nathan, and Temple (2013) and they were inspired by the work of Henderson (1990), Gentry (1989), and Schlagal (1989). The phases we will use in this book are the *prephonemic phase*, the *early phonemic phase*, the *letter name phase*, the *orthographic phase*, the *morphological phase*, and the *derivational phase*. To correlate our phases of spelling development with other writers' phases, please see Table 10.1.

Learning a system of spelling phases is worthwhile for teachers, because looking developmentally at children's progress through phases of invented spelling reveals a great deal about children's knowledge of words; this is important to understand in order to help them learn to read (Hauerwas & Walker, 2004).

THE PREPHONEMIC PHASE OF SPELLING   When children first begin to write, they often fill entire pages with a lot of unconnected letters (see Figure 10.2). Although what the child has written has no meaning, he or she has demonstrated prephonemic spelling. It is a kind of writing that uses letters without regard to their sounds. In this phase, children write down letters at random or possibly with some early notion of how they might represent ideas.

Children at the prephonemic phase of spelling know how to make many letters (and often many more pseudo-letters). They know what writing looks like, and they might know how it is arrayed on the page. But children at this phase have not yet discovered the alphabetic principle: the understanding that spelling represents words by relating written letters to spoken phonemes. If this is the case, then much reading instruction in which children are expected to learn to recognize words by being exposed to them will not be effective yet. Neither will phonics instruction that focuses on learning particular letters and sounds, which requires an understanding of the fundamental idea that words are real, they consist of phonemes, and those phonemes are represented by letters.

THE EARLY PHONEMIC PHASE OF SPELLING   Figure 10.3 represents the work of a child in the early phonemic phase of spelling. This child has used letters to represent some of the sounds in words but not all of them. That is why we call this phase early phonemic: The child is just beginning to represent words by their phonemes. Children at this phase typically represent only the first and last and possibly a middle consonant in the word. They usually leave out vowels unless the whole word is a vowel, such as A. Children who spell in the early phonemic phase sometimes spell the first sound in a word with a sensible choice of a letter, then add random letters to make the word longer and hence make it look like a word (Ferreiro & Teberosky, 1982). But note carefully what we mean by a sensible choice. When children do use letters to represent sounds, rather than to use letters for sounds in conventional ways, they spell intuitively, matching as best they can a letter with a letter name that sounds closest to the sound they want to spell. Thus, for example, they are likely to choose the letter H to spell /ch/, and the letter Y to spell /w/.

If children are spelling in the early phonemic phase, we know that they have discovered the alphabetic principle. They are not yet very proficient, however, at breaking words into phonemes and matching them with letter sounds. Matching letters to sounds contains at least four operations: making the word hold still in the mind, breaking it down into phonemes, matching each phoneme with a letter, and writing down that letter. All of these steps may be difficult for a beginner.

Determining the number of sounds children can represent in their spelling yields important diagnostic information. Bear in mind Ehri's hypothesis that a child's memory for storing images of written words for later recognition consists of a number of "slots" (Ehri, 1991, 1997a). A child with more memory storage "slots" for word recognition will store a more complete memory of that word and will recognize it more accurately when she sees it written down.

Examining a child's invented spelling can yield clues to his or her ability to segment words into phonemes. A child who writes *HK* for *truck* (that is, the early phonemic speller) shows a limited ability to segment phonemes in words. When it comes to recognizing words in print, that child will try to say the word on the basis of very shallow processing, typically looking at the first letter and calling out a word he or she knows that begins with that letter. Because the child does not yet focus on all of the letters and phonemes in the word (Morris, 1998), he or she can easily confuse the words being read with other words that share one or two of the same letters.

Phonemic Segmentation with Elkonin Boxes

THE LETTER NAME PHASE OF SPELLING   At a slightly more advanced phase, a child offers spelling like that in Figure 10.4. This child is in the letter name phase of spelling. Here, Iuliu represented all or nearly all of the phonemes in a word, but he did so intuitively. He made logical judgments when he chose a letter to represent a sound, but that logic still diverged quite a bit from the conventions of English spelling. For instance, Iuliu wrote H for the /č/ or "ch" sound in *Charlie* and *much*, probably because the letter name "*aitch*" contains that sound.

Figure 10.4   Letter Name Spelling

> Hole I like u So moH

"Charlie, I like you so much."

Children use names of the letters of the alphabet as if they were building blocks of sound out of which words could be constructed. In the case of some sounds, the letter name strategy results in spellings that look conventional; in others, the spellings can look bizarre. Especially in these cases, examining children's letter name spellings gives us a window into the ways children think about words and into the eccentricities of the English spelling system.

- *Spelling Most Consonants.* As the sample in Figure 10.4 demonstrates, many consonant letters are spelled intuitively in ways that look conventional. Note the spellings of *L* in *Charlie*, the *S* in *so*, and the *M* in *much*. The names of these letters are close enough to their corresponding phonemes to make the letter name strategy successful or nearly successful.

- *Spelling Non-Intuitive Consonants.* Young children often spell the sound of /w/ as in *went* with the letter Y. In such cases, they choose the Y for the sound of its name. After all, the letter name for W ("double U") doesn't sound at all like /w/, but the name of Y ("wye") is a good fit, so this choice of Y for the /w/ sound is not surprising for the child who is using the letter name strategy.

- **Spelling Digraph Consonants.** Young spellers are troubled by the spellings of digraphs, since they do not know about the conventions for spelling them. Note the invented spelling of the CH digraph in spelling the /č/ sound in *HOLE* (*Charlie*) and *MOH* (*much*). In both cases, the letter *H* was chosen because the name of that letter sounds closest to the phoneme that is usually spelled by *CH*. The letter *H* is often used by children in the letter name phase of learning to spell the sounds of /š/ ("sh") and /č/ ("ch").

- **Spelling Ns and Ms Before Stop Consonants.** In spellings like *YUTS* for *once* and *AD* for *and*, letter name spellers often leave out Ns and Ms when they come before other consonants, especially before what are called *stop consonants* (so called because they briefly stop the flow of air through the mouth) such as /p/, /b/, /t/, /d/, and /k/. The problem is not that children don't know how to spell the /n/ and /m/ sounds. It is rather that they are used to feeling the consonants produced in the mouth as they sound out the word in order to spell it (Read, 1975). When Ns and Ms are pronounced before stop consonants, you cannot feel them in your mouth, because your tongue goes to the same position to form the stop consonant anyway. Say the words *wet* and *went* aloud, and you will see what we mean: The activity of the tongue in the mouth is the same in both cases. What is different when N or M is present is that the whole syllable is pronounced through the nose. The omission of N and M in this position is prevalent in the spellings of kindergarten and first-grade children and in older children who are advancing slowly as spellers.

- **Spelling Word-Final R, L, M, and N: "Syllabic Sonorants."** Spellings such as *FLEPR* for *Flipper* shows another common feature of children's letter name spelling. Unstressed syllables ending in R, L, M, and N often lack vowels when they appear at the ends of words. Thus it is common to see *TABL* for *table*, *LEDL* for *little*, and *BIDM* for *bottom* in the writing of children in the letter name phase of spelling. English has a convention that all syllables must be spelled with vowels. Even though children in the letter name phase represent most vowels, they leave them out of these words, presumably because they expect every letter they write into a word to be clearly sounded, but in these syllables, no distinct vowel sound is heard (Read, 1975).

- **Spelling Long Vowels.** As Iuliu's spelling of U for *you* in Figure 10.4 demonstrated, long vowels in words usually "say their names"; that is, the sound to be spelled sounds much like the name of the letter we would use to spell that sound.

- **Spelling Short Vowels.** Spelling short vowels presents problems to letter name spellers. Short vowels do not sound very much like the "long" vowels spelled by the same letter. There are no vowel letter names that have short vowel sounds, so the speller must choose the letter name that is the best fit with that short vowel. This in practice is the long vowel sound that sounds the most like, or is produced in the mouth in the manner most like, that short vowel sound. This principle explains the spelling of O for the short vowel /uh/ in *much*. It also explains why children write A for /ĕ/ in *bet* and E for /ı/ ("ih") in *bit*.

Children who are letter name spellers represent nearly all of the phonemes (the smaller speech sounds) in words. But they represent those speech sounds intuitively, using a letter name strategy, rather than conventionally, using the kinds of spellings for sounds that are seen in books. Letter name spellers' ability to segment words into all of their phonemes gives them many corresponding "slots" in word memory storage for the parts of the words they see in print. Letter name spellers are usually beginning readers who are making progress acquiring sight words.

Letter name spellers have a means at their disposal to write many words, and children enjoy this freedom to create. Their spelling ability is still limited, of course. Because they spell words by relating letters to their individual sounds, they are not yet taking advantage of onsets and rimes and phonogram patterns. Nor are letter name spellers yet aware of the conventions for marking vowels "long" or "short."

Research shows that the practice of invented spelling is good for kindergarten and first-grade children. Children who are encouraged to invent spellings learn to recognize more words than children who do not use invented spelling. But children should not persist in letter name spelling much beyond the end of first grade. To help them make progress, teachers need to be careful to remind children that invented spelling is "temporary spelling"; it is the way that they can write some words before they learn the way words are spelled in books. Teachers also need to be careful to give students correctly spelled material to read and to take opportunities to call children's attention to standard spelling patterns in print.

CCSS
• Foundational Skills 3: Phonics and Word Recognition

THE ORTHOGRAPHIC PHASE OF SPELLING   Spellers in the orthographic phase are beginning readers who are becoming aware of conventional spellings for sounds. They are learning phonogram patterns (onsets and rimes) and are trying to master the marking systems for long and short vowels, although not always correctly, as seen in Figure 10.5.

Orthographic spellers may be keen observers of the English spelling system, and the difficulties they face in spelling correctly often reflect the eccentricities of the system. For example, orthographic spellers may write *LUV* and *ABUV*. The correct spellings, *love* and *above*, thwart their expectations.

Children who spell in the orthographic phase show us that they have learned many things about the way the English writing system works, and this knowledge can help them both in writing and in reading. These children show a grasp of common onsets and rimes in their writing, indicating that they should be able to use knowledge of these patterns to read unfamiliar words. Children who are aware of onsets and rimes can use the strategy of reading by analogy. For example, if they encounter the unknown word *sill*, they can recognize its similarity to the known word *pill* and will read *sill* by mentally taking away the /p/ sound and substituting the /s/ sound in front of the *-ill* rime. Such reading by analogy leads to more rapid and accurate deciphering of words than does puzzling out words letter by letter.

Spelling in the orthographic phase presents challenges that many students never move beyond. A student who has learned to spell *gate*, for example, might still be unsure how to spell *great*, *bait*, *straight*, or *eight*. It will take a habit of studying words carefully plus an act of memory to master these challenges. Both are encouraged by good teaching.

Figure 10.5   Spelling in the Orthographic State

Stella

We went to the park
we went on a nacher
chrel They hid The
eggs I fond 7 eggs
I fond candy we ate
boby Q we had fun
We playd basball.

Source: Temple, C., Nathan, R., Burris, N., & Temple, F. (1993). *The beginnings of writing* (3rd ed.). Boston, MA: Allyn & Bacon.

THE MORPHOLOGICAL PHASE OF SPELLING   Spellers in the morphological phase are able to spell in stable and correct ways grammatical endings and prefixes and suffixes—items that linguists call *bound morphemes*. Also, with regard to suffixes, the speller is able to consistently spell some inflectional word endings such as *-s* or *-ed* that have alternate pronunciations, depending on the sounds in the syllable to which they are attached. (Compare, for instance, the pronunciation of *-s* in *wants* and *slows*, and the pronunciation of *-ed* in *wanted*, *slowed*, and *hiked*.

Spellers in this phase have learned the common patterns of spelling such as the phonogram patterns and the rules for marking vowels long or short. But the spelling system of English reflects more than sounds. There are grammatical endings and prefixes and suffixes that must be spelled in certain ways, even when they may be pronounced differently from one word to another. Also, when grammatical endings and prefixes and suffixes are attached to other words, they often have the effect of marking a vowel long or short in the root word, which is another complication for a learner to take into account.

The child who wrote the piece in Figure 10.6 shows some of the difficulties posed by the morphological phase. Note his spelling of *chewed*. Note also, the effect of his South Texas accent on his spelling!

THE DERIVATIONAL PHASE OF SPELLING   Moving still further away from the expectation that letters simply spell sounds, learners encounter the derivational phase, in

Teach It! 62

Word Origins and Derivations

Figure 10.6 The Struggles of the Morphological Phase

> Onece there was two dogs he chood on the sofa and inee thang he can git a hode uv.

which spellings must honor the origins of words and their relationships to other words. Some words are derived from other "living" words, and others are derived from common ancient sources (hence the name "derivational"). Many words that are found from fourth grade up, such as *photograph*, *sign*, *doubt*, and *bomb* don't have a very obvious connection between letters and sounds, because these letters relate not so much to sounds as to word histories—or to other words from which they are derived.

When children reach the most advanced phase of word knowledge, they can recognize meaningful chunks of words called *morphemes*, and use them not just for spelling and reading but also as a clue to word meanings. In the derivational phase of word knowledge, children think of words in family relationships, and use their awareness of these relationships to write and read words.

For example, recognizing the relation between *photograph* and *photography* helps a student spell the reduced vowels in both words, because the reduced and unrecognizable second O in *photograph* is stressed and identifiable in *photography*. Likewise the A in the next to last syllable of *photography* is stressed and recognizable in *photograph*. But beyond the help with spelling, recognizing the morpheme *photo* and associating it with the meaning "light" helps unpack words like *photosynthesis*, "coming together with light."

HISTORICAL ODDITIES   Some words defy simple spelling-to-sound relationships because of spelling changes that happened over the centuries. For example, many words from Anglo-Saxon with O before following consonants pronounce that vowel as a short U: *brother*, *mother*, *son*, *love*, *cover*. It turns out the letter O was written in for the original letter U in many of those words by scribes in the tenth and eleventh centuries, to make them easier to read when they appeared in the Gothic script (Scragg, 1974). Medieval scribes also gave us the B in *doubt* (originally it was spelled without the B) to make the word resemble the related Latin word *dubere*. Children are unlikely to discover these things, but it will certainly help if their teachers know them and talk about them.

HOMOPHONES AND HOMOGRAPHS   There are some different words like *deer* and *dear*, *bare* and *bear*, and *waist* and *waste* that sound the same but have different meanings. They are called *homophones* (from *homo-*, meaning "the same," and *phone*, meaning "sound"). There are other words that have the same spellings but have different meanings, like *lead* ("I will lead you to your table") and *lead* ("I put a lead weight on the line"). Sometimes homographs are pronounced the same, but still have different meanings, as in "sock someone in the arm" and "put on a sock." Several homophones and homographs are shown in Table 10.2. Homophones can be funny. Fred Gwynne's *The King Who Rained* and Peggy Parish's *Amelia Bedelia* still delight readers after many decades. Their humor hinges on homophones.

LOAN WORDS   English contains many "loan words" from different languages, and most of them are pronounced according to the rules of the original languages: *taco*, *filet*, *wiener*, *fuselage*, *macho*, *chassis*, *chic*, and *wiki*.

Assessing Spelling Knowledge

Children's knowledge of spelling develops in two ways. One way is the level of words they can spell. For instance, we would expect a second-grade child to be able to spell *train*, *queer*, and *float*, but not *conceive* or *profitable*, while a sixth grader should be able to spell the harder words. Another way children's spelling ability develops is that they work their way through stages of spelling knowledge, and each stage is a way of thinking about the ways written words are structured.

Table 10.2 Homophones and Homographs

HOMOPHONES. These are words that are spelled differently, pronounced the same, and have different meanings.		HOMOGRAPHS. These are words that are spelled the same, but have different meanings. Some homographs are not pronounced the same.	
too	two	dove (bird)	dove (from "dive")
new	knew	close (shut)	close (nearby)
red	read (past tense)	wind (twist)	wind (breeze)
deer	dear	read (present tense)	read (past tense)
there	they're	produce (verb)	produce (noun)
him	hymn	conduct (verb)	conduct (noun)
cent	sent	discharge (verb)	discharge (noun)
reel	real	relay (verb)	relay (noun)
Some Homophones are phrases.		Some homographs are spelled the same and pronounced the same. They still have different meanings.	
I scream.	ice cream	show (verb)	show (noun)
depend	deep end	shift (move)	shift (work period)
will he	Willy	sock (verb)	sock (noun)
		bank (for money)	bank (of a river)

USING WORDS FROM SPELLING TEXTBOOKS Commercial spelling and language arts programs normally provide lists of words children are expected to learn every week. Those lists are arranged at difficulty levels according to their grades. Publishers use various means to level words, including surveys of children's writing and studies of the vocabularies of textbooks and trade books.

If you are using a spelling series, or if you are teaching grade-level-based spelling lists every week, it is important to find children's instructional level in spelling. The range of spelling abilities of a typical classroom of children is very wide. If students in a typical classroom were asked to spell words they had not yet been taught, their scores might range from less than 10 percent to more than 90 percent (Morris, Nelson, & Perney, 1986). But if the lowest scoring spellers were taught words at their instructional level of spelling instead of words at their grade-placement level, they might fill in the foundational spelling concepts taught at lower grades that they are missing but that they need for further learning; in the long run, they would actually make more progress toward learning to spell the harder words. This was exactly what Darrell Morris and his colleagues (Morris et al., 1995) found in an experimental study.

The instructional level of spelling is found by testing children on spelling words they have not been taught and finding the grade level of words where the children score from 50 percent to 75 percent (Henderson, 1990). To assess children's spelling ability for grade-level placement, construct a spelling inventory, consisting of 20 randomly chosen words from each grade level in grades 1 through 6 of the spelling program. (These lists are usually found as an appendix in the teacher's guide.) You can test a whole class by beginning with the words one year below grade level and calling out the words as the children spell them. Then call out the correct spellings, or display them on an overhead transparency, and have the children mark their own errors. Call out words from higher-level lists and have the children continue to spell words until they misspell 50 percent of the words. Children who score 50 percent spelling errors can stop. After you look over their papers, you can go back and privately ask some children to spell words from easier lists if they did not reach the instructional level on the first list you called.

Table 10.3 Stages of Invented Spelling

STAGE	ALSO KNOWN AS	EXAMPLES	TYPICAL AGE
Prephonetic	Preliterate	*bumpy* = R4TSX	Preschool and kindergarten
Early phonemic	Early phonetic	*bumpy* = BP	Kindergarten and early first grade
Letter-name	Phonetic	*bumpy* = BOPE	Early to mid-first grade
Common patterns	Transitional, within-word pattern	*bumpy* = BUPPY	Late first to mid-second grade
Syllable juncture		*batted* = BATID	Mid-second grade through third grade
Derivational constancy	Conventional	*photograph* = FOTOGRAF	Fourth grade and above

Source: Bear, Invernizzi, Templeton, and Johnston (2000); Gentry (1981); Henderson (1990); Schlagal (1989); Temple, Nathan, Burris, and Temple (1993).

ASSESSING SPELLING QUALITATIVELY Students work their way through stages of spelling development that reflect how they think about the structure of words. Those stages are described in Table 10.3. The student's spelling level suggests ways that she or he can be taught to spell.

To assess a child's level of developmental spelling, you can administer a list of words that are arranged to elicit invented spellings at different levels. A typical list of such words is found in Figure 10.7.

Developmental spelling inventories with full explanations are available in *Words Their Way* (Bear et al., 2007), *Word Journeys* (Ganske, 2003), and *The Developmental Literacy Inventory* (Temple, Crawford, & Gillet, 2009). As all of these publications make clear, improving children's spelling knowledge enhances their word knowledge, especially if they are taught to use what they learn in the context of writing and reading.

CCSS

• Language 2: Capitalization, Punctuation, and Spelling

Teaching Children to Spell

Spelling instruction should address three needs:

1. "survival words"—words students will use often in their writing
2. words that contain features children are trying to master
3. ways to generalize from spelling words students know to spelling new words

Teaching frequently used words is done a couple of ways. One is by using Word Walls, in which words that students use regularly in their writing are copied onto index cards and arranged either alphabetically or in semantic groups on the wall. Words chosen for Word Walls should be those that many children use, but struggle to spell correctly. They may be high frequency words, but they may also be words related to units children are studying and writing about in science, social studies, and other subjects. (See the discussion of Word Walls on page 134 in Chapter 5.)

Figure 10.7
Words to Elicit Different
Levels of Invented Spelling

1. lit	6. peeked	11. spacious	16. physician
2. chap	7. sailed	12. design	17. biographical
3. rock	8. shove	13. brilliance	18. sympathetic
4. truck	9. sitter	14. traction	19. adjournment
5. lend	10. batted	15. doubting	20. collegial

Source: Temple, Crawford, and Gillet, *Developmental Literacy Inventory: Reading and Spelling from Emergent to Mature Levels*. © 2009. Reprinted by Permission of Pearson Education, Inc.

Another way to teach frequently used words is to keep a log of commonly used words that individual children struggle to spell. These words are recorded in the student's own *spelling dictionary*, which is made from a small spiral-bound notebook, with pages labeled with alphabetical headings.

A third way to teach frequently used words is to collect them and add them to students' weekly spelling lists. Many commercial spelling programs set aside four or five locally chosen words for the students to learn. Students may nominate words themselves, or you may choose them based on your observations of their needs.

Teaching words that contain features children are trying to master is the basis for most current commercial spelling programs. There is an economy in teaching children words that share not only the same phonogram patterns, such as *pitch*, *stitch*, *hitch*, and *itch*, but also the same spelling features, such as the *-tch* consonant cluster in the previous words and also in *latch*, *match*, *crutch*, *Dutch*, *Scotch*, and *botch*; as well as the *-dge* consonant cluster in *badge*, *ridge*, *budge*, and *hedge*. Of course, there are many other such features. Basal spelling programs teach groups of such words, and so do guides to teaching spelling and word knowledge such as Bear et al.'s *Words Their Way* and Ganske's *Word Journeys*.

Teaching students to generalize from known words to unknown words that share their patterns can be done by using word sorts and Word Walls, both of which are explained in Chapter 5 of this book. You must be careful, though, to call attention to the many exceptions to the patterns. Consider, for example, *post*, *most*, *lost*, and *cost*; or *butch* and *clutch*; or *chase*, *chore*, *chasm*, and *choir*.

The need to teach correct spelling should be taken seriously. It is true that children can invent spellings for most words they write. And inventing spellings form an important part of children's learning about the way words are written and read (see Temple et al., 2013). But inventing spellings for words takes considerable effort. As Steve Graham and Karen Harris (2005) have demonstrated, not having many spellings available in memory is a handicap that impedes students' fluency in writing. Teachers should teach students to spell correctly. It's an important part of teaching them to write.

Specially written dictionaries are available for even the lowest grades, and frequent visits to them should be a feature of all classrooms.

The Writing Process

A model of the writing process was put forward thirty years ago by Pulitzer Prize–winning journalist and writing teacher Donald Murray (1985) and language arts specialist and researcher Donald Graves (1982). That model is now used widely both within schools and in other areas to describe what people do when they write, and also to guide teachers of writing. According to their writing process model, thoughtful writers may go through five steps or phases as they produce their works: rehearsing, drafting, revising, editing, and publishing.

REHEARSING   The process of rehearsing entails preparing to write by gathering information and collecting one's thoughts. Student writers think of what they might like to write about, they survey what they know about the topic, and they begin to plan a way to write about it. Several strategies are available that can teach students to rehearse their ideas before writing:

- ***Brainstorming and clustering.*** Children can jot down in list form their ideas about a topic before embarking on writing about it. As a more elaborate version of the brainstorm, they create a graphic organizer, such as a cluster or semantic web, with the topic listed in the center connected to "satellites" around it (see Figure 10.8).
- ***Interviewing each other to find the story.*** Students can interview a partner. Regardless of whether a writer has already prepared a cluster, it often helps if

The students in this video are writing in their social studies class as they learn about explorers. How does the teacher encourage the students' writing at each step of the writing process?

CCSS

- Writing 4: Production and Distribution

Graphic Organizers

Figure 10.8 A Cluster

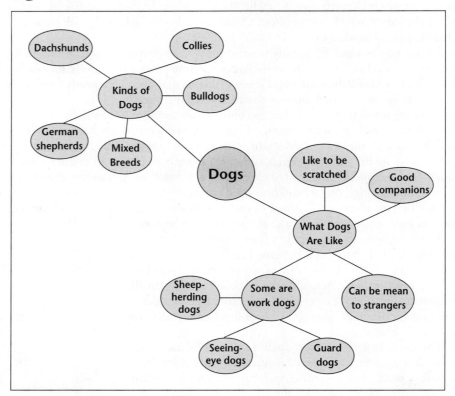

another student asks questions about the topic to help him or her "find the story." The student asks questions such as the following:

"Why did you choose this topic?"

"What most interests you about the topic?"

The student also asks questions about details, things the writer might not realize other people will want to know.

Form Poems

- *Making class collaborations.* When introducing a new kind of writing, such as a poem or a fairy tale, it might be best to ask the students to compose one work together before writing on their own. This is especially helpful for younger students. The teacher can contribute as well to help steer the work in positive directions. If the students have difficulty beginning, offer them a series of choices:

Where does the story take place? In a big city or a small village?

Who should be the main character? A young girl or an old magician?

A young girl? Okay. Then who can describe her? And what is her problem?

- *Researching the topic.* Students are often able to write stories or papers about personal experiences off the tops of their heads, but when they are writing about the real world beyond themselves, they will soon run out of things to say unless they collect information about their topic. They might need to read up on it or interview experts about it, or they might observe carefully and collect details about it. Lucy Calkins and her colleagues in the New York City Writing Project (1994) suggest having students keep notebooks for gathering observations.

DRAFTING Drafting involves setting ideas out on paper. Drafting is tentative and experimental. Students write down their ideas so that they can see more of what they have to say about their topic; often their best ideas do not occur to them until they begin committing thoughts to paper. The phase of drafting is not the time to be critical about spelling and handwriting. Such mechanical concerns are better dealt with later; this is the time for students to focus on getting their ideas onto the page.

Young writers do not have the habit of writing more than one version of a paper. Proficient writers, however, know that good writing is rewriting. Teachers can encourage students to think of writing as drafting in a number of ways:

- Stamp the papers DRAFT or use the backs of recycled office paper. Both measures make it clear to everyone that these versions of their papers are not final.

- Have the students write on every other line. This leaves room for them to add material they think of later on.

- Show students how to use arrows, carets (^), and stapled-on sections to indicate on a draft how it should be rewritten. Unless they are shown, students will not know how to physically mark up and modify a draft and use it to plan the next version of the paper.

- Remind students not to worry too much about spelling, handwriting, and mechanics at the drafting stage. A large advantage to writing more than one draft of a paper is that it frees writers to concentrate on their ideas at first and then worry about form and correctness later. This should be explained to students at the start, and the treatment of their early and later drafts should be consistent with it. Be careful, however, that you do not encourage students to be messy. Bromley (1999) advises against calling an early draft of a paper a "sloppy copy."

REVISING After their thoughts have been written out in draft form, students need to think about stating their ideas more clearly. Most students need to be shown ways that writing can be improved: by having clear beginnings, middles, and ends; by finding a topic and sticking to it; by showing and not telling; and other techniques. Teachers can teach these points through focused lessons (discussed later) and help young writers internalize them by means of conferences. Teachers use two main kinds of conferences in teaching writing.

Teacher-Led Conferences Conferences allow the teacher to assist students in clarifying their writing and also to model ways to ask helpful questions that will encourage other struggling writers, their peers. The teacher needs to ask questions that teach, pulling solutions from the students themselves and always respecting the students' ownership of their writing. The teacher asks students questions to help them focus on areas to improve their writing, and provides checklists of things to watch out for.

Peer Conferences Once the teacher has modeled the process, students can hold conferences with each other. Because many conferences will be going on in the room at one time, it helps if students understand their tasks clearly. The teacher can put together a checklist of good questions to ask as the students review their works-in-progress with each other, such as the following:

In conferences with students, teachers can teach pointers about good writing that students can revisit in their peer conferences and in their writing.

- Did my opening lines interest you? How might I improve the beginning?
- Do I need more information anywhere? That is, where could I be more specific?
- Do you ever get lost while reading my draft?
- Do I stay on topic?
- Do I come to a good conclusion?

EDITING OR PROOFREADING   Once a paper has been drafted and revised, it needs to be reviewed for mistakes. Naturally, proofreading is held off until the last version because whole paragraphs might be cut or added in the revising stage. The habit of proofreading must be taught. It consists of three things:

- Caring that the paper be correct
- Being aware of particular errors
- Knowing how to set those errors straight

A caring attitude toward their writing is probably best developed by publishing what students write. Students are most likely to care about correctness once they realize that writing is not simply done for a grade, but that their works must pass the scrutiny of others, who will be distracted from their ideas if the papers are marred by flaws in spelling, grammar, and handwriting.

Children should be made aware of errors through focused lessons that demonstrate one or two errors of writing at a time. Focused lessons treat errors that one or more students are actually making in their writing. Areas in which children make errors might include the following:

- Beginning each sentence with a capital letter and ending it with terminal punctuation (a period, a question mark, or an exclamation point)
- Making each sentence express a complete thought, avoiding sentence fragments and run-on sentences
- Spelling correctly

After clearly teaching students to be aware of different kinds of errors and how to repair them, the next step is to get the students to proofread their own work. Give them a checklist to guide their proofreading, such as the one shown in Figure 10.9. Each point on the checklist should be carefully introduced, explained, and practiced before students are sent off to use it on their own. Several versions of the checklist might be introduced during the year as new points for correction are added to the students' repertoires. Once the checklist has been introduced, students should practice using it with a partner to go over each other's papers before they are ready to use the checklists by themselves.

PUBLISHING   Publishing is the final stage of the writing process, and it actually drives the whole endeavor. The prospect of sharing what they have to say with an audience makes many students want to write, rewrite, and smooth out and refine, especially if they have seen other students' work received with appreciation and delight. Publishing also lets students see what others are doing. A good idea is contagious; and anything from an interesting topic to a plot structure, to a way to use dialogue, to the habit of taking risks with spelling may be shared from one student to another through the process of publishing. How refined should published works be? Not all writing that is published in the classroom has to be perfect. Age level matters here. If they are to be kept in the classroom community, younger children's publications may be less than completely perfect; if they are going "public" such as out in the hallway, that writing should be corrected up to your grade level standards.

Different Levels of Support for Writing

The writing workshop model assumes students are capable of a fair amount of self-direction and that they understand at least the rudiments of how ideas are put down on paper. It is true that children as young as kindergarten age can participate in writing workshops in some fashion. But teachers find that many young writers—and not just the youngest—sometimes need more explicit support as they learn to write. As teachers adjust the explicitness of their instruction and the fullness of their guidance according to the needs of the

Figure 10.9
A Proofreading Checklist

Source: Reprinted with permission from *Classroom Strategies That Work: An Elementary Teacher's Guide to Process Writing* by Ruth Nathan, Frances Temple, Kathleen Juntenen, and Charles Temple. Copyright © 1989 by Ruth Nathan, Frances Temple, Kathleen Juntenen, and Charles Temple. Published by Heinemann, Portsmouth, NH. All rights reserved.

1. Did I spell all words correctly?

   (Underline words you are unsure of. Try looking some of them up.)

2. Did I write each sentence as a complete thought?

   (This is an incomplete thought: "On the street." This is a complete thought: "The little puppy stood all alone on the street." Note: Sometimes writers use an incomplete sentence on purpose—to create a certain effect. For example: "Not me!")

3. Do I have any run-on sentences?

   (Here is a run-on sentence: "The little puppy stood all alone on the street and he couldn't find his mother and he was so, so frightened that he thought he would die and so he looked around to find a friend and he didn't find one so he walked on and on." This is a run-on sentence, too: "I don't have a pet at home do you?")

4. Did I end each sentence with the correct punctuation?

   (Here is a sentence that has the wrong punctuation at the end: "Could the puppy find his mother." The sentence needs a question mark, not a period.)

5. Did I begin each sentence with a capital letter?

6. Did I use capital letters correctly in other places?

   (Names, days of the week, months, titles, etc.)

7. Did I use commas, apostrophes, and other punctuation correctly?

   (Commas are used between words in lists, before a conjunction introducing an independent clause, after salutations, etc. Apostrophes are used with possessive forms [Jimmy's shoes, the boys' lockers] and in contractions [can't, it's—for "it is"].)

8. Did I indent each paragraph?

   (Whenever you start a new idea, you need a new paragraph. Dialogue [talk between two or more people] also requires a new paragraph each time a different speaker talks.)

learners, they practice "gradual release of responsibility" (Pearson & Gallagher, 1993). The gradual release of responsibility model, as elaborated by Regie Routman (2013), has the teacher providing high levels of direct teaching and support to beginners, and giving more freedom to perform on their own to students who have largely learned the target skills (see Figure 10.10).

Figure 10.10 shows examples of the kinds of activities that are conducted at each level of writing support. Although some of the activities at the more highly supported end of the scale are intended for young children, it is not the case that only younger writers need more support and only older writers need less. At one time or another, writers of all ages can use both support and freedom to create.

MODELED WRITING   In modeled writing, when students need to be shown some aspect of the writing process, the teacher models it for the class. For example, if you wish to introduce the writing process to young students for the first time, you might proceed as follows:

> Gathering the children in front of you, announce that you are going to write about something important. Explain that you are first going to draw your ideas as you talk about them and that you will then write in a space below the picture. Take a piece of chart paper and fold it horizontally so that the crease is about a third of the way from the bottom. When the paper is flattened out, the crease will mark off the space for writing. Now think aloud by naming and talking about your topic: your aging family dog. Using a page of chart paper, draw a picture as you talk, and demonstrate how you can use drawing as a way of rehearsing or thinking out your ideas. Then think of one line you want to write about the dog in the space you left for writing underneath the picture.

Figure 10.10 Gradual Release of Responsibility in Writing Instruction

Demonstrated Writing	Interactive Writing	Guided Writing	Independent Writing
I do. You watch.	*I do. You help.*	*You do. I help.*	*You do. I watch.*
Students mostly observe Teacher mostly demonstrates and explains The **teacher's** level of control	Students add to teacher's lesson Teacher controls the activity	Students create within guidelines set by teacher Teacher structures the activity; students create	The **students'** level of control Students create independently Teacher is observer and resource
Typical Activities			
Modeled writing Focused lesson	Shared writing Interactive writing	Writing Frames Form Poems Graphic Organizers	Writing workshop Independent writing

Source: After Routman, 2013

My dog is old.

> *You say the sentence to yourself several times and then announce that you're going to write the first word, "My," which you pronounce slowly.*
> *"What sound does it begin with?" you ask.*
> *"Muh," you say, "and what letter makes that sound?"*
> *"M," you say and write M on the board.*
> *You then pronounce the next sound and spell it, and you write the other words in the same way. When you are finished, you have the children read the sentence with you and discuss the picture. Ask the children to identify one thing that interests them about the picture and writing and to ask one question. Post the composition on the wall for the children to look at later, and remind the children that they can write down their ideas in the same way.*

Language Experience or Group Dictated Story

SHARED WRITING   In shared writing, the teacher not only models acts of writing, but also engages students in composing the writing. When shared writing is used, the topic needs to be one that both the teacher and the students know about and are excited about. Such a topic might be a shared experience such as a field trip, a story that everyone is reading, or a topic that is under investigation by the class. Completion of a K-W-L chart offers a natural occasion for shared writing. Another kind of shared writing activity is group dictation. Here the writing activity is preceded by some kind of activity that excites the students and stimulates talk about it. The teacher leads a discussion and helps students find things to say, asks the students to offer comments about the topic, and then writes these down on a piece of chart paper. The teacher might lead the students to sound out some of the words and to offer spellings for them.

INTERACTIVE WRITING   By using interactive writing you can help emergent and beginning readers and writers explore the writing system in its details. Developed by Moira

McKenzie at the Ebury Street Centre for Language in London, the method has been incorporated into Fountas and Pinnell's guided reading program because "Interactive writing provides an authentic setting within which the teacher can explicitly demonstrate how written language works" (Fountas & Pinnell, 1996, p. 33).

Interactive writing works very much like taking a dictated account except that the teacher and the children "share the pen." The procedures follow these steps:

Phonics and Phonological Awareness

How do writing activities support development of phonemic awareness?

1. The teacher and a group of six to twelve students share an experience and agree on a topic. The topic might be a retelling of a story or a poem or a song, the daily news, or an idea that the class is studying.

2. The students offer a sentence about the topic. The teacher has the students repeat the sentence many times and even count the words to fix them firmly in their minds.

3. The teacher asks the students for the first word, then pronounces that word slowly, writing its letters.

4. The teacher now asks for the next word and invites a child up to write the whole word, a few letters, or a single letter. The teacher fills in letters the students miss. Each time a word is added, the whole text is read back by the students, with the teacher pointing to the words.

5. To help the students orient themselves to the text and add letters, the teacher might write blanks where the letters should go.

6. The teacher uses correction tape to paste over letters that are poorly formed.

7. The teacher instructs the class about words and print as the lesson progresses, reminding students about words they know or almost know and spelling patterns they have seen before, and prompting them to leave spaces between words and to add punctuation.

GUIDED WRITING   When teachers instruct students about how to create a particular pattern of writing or use a particular strategy, or compose a sample piece as a group, and then ask individuals or pairs of students to produce their own writings according to the form or the strategy, they are guiding student writing. Guided writing is used when students can handle the rudiments of writing—making letters and spelling words—but still need to know some strategies for organizing their ideas on the page.

Many types of the writing lessons described in the next section on writing in the genres lend themselves to guided writing. For example, the form poems of *cinquains* and list poems can be done as class collaborations and then individually by students as guided writing activities.

WRITING FRAMES   Steering young writers' composition in certain productive directions is the job of writing frames. Even professional writers use them. Margaret Wise Brown's *The Important Book* is essentially a writing frame that she uses over and over. On each two-page spread she writes, "The important thing about _____ is _____. It has _____. And it _____, and _____. But the important thing about _____ is _____." Of course, she fills in the blanks with a topic word, descriptive words, and actions. Judy Allen's *Are You a Spider?*, like her *Are You a Butterfly?*, *Are You a Ladybug?*, and *Are You an Ant?*, begins with the question posed by the title, and then proceeds with, "If you are...," and then supplies descriptions of how these creatures look, how they are born, how they grow, where they live, what they eat, and what or who their enemies are. Of course, these same frames can be introduced to young writers by reading one of the books to them. Then the children can be given handouts with the repeated phrases filled in but the details left blank.

Writing frames are often used as a way of scaffolding writing tasks for English language learners, and other students who find writing to be a special challenge. English language learners can be helped by sentence starters, too.

Helping Struggling Writers

The writing workshop is a wonderful forum for many children's creativity, but it has not always served all children well. There are some students for whom the self-direction afforded by the writing workshop seems almost tantamount to neglect, particularly children whose home culture and language differ significantly from those of the school (Delpit, 1996). One explanation of the difficulty is offered by Collins (1998), who points out that writing is a secondary form of discourse normally based on speech, which is the primary form of discourse. If the kind of discourse a child sees in books and is expected to produce with a pencil fairly closely resembles the kind of discourse that is spoken, then the task of learning to write is largely one of discovering or acquiring the relations between speech and writing—that is, to figure out the strategies that enable us to put down on paper what we say in speech. The kind of writing workshop described earlier should serve this child well, for as Collins (1998) tells us,

> When literacy activities involve language forms and functions that are close to one's primary discourse, they can be achieved through a balance between acquisition and learning which favors acquisition. The typical writing workshop shows this balance in favor of acquisition, owing to its pronounced student-centered methods, including student-generated topics and genres for writing, multiple drafts to gradually improve writing, and supportive feedback from teachers and peers. When literacy activities involve ways of using language substantially different from one's primary discourse, the balance shifts in favor of learning. (p. 6)

As you might recall from the discussion of language acquisition and language learning in Chapter 3, *learning* refers to formal, teacher-directed, explicit instruction. *Acquisition* means learning by discovery and inference from being immersed in writing activities. Moving the balance toward learning means explicitly teaching students what they need to know to carry out the processes of writing. Struggling writers do not need to be taken out of writing workshops and given skill sheets to fill out. It is still possible for teachers to teach students strategies for writing that they can use to express themselves to an audience of their peers (Harris & Graham, 1996).

Strategies are explicit procedures. Strategies relate to every aspect of writing, from choosing a topic to deciding which parts of the topic to include and which to leave out, to organizing ideas on paper. Strategies may be taught in two ways. One is by means of focused lessons. In a focused lesson, the teacher makes it very clear to the students when and how to use a particular technique in writing, whether it be a beginning + middle + ending organization for a paper or the way to punctuate dialogue. Another means of teaching a strategy is using writing guides or graphic organizers. For struggling writers, having a graphic organizer to follow, such as a story map or an outline for a persuasive essay, helps to make the writing strategy explicit. When the students understand the steps to the strategy, the teacher gives them guided practice using the strategy and provides feedback on their use of it. After they have learned to use the strategy, they will no longer need to use the graphic organizer.

INDEPENDENT WRITING Types of independent writing include writing in journals, self-initiated writing of all kinds, and writing done in writing workshops. It is important that students of all ages have regular chances to write independently. Doing so allows children to exercise many of their ideas and strategies for writing—from letter formation to the direction of print on a page, to spelling, to the use of illustrations, to the arrangement of ideas in a composition. Good writing ideas are contagious. If you observe students who have spent extended time in writing workshops, you will see that many more ideas emerge from these students and are passed from student to student than the teacher would have had time to think up and teach them during more structured writing time.

Some students will produce writing on their own, but many will not. That is why the writing workshop is so valuable: It combines teacher example and direction with encouragement of children's peers to get them writing. What about students who find writing difficult? See the suggestions in the Differentiated Instruction box.

The Writing Workshop

A popular approach to teaching children to write is the writing workshop, in which students are shown how to use the writing process and are given regular opportunities to produce many kinds of writing. Teachers who teach writing successfully work three elements into their teaching:

Figure 10.11 Daily Schedule of a Writing Workshop

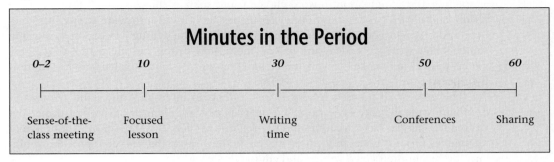

Minutes in the Period

0–2	10	30	50	60
Sense-of-the-class meeting	Focused lesson	Writing time	Conferences	Sharing

- **Time.** Writing workshops should be scheduled at consistent intervals so students know when they will have opportunities to write. When students know that they will have these opportunities regularly, they are more likely to collect ideas during their daily lives that they can write about during writing workshop.

- **Emphasis on communication.** It matters a lot whether students are writing for the teacher (to demonstrate skill or to get a grade) or writing because they want to say something to people who will be interested in hearing it. When writing is real communication, students may engage more of their powers of expression. Students should have opportunities to choose their own topics or—when the topics are assigned—to decide on their own approach to a topic. When conferences are conducted to help students improve writing, their ownership of the work—that is, what they mean to say—must still be respected, with freedom left for them to choose the advice they will follow as they seek to refine a work.

- **Demonstration and direct instruction.** Teaching writing is a studio craft, with attention to the process of creating. The teacher should demonstrate every phase of the process so that students will know how writing is done. The teacher should also teach skills of writing, from organization to correct punctuation, but this should be done in the context of writing for communication so that students will actually come to use them.

How often writing workshops are conducted and how much time they are given varies from one teacher to another. Figure 10.11 shows one plan for managing the time in a writing workshop. This writing workshop lasts an entire 60-minute class meeting, perhaps three days a week, with time set aside for five distinctive activities.

SENSE-OF-THE-CLASS MEETING Assuming that the students are already engaged in writing tasks, the period begins with a brief sense-of-the-class meeting (Atwell, 1986) to find out who is working on what writing topic. Students keep a list of writing topics in a journal or a writing folder; if they do not have a work in progress, they should have a topic ready to be written about. By finding out and recording several interesting things about each child at the beginning of the year, the teacher can have a lively suggestion available if a student comes up empty.

FOCUSED LESSONS The goal of writing workshops is to encourage students to write about things they care about for real audiences and to improve their writing so that it communicates more and more effectively. It is essential to give students time, models, and opportunities to write. But students also need careful instruction on all aspects of writing—from how one carries out the writing process to proper punctuation. Focused instruction helps children in the rehearsal and drafting stages by showing them strategies for writing, and it helps them in the revising and editing stages by giving them criteria or working standards for making their writing better.

Descriptive Writing

Focused lessons may relate to any aspect of writing, from mechanical issues such as spelling and punctuation to word-choice issues such as showing, not telling, to write vividly and clearly, to composition-related issues such as ways to write strong introductions and closings. Focused lessons also may highlight the writing process itself, showing students how writers get ideas and narrow them, how writers put ideas into words, how writers go back and make the work better, and how writers share their work and learn from their peers' comments.

The goal of all focused lessons is for students to internalize the main points and use them while they are reviewing their peers' papers and their own. In other words, the writing teacher tries to work himself or herself out of a job. It is important to conceive of focused lessons not as teaching about writing in the abstract, but rather as providing guidance to the children's own writing and editing processes.

Focused lessons can follow a four-part model for teaching skills in context: demonstration and immersion, attention to detail, guided practice, and independent use. In the writing workshop, focused lessons use those four parts in the following ways.

1. *Finding a text that demonstrates a point or skill you want to teach.* For example, if you want to show children how to write vivid beginnings to stories by jumping right into the action, read the beginning of *Charlotte's Web*:

   > "Where's Papa going with that axe?" said Fern to her mother as they were setting the table for breakfast.
   > "Out to the hoghouse," replied Mrs. Arable. "Some pigs were born last night."
   > "I don't see why he needs an axe," continued Fern, who was only eight.
   > "Well," said her mother, "one of the pigs is a runt. It's very small and weak, and it will never amount to anything. So your father has decided to do away with it."
   > "Do away with it," shrieked Fern. "You mean kill it, just because it's smaller than the others?" (White, 1952/1980, p. 1)

2. *Sharing the example and calling students' attention to the skill it demonstrates.* E. B. White could have begun his story by describing the setting and the characters, but he didn't. He started right in with the action. He decided to have Fern ask that question, hear that terrible answer, and get upset. After just these few lines, it is evident that the main problem of the story will be saving the little pig's life, and readers will want to know what can be done to solve this problem.

   You might ask the students how the beginning made them feel and what it led them to expect. What advice do they suppose E. B. White gave himself that made him begin the story that way? Discuss this example until the point is clear that a good way of beginning a story is to start right in with action that shows readers a problem and makes them care what will happen in the story.

3. *Providing the students with guided practice using the skill.* Ask the students to take out a draft of a story they are writing. Have them rewrite the beginning of the story so that it starts right in with action or dialogue that leads the reader right into the main problem of the story. Have the students pair up and take turns explaining to a partner the changes they made to their paper.

4. *Encouraging students to use the skill in their independent writing.* So that the points taught in the focused lessons enter students' repertoire of writing skills, you might add each point to a writing rubric or editing checklist or to your guidelines for good writing. You can also add that point into rubrics used to evaluate students' writing or into the checklists they use to edit their own and each other's drafts.

WRITING TIME   During much of the writing workshop, all of the students are writing. This is quiet time. The teacher writes for the first five minutes as well, to help establish an atmosphere for quiet independent work. For the next ten minutes, the teacher might move around to individual students, to encourage them as they write. Nathan and colleagues (1988) advise that the teacher go first to those who appear to be having trouble writing.

CONFERENCES   After the students have written for a designated amount of time, a period of conferences begins. The teacher can conduct a conference for the whole class, with one student, or with a small group.

Students may confer with a partner or with a small group. Conferences were discussed in detail earlier. Students who wish to continue writing during this time may do so.

SHARING   The last ten minutes of the workshop are reserved for sharing. The teacher should choose students to share who are far along in a draft or whose work displays an interesting issue. Different students should share each time because only one or two can normally share in a ten-minute period. Some teachers extend sharing time to get in three students a day; that way, every student gets to share every other week.

For English Language Learners

Modifying the Writing Workshop for English Language Learners

English language learners can benefit from instruction using the writing workshop approach, with certain modifications.

- During the rehearsal phase of writing, help them brainstorm English vocabulary they are likely to need, and write these words on the board.
- Allow them to write a first draft in their first language.
- Keep a bilingual dictionary handy, and encourage English language learners to use it as they create finished drafts of their works. Then allow time for them to look up key words using their dictionaries.

Writing in Different Genres

A writing *genre* is a form or pattern of writing related to a purpose. Different kinds or genres of writing pose particular challenges to writers. The main genres of writing include the following:

- *Journals* are personal accounts of events or ideas whose purpose is to record experiences and help writers remember them and think about them deeply.

- *Stories* are fictional accounts of characters in settings who attempt to overcome problems. The purpose of stories is to be outlets for writers' inventiveness and to entertain others.

- *Poems* are compositions that capture and convey emotions and insights while taking liberties with sentence and paragraph construction.

- *Expository accounts* are intended to be careful descriptions or explanations of things in the world.

- *Persuasive essays* convey writers' views of real issues in their lives and try to influence their readers' views.

These genres include important subtopics: A play is a kind of story; a song is a kind of poem; an observation report in science is a kind of expository account, as are biographies and autobiographies; and an advertisement is a kind of persuasive essay. They may also be mixed with each other; sometimes writers describe or explain to persuade readers or to tell them a story. Fictitious journals can be a form of storytelling, as Pam Conrad (1992) ably demonstrated in her novel *Pedro's Journal*, a fictional day-by-day account of the voyage of Christopher Columbus.

Teach It!

Refer to the Teach It! appendix at the end of the book for further activities you can use to reinforce concepts discussed in this chapter.

Teaching Students to Write in Genres: Descriptive Writing

Writing expert Lucy Calkins (1994) suggests that teachers immerse students in genre study, in which they read several published works written in a particular genre and then try their hands at writing in that genre. The format for teaching lessons of genre study is basically the same as that for focused lessons.

In the following sample lesson, teacher Paul Darion has decided to immerse his students in descriptive writing.

- *Share a sample of the writing form.* To demonstrate descriptive writing, Mr. Darion selects the opening paragraphs from Frances Temple's *Tonight, By Sea* (1995) and makes copies of them for his students. He plans to call the students' attention to the author's skill at writing vividly. In this case, the writer has carefully observed a process and shown it to the reader, step by step, and has put the reader in the picture by naming sights, sounds, smells, and tactile sensations.

- *Call attention to the features of the writing form.* Mr. Darion reads the passage aloud as the students read along. Then he invites the students to say aloud what they experienced in reading the passage. He invites one student to retell the process of lighting a fire. Then he invites several more students, one at a time, to name a detail the writer has given and say whether that detail is a sight, a sound, a smell, or a feeling. Mr. Darion has also decided to pass out different colored pencils and ask students to use different colors for words that appeal to different senses. This part of the lesson ends with the students saying aloud how the writer achieved vivid descriptive writing: "Descriptive writing names things exactly, and uses words for sights, sounds, smells, tastes, and feelings."

- *Provide guided practice in using the writing form.* Sometimes, the next thing Mr. Darion does is to have the students observe something carefully in the classroom and describe it in writing. Today, however, he pulls out a mystery bag he created beforehand. It is nothing more than a paper bag containing an object (such as a chess piece, a spark plug, a sewing thimble, or a Christmas tree light bulb). Mr. Darion invites the students, one at a time, to reach into the bag and touch the object. The students then describe it on paper, with the understanding that they must thoroughly describe the object before they name it.

- *Make a poster explaining how to write in that genre.* Mr. Darion has the students create a poster that names the kind of writing, provides an example of it, and includes a graphic organizer that makes clear the instructions for writing in that form or genre. The students will now be able to refer to the poster as they complete their own writing.

- *Encourage the students to write in that genre during their independent writing.* Mr. Darion reminds the students of what they know about descriptive writing and encourages them to describe things carefully with words that appeal to the senses. The term *descriptive writing* enters the students' vocabulary, and the reminder to "use words that name sights, sounds, smells, tastes, and feelings" is commonly heard among the students themselves.

> Kneeling in the sand, Paulie shredded dry seaweed and fluffed it into a heap between the three black cooking stones, half forgetting that she had no food to cook. She broke palm fronds over the seaweed, then propped two pieces of driftwood with their tips just above the palm. Raking the sand together with her fingers, she built up a ring around the outside of the stones, careful to make room for the air to blow in and give life to the fire, a little and not too much.
>
> Paulie leaned back, still kneeling, circling her upper arms in her hands to warm them. Night had come. The tree frogs stopped singing all at once.
>
> "You got matches, Uncle?"
>
> Paulie's uncle was washing in seawater from a bucket, pouring it down his back to get off the sweat and the sawdust, rinsing his arms.
>
> "All the matches gone, Paulie."
>
> "Go see if you can borrow a coal," her grandmother said. Sitting on the steps of her house, a cloth around her thin shoulders, Grann Adeline leaned toward the fire as if it were already lit. She frowned, slapped at a mosquito on her ankle. "Go on, girl. Ask sweetly and somebody bound to give you an ember."
>
> Paulie wandered down the sand path. The small houses clustered under the trees were mostly dark. She could hear voices talking softly, a baby crying. A thin dog came out and sniffed at the backs of her knees. Paulie looked for the glow of a cook fire, smelled the breeze for one. She could feel the sea air, and hear the waves coming in, but it seemed like nobody was cooking.

Source: From *Tonight, by Sea,* by Frances Temple. Scholastic Inc./Orchard Books. Copyright © 1995 by Frances Temple. Reprinted by permission.

Journals and Other Personal Writing

CCSS

- Writing 2: Text Types and Purposes (Explanatory)

CCSS

- Writing 1: Text Types and Purposes (Personal)

Journal writing consists of jotting down thoughts, feelings, and impressions that are close to the writer; the intended audience is the writer herself or himself. Such writing usually comes fairly naturally to young writers because it has few formal demands. Nonetheless, the kind of personal expressive writing found in journals is important for students to use because it serves as a sort of playground or laboratory for the imagination (Britton, 1970). Students may begin ideas in journals that they later turn into more formal pieces.

DUAL-ENTRY DIARY Journals have other important pedagogical uses, too. Response journals are used to encourage students to reflect on their reading and their learning. A simple but powerful approach to response journals is the *dual-entry diary* (Barone, 1992; Berthoff, 1981). In a dual-entry diary (DED), students are asked to divide the page down the middle with a vertical line. On the left-hand side, they record phrases that they found striking, important, or puzzling. On the right-hand side, they write comments on the passages. DEDs can be used to respond to literature or a host of other topics. After the students have written their DEDs, the teacher may write comments in them or may ask the students to share their entries in a discussion group.

DIALOGUE JOURNALS In this form of response writing in journals, students are assigned to pairs by the teacher. After they have read a part of a book or participated in some other learning event, they write their impressions of it in their journals. Later, they have written conversations with each other. One makes a comment in writing and ends with a question for the other. The other answers the question, makes a comment as well, and writes another question for the partner, and so on.

Stories

Most students enjoy writing stories, and because they are surrounded by stories, they find it natural to do so. Yet the structure of stories is fairly complicated, so some instruction in writing stories is helpful. There are many ways to show students how to write stories.

IMITATING AN AUTHOR In the genre study approach, you might read the children several stories by the same author and then ask them to write a similar story. For example, second- and third-grade children delight in writing their own episodes about Amelia Bedelia (Parish, 1992), James Marshall's character Fox (Marshall, 1994), Russell Hoban's character Frances (Hoban, 1995), or Mo Willem's Pigeon (Willems, 2003).

STORY MAPS Outlines that guide students to write stories part by part are called story maps. Story maps are used in reading instruction as devices for calling children's attention to the parts of a plot. In writing, story maps like the one shown in Figure 10.12 can be used as frameworks for planning out a story.

Teach It! 32

Dual-Entry Diary

CCSS

• Writing 3: Text Types and Purposes (Stories)

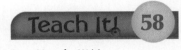

Teach It! 58

Story Maps for Writing

Figure 10.12
A Story Map

| There was a person . . . |
| who wanted . . . |
| So she . . . |
| but . . . |
| (and she . . .) |
| (but . . .) |
| And then she . . . |
| And finally, . . . |
| So . . . |

In a map such as the one shown in Figure 10.12, students fill in the blanks on the right-hand side of the chart. If they are using the map for planning, after the students have filled in the chart, they write the story out, adding details and whatever other twists occur to them as they write.

For English Language Learners

Story Structure and English Language Learners

The familiar story structure that introduces a character in a setting with a problem and attempts at a solution and a resolution of the problem is not the way everyone tells stories. Stories written for children in many countries in Latin America and southern Europe may be wildly imaginative and unpredictable—their charm is in their constant surprises. Even stories told by African American children may be less linear, more episodic, and told with more passion than the linear stories favored by the white middle class (see Cazden, 2001). If a story that follows the traditional story grammar outlined here is what is wanted, the teacher should be careful to teach that structure to all of the children, especially the English language learners.

DIALOGUE STORIES   A simple but effective pattern for structuring stories is the dialogue story. Students can be shown an example of a dialogue story, such as John Archambault and Bill Martin, Jr.'s *White Dynamite and the Curly Kid* (1989). Then ask the students to write their own story in dialogue form. As a rehearsal step, have two students make up an oral story together and each write their own version of it later.

Poems

Styles of poems range from those that put an emphasis on form to those that stress ideas and let form take care of itself. Following are three different approaches to writing structured poems. Even though the form is tightly prescribed, children write poems that are lively and surprising with these frameworks to support them. To teach children to write a form poem, follow these steps:

1. Show the students an example of a well-written poem that follows the form. (You might need to write this yourself or save it from a previous class.)
2. Have the students help you create a poem as a group. Discuss each choice they make so they understand the process well.
3. Have individuals or pairs write their own poems.
4. Share several of the poems, and discuss their qualities. Also call attention to the ways in which the poems followed the structure.
5. Make a wall chart in which you feature several of the students' poems; also outline the procedures for writing a poem with the structure in question.

ACROSTICS   Acrostics can be used simply, as when they spell a person's name. Students write a name in capitals vertically down the left side of a page and then go back and insert a word that begins with each letter. Here is one:

Persistent
Energetic
Never dull
Native of the mountains—
Yes, you will like this person.

On a more ambitious level, students can create acrostics with whole phrases, rhymed or unrhymed, but still have the first letter of the first word of each line spelling a word when read from top to bottom:

Alicia lived through long, cold days
Like an old unnoticed stone
Off the path, far from the crowds
Never seen,
Ever.

In their wonderful book, *Ways of Writing with Young Kids*, Sharon Edwards and her colleagues (2003) explore many ways of using acrostics. A particularly interesting way is to have a poet read her acrostic aloud to the class twice: first as a poem, with attention paid to the sounds, the images, and the tone, and then to uncover the mystery word that is spelled by the poem.

CINQUAINS Christmas tree–shaped poems that look like the following are called cinquains:

Harry
Young, charmed
Studying, flying, surviving
Ron Weasley's best friend
Wizard

Cinquains are surprisingly useful means of encouraging students to think about a concept. They follow a simple pattern:

- The first line names the topic.
- The second line contains two describing words.
- The third line has three action words ending in *-ing*.
- The fourth line is four feeling words, which may be written as a phrase.
- The fifth line is a one-word synonym for the name in the first line.

LIST POEMS Throughout the ages, many fine poems have been developed around the idea of lists. Take this medieval prayer, for example:

From Ghoulies
And Ghosties
And long-legged Beasties
And Things that go bump in the night:
Good Lord, deliver us.

Writers can use the idea by listing all of the things that are:

—dark

—lonely

—round

—scarce

The effect is heightened when writers include in their list both concrete and abstract things. For example,

A pebble in the pond
a policeman's beat
the moon's halo
subway tokens
surprised eyes
a ghost's mouth
and the world—
are round.

Expository Writing

Expository writing includes texts that describe or explain. Focused lessons that share good examples from literature and encourage their imitation can help young writers create expository works. Graphic organizers serve as valuable tools for helping children to write descriptive and explanatory prose. A number of graphic organizers are popular with children from second grade up and have been discussed at various points in the book. As you might recall, graphic organizers are important learning aids in comprehension (see Chapters 7 and 8) as well. This reinforces an important theme of this book about the close connection between the teaching/learning of reading and writing.

Figure 10.13 A Cluster, or Semantic Web

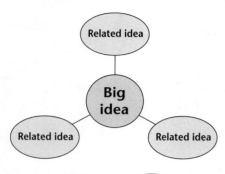

Graphic Organizers

CLUSTERS Clusters, also called semantic webs, are linked circles that show relationships between ideas. The writer starts by naming the topic of the writing in a circle in the center of the page and then writes subordinate topics in satellite circles around the main circle. Aspects of each subordinate circle are written in still more satellites (see Figure 10.13). After the details about a topic have been set out in the form of a cluster, the writer can refer to them in writing out an essay.

VENN DIAGRAMS Venn diagrams are helpful planning aids when writers want to compare and contrast two items, and they consist of two interlocking circles (see Figure 10.14). In the outer left-hand circle is listed everything that is true about Topic X but not Topic Y. In the outer right-hand circle is written everything that is true about Topic Y but not Topic X. In the overlapping part in the middle is written everything that is true about both Topic X and Topic Y.

DESCRIPTIVE ESSAY FRAMES Frames provide boxes that prompt writers to collect and organize their thoughts before writing out an essay; in this way, they can lend structure to a piece of writing. Like all writing frameworks, though, they should be used sparingly: They can become a crutch to be relied on too much and they may take the place of the student's own voice and originality. Figure 10.15 shows one example of a frame for structuring a descriptive essay.

CAUSE-AND-EFFECT CHARTS When students plan to write about cause-and-effect chains, they can organize their ideas before writing using a cause-and-effect chart. A

Figure 10.14
A Venn Diagram

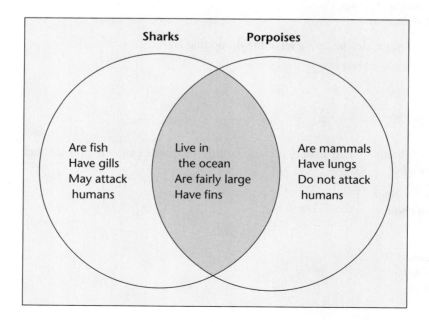

I'm going to write about . . .		
Here is a word that describes my topic:	Here is one example of that word	
	Here is another example	
Here is another word that describes my topic:	Here is one example of that word	
	Here is another example	
Here is another word that describes my topic:	Here is one example of that word	
	Here is another example	
This is how I feel about my topic:	Here is the reason I feel that way	

Figure 10.15
A Framework for a Descriptive Essay

cause-and-effect chart (Figure 10.16) can have few or many boxes. Causes are listed in separate boxes on the left-hand side of the chart and effects are listed on the right. Several causes may contribute to a single effect, which may simultaneously be the cause of several other effects. The chart in Figure 10.16 shows the many causes of air pollution and their related effects.

PERSUASIVE ESSAYS There are many ways to help students produce arguments and shape them into persuasive essays. A popular procedure for helping students formulate their ideas for a persuasive essay is the K-W-L strategy (Ogle, 1986), discussed in Chapter 8. By constructing a K-W-L chart, students consider what they already know about a topic, formulate questions that say what they want to know about it, and later list what they learned about the topic. Having done this activity, you can then construct a new chart labeled like the one in Figure 10.17 that will guide the students to think about and take positions on actions that should follow from those findings.

After the students have completed the chart, they might think about ways to use their entries in an argumentative essay. One way in which the essay can be structured is to enter the information into another kind of format, like the one shown in Figure 10.18.

Writing should be integrated into the reading program early and children should write every day. How can we accomplish these two goals?

Teach It! 47

Know-Want-to-Know-Learn (K-W-L)

CCSS

• Writing 1: Text Types and Purposes (Opinions)

Figure 10.16
A Cause-and-Effect Chart

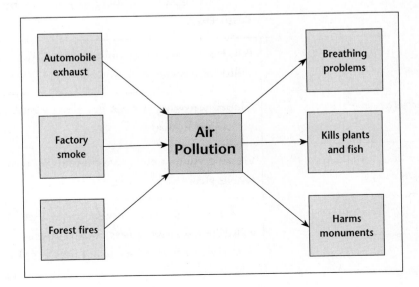

Figure 10.17   What? So What? Now What?

What?	So What?	Now What?
Pollution from automobiles and industrial pollution causes global warming.	Global warming is bad for plants and animals, including humans.	We should reduce automobile pollution by driving less and reduce industrial pollution by using less fossil fuel.

CCSS

Common Core Standards: Writing Position Papers

The Common Core Standards ask that students—beginning in kindergarten and with increasing sophistication as they progress through the grades—be able to write position papers on a host of topics. Position papers often take the form of (1) stating a position, (2) stating two or three reasons for it, (3) supporting each reason with evidence, and (4) restating the conclusion. Active class discussions and graphic organizers can bring out positions for students to take and provide structure for their arguments. But it is important to give students much practice in actually writing out their position papers, too (CCSS Foundational Standards, Text Types and Purposes, 1).

MIXING GENRES: RAFT   A writing-to-learn strategy that calls attention to genres even as it mixes them up is the RAFT procedure, developed by Carol Santa (1988). RAFT is an acronym for **R**ole, **A**udience, **F**ormat, and **T**opic.

Once a *topic* has been established in a lesson, students are invited to adopt different *roles* of people or other characters who have a stake in the issue. For example, if the topic is protecting dolphins, the roles might be fishermen, conservationists, the state wildlife

Figure 10.18   Framework for a Persuasive Essay

What do you believe should be done about _____?	We should reduce automobile pollution by driving less and reduce industrial pollution by using less fossil fuel.
What is one reason why that should be done?	Pollution from automobiles and industrial pollution causes global warming.
(What is a second reason why that should be done?)	Global warming is bad for plants and animals, including humans.
(What is a third reason why that should be done?)	We are ruining our environment by warming the whole planet's climate.
So, say again what you believe should be done about _____.	Therefore, we should reduce automobile pollution by driving less and reduce industrial pollution by using less fossil fuel.

protection people, and (with a little imagination) the dolphins themselves. Once each student (or teams of students) has chosen a role, the student decides who the *audience* is—the people or characters to whom the message will be addressed. For example, conservationists might want to send a message to fishermen on the topic of protecting dolphins. But now the question is what *format* the message might use. Conservationists could write persuasive letters, editorials for the local newspaper, billboard advertisements, or catchy jingles, to name just a few formats. Once the four aspects of the RAFT are decided on—the Role, the Audience, the Format, and the Topic, the students create their works.

As an added twist, Alan Crawford (Crawford et al., 2005) suggests using *Reciprocal RAFT*, in which the original messages are distributed to students in the class, who then adopt the role of the audience and respond to the messages.

Assessment of Writing

Various parts of this chapter have focused on teaching children to revise and edit their own work. Revising and editing are basic forms of assessment of children's writing. Assessing students' writing and providing ongoing feedback are critical in encouraging students to write. However, in assessing students' writing, keep in mind some valuable principles:

- Not everything should be assessed. Most of children's writing should be for communication and should not be graded.
- Assessment should teach; that is, children should learn about writing from the assessment.
- The criteria for assessment should be explicit and clear.
- Children should be involved in their own assessment.
- Assessment should show strengths and progress as well as needed improvements.

USING RUBRICS   *Rubrics* are detailed presentations of quality criteria. They address several aspects of writing at once, and they explain clearly what constitutes a good job. Rubrics may be constructed by the teacher or by the students and the teacher together. They should be closely connected to the qualities of writing that have been stressed in the focused lessons as well as any checklists that have been used to guide the students' revising and editing. Students should be fully aware of the meaning of each criterion (aspect of quality) on the rubric before they produce the work that will be assessed.

Following are the steps for using rubrics:

- Choose four to eight qualities of writing to assess. (Consider having the children suggest qualities of good writing.)
- Make sure the qualities of writing you assess have been carefully explained.
- Describe good work according to each quality. You may also describe fair and poor work.
- Share the rubrics with the students before they write the works that will be assessed.
- Use the rubrics often so that students learn what they mean and are able to use their criteria to guide them when they write.

Six Traits Assessment, a popular evaluation tool, is featured in the Assessment box. Whatever assessment tools you use to evaluate children's writing, it is important to use the same terms in your instruction as you use in evaluation. For example, if you evaluate children's use of written dialogue, you must be sure you have carefully taught them how to do it (Spandel, 2013). Use the same terms in your instruction such as "dialogue"; avoid switching to "write like talking marks" or other terms and phrases that will confuse the children. And make sure your writing lessons and writing workshops are filled with teacher-to-children, teacher-to-child conversations about writing and writing terms.

 Rubrics are an effective way to assess a variety of writing skills. In the video, how did Ms. Sanchez encourage her fourth graders to use rubrics to assess their own writing, and how did she use literature to support their ability to develop rubrics?

CCSS

- Language 1 and 2: Conventions of Standard English

If you use a Six Traits Rubric (see Figure 10.19), be sure your students are familiar with the rubric that will be used to judge them. Read the rubric together and have it available in the classroom. It is sad to say, but often true that children end up hating to write because they have not been given a fair chance to learn well and to prepare for assessment. High quality instruction/assessment will help you avoid mistakes that can be tragic. Your students will be judged all their lives by their writing.

Spandel's text on Six Traits writing assessment (Spandel, 2013) includes many examples of student writing at various grade levels that correspond to each trait, such as word choice, sentence fluency, and punctuation. Direct "how to do it" teacher guidance is provided that shows appropriate instruction to use, for example, if a student overuses words such as "things," writes a series of choppy sentences, or doesn't use adequate punctuation.

Figure 10.19
A Rubric for Assessing Writing: Six Traits Writing Evaluation Sheet

Ideas and Content:

Clear ideas. It makes sense.

The writer has narrowed the idea to a manageable topic.

Good information—from experience, imagination, or research.

Original and fresh perspective.

Details that capture a reader's interest. Makes ideas understandable. ____________

Organization:

A snappy lead that gets the reader's attention. ____________

Starts somewhere and goes somewhere. ____________

The writer continually makes connections within the work. ____________

Writing builds to a conclusion. ____________

The writer creates a memorable resolution and conclusion.

Voice:

Sounds like a person wrote it.

Sounds like this particular writer.

Brings topic to life.

Makes the reader respond and care what happens.

The writer has energy and is involved. ____________

Word Choice:

Words and phrases have power. ____________

Word pictures are created. ____________

Thought is crystal clear and precise. ____________

Strong verbs and precise nouns. ____________

Sentence Fluency:

Easy to read aloud.

Well-built sentences.

Varied sentence length. Some long sentences, some short.

Conventions:

Looks clean, edited, and proofread.

Free of distracting errors. ____________

Easy to read. ____________

No errors in spelling, punctuation, grammar and usage, capitalization, and indentation. ____________

Six Traits Writing Evaluation

The Six Traits model for writing assessment meets all of the principles just identified. Developed by Vicki Spandel and her associates (1996, 2000) at the Northwest Regional Education Laboratory, the Six Traits model seeks to direct teachers' and students' attention to six aspects of writing: ideas and content, organization, voice, word choice, sentence fluency, and conventions.

1. *Ideas and content* amount to the quality of having something to say and saying it clearly to the reader. They include having found out something about the topic before writing about it and having an original point of view. They can include providing details that lend an eyewitness feel to the paper.

2. *Organization* refers to the paper's having a beginning, a middle, and an end. It may include supporting main ideas with details, sticking to the topic, and making clear transitions from one point to another.

3. *Voice* describes the quality of reaching for words that express ideas well, even when this means writing words one has not been taught to use or to spell. A paper with a well-developed voice approaches the writer's oral fluency and expressiveness.

4. *Word choice* is the quality of showing the writer's meaning with precise words and specific details, and using fresh ways of expressing ideas, avoiding clichés.

5. *Sentence fluency* means a reader can easily read the work aloud. There are sufficient numbers of sentences to convey the meaning, and the sentences are varied in their length and form.

6. *Conventions* include spelling, capitalization and punctuation, and grammatical correctness. In later grades, conventions may refer to allocating separate ideas to separate paragraphs.

Children of different ages and levels of development naturally will be more or less advanced in their performance within each trait. Spandel and her associates have listed behavioral descriptors at four levels of development:

- *Exploring writers* are young writers who are experimenting with the whole enterprise of making meaning with graphic communication. Thus, within the trait of ideas and content, exploring writers might use pictures and scribbles to express ideas.

- *Emerging writers* are still young writers, but they have advanced to the point at which they are starting to work the features of conventional writing into their graphic productions. Thus, within the trait of ideas and content, emerging writers may use pictures or both pictures and mock writing in such a way that a reader might be able to guess an approximate meaning.

- *Developing writers,* through a mix of their own inventions and discoveries and overt teaching, can produce written messages that convey clear meaning, with the beginnings of formal organization and attention to some of the conventions of spelling and capitalization. Thus, within the trait of ideas and content, developing writers create stand-alone messages that are more readily decipherable. Their works show some attention to detail.

- *Fluent/experienced writers* express meanings more eloquently in print and take advantage of many features of fluent writing within all six traits. Thus, within the trait of ideas and content, fluent writers create works that show advancing mastery of qualities of writing, including the ability to say things clearly and in fresh and interesting ways, honoring more and more of the conventions of writing.

WORK SAMPLING   Another effective approach to evaluating writing is work sampling. One way to sample work is to choose representative pieces of each child's writings at intervals during the year, but at least once per month. Sit down with the child and discuss the improvements you both see. Ask the child to take the lead in pointing out the improvements. If the child needs help, you might comment on the following:

- The length of each piece
- Organization: sticking to a topic and saying interesting things about it
- The appearance of new features, such as description or dialogue
- Attempts to write in a new genre, such as persuasion or description
- Attention to mechanics, such as spelling, punctuation, and handwriting

Before ending the conversation, ask the child to set goals—writing improvements to make in the next month. Write these down, or have the child write them, with a copy for yourself and a copy for the child. Provide regular reminders of the goals.

Writing to Learn

Writing can be used to boost learning in at least five ways:

1. **Writing requires students to make their thoughts explicit.** Fuzzy thinking leads to fuzzy writing (vague, unfocused, disorganized) and vice-versa. When students learn to read back and reflect on what they write, they have a tool for sharpening their thinking. In the meantime, teachers can reflect with individual students about their writing, and help them clarify their thoughts. As the Brazilian educator Paolo Freire (1976) noted nearly half a century ago, writing can raise our consciousness by enabling us to enter into a dialectic (a sort of creative argument) with our own thoughts.

CCSS

• Writing 9: Research

2. **Writing can lead students to surprise themselves, by expressing thoughts they didn't know they had.** Donald Murray (1982) considered drafting—writing out ideas in an unrestrained fashion—as a means of discovering what you know about a topic. The point is, students often don't know what they know about a topic until they write about it. Of course, writing that will be made public must be revised and shaped for clarity and elegance. But in the early stages of writing, or when writing in a journal, composing constitutes a sort of laboratory for the mind and the imagination.

3. **Writing commits students to ideas.** In a class discussion, some students may be timid and unwilling to state their own views, or they may simply agree with someone else's strongly stated opinion. But teachers can ask students to individually write down what they think about a topic or their questions about it, and insist that they read their own comments aloud instead of deferring to others.

4. **Writing guides inquiry.** Whether the assignment is a brief position paper or a longer research project, teachers can assign formats to guide students' thinking and expression.

5. **Writing calls attention to language.** The act of writing makes explicit many aspects of language that otherwise don't often come to consciousness. Spelling, word choice, sentence grammar, paragraph structure, and larger patterns of the organization of ideas are all laid bare when written down.

Teaching Writing to Learn

CCSS

• Writing 10: Range of Writing

Virtually all of the ideas already presented in this chapter are means of using writing to help students learn. A few additional ideas are given below.

ENTRANCE CARDS   The topic of the next day's class is announced in advance. Students are required to write at least one good question about the topic on an index card, and bring that card as a ticket for admission to the class discussion. The teacher may collect the cards and read the questions randomly, or call on the students to read their questions aloud. Optionally, the questions may be worked into a K-W-L chart.

EXIT CARDS   At the conclusion of a class, students can be given four minutes to fill out an exit card with answers to three questions:

1. What is the most important thing you learned today?
2. What is one question you have about the topic?
3. What is one comment you want to make about today's lesson?

The teacher collects the cards and reviews them before the next class. He or she may choose to open the next class with answers to the questions. In any case, having students name the most important thing they learned from the class leads them to mentally review what happened in the class, and reading students' answers to the questions gives the teacher a window into what the students took from it.

LEARNING LOGS   Learning logs are daily journals the students keep. They provide a way for students to make explicit their thoughts about what they learned (or think they learned) in a class.

Often they take the form of "Write a letter to _____ (an absent class member) and explain exactly how we solved the problem we studied today." The teacher reviews the journals periodically to see what the students are understanding and where their difficulties are.

Other learning logs may be structured with questions to guide students' responses. The teacher can ask what students' favorite part of the lesson was, what the hardest part was, how they felt about it, what would make the lesson more productive for them, or what they were doing to understand the material.

I-SEARCH PROJECTS   As a way of guiding inquiry and making it more personal, writing teacher Ken Macrorie (1988) developed the I-Search procedure. The I-Search procedure follows the format given in Figure 10.20, with variations to make it less sophisticated for younger students.

Family Literacy

How can you recruit the help of families in supporting students who are learning to write?

CCSS

Common Core Standards: Writing Research Papers

The CCSS ask that students by grade 3 be able to conduct research projects and build knowledge about a topic. (Foundational Writing standards: Research to Build and Present Knowledge, 7)

CCSS

• Writing 7 & 8: Research

Figure 10.20
Writing an I-Search Inquiry

What you want to know

(Write this section at the very beginning of your project.) Tell us the question you want to find out about. Say what you already knew about this question when you began your search. Tell us why you cared about or were interested in this question.

How you will find out

(Write about these questions when you begin your search.) What will you do to find answers to your question? Who will you talk to? What will you ask them? What will you read? What Internet sites will you visit?

(The teacher usually specifies what kinds of sources the student is expected to use.)

What did you learn?

What are three or four major things you found out? State your findings one at a time, and support each one with examples, stories, or arguments that will help the reader understand how you arrived at those conclusions. Try to connect your findings with your original questions.

Lessons for the writer

In this part of the paper, tell the story of your investigation and what you learned in the process. Did other questions occur to you in the course of the investigation? Did some sources turn out to be more useful than others? Did you discover new sources of information as you went along? If so, how? Did you find trends of agreement in your sources? Were there any disagreements among them? How did you decide what to conclude?

References

At the end of the paper, write out the references you consulted, using the form your teacher tells you to use.

Involving Families in Their Children's Writing

Families can be partners in all stages of children's growth as writers. Research has shown that children who are drawn into family literacy activities, and especially into letter writing activities, make more progress as readers and writers (Clay, 1987).

Family Writing for Young Children

When children in kindergarten and first grade begin to explore the writing system, it helps if parents give them reasons and opportunities to practice their early writing, even when it bears only a slight resemblance to adult writing. As discussed in earlier chapters, children make progress both as readers and as writers if they are allowed to produce pretend versions of writing. Indeed, with a little training, it is possible to ensure that important concepts about print are discovered and practiced through early writing experiences, even scribbling and invented spelling. Families of younger children can invite children to write some of the following:

> Greeting cards to relatives
>
> Grocery lists
>
> Captions on their drawings
>
> Refrigerator notes to the rest of the family

You might need to explain to parents the importance of encouraging young children to write even before they have learned to do so conventionally. Many parents may worry that early untutored writing could reinforce incorrect habits. Assure them that this is not the case. However, you must then observe some safeguards in your classroom, such as making sure that the materials displayed for children to practice reading are written conventionally.

Family Writing for Older Children

When children are able to spell words and write sentences, they should be encouraged to do meaningful writing at home. Writing at home might include the following:

- Writing up family stories to share on special occasions, as in family letters to relatives
- Lyrics to favorite songs
- Titles of favorite TV shows to records
- Writing to a safe circle of friends via a computer-based instant messaging service

Children will be inspired to write if they see family members writing. Some families make a custom of compiling and writing down family stories that occur during the year: the most outrageous camping trip, the funniest family event, and so on. These can be a fine addition to a family photograph album, and can be written by all—children included.

For Review

Stressing writing in the elementary grades helps students think, learn, and make better use of language. The first aspect of writing dealt with in the chapter was spelling, and we saw stages or levels of strategies that students typically use as they learn to spell, which are to be matched with carefully planned teaching.

Then the chapter looked at the writing process, consisting of rehearsing, drafting, sharing, revising, editing, and publishing. Writers at different ages and levels of learning need different levels of support. In this chapter we used the model of the "gradual release of responsibility" to guide us from teacher centered modeling, to scaffolded productions by children, to independent writing.

The products of writing are arranged into genres. Genres include expressive writing such as journals, stories, poems, expository writing, and persuasive essays. Suggestions were given for helping students write in each genre. Children sometimes need more explicit support than the writing workshop gives them. Different levels of support for children's writing include modeled writing, shared writing, interactive writing, guided writing, and independent writing. The special problems of struggling writers were also addressed, and it was suggested that strategies for writing be introduced to them through focused lessons and graphic organizers and that these be regularly practiced. Assessment is an important part of teaching children to write. Assessment should teach—by employing means that communicate clearly what the children are doing well and what needs work and by involving the children in assessing their own work.

Writing can be used to support learning across the disciplines. The Common Core Standards insist that it be used for that purpose. We suggested that writing can aid learning in five ways, and in addition to the many relevant teaching strategies already presented in this chapter we added a few more.

Families have a role to play in supporting students' writing, and suggestions were given for families of younger children and older children.

For Your Journal

1. Try out the writing process for yourself with the assistance of a partner, although you can do this activity alone.
   - Make a list of five topics you might write about. These should be topics you might share with children in grades 1 though 5.
   - Ask yourself or have a partner ask you what interests you about each topic. Find your story!
     - Write a draft of your paper. Write for eight minutes without stopping.
     - Read back over your paper, or have a partner read it, and consider areas you need to revise.
   - Write about this writing experience in your journal, reflect on what happened in the process, how you felt about writing this way, and if it was different than previous writing you've done.

2. In helping children learn to write, where do you think the proper balance can be found between the need to encourage children to feel ownership for their writing and take initiative for their learning and the need to teach them to write better—that is, more coherently and correctly?

Taking It to the World

1. The writing process described in this chapter—rehearsing, drafting, revising, editing, and publishing—is often described as the way professional writers create. But is it? Find and interview at least two writers. If possible, look for writers of fiction and poetry as well as writers of nonfiction. Ask them what they do when they write. (*Hint*: Don't mention the writing process or talk about the steps. See whether they mention those themselves.)

Compare your notes with those of your classmates. Do the writers do similar things as they write? Does the process they use seem to depend on whether they are writing fiction or nonfiction? Do their processes resemble the process described in this chapter?

2. The writing workshop described in this chapter is widely regarded in the educational literature as a valuable development. Many teachers use the workshop approach successfully and many children seem to have internalized the steps of the writing process, but maybe not as many as reading the literature might suggest. Visit an elementary school, and ask the teachers whether they use writing workshops with their children. If so, how often? What do they like about it? Does it work for all students? If not, what modifications must they use for the children who struggle? If they don't use the writing workshop, why don't they? What approach to writing instruction do they use?

New Literacy Connections

Check out the online magazine for writing for and by children called Cyberkids <www.cyberkids.com>. Investigate the Creative Works gallery. How might you be able to use this site to help you teach children to write?

MyEducationLab™

Go to Topic 6 (Writing) in the MyEducationLab <www.myeducationlab.com> for your course, where you can:

- Find learning outcomes for Writing along with the national standards that connect to these outcomes.

- Complete Assignments and Activities that can help you more deeply understand the chapter content.

- Apply and practice your understanding of the core teaching skills identified in the chapter with the Building Teaching Skills and Dispositions learning units.

- Check your comprehension on the content covered in the chapter by going to the Study Plan in the Book Resources for your text. Here you will be able to take a chapter quiz, receive feedback on your answers, and then access Review, Practice, and Enrichment activities to enhance your understanding of chapter content.

- Visit A+RISE. A+RISE®Standards2Strategy™ is an innovative and interactive online resource that offers new teachers in grades K-12 just in time, research-based instructional strategies that meet the linguistic needs of ELLs as they learn content, differentiate instruction for all grades and abilities, and are aligned to Common Core Elementary Language Arts standards English language proficiency standards in WIDA, Texas, California, and Florida.

Assessing Literacy

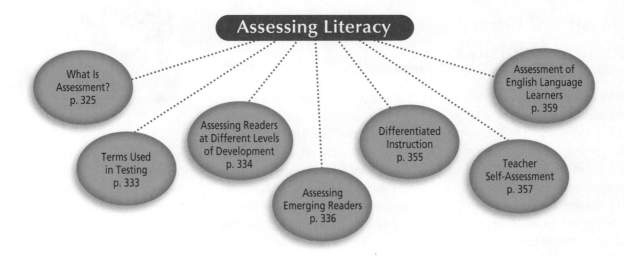

Assessing Literacy

- What Is Assessment? p. 325
- Terms Used in Testing p. 333
- Assessing Readers at Different Levels of Development p. 334
- Assessing Emerging Readers p. 336
- Differentiated Instruction p. 355
- Teacher Self-Assessment p. 357
- Assessment of English Language Learners p. 359

Anticipation Guide

The following statements will stimulate your thinking about the topics of this chapter. Answer *true* or *false* in response to each statement. As you read and learn more about the topics in these statements, double-check your answers. See what interests you and prompts your curiosity toward more understanding.

_____ **1.** Assessment of literacy is done at different times and for different purposes. At the beginning of the year, screening assessment is done, followed by diagnostic assessment for those who need it. All during the year all students are subjected to monitoring assessment, and at the end of the year, most face outcomes-based assessment.

_____ **2.** High-stakes assessment has so alarmed and angered the American public that it probably won't be around by the time this book makes it into print.

_____ **3.** The concepts of validity and reliability are not just of interest to researchers; teachers also need to be concerned with the validity and reliability of the instruments they use.

_____ **4.** Informal assessments are only given on weekends, preferably at a cookout with everybody dressed in old clothes.

_____ **5.** An important piece of information yielded by assessment concerns children's independent, instructional, and frustration reading levels.

_____ **6.** It is usually harder for a child to read words in the context of a meaningful passage than to read them off lists.

_____ **7.** The online management and reporting of children's assessment data are becoming something of an industry in the United States.

_____ **8.** All assessment should be done using scientifically tested instruments.

_____ **9.** Readability measurement is an exact science. It is possible to pinpoint precisely the level of challenge any piece of text will pose to any reader.

_____ **10.** Assessment is for children. There is no earthly reason why teachers should ever assess themselves.

A Classroom Story

Assessment Drives Teaching Decisions

John Samuels teaches a diverse group of first graders at a small elementary school in a farming community. Of his 27 students, 7 speak Spanish at home. The parents of 8 of the children (including two of the Spanish-speaking families) are scientists at a nearby agricultural experiment station. Some children are from families of farm workers, and others are from families on public assistance. John believes very strongly that his job as a teacher is to help all of his children be as well prepared for a happy and successful life as he can make them.

At the beginning of the year John, the school's reading teacher, and the three other first-grade teachers in his school administer a screening test of early reading abilities to the entire first grade. They test the children's letter knowledge, their concept of word, their phonemic segmentation and phonics (through an invented spelling task), and their recognition of both environmental print and decodable words. The results for John's class are given in Table 11.1 on page 325.

Family Literacy

How is John partnering successfully with his students' families?

John and the other three teachers look through all of the scores together. They decide that the top scoring readers in John's groups are probably beginning readers already. The middle group still needs a moderate amount of support in emergent literacy skills and concepts. The group with the lowest scores will need special intervention to help them profit from reading instruction during the year.

During the first two weeks of the school year, John gives further diagnostic tests to his students. The children with the lowest scores have their concepts about print assessed as well as their awareness of phonemes in words. The early screening already showed him which letters of the alphabet each child still needs to recognize and be able to produce, and their other scores suggested that they will need a holistic introduction to reading, with frequent sessions of listening to read-alouds, lots of dictation and shared book reading, and shared writing. They will need the whole sequence of systematic phonics instruction.

But John is also a good "kidwatcher." He observes the children carefully as they participate in his early lessons. He is pleased to see them singing along to "Down By the Bay" and smiling as they clap along to the rhythm. He watches to see whom they interact with on the playground.

He has already visited with their families before school started. The parents want their children to learn, and they make it clear that they are counting on his suggestions for ways to help their children. One of the fathers and two of the mothers are unemployed. They seem skeptical when John suggests that they might come into the classroom to help out, but John thinks at least the father and one of the mothers can be persuaded.

John finds time to read a simple book with each of the top- and middle-scoring children, and he keeps a running record of their abilities. He has learned to be a little skeptical of test scores, and he watches carefully to see if their performance in a real reading task lives up to what the test predicted. He is "roaming around the known," as Marie Clay (1993) puts it. Soon he has determined a reading level for each child and is ready to place the children in their first group for guided reading.

Struggling Reader

What is John doing to support his struggling students?

As he makes running records of the middle-scoring children's reading, he finds levels of books they can read at the instructional level, too. He notes they have developed some sight vocabulary and are developing some phonics skills. They are not fluent readers—they read word by word, without inflection. He will see if he can match them up with tutors from the nearby college's service learning project.

Assessment is an essential part of doing anything well, including the teaching of reading. The topic of assessment is getting more attention in reading instruction now than ever before. With the current emphasis on "research-based reading instruction," educators are paying more and more attention to how children are learning, what works and what doesn't, and why.

Table 11.1   Scores of First Graders on the Early Reading Screening Inventory

STUDENT	ALPHABET KNOWLEDGE (%)	CONCEPT OF WORD (%)	INVENTED SPELLING* (%)	WORD RECOGNITION (%)
High-scoring group				
Janice	100	100	92	80
Ephraim	92	100	88	75
Ignacio	98	100	90	80
Topaz	96	90	92	82
Middle-scoring group				
Peter	70	80	65	50
Carla	65	88	60	55
Laticia	68	80	70	60
Low-scoring group				
Juana	52	40	35	20
George	55	45	30	24
Alexia	40	40	20	10
Amanda	30	30	16	5

*Includes phonemic segmentation and early phonics.

What Is Assessment?

Assessment in reading entails gathering, analyzing, and interpreting information to determine how well a student reads. Assessment covers everything from informal observations of a student's reading to the use of commercial tests. Assessment practices include:

- Deciding what we need to know about a child's or group of children's reading.
- Deciding what measures will tell us what we want to know.
- Gathering information with those measures.
- Interpreting the information.
- Making decisions about what to do next, based on the new information.

Why Do We Assess?

There are different purposes for assessment and also different audiences for the information that assessment brings to light.

1. *We assess to guide our instruction.* We may assess to:
   - *Identify reading levels* (*independent*, *instructional*, and *frustration*) so we can place students in materials at the right level.
   - *Investigate children's readiness or prior knowledge* before starting instruction. Many aspects of learning to read and write are developmental, and in order to give the right instruction, teachers need to know where learners are in their development. For example, emergent readers need to develop the ability to

segment phonemes and also develop a concept of word before more advanced phonics lessons will make sense to them.

- *Locate children's strengths and areas of need* so we can steer our instruction toward appropriate targets. There are many aspects of children's literacy development, and if there are some aspects in which they are not progressing adequately, we need to locate these so we can offer specially tailored help. For example, a child may have learned many sight words, but have low reading fluency. We need to know that, so we can work on the student's fluency.
- *Identify children's literacy strategies* so we can strengthen appropriate ones and direct a child away from inappropriate ones. For example, good readers preview texts and set purposes for reading to help them understand better. Does each child know how to do this? Some immature readers look only at the first letter of a word and guess any word they know that begins with that letter. We can direct that child's attention to more letters and letter combinations in words.

2. **We assess to make sure our instruction is succeeding.** Some approaches work better than others with individual children, or with whole classrooms of children. We assess to:
   - *Find out if a teaching approach or set of materials is working for a child.* For example, to build reading fluency, teachers may use "buddy reading" or a computer program. But does the child know how to take advantage of these activities? Or in teaching word study, the teacher wants each child to study words that are right at his or her level of development of word knowledge. Is this the case? In guided reading, we want children to read some texts that are moderately challenging and some texts that are easier. Is each child placed with the right materials?
   - *Find out what strategies seem best suited to whole groups of students.* Research shows that schools that are most effective in helping all children learn to read and write are those in which teachers monitor how well instruction is working, and then use this information as they work with other teachers to find ways to improve instruction (Cunningham & Allington, 1994; Taylor, et al., 1999). Teachers may monitor a host of factors, from classroom routines and management strategies to teaching methods, to materials, to ways of working with instructional aides and parent volunteers, to ways of assessing children.

3. **We assess to give feedback to students and their parents.** Findings from assessments should be communicated to children and their parents, so both can work toward the children's success. We assess to:
   - *Show students what they are doing well and what they can do better* by communicating information in a way that helps them become aware of those strategies they are using successfully; this can point the way toward improvements.
   - *Help students set goals for better performance* and monitor their progress toward meeting those goals.
   - *Help parents understand how their children are performing* in learning to read and what they can do to help.

4. **We assess to make sure all students are meeting state standards for learning.** The federal No Child Left Behind law that passed in 2002 mandated that every child in America be tested in reading from grades 3 to 8, with tests developed by the individual states. Beginning in 2014, new tests developed by the Partnership for the Assessment of Readiness for College and Careers (PARCC) will assess students' achievement of the Common Core Standards—at least they will in the 45 states, two territories, and the District of Columbia, where the CCSS have been formally adopted. Because the standards-based tests have significant consequences, many teachers are giving more frequent assessments throughout the year to monitor their students' progress toward meeting the standards on which their state tests are based.

5. **We assess to make decisions on the placement of students in special instructional services.** All children in the United States are entitled by law to special education services as they need them, and they are also entitled to special support to learn the English language, if necessary. Parents may request that their children be screened for such services, but teachers may also identify students who need more support than what is likely to be available to them in the regular classroom. In either case, special screening is called for, including specialized tests that are normally administered by school psychologists. But the teacher's own observational records and assessment results play a useful role in these decisions.

6. **We assess ourselves as teachers or as teachers-to-be.** We make sure our professional knowledge is up to date, and that our practices are serving our students as best they can. We assess our professional knowledge, both to keep ourselves current and to meet teaching licensing requirements.

Approaches to Assessment

With the many different purposes for assessment comes a variety of means to measure and investigate children's reading and writing abilities.

NORM-REFERENCED TESTS   Standardized or norm-referenced tests of reading compare children's performance with that of large numbers of other students. For example, tests such as the Stanford Achievement Test and the California Achievement Test report children's reading performance in comparison to other students at their grade level. The tests are given under rigorously controlled conditions so the results will be comparable. Norm-referenced tests are typically used, along with other data, to inform decisions about placing a child for special reading services. But these tests traditionally have lacked an obvious connection with any school curriculum, so it is difficult to tell what aspect of a school's instruction has contributed or failed to contribute to a child's performance.

STANDARDS-BASED TESTS   Standards-based tests have come about in recent years as individual states have set standards for achievement in reading and other subject areas at each grade level, as they have been required to do by the federal No Child Left Behind Act and will shortly be required for the many states (all but five) that have adopted the Common Core Standards.

Standards-based tests are meant to assess each student's performance on the standards set by the states. Students may be promoted to another grade or held back, depending on their performance, and schools may suffer sanctions if they do not make "adequate yearly progress." Standards-based tests are sometimes called *high-stakes tests*, because a child's performance on such a test can determine whether she or he is promoted to the next grade, and the performance of many children can determine if a school is achieving or underachieving.

CURRICULUM-BASED MEASUREMENT (CBM)   As the term *high-stakes testing* implies, by the time a student takes a standards-based test, it is usually too late for the teacher to do anything more for the student that year. To make sure that children are making good progress toward meeting the standards measured on the high-stakes tests—and indeed, to better teach children to read—many educators are turning to the practice of curriculum-based measurement (Fuchs, Deno, & Mirkin, 1984; Shinn, 1989), a set of practices and instruments that have been borrowed from the special education field. These measures are normally based on the skills students are expected to acquire according to the state standards for learning, but they have the advantage of being given repeatedly—sometimes as often as weekly—throughout the school year so the teacher can still take corrective action as needed. Curriculum-based measurements are very brief samples of behavior, deliberately so because a teacher may have to test 25 or more children individually several times during the year. To test oral reading, for instance, a teacher may have a student read three passages aloud for one minute each and average the speed and accuracy of the reading. Nonetheless, even such brief measures of oral reading have been shown to predict students' later performance on different states' high-stakes standards-based tests. Although curriculum-based measures have many uses, among the most promising is that they facilitate continuous monitoring of a student's performance in reading throughout the year, to ensure that both the student's learning strategies and the teacher's instruction are working well.

Curriculum-based measurements may be designed by the teacher (see Jim Wright's guide on CBM at <www.jimwrightonline.com/pdfdocs/cbaManual.pdf>), or they may be purchased commercially. For grades 5–8, Timothy Rasinski and Nancy Padak (2005) offer a series of Three-Minute Reading Assessments: Word Recognition, Fluency, and Comprehension. Many states are using DIBELS, the Dynamic Indicators of Basic Early Literacy Skills, and studies have shown scores on DIBELS predict later performance on the standards-based tests of some states, including Arizona (Wilson, 2005), Florida (Buck & Torgesen, 2003), North Carolina (Barger, 2003), and Oregon (Shaw & Shaw, 2002).

DIBELS was created with public funds, and it is available for free on the Internet (at <http://dibels.uoregon.edu/index.php>). However, for a fee, the providers of DIBELS offer an electronically based data management and reporting service that keeps track of each child's scores on each part of the test, follows the child's progress on each of several indicators over time, and makes available a number of verbal and graphic ways to display results.

The Developmental Reading Assessment (DRA) is published by Pearson. Based on the model of an Informal Reading Inventory (see below), the DRA provides a range of assessments for screening, diagnosis, and monitoring. For a fee, the DRA enables teachers to manage the test scores online and perform a number of tracking, comparing, and reporting functions (see <www.pearsonschool.com>).

INFORMAL READING INVENTORIES Informal Reading Inventories (IRIs), developed nearly 70 years ago by Emmett Betts (1946), are comprehensive measures of students' reading ability. IRIs are administered to individual children to create diagnostic profiles: a picture of individual readers' word recognition, reading fluency, comprehension, and overall reading levels. In contrast to standardized reading tests, IRIs have not been normed by elaborate field testing with hundreds or thousands of children. Hence they are called "informal" reading inventories.

IRIs are created from samples of grade-level texts, either taken from basal readers at ascending grade levels or written by the test authors and matched to grade levels according to readability formulas. IRIs consist of lists of words and text passages of graduated levels of difficulty—usually from early first grade or preprimer through grade 8 or higher.

Teachers may create their own IRIs, but many good ones are commercially available, including the Qualitative Reading Inventory (Leslie & Caldwell, 2005) and the Classroom Reading Inventory (Silvaroli & Wheelock, 2000). The Developmental Literacy Inventory, written by some of this book's authors (Temple, Crawford, & Gillet, 2009), combines an Informal Reading Inventory with assessments of emergent literacy.

RUNNING RECORDS Developed by Marie Clay (1993) to support her Reading Recovery Program, running records are teacher-made assessment devices administered to individual students to monitor their fluency, word recognition accuracy, and reading levels. Running records are usually carried out in the first two grades with younger readers, with whom they may be used every month or more frequently, both for diagnostic testing and for monitoring.

The teacher chooses simple texts that he or she suspects are at several difficulty levels for the child: one moderately challenging, one easy, and one more challenging. Clay suggests that an easy book be one that the child has read before with the teacher, and of which the child can read more than 95 percent of the words. A moderately challenging text would normally be one that the child had seen before but not studied with the teacher, and whose words the child can read with 90 to 95 percent accuracy. A difficult text would be one the child had not seen, and whose words the child could read with 80 to 89 percent accuracy.

Teach It! 25

Repeated Reading

New Literacies

Research DIBELS online and describe what you've found.

The teacher's role is to observe carefully and record what the child says as she or he reads the book. It is best to construct a form for recording the student's performance, like the one shown in Figure 11.1, but in a pinch you may sit close enough to the child to see the words as they are read, and make notes on a piece of paper.

Figure 11.1   Running Record Sheet

Name: _____				Date: _____	
School: _____				Teacher: _____	

Text Titles	Running Words Errors	Error Rate	Accuracy	Self-Correction Rate
Easy (100%–95%)		1:	%	1:
Instructional (94%–90%)		1:	%	1:
Hard (89% and lower)		1:	%	1:

Analysis of Errors and Self-Corrections

Information used or neglected [Meaning (M), Structure or Syntax (S), Visual (V)]

Easy: _____

_____

Instructional: _____

_____

Hard: _____

_____

Teacher Observations:				
Analysis of Errors and Self-Corrections				
			Information used	
Page	E	SC	E	SC
			MSV	MSV

The running record shown in Figure 11.1 allows the teacher to observe the following:

- The error rate
- The self-correction rate
- The kinds of miscues (incorrect word identifications) that the child makes: visual, structural, or meaning-based
- Other behaviors, such as the direction in which the student reads, the number of repetitions of words, and so on.

The characterizing of miscues as *meaning-based, structural, or visual* is intended to bring to light the kind of information a child is tracking in a text. Clay writes:

Meaning: Does the child use meaning (M)? If what he reads makes sense, even though it is inaccurate, then he is probably applying his knowledge of the world to his reading.

Structure: Is what he said possible in an English sentence (S is for syntactically appropriate)? If it is, his oral language is probably influencing his responding. If it is not . . . [he] is paying close attention to detail, or to word by word reading. . . .

Visual information: Does he use visual information (V) from the letters and words or the layout of print? [In a footnote, Clay adds, "Whether the child is relating visual information to sounds (phonological information) or to orthography (information about spelling) is a refinement of using visual information not distinguished in this analysis at this time."] (Clay, 1993, p. 31)

A running record is a quick way to verify that a particular book is written at a child's instructional or independent reading level. It should be supplemented, though, by other kinds of assessments when you need more detail on a child's word knowledge (see Chapter 5). Running records are used most often with beginning readers; however, when children reach a level of reading where both fluency and comprehension become issues—and teachers are rightly becoming concerned about both of these even with young readers—you will want to use measures for those aspects of reading, too. Many teachers follow a running record with a retelling task (i.e., the child is asked to retell what he or she just read, and the teacher may tick off items from a pre-prepared list of main ideas and details) (see the World of Reading feature).

AUTHENTIC ASSESSMENT Sheila Valencia and her colleagues (Valencia, Hiebert, & Afflerbach, 1993) popularized the idea of the authentic assessment of literacy. Authentic assessment addresses the problem that most assessment methods have students carry out contrived tasks that are not always representative of what they do in purposeful reading and writing. Contrived tasks may not yield the full picture, including what they have achieved, how they think about literacy, their interests and motivations, preferences, strategies, or likes and dislikes. Authentic assessment thus involves both informal and structured observations (sometimes called *kidwatching*) and work-sampling, including portfolios. Authentic assessment also includes the use of rubrics.

KIDWATCHING *Kidwatching* is a term coined by influential literacy educator, Yetta Goodman (Goodman, 1985; Owocki & Goodman, 2002), to refer to a host of observations, ranging from observations quickly captured on stick-on notes to home visits, to more formal assessments.

Kidwatching Is Informed Teachers learn more from observing children in the daily life of the classroom if they know a good deal about language and literacy processes, as well as how children talk, read, think, investigate, and interact with each other and the world.

The World of Reading

The Three-Cueing System

Both the Reading Miscue Inventory and running records highlight the importance of the *three-cueing system* in children's word recognition. The three-cueing system is the idea that children use visual (or graphophonic), structural (or syntactic), and meaning-based (or semantic) information to recognize new words.

There is no doubt that readers use the surrounding context to help identify a word. For example, any time you administer an Informal Reading Inventory, you expect students to recognize more words when the words appear in the context of meaningful passages than when they appear in isolation, such as on lists (see Table 11.2).

The argument arises over *when* the context matters. In the early days of the Reading Miscue Inventory, its advocates thought readers read words by sampling enough visual information from the text to create a sense of the meaning. Once they had a sense of the meaning, they needed only to sample the print to confirm or disconfirm what they thought the text must be saying. As long as they could assume what the text must be saying from the meaning that was forming in their heads, they had a reduced need to take in the visual information (the strings of letters) from the page. When it was unclear what the text was saying, they focused on more of the letters in the words.

But that view of reading aroused a chorus of criticisms. Perfetti (1985), for example, found that readers always read the words and the letters, and the most fluent comprehenders were the best at word recognition, because fluent word recognition freed up the brain's available attention for making sense of the text.

All of this matters because if you believe readers should rely heavily on context to read words, you are more likely to emphasize that approach as you help struggling readers. And if you believe that well-developed word identification skills, including decoding ability, are the key to successful reading, you are more likely to teach accordingly.

The National Reading Panel (2000) clearly endorsed the view that reading requires the reading of words, and not guessing words from context, and readers need to know the relations between letters and sounds to help them read words. Marilyn Adams (1998), a member of the National Reading Panel, has elsewhere expressed doubts about the idea of the three-cueing system, first because so many educators seem to follow it and yet nobody is sure where it came from, and second, because the model doesn't underscore the primary importance of reading words or give much guidance to the teacher on what kind of correction is best if a child depends too much on one cueing system versus another. Other educators strongly argue that the larger context of information should be kept in mind when teaching reading (see Margaret Moustafa's summary of these articles at <http://instructional1.calstatela.edu/mmousta/Research_on_Effective_Reading_InstructionK-4.htm>).

So when you pick up a Reading Miscue Inventory or a running record, or nod your head when you read an article about the three-cueing system, controversy may be lurking just around the corner.

Kidwatching Is Nonjudgmental Teachers record events or pieces of language as they occur, without filtering them through judgments. Planning what to do on the basis of the collected evidence will happen later, preferably after many different kinds of information have been collected. Here is an example of one kidwatcher's observation:

> *Notes on Erin (11/19) age 5-1/2 in the library corner: Erin is turning the pages of Fruits Good to Eat in order, at a regular pace. She gets to the page with a pineapple on it, looks at it closely, turns to Robin, and asks, "Is this a pineapple?" Robin replies, "I think so, but let's ask Ms. B." They come to me. I ask Erin what she thinks, and she says, "I think so, but what does this say [pointing to the print]?" When I ask her what she thinks, she says, "I think it says pineapple because that's in the picture and there's a p." (Goodman, 2006)*

Note that this kind of written observation is also called an *anecdotal record*.

Table 11.2   Scoring Word Recognition on an Informal Reading Inventory

	INDEPENDENT READING LEVEL	INSTRUCTIONAL READING LEVEL	FRUSTRATION READING LEVEL
Word Identification in Isolation	90% +	70%–89%	Below 70%
Word Identification in Context	97% +	90%–96%	Below 90%

Kidwatching Uses Diverse Sources of Information   Goodman (2006) writes, "Kidwatchers use a variety of tools to document their observations, including informal conversations, formal interviews, check sheets, observation forms, field notes, portfolios, and home visits." Using many sources of information, including not only the teacher's observations but also the child's and the family's points of view, as well as more formal assessments, allows teachers to make small adjustments—and sometimes larger ones—to instruction and classroom procedures.

Teach It! 32

Dual-Entry Diary

PORTFOLIOS   Portfolios are collections of children's works gathered according to the objectives of the teacher's instruction. They may be maintained by the teacher as a way of keeping a diverse collection of artifacts related to a child's progress in learning to read and write. But usually they are maintained in collaboration with each child. The teacher and the child should decide in advance the sorts of items that should be kept in the portfolio. These might include:

- Lists of books read
- A reading journal
- Repeated reading score sheets
- Written works chosen as indicative of the child's best work and range of work during a particular time period
- A list of topics for the child's writing
- Learning logs
- Running records

Periodically—at least once a month or once each marking period—the teacher schedules a conference or interview with the child. Ahead of the conversation, both the child and the teacher should look through the portfolio to find signs of progress and areas that need work. During their conversation, the child describes what he or she has learned during this period and sets goals for improvement during the next period. The teacher may ask questions to find out what things the child likes and doesn't like to read, what strategies he or she is using in reading, and aspects of the reading instruction that might be changed. The teacher makes suggestions to help the child learn.

RUBRICS   According to Andrade (2002)*,

> A rubric is a scoring tool that lists the criteria for a piece of work, or "what counts" (for example, purpose, organization, details, voice, and mechanics are often what count in a piece of writing); it also articulates gradations of quality for each criterion, from excellent to poor.

Rubrics have the advantage of allowing teachers to observe and evaluate an authentic performance, such as a child's oral reading, or a piece written for a real purpose other than testing. They also have the advantage of pointing out to the students the aspects of reading and writing that we consider important. Especially when rubrics are shared with a student before he or she carries out a task, the rubrics tell the child what the important tasks are, and how to do them well.

Rubrics may be already designed by educational experts, such as the Multidimensional Fluency Scale for measuring reading fluency and the Six Traits rubric for evaluating writing. Rubrics may also be developed by teachers, or even by the students themselves. When students participate in designing a rubric, they may become more strategic in reading—that is, they have a better idea about how they should try to perform.

It helps to think of a rubric like a chart. Each row names an important aspect of performance on a task, and in the boxes under each column are descriptions that range from unsatisfactory to satisfactory to excellent performance on that aspect.

---

*Originally published in *Educational Leadership*, December 1996/January 1997 | Volume 54 | Number 4 Teaching for Authentic Student Performance Pages 14–17. © Heidi Andrade, Used by permission of Heidi Andrade. <http://www.ascd.org/publications/educational-leadership/dec96/vol54/num04/Understanding-Rubrics.aspx>

Terms Used in Testing

Students' performance on norm-referenced tests are usually reported in three ways. First, they are given *raw scores*, which simply report the number or the percentage of items on the test they answered correctly. Raw scores mean little, though, without the understanding of how a particular child's score compares with those of other children in the same age group. Therefore, scores are presented in two additional ways. *Percentile scores* are based on a 99-point scale, and they tell a child what percentage of the children in a comparison group received a lower score than his. *Stanine* scores may also be used to report performance on a test, especially when they are also used to eliminate the fine distinctions reported in percentiles that don't mean much. Stanine scores are reported in whole numbers on a 9-point scale. The spread of scores represented by each number is based on a *normal curve of distribution*. Scores of 4, 5, and 6 are average. Scores of 1, 2, and 3 are below average. Scores of 7, 8, and 9 are above average. *Grade-equivalent scores* are what they sound like: indications of what grade-level material an average reader would read at an instructional or independent level based on her performance on this test. Thus if a fourth grader's grade equivalent score on a reading test is 7.5, that means he scored the way an average seventh grader would have scored on the material in that test. (But that doesn't mean the child is ready to be promoted to seventh grade; just because he read material on a test intended for fourth graders like an average seventh grader would doesn't mean that he will be able to read seventh-grade materials like an average seventh grader.)

Tests are often described in terms of their validity and reliability. *Validity* refers to the extent that the tests measure what they claim to measure. Because all tests take a sample of a child's performance and claim to generalize from that sample to the child's more global level of performance, it is important to know if the test really does tell you what it says it does.

Educators often speak of different kinds of validity.

- *Content validity* is the degree to which a test measures what it says it does. If a test of reading comprehension asks students to answer questions about a passage after reading it, that test can be said to have content validity because answering questions is a reasonable demonstration of comprehension. But if the test asks students to locate all the words in a passage beginning with *B*, it would not have content validity as a test of comprehension.

- *Predictive validity*, also called *assessment-criterion relationship validity* (Linn & Gronlund, 2000), refers to the power of the test to predict the student's future performance on related tasks. Predictive validity is of great importance with screening assessments and monitoring assessments because a key purpose of those measures is to use students' present performance on early reading tasks to predict their future reading ability. Note, too, that the predictive validity of a test may depend on when—that is, with what age child—it is used. For example, a test of phoneme awareness given to five-year-olds is not a very good predictor of future reading performance (Snow, Burns, & Griffin, 1998). The same test given in first grade may have greater predictive validity because a greater number of six-year-olds versus five-year-olds display some phonemic awareness.

Reliability has to do with the likelihood that the results of the test are stable and dependable; that is, if the same test were given to the same child by two different people, or on two different days, would the results be similar? There are different ways reliability is used.

- *Test-retest reliability*, in which the same students are given the same test within a short interval, to see if the results are similar

- *Split-half reliability*, in which samples of a student's performance on different items of the same test are compared with each other
- *Inter-rater reliability*, in which an instrument such as a rubric is used by different raters to assess the same student, and the results are compared

The terms *validity* and *reliability* are usually applied to standardized tests, but they are worth considering regardless of the kind of assessment being done. Since 2002, the federal No Child Left Behind Act has required that assessments be scientifically validated, which means that assessment instruments must have demonstrated validity and reliability. But a caution is in order—many valuable ways of collecting and making judgments about children's reading and writing do not have demonstrated validity and reliability. Informal observation of students' reading is one; all types of Informal Reading Inventories are another.

- *Formative and Summative Assessments.* Formative assessment is done while instruction is going on, in order to see how well the instruction is working. Summative assessment is done and after instruction is completed to see what the instruction accomplished.

Assessing Readers at Different Levels of Development

We need to assess and monitor many things with respect to what children are learning about literacy.

Phonics and Phonological Awareness

Why is it important that children understand what literacy is about, and what books are for?

Emergent Readers

Emergent readers are usually preschool, kindergarten, and first-grade children who are developing concepts about language and print and knowledge of the alphabetic writing system that form the foundation on which later reading is built. Children develop all these concepts at different rates and to different extents. Giving children special, finely tuned intervention early on can help many of them avoid reading failure and make progress as readers and writers. Assessment of children's early literacy is essential. So what do we need to know? Effective early literacy assessments focus on several areas.

- *Concepts about print.* The more developed holistic sense children have of what literacy is about, the better they will be able to focus their attention on the details they must understand in order to read. Without an orienting sense of what literacy is and what books are for, early literacy instruction may be confusing for some children.
- *Knowledge of the alphabet.* Children must know many letters of the alphabet to begin to develop the ability to read. Knowledge of the alphabet is an indicator of the amount of print exposure they have had (the more letters they know, the more print they are likely to have seen). But knowing letters is also important in itself because the more letters they know, the more successfully they can explore how print and speech go together. There is a difference between letter identification and letter retrieval. Because some readers with disabilities have difficulty naming letters quickly (Katzir & Pare-Blagoev, 2006), a number of assessments of early literacy include a timed letter identification task.

- *Awareness of sounds in language.* Writing represents spoken language, and in English, writing represents language at the level of words, onsets and rimes, and phonemes, as we saw in Chapter 3. The problem is that in speech, children can use language without thinking about it; but when they learn to read and write, children must be conscious of words, rimes, and phonemes. Those aspects must be real for young learners, because they will need to think hard about the relations between spoken units of spoken language and units of print.

- *Knowledge of some words.* Virtually all children in America are exposed to print before they begin formal reading instruction. Many of them learn to identify some words: their own names, names of fast food restaurants, words from favorite book titles. The number of words they can identify while still prereaders is a sign of emergent literacy.

- *Listening comprehension.* Children need to have receptive language developed to the degree that they can follow books read aloud to them by the teacher and also comprehend texts themselves when they become readers. Some, but not all, emergent literacy assessment instruments include measures of listening comprehension.

- *Knowledge of letter-to-sound correspondences (phonics).* Children need to develop ideas about the relations between letters and sounds to learn to read. Children's understanding of letter-to-sound correspondences can be assessed beginning in kindergarten and continuing through first grade. (Phonics knowledge will continue to be assessed in beginning readers and in older struggling readers.)

Phonics and Phonological Awareness

When can children's understanding of letter-to-sound correspondences begin to be assessed?

Contemporary assessment of early literacy, then, tracks the development of concepts about print, awareness of sounds, awareness of letters, knowledge of words, and (sometimes) listening comprehension.

MEASURES OF EMERGENT LITERACY Teacher-made measures of emergent literacy can be fashioned after the Early Reading Screening Inventory (Morris, 2000) and the Print Concepts Assessment (after Clay, 1999). The Early Reading Screening Inventory, as the name implies, has been widely used to identify young readers in early first grade who will need additional help to learn to read. Other emergent literacy assessment programs are in use around the United States, some of them promoted by individual states. The Phonological Awareness Literacy Survey (PALS) <http://pals.virginia.edu/> is provided to school districts in Virginia and is widely used elsewhere as both a screening and a monitoring tool. The Illinois Snapshot of Early Literacy is promoted by that state as a screening tool. The Texas Education Agency developed the Texas Primary Reading Inventory <www.tpri.org/About/>, with versions for kindergarten through third grades, which can be administered as a screening, diagnosis, and monitoring tool.

At the University of Oregon, the Dynamic Indicators of Basic Literacy Skills (DIBELS) was developed with a federal grant and is available to teachers for free online. This test, which can be used as a screening, diagnosis, and a monitoring tool, begins with a preschool version that assesses initial sounds or onset fluency. At the kindergarten level are added tests of phonemic segmentation fluency, letter naming fluency, and nonsense word reading fluency. These continue through first grade, where an oral reading fluency measure is also added, and continues through third grade. These are called fluency tests because children's responses are timed, and the speed of the child's responses is noted in addition to accuracy (see <http://dibels.uoregon.edu/measures.php>).

Emergent readers can be young children who are developing a foundation upon which later reading is built.

Assessing Emerging Readers

In this section we will look first at the assessment of children's concepts about print. Next, we will turn to assessing children's ability to break speech down into small units (phonological awareness). Then, we will look at oral language development, and finally, at comprehension.

Assessing Print Concepts

CCSS

• Foundational Skills 1: Print Concepts

Marie Clay's Concepts About Print Test measures:

- Book orientation knowledge.
- Principles involving the directional arrangement of print on the page.
- The knowledge that print, not the picture, contains the story.
- Children's understanding of important reading terminology such as *word*, *letter*, *beginning of the sentence*, and *top of the page*.
- Understanding of simple punctuation marks.

Assessment of print concepts can be done with a simple illustrated children's book, so long as the child being tested has not seen it before. Marie Clay's Concepts About Print Test has two specially made books (*Sand* and *Stones*), but teachers can get much of the flavor of the procedure with a book of their own choosing. Here are the steps:

1. *Knowledge of the Layout of Books.* Hand the child a book, with the spine facing the child, and say, "Show me the front of the book." Note whether the child correctly identifies the front.

2. *Knowledge That Print, Not Pictures, Is What We Read.* Open the book to a double spread with print on one page and a picture on the other. Then say, "Show me where I begin reading." Watch carefully to see if the child points to the print or the picture. If the pointing gesture is vague, say, "Where, exactly?"

3. *Directional Orientation of Print on the Page.* Stay on the same set of pages, and after the child points at some spot on the printed page, say, "Show me with your finger where I go next." Then observe whether the child sweeps his finger across the printed line from left to right or moves it in some other direction.

   Then ask, "Where do I go from there?" and observe whether the child correctly makes the return sweep to the left and drops down one line.

   Note that a correct direction pattern is like this:

   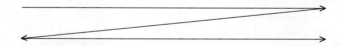

   If the child indicates some other directional pattern, make a note of it.

4. *Knowledge of the Concepts of* **Beginning** *and* **End.** Turning now to a new page, say, "Point to the beginning of the story on this page" and then "Point to the end of the story on this page." Observe whether the child interprets both requests properly.

5. *Knowledge of the Terms* **Top** *and* **Bottom.** Turning to another pair of pages that have print on one page and a picture on the other, point to the middle of the printed page and say, "Show me the bottom of the page" and then "Show me the top of the page." Then point to the middle of the picture and say, "Show me the top of the picture" and then "Show me the bottom of the picture." Note whether the child responds accurately to all four requests.

6. **Knowledge of the Terms** Word **and** Letter. Now hand the child two blank index cards and say, "Put these cards on the page so that just one word shows between them" and then "Now move them so that two words show between them. Now move them again so that one letter shows between them" and then "Now move them so that two letters show between them." Make note of the child's response to all four requests.

7. **Knowledge of Uppercase and Lowercase Letters.** Find a page with both uppercase and lowercase versions of at least two letters. Point to a capital letter with your pencil and say, "Show me a little letter that is the same as this one." Next point to a lowercase letter and say, "Now point to a capital letter that is the same as this one." Repeat this procedure with other pairs of letters.

8. **Knowledge of Punctuation.** Turn to a page that has a period, an exclamation point, a question mark, a comma, and a set of quotation marks. Pointing to each one in turn, ask, "What is this? What is it for?"

It is advisable to make up a record sheet that provides for the quick recording of information yielded by the assessment.

ASSESSING ALPHABET KNOWLEDGE   When testing students' alphabet knowledge, ask them to recognize all of the letters of the alphabet in both uppercase and lowercase. We also ask them to write all of the letters once each, without specifying uppercase or lowercase. The letters are always presented in a scrambled sequence so that the children cannot use serial order as a cue to identifying a letter.

For a Letter Recognition Inventory, prepare a sheet of randomly arranged lower- and uppercase letters (see Figure 11.2). That is the version to show to the student. Prepare another copy to use as a record sheet. As you proceed from left to right across the line, point to each letter and ask the child to identify it. Enter on the record sheet only a notation of what letters were misidentified or unnamed. Then, call out the letters slowly and ask the child to write each one. Score a letter correct whether it is written in uppercase or lowercase.

ASSESSING THE CONCEPT OF WORD   To assess a student's concept of word, follow this procedure designed by Morris (1998).

Teach the student to memorize the poem shown below orally, *without showing her the written version.*

My little dog Petunia
Is a very strange dog.
She bellows like a mule
But she leaps like a frog.

Figure 11.2   Alphabet Recognition Assessment—Student Version

```
R   M   P   G   F   A   Z   S   T   N   B   I   W

Q   O   K   X   C   U   L   V   J   D   Y   E   H

+++++++++++++++++++++++++++++++++++++++++++++++++++++++++++

r   m   p   g   f   a   z   s   t   n   b   l   w

q   o   k   x   c   u   l   v   j   d   y   e   h

+++++++++++++++++++++++++++++++++++++++++++++++++++++++++++
```

Figure 11.3   Concept of Word Assessment

Concept of Word Assessment

Student: _____   Grade: _____

Teacher: _____   School: _____

Date: _____   Examiner: _____

	Voice-Pointing	Word Identification
My little <u>dog</u> <u>Petunia</u> 1 2	_____	_____
Is a <u>very</u> <u>strange</u> dog. 1 2	_____	_____
She <u>bellows</u> <u>like</u> a mule 1 2	_____	_____
But <u>she</u> leaps like a <u>frog</u>. 1 2	_____	_____

Voice Pointing: _____ _____ (of 4)

Word Identification: _____ _____ (of 8)

Total Concept of Word (Voice-pointing plus Word identification): _____ (of 12)

+++

Once the student can recite the words from memory, show her the written poem and explain that these written words say the poem just learned.

Now, read through the poem at a slow natural rate, pointing to each word with your finger as you read it. Explain that you want the student to read the poem the way you did, but one line at a time.

Ask the student to say the first line, pointing to each word as she says it. On the record sheet shown in Figure 11.3, enter a score of 1 under *voice-pointing* if she points to every word in that line correctly, and a score of 0 if she incorrectly points to any word in that line. Next, ask the student to point to the word *little*. Enter a score of 1 under *word identification* if she points to it and 0 if she does not. Now ask her to point to the word *Petunia*. Enter a score of 1 under *word identification* if she points to it and 0 if she does not.

Now go to the second line and repeat the process, testing first the student's voice-pointing and then the student's word identification. Award a score of 1 if the student points to every word just as she says it, and a 0 if the student makes any errors. Then ask her to point to *very* and then to *strange*. Award a score of 1 for each word the student correctly points to, and a 0 for each error. Repeat these instructions for lines 3 and 4.

ASSESSING PHONOLOGICAL AWARENESS   Phonological awareness—the awareness of speech sounds at the phoneme level—can be indicated may ways. They include

CCSS

• Foundational Skills 2: Phonological Awareness

CCSS

• Foundational Skills 3: Phonics and Word Recognition

comparing phonemes, isolating them, adding them, deleting them, and separating them. Here we will demonstrate phoneme segmentation.

Phoneme Segmentation   The Yopp/Singer test of phoneme segmentation is done as follows. You say:

> *Today we're going to play a word game. I'm going to say a word, and I want you to break the word apart. You are going to tell me each sound of the word in order. For example, if I say old, you will say o-l-d. Let's try a few words together.* (Yopp, 1988, p. 166)

You follow with three more demonstration words: *ride*, *go*, and *man*. Praise the child if she is right, and correct her if she is wrong. After the trials, read the 22 words to the child, and have her break each word apart as it is read. You should give praise or correction after each word. Note that the number of phonemes or separate sounds in each word is given in parentheses after the word. Score each word "1" if the child separately pronounces all of the phonemes in the word, or "0" if she does not. The words are shown in Figure 11.4.

Assessing Phonemic Awareness by Means of Invented Spelling   Another way to observe whether a first-grade child has phonemic awareness is to ask him to spell words that he does not already know. When a child is asked to spell unknown words, he must rely upon his *invented spelling*, the inner capacity to forge connections between letters and

Figure 11.4   Words for the Yopp-Singer Phoneme Segmentation Test

---

Words for the Yopp-Singer Phoneme Segmentation Test

Student: _____   School: _____

Date: _____   Examiner: _____

1. dog (3) _____	12. lay (2) _____
2. keep (3) _____	13. race (3) _____
3. fine (3) _____	14. zoo (2) _____
4. no (2) _____	15. three (3) _____
5. she (2) _____	16. job (3) _____
6. wave (3) _____	17. in (2) _____
7. grew (3) _____	18. ice (2) _____
8. that (3) _____	19. at (2) _____
9. red (3) _____	20. top (3) _____
10. me (2) _____	21. by (2) _____
11. sat (3) _____	22. do (2) _____

Score (number correct) _____ /22 Percentage score: _____

Figure 11.5   A Spelling Test of Phoneme Awareness

A Spelling Test of Phoneme Awareness

bite   (three phonemes: BIT = 3 points; BT = 2 points, BRRY, etc. = 1 point)

seat   (three phonemes: SET or CET = 3 points; ST, CT = 2 points)

dear   (three phonemes: DER = 3 points; DIR or DR = 2 points)

bones   (four phonemes: BONS or BONZ = 4 points; BOS or BOZ = 3 points)

mint   (four phonemes: MENT or MINT = 4 points; MET or MIT = 3 points; MT = 2 points)

rolled   (four phonemes: ROLD = 4 points; ROL or ROD = 3 points)

race   (three phonemes: RAS, RAC, or RAEC = 3 points, RC or RS = 2 points)

roar   (three phonemes: ROR or ROER = 3 points; RR = 2 points)

beast   (four phonemes: BEST = 4 points; BES or BST = 3 points; BS or BT = 2 points)

groan   (four phonemes: GRON = 4 points; GRN = 3 points; GN = 2 points)

TOTAL: _____ / 35 points, for 35 phonemes represented.

---

sounds. Children have an amazing intuitive ability to invent spellings, and we can learn much about their word knowledge by looking at their invented productions.

A procedure for testing phonemic segmentation (after Morris, 1993), then, is to have the child spell the list of words in Figure 11.5 as you call them out. Then you can count the number of phonemes the child reasonably attempted to represent. (Guides to scoring each word are presented in parentheses.)

Explain to the child that you are going to ask him to spell some words you know he doesn't know how to spell. He will have to figure out the spellings as best he can. After you call out each word (at least twice, and as many more times as he requests), ask him to try to spell each sound in the word. If he says he can't, ask him to listen to the way the word begins. What sound does it start with? Ask him to write down a letter for that sound and letters for any other sounds he can hear. If the student is not sure how to spell a sound, ask him to write a little dash (—).

After reading all 10 words (fewer if the test seems too arduous for a particular child), count the number of reasonable letters the child wrote for each word and compare that to the number of phonemes in the word. A child who consistently writes three or four letters that show some reasonable connection to the sounds in the word appears to be able to segment phonemes. Assuming the child is making an effort, if he writes nothing or strings together many letters indiscriminately we assume he is not yet able to segment phonemes. And if he writes one or two reasonable letters per word, we assume he is just beginning to segment phonemes. You can calculate a score for phonemic segmentation by scoring each word according to the guide at the right of each word and then comparing the total number of points the child receives to the total possible.

WORD RECOGNITION   Emergent readers can often recognize a few words. The following assessment of word identification (after Morris, 1998) tests both high-frequency words and decodable words.

Show the student the lists of words in Figure 11.6 and ask her to identify them.

Figure 11.6 Word Recognition for Emergent Literacy

Word Recognition for Emergent Literacy

First List	Second List
bed	and
sad	good
ride	you
pin	the
pole	one
tub	come
got	is
duck	said
ball	play
rule	look

Mark the student's responses on a response sheet such as the one shown in Figure 11.7. Award the student one point for each word the child can name correctly.

"ROAMING AROUND THE KNOWN." How accurate are all of these measures? According to Snow et al. (1998), the correlations between the component measures listed earlier in this section and children's later success in learning to read are in the 30 to 50 percent range. Scores in this range suggest that the factors are important in reading, but there is a very real chance that a child will be more or less successful in learning to read than these tests predict. With these limitations in mind, prudent teachers avoid making important decisions about children's education on the basis of one of these tests alone. Many use the practice of following the testing with "Roaming around the Known" (Clay, 1993); that is, taking the findings from the assessments as suggestions only, and teaching the child for several days to see how she or he responds to actual instruction—in other words, teaching with the idea that the assessments may very well be wrong.

Beginning Readers and Beyond

Beginning readers are starting to read words in connected text. Just as it is important to know that they have their emergent literacy concepts and abilities in place, it is also critical to know if each child is making progress in all aspects of beginning reading. These aspects include word recognition—including having a sight vocabulary stored in memory, decoding skills so that the child can read a word he didn't know before, and the ability to use context to help identify words. Their reading fluency—their accuracy, rate, and intonation—needs to develop apace as well. Their vocabulary should be growing by thousands of words each year, and they will need to learn vocabulary from reading. Comprehension is the ultimate goal of reading, and we want to know how this ability is growing, too. As we saw in Chapters 6 and 7, comprehension is a complex of many factors including having and using world knowledge, getting main ideas, making inferences, having metacognition

Figure 11.7 Word Identification Response Sheet

Word Identification Response Sheet

Student: _____ School: _____

Date: _____ Examiner: _____

Decodable Words   High-Frequency Words

bed   _____   and   _____

sad   _____   good   _____

ride   _____   you   _____

pin   _____   the   _____

pole   _____   one   _____

tub   _____   come   _____

got   _____   is   _____

duck   _____   said   _____

ball   _____   play   _____

rule   _____   look   _____

Total _____ /10   Total _____ /10

++

---

or cognitive monitoring—that is, knowing if the text is making sense—and following the patterns of different kinds of fictional and informational texts to construct meaning. We also care about their attitudes toward reading and what kind of text and how much of it they read. But one measure that combines all of these factors is their reading levels.

READING LEVELS: INDEPENDENT, INSTRUCTIONAL, FRUSTRATION It is possible to measure students' *reading levels*, the levels of text they can read for different purposes. To talk about reading levels implies two things: that texts have levels of difficulty and that readers have levels of ability. To speak of levels of difficulty of texts implies that some are written on a first-grade level, some on a second-grade level, and so on. These levels of difficulty are referred to as *readability*, and we will say more about that later. When we speak of the reading levels of individual readers, it helps to ask what the reading task is: Will they be studying a book in a group under the teacher's supervision, reading a textbook for homework, or reading for pleasure? Depending on the answers to those questions, it is proper to speak not of one reading level but three: the independent level, the instructional level, and the frustration level.

Independent Reading Level If the student is to read material on his or her own, without the support of a teacher or other more skilled readers, then the material should fall within the student's independent level of reading ability. In material written at the student's independent level, the student should encounter no more than three or four unknown words in a hundred and should enjoy nearly total comprehension.

Books that fall within students' independent level include those students choose to read for pleasure and textbooks they use independently for homework. Regardless of a student's grade placement, if the books are above the student's independent level, then the student should be given easier books or should be offered support for reading such as buddy reading, study guides, or recorded text. Conversely, teachers sometimes have to prod students to read more challenging material that falls within their independent level.

Instructional Reading Level   In the classroom, teachers often work with students using material that is moderately challenging for them so they will learn from the supported practice. Material used for this purpose should fall within the student's instructional level of reading ability. Such material presents the student with unknown words at a rate of up to one in ten, and language and concepts that are not fully comprehended—at least not at first. The intention is that with guided practice in materials written at the instructional level, students will learn the unknown words and come to comprehend the once-challenging language and concepts. The instructional level corresponds to what Russian psychologist Vygotsky (1976) called the *zone of proximal development*, the area of moderate challenge that is just at the threshold of a reader's growing abilities. It is here that teachers most often practice scaffolded instruction, providing temporary support, including teaching strategies that will help the student learn on his or her own in the future.

Again, a particular student's instructional level often falls above or below that student's grade placement level. Because of the value of working in moderately challenging materials when teaching a student to read, it is very important to locate a student's instructional level wherever it may fall.

Frustration Reading Level   If the material is too challenging—that is, if it contains more than one unfamiliar word in ten, and language and concepts that substantially resist comprehension—the material is said to be written at the student's frustration level. The frustration level is not actually a reading level because students do not practice successful reading there. It is used rather to define the limits of a student's instructional level. Teachers can assign reading material during closely supervised instructional tasks that approach, but do not cross into, the frustration level.

As the name implies, frustration level text is so challenging to a student that the challenge of reading it is burdensome and disagreeable. Students may actually progress faster in learning to read and learning to spell when they are placed in instructional-level text, even though that is easier than frustration-level text.

Students' reading levels are often determined by administering an Informal Reading Inventory. When an IRI is used, it will normally tell you how many errors a student can make in each part to be classified as independent, instructional, or frustrated at that level. If an IRI is not used, you can still get a rough idea of a student's reading level if you know the reading levels of several short texts. Have the child read a passage of at least 150 words. Mark each reading error as an *omission* (leaving out a word), a *substitution* (reading a word other than the word supplied in the text or misreading the word in the text), or an *insertion* (adding a word or words that were not in the text). Each counts as one error every time it occurs. *Proper names* that are misread count as one error, regardless how many times they are misread. *Reversals* (reading two words in the wrong order) count as one error. Repetitions do not count as errors, and neither do self-corrections or long pauses.

Using those criteria, here is how the scores are interpreted:

Independent level: 97 to 100 percent of the words are read correctly.

Instructional level: 90 to 96 percent of the words are read correctly.

Frustration level: Fewer than 90 percent of the words are read correctly.

These criteria are taken from Betts (1946).

READING LEVELS AND READABILITY   Applying the concept of reading levels that was just presented, a teacher might test a particular third-grade student and find that his independent level is second grade, his instructional level is third grade, and his frustration level is fourth grade. For this information to be useful to the teacher, we must assume that reading material is available that is written at the second-, third-, and fourth-grade reading levels. This is a reasonably safe assumption, but there are some problems with it. Most importantly, we now know that whether a reader comprehends a particular text depends to some extent on what is already in the reader's head and not solely on what is in the text (Alexander, 2000; Pearson & Anderson, 1985). Two third-grade readers may read a text about a game of basketball, and even though they have equivalent reading abilities, if one happens to be a passionate player of the game, that student may understand the text better than the other student.

The determination that a text is written at a particular grade level is usually based on surface features of the text, such as the length of the sentences and the number of syllables in the words. The readability level might also be determined by trialing the text with a group of sample readers of different ages. Either way, a particular reader may have a harder or easier time reading a particular text, depending on that reader's background knowledge of, and interest in, the topic of the text.

MEASURING READABILITY. In the 1940s, an Austrian immigrant to the United States wrote a doctoral dissertation in which he developed a mathematical formula for estimating the readability level of written language. Soon Rudolph Flesch's formula and many others like it were being used to help publishers adjust the level of difficulty of their products, be they textbooks for children, newspapers and magazines for the general reader, or government publications aimed at special audiences such as farmers, cooks, or sanitation workers. Now readability formulas are available for most of the world's languages.

One of the simplest readability devices for English was developed by Edward Fry, now a retired professor of literacy at Rutgers University in the United States. Fry's procedure is to take three separate 100-word samples from a work to be studied, count the number of sentences in each sample to the tenth place, and then count the number of syllables in each sample. The sentence counts and syllable counts are averaged, and the results are plotted on the graph presented in Figure 11.8.

Fry's graph resembles other formulas in that it considers the length of sentences and the length of words as the variables that affect readability. The logic here is that longer sentences tend to be more grammatically complex, and more grammatically complex sentences are harder to read. Longer words tend to be more sophisticated, more rare, and encountered later in schooling. Combining the two measures of sentence length and

Figure 11.8
Fry Readability Graph

Source: Fry Readability Graph, from Edward Fry, *Elementary Reading Instruction* © 1977, by The McGraw-Hill Companies, Inc. Reprinted by permission.

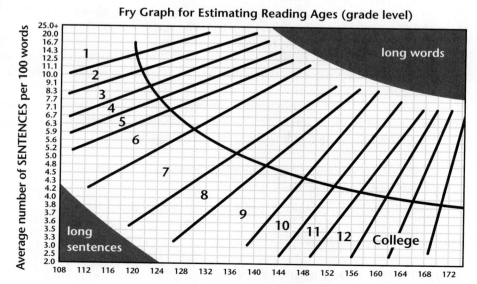

Fry Graph for Estimating Reading Ages (grade level)

Average number of SENTENCES per 100 words

Average number of SYLLABLES per 100 words

Teach It!

Refer to the Teach It! appendix at the end of the book for further activities you can use to reinforce concepts discussed in this chapter.

The Fry Readability Graph

Try the Fry readability graph on a sample of this text. For a short exercise, instead of taking three 100-word passages and averaging the results, you can take just one 100-word passage. Count off 100 words, then count the number of syllables in that sample. Count the number of sentences to the tenth place. Plot the results on the graph. Are you surprised at the results? Try the readability graph on a children's book. Try it on an article from your daily newspaper. If you can, find a memorandum to parents from a local school and try it on that. Try it on the warranty statement of the next electronic item you buy, or on the user's agreement of the next software program you download.

If you are in a classroom, have students bring in some written materials that come in the mail at their house (with their parents' permission, of course!). Have them look at the fine print on an application for a credit card. Or have them go online and look up information on applying for U.S. citizenship through the U.S. Immigration and Naturalization Service. In pairs or triads, have them compute the readability levels.

What conclusions can you draw about the reading demands faced by citizens in your community? What levels of reading ability allow people to understand what kinds of communications? What are some of the consequences of having a low reading level?

word length yields a more reliable estimate of readability than one measure alone (see the Teach It! box).

Other readability formulas are Flesch-Kincaid (which is folded into most versions of Microsoft Word [go to *Tools → Spelling and Grammar → Options → Check Readability Level*]), Dale-Chall, and SMOG ("Simplified Measure of Gobbledygook").

What has rapidly become a widely used system for establishing readability level is the Lexile Framework (Lennon & Burdick, 2004). The Lexile system, developed with federal funds by Metametrics, Inc., measures both readability of text and reading ability of readers. Readability measures are based on semantic (word-based) and syntactic (sentence-based) features of the text. The semantic score is calculated from the frequency or commonality of the words in the text and the length of the sentences. A computer program compares the words in a particular text to a dictionary that has a score for the frequency with which each word is typically encountered ("the" would be a common word; "Zoroastrianism" would be an uncommon one). The syntactic score is based on the average length of sentences in the text, and the two factors together yield a Lexile score of between 200 (for a very easy text) and 1,700 (for a very challenging one). The Lexile Framework is also used to assess a reader's ability to read a text. Using Lexile scores to match readers with books can be more accurate than establishing a child's reading ability in grade equivalents, and then matching the reading score with the readability score of a book. Students with a Lexile score of 300, for instance, would be expected to read with 75 percent comprehension a book with a Lexile score of 300. Information about the Lexile Framework is available online at <www.lexile.com>. Reading difficulty of text is now measured in grade equivalents, Lexiles, Reading Recovery levels, Fountas and Pinnell levels, and others (see Table 11.3).

Somewhere between a readability formula and a comprehension test is the cloze procedure (Bormouth, 1968; Taylor, 1953). The cloze procedure tests a reader's ability to read a particular text at the independent, instructional, and frustration levels. Thus if you are fairly sure of the difficulty level of the text, you can use the cloze procedure to get an idea of the reader's independent, instructional, and frustration levels. And if you are fairly sure of the reading ability of the group of people who take the test, you can use their performance on the cloze procedure to get an indication of the readability level of the text.

To conduct the cloze procedure, select a passage of more than 260 words. Leave the first sentence intact. Then go through and mark every fifth word thereafter until you reach 50 words marked. Then leave the sentence after the fiftieth word intact. Retype

Table 11.3   Comparing Readability Levels

Several different systems provide ratings of the difficulty levels of texts. Readability formulas such as the Fry, the Dale-Chall, and the Flesch-Kincaid report scores in terms of grade level equivalents. Most informal reading inventories report results as grade level equivalents, also. Recently, other systems have proliferated. In addition to Lexiles, which range between 200 and 1700, Reading Recovery (Clay, 1993), Fountas/Pinnell (2005), and Developmental Reading Assessment or DRA (from Pearson Education <http://plgcatalog.pearson.com/program_multiple.cfm?site_id=2&discipline_id=807&subarea_id=1000&program_id=23661>) provide fine gradations of difficulty for readers in the primary grades. This chart shows how scores from the different systems compare to each other.

GRADE LEVEL	INFORMAL READING INVENTORY SCORES	FOUNTAS/PINNELL GUIDED READING LEVELS	READING RECOVERY LEVELS	LEXILES	DRA LEVELS
K		A	A, B		A
			1		1
		B	2		2
	Pre-primer 1	C	3		3
1.1	Pre-primer 2		4		4
	Pre-primer 3		5		
		D	6		6
			7		
		E	8		8
1.2			9		
	Primer	F	10		10
		G	11	200–299	
			12		12
			13		
	Grade 1	H	14		14
			15		
		I	16		16
2	Grade 2	J	18	300–399	20
		K	19		
		L	20	400–499	28
		M			
3	Grade 3	N	22	500–599	30
		O, P	24	600–699	34
					38
4	Grade 4	Q, R, S	26	700–799	40
5	Grade 5	T, U, V	28	800–899	44
6	Grade 6	W, X, Y	30	900–999	
7	Grade 7	Z	32	1000–1100	
8	Grade 8	Z	34		

Source: After Salt Lake City School District, 2006.

the passage, and replace every word you marked with a blank of equal length. Have the students read the passage and fill in the blanks. Cloze tests are scored as follows:

The independent reading level = 60 percent and greater correct responses (30+ words)

The instructional reading level = between 40 and 59 percent correct responses (between 20 and 29 words)

The frustration level = fewer than 40 percent correct responses (fewer than 20 words)

More information about readability is available on the Internet. For a good introduction and links to other sites, you might begin with the article in Wikipedia, the free encyclopedia, at <http://en.wikipedia.org/wiki/Readability>.

WORD RECOGNITION   Word recognition has several aspects to it:

- *Sight vocabulary.* These are the words a reader has stored in memory—words that can be recognized instantly. Sight words are learned from reading. Words that may initially be decoded or figured out from context become sight words after repeated exposures.

- *Decoding ability.* Young readers frequently encounter words they do not have stored in memory. One way they can read them—which the National Reading Panel and the No Child Left Behind Act have indicated is the most important way—is to decode the word, or work out its identity by matching its letters and its sounds. Children differ in their ability to decode, and a task of assessment is to measure their ability to do it.

- *Identifying words from context.* When unrecognized words occur in meaningful texts, readers have two other ways besides decoding to figure out what they are. One is the syntax of the sentence. For example, if we read, "Give me the _____ ," we can be pretty sure that whatever fills that blank is a noun, or something that can function like a noun. But suppose the text said, "It was midnight. The safe cracker had opened the safe and taken the money. Just as he reached the door, the lights went on and a voice said, 'Stop. Now turn around slowly. Give me the _____ .'" Now we would probably guess that the missing word was not only a noun, but *money,* because the meaning of the text limits our choices to that word. Both of these examples go under the name of *using context to support word identification.* However, Marie Clay's *running records* procedure keeps track of each kind of context support by distinguishing *structural cues* from *meaning-based cues.* Both of those are distinguished from *visual* or graphophonic cues.

Phonics and Phonological Awareness

What's the difference between sight word reading and decoding?

ASSESSING WORD RECOGNITION AND PHONICS   There are several ways to assess word recognition. Assessments of reading fluency in the repeated reading task measure students' accuracy in word recognition. If you know the reading level of the book, and you know the student's accuracy score on at least a 100-word passage (the score, in percentages, is derived by dividing the number of errors by the total number of words), you can compute the student's level of word recognition in terms of grade-equivalents as follows:

Independent: 97–100 percent correct

Instructional: 90–96 percent correct

Frustration: Below 90 percent correct

Word recognition rates can also be measured by means of an Informal Reading Inventory. Many IRIs measure word recognition three ways. First, they give a measure of a child's *sight vocabulary,* the words a child has stored in memory and can recognize instantaneously. They do this by "flashing" (exposing very briefly between two index cards) words from a list (see the Assessment box on pages 348–349).

Second, they give a measure of a child's *decoding.* They do this by giving a long exposure of any words the child could not recognize instantly, and allowing the test administrator to compare the difference between the "flashed" and the "untimed" scores. The difference in favor of the untimed score demonstrates the power of the child's decoding ability because it shows how many words he could not recognize instantly, but could sound out given the time to do so.

Word Recognition Inventory

The word recognition inventory has two parts: a display list, which is shown to the child one word at a time, and a recording sheet for the child's answers.

To administer a word recognition inventory, you have two options. You can simply point to the words one at a time and have the child read them, putting a checkmark on the recording sheet for each word that is correctly identified. You may record what the child says when he or she misreads a word if you want to study those errors later. Count the number of words read correctly, and multiply by five points to yield a percentage score.

As an alternative, you can hold two index cards over the word and briefly expose the word (expose for about a quarter of a second) to the child. If he or she reads the word correctly, place a checkmark in the "flashed" column of the record sheet and go on to the next word. If the student fails to read the word correctly, record whatever he or she says in the "flashed" column and then open up the cards to expose the words. If she now reads the word correctly, place a checkmark in the "untimed" column; if not read correctly, record whatever the student says, or enter a zero if he or she says nothing. Calculate the scores for both columns by multiplying the words correctly identified by five points.

The scores can be used as follows to identify the child's independent, instructional, and frustration levels, as follows:

Independent level: 90 to 100 percent correct
Instructional level: 70 to 89 percent correct
Frustration level: Below 70 percent

Display List

cards	station
above	ought
library	idea
brave	coach
instead	type
dear	damp
press	elbow
popcorn	mystery
pretty	yourselves
monkey	midnight
feather	motorcycle
become	insect
grandfather	study
hair	easier
people	headache
kept	match
mountain	quit
pass	alive
seem	moment
anyway	range

Third, IRIs also give a measure of children's power to recognize words in context. The child reads aloud words from a text passage as the teacher listens carefully and records and scores the errors. The percentage scores of words correctly read in context are interpreted using the same criteria used in the fluency measure.

Recording Sheet

	Flashed	Untimed		Flashed	Untimed
cards			station		
above			ought		
library			idea		
brave			coach		
instead			type		
dear			damp		
press			elbow		
popcorn			mystery		
pretty			yourselves		
monkey			midnight		
feather			motorcycle		
become			insect		
grandfather			study		
hair			easier		
people			headache		
kept			match		
mountain			quit		
pass			alive		
seem			moment		
anyway			range		
Total Errors:			**Total Errors:**		

0–2 errors = independent level
3–6 errors = instructional level
7 + errors = frustration level

Source: From C. Temple, A. Crawford, and J. Gillet (2009). *Developmental Literacy Inventory: Reading and Spelling from Emergent to Mature Levels.* Published by Allyn and Bacon, Boston, MA. Copyright © 2009. Reprinted by permission of Pearson Education.

Assessing phonics knowledge can also be done by carefully observing the kinds of errors children make when they are recognizing words. The Assessment box on page 350 presents a system of categorizing errors that shows whether a child's word reading is in the logographic, alphabetic, orthographic, or derivational stage.

Some tests, including DIBELS and the Woodcock-Johnson-III Basic Reading Battery, assess phonics knowledge by testing children's reading of nonsense words, like *VAJ, KOL, NAK,* and the like. The advantage to having children read nonsense words is that we are assured they have never seen them before, so the words must be read by pure decoding. The disadvantage is that, because they are nonsense words, the children don't have the normal self-correction to them that comes from arriving at a word they know in their speech. Another disadvantage is that some of the nonsense words do not conform to English orthography. For example, DIBELS uses *doj, ol,* and *huf,* even though these spellings are not allowable in English; that is, there are no single-syllable words in Standard English that are spelled that way.

Word Knowledge Levels by Error Type

Once you have become accustomed to thinking about children's development through phases of word knowledge, you can observe their reading errors and estimate a child's level or phase of word knowledge. This can be done in a structured way. Ask a child to read 100 words of text written at her instructional level—that is, a piece of moderately challenging text of which the child misreads about one word in ten. Then write down the errors, with the target word (the word the child was attempting to read) next to each error. Compare the errors to the responses in the chart below. If half of a child's errors fall within a phase, according to the chart, this is a reasonable indication that the child is reading words using strategies from that phase.

LEVEL OF WORD KNOWLEDGE	TARGET WORD	TYPICAL ERROR	DESCRIPTION OF THE ERROR TYPE
Logographic Reading	plant right	*Larry. He has L.* _____	Student typically looks at one letter and calls out any word it reminds her of.
Alphabetic Reading	plant right	*pal ?* *rye gut?*	Student reads through words one letter at a time, making a sound for each letter. Early in the phase, only a few letters are read.
Orthographic Reading	plant right	*pl, pl, ant, plant!* *ruh, ruh, -ight, right!*	Student begins to see words as clusters of onsets and rimes.
Morphological Reading	ticked surprising unfed	*tiked, tick-ed, ticked!* *surprise, surprising!* *oonfd, oonfeed, unfed!*	Student begins to recognize prefixes, suffixes, and grammatical endings—and to see that they have consistent spellings even when they have different pronunciations.
Derivational Reading	*assign*	*assigg—No, assign!*	Student recognizes that the target word is derived from a familiar word.

Writing and Reading Connections

Why has reading fluency become an area of such intense interest to educators?

CCSS

• Foundational Skills 4: Fluency

Another test of phonics knowledge is done by means of children's spelling. The assessment inventories built into Kathy Ganske's (2000) *Word Journeys* have children spell challenging words, and then give teachers advice on (1) analyzing the spelling error to assign the child to a probable level of invented spelling and (2) pinpointing the aspect of phonics knowledge that the child needs to learn.

ASSESSING READING FLUENCY   Reading fluency has moved from being a neglected skill (Allington, 1983) to an area of intense interest. In *Put Reading First*, Armbruster, Lehr, and Osborn (2001) define reading fluency this way:

Fluency is the ability to read a text accurately and quickly. When fluent readers read silently, they recognize words automatically. They group words quickly in ways that help them gain meaning from what they read. Fluent readers read aloud effortlessly and with expression. Their reading sounds natural, as if they are speaking. (p. 22)

Assessing reading fluency is most simply measured by counting the number of words children read per minute minus the errors. This yields a measure called *words correct per minute* (WCPM), which is calculated using this formula:

$$\frac{(\text{Total words read, minus words read incorrectly}) \times 60}{\text{Reading time in seconds}} = \text{WCPM}$$

Thus, for example, if a third-grade student reads 125 words in one minute but makes five reading errors, we would calculate her fluency rate of WCPM as:

$$\frac{(125 - 5) \times 60}{60} = \frac{120 \times 60}{60} = 120 \text{ WCPM}$$

For a third grader in the middle of the year, that would be a normal reading rate (see Table 11.4).

Reading fluency consists not only of speed and correctness, but also of reading with expression and proper phrasing. Zutell and Rasinski (1991) developed the Multidimensional Fluency Scale (see Table 11.5) to help teachers observe several dimensions of fluency at once. These factors are expression and volume, phrasing, smoothness, and pace. The scale is a rubric to guide teachers' judgment. To carry out the procedure, the teacher selects a passage of at least 100 words that should be written at the students' grade level or a year below. The student reads the passage and the teacher records it. The teacher then plays the recording back and evaluates the student's reading for each of the factors of accuracy, phrasing, smoothness, and pace.

ASSESSING VOCABULARY   Vocabulary development is recognized more and more as a critical variable in learning to read. But how do we know how many words a child knows? As we saw in Chapter 4, it depends on what we mean by "know." Does the child have a vague idea what the word means? Can the child understand the word when reading it or hearing it, but not when using it? Does the child know all of its meanings? These questions show what a complicated thing it is to assess vocabulary. Vocabulary has often been assessed as part of an IRI and other reading tests. But with the advent of No Child Left Behind and Reading First, teachers are being called upon to assess children's vocabulary knowledge more systematically.

CCSS

• Language 4: Vocabulary

Table 11.4   Oral Reading Fluency Norms

GRADE	PERCENTILE	FALL WCPM*	WINTER WCPM*	SPRING WCPM*
2	75	82	106	124
	50	53	78	94
	25	23	46	65
3	75	107	123	142
	50	79	93	114
	25	65	70	87
4	75	125	133	143
	50	99	112	118
	25	72	89	92
5	75	126	143	151
	50	105	118	128
	25	77	93	100

*WCPM is words correct per minute.
The 50th percentile for upper grades is 125–150 WCPM.
Source: Republished with permission of The Council for Exceptional Children, from *Teaching Exceptional Children*, by J. Hasbrouck and G. Tindal, 1992, 24, p. 42 © 1992 by The Council for Exceptional Children; permission conveyed through Copyright Clearance Center, Inc.

Table 11.5 Multidimensional Fluency Scale

	1	2	3	4
Expression and volume	Reads in a quiet voice as if to get the words out. The reading does not sound natural like talking to a friend.	Reads in a quiet voice. The reading sounds natural in part of the text, but the reading does not always sound like talking to a friend.	Reads with volume and expression. However, sometimes the reader slips into expressionless reading and does not sound like talking to a friend.	Reads with varied volume and expression. The reading sounds like talking to a friend with voice matching the interpretation of the passage.
Phrasing	Reads word-by-word in a monotone voice.	Reads in two- and three-word phrases, not adhering to punctuation, stress, and intonation.	Reads with a mixture of run-ons, midsentence pauses for breath, and some choppiness. There is reasonable stress and intonation.	Reads with good phrasing, adhering to punctuation, stress, and intonation.
Smoothness	Frequently hesitates while reading, sounds out words, and repeats words or phrases. The reader makes multiple attempts to read the same passage.	Reads with extended pauses or hesitations. The reader has many "rough spots."	Reads with occasional breaks in rhythm. The reader has difficulty with specific words and/or sentence structures.	Reads smoothly with some breaks, but self-corrects with difficult words and/or sentence structures.
Pace	Reads slowly and laboriously.	Reads moderately slowly.	Reads fast and slow throughout reading.	Reads at a conversational pace throughout the reading.

Source: Zutell, J., & Rasinski, T. (1991). Training teachers to attend to their students' oral reading fluency. *Theory into Practice, 30,* 212–217, Taylor & Francis Ltd.: <http://www.informaworld.com>. Used with permission.

When states specify that teachers use scientifically based tests of vocabulary—that is, tests with proven validity and reliability—the choices are rather limited. A group commissioned by the U.S. Department of Education to approve assessment instruments for use with federally funded programs yielded a very short list of approved instruments for assessing vocabulary at the points of screening, diagnosing, monitoring, and outcomes-based assessment.

According to the *Final Report: Analysis of Reading Assessment Instruments for K–3* <http://www.ecs.org/html/Document.asp?chouseid=4414>, one instrument, the *Peabody Picture Vocabulary Test-III,* was approved for all purposes for levels kindergarten through grade 3. This test costs well over $400, and is administered by school psychologists. Other tests such as the *Expressive One-Word Picture Vocabulary Test,* the *One-Word Picture Vocabulary Test Revised,* the *Texas Primary Reading Inventory,* and the *Expressive Vocabulary Test* were approved for limited applications in certain grades. Recently, however, the U.S. General Accounting Office has questioned the propriety of some of the procedures the Department of Education uses to decide what materials and approaches are to be allowed for federal support. Vocabulary development is included among the Foundational Reading Skills of the Common Core Standards, so we can expect less expensive tests of vocabulary development in the near future.

Teachers who wish to construct their own vocabulary tests would do well to follow the advice of Barone, Hardman, and Taylor (2006) and create devices that ask children to:

- Select the meanings from a set of possibilities when a target word is given.
- Select a target word from a set of possibilities when a meaning is given.
- Classify words into categories.
- Tell which word from a group of words does not belong.
- Use visual and contextual clues to understand difficult words in sentences.

- Choose the correct word meanings, an antonym, or a synonym from a set of possibilities.

- Show an understanding of root words, prefixes and suffixes, historical morphemes, or grammatical endings.

- Choose correct meanings for homophones (words that sound the same but have different meanings: *read a book*; *a reed in a pond*) and homographs (words that are spelled the same but have different meanings: *lead the way*; *a lead pipe*).

- Complete a sentence with a correct word choice from alternatives.

- Demonstrate dictionary skills.

ASSESSING COMPREHENSION   Reading comprehension consists of several abilities. Students' prior knowledge (sometimes called world knowledge) is needed to contextualize the new information they gain from the text. And students need to read actively, using their prior knowledge and clues from the text to set purposes and raise questions to answer while reading. They need the ability to find main ideas and supporting details and recall them later. They also need to be able to make inferences to construct meanings when ideas are not explicitly stated. They need to be able to follow the patterns of different kinds of texts, both fictional and informational, as guides to constructing meaning. And they need to keep building their inventory of vocabulary. They must do all this while reading aloud and silently.

That is a lot for a teacher to assess! In practice, when teachers want to observe this many factors, they often rely upon IRIs because they provide comprehensive measures.

ASSESSING COMPREHENSION WITH AN INFORMAL READING INVENTORY
IRIs allow teachers to assess comprehension by using meaningful text passages written at ascending levels of difficulty. Questions are asked before and after the reading, and the child's behaviors are closely observed during reading.

Before reading a passage on an IRI, students may be asked a set of optional questions to ascertain what they know about the topic, to get an indication of the extent of their *prior knowledge* about the topic. Some examples, all taken from Temple, Crawford, and Gillet (2009), are in the following paragraphs.

After they have read the passage, students are asked a series of questions of different kinds. Some questions may also ask a student to summarize a main idea that has been stated in the text. For example, in a second-grade passage, the text says:

Jan lives in the city. The city has many big buildings. People work in some of the buildings. People shop in other buildings. Some buildings have apartments. . . . There are many cars, trucks, and buses in the city. They make a lot of noise. Many people walk on the street. Some people ride on the bus. There are many people on the bus.

The question asks: *What did this story say that it was like in the city?*

Some of the questions require the recall of important details. For example, the text says: *In Israel, the birthday girl or boy gets a beautiful crown of flowers. The mother places the royal crown on her child's head.* The question asks: *According to this passage, in what country does the birthday child wear a crown of flowers?*

Questions may require that readers make inferences to construct meaning where ideas are not stated explicitly. In narratives, some inferences require that the readers infer motives for behavior. For example, in a sixth-grade passage, the text says:

Finding time to assess individual students takes ingenuity, but the payoff in better understanding of each student's reading processes is well worth the effort.

"Cast near the trunk. Watch out for the branches."

"I know, Dad," said Paco. But his first cast landed on top of the trunk. Without commenting, his father paddled the canoe to the other side of the dead tree, pried the lure from the bark, and gently tossed it into the water.

The question asks: *How did Paco feel about his father's advice? How do you know?*

When the text is informational, inference questions can require readers to derive an answer by applying logic to pieces of information that are given, although the answer to the question is not explicitly stated. For example, in a middle school–level passage the text says:

Industries like the textile industry have had to shut down because of increased competition. They could no longer compete in the global economy. Increased competition often leads to lower prices for consumers. But lower prices can sometimes cause lower profits for industries.

The question asks: *From what the article said, do you think you pay more or less for a shirt now that we have a global economy?*

Questions may assess *vocabulary*, too. One kind of vocabulary knowledge is the knowledge of words and their meanings that is stored in memory. Another kind is the ability to infer word meanings from context. As an example of assessing words and meanings stored in memory in a second-grade passage, the text says, *Jan lives in the city. The city has many big buildings. People work in some of the buildings. People shop in other buildings.* The question asks, *When the text said "People shop in other buildings," what does "shop" mean?* As an example of assessing a child's ability to infer vocabulary meaning from context, in a fourth-grade passage the text says, *The wings quiver as they slice through the turbulent air.* The question asks: *In the sentence, "The wings quiver as they slice through the turbulent air," what does "turbulent" mean?* A student who did not already know that the word meant "stormy" or "stirred up" might infer the meaning from the context because it is obvious that *turbulent* refers to air that an airplane is flying through, and it is a condition that makes the wings of the airplane tremble.

For the purpose of scoring, correctly answered questions are counted as a percentage of the total number of questions the child is asked. The scores are interpreted as follows:

Independent reading level = 90 and greater percent correct responses

Instructional reading level = 70 to 89 percent correct responses

Frustration reading level = below 70 percent correct responses

Most IRIs contain both narrative and informational texts, so teachers can assess reader success in dealing with all of the factors just mentioned in different patterns or genres of text. For example, the inference question we saw before from the narrative passage about Paco fishing with his father relied upon the reader's prior knowledge of relationships between parent and child to make a successful inference. The inference question regarding the informational passage about globalization, however, requires the reader to consider information about a generalized situation (cheap labor brings down prices on consumer goods) and to draw a conclusion about the way it affects the reader personally (how much he will pay for a shirt).

IRIs also allow teachers to assess students' listening comprehension in contrast to their reading comprehension. In the case of developing readers, listening to a text is usually easier than reading it—the activity of recognizing written words and constructing understanding from them is less practiced than listening to speech and constructing meaning from it. In reading assessment, testing listening capacity offers an indication of readers' potential for comprehending a text, and may serve as a goal against which their reading comprehension of a text can be measured.

OTHER MEASURES OF COMPREHENSION IRIs afford a great deal of insight into a reader's comprehension, but they do so at a high cost of time. Also, they must be administered to one child at a time, and completing one with a child in third or fourth grade can take an hour. They are most useful for diagnostic testing, to identify strengths and weaknesses of a child's reading ability to guide instruction. Even when a full IRI is not administered, questions of the type just described can be made up by the teacher and used with any text passage, of course. Many teachers include a variety of questions like these during informal observations. For the more frequent testing that's used to monitor children's progress in learning to read, teachers rely on other, quicker means of assessing comprehension. These include oral retellings and fluency measures.

After a child has read a passage, the teacher asks the child to give an *oral retelling*—that is, to retell the passage in his own words. The teacher then makes a mental calculation of how much of the information from the text the child retold. For a slightly more exact way of evaluating the retellings, teachers may use a retelling checklist, which is a list of pieces of information contained in the text, prepared in advance. The teacher checks off the pieces of information that the child retold and then computes the score as a percentage of the whole list of items.

Another way of assessing reading comprehension is to use a structured observation procedure. The teacher sits alone with a child and has the child read a passage aloud. The teacher may ask the student questions before, during, and after the student reads. A checklist for guiding observations may then be used, such as the one shown Figure 7.7 in Chapter 7 (see pages 208–209).

MEASURING ATTITUDES AND INTEREST   It has long been noted, and was recently very eloquently affirmed (Allington, 2005), that children learn to read by reading. Children differ enormously in the amount of reading they do, and as Stanovich (1992) has pointed out, those who read more benefit enormously in increased vocabulary, increased world knowledge, better spelling, and even greater measured intelligence. Somewhere between reading ability and the amount of reading that actually gets done is the will to read, a positive attitude toward reading, and a deep interest in books and reading. Where that motivation and interest is lacking, we have a problem. Teachers would do well to assess students' attitudes toward reading.

Surveys can look into children's general attitude toward reading. The Elementary Reading Attitude Survey (McKenna & Kear, 1990) is one widely used instrument that reveals how students are feeling about reading and reading instruction in general. This instrument can tell if a school or a classroom is succeeding in promoting an interest in reading among groups of children, as well as an individual child's attitude. It has also been used in research to track the attitudes toward reading of large groups of students over time.

Reading interest inventories are intended to discover individual students' interests and preferences, and to help teachers and librarians match them up with books and learning experiences they will enjoy. A reading interest inventory from a librarian in Michigan is found in Figure 11.9.

Teach It! **20**

Analytic Phonics Lesson

Teach It! **26**

Fluency Oriented Oral Reading

Differentiated Instruction

Differentiated instruction begins with good assessment. *Screening assessment* indicates which students are where they are expected to be, which are above grade level, and which need additional support. *Diagnostic assessment* indicates how strong each student is in different aspects of reading and writing development. Based on diagnostic assessment, students will have different kinds of instruction designed for them. They will be assigned different levels of books for guided reading. They will be given different groups of words for word study and possibly will be placed in different points in the sequence of phonics instruction. The teacher will construct focused lessons on aspects of comprehension—on setting purposes for reading, summarizing, visualizing, making inferences, understanding vocabulary from context, learning new information, and interpreting the text. The students will be placed in groups that read different levels of text for fluency practice. They will be placed at their instructional level of spelling words to learn, even if that falls a year above or below their grade-placement level. The assessment picture will be rounded out

Figure 11.9 Reading Interest Inventory

Source: Reading Interest Inventory, from "But There's Nothing Good to Read," by Denice Hildebrandt, *Media Spectrum: The Journal for Library Media Specialists in Michigan*, Vol 29, Fall 2001, pp. 34–37. Used by permission of MAME Sue Lay President and Executive Board.

1. Do you like to read?
2. How much time do you spend reading?
3. What are some of the books you have read lately?
4. Do you have a library card? How often do you use it?
5. Do you ever get books from the school library?
6. About how many books do you own?
7. What are some books you would like to own?
8. Put a check mark next to the kind of reading you like best. (topics you might like to read about)

   _____ history   _____ travel   _____ plays

   _____ sports   _____ science fiction   _____ adventure

   _____ romance   _____ detective stories   _____ war stories

   _____ poetry   _____ car stories   _____ novels

   _____ biography   _____ supernatural stories   _____ astrology

   _____ humor   _____ folktales   _____ how-to-do-it books

   _____ mysteries   _____ art   _____ westerns

9. Do you like to read the newspaper?
10. If 'yes', place a check next to the part of the newspaper listed below you like to read.

    _____ Advertisements   _____ Entertainment   _____ Columnists

    _____ Headlines   _____ Comic Strips   _____ Political Stories

    _____ Current Events   _____ Sports   _____ Editorials

    _____ Others: (please list)

11. What are your favorite television programs?
12. How much time do you spend watching television?
13. What is your favorite magazine?
14. Do you have a hobby? If so, what is it?
15. What are the two best movies you have ever seen?
16. Who are your favorite entertainers and/or movie stars?
17. When you were little, did you enjoy having someone read aloud to you?
18. List topics, subjects, etc. which you might like to read about.
19. What does the word 'reading' mean to you?
20. Say anything else that you would like to say about reading.

by other information gained from interviews with the students to determine the topics they are interested in, the kind of reading they most prefer, the conditions they need to help them learn.

Once courses of instruction have been established for all students, they are given periodic monitoring assessments. Unlike the daily observations, these are more formalized and done on a schedule. The results may be shared with other teachers or with the reading specialist, and provide guidance for determining whether the present plan of instruction should be followed or if different strategies should be tried to improve a student's learning. In addition, the teacher should practice kidwatching by making a habit of selecting a small number of children every day, and asking how they are working, what exactly they are doing when they read and write, what they appear to be interested in, what kinds of tasks they are succeeding in, when they work best, and when they get off task, and in sum, how the teacher can help each one be successful in this class.

Different Assessments for Different Phases of Instruction

Teachers use different kinds of assessments for different purposes at different points in the year. Commonly, schools administer assessments in these four "moments" or phases of instruction: *screening assessment, diagnostic assessment, monitoring assessment,* and *outcomes-based assessment.*

Screening Assessment. Before instruction begins at the start of the year, teachers may administer screening measures to determine which children are at risk for reading difficulty and may need more support during the year. The screening instruments they use are as economical as possible, because they may be given to an entire class or an entire grade. So they typically examine only a few key aspects of literacy, just enough to identify the children who need extra attention.

Diagnostic Assessment. Another kind of assessment is used to identify more precisely a student's needs, so that the teacher can develop a teaching plan that is right for that child. If children have been identified by the screening tests as needing special help, the diagnostic instruments take up where the screening instruments left off. They not only tell that the child needs to know more letters of the alphabet but also which ones; not only that she is a struggling reader, but also that she is weak in comprehension, especially in making inferences. Individual diagnostic instruments may test specific skills, such as a test of phonemic segmentation or a test of reading fluency. Others are more comprehensive and test many areas of reading ability, such as an Informal Reading Inventory.

Monitoring Assessment. Sometimes called formative assessments because they occur while work is in progress, monitoring assessments are used once the teacher has a plan for instruction for a group of children to make sure the instruction is working and each child is making adequate progress. Monitoring assessments range from informal observations to formal probes. Reading First schools and many school districts may require that monitoring assessments use formalized instruments. If so, you must find an instrument with several alternative forms for each level. Informal assessments may consist of records of children's repeated reading scores, records of the numbers and levels of books read, and collected writing samples. Of course, teachers may observe other important behaviors that a test would miss: a child's favorite subjects, who her most productive workmates are, and her difficulties with concentration and how they are best handled.

Monitoring assessments are best done at regular intervals—every month or every quarter for most students, but more often for students who seem to have more difficulty learning. It is advisable that monitoring assessments be designed with the end-of-year assessments in mind. Because of No Child Left Behind, nearly all children in American public schools are now tested at the end of their third through their eighth years, so the monitoring assessments should see how much progress children are making toward meeting the standards embodied in those tests, while changes in instruction can still be made.

Outcomes-Based Assessment. Outcomes-based tests are also referred to as grade-level reading standards-based assessments because the desired outcomes of a year's teaching are reflected in each state's learning standards. Yet another more general term, *summative assessments,* may be applied to them, because they come at the conclusion of or the summation of the period of learning that is being assessed. Standards-based assessments are used to test the skills that are named on the state's standards for learning in literacy.

Late in the year come the outcomes-based assessments, which are based on the state learning standards—for most states, the Common Core Standards—for each grade level. This is a serious accountability event. While the daily informal assessments and the periodic monitoring assessments focus on children's development as readers, writers, and learners in general, these assessments also have one eye on the outcomes of instruction. In 22 states, by the 2014–2015 school year, a common assessment called the PARCC will begin to be administered at year's end to students in grade 3 and up, covering 24 million students in all, to measure what they know about reading and writing (see <http://www.parcconline.org/about-parcc>).

Teacher Self-Assessment

As new entrants to a profession, beginning teachers must have the professional knowledge they will need to be successful in the classroom. Experienced teachers, too, have the obligation as professionals to keep abreast of developments in the field of literacy and other domains of knowledge that impact their classroom and to continually perform teacher self-assessment activities.

Donald Schön (1983) developed the influential model of the *reflective practitioner*, a professional who is able to learn from experience and create his or her own practical knowledge and skill. This model is still useful today. Professors in your teacher education classes undoubtedly encourage you to observe as closely as you can individual children and whole classrooms, to sense patterns and find possibilities for action.

Becoming a reflective practitioner is not a solitary activity, however. As Taylor and Pearson (2005) noted, in "schools that beat the odds," where students outperform what is predicted for them, teachers come together to share information about their students, about teaching, and about what works in their schools.

Following is an example of a second-grade teacher's observation/assessment discussion with her team teachers:

> *I worked with Michele today. She is putting extra vowels in some words and leaving needed vowels out in others. Today, she spelled chin as CHIAN and cream as CREM; this is a pattern for her. I looked it up in a textbook, and this means that she is using but confusing vowel- and consonant-patterned words. Easy to see, but now what? She is on the verge of getting it but needs help. Here is what I am thinking. First of all, I don't think she can read the words she is trying to spell—chin and cream are not known words for her. I need to step back to a point at which she can succeed. What do you think? Give me some feedback.*

This teacher received suggestions from the team on increasing assessments of Michele's understanding of the words she attempts to spell. They also suggested she give Michele more opportunities to write. Someone suggested word sorting by patterns—*chin, pin, tin, in*. They made a date for her to try some of these suggestions and report back to the group.

Teachers benefit from comparing and contrasting their ideas with those of others and from using multiple assessment measures. If the opportunity for collaboration does not exist in your building, you should create it with at least one other teacher. With teachers in your building, create regular meetings to talk shop before or after school, at planning times, or during working lunches.

Because of their many variables, teaching and learning are always in flux. Assessment helps to make order and sense of teaching and learning. For direction and planning, you will learn what children know on a daily basis. When physicians prescribe medication, they are following a routine that is grounded in research on groups of people. In addition, however, physicians tell patients, "Get back to me if this doesn't help within three days, and call me if you have any serious side effects." Modern medicine is wonderful, and much of its success depends on knowing what generally works and on the individual's responses. There is no silver bullet in either the practice of medicine or the practice of education. However, we have good evidence about more successful medical and teaching practices that we must use to improve.

Professional organizations have had their say about the assessment of teachers, too. The International Reading Association (IRA) and the National Council for the Accreditation of Teacher Education (NCATE) jointly published a set of Standards for Reading Professionals (2006) that outlines what a committee of reading educators believes teachers of reading should know. The standards are available online at <http://www.reading.org/resources/community/ncate_standards.html>.

The IRA/NCATE standards have been incorporated by many schools of education to guide their curricula. James Zarrillo has written a self-administered guide based on the standards entitled *Are You Prepared to Teach Reading?* (2010). It includes a sample written test at the end of the book.

Professional Assessment of Teachers

In more and more states, teachers' professional performance is being measured in ways that go beyond long-used paper and pencil tests such as PRAXIS and individual states' teacher competency tests. In many states, college graduates seeking teaching certification are now asked to submit portfolios related to their teaching, along with videos of live instruction of students in classrooms. Student teachers may be asked to show evidence that they had a positive impact on the students they taught. Practicing teachers also are having their performance evaluated in new ways that include measures of their impact on students' learning as demonstrated in performance on tests, observations, and other ratings of professionalism.

Programs of the professional assessment of teachers still vary from state to state and sometimes from school district to school district (for a comprehensive review, see Doyle and Han, 2012.) By the 2013–2014 school year, programs for assessing teachers' knowledge and competence in reading instruction are being administered in most of the United States. Prominent among them is the edTPA, program, developed by SCALE, the Stanford Center for Assessment, Learning, and Equity (see <http://www.edtpa.com> for more information).

Assessment of English Language Learners*

The Federal No Child Left Behind law of 2001 mandated that all states annually test English language learners' English Language Proficiency (ELP), and that they include their scores reporting school-wide achievement in reading, mathematics, and science. Years later, states were still scrambling to come up with valid and reliable assessment procedures for their English Language Learners (Wolf et al., 2008).

The Common Core Standards are keeping up the pressure that the No Child Left Behind Act placed on schools. While the promoters of the CCSS suggest that English language learners receive extra support, they also make it clear that these students should meet the same standards as everyone else:

> *The National Governors Association Center for Best Practices and the Council of Chief State School Officers strongly believe that all students should be held to the same high expectations outlined in the Common Core State Standards. This includes students who are English language learners (ELLs). However, these students may require additional time, appropriate instructional support, and aligned assessments as they acquire both English language proficiency and content area knowledge.* **

Meeting the standards will be a challenge, though, since English language learners as a group (and they are, admittedly, a heterogeneous group), currently score nearly 20 percent lower than average on tests of reading and mathematics (NAEP, 2011).

Research on the use of wide-scale reading and content area tests in English has revealed that culturally and linguistically diverse students' performance is adversely affected by the fact that, because such tests are designed for monolingual speakers of (Standard) English and do not take into account minority students' linguistic and cultural background, they are often linguistically and/or culturally biased (Abedi, 2002; Garcia, 1991; Pomplun & Omar, 2001; Stevens, Butler, & Castellon-Wellington, 2000). For example, one of the factors that negatively affects minority students' performance is their lack of familiarity with the passage topics and vocabulary of test questions. If they were given the opportunity to respond to test questions in their home language or if the questions were posed to them in their first language, English language learners might demonstrate much greater comprehension of the test passages than indicated by their answers on a standardized test (Garcia, 1991).

Language and Diversity

What do classroom teachers and reading teachers need to know about the reading assessment of English language learners?

---

*By Codruţa Florin Temple (From *Understanding Reading Problems*, 8th edition, Gillet, Temple, Crawford, & Temple. Pearson, 2012).

English language learners tend to perform better in science and mathematics than in reading, a difference that may be attributed to the higher language demands of reading tests compared to science and mathematics tests. Nevertheless, the linguistic complexity of test questions adversely affects these learners' performance even on mathematics tests (Abedi, 2002).

Such findings raise a serious question about the validity of standardized tests when used with culturally and linguistically diverse students. Do these tests really measure what they claim to measure, that is, reading comprehension or knowledge in the content areas, or do they measure students' proficiency in academic English and familiarity with mainstream American culture? Admittedly, it is hard to devise test questions even in science and mathematics that do not require knowledge of the language of the test, just as it is virtually impossible to design a reading comprehension test that is culture-free. Nevertheless, the question remains, and can be asked not only of standardized tests, but of classroom assessments as well.

What can be done to reduce the linguistic and cultural bias of tests? First and foremost, English language learners must be included in the design and piloting of these tests (Abedi & Lord, 2001). Then, testing accommodations must be provided for them. Research has shown that the one accommodation that narrows the gap between English language learners' test performance and that of other students is the linguistic modification of test questions with excessive linguistic demands; other accommodations increase scores for *all* students (Abedi, 2004; Abedi, Hoffstetter, & Lord, 2004). Figure 11.10 includes a list of guidelines for simplifying test questions that can be used by both test designers and classroom teachers in constructing tests (adapted from Cloud, Genesee, & Hamayan, 2009).

To avoid linguistic bias when assessing English language learners' listening or reading comprehension, teachers can use close-ended or limited-response formats that make minimal demands on students' expressive skills (e.g., illustrations of possible answers that students need to choose from), and which allow teachers to determine whether students understand what they read even though they cannot express their understanding orally or in writing. If teachers speak the students' first language, they may also choose to allow English language learners to answer comprehension questions in that language.

More often than not, teachers assess their English language learners' literacy skills and development using assessment instruments that have been devised for monolingual English children. While understandable, this practice may be problematic because it ignores certain characteristics of bilingual children's knowledge and development and thus yields inaccurate assessment information.

For example, if an English language learner's vocabulary is assessed using an English vocabulary test, the results will indicate the child's vocabulary knowledge *in English* as opposed to her overall vocabulary knowledge, since bilingual children often know different words in each of their languages (Fernandez et al., 1992). Similarly, using running records or informal reading inventories with English language learners may lead to misleading conclusions about children's reading ability if, for example, pronunciation errors are marked as miscues. Such errors may be due to phonological · or orthographic differences between English and a child's first language, and they do not necessarily indicate that the child does not recognize or understand the mispronounced words.

Assessment results yielded by fluency measures such as the DIBELS should also be interpreted with caution. Because English language learners often struggle with the pronunciation of English words (even when they know their meaning), their fluency rates often lag behind those of native speakers, even though they may have good comprehension (Lems, Miller, & Soro, 2010). The reverse may also be true, in that some students may be misidentified as good readers based on their scores on fluency measures, when in fact their comprehension of the text may be low (Samuels, 2007).

When assessing English language learners' spelling, teachers may benefit from being familiar with some of the ways in which English language learners' spelling development differs from that of monolingual English children (adapted from Helman & Bear, 2007):

Figure 11.10 Guidelines for Simplifying Test Questions

Guidelines for Simplifying Test Questions

- Replace low-frequency words (e.g., *depreciate*) with common words (e.g., *lose value*).

- Repeat words and avoid synonyms. For example, in the problem,

    "Daniel's print shop bought a new printer for $3,500. Each year it depreciates at a rate of 5%. What will its value be at the end of the fourth year? How much value will it have lost by then? If the printer were to be sold after three years and a new one were to be purchased for $3,000, how much money would Daniel have to spend?"

    the word *depreciates* can be replaced by *loses value*, and the word *purchased* by the word *bought*.

- Make sure that all pronouns have clear antecedents—that it is clear which noun a pronoun refers to. For example, in "Daniel bought a new $3,500 printer for his print shop, which depreciates each year at a rate of 5%," it is not clear whether the pronoun *which* refers to the *printer* or to *the print shop*. To avoid the ambiguity, the sentence can be rewritten as "Daniel's print shop bought a new printer for $3,500. Each year it depreciates at a rate of 5%."

- Remove unnecessary expository material. For example, in "[Daniel owned a print shop that had to replace its printers every 3–4 years. One year,] Daniel's print shop bought a new printer for $3,500...," the words in brackets are unnecessary for students' understanding of the question.

- Replace passive structures with active structures. For example, *If the printer were to be sold after three years and a new one were to be purchased* should be replaced with *If Daniel sold the printer after three years and bought a new one.*

- Separate long sentences into shorter ones. For example, the sentence *"If the printer were to be sold after three years and a new one were to be purchased for $3,000, how much money would Daniel have to spend?"* could be rewritten as *"After three years Daniel wants to sell the printer and buy a new one. The new printer costs 3,000. How much money will Daniel have to spend?"*

- English language learners progress through the same stages of spelling development as English-speaking children; however, because they are also learning the language as they are learning to read and write, their progress through the stages takes longer than that of their monolingual English peers.

- Some of the misspellings of English language learners may be standard developmental errors, while others may mirror phonological and orthographic differences between English and the students' first languages. For example, spelling *hot* as *hat* may be due to the fact that the vowel sound in *hot* is represented by the letter *a* in a child's first language. Consonant sounds that do not exist in learners' first languages are also likely to be misspelled (e.g., *than* may be spelled as *van* or *dan* by speakers of many languages).

- Presumably because of the system of sounds in their first language, English language learners often do more sounding out than native English speakers, which results in certain words being spelled with more letters than expected. For example, the first vowel sound in *blade* is perceived as a diphthong (a combination of two vowels) and represented by two letters (*ei* or *ey*) in Spanish, which may account for a Spanish-speaking child's spelling the word *lady* as *leidy*.

- Because of the differences between the English vowel system and that of other languages, and because internalizing the English vowel sounds takes a long time, there is greater variability in the vowel substitutions that English language learners make as compared to native English speakers. For example, a Spanish-speaking child may spell the word *dirt* as *dart*, *dert*, or *durt*, substituting Spanish vowels for the English vowel in *dirt*, which does not exist in Spanish.

- Grammatical morphemes (e.g., the past tense ending -*ed* or the plural ending -*s*) may be omitted in English language learners' spelling before the grammatical structures that the morphemes represent become part of children's oral language.

To sum up, when assessing English language learners' literacy skills, teachers need to be very clear about what it is that they want to find out, aware of the ways in which these students' literacy development may differ from that of monolingual English children, alert to possible cross-linguistic influences, and careful in interpreting and using the assessment results. This is particularly important in situations where students are considered for special education services. Those English language learners who are poor readers and writers because of their limited English proficiency can easily be labeled as having a learning disability, even though what they need is not special education, but oral language development and literacy instruction that match their level of English language proficiency.

While standardized tests often fail to reveal the progress made by English language learners in developing English language and literacy, the insights yielded by ongoing assessments and captured in teacher observations, samples of student work, and student portfolios can be extremely useful in documenting such progress. These insights should be shared with the students, their parents, other teachers, and school staff and administrators when making program placement decisions for English language learners. Unlike standardized tests, they will often show that English language learners *are* making progress even though their test scores may not demonstrate it. Moreover, ongoing assessments are likely to be much more useful than standardized tests in helping teachers make informed instructional decisions for their English language learners.

For Review

Assessment is used in this chapter as a term to cover deciding what we need to know about children's learning, considering what means we will need to use to get the information and possibly designing our own, collecting the information, and interpreting the information to help us make instructional decisions to help the students.

With the federal No Child Left Behind Act and, particularly, with the Reading First program has come an intensified interest in assessment. Reading First requires that teachers assess children at four moments: for screening, for diagnosis, for progress monitoring, and to assess outcomes. Assessment of students' literacy is becoming standardized across the United States and U.S. territories via the Common Core Standards.

Several different kinds of assessment instruments are available to teachers. Standardized or norm-based tests compare children to other children; and standards-based tests look at their accomplishment of curricular standards. Curriculum-based measurement takes brief snapshots of learning, usually for monitoring purposes, and these are closely tied to the outcomes that are desired at the end of the year. Informal assessments such as the Informal Reading Inventory, the Reading Miscue Inventory, and running records reveal a rich array of information about children's reading. However, teachers need to pay attention to the validity (the extent to which the test measures what it claims to) and reliability (the extent to which the findings of the text are stable) of tests they use.

Assessments are done of various aspects of emergent literacy, including print concepts, language awareness, and letter knowledge. Once children can begin to read, we can assess reading levels (independent, instructional, and frustration) as well as their word recognition, fluency, vocabulary, and comprehension. The readability of texts can be assessed by means of a readability formula or the cloze procedure. Teachers and teachers-to-be are now expected to pass competency tests, most of which are derived from and coordinated with the Common Core Standards.

For Your Journal

1. Now that you have read the chapter, return to the anticipation guide at the beginning. What differences are there in how you would answer those questions now?

2. Choose a grade that you would like to teach, or that you do teach. First, describe what aspects of reading and writing you would want to test for in your screening and diagnostic assessments. Second, explain what instruments you would use and why.

3. Go online and find your state's standards for literacy at your chosen grade level. Read the information about the outcomes-based assessments given. Then, for each set of abilities and concepts that they list, describe the way you would monitor students' progress toward achieving those outcomes.

Taking It to the World

The Common Core Standards were adopted by most states in very short order. Forty-five states and the District of Columbia will be preparing to conform to them during the life of this edition of *All Children Read*. If your state did not adopt them, find the arguments about why not. If your state is among the great majority that did adopt them, what steps are your schools taking to meet the standards?

MyEducationLab™

Go to Topic 8 (Assessment) in the MyEducationLab <www.myeducationlab.com> for your course, where you can:

- Find learning outcomes for Assessment along with the national standards that connect to these outcomes.

- Complete Assignments and Activities that can help you more deeply understand the chapter content.

- Apply and practice your understanding of the core teaching skills identified in the chapter with the Building Teaching Skills and Dispositions learning units.

- Check your comprehension on the content covered in the chapter by going to the Study Plan in

the Book Resources for your text. Here you will be able to take a chapter quiz, receive feedback on your answers, and then access Review, Practice, and Enrichment activities to enhance your understanding of chapter content.

- Visit A+RISE. A+RISE® Standards2Strategy™ is an innovative and interactive online resource that offers new teachers in grades K-12 just in time, research-based instructional strategies that meet the linguistic needs of ELLs as they learn content, differentiate instruction for all grades and abilities, and are aligned to Common Core Elementary Language Arts standards English language proficiency standards in WIDA, Texas, California, and Florida.

Putting Effective Literacy Instruction into Practice: Grades K to 2

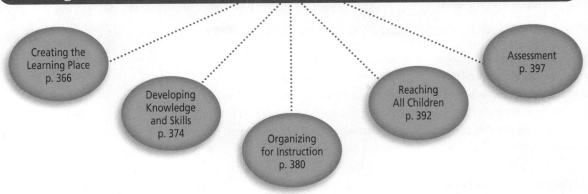

Creating the Learning Place
p. 366

Developing Knowledge and Skills
p. 374

Organizing for Instruction
p. 380

Reaching All Children
p. 392

Assessment
p. 397

Anticipation Guide

The following statements will help you begin thinking about the topics of this chapter. Answer *true* or *false* in response to each statement. As you read and learn more about the topics in these statements, double-check your answers. See what interests you and prompts your curiosity toward more understanding.

_____ **1.** Establishing a friendly and supportive psychological/social climate in the classroom should be a teacher's first concern in teaching early literacy.

_____ **2.** It is more important for children to learn to follow the teacher's rules than to manage their own behavior.

_____ **3.** In classroom management, it is useful to make a distinction between teaching children procedures and enforcing discipline.

_____ **4.** When children practice learning procedures, these procedures eventually become routines.

_____ **5.** Reading to children is valuable in kindergarten when most children cannot read for themselves, but it has little value after that.

_____ **6.** The "five-finger test" is a way of telling if a book is too difficult for primary grade children to read: If children miss five words on a page, the book is probably too hard.

_____ **7.** Children can learn about phonics from writing and using invented or temporary spelling.

_____ **8.** Children who are English language learners will not profit from formal instruction in English reading until they reach an intermediate level of proficiency in English.

_____ **9.** Young children don't benefit from reading and having non-fiction books read to them. They are much more comfortable with fairy tales and stories.

_____ **10.** Learning centers should be carefully designed to teach only reading or writing skills. It is not advisable to mix content from other subjects such as social studies or science into them.

A Classroom Story

Literacy Activities in a First-Grade Classroom

It's October. Nineteen children are looking at books while Ana Lopes sets the non-fiction big book, *Bread, Bread, Bread* (Morris & Hevman, 1989) on the easel. Her students come from diverse backgrounds; all the children can connect meaningfully with this information book. There are actual photos of people making and eating bread—including Mexican tortillas, Indian nan, French baguettes, and others.

Ms. Lopes speaks to a small group of children who are not scheduled to participate in this lesson. She offers them a choice of two literacy activities: They can work on creating a poster for a science project or in the classroom interest center. Once they are settled, Ms. Lopes motions to the other children to join her on the reading rug. She asks them to look at the pictures first, and then whisper their ideas about the book to one another. Now actively involved, children in the larger group whisper and then talk with Ms. Lopes about bread.

Before she reads the book, she points out the author and illustrator names and has the children repeat them. She also asks that they pay attention to the pictures and decide if they depict real people and if they show something meaningful. As she reads the book aloud, she uses a long pointer to indicate each complete word (emphasizing that the groups of letters separated by a space are words) while she encourages the children to read with her.

Ms. Lopes stops reading to spark comprehension-supporting discussions—sometimes about the book and other times about the writing. She says, "I really like the way this author talks about making bread. Who is this author? Let's see that name again." Ms. Lopes prompts pointing out the author's name as the children read it together. Ms. Lopes points out that this book tells us the chronology, that is, the steps to follow in making bread. "Do any of you know something about making bread?"

One child says, "I like the way it smells!"

"Oh yes, and I like the way you are listening! Does anyone else have something to say?" says Ms. Lopes. Several children raise their hands and again engage in conversation. Next, the children who didn't get a turn at speaking are invited to whisper what they know about bread making in one another's ears. Everyone is included!

By drawing the children into talking about the meaning of the text and the nature of the written presentation, Ms. Lopes is teaching good reader behaviors and encouraging the children to think, comprehend, and relate personally to books. She also shows the children that she is interested in what they know or are thinking. She and the class discuss the photos showing people all over the world making bread. The point of this discussion is that the photos sometimes tell more or the same thing that the words say.

After reading, children are encouraged to identify words they know. Ms. Lopes points out that some words begin with two consonant blend letters, such as /br/ in *bread*. As the lesson continues, Ms. Lopes points out that some words with consonant blends are repeated, such as "bread, bread, bread." She asks the students to find other words that are repeated. A child responds, "I see the word eat. And we saw it before, too."

"Excellent word watching!" Ms. Lopes responds. "Now let's see if we can spot the word eat repeated again."

This teacher draws the children into more focused reading by asking them to think about the book's words as she points to words on the word wall (see page 383) that share features with the words in the book; for example, they end with the same phonogram pattern, or they begin with consonant blends.

As Ms. Lopes brings the lesson to a conclusion, the children move into dramatic play as they pretend to make and eat bread. While they are engaged in play, Ms. Lopes returns to her desk to make quick notes on her observations of children who actively participated and those who needed nudging into the lesson. She also makes notes on the sense children seemed to make about letter-to-sound relationships. Then she motions for all the children to return to their seats.

Creating the Learning Place

CCSS

• Common Core Standards for Informational, Text K–5, standards 5, 6

School beginnings are important. Teachers focus first of all on setting up a learning place: a classroom environment and instructional procedures that support learning. In the complex act of teaching, we strive for children to become *readers* who not only "know the words" but also engage their whole minds. The goals of early-grade literacy instruction are to nurture children intellectually, emotionally, and socially as we immerse them in spoken and written language, instill concepts about print, and develop their joy in reading and writing (IRA & NAEYC, 1998). Effective teachers create a *learning place* as they carefully craft their lessons so that children experience success and come to believe in themselves as competent learners on the path to literacy. Because nothing succeeds like success, your students' success ensures your success.

A learning place is created in a classroom that is steeped in mutual respect and responsibility. Young children come to school believing that they will learn to read and write. The effective and caring teacher in the early grades can go a long way toward fulfilling that expectation. Teaching requires sustained energy and dedication, which becomes self-sustaining in the teacher when it is supported by certain attributes:

CCSS
• Foundational Skills 1: Print Concepts

CCSS
• Informational Text 7 and 8: Integration of Knowledge and Ideas

CCSS
• Foundational Skills 2 and 3: Phonological Awareness; Phonics

- Strong principles
- A strong sense of responsibility for student learning and motivation
- A desire to search for personal strengths
- An enjoyment of interactions with students and an abiding compassion for them (Ayers, 1993).

Classroom Management

As they set about creating a productive classroom, many teachers, especially beginning teachers, think first about classroom management. Even the most creative teaching can achieve little unless it takes place in a well-ordered environment in which children can focus on learning and discovering.

In order to achieve a well-ordered classroom, it is useful to distinguish between establishing *routines* and maintaining *discipline* (Wong & Wong, 2009). Having routines ensures that children know what to do at all times during the school day so that many young people occupying the same space at the same time can work productively and enjoyably. Routines apply to such things as coming into the classroom in the morning and getting to work, working in learning centers, feeding the fish, watering the plants, walking to and from the classroom library, hosting visitors to the classroom, rotating assignments and carrying out classroom tasks, reading with a partner, settling disagreements, borrowing books and returning them, distributing hand-outs, reading with a partner, participating in a guided reading group, cleaning up after art work, and getting ready to leave at the end of the school day. Having well-understood routines helps ensure that children are able to control themselves peacefully. Behavioral routines also deal with the limits of what is acceptable and what happens when behavior is unacceptable.

ESTABLISHING ROUTINES   It takes the first few weeks of school to establish procedures that will become routines. There are many procedures that students must learn to carry out; teachers must prioritize and select just a few to teach at first, and add more as the year goes on. Some of the procedures have to do with general classroom order, such as:

- Entering the classroom in the morning
- Going over the day's schedule
- Performing tasks assigned for the day and learning week-long tasks
- Taking turns speaking
- Moving about the classroom or asking to be excused
- Getting ready to leave for recess
- Moving as a group through the hallway
- Cleaning up after artwork and other tasks that involve materials
- Getting ready to go home

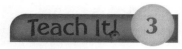

Teach It! 3

Morning Message

Teach It! 52

Shared Writing

Elementary school teachers discuss reasons why young children may struggle with socially acceptable school behaviors and share strategies to encourage appropriate behavior. After watching the video, reflect on the strategies you have learned and when you have seen them implemented with children in grades K to 2.

Other procedures are more specific to language and literacy instruction:

- Coming to the reading circle and participating in an interactive read-aloud
- Listening to the morning message
- Participating in a guided reading lesson
- Using the quiet reading area
- Choosing and using books from the classroom library, and returning them
- Reading with a partner
- Learning what to do during independent reading time
- Learning what to do during independent writing time
- Sharing writing
- Working in a learning center
- Learning what to do when you come across an unknown word in reading
- Learning what to do when you need to spell an unknown word in writing
- Participating in group work
- Sharing and critiquing written work

To teach a procedure, you should carefully explain and demonstrate it to the class. You may end the lesson by showing the students a poster with the procedure explained in bulleted steps (for younger children who cannot yet read many words, the steps may be identified by graphic symbols). The posters will be hung around the room. See Figure 12.1 for an example of a classroom procedure.

After you teach the procedure, be sure to practice it. Just as schools have many fire drills early in the year and a few periodically thereafter, many wise teachers provide guided practice in carrying out a procedure until every student knows how it is done. Remind the students from time to time how to do the procedure, especially if problems arise with children not performing it properly. But even if it goes well, make sure the procedure is well engrained in the students' behavior. Once the procedure is so well learned that it is second nature, it becomes a routine.

Teaching procedures is a good way to gradually place responsibility on the students to control their own behavior. As they learn, let them know that you have confidence in their ability to manage themselves. Guide children toward self-management. Take whatever time is needed.

ESTABLISHING AND MAINTAINING PRODUCTIVE BEHAVIOR   Before children arrive in your classroom, you should have in mind ways in which you will help them learn

Figure 12.1   Procedure Poster

When Mr. Acevedo Reads a Book Aloud

1. Listen and watch

2. Keep your hands to yourself

3. Make pictures in your mind

4. Wonder what will happen next

5. Be ready to say what the book makes you think of

to manage their own behaviors. For example, generate a few simple classroom rules or guidelines for the first days of school and show great appreciation for the children's efforts to comply with them. Be generous with time and respect. Some kindergarteners may have been to preschool, and others have not; some have traveled and known various people and places, and others have had none of these experiences. Some have siblings in other grades, others have not.

A useful strategy in the first weeks of school is to use a form such as the Teacher Observation Form (Tattershaw & Prendeville, 1995) for recording observations to identify where some trouble spots may arise (see Figure 12.2). Often children do not know what to do in school; in fact, learning to "do school" for the first time or in a new classroom is quite a challenge for many of them. Some children may need frequent redirecting to learn what is expected of them. After carrying out structured observations, you can tell at a glance who needs more of your guidance.

BEHAVIOR CONTRACTS   If you repeatedly demonstrate for the child, both physically and verbally, what to do, but are still unsuccessful, you may try writing a contract. A simple written document nicely integrates literacy into a way for children to learn to control their own behavior. One copy for the child and one for the teacher is a good idea. Here are some simple ideas you may find useful:

- List the child's name and yours, using one piece of paper or several pieces stapled together.
- Insert a line about the daily meeting that will be dated by both you and the child. Pick a moment right before school starts or ends and show the child your notes on one, two, or three behavior(s). Insert a line for the child to check off or write in the good behaviors achieved that day. Make this part of your talk very upbeat and enjoyable, celebrating the smallest positive move. Also insert a space where you can list what the child and you want her to work on every day. Finally, read over the contract together.

Contract writing is particularly helpful with students who have difficulty adjusting to the class routine or controlling negative behaviors, as well as those who have learning challenges. Keep your teacher observation forms and contracts as needed in children's files.

From the first day of school, talk with the children about what will happen during the day. It's a mystery to them! Post a daily schedule on a large chart; knowing what will happen next will create comfort in the classroom. Note that in doing this you are also inviting the children into literacy. Strive for all classroom routines to have some written language aspects. Reviewing the day's routine again and again, providing special attention as needed, and drawing the children into play and song activities all help calm anxiety, particularly for the youngest children. By second grade or even perhaps in first grade, you might want to include students in your planning; this encourages them to take on more responsibility.

Writing and Reading Connections

How can the teacher motivate young children to begin to manage their own behavior?

"I HAVE A PROBLEM."   Regardless of your careful work, children will have problems that can interrupt the classroom. A literacy strategy that helps teachers and children deal with conflict and think critically through reasoning and evidence is an "I have a problem" writing place. Post a sign, and provide writing materials and a "problem basket." Assure children that the two of you will read their writing and solve the problem together. Figure 12.3 is an example of the kind of message that you might get.

Learning Centers

Learning centers are spaces set aside in the classroom where individuals, pairs, and small groups of students engage in activities that extend their learning. A learning center can be arranged on tables with space for children to work on both sides. It can also be a big book on an easel and space for students to work, or a pocket chart and task cards hung in a quiet

Figure 12.2 Teacher Observation Form

Teacher Observations

Student's name: _____ Date: _____

Teacher's name: _____

Please use the following statements to guide your observations of the child on a typical school day. Write your comments after each statement.

1. The child seems to know the order of events in a typical class day.

   Yes   No   Comments: _____
   ☐   ☐   _____

2. The child looks in your direction when you are standing in your usual teaching spot.

   Yes   No   Comments: _____
   ☐   ☐   _____

3. The child responds appropriately and in a timely manner to your signals for attention.

   Yes   No   Comments: _____
   ☐   ☐   _____

4. The child can usually restate directions that you have given in his or her own words when asked to do so.

   Yes   No   Comments: _____
   ☐   ☐   _____

5. The child restates only the first part of directions.

   Yes   No   Comments: _____
   ☐   ☐   _____

6. The child restates only the last part of directions.

   Yes   No   Comments: _____
   ☐   ☐   _____

7. The child responds appropriately to your signals for transitions. (For example, the child puts away materials used for prior tasks, gets out materials for the new activity, or looks at you with apparent readiness for the new information or activity.)

   Yes   No   Comments: _____
   ☐   ☐   _____

8. The child seems to have difficulty leaving a project or task when you signal a transition.

   Yes   No   Comments: _____
   ☐   ☐   _____

9. The child seems to look at and follow peers' actions rather than respond independently to your signal for transitions.

   Yes   No   Comments: _____
   ☐   ☐   _____

10. The child's comments are appropriate for the topic under discussion.

    Yes   No   Comments: _____
    ☐   ☐   _____

11. The child seems able to understand and follow the rules and procedures of a game or classroom activity.

    Yes   No   Comments: _____
    ☐   ☐   _____

12. The child follows the class rules for behavior without reminders.

    Yes   No   Comments: _____
    ☐   ☐   _____

Source: From *Using Familiar Routines in Language Assessment and Intervention* by S. Tattershaw and J. Prendeville. Copyright © 1995. Permission granted by Sandra Tattershaw.

Figure 12.3 "I Have a Problem" Note

> simon   5/17/02
> I have a problem.
>
> Today Bob pushed me into
> the lunch line and sed bad
> wards. I told him to stop he din't
> stop

corner. Many teachers create learning centers in tubs of various sizes. Or one could be a space by the window where plants grow, with a reading/writing area and various levels of science books and rulers for measuring plant growth. It can be a puppet theater, or a dramatic play area decorated according to the theme of the fiction and non-fiction books the class is reading, which range from easy to challenging levels.

Depending on the grade level, K, 1, or 2 learning centers will include a number of Common Core standards. For example, given the structure and focus of the center, it will include several standards for any of the primary grades. For example, the range of easy to challenging texts meets the goals of using literature and/or information books in your teaching. In like manner, for example, in a center that includes writing, students' discussions will include the teacher's focus on various Common Core Standards for Writing, Speaking, and Listening, and Language Standards K–5 without excluding Reading Standards.

Most center materials can be purchased, but many teachers enjoy the creative act of making their own—going to garage sales and collecting books and other materials from retiring teachers or friends works well, too. Book collections are built more easily by sharing with other teachers. This may come about as you engage in mapping curriculum (Jacobs, 1997, 2006). Centers may focus on areas of study such as the first-grade unit, Life Lesson, described in Common Core Curriculum Maps (Common Core, 2010). This unit helps meet Common Core State Standards (hereafter CCSS).

There are multiple criteria to keep in mind as you prepare learning centers:

1. They should address standards' objectives from at least one content area and always include literacy skills and strategies.

2. Learning center activities should be planned so that they can synchronize with other activities being conducted at the same time.

3. The procedures should be straightforward and, once they are well taught, should require neither elaborate explanation nor direct supervision.

4. There should be some end product or other indication that the student has completed the center. Most of these should be suitable for ongoing assessment.

5. Learning centers should be long on use and reasonably short on preparation. Some are set up in an hour or two after school, others require much more time. Learning centers should be engaging enough and variable enough for children to rotate through the same one at least several times over several weeks or

CCSS

- Literature and Informational Text 10: Range of Reading

To create a literacy-rich classroom, it's important to include an array of books that appeal to all children's needs and interests.

Integrating Across the Curriculum
Teaching Science in a Learning Center

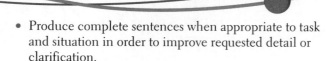

The second grade is engaged in an inquiry science unit. Their teacher has carefully planned the materials and activities to support the CCSS and learning science <www.scoe.net/castandards/agenda/2010/ela_ccs_recommendations.pdf>. The center's theme is "What Do Plants Need to Grow?" Among other materials, we need the following items: A table large enough for children's work; radish seeds; soil; paper cups; rulers; markers; paper for children to record their findings, including a large piece of graph paper on the wall with 1-inch squares (each pair or small group of students working together needs its own column on the graph paper).

Focus Standard

Reading—Literary Texts
- Compare and contrast two or more versions of the same story by different authors.
- Ask and answer such questions as *who, what, where, when* and/or *why* that demonstrates understanding key details.

Reading—Informational Texts
- Compare and contrast important points presented by two texts on the same topic.
- Identify the main purpose of a text, including what the author wants to answer, explain, or describe it.

Reading—Foundational Skills
- Recognize and read grade-appropriate irregularly spelled words.
- Read on-level text orally on successive readings.

Speaking and Listening
- Build on others' talk in conversations by linking their comments to the remarks of others.

- Produce complete sentences when appropriate to task and situation in order to improve requested detail or clarification.

Language
- Use knowledge of language and its conventions when writing, speaking, reading, or listening.
- Demonstrate understanding of word relationships and nuances in word meanings.

Writing
- Participate in shared research and writing projects (e.g., read a number of books on a single topic to produce a report; record science observations).
- Write opinion pieces in which they introduce the topic or book they are writing about, state an opinion, supply reasons that support the opinion, use linking words (e.g., *because, and, also*) to connect opinion and reasons, provide a concluding statement or section.

Management and Objectives

Provide task cards with instructions ranging from some with illustrations to cards written at rigorous levels. Many learning center activities are cooperative in nature, so children work together to solve problems, use literacy skills, and learn science. The teacher introduces the science center and helps children learn how to use it before they begin on their own. Completing some cards will require adult supervision—a paraprofessional or a parent volunteer can help with more complex tasks in the first few days, for example, the graphing task. In time, the children will become independent. At times, you will conduct ongoing assessments and redirect children to repeat, correct, share, or discuss a task. Thus, you are always teaching and assessing. Daily effective teaching combines both!

(continued)

quarterly. Alternatively, some center(s) could have durable frameworks (same design, similar instructions, and same space) set up for different content that is changed more frequently.

Scheduling and monitoring students' progress through learning centers requires a well-designed system.

- A wall chart can specify which students will be assigned to various centers weekly.
- Each child can have a pocket folder with a "center schedule" anchored in the middle with brads. For younger children, an icon representing each center can be

Here are samples of task card instructions; they include examples of instructions for growing/studying plants and examples of tasks more explicitly related to standards. In each instance, task cards are written at various levels and students are guided to work with the range of cards and to use them individually, with a buddy, and/or in small group:

- After you plant your radish seed in the cup, be sure it has everything it needs to grow. Draw a picture of the seed. Draw a new picture of your plant once a week; write the date under each picture.
- Check through the center puzzles, or illustrations that show how plants look when they are growing. Compare these drawings to your plant's growth, write about what you notice, and tape your writing to the drawing you like best.
- Fill in one square on your graph on the day your plant reaches another inch-date.
- Each week, read one center easy book and one challenging book with a buddy, record and date books read on your center folder, write your answer to the question, "Why were these books alike or not alike?"
- Look through science books and make two lists, one for what plants need to grow and one for what is harmful to plants. Compare these lists with a buddy. Write about your findings. Draw a picture of a healthy plant and one that is not.
- Choose an important part of the challenging book, think about what you want to teach a buddy about what you have read, reread the important part over three times, and write down what you want to say.
- Listen to the *Jack in the Beanstalk* audio book, think about the characters, and answer these questions: "What did Jack do? What did the giant do? and Why did they do it?" Next, read the same book, think about both books, and write sentences about details you liked in the audio book and that you liked in the book you read.
- Write a page about the author's main purpose in writing a book that you enjoy reading.
- Listen to the *Jack and the Beanstalk* book and write about your favorite parts; tell why you like them. Then read the book *Trust Me, Jack's Beanstalk Stinks!* Write about your favorite parts of this book. Write about how these books are the same and different.

- Listen to a song, then watch a video; write your answer to these questions: "What is the same in these two media and what is different, and which do you like best?"

Learning centers provide an excellent opportunity to teach literacy across the curriculum and in accord with the standards. Beyond reading and writing materials, this center includes games, a video viewing place, and a listening place.

Suggested Works
INFORMATION TEXTS

How plants grow (Angela Royston, Heinemann-Raintree) (Lexile 299–399)

From seed to plant (Allan Fowler) (Lexile 299–400)

Read aloud/independent cross-over book—information in story format

The Magic School Bus Plants Seeds: A Book about How Living Things Grow (J. Cole, Scholastic) (Lexiles 299–499)

LITERARY TEXTS

Trust Me, Jack's Beanstalk Stinks! The story of Jack and the beanstalk as told by the giant (Eric Mark Braun, Harper Collins) (Lexiles 299–499)

Mama Miti (Wangari Muta Mattha, Simon & Schuster) (Lexiles 300–499)

Poem

Oats, peas, beans and barley grow (Tony Barbani) (Lexiles not available)

Art, Play, Media, and Teaching Materials

Jack and the Beanstalk (Keepsake Stories) Audio Book CD (Carol Ottolenghi)

<www.neok12.com/Plants.htm>—see for K–2 children's videos, manipulative puzzles, games, teacher-created presentations and students' project presentations
<www.neok12.com/quiz/PLANTS01>
<www.youtube.com/watch?=OQT6piZOX7c>
<www.songsforteaching.com/curriculumrocks/aplantwillgrow.htm>

---

printed on the schedule, with instructions for the child to color the icon as soon as she has completed the center. Worksheets or other written products can be kept in the folder all week, and handed in at the end of the week to be graded <www.mrsmcdowell.com/centers.htm>.

- Each child can have a "center lariat" to hang around his or her neck, with icons printed on it that correspond to the centers. The students check off or color each icon once the center has been completed.

Time for students to work in learning centers is scheduled in rotation with small group instruction with the teacher, independent reading time, and perhaps independent

Teach It! 13

Working with Names to Teach the Alphabet

writing time. Begin small group reading and writing instruction and start using learning centers as soon as you have the whole class well organized and the day running smoothly.

Learning centers should begin in kindergarten, before all children are reading and writing well. These centers usually focus on such topics as alphabet learning (opportunities for children to copy and write letters, write, experiment with writing names, create labels for areas of the classroom, and so on), blocks (a great old standby that interests boys and girls in building and learning spatial concepts), math (primarily counting and sorting), dress up (dramatic play), art (clay/play dough), and home living. Special centers such as a grocery store or post office are popular kindergarten learning centers. Within your effective literacy teaching, weave objectives and activities according to your state's standards. The old standby centers such as housekeeping are valuable in the healthy development of young children (Christie, 1991; Christie & Roskos, 2001; Morrow, 2003). They provide important "stress-free periods" from regular literacy work and the integrated curriculum. Much learning occurs in centers. Make no mistake: Young children learn a great deal in productive play. Various activity and interest centers should be part of the schedule each day or week, depending on the children's maturity and needs.

Integrated Curriculum

Throughout this book we stress the importance of multiple, repeated, and meaningful opportunities for children to read, write, speak, and listen at more and more challenging levels, whether they are learning science, social studies, or math. Everything children are learning in the twenty-first century classroom—from recognizing the English alphabet to the new literacies and technology—are a must for the college and career preparation they have a right to. It is critical for all students to experience as much varied, well-integrated literacy practice as possible. From kindergarten through middle and high school, students must be reading, writing, speaking, and listening at their grade level and beyond.

Just think about what your learning centers, over and above your grouped integrated curriculum lessons, will offer when each and every center integrates all language arts modalities, including:

"Word Conversations" for Primary Grades

- Oral language and listening to language (remember, a silent primary classroom is a boring, frustrating place and it cannot achieve the CCSS)
- Music, writing, drawing, and building using a range and variety of tools, including technology, to create meaningful images and thought
- Writing and reading as tools for learning and success in school, such as the use of behavior contracts and wall charts and signs

See the feature "Integrating Across the Curriculum: Teaching Reading and Writing through Science in a Learning Center" for an example.

Developing Knowledge and Skills

CCSS

• Common Core Standards for Informational Text K–5, standards 1–10 (depending on the instructional design and implementation)

As a primary teacher, you might ask, "What are the most important learning opportunities teachers should provide for children in the earliest years of reading instruction?" First, children must learn to love school and reading materials of all sorts—from the words in a song to videos with subtitles, books, or online readings—and they must learn basic skills of literacy. Second, the teacher must know the reading process and understand well the developmental changes that new readers experience. You have read a good deal about literacy development previously. If you become a K–2 teacher, that learning and this material will serve you well. Use it for teaching support, for classroom design, and for your own family's and friends' enrichment!

Instruction in grades K–2 focuses not only on the five elements of reading that the U.S. Department of Education emphasizes—awareness of sounds in words, awareness of letter-to-sound relationships, fluency, vocabulary, and comprehension—but also on developing children's oral language (Ogle & Beers, 2009) and helping them think of themselves as readers. Written language is grounded in oral language, and for young children, song and poetry play key roles; children are wonderfully attracted to rhythm and they delight in learning to read the words to songs and poems they like! Language development is supported by teachers' reading aloud, dramatic action, social interactions, and their own talk—lots of talk about literacy work and classroom life! A silent classroom is a barrier to learning. As children move through the stages of reading development, the goal is that they all arrive at fluent oral reading and silent reading on grade level and beyond it by the beginning of third grade. Some will gain these abilities by the end of first grade and many by the end of second grade. Children become better readers as a result of:

- High-quality guided reading instruction
- Reading a great deal of easy materials in beginning reading and increasingly challenging and varied materials as time goes on. Good teachers nudge children along by structuring their choice of a challenging book each week or two
- Becoming more aware of reading strategies and how to use them
- Building more independent action and having the willingness to take on challenging reading

Critically, this willingness is developed when teachers consistently demonstrate that risk taking is held in high regard and that students do not suffer feelings of failure when their reading is not "word perfect" (Allen & Mason, 1989).

See The World of Reading box for an example of teachers' critical thinking and questioning. Figure 12.4 provides an example of children's self-directed practice in word identification strategies.

Helping children learn good strategies builds metacognition and extends skills to all areas of their educational and personal lives. These skills open up the world to children. Kathleen and Katie explain just what those strategies are in Figures 12.5A and 12.5B.

Reading Aloud

Teacher read-alouds in grades K–2 should be the most common teaching practice in the United States and throughout the world. And reading aloud should continue through high school (Trelease, 2006). Reading aloud reinforces children's literacy growth (Adams, 1990). Reading aloud supports children with risk factors, such as living in poverty, having less parent involvement, and having limited language development (Temple & Makinster, 2005).

Reading Aloud

Figure 12.4   Word Strategies

Name _Will_____ Date _May 14, 2001_
What you read today _The town mouse and county mouse_

Word Strategies

1. List the strategies you used to figure out words when you were reading today.
   CHunK,   sKip,   sounl

2. Write down a sentence that had a word you had trouble with and underline the word.
   She had never seen such delicacies

3. Tell what you did to figure out what this word meant.
   I cHunKed the wild out

Figure 12.5A *I Am a Good Reader*—Kathleen

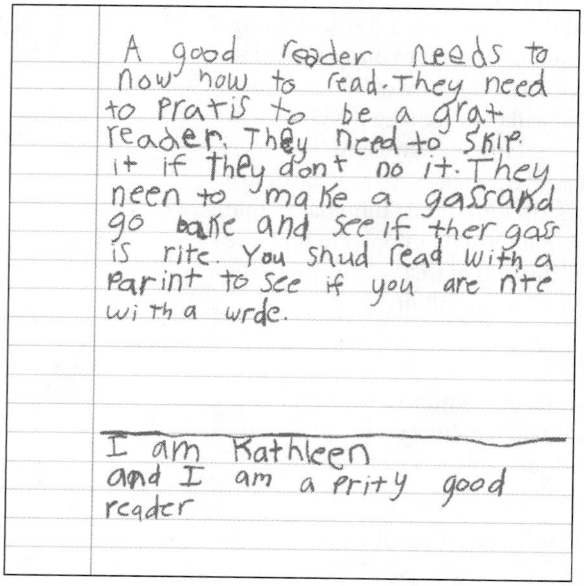
A good reader needs to now how to read. They need to pratis to be a grat reader. They need to skip it if they don't no it. They neen to make a gassand go bake and see if ther gass is rite. You shud read with a parint to see if you are rite with a wrde.

I am Kathleen and I am a prity good reader

Figure 12.5B *I Am a Good Reader*—Katie

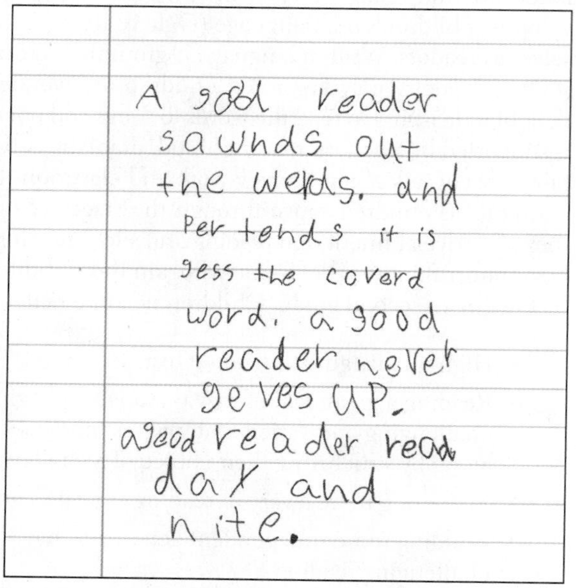
A gobl reader sawnds out the werds. and pertends it is gess the coverd word. a good reader never geves up. agood reader read day and nite.

Teachers in grades K–2 read aloud three to five times daily for sheer pleasure and for vital instructional conversations that are particularly helpful to English language learners and struggling readers. Reading aloud often makes connections to children's lives (Sipe, 2000). Making it real is very important! Through an analysis of the oral and written language of well-read-to young children, Victoria Purcell-Gates (1991) found that those children understood the vocabulary and structures of written language even before they learned to read. Thus, children who have had extensive read-aloud experiences before starting school have an important advantage. In another study with low-income children who had not been well read to before starting school, and who then received extensive teacher read-alouds in kindergarten and first grade, Purcell-Gates, McIntyre, and Freppon (1995) found that by the end of first grade, their knowledge of written language was comparable to that of upper- and high-middle income, well-read-to children. It is reasonable to infer that teachers' read-alouds compensated for the children's limited reading experiences prior to school.

Competent middle school teachers value and practice reading aloud (Alley, 2008; McEwan-Adkins, 2001), and many effective high school teachers are finding successful instructional strategy in reading aloud. McEwan-Adkins (2001) reports raising middle and high school reading achievement by reading aloud.

Interactive reading aloud demonstrates to children that reading is *comprehending*; that is, that reading is thinking and making sense. It prompts children to engage in comprehending as they hear sophisticated vocabulary. Importantly, having words in their listening vocabulary provides a significant boost in learning new words (Beck, McKeown, & Kucan, 2002; Silverman 2007). All this and more happens when teachers regularly read aloud and ask open-ended questions. Naturally, reading aloud comes alive with meaning for students and teachers when it's interactive.

These examples show that "value-added" teaching is done explicitly and implicitly in reading aloud. Reading aloud is also useful in organizing and managing classrooms in the following ways:

- Getting the day or period off to a good start
- Changing classroom activities in an orderly way such as getting ready for the next class, next lesson, recess, or lunch (just start reading the current read-aloud and see what happens during transitions)

CCSS

- Common Core Standards Literature or Informational Texts Reading Skills, K–5, standards 1–10 depending on your teaching focus

The World of Reading

Teacher Questioning

Good questioning promotes critical thinking in children and provides high-quality oral language teaching and practice. Critical thinking questions are open ended; they require children to infer, reason, use language to express thought, and think deeply. Open-ended questions call forth more thinking and expressive oral language. Such questions might include: Why do you think that? Why did the author of our story write about ____? What do you think will happen? What would you do? Can you tell me more about that? What is your prediction? Show how you can confirm or disconfirm your prediction. How do you think this problem can be resolved? Consider the following examples of open-ended questions and the child's answers.

TEACHER	CHILD
What did the princess do to help?	She went off on her own to take care of the dragon.
Why did she do that?	She just did. Cause the prince wouldn't.
How could she do that?	She was brave, and she wasn't afraid.
How did the princess and prince dress?	Well, the prince was in nice prince clothes, but all the princess had was a dirty paper bag.
Why?	Because of the dragon. He burned up everything even her clothes.

What did the prince do?	He just stayed in the cave and said her clothes were a mess. And her hair too. That wasn't very nice.

Notice the child's vocabulary and textlike phrasing use: *brave, nice, prince,* and *clothes.* Notice the length of the sentences and the clarity of thought, and consider the critical thinking that occurs in the child's last sentence. "That wasn't very nice." This response demonstrates the use of inference.

Now consider this same discussion, but with the teacher using closed questions that do not call for critical thinking.

TEACHER	CHILD
What happened to the princess?	She ran away.
The prince was no ____?	Help
Who was the prince afraid of?	The dragon.
What did the princess do to the dragon?	Made him tired.

Children can respond "correctly" to constrained/closed questions, yet totally miss the real meaning in the book. With practice, teachers learn good questioning. Some examples of such questions should be kept with as you teach. It is important to pre-read all that children read—know the literature you teach.

- Building a love of reading
- Promoting motivation to read
- Appreciating and knowing books in various genres and authors
- Ending the day on a positive note

Phonics and Phonological Awareness

Why is it important to teach phonics in context of children's needs?

CCSS

- Foundational Skills 3: Phonics and Word Recognition

Phonics Knowledge and Skills

As you know, phonics knowledge is a necessary, but not sufficient condition for learning to read. In literacy lessons, phonics shares attention with oral language development, concepts about print, vocabulary, fluency, comprehension, instantaneous word recognition, and the habit of reading.

Phonics is certainly an important part of balanced literacy instruction. As much as a total of thirty minutes a day in the early grades may be spent on various kinds of phonics instruction.

Phonics instruction should be *systematic*; that is, the teacher should have in mind a set of concepts and specific standards about the English spelling system and she or he should make sure that they are being taught and learned.

Teach It!

Refer to the Teach It! appendix at the end of the book for further activities you can use to reinforce concepts discussed in this chapter.

Reading Aloud

We suggest following these steps for successful reading aloud.

1. **Read the Book.** Read through the book yourself before you read it to children. Decide whether it is suitable for your group. Does it have enough excitement or depth to hold the interest of a whole group? If it is suitable, decide how you want to read it—with humor, with drama, with questions to whet curiosity? If there are voices to bring to life, determine how you want to make each one sound. If you decide to stop reading to ask for predictions or discussion, choose where the stopping places should be. If there are any words or ideas that will be unfamiliar to the children, make a note to pronounce them carefully and explain them to the children.

    If the book has illustrations large enough for the children to see, practice reading the book through while you hold it facing away from you, where the children will be able to see it.

2. **Prepare the Children.** Make sure the children are seated comfortably where they can see and hear you. Most teachers prefer to have the children sit on a carpet or cushions in front of them. As needed, remind the children of the behavior you expect of good listeners: hands to themselves, eyes on the teacher, and ears for the story.

3. **Begin to Read.** Show the children the cover of the book. Ask them what they know about the topic. If you want to arouse more curiosity, quickly show them some other pictures in the interior of the book (not the last pages—keep the suspense going). Ask the children to make predictions about what will happen or what they expect to find out in the book.

    Read the author's and the illustrator's names. Talk about what they contributed to the book. The children should know that the author and the illustrator have important things to do to bring the book into being. Remind the children of any other books they know by this author or this illustrator.

4. **While Reading.** As you read the book, ask for comments about what is going on. For example, how is the character feeling? What is the character's problem? What do they think the character can do to solve the problem? Ask the students to predict what will happen. Read a few pages; then stop again. Ask how things look for the character now. What is the character doing to solve the problem? Do you want to change your prediction? What do the children think will happen now? Why do they think so? Stop before the end and ask for last predictions. Use the terms *confirm* or *disconfirm* in your discussions. Children should be guided to realize that predictions are not wrong if they are not confirmed. Confirming and disconfirming is a critical thinking process we strongly encourage!

5. **Follow Up the Reading.** Ask the children whether the book turned out the way they thought it would. What made them think it would turn out that way, or why were they surprised? What did they like about the book? How did it make them feel? Why?

6. **Reread the Book.** Read the book through a second time. This time, you might want to take more time to look at the ways the illustrator pictured the action. Ask questions about characters, motives, and other things you and the students find interesting about the book.

7. **Leave the Book Available to the Children.** Put the book on display, and encourage children to read it later during scheduled time in the reading center or between other activities. Encourage them to read it to one another.

Phonics instruction should be *developmental*; that is, the teacher should recognize that at an early level, phonics instruction makes children aware of words themselves, and the sounds within them. Then, it focuses on the matches between letters and sounds. At a later level, it focuses on relations between larger chunks of sound and clusters of letters. Beyond that, it emphasizes what happens when vowels in words are "marked" long or short, or when morphological endings are added to words. And still later phonics instruction explores etymologies of words.

Phonics instruction should also be done in the context of reading or writing. Dahl and colleagues (2001, p. ix) write, "Phonics in context means: in the context of children's needs, in the context of children's developing language knowledge, [and] in the context of classroom reading and writing activities." Encouraging young children to write and to use invented or temporary spelling calls their attention to the alphabetic nature of English spelling and leads them to explore letter-to-sound relations (Templeton & Morris, 1999).

Teach It! 5

Language Experience with Authentic Children's Literature

Teach It!

Refer to the Teach It! appendix at the end of the book for further activities you can use to reinforce concepts discussed in this chapter.

Phonics in the Context of Children's Needs

Daniel Woo is teaching a group of eighteen children in a transitional first grade. They have completed kindergarten, but are not yet ready for first grade. Most of the children struggled in kindergarten, and some are English language learners. Mr. Woo's school and its teachers recognize the need for an additional year of expert teaching before first grade to prevent later failure.

In the following lesson, Mr. Woo engages the children in explicit word study that is highly interactive and appealing to them. He has arranged for half of his class to go to music in the morning and half in the afternoon. In this way, Mr. Woo can provide more focused attention to specific children with similar needs in a smaller group. His needs-based lesson follows:

Mr. Woo asks the children to raise their left thumb if they are ready for word play. The children love word play and eagerly help one another find their left thumb.

He then asks the children to give him their "important" word, cautioning them that it must be a real word. This activity is similar to key vocabulary teaching. Mr. Woo says, "Tell us your word and new letters you want to try."

Taking turns, the children say their words and letters they want to substitute as the beginning letter. A child volunteers the word Lex (his dog's name) and the letters D and B.

Mr. Woo writes the word Lex on the board; then the children spell Dex and Bex. Mr. Woo then writes these words on the board. Next, he asks

the children to work with the two words bat and big, and he writes these words on the board. He and the class change the beginning letters to make new real words, with the children leading the conversation.

Mr. Woo guides the instructional conversation, but makes every effort to "lead from behind." He employs scaffolding actions—warmth and responsiveness, coming to shared understandings with children, staying in their zone of proximal development—as he teaches.

For consolidation, he guides the children's participation in word learning practice. He chants, "If I know pig, I know jig." The children read this refrain with him from chart paper. The teacher and the children continue: "If I know day, I know play. If I know...."

As an application and extension of the lesson, Mr. Woo distributes word cards that have the letter/sound patterns just taught and has the children engage in exclusive word learning practice in partner groups and individually.

As part of his ongoing assessment, Mr. Woo takes notes on several children after he has observed and interacted with them as they sort through the word cards. He makes a note to do a formal phonemic awareness test with three children he is worried about.

Source: Contributed by Linda Headings, M.Ed. Used with permission.

Reading Comprehension

Should we teach even kindergartners reading comprehension? Yes, of course; we should teach comprehension at all ages! Comprehension taught both explicitly and implicitly is as important as phonics and vocabulary—just recognizing and saying words is not comprehending. McKeown, Beck, and Blake (2009) argue that contextualized talk with open-ended, critical thinking questions is as important as comprehension strategies. In your highly interactive, lively classroom you will have it, provided you learn *how* to guide such discussions and ask high-quality, critical thinking questions. Be sure to review examples of teacher talk and questioning throughout this book and make a resolution to learn how to engage your children. Classroom vignettes and examples of student/teacher interactions provide models of what teachers need to learn. Moreover, when children are read to and when they read themselves, they must "do something" with the text. This is also true when listening to songs, poems, and books, as well as when reading computer screens and reading materials. Explicitly teach children to internally picture the events and characters and to make personal connections to texts when they read and during reading discussions (Bean & Freppon, 2003; Langer, 1990; Purcell-Gates, 2009). Some children will not automatically do this—in particular, those who struggle and some who are English language learners. "Getting the words" can easily dominate their thinking. The following list of tasks and questions provides remarkably easy, effective comprehension strategies that you can select from and incorporate into daily reading lessons; responses may be written or oral. Importantly, critical thinking occurs during sustained silent reading when readers "do something with their reading." The point is that they can't *just* read, they *must process* their reading using strategies. Children who struggle need this even more.

CCSS
- Literature 1–9: Key Ideas; Craft and Structure; Integration

CCSS
- Foundational Skills 1 and 2: Print Concepts; Phonological Awareness

CCSS
- Informational Text 1–9: Key Ideas; Craft and Structure; Integration

Guiding Student Self-Assessment

Picture the teacher in May—he has observed his kindergartners during a rhyming word lesson and has decided to work with a few children who avoided participating or seemed lost during the activity. For a ten-to-fifteen-minute informal assessment, he gathers a selection of rhyming word cards (single syllable and consonant blend) including words from a lesson just taught: table, able, chair, Blair, rag, bag, tag, goat, boat, float. The children sort the words into rhyming matches independently—they are seated spaced apart at a table.

Having told the children he would make some notes, he watches for accurate matches, mistakes, self-corrections (a sign of confidence and great thinking), and signs of uncertainty. With a small group of four or five children, the teacher is able to make notes on each child. After this brief word sort, he asks the children to move together. Of course, the cards are mixed up as they are slid across the desks, but this gives the children another opportunity to quickly arrange their rhyming matches.

Beginning with accurate matches, the teacher asks why they are matches. He guides children to identify rhyming patterns ("It's the ending letters!") and to encourage self-assessment. Through dialogue, the teacher and children discuss "good matches" and engage in "good fixes." This brings the assessment to a dynamic level; learners self-correct and feel accomplished. During this conversation the teacher affirms, repeats children's accurate reasoning, and corrects as needed. Some direct correcting is needed, but not very much because since the activity began with talk about accurate matches and why they are accurate, incorrect ones are more readily identified and corrected by the children.

Assessment notes are filed in children's folders as they return to their seats. Which is more informative, an assessment such as this or corrected worksheets? Which helps meet standards more? Which is a better use of the teacher's and the students' time? Which is more interesting to you as a professional reading teacher?

- Which part of was your favorite? Create a picture or a poster about your favorite part. Say why you like it.
- What character in _____ was like someone you know? How is this character like someone you know?
- Pretend you are telling someone about _____ and you want them to read or hear it. What will you say?
- What part would you like to change or make better? Describe it and create illustrations as you wish.
- Did you ever read, hear, or see something like this _____ before? How are they alike; how are they different?
- How is this text like another one, or like a TV show, movie, or what you have seen on a computer?
- Design a new cover and tell the reader why you like this image. What makes it meaningful?
- What has happened in this text, or computer program, movie, or TV show that has happened to you? Describe it and illustrate it.
- Make a new title for a song, poem, computer program/game, or book you like. What makes your title meaningful?

These strategies are used during or after reading. Teach the strategies and assign them during silent reading time and of course in other lessons. Depending on your teaching focus, document the specific CCSS or other state standards included in the lessons. Children's responses can be oral, talking to a peer or to the teacher, or written to a peer or teacher and discussed together.

Organizing for Instruction

Nearly all young children benefit from and enjoy learning with peers. They approximate literate reading and writing behaviors through pretend-reading and pretend-writing for some time before the behaviors become a reality. Not all children enter school with the

A Rural Primary Classroom

Plans for a week of reading lessons in a Readers' Workshop.
One lesson set supports children at several developmental levels, another provides for two interest groups, and another gives children opportunities to read their weekly "challenge" books. In teaching, focus on reading comprehension, fluency, and word recognition skills (vocabulary and phonics), as well as children's enjoyment. As you can see, Readers' Workshop helps you teach important standards. Which CCSS standards can you identify in one example here?

For the guided reading groups, get multiple copies of the following books:

- Books for more emergent readers:
  Wake Up, Dad (Randell, 1996c)
  At the Zoo (Peters, 1995)
  The Animals Went to Bed (Theodorou, 1996)

- Books for the solid beginning readers:
  Mrs. Wishy-Washy (Cowley, 1990)
  Baby Bear Goes Fishing (Randell, 1996a)

- Books for those farther along:
  Happy Birthday, Sam (Hutchins, 1978)
  Henny Penny (Galdone, 1968)
  Leo the Late Bloomer (Krauss, 1987)

For interest groups, have several new books. For primary literature texts, include *Ace Lacewing: Bug Detective, Mr. Tuggle's Troubles,* and *Russell the Sheep.* For informational books, include *Jose! Born to Dance, Brave Dogs, Gentle Dogs: How They Guard Sheep,* and *Recess at 20 Below.* During the week, children will have several opportunities to take turns reading these books alone and in pairs. As with all reading groups, attend to comprehension strategies and word recognition skills.

Have the children select challenge books from the classroom or school library. While you teach the guided reading group, instruct the students who are not in the group to read their self-selected books at their tables (or desks pushed together). Later in the day, meet and observe several readers. Something is always gained with the self-selected books, including new vocabulary and increased motivation for the students to read. You gain, too, by learning what your students can do given varied and flexible opportunities to read with your guidance.

---

same abilities. Some children have been in preschool for three or four years, while others are having their first school experience (Riley, 2007). Some might have disabilities, some might read independently, others might have literacy skills typical of a three-year-old, and for some, English is a second or third language. Therefore, instruction must have breadth and great flexibility. In the early years, teachers need to know what to expect in children's development, be able to recognize differences, manage a broad range of development, and use research-based strategies that are designed for a range of development. (See the Differentiated Instruction box.)

Differentiate Instruction Through Grouping and Planning

Grouping children and planning for instruction are major teaching strategies designed to address differences in children's learning. Traditional grouping, which identified students as having high, medium, or low ability, nearly guaranteed underachievement for many children and teachers. How could teachers be effective and still have the same children in the same low-ability group for nine months? For years? This concept is based on an invalid deficit learning model, and it invites a "blame the kid" attitude (Pressley et al., 2001, p. 233).

Research shows that once a child has been assigned to the low reading group, it is highly unlikely he or she will ever be moved to a higher group (Good & Marshall, 1984; Hiebert,1983). Children in low groups often have poor self-esteem and receive instruction with fewer opportunities to think and work with meaning (Allington, 1983; Allington & McGill-Franzen, 1989; Eder, 1983).

Two well-known approaches offer grouping ideas that are designed to help avoid the pitfalls of traditional grouping. Each approach makes a distinction between organization and the kind of instruction conducted. Grouping strategies are not prescriptions for effective teaching. Rather, what teachers *do* in these time blocks is of greatest importance. However, a well-designed lesson structure is essential to managing the classroom, which, of course, frees you to teach your personal best!

DYNAMIC GROUPING   Fountas and Pinnell (2001, 2007) developed the concept of dynamic grouping as a way to target guided reading opportunities. Dynamic grouping involves several kinds of reading and writing groups that work together and receive instruction over the course of a school day. For example, dynamic groups allow for non–ability-based interest groups, peer tutoring and cooperative learning pairs, cross-grade buddies, and needs-based small groups (flexible and ability based). In needs-based groups, children are moved regularly so that no child is stuck in any one group all year.

GUIDED READING AND FOUR BLOCKS   As described earlier, *guided reading* often takes place within a *four-blocks* language arts period. However, guided reading could take place in other organizations. For example, a wise and creative teacher effectively guides children's reading using basal texts if required to use them, and teaches just as effectively with a range of texts/ materials required by CCSS. This happens because by definition guided reading creates "a context in which the teacher supports each reader's development of effective strategies for reading at increasingly challenging levels of difficulty" (Fountas & Pinnell, 2001). Provide first and second graders with opportunities to select their own challenge books. This helps ensure high interest. We surely don't want to force young children to read difficult materials they don't find interesting. Such a practice will not a reader make! And it could cause behavior problems.

Four blocks is a well-balanced instructional structure. It describes four specialized reading periods that address some of teachers' most challenging issues. No matter what reading program is used, all teachers are faced with the responsibility of teaching a class of twenty to thirty students in ways that meet their individual needs, without having some children labeled and taught as "low-ability" all year. Strive for about half of all reading materials to be literary and half non-fiction or informational texts. Additionally, the question of how to grade young children looms large. Cunningham, Hall, and Sigmon (2007) and Cunningham, Hall, and Defree (1991) created a framework to address these questions and issues and to provide guidelines for organization, planning, teaching, and grading. (Grading is discussed later.) The four blocks provide varied and ample opportunities for primary grade children to learn and for teachers to teach reading and writing.

The framework of four reading periods occurs during the school day and includes (1) guided reading, (2) self-selected reading, (3) working with words, and (4) writing. Within each block, specific structured activities take place. A major goal of four blocks is to give children a balance of reading, writing, and word instruction. Four-blocks structure provides what is necessary for teachers to make each block as multileveled as possible. *Multileveled groups* help include all children at some success level (Cunningham & Allington, 1999; Cunningham, Hall, & Defree, 1991). *And nothing succeeds like success!* These four blocks contain the following key elements:

Guided Reading and the Four Blocks Approach

- *Guided Reading.* For 30 to 40 minutes, with teacher guidance, children read various texts and are taught reading strategies. The lesson focus is also on developing prior knowledge; oral language; word identification including guessing with letter/sound relationships and sensible word meanings in the sentence; vocabulary; self-confidence; motivation; and critical thinking. There is no doubt that small-group reading instruction is superior to whole-class instruction. For this reason, it is critical that your students manage their behavior well in centers! Within guided reading periods, children often engage in shared reading—the teacher reads aloud first, children read the same text with the teacher in unison, and they turn take reading to one another while the teacher listens to selected individuals reading alone. Children read a big book or sets of the same little books. Following instruction, children read with their partners (often two children who read at somewhat different levels, but who are compatible enough to read together) and the teacher watches partners closely, intervenes to stress use of strategies, and encourages. Next, the group comes together again for discussion. The children or both the teacher and the children usually write, or draw and label something about their reading.

- **Self-Selected Reading.** The goal of self-selected reading is to share different kinds of texts, albeit paper or electronic, and build motivation. The teacher encourages, provides developmentally appropriate books, and "coaches" selected children's reading. Children read with help as needed and confer with the teacher individually. They also select and use a reading comprehension strategy listed on a wall chart. This block lasts about thirty minutes.

- **Working with Words.** For about thirty minutes, the teacher and the children engage in various word-related activities, such as reading both familiar words on the word walls and the new ones that are added weekly (approximately five). The teacher coaches through reviews of the words such as those found in units of study, high-frequency words, and sight words, and talks about their importance. Children write words, say the words, look for patterns in words, and discuss and practice the words' spelling patterns. The teacher writes words, showing how the letters and words are formed and pointing out word patterns (rhyming, blends, diagraphs, short or long vowel words, and so on) according to children's literacy development. The children practice making words and sorting them with games and word cards.

- **Writing.** A mini-lesson occurs in writing workshop. It begins each writing period, which lasts forty-five to sixty minutes, depending on how young children get along in an extended time period. Goals vary from kindergarten to second grade; for example, first graders may focus on having every sentence make sense and using capital letters and punctuation to end a sentence. In addition, the writing block focuses on spelling. Children write during the mini-lesson, on their own and with partners. This is an easy block to teach on multiple levels. Children write books, stories, and information pieces; illustrate their writing; and have conferences with the teacher for individual instruction. The word wall helps children to find words they need and to work on spelling. Writing time concludes with sharing writing in the author's chair. Be aware that different teachers use different formats and structures for writing workshops. What is important is that all writing workshops include the basic essentials—time to write, writing and spelling instruction, strong support, and a warm and inviting work environment. Cunningham and Allington (1999) provide some basic guidelines to consider in using four-blocks teaching:

  - Long-term planning for four-blocks teaching is organized around units of study such as inquiry units in science, math, and social studies; four-blocks teaching also contributes greatly to integrated curriculum. Short-term planning is laid out in both daily and weekly descriptions. This is the time when some of the arts and media may also be integrated into the already integrated curriculum.

  - Oral language is not a formal part of the four blocks, but many conversations take place during all four blocks that help ensure that CCSS speaking and listening objectives are met.

  - Four-blocks teaching does not eliminate the need for interventions such as Reading Recovery; it is not an add-on and it can be used with other approaches such as response to intervention (RTI).

  - Volunteers and paraprofessionals may help support four-blocks teaching.

  - The four blocks can be arranged in any order that works in your classroom.

  - Finally, it is fine to do whole-class instruction as well; for example, reading big books, or combining reading with music, movement, and song. Whole-class lessons take place as time permits during the four-block day.

The content of four-block lessons is planned to include a variety of CCSS objectives, for example, foundation skills about syllables, letter-sound correspondence, and prefixes and suffixes in word study.

CCSS

- Common Core Writing Standards, K–5, standards 1–3 and 5–8 specific to your teaching goals and the children's developmental level

Lesson Structures

Because children need frequent and varied learning opportunities, teachers use different types of lessons to accomplish desired outcomes. In all lessons, the teacher uses the ABC structure. For example, there is an introduction to the lesson (**anticipation**), a period in which the heart of the lesson is conducted (**building knowledge**), and an end where **consolidation** occurs by extending and/or applying the lesson's focus. Each lesson has structural aspects that help teachers meet their goals. That is, some lessons are more comprehensive and include a strong focus on word study, while reading or writing is also taught. Other types of lessons include mini-lessons, teachable moments, and think-aloud modeling.

MINI-LESSONS   Mini-lessons require fewer materials and are planned and taught fairly quickly. A mini-lesson is often taught at the beginning, and it focuses on one or two teaching points, such as self-monitoring one's comprehension and metacognition, providing the anticipation and focus of the lesson. The following is an example of a writing mini-lesson conducted by teacher Dr. Jill Dillard. She begins the conversation by talking about the previous lesson and by reminding the children that they should think of their audience and use correct punctuation and descriptive words when they write.

Recess is over and the second graders are either reading or sitting at tables playing word games. Dr. Dillard asks the children to get ready for writing workshop. They gather around her and she talks with the children about yesterday's topic lesson, "I'm an expert." Several children generated new topics after that mini-lesson: Jarad selected a pet story; Sammie Ann selected a soccer story; and Kyle selected a story about his baseball team (see Figure 12.6A and Figure 12.6B). Dr. Dillard invites the children to talk to a neighbor about their writing topic. During this time, she circulates among the children, prompting and encouraging. She confirms the children's ideas for stories and information composition and then asks the class whether they are ready to begin. With the children's consensus, she calls Monday's small writing group to meet with her to talk about their writing before Annie, the high school volunteer, arrives.

Figure 12.6A   *I Am an Expert*—Kyle

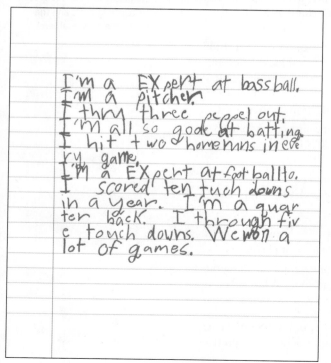

Figure 12.6B   *I Am an Expert*—Sammie Ann

TEACHABLE MOMENTS   Teachable moments are lessons in which the teacher seizes on an incident or observation to reinforce a concept. For busy teachers, teachable moments are superior opportunities for providing individual instruction in the context of a child's need. The next example demonstrates how much a good teacher can do in a very short time.

> *First-grader Ransika is working in the writing center. As Mr. López walks by to check on him, he notices that Ransika is putting capital letters in the middle of some of his words. Mr. López intervenes immediately, asking Ransika if he is using capital letters. Ransika nods yes, and Mr. López reviews the morning talk about when to use capital letters. With a sheepish grin, Ransika realizes his errors and begins to erase. Mr. López nods approval and turns to help another child.*

With this interaction, Mr. López was able to reinforce the morning's lesson quickly and positively. And, importantly, his speaking to Ransika reminded him and Ransika self-corrected! Self-correcting is powerful stuff for all of us—especially young learners.

THINK-ALOUDS   Think-alouds are lessons that demonstrate and model. They often show children how to think like a reader, writer, or speller. The following is an example of a reading comprehension think-aloud.

> *Ms. Novacek rereads* Sheila Rae, the Brave *(Henkes, 1987) to her first and second graders in a multiage classroom. This book is a favorite, as is* Lilly's Purple Plastic Purse, *also by Henkes (1996). The children and Ms. Novacek discuss the topic of bravery, which the children think is the book's theme. For discussion among the children, Ms. Novacek has paired a slightly less experienced reader with a somewhat more experienced reader. Ms. Novacek's goal is to help the children work toward understanding a deeper meaning, one that has to be inferred.*

Henkes's books provide opportunities to teach children to infer meaning, and the implied meaning in *Sheila Rae, the Brave* is about sibling relationships. Ms. Novacek engages in the following think-aloud: "Class, I've been thinking about this book and what Sheila Rae is like. I'm going to read a bit and keep thinking." Ms. Novacek reads and says, "I make a connection with Sheila Rae. When I was a child, I had a little brother, and I wasn't always nice to him. Sometimes I'd say mean things. What do you think about this?" The children discuss the idea, and Ms. Novacek picks up on their levels of understanding and carefully guides them to make inferences.

 It is necessary for teachers to establish effective routines if they are to successfully manage their students and the instructional day. Identify the routines found in the video and reflect on how teachers use them to promote independence and structure in their classrooms.

The use of wall charts for things such as lunch schedules and attendance helps students learn classroom routines. How does this carry over to benefit children's learning and your classroom management?

Daily Routines in K–2 Classrooms

As mentioned earlier, well-balanced daily schedules help young children to adapt more quickly and happily to the school day. The following routines and lessons serve as examples of systematic routines that provide opportunities to work on important skills, such as word recognition and reading comprehension, in highly authentic situations.

KINDERGARTEN ROUTINES A typical day in a kindergarten class would include many, if not all, of the following routines (Vukelich, Christie, & Enz, 2002, pages 45, 54–57):

Teach It! 11
Shared Reading

Teach It! 52
Shared Writing

- *Morning Greeting.* Engage in one-on-one conversations with the children to provide time to observe how children talk with each other and which learning centers they self-select. This allows you to check for children's interest and avoidance.
- *Taking Attendance.* Use a creative technique to take attendance, such as singing a song that includes the children's names. Children sing along and learn one another's names. Use large name tags that children read and hang on the attendance chart during the singing. Point to the words on chart paper as they are sung.
- *Shared Reading.* Read aloud predictable books with repeated phrases. As the children become familiar with the words and phrases, they join in. Figure 12.7 provides a typical read-aloud lesson plan.
- *Shared Writing.* Model writing such as letter formation, thinking about what to say, or using conventions such as periods and capital letters. Inviting children to take turns writing letters and words provides high-level scaffolding.
- *Writing Center.* Encourage use of the writing center where children can self-select, write on their own, and experiment with invented spelling and letter formation (see Figure 12.8).
- *Group Time.* Use group time to emphasize oral language. Demonstrate purposeful speaking, good listening, taking turns, and idea sharing. Use it to discuss the daily schedule and some center assignments. After assignments have been made, invite a group of approximately six children to sharing time.

Figure 12.7 Reading Aloud Lesson Plan as Described in the ABC Model

Objectives: Engage the children/establish anticipation (through a conversation and shared reading).

Goals: Provide rich oral and written language experiences. Demonstrate the joy of reading.

Increase intrinsic motivation (Guthrie & Wigfield, 2000).

Materials: Big book copy of The Wheels on the Bus (Kovalski, 1987), drawing paper, and crayons.

Demonstrate what is going to happen—initiate the building knowledge phase.

Immerse children in the literacy event by discussing illustrations.

Provide Word Study, and Guided Practice by reading the book, rereading children's favorite parts, building knowledge by singing and rereading.

Apply and Extend by having children draw their favorite part of the story—initiate the consolidation phase.

Share several new little Wheels on the Bus books; invite children to read them as much as they wish.

Ongoing assessments: Write and file notes on level of participation, enjoyment, skills, and interest on the three to five children you select as focal for the week. This schedule helps you avoid a hit and miss routine and become overwhelmed.

Figure 12.8   Topics of Interest. Invitation to Fisher David Cook's Pirate Party!

- *Sharing Time.* In smaller groups, children can be more at ease and engaged than they are in larger groups. You also have opportunities to ask natural questions, such as "What happened next, Mark?" or "Does anyone have a question for Michael?" (Moffett & Wagner, 1991).

Beginnings are important, and good teachers teach children many things on the first day of school. The Teach It! box on page 388 provides a model of how one teacher organizes her first day of kindergarten.

FIRST-GRADE ROUTINES   Routines that incorporate authentic reading and writing in kindergarten also work well with first and second graders. For example, taking attendance, lunch count, and accounting for classroom jobs require children to read and think. Wall charts used as tools in everyday teaching also serve children well. Early in first grade, children need the support of illustrations and photographs to comprehend their reading. Later, these supports are removed as children become better able to read without them.

Each day, at some point during the day, all children engage in the following: guided reading, being read to, self-selected reading, peer or buddy reading, and writing. Read-alouds introduce more informational books on science or social studies topics. Far too often, the primary grade curriculum is strongly based on storybooks (literary). Providing plenty of reading from informational books in the early school years helps prepare children for the heavy reading of this type of book they will need to do in later grades. Children really enjoy informational books, and often these books pave the way to reading for boys (Duke, 2000; Duke & Bennett-Armistead, 2003).

Establish learning centers where children can focus on particular reading and writing skills. Centers might include a writing area, an inquiry study area, a listening area with audio books, a computer area with options for self-selecting from two or three activities posted on the computers, a word work center, and, perhaps, an interest center. These centers, along with the teacher's guidance, provide vital reading experiences. Children should be rotated through the learning centers, and these assignments should be charted for children's self-guidance. They can check the chart for center assignments and go to work while you teach small-group blocks.

SECOND-GRADE ROUTINES   On the first day of second grade, you and the children might follow a schedule that is highly similar to the one used in first grade, but with more advanced materials and activities. Table 12.1 models part of a weekly schedule for second grade. Creating such schedules helps to ensure that many varied learning opportunities are included daily.

Second-grade planning proceeds until all children are scheduled for a week. The teacher's long-range plans need to be open to change and should include daily read-alouds, small-group reading, children's self-selected reading, spelling and word work, and at least twice-weekly comprehensive writing workshops with daily writing activities. You might also incorporate a block of pleasure reading with several varieties of texts, perhaps

Teach It! 55

The Writing Workshop

Teach It!

Refer to the Teach It! appendix at the end of the book for further activities you can use to reinforce concepts discussed in this chapter.

First Day of Kindergarten

The following schedule was contributed by Linda Headings, M.Ed., a highly effective kindergarten and first-grade teacher. Used with permission.

Half-Day Kindergarten Schedule

To begin, the children come to school in small groups until all are transitioned into classroom life. The teacher welcomes the children, teaches about learning centers, how attendance and lunch charts work, photographs each child for the "Our Class" poster, and discusses and points out classroom routines posted in large print. Photos are later glued to individual name tags printed on sentence strips.

Goals: (a) relationship building, (b) establishing daily routines, and (c) gathering data by observing children's interactions with environmental and class-created print and read-alouds.

First Day of Kindergarten with All the Children

Greeting: Happily greet children by name at the door at their eye level. Belongings are stored, lunch selections made, and children gather on the rug. {*guide using warmth, caring, and support*}

Demonstrate and Immerse

Review the Daily Schedule: Tell children exactly what is going to happen throughout the day. [Use a schedule chart at children's eye level; talk and point to the words.] Review the daily schedule as frequently as needed, especially with anxious children. {*provides reassurance, demonstrates that print carries meaningful information*}

Working with Words

Attendance and Reading: Take attendance by holding up each large name tag (now with a photo on it). When children read their names, they put the tag on the name chart. As each name is read, the class repeats it and says " Hello____ "

Apply and Extend

- Small groups practice sorting with name tags; circulate to guide and instruct about beginning, middle, and ending letter/sounds
- Read aloud and engage in lively instructional conversations

- Children share their "lovey" from home in pairs and with the class: {*demonstrates warmth and caring*}

School tour: Physically walk the following locations: restrooms, principal's office, lunchroom, and playground. Prepare to work in recess when the class is calm.

Center time: Stand by centers and the posted rules: (1) Only five children in a center at one time and (2) children put their names on a waiting list. Role-play using waiting lists. {*demonstrates the function and power of print and class behaviors*} Review option activities when waiting for a turn; role-play frequently.

Centers and Materials

- Writing center: Pencils, markers, note cards, name word cards, a variety of paper, stamps, etc.
- Reading center: Big and little books, manipulative charts, audio books, magnetic letters on cookie trays, flannel board story
- Dramatic play center: Dress-up clothes, shoes, hats, and various props
- Math center: Blocks, Unifix cubes™, puzzles, sorting items, counting games
- Science center: Magnets, experimental metals, a scale, and writing materials add more materials as time goes on.

Monitor and observe who works well together, who engages, who works alone, and other group dynamics. Manage and problem solve as children use centers.

Transitions

- Signify transitions by bell ringing, singing softly, or playing music.

End of day: Have the class meet on the rug, review the day, entice with something interesting coming up tomorrow, close with singing "The More We Get Together" (Raffi, 1996), written on chart paper—do voice print matching with the pointer. {*demonstrates meaning and enjoyment of print*}

Dismiss

- Names are called, children gather their gear, and line up.
- Take a quick break—prepare for the afternoon group.

every Monday, Wednesday, and Friday for twenty minutes right before the end of the day. Reading for pleasure is one of life's greatest joys!

Providing Appropriate Materials

Before the children come through the door on the first day of school, teachers have prepared the classroom for learning. They have also thought about the materials they will need to assist them.

Teach It!

Refer to the Teach It! appendix at the end of the book for further activities you can use to reinforce concepts discussed in this chapter.

First Day of First Grade

Goals: Building relationships, establishing routines, gathering literacy data

Greeting: At the door, greet children at eye level. Ask them to place their personal items on any table or set of desks pushed together and then sit on the rug. Take attendance and lunch count. Children stand and point to their names on the attendance chart and point to words.

Opening: Share personal objects that tell about yourself, draw and discuss a large graphic organizer that links these objects and you together {*provides a visual to organize ideas, personal story, and building relationships*}

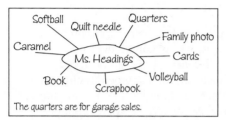

The quarters are for garage sales.

Graphic Organizer: Pillowcase

Welcome: Welcome children by doing some sorting activities and writing them down on large pieces of white construction paper in full view. {*introduce making a class big book*} Use one page for each pair of children. {*literate collaboration begins*}

Sorting examples that create the first class-made book are:

- Number of children in classroom enrolled along with number of boys and girls
- Number of children who walk to school, who ride the bus, who are dropped off
- Types and number of pets children own
- Favorite foods
- Favorite holiday

After sorting topics, pairs of children dictate pages, write each page, read it together, and point at each word. {*later record observed participation, cooperation, and oral language development*}

School tour: The bathrooms, lunchroom, office, nurse, music, gym, and art room.

Read aloud: Introduce an author study—encourage lively participation and teach literacy skills and strategies.

Work on book illustrations: Distribute class book pages to child pairs for illustrating. {*collaboration in action*} Discuss and demonstrate large-size illustration—fill up the space brightly!

Classroom explorations: Small groups explore the classroom's various literacy, math, and science learning centers—introduce computers later in the week. Holding up name cards signals lining up for lunch time. After lunch, read aloud another book in the new author study.

Journals: Introduce and illustrate journal writing with a PowerPoint or other technology and teacher think-aloud. Divide the class in two groups: one does journals and the other does center work. Circulate among these groups. Expect hesitation and questions—journal writing is *new*—work in 20-minute blocks and then switch group tasks. Observe and record behavior. Children create journal folders to store their writing. In closing, children take turns and read their writing to you; teach voice/print matching, and observe and record impressions.

Science: The sink and float experiment.

Gather students around a shallow tub of water and ask them to hypothesize which specific object will sink and which float. {*taps prior experiences and supports oral language*} Children's thumbs up means it floats; thumbs down means it sinks. {*watch for interactions—who is in and out of the lesson*} Discuss objects that floated and sank and why they made judgments about what would happen. Sometimes science results surprise us! Write the class's conclusions on chart paper. {*first inquiry study*} Extend and apply through child illustrations and writing, and post their work for all to see.

Closing: Review teacher-made attendance and lunch charts, have children store their name tags to be put on the attendance chart along with charting lunch requests tomorrow.

Homework assignment: Bring a personal item to school tomorrow—distribute a parent/ caregiver note on this. Tomorrow students' personal items are shared and discussed. {*introduces sharing, inclusion, and building community*}

Dismiss: Hold a take-home folder for each child. Say, "I'm holding a homework folder for a boy whose name begins with the sound of /ch/." {*supports children's recognition of letter/sound patterns*} Observe and record their responses.

CLASSROOM LIBRARIES Classroom libraries are essential in a literacy-rich classroom. Teachers and children use many varied text collections for lessons, pleasure reading, and inquiry lessons. This supports an *integrated curriculum* that includes all the language arts in science, math, and social studies. Work with your school librarian to build your collections. In addition, join book clubs that offer good children's literature at reduced prices; leave no garage sale, yard sale, or library sale unexamined; find used bookstores; and contact the

CCSS

- Writing 2: Text Types; Writing 7: Research

Table 12.1 Daily Schedule

OCTOBER	WEEK 1	GUIDED READING	BUDDY READING	INQUIRY CENTER
Daily read-alouds	Monday	Ben, Shealee, Sam, Tessa, Mark, Jenny	Books of choice (oral language practice)	Book research: work with frog facts (write findings)
Reading and writing	Tuesday	Joe, Michael, Dan, Angela	Listening center and read together	Report writing: science
Literature study		Jerriann, Nicki, Don		
		Helen, Jane, Chris, Mickey	Oral language practice	Author study (write and share)

Source: Adapted from Fountas and Pinnell (1996).

local public library to see if they have a program for obtaining children's books on a regular basis. Involve parents in helping to find ways to obtain reading materials. A good source for identifying great books is *The Reading Teacher*, which can be accessed at <www.reading .org/choices/>. Provide a wide variety of materials such as brochures from stores, automobile sales offices, community information centers, and the local police and fire departments, in addition to books and children's magazines. As you already know, children's own writing and published books and whole-class–created books make excellent reading materials!

LEVELED BOOKS   Review the leveled books your school has to offer. A conversion chart that provides lexiles is included in this book. These books provide excellent materials for reading lessons, children's self-selected reading, and books you ask children to read repeatedly. Leveled books help you consistently guide children into more challenging reading. Once they are at the mid to late point as readers (finger pointing), children need large amounts of easy reading at their level in order to gain fluency and confidence. One way to encourage repeated readings is to use drama. Children will gladly practice scripts to learn their parts! The following is another way to encourage repeated reading especially for struggling readers.

- Write up a simple contract that structures children's opportunities to read to others, such as the principal, cafeteria staff, custodian, or children in other classrooms (cleared with the teachers first).
- Decide on a reasonable date for the child to leave your classroom for the "performance reading."
- Encourage children to practice reading until they are performance perfect.
- Provide a time for a rehearsal with you or with classmates.
- Arrange for the child or children to leave the classroom on the appointed day.

Children will practice long and hard for the privilege of doing performance reading. Excellent Web sites for leveled books and many other excellent materials are <www .readinga-z.com> and <www.starfall.com>. These sites require membership, but they are well worth it (specific grade levels could share a membership). Struggling readers will gain significantly through performance reading.

Importantly, be aware of each child's independent reading level and furnish books at one or more higher levels to nudge readers forward. High-interest, higher-level books provide essential support in moving all children along. This can take time with some children, but nearly always, patience, excellent instruction, and much encouragement works wonders.

Leveled books are rated by a child's reading development stage, not by age or grade. Basal readers and other texts are often leveled only by grade. Often grade-level ratings are not sufficiently helpful. If a basal series is required, you can use Reading Recovery leveled books, or Fountas and Pinnell (1996, 2001, 2007). With state adoption of the CCSS, use lexiles to target readability or level. The following factors determine readability but do not account for interest.

- Sentence complexity (length of sentence)
- Vocabulary (number of high-frequency words)
- Print features (length of book, illustrations, format of the book)
- Language features (similar to oral language, high-level written language)
- Content (fiction, information, genre)

Assessing Book Levels   Some children need guidance when self-selecting books. Offer an array of books and ask the children to select from them. The "five-finger test" offers one simple method: The child holds up fingers and thumb, reads the book, and turns down one finger for each word missed on a page. If the child gets to the thumb, the book is probably too difficult. However, children should be encouraged to read books they self-select regardless of level of difficulty—this builds interest! Children should not continue to read a book they do not like. There are far too many wonderful books available for that to happen. Be aware of easy books that might hold high appeal for struggling readers and diverse language learners so that they can experience success. Nothing succeeds like success! All readers can make progress; some just need more time and support than others.

NEW LITERACIES   Computers are an important component of today's classroom materials. It is necessary that every primary classroom has them. Computer grants are still fairly easy to get, and even the youngest school child should have computer access. The importance of new literacy skills is evident even in the first few years of school as the following situation illustrates.

> *Picture a second grader stopping a visiting teacher in her classroom. The child is poised to sit down at a computer to take her turn, and she asks for help. She has to do research on animals and doesn't know where to look. The visitor says, "Well try <www.animals.org>," the child types in this address and says, "Great, I've got what I need now, thanks."* (Personal communication Dr. Jill Dillard, May 14, 2009)

We will never know how this research project turned out, but we do know the challenge it can be to search for information. The fact is that by second grade, children need a number of computer skills. Be very explicit in your teaching. Know that it requires much patience, and that early on, children's "playing around" on the keyboard or screen is a good way to learn. We have all learned computing this way.

A brief list of computer skills, dispositions, and goals that need to be integrated into your practice starting in kindergarten and through the primary grades follows:

- Small muscle motor coordination for (1) booting up or turning on, and logging off, (2) navigating with the mouse, and (3) beginning keyboarding. Teachers should set aside time and use patience to teach these skills. Fortunately, children are usually very eager to have time on the computer, and those with some home technology experience will learn more quickly. Your classroom learning place's open and democratic environment will help children learn to take turns and share.
- Simple keyboarding and on-screen looking, not only left to right, but in various directions in order to point and click and solve search problems are essential activities as children mature. Knowing where to look is not always obvious! Teachers should model and demonstrate skills, and allow time for children's sufficient low-key practice (being hurried will frustrate them). Work out a weekly schedule so all children have their time "on" all year.
- In first grade, facilitate children's learning to share playing a game or working on a reading activity on the same computer and finding the help they need from computer center charts of directions or from another child. Children can begin to buddy up on the computer, thus doubling their practice time.

New Literacies

Why should we begin to help children be comfortable and learn how to navigate on the computer screen in the primary grades?

CCSS

- Literature and Informational Text 7: Variety of Media

- By the end of second grade, classroom technology instruction and practice should enable students to: (1) look, search, and click successfully in appropriate software without stress; (2) follow the text while they read it and click on unknown words; (3) think about and experiment with key word searches; and (4) navigate with the mouse in order to conduct specific searches and get support when they need it (from classroom charts, other children, and sometimes the teacher).

Reaching All Children

There is little doubt that you will have English language learners and struggling readers in your classes during your teaching career. Teaching these children is one of your primary responsibilities.

Language and Diversity

How can we address the needs of English language learners?

English Language Learners

As with older students, young English language learners' English listening comprehension is more advanced than their ability to speak the new language, let alone read and write it. Much of the focus in the early years needs to be on oral language development. Helpful teaching includes the following, which reviews some of what you have already read about:

- Warm acceptance and valuing differences
- Reading (or read-alouds of) the same book(s) in the English language learners' mother tongue and later in English
- Using parents and paraprofessionals, community volunteers, and anyone available in the school (all other support staff) to read and write with the children in their mother tongue
- Playing naming games of classroom objects in both languages, but in one language at a time
- Singing songs and listening to music in two languages
- Providing many positive experiences with cultural differences—strive for classroom experiences that focus on universally important aspects of life such as food, home, dramatic play, family, friends, birthdays, animals/pets, and homelands.

Language Experience with English Language Learners

Volunteers who include parents and business and community people can provide much-needed support if they speak the children's mother tongue.

ENGLISH LANGUAGE LEARNERS IN KINDERGARTEN For children who come to school with some English proficiency, learning will move more rapidly than for those with little or no English proficiency. A few might be ready for phonemic awareness activities in English by late kindergarten, but probably not before, and certainly not before they reach an intermediate level in spoken English. For a quick assessment of the intermediate level, try the following strategy:

- Read a predictable book in English to a small group of children.
- See if they can respond well to most comprehension questions.
- If so, try some simple phonemic awareness picture sorts.
- If children are successful, continue instruction.
- If children are not successful, step back and continue oral language development, and perhaps try the language experience approach (LEA).
- Repeat the cycle of teach, assess, and proceed accordingly.

Few English language learners will reach the intermediate level at a young age unless they speak English in addition to their mother tongue at home. As critical as explicit instruction is, other high-quality learning happens in the well-managed classroom, which is confirmed in a study by McCafferty and Iddings (2001). Notice how classroom organization provides for meaningful and frequent oral language practice in the following example:

> *Picture two Hispanic kindergarteners, one more advanced in English than the other, seated in the housekeeping center. Nicole (the more experienced English language learner) is reading a very well-known children's book in English to Jorge (as assigned by the teacher). Nicole knows the story by heart, and despite the fact that this lesson is appropriate for these children, they soon become less and less engaged and eventually toss the book aside. Nicole then stands up and begins to pretend that she is preparing food for Jorge. She speaks in English as she makes a sandwich, and Jorge responds. He immediately joins in the pretend play. The two children engage in an extended English conversation in which Jorge actually speaks more English than Nicole!*

Productive play episodes such as this are exactly what Jorge needs to gain the oral proficiency necessary for moving into written language instruction. "Real-life" pretend-play situations provide rich opportunities, and sometimes being "off-task" provides valuable support. In play, young children learn to infer, and they will engage in useful language experiences (Christie & Roskos, 2009). Productive play is most likely to occur when the teacher has encouraged it. Centers such as housekeeping, puppet theater, post office, restaurant, and others are present, and there is time for children to engage in them.

Moreover, children respond well to vocabulary words of personal significance to them, and book reading is a perfect place to teach vocabulary. Provide personal dictionaries (for home and school) in which children's favorite words may be kept. When your English language learners are ready for reading instruction, use *voice-to-print matching* (matching voice to print or word, focusing on word after word in order, and pointing to each word read), with small groups and frequent instructional conversations.

Children may be ready for phonemic awareness activities in their mother tongue, but not yet in English. Here is an example of an ESL lesson for intermediate English language learners who speak Spanish.

- Read a book in English that the children already know in their mother tongue (you, or someone else might have read the Spanish version to them). For example, *The Very Hungry Caterpillar* (Carle, 1987) is also available in a Spanish language version entitled *La Oruga Muy Hambrienta* (Carle, 1994).

- Engage the children in an enjoyable conversation; then reread the book using children's suggestions for their favorite parts and highly supportive discussion. With an English big book version or the same text on large chart paper, use voice-to-print matching and more discussion. Demonstrate how to identify a word, and help children identify words. To teach the concept of word, put your fingers and then their fingers at the beginning and end of a word. Make both book editions available for children's use in other explicit lessons and for self-selected use in pleasure reading and partner reading. The shared reading techniques described throughout this book help extend the lesson. Use shared writing in similar ways with both languages as much as possible.

ENGLISH LANGUAGE LEARNERS IN FIRST AND SECOND GRADES   Remember that some English language learners might enter your classroom having had no previous school experiences. As such, they are many months away from being ready for phonemic awareness activities in English. They greatly need a strong emphasis on ESL lessons. Having developed English only at the level of basic interpersonal communication skills, a conversational level (Cummins, 2001), pronunciation difficulties often complicate letter-to-sound relationships and phonics learning.

Teachers can celebrate English language learners' home languages and also teach other children that the world's languages use different words for the same ideas, and even use different symbols to represent words.

Many English language learners must learn to read first in English because of schools' limited resources to teach more effectively in their mother tongue or because of state or district policies. Unfortunately, they have probably not mastered English at an oral level sufficient to support academic instruction in English. Therefore, the primary focus of your reading instruction should be on word recognition and comprehension.

Phonics will be the English language learners' weakest modality in learning to read. A phonetic approach is based on knowledge of the sound system, and English language learners probably speak English with a heavy accent—a very strong indicator that they have not yet mastered the sound system of English.

Does this mean that you cannot teach these children to read until they master the phonetic approach? Not at all! Lessons discussed throughout this book provide varied and reliable instruction for teaching these children. Here are some helpful hints:

Word Wall Activities

- Focus on children's dictated texts (the language-experience approach [LEA]). Work with teacher- and child-selected sight words for practice.
- Focus on *meaning*; use word walls, sorting cards, word hunts, and games (all described previously).
- Work on *vocabulary*. Your English language learners might know the word *big*, but not *huge*, *gigantic*, or *enormous*.

Using Questions to Teach English Language Learners

Using children's "favorites" in an LEA activity is a meaningful way to provide guided reading instruction to young children at the emergent or beginning phase of reading.

Above all, involve the children and engage in conversations throughout the day—make it real for them! Often, children making the transition from their mother tongue to English have periods of stuttering or other issues, such as pronunciation and articulation difficulties. However, these periods do not usually signal a language disorder. Eventually, most children improve. If they don't show improvement over time, seek help from school experts and work with parents who may not know where to turn for help. It is important to keep in mind that English language learners are no different than any other populations of children; and, just as with English speakers, a few may have problems with literacy learning (even in their mother tongue). However, the vast majority simply speak a language other than English. They have many challenges to overcome as they develop English proficiency.

Struggling Readers

Struggling Reader

How can Elkonin boxes provide extra support to struggling readers?

Young children who do not show steady reading, writing, and spelling growth close to that of their peers need careful evaluation and immediate intervention through the Response to Intervention (RTI) process. RTI emphasizes differentiated approaches and the need for integrated instructed (2012). The causes of delayed development may include a lack of early literacy experience, or lags in neurophysiological, psychological, and cognitive development.

Interventions such as Reading Recovery and the *Elkonin box* strategy (Clay, 1985) provide support for struggling first graders. Well-implemented RTI, and high-quality summer programs and tutoring are also recommended. The Elkonin box may well be an intervention used even in kindergarten with children who have been screened for possible problems in the RTI program. The Elkonin box strategy focuses children's attention on letter-to-sound relationships. The routine goes as follows: The teacher might begin by asking a child to identify the problem word. When the child points to the word, the teacher writes the word.

got

Then, together, they segment the word into chunks of letters and draw boxes around each letter chunk as they have a good deal of discussion about the letter-to-sound relationships. A variation on this would be for the teacher to draw the boxes first and then coach the child to write the letters in the boxes as he or she works through the letter-to-sound relationships.

If the child cannot pronounce the word, the teacher provides support by saying the word first. To consolidate the lesson, the student and teacher write the word in a sentence and then use it orally in a sentence.

The Elkonin box strategy fills several needs. For older children who still need help, the strategy clarifies segmenting and manipulating letter-to-sound relationships. It can also be used as a visual aid in working with multiple-syllable words. For young children, the Elkonin box strategy is extremely helpful for those needing help with phonemic awareness and who struggle in perceiving and matching letter-to-sound relationships. See Figure 12.9.

Making a book available in your students' mother tongue as well as in English can help them make the connection between the languages.

Interventions

The earlier the intervention begins, the better the potential outcome. However, children in intervention programs are rarely able to function well for long at grade level after the intervention stops (Bronfenbrenner, 1974; Spache, 1981). Gaskins (1998, p. 534) states that there is "more to [helping] delayed readers than good instruction." Here is a list of insights and recommendations provided by Gaskins and the teachers at Benchmark School in Media, Pennsylvania:

- Engage in extensive reading instruction.
- Show respect and teach the children self-monitoring and self-directing.
- Hold on to the idea that <u>all</u> teachers can change is their own approach to children and that children change as a result of teaching changes.
- Focus on academic and nonacademic roadblocks (issues with engagement, having a disposition for learning, self-esteem).
- Work with other teachers, school experts, outside services, and parents to plan and achieve goals.
- Realize that long-term intervention is critical; most delayed readers need help from kindergarten through middle school and high school.

At Benchmark, the teachers work with children's dispositions or characteristics, such as attentiveness, organization, and conscientiousness. Research indicates that accelerating reading ability was not sufficient for at-risk learners. They must also acquire a disposition for learning (Dahl & Freppon 1995; Freppon, 1995) and other affective or cognitive abilities. Among the many instructional foci used at Benchmark, one of the most important is teaching the *active search for meaning*. Graphic organizers, rich discussion, and other techniques need to be used intensively over time with struggling readers. If a child receives intervention, the specialist's instruction and the teacher's instruction must be in accord (Gaskins, 1998). Children are often put *more at risk* when the specialist teaches in one way and the classroom teacher in another. Teachers and specialists must learn well from one another.

Figure 12.9 Elkonin Box

Elkonin Box Teacher and Child Conversation

Teacher: That was a wonderful job retelling that story. What would you like to write about that story?

Child: I want to say, "The crocodile got on."

T: That will be a fun sentence to write. [Here is where the teacher can encourage a more complex or a simpler sentence, depending on the needs of the child.] How would you begin the sentence, "The crocodile got on."?

C: With 'the.' I know 'the.'

T: I know you do! Write it on our book writing page. [The book writing page is the page where everything appears correct.]

[*Child writes the word 'The'.*]

T: I noticed you put a capital 'T'. Why did you do that?

C: 'Cause it starts the sentence.

T: You are just learning so much about writing! OK, say your sentence again.

C: The crocodile got on. I need crocodile.

T: Yes, let's see if we can work on that one together. What sounds do you hear in 'crocodile'?

C: Is it a 'c' or a 'k'?

T: What do you think?

C: 'c'

T: You got it! What else do you hear?

C: [*child stretches word*] 'r' and another 'c'

T: There is an 'r' and a 'c'; put the 'r' down and listen as I say the word. What do you hear before that other 'c'? [*Teacher stretches word*]

C: Oh! I hear an 'ah'. Ah, ah, octopus! 'O'!

T: You are really listening carefully for those sounds. OK, write 'o' and the 'c' you heard. What does that much say?

C: The croc

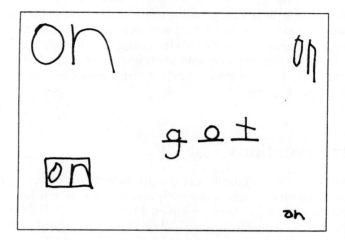

T: Yes, let's finish this word together [*Teacher and student sound word together and collaborate on writing letters—student supplies all but the silent e, which the teacher adds*] So now we have The crocodile; we need to finish the sentence. What did you want to say?

C: The crocodile got on. I need got.

T: I want you to work out got by yourself. I know you can do it! I'll tell you that 'got' has 3 sounds. [Teacher draws 3 lines on the try page; some teachers use boxes]

C: I know it starts with 'g'.

T: Yes, sir! What do you hear next?

C: [*Stretches word*] A 't'!

T: 'T' is in that word! But where do you hear it? Say it again and listen.

C: 'Got'—it's at the end. 'Got'. Oh, I know! It's 'o' again! G-o-t

T: Wonderful work! I could just see your brain in action! Now, what do we need to finish your sentence?

C: The crocodile got on. We need on, a –n, right?

T: Let's think about it. You just told me crocodile had an 'o' for the 'ah' sound; and got had an 'o' for the 'ah' sound. So what do you think makes the first sound in ah-ah on?

C: 'o'!

Source: Elkonin Box Teacher and Child Conversation, contributed by Karen Morrow Durica. Used with permission.

Cunningham and Allington (1999) suggest the following strategies for providing struggling readers with extra practice:

- Organize an after-lunch bunch in which you work with these children for ten or fifteen minutes, reading easy books just for fun.

- Organize an easy reading time for ten or fifteen minutes after school using the same strategies as with the after-lunch bunch.

- Create a learning center with materials such as Legos™, puzzles, computer games, word board games, math and science manipulatives, Play-Doh™, chalk (slates), markers, pencils, stickers and stamps, children's magazines, and a TV connection for watching *Reading Rainbow* or other educational videos.

Using sound reading instruction with young at-risk readers can result in tremendous benefits years later.

Remember that children who struggle can easily become defensive and lose interest in learning. Sometimes fear of failure can be traced to instruction that focused on right answers at the expense of making sense or to teachers' lack of knowledge, persistence, and skill.

Some children engage in negative behaviors, such as refusing to turn in their homework, because of a deep fear that it will be incorrect or because of a family problem. Children who are troubled often engage in behaviors that are self-destructive. These children need help, not blame. Children with struggles need the entire school system working for them. Beyond the risk of reading failure for students, their failures deeply hurt teachers, parents, and families (Dudley-Marling, 1990, 2000). Failure is suffering that no child, family, or teacher should have to experience.

Assessment

Screening for possible learning difficulties will likely begin in kindergarten. Response to Intervention (RTI) is adopted by an entire district; thus, every school and classroom must implement RTI. Screening may not occur until first or even second grade, and often these testing materials are from the Reading First program. However, some school districts decide to elect their own, scientifically grounded screening tests. The following are some additional RTI-related points that you will find useful in your teaching:

- A leadership team (LT) consists of about six to eight highly competent teachers and sometimes the principal or special education teacher.

- The LT is responsible for supporting the classroom teacher to ensure implementation of the reading program, such as four blocks with guided reading; it monitors the classroom teaching to ensure that there is fidelity and consistency in this instruction. (Writing is also taught and monitored according to sound principles.)

- If, as a result of thorough screening and teacher input, a child is found to be struggling, an RTI "Tier One" phase is begun. Tier One means that specific high-quality, comprehensive instruction such as is described in this book is carried out for a specific time by the classroom teacher (progress is monitored and records are kept).

- If a child's progress is still not satisfactory, "Tier Two" is begun. This tier is similar to Tier One, but it has a longer timeline and more intensive classroom teacher instruction; more intensive support from the LT should also occur.

- If, after high fidelity to RTI practice it is found that the two previous Tiers are unsuccessful, Tier Three is begun, with serious collaboration taking place among teachers, the LT, and parents. It is possible that if Tier Three is unsuccessful, the child will be placed in special education classes.

Grading

Because grading is a challenge and a trial, Cunningham and her colleagues hold that the concept of grading young children in the typical sense is simply not realistic. Putting a number or letter grade on young children is not informative or helpful because children vary so much. In traditional grading, the struggling reader or English language learner will almost always receive lower grades (marking them as "not as good as others"), and the more experienced and privileged children will almost always receive higher grades (marking them as "better than others").

Teachers must work hard to communicate to parents and school administrators that grades should reflect individual *effort* and *growth*. What matters most in teaching is that children are developing and making progress. Avoid marking any child as a learner with static ability. In *Classrooms That Work* (1999), Cunningham and Allington argue that we must change the way grades are determined. The typical grading system tells children who struggle: "You are a failure."

Many schools throughout the country do not assign letter grades to young primary children, focusing instead on their development. Even if you must work with a mandated traditional grading or report card system, you can maintain an encouraging attitude that is explicitly conveyed to children. Donald Graves (1983, p. 93) states, "Grading is a fact of life. It's the most difficult responsibility placed on teachers." He advises teachers to use grades to encourage children and to document well what children do in class.

Caldwell (2002) cites the limits of most report cards. She suggests adding to report cards in ways that show the children's growth and hard work. Here are some examples of this:

- Add a list of good comprehension strategies the child is working on and uses.
- Do something similar for word learning.

To keep grading records such as these, divide the grade book into sections labeled with your teaching emphasis—for example, *predicts in reading, connects self and the world to books, is learning sight words*. If you have a narrative report card, divide the report into categories, and keep information on all children in the same categories (reading comprehension, letter-to-sound relationships or phonics, spelling, etc.). In this way, you provide continuity in your report cards and even-handedness for all the children (Afflerbach, 1993).

Anecdotal Notes

Another tool that is vital for evaluating children's progress is the use of teachers' anecdotal notes. Anecdotal notes are narrative notes written while observing a child or children (E. McIntyre, personal communication, September 10, 2005). They are descriptive (avoid a rush to judgment). They often pose questions ("Why is he doing that?") and hunches ("I wonder if he understands the flexibility of writing?"). Anecdotal notes are based on what is actually seen and heard. They ask good questions, such as: Where is the child on meeting identified aspects of the first-grade standards? Is he successful with help? What do I need to do?

Teachers take anecdotal notes to understand children's development and plan instruction, and to demonstrate accountability when called upon. Teachers write about what happens when they intervene, reteach, and provide high-level scaffolding, such as the Elkonin box. It is hard to imagine effective instruction without data gathered and analyzed, and this data should be based on frequent notes and work samples. In this way your instruction is evidence based.

Teachers who write anecdotal notes on children's demonstrations of CCSS knowledge and skills will have very important information at their fingertips for lesson planning, report cards, parent meetings, and meetings with other school experts. For example, a child might meet a standard regularly, sometimes, or rarely. This observation, with a line or two of description about what the child is doing, creates reliable data when carried out consistently.

In the beginning, it is often difficult to know when to write, so carry a clipboard or pack of sticky notes with you so that you can write anecdotal notes throughout the day. Use your notes to look for patterns. For example, identify a child who never seems to know short or long vowel words, who wanders around the room, or who is consistently left out of social activities. Recognizing patterns is the first step in intervention, and knowing patterns provides critical information for assessment.

For Review

Our discussions connect research-based information on children's learning with effective teaching from kindergarten through the second grade. It provides practical information for new and practicing teachers. A significant portion of this material is devoted to practice that develops both the knowledge and skills of young children as well as your own. Discussion of routines that teach and "first day of school" illustrations provide concrete guidance. Organization and management of the classroom learning community includes helping children learn to manage their own behavior. Included also are discussions of family, materials, leveled books, Response to Intervention (RTI), the CCSS, Critical Thinking, and New Literacies connections.

For Your Journal

Write the notes below in your journal. Then analyze each for its value as anecdotal notes made when observing children.

1. Victoria is driving me crazy. I think her mother is at the root of this. Mom works and is never home!

2. Cody pretend-read *Frog and Toad* to me today; he uses a lot of text-like phrases and his own mix of oral language. This little guy maintains a story formation with a beginning, middle, and end. He even connected the real frog he once had with Frog in the story!

Taking It to the World

Develop a home literacy project that will help make school life more authentic and draw families into the school community. For such a project, it is wise to connect homework activities with inquiry projects and to have culminating activities in the classroom to which parents and caregivers are invited. Identify an inquiry project that would provide an excellent forum for family member or caregiver involvement. Create questions the children could use for interviews, and plan for how they might be able to supplement the information with photos, toys, or perhaps articles of clothing. How would the children be able to tell their stories?

New Literacies Connections

1. Children in grades K–2 nearly always go through a period of intense interest in dinosaurs. Build on children's natural interest in dinosaurs and increase your teaching opportunities by using the following Web sites and books to enhance pleasure reading:
   * <www.enchantedlearning.com/subjects/dinosaurs> (an interactive child-friendly site with basic information about dinosaurs and extinction)
   * <www.fieldmuseum.org/sue> (a site dedicated to Sue, the largest *Tyrannosaurus Rex* yet discovered)

2. Explore the following Web sites, and identify one that might work well with younger children (K–2). Add your views on why you think they would be useful.
   * <www.youthtrust.org>—then click on "e-mentoring"
   * <www.itown.com/athens/mentor>

3. Try these Web sites for teaching practices:
   * Teaching Reading K–2 Workshop at <www.learner.org/resources/series175.html>
   * Teaching Reading K–2: A Library of Classroom Practices at <www.learner.org/resources/series162.html>

MyEducationLab™

Go to Topics 1 and 2 (Emergent Literacy and Phonemic Awareness/Phonics) in the MyEducationLab <www.myeducationlab.com> for your course, where you can:

- Find learning outcomes for Emergent Literacy and Phonemic Awareness/Phonics along with the national standards that connect to these outcomes.

- Complete Assignments and Activities that can help you more deeply understand the chapter content.

- Apply and practice your understanding of the core teaching skills identified in the chapter with the Building Teaching Skills and Dispositions learning units.

- Check your comprehension on the content covered in the chapter by going to the Study Plan in the

Book Resources for your text. Here you will be able to take a chapter quiz, receive feedback on your answers, and then access Review, Practice, and Enrichment activities to enhance your understanding of chapter content.

- Visit A+RISE. A+RISE® Standards2Strategy™ is an innovative and interactive online resource that offers new teachers in grades K-12 just in time, research-based instructional strategies that meet the linguistic needs of ELLs as they learn content, differentiate instruction for all grades and abilities, and are aligned to Common Core Elementary Language Arts standards English language proficiency standards in WIDA, Texas, California, and Florida.

Putting Effective Literacy Instruction into Practice: Grades 3 to 5

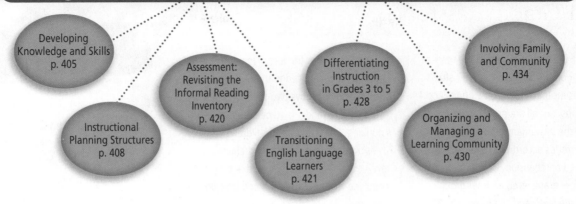

Putting Effective Literacy Instruction into Practice: Grades 3 to 5

- Developing Knowledge and Skills p. 405
- Instructional Planning Structures p. 408
- Assessment: Revisiting the Informal Reading Inventory p. 420
- Transitioning English Language Learners p. 421
- Differentiating Instruction in Grades 3 to 5 p. 428
- Organizing and Managing a Learning Community p. 430
- Involving Family and Community p. 434

Anticipation Guide

The following statements will help you begin thinking about the topics of this chapter. Answer *true* or *false* in response to each statement. As you read and learn more about the topics in these statements, double-check your answers. See what interests you and prompts your curiosity toward more understanding.

_____ 1. When children enter the third grade, there is little change from the first grade in the use of literature, in word recognition instruction, in reading in the content areas, and in writing.

_____ 2. Teachers in grades 3 to 5 devote much less attention to phonemic awareness and phonics than teachers in grades K to 2.

_____ 3. When children move from grades K to 2 to grades 3 to 5, the balance between oral reading and silent reading is about the same.

_____ 4. As children reach higher grades, there is a greater range between their achievement levels, resulting in the need for careful grouping for instruction.

_____ 5. The child's home can be the source of many family literacy activities.

_____ 6. When children are reading orally for fluency, it is not possible to judge their comprehension.

_____ 7. Formal assessment processes such as standardized testing do not provide information that is valuable in diagnosing the needs of individual students.

_____ 8. Teaching English phonics to English language learners is the same as teaching it to native English speakers.

_____ 9. Most children go through similar stages of spelling development.

_____ 10. Computer technology is more useful in writing instruction than in reading instruction.

A Classroom Story

Literacy Activities in a Third-Grade Classroom

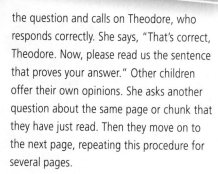

Chantell DeLaney is a third-grade teacher in a suburban classroom. Her 27 students represent many different cultures and ethnic groups, but all are proficient in English. Today she has organized her students into three groups according to their levels of reading comprehension. One group reads slightly below grade level, another group reads at grade level, and some children read at fourth- and fifth-grade levels. Ms. DeLaney's children come together in these groups from time to time, but her overall approach to grouping for instruction is flexible, according to the children's needs and to the goals and standards she is addressing.

In today's lesson with a group of 12 children who are reading at grade level, Ms. DeLaney's plan reflects a three-stage structure: anticipation activities, building knowledge, and consolidation. She begins with two anticipation strategies. She first conducts a read-aloud of the story title and the first page of the story, asking the students questions about the illustration on the page, which she shows them from her copy of the book. She asks, "Based on the title and the illustration on this page, what prediction can you make about the story?"

Vinh says, "It's about a big animal. What is it?"

"Who knows?" asks Ms. DeLaney.

Theodore responds, "A hippopotamus!"

"How large is a hippopotamus?" asks Ms. DeLaney.

"Really big!" they shout.

She then introduces two new vocabulary words from the story, "huge" and "gigantic," with a t-graph, a graphic organizer.

For the part of the lesson in which the children build knowledge through reading, Ms. DeLaney employs two strategies that are often used in tandem: guided reading and chunking. She focuses the children's reading by asking a higher-order (comprehension-level) question before they read and by chunking the amount of reading they do after she asks the question, usually a single page, occasionally more than one page, or sometimes only a paragraph or two in difficult material. After she poses the purpose-setting question, the children read silently to find the answer and then discuss what they have found out. Ms. DeLaney then proceeds to the next question and the next chunk. She uses the questions as a scaffolding strategy in a Directed Reading Activity (DRA). Placing the focus on the children's reading comprehension of what they read silently instead of only on accurate pronunciation and speed strengthens the children's abilities to understand what they are reading.

Ms. DeLaney's procedure is as follows: "Boys and girls, we are going to read a story about a girl who tries to hide from her mother the pet hippopotamus she found. Look in the table of contents for the story, turn to the first page, and close your book with your finger in the place. I am going to ask you a question before you read, and I want you to read to find the answer. How does Kamesha solve the problem of feeding her new pet so that her mother doesn't find out about it? Please read silently to find the answer." The children read silently and, one by one, they raise their hands as they find the answer. Ms. DeLaney repeats the question and calls on Theodore, who responds correctly. She says, "That's correct, Theodore. Now, please read us the sentence that proves your answer." Other children offer their own opinions. She asks another question about the same page or chunk that they have just read. Then they move on to the next page, repeating this procedure for several pages.

In a consolidation activity after the children have read about half of the story, Ms. DeLaney asks them to retell the story so far in their own words, with each child contributing part of the retelling. She asks, "How did our story begin?"

Tran contributes, "Kamesha found a huge hippopotamus at the park."

Nestor adds, "Her mother will be angry if she sees it."

"Why?" asks Ms. DeLaney.

"Because it will eat a lot of food," responds Nestor.

The children continue, negotiating with each other when there are disagreements or something is left out. Ms. DeLaney then asks the children to write two or three sentences predicting what Kamesha's mother will do when she discovers the hippopotamus. They can choose to read a library book or play one of the many reading games available to them as independent activities after they finish their writing. They will finish the story the next day, but with only a brief review activity before the children continue reading.

As children move into grades 3 through 5, they have acquired a concept of print, and most can decode the majority of the words they encounter—especially when the words are contextualized in connected text. The children are reading silently, are understanding what they read, and are expressing themselves in writing. The purpose of Chapter 13 is to weave together the major elements of a comprehensive and balanced reading program for implementation in self-contained classrooms in grades 3 through 5.

Developing Knowledge and Skills

As you saw in earlier chapters, there is much variation in beginning reading programs for kindergarten and first and second grades. The range extends from scripted, direct instruction, one-size-fits-all programs of explicit phonics to literature-based programs in which shared reading of authentic connected text is a major activity. Phonemic awareness and phonics are taught in the context of words the children have already learned to recognize. A basal reading program is also frequently employed. Such programs are less scripted than formal code-emphasis programs, but have more connected text for the children to read. Phonics elements and skills are systematically sequenced and presented explicitly. The text they read might be authentic in the case of anthologies of original versions of children's literature, but less so in the case of traditional basal readers. In these programs, text is often manipulated to conform to various criteria.

Consolidating Primary-Grade Gains in Grade 3

Teachers in grades 3 to 5 must organize reading instruction according to the experiences the children had in kindergarten and first and second grades and according to their degree of success there. Several very basic changes from children's initial reading experiences begin to appear in their reading instruction in the late second grade, continuing into the third grade. Individual differences among children not only continue to exist, but also to grow into even greater differences. Some children have not been successful in kindergarten through second grade, most have been moderately successful, and others are leaping ahead in their abilities to process and benefit from both narrative and expository text. The result is an increased need for flexible grouping according to different needs. There is also an increased need for a variety of instructional materials on several levels, as well as for more sensitive instructional strategies, especially for children who are not meeting expectations for the grade level. Although this process might not always be under the control of the individual classroom teacher, he or she should have the knowledge and skill necessary to develop such a program where that opportunity exists or to adapt and augment the adopted program where possible.

USING CODE-EMPHASIS PRIMARY-GRADE PROGRAMS A trend in some school districts is a reading program through which all children proceed at the same pace. Differences in home language, proficiency in English, previous experiences or lack of experiences with print, knowledge of the sound system of English, availability of print in the home and community, and parent roles in providing emergent literacy experiences are *not* considered. Typically, these programs focus on phonemic awareness and explicit decoding skills, with text reading occurring in decodable text or fragments of text that are written specifically to provide regular practice in decoding. The major goal of such programs is for the children to achieve *automaticity*, which involves rapid and accurate pronunciation of words that follow phonic generalizations. Children may be discouraged from using cueing systems other than the graphophonic system. The obvious strength of such a program is seen in the formidable decoding skills of successful students when they attack regular words. But there are also problems with such a methodology:

Teach It! 15

Word Sorting

- The focus of instruction is on accurate and rapid pronunciation, not on comprehension.
- Motivation is a frequent problem in that decodable text tends to be less interesting than authentic literature.
- Because of the systematic and sequential nature of instruction, children who fail to master some skills and elements have difficulty learning subsequent skills and elements that are based on previous teaching. Similarly, some children are already able to decode virtually any unknown words through skilled use of all cueing systems, but they are required to follow the program nonetheless.
- Many children have difficulty in the application of phonics generalizations to words that are not regular, especially if they lack experience in using other cueing systems as tools in the decoding of unknown words.
- Many English language learners must try to learn to decode in a language they do not understand and in which they have not mastered the sound system.

These children will benefit from additional emphases in their later reading instructional experiences:

- Extensive reading of authentic children's literature and expository text
- Instruction in strategies from other cueing systems for use with new words that do not yield to analysis with regular phonics generalizations, such as using context clues, ignoring unknown words and reading on, using structural analysis skills, and questioning whether or not the word makes sense in the passage
- An increasing focus on silent reading as children gain proficiency in the middle grades, with questions to scaffold or guide that silent reading, followed by discussion

This situation was very much on Ms. DeLaney's mind when she planned her third-grade reading program. In grades 1 and 2, her children's teachers used a code-emphasis reading program that was characterized by explicit and systematic phonics in a highly scripted, direct instruction approach.

To meet their comprehension needs, Ms. DeLaney selected a basal program that has particularly attractive and interesting literature. She continued to build their phonics and related word recognition skills from the program, but she drew those brief lessons out of the literature that the children were reading in the program in a process called "breaking the lockstep." She taught the components in the program, but not always in the order in which they occurred in the teacher's manual.

Teach It! 17

Making and Breaking Words

USING BASAL PRIMARY-GRADE PROGRAMS   Basal reading programs tend to be broad and eclectic. They provide detailed teachers' manuals, often to the point of being scripted. Attention to phonemic awareness and phonics is usually ample. Instruction in the use of reading strategies such as decoding, comprehension, and content reading skills is provided in a sequence linked with the text to be read. Teachers often need to break the sequence by providing additional instruction related to a skill that is presented with a given story. This instruction might take several days. In the meantime, the children continue their reading of stories apart from this instruction, sometimes falling behind with respect to the skills presented with each story. A teacher might wisely decide to skip some direct skill development for children who have already demonstrated these abilities.

As children move into the middle grades from a basal reading program, you might choose the following options:

Teach It! 19

Word Wall Activities

- Augment with multiple copies of trade books and expository texts, apart from the basal reader or anthology.
- Provide scaffolding activities beyond those recommended in the basal reader when the children lack background knowledge about a story theme.

- Supplement skill development in decoding when gaps are encountered in the children's knowledge and skills, sometimes by reviewing word recognition lessons from previous levels of the program and sometimes by preparing new brief focused lessons.

USING LITERATURE-BASED PRIMARY-GRADE PROGRAMS   Some children might have had a less structured experience in the primary grades, such as those who have been in a language-experience approach or a literature-based program. Children who were in a literature-based program have often had extensive experiences with shared reading in the primary grades. Their texts are often group sets of authentic literature, for example, multiple copies of *The Very Hungry Caterpillar* (Carle, 1987), that a group of children works with for a week or two before moving on to another piece of literature. These books are often leveled, with their difficulty having been assessed and taken into account before they are selected for use (Pinnell, Bridges, & Fountas, 1999).

Decoding skills are sometimes taught opportunistically rather than systematically. For example, teachers using this approach might notice several words in a piece of text that begin with the same sound/letter correspondence. It might be an element that the children have not examined formally, such as the consonant blend *spl*. The teacher develops a lesson on this sound/letter correspondence that has emerged from words the children have encountered in the story.

When you teach a group of children who have such an experiential background, there might be a need for a more systematic approach to word recognition to augment their earlier instruction and for exposure to many types of comprehension scaffolding strategies.

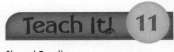

Shared Reading

Moving Toward Independence in Grades 4 and 5

As children move further into the middle and upper grades, the same elements of the reading framework are in place, but the emphasis in each area and within the content changes. First, much more independent work takes place now that the children can read and write on their own. They still need support from the teacher, but they are much more self-sufficient.

Second, there is a diminished focus on skill development because the children have now mastered most of the word recognition skills they need to acquire. The focus on working with words in the four blocks is now more on vocabulary study than on letters and sounds, although occasional lessons are taught on letter/sound correspondences that are less regular or less frequently encountered, such as the silent consonants in *knee, write, pneumonia,* and *psychology* or prefixes of Greek origin, such as *poly-* and *biblio-*.

A third major change is that more instruction emphasizes reading in the content areas of the curriculum, with some lessons focusing as much on science or social studies as on reading. Writing activities are also broadening out from early narrative efforts into various aspects of expository writing, including persuasion and argumentation.

Teach It! 62

Word Origins and Derivations

Building Fluency in Reading

Although the reading fluency of many children is well established by the end of second grade, some children will benefit from continuing emphasis in this area. According to the report of the National Reading Panel (2000), children should read orally with appropriate timing, expressiveness, stress, and intonation (prosody). When necessary, fluency can be promoted through the following contextualized activities in grades 3 to 5:

- Providing daily self-selected reading of easy books at the children's independent levels
- Asking children to rehearse by reading to themselves before reading aloud

CCSS

• CCSS Foundational Skills 4: Fluency

- Discouraging children from interrupting and correcting each other's oral reading
- Disregarding errors that do not change the meaning of the text and providing time for self-correction
- Focusing on comprehension by asking whether what was read incorrectly made sense when correction is needed
- Incorporating daily writing and encouraging invented spelling

Helping struggling readers to develop fluency in the middle grades is always a challenge because they already might be discouraged and they do not want to be perceived as needing to read easy books. Fielding and Roller (1992) suggest that the teacher can sometimes make more difficult books accessible to such children by doing the following:

- Having the children read to themselves first before reading aloud
- Providing paired reading opportunities in which a stronger reader supports a weaker reader (Caution: This can be overdone to the detriment of the more able reader.)
- Building background knowledge with easier books
- Having older troubled readers read easy books to younger children, which provides a good rationale for using less challenging materials at their independent reading levels
- Having children read the text in their mother tongue before reading orally in English (Crawford, 1993)

Paired Reading

Using these strategies to build fluency in the middle grades can also be an important aspect of Tier Two of RTI (Friedman, 2010).

Finally, older children need extensive time for free-choice sustained silent reading, the self-selected reading aspect of the four blocks model. Worthy and Broaddus (2002) suggest beginning with about ten minutes each day, increasing to about 35 minutes each day as the children become capable of maintaining their attention and motivation for longer periods of time. Of course, the students need large numbers of high-interest books in a wide variety of genres.

Struggling Reader

How can Tier Two RTI be strengthened in the middle elementary grades?

Instructional Planning Structures

Throughout this book, you have seen and will continue to see numerous strategies that support various aspects of reading instruction. Teachers must make decisions daily, and sometimes by the hour and minute, about which strategies to use, when to use them, how to sequence them, why to use them, and even how many to use.

A major factor in planning reading instruction relates to the type of program being implemented. A highly scripted program requires little planning in the sense of organizing instruction, but it might be necessary to prepare charts and other materials to be used with the lesson from the manual. Basal programs are also highly organized with many activities, usually more than can be accomplished during a typical lesson.

The task, then, is to plan the comprehensive reading program, assuming you have the latitude to combine elements and strategies from many sources to provide instruction that addresses the needs and interests of your students and the standards established for the school. When that latitude is limited or does not exist at all, the opportunity to address children's individual needs precisely is diminished.

Planning at the Daily Level

When planning daily reading lessons, consider the elements recommended in the four blocks approach:

1. Demonstration of authentic acts of reading and writing in meaningful literacy activities
2. Attention to working with words and developing students' knowledge of the structure of written language
3. Guided practice in meaningful reading and writing so that the children internalize effective strategies
4. Carrying out independent activities in which children apply and extend their reading and writing abilities and develop lifelong habits of literacy

Common Core Curriculum and other state standards should also be reflected in lesson elements.

In grades 3 through 5, there will likely be more than one reading group in the classroom, sometimes three or four. Furthermore, one or more of those groups might be learning to read in Spanish or another language before moving into reading English later. The amount of planning that is necessary can be daunting for a beginning teacher, but just a year of teaching experience will lead to efficiencies that facilitate the planning process.

Most lesson plans contain several common elements:

- One or more student objectives that emerge from student needs and Common Core Curriculum and other state standards
- Necessary text and instructional materials
- An estimated amount of time planned for the lesson
- The body of the lesson, which includes:
  - Anticipation activities to motivate and to activate or introduce needed background knowledge and vocabulary
  - Reading activities to build knowledge for guiding and scaffolding the students' reading and comprehension of the text
  - Consolidation activities, in which students apply new knowledge, often by writing
- A brief focused word study lesson, usually an element that is related to or emerging from the text to be read
- Assessment, often incorporated into a consolidation activity after reading, and also part of an ongoing process of observation and record keeping described in Chapter 11

The Common Core Standards and Literacy box illustrates a lesson plan that might be designed to address some version of Little Red Riding Hood, a story that is familiar to most children. There are three objectives in the lesson, each emerging from one or more state standards—from the state of California in this case (California State Department of Education, 2010). A description of materials that the teacher will need is provided, along with an estimated amount of time scheduled for the lesson.

The body of the lesson contains the three elements that make up most reading lessons. The prereading anticipation activities are brief and simple because the story is well known to most children. The activities to build knowledge during reading are focused on higher-order questions. The children read silently to find information needed to answer the teacher's questions, and they occasionally read evidence aloud to support their responses. The postreading consolidation activities allow them to negotiate the story during the oral retelling. They enjoy the authentic writing activity at the end. They are writing to a real audience—the judge (their teacher)—and they have an authentic purpose for writing. They will enjoy reading the teacher's judgments about the culpability of the wolf.

Phonics and Phonological Awareness

How can phonics instruction emerge naturally from children's reading?

The assessment of the children's achievement during the lesson is also authentic because the teacher is observing their actual listening, reading, thinking, and writing behaviors.

This teacher has incorporated a brief focused lesson on phonics that reflects a need of the children and uses vocabulary from the story as a base for the phonics mini-lesson. In this case, the unvoiced final sound of /th/ is the focus of the lesson, and the teacher will check phonemic awareness, even though the children will undoubtedly have no problem with this aspect in the third grade. Then the teacher moves from the sound to words the children already know that end in the element, some of which come from the story they have read. Finally, the children combine their background knowledge about the sound and the letters that make up the consonant digraph and draw a conclusion about the sound in that position in new and unknown words. The focused lesson on phonics is brief and explicit, only about five minutes, but it is related to and emerging from the literature they have read. It is in the analytic or whole-part-whole mode.

CCSS

Common Core Standards and Literacy Sample Lesson Plan
Daily Lesson Plan: Third-Grade Level

Little Red Riding Hood

Reading—Literature 1 and 3: Key Ideas and Details—Characters
Reading—Foundational Skills 3: Phonics and Word Recognition
Language Standard 2: Standard English Punctuation, Capitalization, and Spelling
Speaking and Listening 1 and 2: Comprehension and Collaboration

Body of Lesson Plan

Anticipation reading activities: The teacher shows the book cover, and the children immediately recognize a familiar story. The teacher asks one or two students to share the beginning of the story before they begin reading. The teacher introduces two vocabulary words using the context of the sentences in which they occur: *hood* and *forest*.

Building knowledge through reading activities: guided silent reading, chunking, and discussion.

Read the first two pages to find out how the author told you that Little Red Riding Hood was a disobedient girl.

How did you know that the wolf was hungry? Please read the sentence that proves your answer. Let's read the next page to find out the effect on the wolf of his great hunger.

When Little Red Riding Hood returns home, what will her mother say to her? Why?

Read the next page to find out what kind of man the hunter was. How do you know that?

How do you know that this is a fantasy story?

Consolidation Reading Activities

Oral retelling of the story: The children retell the story in their own words.

Writing activity: The teacher appoints each child to be an attorney for the wolf, who is in jail. Each child is to write a letter to the judge, asking for the release of the wolf. The teacher is the judge who will decide the wolf's fate in response to each letter. RAFT: Role is attorney; Audience is judge; Format is formal letter; Theme is getting the wolf out of jail (Buehl, 2001).

Oral language activity: The students read their letters aloud to the teacher and the class/reading group.

Read another fairy tale of your choice: Find two story elements that are similar to Little Red Riding Hood and two that are different and make notes about them. Be ready to discuss them tomorrow.

Brief Focused Lesson on Phonics Element

Step One: Students listen to words that contain the final unvoiced consonant /th/, such as *teeth* (the wolf's teeth from the story), *both*, and *bath*. The teacher asks how the words sound alike, as well as other questions that focus the children on the target sound.

Step Two: The teacher shows known words that contain the sound, asking how the words look alike. The teacher asks the students to focus on the letters that make up the sound and where they are.

Step Three: The teacher shows new words that contain the same element in the final position and asks the children to pronounce them. The teacher then asks the children to make a rule about the letters and the sound they have pronounced.

Assessment

Reading comprehension during reading: Success of the children in responding to inferential questions about the story and giving evidence for their answers.

Writing assignment: Coherence and persuasiveness of the argument to release the wolf; attention to the conventions of spelling, punctuation, and syntax.

Focused lesson on phonic element: Success of the children in decoding new words and correctly pronouncing the final sound of /th/ in them.

As this lesson plan is examined in terms of the four blocks multimethod, multilevel approach (Cunningham, Hall, & Sigmon, 2007), each of the four blocks—guided or directed reading, writing, self-selected reading, and working with words—is found. What is not readily seen in this example is the multilevel aspect of the four blocks approach. This could be accomplished by teaching the lesson to the entire class, making the text accessible to all students with multiple readings involving read-aloud, paired reading, and small flexible groups. There would be no problem in incorporating the writing and self-selected reading blocks of the approach, but the word study block might be less successfully applied in this example for grades 3 to 5. Some lower-achieving students still might not be comfortable with the unvoiced /th/ in the initial position, which they should probably know before moving on to that phoneme in the final position. And some children might have learned the sound/symbol correspondence of the final unvoiced /th/ years before.

Strategies to Integrate into Daily Lessons

The rich variety of instructional strategies we introduced in earlier chapters can be used as scaffolding strategies to support children's reading comprehension for use in reading lessons (see Table 13.1). Scaffolding is the temporary support provided by teachers when children are engaged in a task within Vygotsky's "zone of proximal development." Bruner (1978) has described scaffolding as a temporary launching platform designed to support and encourage children's language development to higher levels of complexity. Pearson (1985) later described the temporary nature of scaffolding as the gradual release of responsibility. Good teachers intuitively use such scaffolding strategies to help children maintain their participation in learning activities (Crawford, 1994a).

Some strategies are appropriate as anticipation activities to prepare children for the reading they will do. Others might be helpful for building knowledge during their reading, supporting their comprehension, engaging them in the ideas they will encounter, and providing them with a structure to share their ideas with other students and the teacher. Others are most appropriate as consolidation activities to be completed at the conclusion of a lesson or even as homework. Some anticipation strategies, such as semantic mapping and semantic feature analysis, can be revisited as consolidation activities at the end of lessons for additions and revisions of initial predictions.

As you think about how these many strategies can be used in lessons, first consider that, as in choosing a meal in a cafeteria, you will take from each category the strategies that support your instruction, but not so many that the lesson becomes confused. Over the period of a year, you will likely use most or all of these strategies, but there is no need to use each one every week or even every month. As in all things, moderation is important. The most important activity in every lesson is the reading of connected text.

The recommended strategies that follow will provide the underlying support, or scaffolding, needed for reading comprehension. It is the isolated skills development that you should consider carefully. Skill development should be viewed as an outcome of learning to read, not as its cause. When a child's needs suggest that a directed skill lesson is needed,

Table 13.1   Examples of Scaffolding Strategies to Support Reading Comprehension

ANTICIPATION ACTIVITIES BEFORE READING
Teacher read-aloud of beginning or selected parts of text
Discussion and predictions from book cover, title page, illustrations
Motivation by relating text to students' previous experiences
Think-pair-share
Quick-write
Introduction of new vocabulary with semantic map, contextualized discussion
Activation or installation of background knowledge with semantic map, semantic feature analysis, advance organizer, shared discussion

ACTIVITIES TO BUILD KNOWLEDGE DURING READING
Guided or directed silent reading
Oral reading (generally limited to plays, dramatic activities, puppet shows, reading for expression, providing evidence)
Silent sustained reading
Think-aloud
Specific strategies, such as K-W-L, reader response, literature circles, the ReQuest procedure, reciprocal teaching, and questioning the author

CONSOLIDATION ACTIVITIES AFTER READING
Oral retelling
Written retelling
Review and elaboration of semantic map, semantic feature analysis from anticipation activities before reading
Writing workshop
Role-audience-format-theme (RAFT)
Reader's theater
Paired reading
Silent sustained reading
And more reading
And yet more reading

you can seek out an appropriate one in the teacher's editions and workbooks of traditional reading and language arts programs.

Finally, the structure of the following strategies has been applied to the narrative text in the chapter-opening vignette, but it can also be applied to expository text in science and social studies textbooks and related readings. Reading can be taught in many other subject areas of the curriculum.

ANTICIPATION STRATEGIES BEFORE READING   An examination of Ms. DeLaney's lesson in the opening vignette makes it clear that she has given deep thought to organizing her instructional program in reading. She has identified the children's needs and has planned a program that addresses them carefully. She includes anticipation activities before the part of her lesson during which children read so they can activate background knowledge about the story and become familiar with the meanings of any new vocabulary words that might be needed. There are many strategies that she could use for these two purposes, but she uses only two to move the lesson along to the most important part: the reading.

Many strategies can be used to prepare children to read the text selected for a reading lesson. Two important factors affecting their readiness for reading are the background knowledge they bring to the task and vocabulary. Literature or expository text can be grouped into three levels of challenge with respect to these factors (see Table 13.2). The first category of text is not challenging because the background knowledge and vocabulary needed to understand it are present in the culture and language of the children who will read it. In addition, the story might be in their oral tradition, or they might have been exposed to it in a read-aloud or storytelling activity before their reading. In this case, you might elect to skip unneeded preparation activities that are provided in the teacher's manual of the typical basal reading program. When English language learners have read a story in their mother tongue in a parallel version of their reading program, the story might fall into this category.

The second category of text requires some activation of background knowledge and introduction of new vocabulary, and these anticipatory activities are usually provided for in the teacher's manual. If not, you can develop the needed activities, as Ms. DeLaney did.

The third category of text is very difficult because the children have little background knowledge about it, and new vocabulary is extensive and challenging. Although anticipatory activities are provided in the teacher's manual, you might decide that they are insufficient or inadequate. One option is to skip the story or text and move on to the next one. Another is to augment the anticipatory activities before reading, especially in areas of need for the children. How do you know into which of the three categories the text falls? That decision requires a professional judgment based on your knowledge of the children's strengths and needs, and on your analysis of the text before they begin reading.

Terms in Advance

Table 13.2   Choosing Reading Texts Based on Readiness

| | READINESS CRITERIA | | |
TEXT LEVEL	VOCABULARY	BACKGROUND KNOWLEDGE	TEACHER ACTION
easy	Part of oral traditions	Present in daily culture Part of oral traditions	Preparatory activities may not be necessary
1			
2	Introduces some new vocabulary	Some activation of background knowledge	Some activities necessary to introduce new vocabulary
3			
difficult	Extensive new vocabulary Very difficult	Little activation of background knowledge	Augment anticipation activities as necessary

All children have acquired background knowledge, but there is often a discontinuity between the background knowledge a child actually has and that assumed by the authors of instructional materials or literature used in the classroom. Crawford (1994a) indicates that the discontinuity between the assumption and the reality is deeper when the child comes from another culture or speaks a language different from that of the children for whom the materials are designed or intended—usually middle-class native English speakers. A very effective anticipation strategy for activating and developing background knowledge is semantic feature analysis (Pittelman et al., 1991). This strategy involves helping students build knowledge about a new topic by comparing it to knowledge of related topics about which students do have background knowledge. The Teach It! box illustrates this effective anticipation strategy.

READING STRATEGIES FOR BUILDING KNOWLEDGE DURING READING   Children learn to read by reading. This fundamental idea should underlie your thinking about how children's time is best spent during reading instruction. Rather than having children study

Teach It!

Refer to the Teach It! appendix at the end of the book for further activities you can use to reinforce concepts discussed in this chapter.

Semantic Feature Analysis

Students in a suburban school may have limited background knowledge about the falcon, the topic of expository text from a science book. Related areas about which students in a suburban school would already likely have background knowledge might be *parrot, chicken*, and *crow*. These topics are listed on the *x*-axis of a chart (the top) and generic elements that relate to parrots, chickens, crows, and falcons are listed on the *y*-axis (the left) (see the chart on the right). The teacher prepares the chart before the lesson and presents it on the board, a transparency, or a large piece of paper. Information about the falcon should be available in the text to be read. In a prereading group activity led by the teacher, the students discuss, marking a plus (+) where they know that a relationship is true, a minus (–) where they know that it is not true, and a question mark (?) where they do not have information or do not agree.

On the sample chart, the prereading predictions of a student group are listed and marked accordingly. The students then read the text on falcons, looking for information about elements from the chart.

At the conclusion of the reading, the students discuss the text and return to the semantic feature analysis chart as a consolidation activity. They discuss again, change incorrect predictions, providing evidence they have found in the text, and fill in areas where question marks were indicated.

Unlike some other text-based strategies, semantic feature analysis lends itself well to reading expository text in mathematics and the sciences. For example, a mathematics teacher might list the following elements in the left column: triangle, isosceles triangle, parallelogram, trapezoid, square, rectangle, right triangle, equilateral triangle, and circle. Across the top, the teacher might list such elements as parallel lines, nonparallel lines, straight lines, no straight lines, equal lines, pairs of equal lines, angles, equal angles, pairs of equal angles, and right angles.

Semantic Feature Analysis Chart
The Falcon

	parrot	chicken	crow	falcon
What color are they?				
Brilliant colors	+	–	–	?
Brown	–	+	–	?
Blue	–	–	–	–
Black	–	–	+	?
What do they eat?				
Meat	–	–	+	?
Fruit	+	–	+	?
Seeds	–	+	–	+
Where do they live?				
In the jungle	+	–	–	?
In the mountains	–	–	–	?
On the farm	–	+	+	–
In the desert	–	–	–	?
In the city	–	–	+	?

Table 13.3	Reasons for Minimizing Round-Robin Oral Reading

- It diminishes the amount of actual reading that children do.
- The focus is on pronunciation, not comprehension.
- Strong readers love to perform by reading orally, but they could read more, and faster, by reading silently.
- Poor readers hate to read aloud, disclosing their reading problems for the whole class to hear.
- Both children and teachers dislike listening to the agonizing efforts of poor readers.
- Although teachers can informally assess student outcomes during oral reading, a more systematic approach is needed (see the informal reading inventory discussed in Chapter 11).
- Teachers sometimes convert an oral reading lesson into a phonics lesson that interferes with comprehension.

about reading by mastering skills, maximize the amount of reading they do. Some obvious counterproductive strategies are pencil-and-paper exercises. Another is the still-common practice of round-robin oral reading, in which each child takes a turn reading aloud to the group or class. This usually consists of having a child laboriously reading aloud a passage she or he has never before read, even silently, while the rest of the children in the group pretend to listen or read along. You might have memories of counting the children ahead of you in the first grade so that you could determine which paragraph you would read, although some wise teachers skipped around to thwart that strategy.

The child reading aloud usually focuses on pronunciation, not on understanding what is being read. The other children are either bored or preparing to read when their turn comes. This practice is especially deceiving in regard to children who learned to read first in Spanish, for example. They can read orally with confidence in English, albeit with a Spanish accent and no comprehension. They are, in fact, pronouncing and not reading. Table 13.3 identifies various reasons why round-robin reading should be kept to a minimum.

There are, however, some excellent uses for oral reading: reading a sentence aloud to provide evidence for a response to a question; reading poetry; reading roles in puppet shows and readers' theater; assessment; sharing writing; buddy reading or paired reading as a practice activity; read-alouds to parents, grandparents, or siblings; and improvement of fluency. Otherwise, valuable instructional time in grades 3 to 5 should be used for guided silent reading and comprehension development.

Readers' Theater

It is more difficult for teachers to provide extra support to English language learners because their need for assistance might be less obvious during the largely independent activity of reading silently. The need should be based on children's abilities to interact with the teacher and each other about what they have been reading—that is, their comprehension of what they have been reading.

Guiding children's reading with questions, a variation on DRA, provides valuable support in maintaining comprehension (Crawford, 1993). The teacher needs to precede the children's reading of a page or passage from a piece of literature by asking a higher-order question, that is, an open-ended question whose answer requires the child to use background knowledge and combine it with information from the selection to be read. An example of such a question is "Why is the main character worried? Please read page 71 and let me know." Students will read page 71 to find the answer to the question. It focuses them on comprehension, not on production and accurate oral reading.

Directed Reading-Thinking Activity (DRTA)

This questioning strategy brings key story concepts to children's attention as they read, and, perhaps more important, it provides moral support, interest, and motivation from someone who cares about them: the teacher. Children who cannot or will not read a lengthy selection alone might do so in chunks, a paragraph or a page or two at a time, within the security of a supportive teacher-directed group. These chunks are manageable

Table 13.4 Examples of Different Levels of Questions from "Little Red Riding Hood"

LOW-LEVEL RECALL QUESTIONS

Tell what happened on the first page of the story.

Where did the wolf first see Little Red Riding Hood?

What color is Little Red Riding Hood's cape?

Where is Little Red Riding Hood taking the food basket?

HIGHER-ORDER COMPREHENSION QUESTIONS

How did the author tell you that Little Red Riding Hood was a disobedient girl?

How did you know that the wolf was hungry?

What was the effect on the wolf of his great hunger?

When Little Red Riding Hood returns home, what do you think her mother will say to her? Why?

Why did Little Red Riding Hood go to Grandmother's house by the forest road?

What kind of man was the hunter? How do you know that?

What advice would you give to Little Red Riding Hood for the future? Why?

and comprehensible sections, and questions can be used very effectively and naturally to accomplish this chunking. You can structure children's reading with questions that elicit predictions, with timely resolution of those predictions through discussion and any needed mediation.

Although there is considerable debate about the value of teaching reading comprehension skills through direct instruction, there are enough other reasons to guide silent reading with higher-order or comprehension-level questions. Table 13.4 provides some examples of poor low-level questions and strong higher-order questions. It takes no longer to formulate and ask a higher-order comprehension question than a low-level recall question before asking children to read to find the answer. Guided silent reading provides an opportunity for children to make inferences and predictions, identify cause-and-effect relationships, and apply other higher-order critical thinking skills when their comprehension is supported (Crawford, 1993). This is seen in Ms. DeLaney's lesson in the chapter-opening vignette. Her students are now in the third grade, and they need to read silently with a focus on comprehension. But their abilities in this area are still limited, and she therefore scaffolded their comprehension by guiding their silent reading with carefully formulated higher-order questions. She also limited how much they read after each question to an amount they could understand and remember for the discussion that followed each chunk. Ms. DeLaney provided occasional opportunities for oral reading, as described in her lesson. She often asked children to read aloud the sentence or sentences that provided evidence for their responses to her higher-order questions.

CONSOLIDATION STRATEGIES AFTER READING   Ms. DeLaney concluded her lesson with two consolidation activities. She integrated an oral retelling and a small authentic writing assignment into the closing part of the lesson—part to be done while she was with the group and the rest to be done after she left them. She collected the children's written predictions and later responded briefly in writing to the content of each one. If she noted a spelling error in a child's prediction, she used the word correctly in her response to that child. She also reviewed their papers for common problems, such as the correct use of the comma in a series. Instead of correcting that error, she would plan a mini-lesson on the element or detail for the next day. The children could then examine their own work and make needed changes or corrections.

Writing and Reading Connections

How can writing be incorporated into the consolidation activity of retelling?

Retelling is an excellent consolidation activity after reading. An oral retelling provides children with the opportunity to negotiate with each other about the meaning of the selection and requires them to listen very attentively to each other (Brown & Cambourne, 1990). Through this process, children can often incorporate new information gained through reading into existing background knowledge. They also observe that retelling promotes multiple readings of text as a part of the negotiation process. Koskinen et al. (1988) found that the verbal rehearsal that occurs in the retelling process also serves to improve the reading comprehension of less proficient readers. English language learners might elect to retell in their mother tongue what they read or heard in their second language (Crawford, 1993).

Retelling also provides a means for integrating writing into the program. Either through a cooperative learning process or through individual or paired writing, children can prepare a written retelling (Strickland & Feeley, 1985). As a result of their earlier discussion, the knowledge they gained through reading, and such prereading activities as semantic mapping and the examination of story grammar, children are better prepared to write a well-structured retelling. Like the demonstration that they provide during read-alouds, teachers should also model retelling with an actual example.

The most obvious consolidation activity after reading should not be overlooked: more reading. If you are successful in providing high-quality literature that children will choose to read and in supporting their comprehension, then you can expect gains in all areas of the language arts. Reading is more powerful than direct instruction in developing vocabulary, grammar, spelling, and reading comprehension, especially for English language learners. Provide extensive free voluntary reading with messages that are easily understood in low-anxiety situations. Good writing is promoted more by extensive reading than it is by writing (Krashen, 1985, 1993).

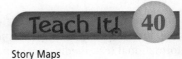

Story Maps

CCSS

• Speaking and Listening 4: Retelling a Story

Long-Term Planning Using Common Core Curriculum Standards and Maps

The use of Common Core Curriculum Standards is a recent trend that constitutes an elaboration on and expansion of the earlier thematic literature unit concept. The Common Core Curriculum Standards expand the thematic literature unit in that they:

CCSS

• How do Common Core Curriculum Standards build on state standards?

- Address both skills and content (Achieve, 2010; Pearson, 2012)
- Incorporate extensive expository text, in addition to literature, as well as other modalities of acquiring information from digital sources, music, art (Hiebert, 2011–12)
- Raise the bar to critical thinking and problem solving in order to prepare children for college and careers in the twenty-first century (Hiebert, 2011–12)
- Are built on the strengths of existing state standards (Pearson, 2012)
- Are informed by countries with high achievement levels on international measures (Pearson, 2012)

The Common Core Curriculum Standards Map that follows provides a variety of narrative and expository texts on the unit theme, Dolphins and Other Cetaceans, as well as poetry, music, art, and Internet sources. They range in difficulty from below grade level to well above grade level, providing text for everyone to read as well as challenges for all. Listening comprehension, speaking, reading, and writing activities are incorporated in such a way that all of the English language arts are addressed. The unit is designed to be taught over a period of one to two weeks and represents one such unit among the three or four that might be implemented during the fifth-grade level. It provides for the kind of multi-perspective text resources that promote critical literacy (Clarke & Whitney, 2009).

Integrating Across the Curriculum
Endangered Dolphins and Other Cetaceans:
A Common Core Curriculum Standards Map for Grade 5

Overview

This four-week Common Core Curriculum Standards map for the fifth grade explores novels, stories, poetry, informational text, media, magazine articles, music, and videos about the life of dolphins and related cetaceans. They relate realistic fiction to informational texts about dolphins and other cetaceans, as well as to gathering information from poems, labels on cans in supermarkets, songs, art, and other Internet sources. Based on attitudes and emotional points of view gained from the narrative sources and information gained from expository texts, they draw conclusions and form opinions about the value of dolphins and cetaceans in our lives. They develop the means to share those conclusions and express those opinions through writing and other media. This exemplar map is based on models from Common Core (2012).

Focus Standards

The focus standards for this unit are from the Common Core State Standards, Grade 5, California State Department of Education, August, 2010. <www.scoe.net/castandards/agenda/2010/ela_ccs_recommendations.pdf>

Reading—Literature
- Determine a theme of a story, drama, or poem, from details in the text, including how characters in a story or drama respond to challenges or how the speaker in a poem reflects upon a topic; summarize the text.
- Describe how a narrator's or speaker's point of view influences how events are described.

Reading—Informational Text
- Describe the connection between a series of historical events, scientific ideas or concepts, or steps in technical procedures in a text.
- Compare and contrast the most important points presented by two texts on the same topic.

Reading—Foundational Skills
- Read with sufficient accuracy and fluency to support comprehension.

Writing
- Write opinion pieces on topics or texts, supporting a point a view with reasons and information.
- With guidance and support from peers and adults, develop and strengthen writing as needed by planning, revising, editing, rewriting, or trying a new approach.

- Conduct short research projects that use several sources to build knowledge through investigation of different aspects of a topic.

Speaking and Listening
- Summarize the points a speaker or media source makes and explain how each claim is supported, by reasons and evidence, and identify and analyze any logical fallacies.

Language
- Demonstrate command of the conventions of standard English capitalization, punctuation, and spelling when writing.
- Demonstrate understanding of figurative language, word relationships, and nuances in word meanings.

Selected Student Objectives

- Compare and contrast the main characters of *Island of the Blue Dolphins* and *Moby Dick*; describe how both characters were developed by the authors as they met major challenges.
- Research the controversy of dolphin protection from the point of view of fishermen and of environmentalists on the Internet; write a rationale for either point of view and defend it.
- Describe how dolphins, porpoises, and whales are more like dogs and cats than sharks and salmon; illustrate and label one cetacean, any fish, and any four-legged mammal.
- Research the importance of whale oil 150 years ago, and make an oral presentation about it.

Selected Sample Lesson Activities That Focus on State Common Core Curriculum Standards and That Reflect Available Resources

- Read-alouds of stories and informational sources and other scaffolding activities to support struggling readers for whom leveled text is too difficult, but who also benefit from exposure to challenging text (Glasswell & Ford, 2010)
- Directed reading lessons of appropriate narrative and informational texts differentiated at reading levels of groups of students according to Lexiles
- Conducting Internet searches for information about dolphins and other cetaceans, taking notes about ideas encountered, and organizing those notes into written communications to share with other students

- Based on Internet sources, class discussions about the relative values of dolphins and other cetaceans to fishermen and environmentalists, and other stakeholders in which students must present and defend their points of view
- Preparing posters and text to illustrate points of view about the importance of dolphins and other cetaceans in the environment

Selected Works

(E) – CCSS exemplar text; (EA) other text from authors with works on the CCSS exemplar list

LITERARY TEXTS

Stories

Island of the Blue Dolphins (Scott O'Dell, Sandpiper) (Lexile 1000)
Dolphin Song (Lauren St. John) (Lexile 980)
Moby Dick (Herman Melville) (Lexile 790–840)

Poems

In Dolphin Time (Diane Farris, Simon & Schuster) (Lexile not available; K–3)
The Dolphin Song (lyrics) (Olivia Newton-John)— <www.sing365.com/music/lyric.nsf/Promise-Dolphin-Song-lyrics-Olivia-Newton-John/20E90F85EA0A6EE048256 A39000FC47A>

INFORMATIONAL TEXTS

Science/Social Science

Amazing Whales! (Sara L. Thomson, Harper Collins) (E) (Lexile 630)
Threats to Dolphins—<http://library.thinkquest.org/17963/threats.html> (Lexile not available)
Threats to Whales and Dolphins—<www.dolphins.org/marineed_threatstodolphins.php>
Dolphins: What They Can Teach Us (Mary M. Cerullo, Scholastic) (Lexile 1150)
Habitat Destruction—<www.aqua.org/dolphins/threats-to-dolphins.html>
The Tuna-Dolphin Issue—(Lexile not available) <http://swfsc.noaa.gov/textblock.aspx?Division=PRD&Parent MenuId=228&id=1408>
Dolphin Safe Tuna—<www.earthisland.org/dolphin SafeTuna/consumer/> (Lexile not available)
Whales are people, too: A declaration of the rights of cetaceans. *The Economist*, February 25, 2012, pp. 92, 94. (Lexile not available; difficult text for read-aloud, very advanced readers)

Reference

Diving Dolphins (Laura Hamilton Waxman, First Avenue Editions) (Lexile 740)

Dolphin Intelligence Explained—<http://news.discovery .com/animals/dolphin-intelligence-explained.html> (Lexile not available)
Whales, Dolphins, and Porpoises (Mark Carwardine, Collins) (Lexile not available)

ART, MUSIC, AND MEDIA

Art

Drawing Whales and Dolphins (Troll Communications) (All levels)

Music

The Dolphin Song (Olivia Newton-John)—<http://www .youtube.com/watch?v=p6FCSVAZJHM>
Dolphin Sounds (sound samples section)—<www .dolphinear.com/data/dolphin_sounds.htm>

Media

Dolphins: The Wild Side—National Geographic video
Dolphins Save Surfer from Being Shark's Bait—<http://today.msnbc.msn.com/ id/21689083/ns/today-today_people/t/ dolphins-save-surfer-becoming-sharks-bait/>
Spinner Dolphin footage—<www.oceanfootage.com/ stockfootage/Spinner_Dolphin>

ADDITIONAL RESOURCES

Graphics and text on cans of tuna and other fish products from a class visit to supermarket

SELECTED VOCABULARY

- cetacean
- whale
- porpoise
- dolphin
- vertebrate
- mammal

MAKING INTERDISCIPLINARY CONNECTIONS

Art
- Illustrating dolphins and cetaceans

Music
- Listening to *The Dolphin Song*, analysis of lyrics
- Listening to dolphin communications

Science
- Learning about animal species—characteristics of mammals and fish, and differences between them

History/Geography
- Oceans of the world
- Whaling in the nineteenth century

Assessment: Revisiting the Informal Reading Inventory

Language and Diversity

What is the effect of language and dialectical differences on the interpretation of oral reading errors in the informal reading inventory?

Although there are already differences in achievement among children at each level from kindergarten to second grade, there is a much broader range of levels of proficiency in reading and writing in grades 3 through 5. Most states and school districts now conduct an annual or biannual assessment of children's reading achievement at several grade levels, but the data that those standardized tests yield are not designed for use in planning instruction for individual children. Teachers need to gather information about the individual strengths and needs of each child in order to plan instruction, select appropriate instructional materials, and group children.

In the chapter-opening vignette, Ms. DeLaney had divided her students into ability groups for that part of her instruction. According to results from the informal assessment she administered during the first week of school, the reading levels of the 27 students in her classroom ranged from second to fifth, with one group reading slightly below grade level, one group reading at grade level, and some children reading at the fourth- and fifth-grade levels. And as a part of the Common Core State Standards initiative, children who read at different levels will need access to literature and expository text at those levels, or through such differentiated strategies as read-alouds, directed reading lessons, and free reading.

Interpreting IRI Results for Linguistically Diverse Students

Most assessment strategies used with English speakers function well in other languages and also in English with English language learners. Some adaptations are indicated, however. For example, one element of evaluating oral reading accuracy in the informal reading inventory is mispronunciation, each occurrence of which is counted as an oral reading error or miscue. When a mispronunciation error can be attributed to a conflict point with the mother tongue or dialect of English and when it does not interfere with comprehension, a short *i* pronounced as a long *e*, for example, then an error would not be counted (Wheeler, Cartwright, & Swords, 2012).

Kenneth Johnson (personal communication, 1977) provides a test sentence to illustrate this principle for the African American child whose mother tongue is African American Vernacular English. The sentence often elicits a mispronunciation that has the potential to interfere with comprehension. The child is asked to read the following sentence aloud: "As I passed the sign, I read it." In conformance with African American Vernacular English, the African American child sometimes pronounces *passed* as *pass*, dropping the *-ed* suffix that is also a past tense marker. If the child comprehends the marker, that is, understands that *passed* is in the past tense even though he pronounced it as in the present tense, then the child will pronounce *read* in the past tense. If not, the child will pronounce *read* in the present tense. According to Johnson, these children invariably correctly pronounce *read* in the past tense. In a study of teachers who administered IRIs to Spanish-speaking children, Lamberg, Rodríguez, and Tomas (1978) concluded that to avoid such problems, teachers need special training to use them with English language learners.

Reading assessments can help identify a child's reading level as well as comprehension. How can a teacher use this information to plan for instruction?

Other Informal Measures of Reading and Writing

As you saw in Chapter 11, there are many informal measures that teachers can use to assess their students' progress through the developmental processes of learning to read and write. Chantell DeLaney, the teacher in the chapter-opening vignette, uses many of these measures daily. Although she makes effective use of the informal reading inventory periodically for all students, and when needed for individual students, she can observe the frustration level in her students' physical behaviors. She might note that some children rarely participate in discussion activities after silent reading, even with the support of the many scaffolding activities she provides. She takes careful notes about these observations and uses them in planning future instruction.

Each student in Ms. DeLaney's classroom has a portfolio of writing products. She urges them to add a sample of writing to their portfolios from their work each week. This can be used as a motivation tool when students are able to observe their progress as they page through the portfolio, week after week. It is also a valuable tool for use in parent conferences to document for parents the progress their children are making.

Transitioning English Language Learners

It is often during grade 3 that English language learners who have been in a mother tongue bilingual education reading program since first grade begin a process of transitioning to English language reading instruction. This may occur earlier or later for some children, depending on their age when they arrived. When children speak and understand English at an intermediate level, and when they are reading confidently in the mother tongue at least at a second- or third-grade level, they are ready to begin a formal transition to English, although they will have had many English language reading experiences before the formal transition. How can teachers help English language learners begin to make the transition into English language reading instruction? What can you do to help your ESL students make the transition to English-language reading instruction?

Using the Language Experience Approach in English

In the past, it was commonly held that second-language learners should not begin learning to read and write at all in the second language until they had reached an intermediate level of fluency in speaking it. Teachers now recognize that informal processes of reading and writing in the second language can begin early in the English language acquisition process, especially for children who have developed literacy skills in their mother tongue. This early reading instruction is informal and incidental; it is not a formal English reading program. In addition, this incidental instruction should not be substituted for mother tongue instruction when it is possible to provide it.

Bilingual teachers who teach reading in their mother tongue recognize that children's motivation to begin reading and writing in the English language is strong. It has already been noted that, where possible, it is most beneficial for children to learn to read and write first in their mother tongue, but teachers can begin a cautious, early introduction to literacy in a second language to take advantage of that motivation. Although it is employed mostly with young children, the language-experience approach (LEA) can also be used in grades beyond second grade when children are just beginning to learn to read in English or when older preliterate children need more time at the earliest stages of English reading, especially if they are unable to read in their mother tongue. Some migrant children or the

The World of Reading

Using the IRI Capacity Level as a Measure of English Language Proficiency

Many commercial instruments are available for assessing English language proficiency. Most examine pronunciation, knowledge of syntax, vocabulary knowledge, and other discrete skills. Because state and federal funds are often involved for qualifying students, English language learners are usually assessed for redesignation as fluent English speakers in a very formalistic and legalistic process. The information gained from this type of assessment is less useful for instructional planning. To teach English language learners to read in English, teachers need to know how well they comprehend English.

According to A. Crawford (1982, 2000), teachers can use the reading capacity level, another level yielded by an informal reading inventory, as a measure of listening comprehension that is a useful reflection of English language proficiency. They can use the IRI to make an informed decision about readiness for English language reading instruction in given materials by reading a selected passage aloud to the child. Crawford reported that children who read in their mother tongue and also respond correctly to 75 percent of comprehension-level questions about the material read to them in English usually have

sufficient second-language proficiency to begin learning to read at the highest level at which they successfully respond to those questions.

For example, a second-grade teacher who believes that an English language learner may be ready for formal English reading instruction would read a passage of 100 to 200 words aloud to the child from the second-grade text used for teaching English reading in the classroom. Children who can respond correctly to three of four comprehension-level (not recall) questions about the text in English when it is read to them are providing evidence that they are ready to begin formal reading instruction in English at the second-grade level. This level is described as one of cognitive academic-language proficiency (CALP), explained in detail in Chapter 15. For those children learning to read in their mother tongue in a bilingual program, this is often at or near the grade level at which they are reading in that mother tongue. They will need all of the scaffolding support described in this chapter. The levels of their English vocabulary and syntax will in no way correspond to those of children who have been communicating in English since birth.

Language Experience with English Language Learners

Language and Diversity

How can teachers help English language learners with beginning reading in English?

Making and Using Word Banks

children of refugees might never have been in school, even though they are ten or twelve years of age, or older.

There are many LEA activities that can be adapted for English language learners. For example, multiple readings of the text are helpful (Crawford, Allen, & Hall, 1995). Using a copy of the text with empty spaces where words have been left out, children can practice reading the text and try to predict what words should be in the spaces. This practice is known as an *oral cloze procedure*. When reading the text with the children, the teacher can pause briefly upon encountering each missing word, and then write in those words as the children identify them.

Children may accumulate new words they learn, with these collections serving as their personal word files. After they have 15 or 20 words, they can do sorting activities with their word files (Bear et al., 2007). Finding words that start with the same letter and sound is a way in which some children learn to associate letters and sounds, allowing them to learn best about letters and sounds from words they already know. They can look for words that are names of people, places, animals, colors, foods, and clothing.

If children are collecting the words they can read, they can try to build sentences with them. You might need to demonstrate this before asking them to try it. Read their sentences to them if they cannot read them independently. Children can also try to reconstruct the same sentences they have used in their dictated texts.

One nonthreatening way to elicit text that reflects more mature syntax and vocabulary is an adaptation called the *collaborative chart story*. When children are dictating and beginning to read with confidence later in the process, ask them to negotiate their suggested text with the group. You can invite questions from other children about a suggested sentence, for example, by asking how they feel about the way it is stated and how effectively the vocabulary provided expresses what the group wants to say. When children who have dictated sentences with grammatical errors hear suggestions from other children about how it might be said in another way, they invariably agree to the change. The children do not view this collaboration as correction, but rather as reflecting the contributions they all make together in communicating with the audience that will read their text later. It is probably better to accept exactly what is dictated at the beginning of the LEA process so that children can see the direct links among what they say, what you write down, and what the group reads back later.

The language-experience approach can be used with students who are learning to read in English as their second language as a way to initiate students into print that is of interest and relevance to them (Dixon & Nessel, 1983; Moustafa & Penrose, 1985; Nessel & Jones, 1981; Winsor, 2009). According to Crawford (1993), the language-experience approach also provides a means through which students can experience authentic literature in English that is above their ability to read and comprehend for themselves. After you tell or read a story aloud, the students can then dictate the story back, that is, retell it for you to record, although probably in a less complicated version than the original.

Beginning a language-experience approach activity with a piece of authentic literature will often result in a better structured dictation than the random list of sentences that often results from LEA dictations stimulated by an illustration, a manipulative, or other prompts. Peck (1989) suggests that listening to read-aloud stories helps children to develop a sense of story structure, which should be reflected in their dictated version, and it enhances their abilities to predict in this and other stories. The dictated text allows children to think, talk, read, and write about the piece of literature and to be exposed to its valuable cultural content. At the same time, they are actively interacting with it at a level of comprehension and of second-language proficiency appropriate for their stage of development.

Vocabulary Development

Reading is also a major factor in the vocabulary development of English language learners. Second-language acquisition and literacy in English can contribute mutually to each other's development for intermediate English language learners. In keeping with a meaning-based approach to teaching English language learners, Harmon (1998) provides an excellent contextualized strategy for vocabulary development. She provides two examples of how a teacher uses a new term and then elaborates and expands its meaning immediately:

CCSS

• Language 4: Vocabulary

> *"Let's start <u>recounting</u> the events of the story. <u>Let's tell about the beginning, middle, and end.</u>" "This is an <u>excerpt—a small part.</u>"*

In another strategy described by Nagy and colleagues (1993) and by Cummins and Corson (1997), Spanish-speaking students can use cognates they recognize from Spanish and English to support their reading comprehension in English. Words such as *general* are the same in spelling and meaning in both languages, and many other cognates are the same in meaning and similar in spelling, such as an example provided by Nagy and colleagues: *transform* in English and *transformar* in Spanish. But looking beyond their study, children must also be taught to be wary of such false cognates as *actual*, which means "nowadays" in Spanish, and *dime*, which means "tell me."

When children read, their lack of vocabulary knowledge is often an obstacle to comprehension. Because they may have insufficient academically related background knowledge and vocabulary development in their mother tongue that would accompany it, this can be an even greater problem for children who must read in their second language. Although vocabulary is an aspect of background knowledge in prereading, it is treated separately here so we can examine several concepts that relate more specifically to this topic.

What can you do to help your ESL students make the transition to English language reading instruction?

One aspect of vocabulary development relates to the richness of language that surrounds children. It is well recognized that children become familiar with the meanings of words when those meanings are highly contextualized, not when they are studied in isolation as new vocabulary words. It follows, then, that a richer language environment should result in increased exposure to contextualized vocabulary and therefore to greater understanding of meanings (Crawford, 1994b).

Schools often postpone or even eliminate instruction for at-risk children, however, in the very areas of the curriculum where new vocabulary words will be offered in the most highly contextualized ways—in science, social studies, art, music, health, and other areas of the curriculum. This is even more common for children who are learning in their second language. According to Crawford (1993), teachers must ensure that these areas of the curriculum are provided for all children, including English language learners, and that they are presented in such a way that contextualized exposure to a rich vocabulary is promoted.

Another aspect of vocabulary is the issue of direct instruction. Although many vocabulary words will be acquired incidentally, some literature or content selections will contain a few vocabulary words that must be clearly grasped if the text is to be understood. There will be other words not known to the children that do not need to be addressed through direct instruction because they are not critical to understanding the selection or because they can be quickly analyzed through the context in which they appear.

Many of the strategies recommended for the activation or development of background knowledge constitute direct approaches to vocabulary instruction. Semantic mapping is one of these strategies, but its application should be limited to those key and conceptually difficult vocabulary terms that are more in the realm of background knowledge. Otherwise, there will be little time left for reading following the completion of anticipation activities before reading.

Teach It! 21

"Word Conversations" for Primary Grades

Adapting Phonics and Decoding Strategies for English Language Learners

CCSS

• Foundational Skills 3: Phonics and Word Recognition

English language learners bring to the classroom phonemic awareness of sounds in their mother tongue. They should first learn phonics in their mother tongue out of the context of words they already recognize on sight, probably acquired from their print environment and from language experience charts and big books. English language learners who learn phonics in their mother tongue generally have a much easier time learning phonics in English than do children who must learn phonics first in English. Some languages, such as Spanish and Korean, are very regular in their sound/letter relationships. Not only is phonics easier to learn, but children have more confidence in the process than do children who are learning to read in a language in which sound/letter relationships are not regular, such as English.

The language-experience approach and shared reading are holistic strategies for teaching reading. In these strategies, teachers do not begin with phonics. But learning about letters and sounds (phonics) is a part of learning to read in all methods, including these. In a developmental approach to teaching about letters and sounds, children should learn about reading first. They should dictate many LEA charts and read them, learning to read some 100 to 200 words on sight. They should have many shared book reading experiences, and then they will be ready to learn about letters and sounds using words they already know in English.

The real dilemma for English language learners is when they must learn phonics in English first. Although they might have learned to speak and understand English, they still lack the phonemic awareness skills in English that a native speaker has. For example, a native Spanish-speaking child will speak the 43 sounds of English using the 25 sounds of Spanish. There are only 5 vowel sounds in Spanish, but 15 in English. This accounts for the difficulty that Spanish-speaking children have in pronouncing short vowels in English, especially the schwa; they have similar difficulty in "reading" (correctly pronouncing)

Language and Diversity

What advantages may English language learners have in learning phonics in English if they first learn to read in the mother tongue?

these sounds in a phonetic approach to reading. Although there are variations in the differences between other languages and English, similar difficulties arise for children who speak those languages. However, for children who learn phonics in their mother tongue, the process of learning English phonics is much easier because they have already figured out how the process works. The process transfers from the mother tongue, even if many of the sounds do not.

Finally, Sleeter and Grant (2007) remind teachers that they need to distinguish between mechanics and meaning when teaching students whose mother tongue is not English or standard American English. They concluded that teachers should not be bogged down in remediation whenever they encounter gaps in student learning that relate more to mechanics than to understanding.

Writing and Spelling

A major principle of a developmental view of literacy is the interdependence of listening, speaking, reading, and writing. Hudelson (1984) observed that English language learners address the four language processes as a totality, not as separate entities. According to Fitzgerald (1993), writing begins when children can draw, and there is no need to wait for reading. These ideas can be extended to English language learners, who should be encouraged to write in the second language early, especially if they have writing skills in their mother tongue. The errors they make should be viewed in the same way that errors in oral production are viewed: as a part of the natural processes of approximation and acquisition (Crawford, 1994a).

For English language learners, writing can flow out of a variety of language acquisition activities, including the key vocabulary and language-experience approaches to reading and the consolidation strategy of written retellings after reading text. The structuring of their writing or their selection of vocabulary may be further supported through the use of semantic maps.

Spelling is another area in which instructional strategies must be adapted for English language learners. Consistent with the communicative approach principle of minimizing error correction and with the developmental nature of second-language acquisition and literacy, described in Chapter 15, teachers of English language learners, like teachers of English speakers, should accept the invented spellings of their students as a very natural aspect of their developmental growth in writing. There are differences, however, in how English language learners will progress through some of the developmental stages of invented spelling.

In the letter name–alphabetic spelling stage of Bear et al. (2007), English language learners begin to approximate an alphabetic orthography and to conceptualize the alphabetic principle (see Chapter 5). They begin to demonstrate the relationship between sound and letter, and they sometimes use letter names as words. They begin to understand the left-to-right convention, and they may begin to segment words. Differences in the nature of invented spelling between languages will appear. The use of consonants tends to predominate over the use of vowels when children write in English as a mother tongue, for example, but vowels predominate over consonants when children write in Spanish as a mother tongue (Ferreiro & Rodríguez, 1994).

In the within-word pattern spelling stage of Bear and colleagues (2007), children have learned most basic rules of the orthographic system. They are aware of such word structures as prefixes, suffixes, contractions, compound words, and homonyms, and they continue to learn some less common spelling patterns and rules. It is at this stage that they begin to recognize when a word looks correct, a phenomenon that corresponds to the natural approach characteristic in which second-language learners begin to recognize when something sounds right or feels right. They are able to spell a large number of words automatically.

English language learners who are literate in another language will tend to move much more rapidly through developmental stages of spelling in their new second language of English than they did in their primary language. Nathenson-Mejia (1989) found

Language and Diversity

How can we support the development of writing in English for English language learners?

CCSS

- Language 2: Conventions of Standard English

Teach It! 53

Interactive Writing

that Spanish-speaking children in the beginning stages of English spelling made extensive use of Spanish pronunciation in their invented spellings in English writing. Edelsky (1982) made the same observation in a more generic sense when she adopted the positive point of view that children are applying some mother tongue writing skills to the second language rather than the negative point of view that it reflected interference from the first language on the second.

Scaffolding Strategies for Improving Reading Comprehension

CCSS

• Language 4: Vocabulary

Your own experiences in learning another language might remind you of the importance of reading for comprehension as opposed to word calling. Remember that comprehension and communication are the focus of reading and writing. There are many reading strategies that will help to ensure that children focus on comprehension instead of only on correct pronunciation.

The use of scaffolding strategies to support the comprehension of children in general is of great importance; but for English language learners, it is the difference between success and failure (Crawford, 1994a). There has been a tendency to place some English language learners in perpetual compensatory or remedial programs. There, teachers expect them to learn to read and write by acquiring isolated skills through interaction with incomplete fragments of language. These children rarely move successfully into the mainstream curriculum; more frequently, they leave these programs only when they complete their schooling—all too often as dropouts. Scaffolding strategies sometimes resemble most closely the enrichment activities that teachers of English language learners never seem to have time for because they are busy teaching the isolated skills that the children appear to lack. Variations of two common comprehension strategies are especially effective in working with English language learners.

THE CUMULATIVE SEMANTIC MAP   Ordinarily, a semantic map is used for activating background knowledge or introducing vocabulary as an anticipation activity before reading. It is developed and completed for one or two related lessons and not referred to subsequently. Teachers often find, however, that they are dealing with some language topics on repeated occasions. Therefore, it can be useful to return to a semantic map on such a topic, to add to it, and to contrast new additions with earlier ones. Crawford has identified this semantic mapping strategy as the cumulative semantic map (Crawford, 1994a).

Figure 13.1 shows a cumulative semantic map on the theme of feelings and emotions that has been augmented periodically during the first few weeks of school (Crawford, 2000). A teacher might introduce the new word *furious* from a piece of literature the class is about to read and ask children where it should be added to the existing cumulative semantic map for words about feelings and emotions. At that point, the children can discuss how much anger the word *furious* implies, as compared to *miffed*, *enraged*, and *upset*, which had been added to the semantic map on earlier occasions. They add the new word *furious* to their cumulative semantic map. Many weeks later, the map has been elaborated, as seen in Figure 13.2, and, of course, this process continues through the school year.

When written on sticky notes, the various words in a cumulative semantic map can be arranged and rearranged in ascending order of increasing anger as children negotiate the meanings with each other. Moustafa (1997) suggests placing words on cards for charts with sticky tape across the top. The teacher can use the same piece of tape over and over by affixing the cards to a large wall chart made of plastic shower curtain material. This strategy can be adapted to the cumulative semantic map, which facilitates moving words from one place to another on the chart or making room for a new word to be added.

In a writing assignment perhaps several months later, English language learners might refer back to the cumulative semantic map on the wall when they want to select just the right word to convey the degree of anger they have in mind (Crawford, 1994a). Discussing the choice of word with the teacher or with other children will be particularly helpful.

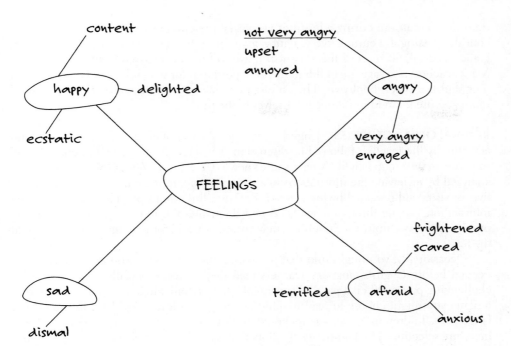

Figure 13.1
A Cumulative Semantic Map

When children are ready to add yet another synonym for *angry* a week or a month later, they will have the opportunity to review other words or expressions for the same feeling, but within a context of known or somewhat familiar vocabulary. Teachers can view a well-developed cumulative semantic map as a "graphic thesaurus." Other suitable topics for cumulative semantic maps might include *see* (*stare, peek, glare,* etc.), *motion* (*crawl, creep, dawdle, dash, poke along, lope,* etc.), and *touch* (*poke, tap, jab, stroke,* etc.). Only the topics come from the teacher; the source of vocabulary is the literature the children are reading.

If your classroom has a word wall, this might be the place to attach several cumulative semantic maps that are used frequently. If there are so many that they do not all fit, several might be mounted on top of each other on the wall or an easel with a way of folding them

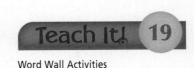

Word Wall Activities

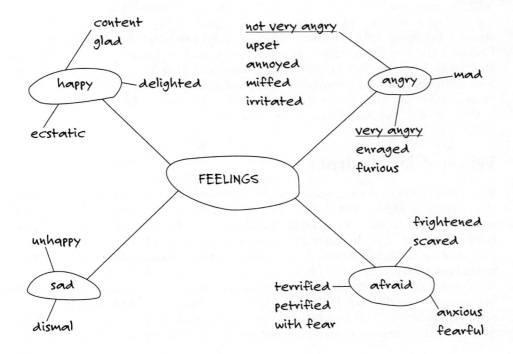

Figure 13.2
An Elaborated Cumulative Semantic Map

up so the one in use during a lesson is visible. At the end of the school year, you might consider passing the cumulative semantic maps on to the children's teacher for the next grade, especially if most of the class will move to the new classroom intact as a group. Many teachers also save the children's writing portfolios for the children to pick up when they start the next school year. The children can take their portfolios to their new classroom and use them to introduce themselves to the new teacher.

READ-ALOUD ACTIVITIES   English language learners often benefit from read-aloud activities by the teacher, followed by discussion. Vocabulary is presented in context, and someone in the group will likely have some knowledge of most words. Other words may be analyzed by reviewing the illustrations in a story or an appropriate illustration, manipulative, or visual aid provided by the teacher. Because illustrations provide important visual information, paging through a selection and discussing the illustrations before reading provides an opportunity for presenting new vocabulary and for making predictions about the text.

Occasionally, you might find that presenting the entire selection as a read-aloud is needed before English language learners read themselves, especially in a particularly challenging piece. When a parallel version of a text is available in the children's mother tongue, you might choose to read it aloud before the children read later in the second language. Children in school are not bored or disturbed by several exposures to the same literature selection. The familiarity of a story that is an old friend becomes a real comfort. Familiarity with the background knowledge and structure of a story permits children to read with better comprehension and with fewer time-consuming visual cues, especially for children's early literacy experiences in English. The read-aloud activity also provides the teacher with the opportunity to demonstrate and model predicting, thinking about context, and other metacognitive strategies in a think-aloud during the teacher's oral reading.

Literacy expert Dr. MaryEllen Vogt discusses differentiated instruction and how it can be successfully implemented. After watching the video, describe what you have learned about differentiated instruction and how you can implement it in grades 3 to 5.

Differentiating Instruction in Grades 3 to 5

By now, you have doubtless concluded that a one-size-fits-all approach to teaching children to read is most inappropriate. Each child needs instruction at an appropriate level, but, fortunately, there are usually many children who have needs in common. Grouping children for instruction is a tricky proposition, but it addresses the need for appropriate instruction for all children. Some advocate for teaching the entire class at one time, a strategy that can be very effective in some areas of the curriculum. For example, placing students in small groups according to individual needs is not a common practice in the areas of science, social science, art, and music.

Whole-Class Instruction

When instruction in reading is consistently conducted with the whole class, it is often characteristic of highly scripted and sequenced direct instruction reading programs. The use of this type of approach implies that all children are the same and that a single program is adequate for all. In reality, this means that every time a lesson is taught, it is just right for some children, too difficult for children who were unsuccessful in earlier lessons and did not attain prerequisite skills, and repetitious and boring for children who mastered the material weeks, months, or years before. Instruction should be planned to meet individual needs. This does not imply a separate lesson for each individual child, but it does permit children with similar strengths or needs to be grouped together for appropriate instruction. There are some reading/language arts activities that can be conducted with the entire class, such as a review of how to avoid run-on sentences in writing when almost all children show the need, teacher read-aloud activities, library visits, using a video of a story, conducting a poetry hour, and readers' theater (Burns, Roe, & Ross, 1999).

Grouping: Why and Why Not?

Schools are sometimes tempted to group students homogeneously by reading ability on a classroom basis across an entire school. If there are five fourth-grade classes, why not place the students who are nonreaders in one classroom, those reading at grade level in another, those above grade level in yet another, and so on? The assumption is that each teacher will need to plan only a single reading lesson for the entire class. Teachers need to recognize that one result will often be racial, linguistic, and gender isolation. Another outcome is the classroom at each grade level with the lowest achieving children—25 of 30 children are likely to be boys, and many of them will display behavior problems. English language learners often end up in the same class, despite their need to associate with native English speakers.

When all of these children with important needs are placed in the same classroom, the challenges for the teacher are extreme. The management of behavior in this classroom requires the most able and experienced teacher in the school, but all too often, this class is assigned to the newest teacher. The result can be negative attitudes, low self-esteem, and continuing low achievement. The classroom with the highest achievers will tend to have a preponderance of girls, along with much of the student leadership potential on the grade level. Although this classroom might seem to be an attractive assignment for most teachers, it is also a challenge.

There is really no such thing as a homogeneous group. Even children who have similar levels of achievement at the beginning of the school year will be very different from each other after a few months of instruction, as some will gain more than others. In addition, teaching a reading lesson to a classroom-size group might not be the best way to provide effective instruction to them. If 20 children in a classroom are really reading at the same level and have similar strengths and needs, most experienced teachers would divide them into two groups and teach similar lessons to each smaller group to maximize individual attention.

In many countries, children are promoted from one grade to the next on the basis of their achievement, not their age. The tradition in the United States has been to promote on the basis of age because of research indicating that children do not benefit from being held back (Wheelock & Dorman, 1988). According to the Texas Education Agency (1996), being older than other students in your grade is a better predictor of future dropping out than underachievement is. In some states, attempts have been made to hold children back if they do not reach a standard for their grade level, but most of these efforts are quickly abandoned when the numbers of children retained are much larger than was expected. The result is that children are usually grouped for instruction in reading to better address their different needs.

Grouping is most common in reading and mathematics. The higher the grade level, the greater is the need for grouping children as some fall behind and others forge ahead. In a first-grade classroom, as you have seen, most children are not reading, they are reading some, or they are reading well at a first-grade level. But in a fifth-grade classroom, the children might range from those not reading at all to some reading at a college level. Those who are not reading at all will tend to be children with severe reading disabilities or occasionally immigrant children with no school experience or very limited school experience.

Grouping children within the classroom can also have negative consequences. It does not matter what names the groups have; the children recognize that there are high groups and low groups, and they know which group they are in. This sends an unmistakable message to children in the "low" group. These expectations often become a self-fulfilling prophecy. Children in the "low" group in the first grade are all too often still there in the fifth grade.

Grouping Students Without Tracking

The dilemma is how to meet individual cognitive and affective needs while avoiding the negative effects that can result from grouping by ability. Children need to receive reading instruction at their instructional levels, and so teachers must form groups that permit children to read at levels where they will be successful, interested, and engaged. Some fifth graders will be learning beginning reading concepts in the language-experience approach, and some in the same classroom will be reading and enjoying Shakespeare. It is difficult to put children from these two levels together when they are in guided reading lessons. There are two possible solutions to the dilemma, and they can be used at the same time: non-ability-based groups and dynamic groups.

Guided Reading

GROUPS NOT BASED ON ABILITY AND ACHIEVEMENT   The interest group structure is not based on ability and achievement, but rather a common interest—perhaps a group of children who enjoy fairy tales. They can all read fairy tales, even the same fairy tale in the same lesson, but from books written at different levels or from the same book, but with different levels of teacher support. This allows students who are working at a lower level to work with students reading at higher levels from time to time so that they are able to say, "Sometimes I am in the same reading group as Janie." Interest groups might meet one day a week instead of every day, and they might meet for a month before dissolving so that students can form new and different interest groups. Fountas and Pinnell (2001) add other structures to introduce flexibility, including peer tutoring, cooperative learning pairs, and cross-grade buddies. In literature circles, children who have decided to read the same book, poem, or other text compare and share ideas about what they have read (Daniels, 1994).

DYNAMIC GROUPING   Occasionally, the teacher should recognize that certain students need to work with a reading group other than their own for specific reasons. A bright but troubled and struggling reader might advance to a higher ability group to read a story for three days because the story will be of great interest to him and he has much background knowledge about the subject. An otherwise high-achieving reader who has trouble decoding words with prefixes might join a lower-achieving group that happens to be working on that specific skill for a few days.

The ability grouping in Chantell DeLaney's third-grade classroom is what Fountas and Pinnell (2001) refer to as *dynamic grouping* (see Chapter 12), bringing students together for a period of time when they have abilities and needs in common. The most capable students, reading at fourth- and fifth-grade levels in Ms. DeLaney's classroom, occasionally join the group working at the third-grade level, perhaps to learn or practice a needed word recognition skill or comprehension strategy. Often, however, they are working on individualized reading and on projects of interest, periodically meeting with Ms. DeLaney as a small group or conferencing with her.

Organizing and Managing a Learning Community

The lesson in the chapter-opening vignette seemed relatively simple and straightforward, but, of course, Ms. DeLaney doesn't just come in each morning and begin teaching. She has planned activities for students who are not working directly with her as she teaches small groups, she has arranged the furniture in the classroom, she has carefully selected instructional materials, she has scheduled precious instructional time, and she has made decisions about how to assess the outcomes of her teaching for the day.

Children's Identity and Motivation

In Ms. DeLaney's lesson on "Little Red Riding Hood," the focus was only on the group of children she was teaching. Over the period of a week, an observer in Ms. DeLaney's classroom sees a very complicated structure. She is usually working with one of several groups while the other two groups complete independent work, read trade books from the classroom library, write letters for the classroom postal system, work on projects in which reading and writing activities are integrated across the curriculum, use the classroom computers, and work in learning centers. There is much movement of students between groups, orchestrated by Ms. DeLaney as she assesses needs and asks students to join groups for a single lesson, a week, or even a month for activities to meet those needs.

A very important part of her planning involved the other two groups that were working independently while she was teaching the lesson to this group. The other large group that reads slightly below grade level needed much guidance and supervision. They had an independent assignment from the previous day's lesson to complete, but she also had learning centers that they could work in and a large variety of trade books at many levels for them to read. The group that was reading above the third-grade level required less direct supervision. Many of them were working on independent projects from social studies and science, and they were also deeply engrossed in library books that they were reading independently.

During Ms. DeLaney's guided reading lesson, there were intervals in which the children read silently for a few minutes. Ms. DeLaney took advantage of their focus and walked around the classroom to help children with questions. They knew that she would come around during the lesson and that they should not interrupt the group's work. In addition, she used her walks as a preventive classroom behavior management strategy, settling down children who were noisy or off task. But she always did this with a touch on the shoulder, a gentle tug on a pigtail, or a smile that said, "I caught you—back to work now." By the time the lesson group had finished the chunk they were reading, after just a minute or two, Ms. DeLaney was back with the group and seated, ready to continue with them until they read the next chunk of text.

On alternate Fridays, the children participate in an individualized reading program based on the many books Ms. DeLaney has accumulated for her extensive classroom library. They range from large-format picture books and simple stories to novels and nonfiction materials at upper grade and secondary levels. Self-selected silent sustained reading (SSR) characterizes the Friday program. As a good model for the children, Ms. DeLaney demonstrates how she reads for her own pleasure during part of the reading period, but she also spends much of her time conferencing with individual children about what they have been reading and encouraging them.

Managing Students and the Classroom for Learning

One important set of decisions teachers in grades 3 through 5 must make concerns how to set up the classroom for instruction in reading and other subject areas. Some elements are inflexible, such as the positions of doors, windows, chalkboards, fixed cabinets, computer network connections, and the sink. But other elements indicate much about the philosophy of the program. Think about the difference between two university classrooms: one with chairs set up in straight rows facing the front, where a podium has been placed for the instructor, and another where there are round tables with chairs around them and no podium or front to the classroom.

One possible middle grade classroom arrangement for reading/language arts instruction and also instruction in other areas of the curriculum would include the following:

- A U-shaped or kidney-shaped table for small-group lessons, with the teacher seated with her back to the wall to be able to observe the entire classroom while teaching

SIOP®
Sheltered
Instruction
Observation
Protocol®

Providing Trade Books and Informational Texts at the Independent Reading Level

Self-selected reading is an element of the four blocks approach to reading (Cunningham et al., 2007) that requires differentiated instruction, just as the more obvious teacher-directed aspects of reading programs do. Most self-selected reading activities are carried out by children individually, occasionally in paired reading. How then can teachers differentiate instruction in this part of the program?

One of the most important strategies is to provide text in the form of trade books or other reading matter that is at each child's independent level. For example, if a student has an instructional level at the third-grade level, but an independent level at the second-grade level, the teacher will provide formal and directed instruction at the instructional level, which is appropriate given the scaffolding support that the teacher will provide during the lessons: the introduction of new vocabulary, activating background knowledge, perhaps guiding reading with questions, and finally consolidation activities that allow the child to apply new knowledge. Because of the new Common Core curriculum trend, these texts should include both narrative and expository selections.

But when the child selects a trade book to read for silent sustained reading (SSR) or self-selected reading, whether in the classroom or at home, that scaffolding support is often absent. The appropriate level of book then will usually be one or two grade levels lower for most children. By providing trade books for the classroom reading center at a variety of levels, a skilled teacher ensures that abundant books are available at the independent levels of all children.

But the teacher should also communicate the need for reading material at the independent level to parents. They will often provide books at home that are at the child's grade level, not the independent reading level. Librarians can help parents and children select books at an appropriate level for independent reading, and so can sales staff at specialized children's bookstores. At chain bookstores or on Internet sources, however, parents may need guidance from the teacher about appropriate books. If motivation is high because a child has just developed a new interest, such as collecting insects, then a capable and highly motivated child might struggle and read successfully at the instructional level or even at the frustration level. But these are not the usual circumstances.

Teachers will find valuable information about the levels of thousands of trade books and other books in Fountas and Pinnell's *Leveled Books K–8* (2009) for a fee; the log-in site is at <www.fountasandpinnellleveledbooks.com/Marketing/order.aspx>. Individual publishers also provide information about the levels of their books, as does Amazon.com.

Echevarria, Vogt, and Short (2014) provide scaffolding suggestions to assist English language learners and other at-risk students in reading in the self-selected mode with books at the independent level. One recommendation is for the teacher to conduct a partial read-aloud of the piece of literature with the student or students who will read it. They can then pair up or work in small groups to continue through the material. Teachers can also scaffold by pointing out the text structure of what they are going to read—chronological in a biography or historical piece, for example.

- Movable individual children's desks that can be quickly and quietly rearranged when groups or activities change (two-student desks are only slightly less convenient)
- A library center with numerous trade books at many levels and places to sit, such as cushions on the floor, pillows in an old bathtub (for reading only), or a sofa (check the fire regulations)
- A computer center with at least two or three computers in the classroom that are connected to the Internet
- The author's chair (Hanson & Graves, 1983), a very special chair in which children sit only when sharing their writing with others
- Other learning centers for individual or paired work, such as science, writing, or mathematics, with task cards that require children to read, write, and discuss
- A word wall above the writing center
- A listening center with earphones and a player for audiotapes, videotapes, and/or CD-ROMs
- Easels that can be moved from place to place, even for grades 3 to 5

Most teachers find it necessary to control or limit access to learning centers, which can often disrupt lessons. This can be done by doing the following:

- Limiting the number of students who can work in a center at the same time

- Limiting the amount of time each student can work in each center
- Assigning centers every day, with children rotating each day to a different one
- Occasionally informing children who misbehave when together that they cannot work in a center at the same time until they demonstrate more maturity

All of these controls have negative effects on children's spontaneity and their interests. Most teachers find that they can relax and even eliminate these controls over time, but they are very helpful early in the school year.

Selecting Appropriate Materials

There is a big difference between texts used to teach reading at the primary-grade levels and at the fifth-grade level. It is partly in the quantity. Fifth-grade students will be able to read more text during a reading lesson than primary-grade students will, but the difficulty of the material is also a major factor. It is easy to observe that text in basal readers at the third-grade level has fewer difficult words and less complex sentences than text has at the fifth-grade level. There is a difference between text included in basal readers and that in authentic literature. The biggest difference between authentic literature and basal reader stories or so-called decodable text is the variety of vocabulary that skilled authors use when they select the precise word needed to best express an idea. This increases the difficulty of the text, but also the interest levels of the students (Crawford, 2000).

LEVELED BOOKS After the teacher determines student reading levels using an informal reading inventory, it is then helpful to be able to identify the levels of textbooks and especially of trade books so that they can be matched appropriately to the children. Many thousands of children's trade books have been leveled for the text gradient, a measure of text difficulty now available on a Web site for a fee (Fountas & Pinnell, 2008).

According to Fountas and Pinnell (2001), text difficulty is a function of the following factors:

- Book and print features, such as length, print, layout, illustrations, graphic features, and organizational aids
- Themes and ideas, such as interest, sophistication, and maturity
- Language and literary features, such as literary and figurative language and dialogue
- Vocabulary, such as multisyllabic words and content-related words
- Sentence complexity, including length, embedded clauses, and punctuation
- Content, including topics, organization, and special graphic features
- Text structure, including fiction (narrative literary devices such as flashbacks) and nonfiction (compare and contrast, cause and effect, description, temporal sequence, and problem/solution)

As we saw in Chapter 12, the resulting text gradient ranges from A (kindergarten) through Z (grades 7 and 8). Grade-level ranges for typical children are assigned to each letter, which allows teachers to select books that are in the so-called Goldilocks range—not too difficult, not too easy, but just right. They are also within Vygotsky's zone of proximal development. Fountas and Pinnell provide lists of thousands of leveled books in their many publications (Fountas & Pinnell, 1996, 1999, 2001, 2008, 2009; Pinnell & Fountas, 2001).

USING TECHNOLOGY IN GRADES 3 TO 5 Possible roles for technology in grades 3 to 5 will be examined in two dimensions: reading and writing.

In Reading In the area of Web text reading, as contrasted to print text reading, Sutherland-Smith (2002) reported that students needed to use different reading strategies to

New Literacies

How can technology enrich reading and writing instruction in grades 3 to 5?

Writing and Reading Connections

How can teachers incorporate a simplified approach to word processing into the writing program?

acquire meaning from the two sources. She based this on student comments about the need to work fast on the Internet, in contrast to a more leisurely style of reading from books. She found that Web text reading was less linear, less hierarchical, and less sequential than print text reading. It was more interactive, allowing the reader to add, change, or move text, blurring the relationship between reader and writer. She described several strategies to help students in their Web text reading, all of which support the inquiry-based technology strategies already offered in Chapter 8:

- Encourage "snatch-and-grab" reading, scanning, or reading superficially to find pertinent information and returning to it later if it survived the culling needed when large quantities of information are found
- Help students to focus on finding keywords for searches as an important skill
- Encourage students to refine or delimit their problem or question so they are not overwhelmed by the amount of information they encounter
- Provide "sure-thing" links to students for their initial forays into the Internet
- Help students to differentiate between informative text and impressive visual images that might offer little information

In a related vein, Henry (2006) identifies new reading comprehension needs when reading on the Internet. For example, students need to read search engine results critically before clicking on them to read the actual Web site. Otherwise, they waste valuable time reading something in depth that will not be useful. Students need to recognize the need to evaluate entries quickly when they might turn up over a million somewhat relevant sites for each request. They also need to consider different kinds of results that particular search engines provide and select accordingly. When information is located, students need to consider whether the information is accurate, whether the author is an authority on the topic, possible biases of the author, whether the information is current, and how it compares with information found in other sources. These skills are clearly within the realm of critical thinking.

Baildon and Baildon (2008) recommended a set of resource questions for guiding the selection of a research source. First, the reader should consider the readability of the source, not in the sense of a Fry-type readability score, but rather whether the source is written at a level that is comprehensible to the student. Reading on the Internet is usually an independent activity, without the support systems that teachers provide during formal lessons. Second, the reader should ascertain if the source is trustworthy. Is the author known to be an expert on the subject? By checking the date, they can determine the currency of the source. They might also try to verify the accuracy of the information by locating another source that provides similar information or a similar point of view. Third, students should consider the usefulness of the information. Does it provide the information called for in the purpose of their project or paper? Does it meet their need?

In Writing   A very effective use of technology in teaching writing in grades 3 to 5 is in the area of word processing. Several word processing aids are available for children, including *Printmaster 18.1* from Broderbund. Many teachers find that they can use Microsoft Word with children, teaching only the aspects that are needed for their writing. The appearance of the screen can be simplified by suppressing some of the toolbars and reducing the numbers of functions in those that remain to what is necessary for that grade level.

Involving Family and Community

Adults other than teachers play major roles at home and at school in supporting literacy instruction, even in the middle grades.

At Home

Authentic environmental print is a valuable resource that teachers can exploit in the home. Purcell-Gates, L'Allier, and Smith (1995) provide valuable print-embedded family literacy activities that are especially useful for children in grades 3 to 5 because they are authentic. Among them are the following:

- Daily living routines, such as shopping lists, reading recipes, and cooking together
- Entertainment, such as reading novels, storybooks, or television program descriptions
- School-related activity, such as homework or school assignments
- Interpersonal communication, such as notes on the refrigerator, e-mail
- Religion, including reading stories from the Bible, the Torah, the Koran, and other religious books treasured by the family
- Participating in information networks, such as sharing scores of sporting events, news of interest, and reactions to new films
- Work-related tasks, such as reading instructions, pay-stub information, and catalogs

Teachers often give students a consolidation or application activity to complete at home after their daily reading lesson. This activity may involve reading aloud to parents, siblings, or others who live in the home. When students are asked to read aloud, they should read something they have already read and practiced in the classroom. If they are to read something new, it should ordinarily be at their independent level, not at the instructional level (see the Differentiated Instruction box earlier in this chapter). When children struggle with reading aloud (which is potentially a very positive experience at school and one the teacher wants the child to have), it can turn into a negative experience with a well-meaning parent who tries to help by criticizing or by teaching a phonics lesson.

Similarly, the teacher might send the parents a note asking them to listen to the child read for 10 minutes from an assigned book. The parent wants to do more and asks the child to read for 30 minutes from a more difficult book. Again, the well-meaning parent is trying to help the child, but fails to understand the importance of following the teacher's directions carefully.

Family Literacy

How can teachers take advantage of home literacy opportunities to enhance reading instruction in the classroom?

Teach It! 2

Dialogic Reading

Children enjoy reading in a comfortable, secure, and accepting place.

At School

The presence of other adults in the classroom can be an important asset. Teacher assistants or instructional aides are paid paraprofessionals who may work all day or part of a day to support the teacher. They might range from a minimally educated community resident to a university student who is ready for student teaching. Paraprofessionals are particularly important in working with English language learners.

Another source of adult support in the classroom is the parent volunteer, who might also be a grandparent or other extended family member or caregiver. Tinajero and Nagel (1975) suggest that you need only invite participation. They recommend that you ensure in advance that family members have the needed skills to accomplish assigned tasks and that the activities you request are culturally appropriate. You might find it helpful to demonstrate for adult volunteers so their roles are clear. Adult volunteers can make many important contributions, including sharing information in oral discussions; tutoring; participating in journal activities by responding to children's entries; reading aloud to students, including in their mother tongue other than English, where appropriate; helping with homework assignments in after-school study; storytelling; and sharing life events, personal oral histories, and job experiences.

Teach It! 1

Reading Aloud

For Review

The reading program for most children changes as they proceed through the grades, with more emphasis on reading comprehension, silent reading, reading in the content areas of the curriculum, and writing in grades 3 through 5. There is still attention to phonics and other aspects of word recognition, but it occupies less time than it does in the primary grades. Developing fluency and automaticity may still receive some attention in the third grade.

The organizational structures for teaching reading are based on the four blocks framework that includes guided reading, working with words, self-selected reading, and writing. Teachers can use three typical stages of reading lessons for planning that reflects this framework: anticipation activities to build interest and connect students to background knowledge, guided reading activities to build knowledge through scaffolding students' reading and comprehension of text, and consolidation reading activities in which students apply new knowledge and have opportunities for writing and self-selected reading. These stages are supplemented with mini-lessons focused on word study or another specific skill that usually has emerged from the text to be read in the lesson.

Long-term planning can be systematized with Common Core Curriculum State Standards maps, which are thematic units that incorporate both narrative and expository text along with poetry, digital sources, music, art, writing, and other media. Access to all text for all students is ensured by the use of leveled texts and support strategies that scaffold comprehension for all. This new process is designed to prepare children for higher education and careers of the twenty-first century.

There is more variation in the reading levels of students in the middle grades than in the primary grades, and the need for grouping for instruction arises. Most useful is dynamic grouping that is flexible and includes multiple structures for instruction, including small ability groups, interest groups, buddy reading and cooperative learning pairs, peer tutoring, occasional whole-class instruction, and the frequent formation of temporary focused groups to address common weaknesses of students from all ability levels.

Most English language learners who have learned to read in their mother tongue are by now able to understand and speak English at an intermediate level. They are also often ready to begin a transition to English language reading in the third grade. Many scaffolding and support activities are particularly important for these students as they begin reading in their new second language, English.

You have now seen that students' abilities to understand text vary widely and students are grouped accordingly for some important comprehension instruction. Teachers must then be able to find textbooks, literature, and trade books that reflect those levels. Many thousands of books have been leveled on a gradient of difficulty, and teachers can quite accurately select books for students for whom they have assessment data. There is a growing role for the effective use of technology in the classroom in the middle grades. Children can do extensive reading on the Internet, but they must be prepared to deal with the immense amounts of information returned in the typical search. The introduction of new reading skills, such as identifying descriptors and criteria, scanning titles of returned references, and delimiting problems or assignments done on the Internet will assist in their effectiveness.

For Your Journal

1. Using the lesson plan and the strategies illustrated in the chapter and the strategies you would like to incorporate from throughout this book, plan a similar lesson for the "Three Little Pigs," another story that most children know. Working with a partner should enrich your thinking as well as speed up completion of the task.

2. Identify a theme you could introduce to a class, such as "change." Visit the children's section of your local bookstore or public library, or look on a search engine for books, such as the one at amazon.com. Try to find three trade books at about the same grade level that fit into the theme of your unit. Develop activities and assessment tools for integrating these books into the unit.

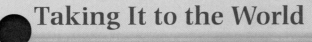

Taking It to the World

1. Now that you have moved into grades 3 to 5, you have found that most children have acquired a concept of print; they are able to decode many words they encounter, especially when they are contextualized in connected text; they are beginning to read silently; they are understanding what they read; and they are beginning to express themselves in writing. What changes from a second-grade reading program do you now expect to find in the use of literature, in word recognition instruction, in reading in the content areas, and in writing as children enter the third grade?

2. Write down one or two thoughts with respect to each of these elements of literacy, and compare notes with another student. Try to agree on a single list of how the focus on these elements might be different from working with K–2 students.

New Literacies Connections

1. Using a search engine, such as Google <www.google.com>, complete an Internet search for reviews on *Kid Pix*. What do the reviews say about this product for children? How could it be used in grades 3 to 5?

2. Visit Education World's "The Reading Machine Archive: Reading Games" online at <www.educationworld.com/a_tech/archives/readingmachine.shtml>. Identify at least three technology activities recommended by Education World's tech experts as appropriate for students in grades 3 to 5. What do the experts say about these products?

MyEducationLab™

Go to Topics 3, 4, and 12 (Fluency, Vocabulary, and Media/Digital Literacy) in the MyEducationLab <www.myeducationlab.com> for your course, where you can:

- Find learning outcomes for Fluency, Vocabulary, and Media/Digital Literacy along with the national standards that connect to these outcomes.

- Complete Assignments and Activities that can help you more deeply understand the chapter content.

- Apply and practice your understanding of the core teaching skills identified in the chapter with the Building Teaching Skills and Dispositions learning units.

- Check your comprehension on the content covered in the chapter by going to the Study Plan in the

Book Resources for your text. Here you will be able to take a chapter quiz, receive feedback on your answers, and then access Review, Practice, and Enrichment activities to enhance your understanding of chapter content.

- Visit A+RISE. A+RISE® Standards2Strategy™ is an innovative and interactive online resource that offers new teachers in grades K-12 just in time, research-based instructional strategies that meet the linguistic needs of ELLs as they learn content, differentiate instruction for all grades and abilities, and are aligned to Common Core Elementary Language Arts standards English language proficiency standards in WIDA, Texas, California, and Florida.

Putting Effective Literacy Instruction into Practice: Grades 6 to 8

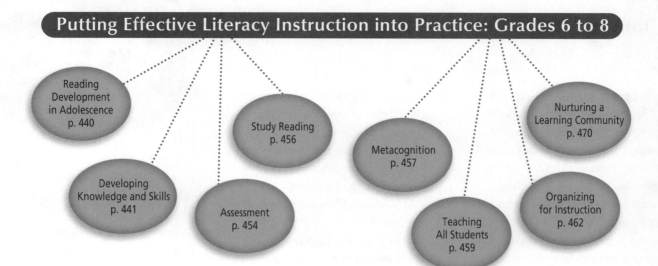

Putting Effective Literacy Instruction into Practice: Grades 6 to 8

- Reading Development in Adolescence p. 440
- Developing Knowledge and Skills p. 441
- Study Reading p. 456
- Assessment p. 454
- Metacognition p. 457
- Teaching All Students p. 459
- Nurturing a Learning Community p. 470
- Organizing for Instruction p. 462

Anticipation Guide

The following statements will help you begin thinking about the topics of this chapter. Answer *true* or *false* in response to each statement. As you read and learn more about the topics in these statements, double-check your answers. See what interests you and prompts your curiosity toward more understanding.

_____ **1.** Schools can safely stop teaching reading by the time students reach the middle grades. Virtually all students will have learned to read adequately by then.

_____ **2.** Middle grade students should be assured daily opportunities to read because reading ability grows with practice.

_____ **3.** Having students post new words they have learned on a vocabulary bulletin board is effective because it helps for students to take ownership of their learning.

_____ **4.** "Possible Sentences" is a method of fitting punishments to crimes, and "Personal Clues" is a means of locating criminals.

_____ **5.** Reading aloud to students and encouraging them to listen to audiotapes and CDs is important because it provides an internal model of fluent reading.

_____ **6.** Integrated instructional units help students build connections between literature and content learning in social studies and science.

_____ **7.** An important form of assessment is for the teacher to learn to look and listen carefully as students read.

_____ **8.** Part of a teacher's responsibility is to help students organize their time to afford more time for reading and studying.

_____ **9.** It is pointless to ask students to reflect on their strategies when they read because fluent readers are simply unaware of what they are doing.

_____ **10.** Teachers should be sure to give English language learners extra mini-lessons on reading materials before that material is discussed in class.

A Classroom Story

Integrated Reading Instruction in a Sixth-Grade Classroom

As part of an integrated unit on the Middle Ages, Rasheed Graham's sixth-grade students had the choice of reading one of Karen Cushman's books: *The Midwife's Apprentice* (2012) *or Catherine, Called Birdy* (2005). Mr. Graham was concerned that some of the students might encounter difficulty with the setting and he wanted to revisit a scene to emphasize its meaning and check for their understanding early on in the reading of one of the books. During Friday story share, Mr. Graham has students sit in a circle on the floor while he reads from what he considers a pivotal chapter in *The Midwife's Apprentice*—where the main character is shopping at a medieval market. The students follow along with the text as he reads aloud. Mr. Graham's goal is to make sure the students reflect on the significance of this section. While reading aloud, he stops to comment and ask the students for their thoughts on the content, and then he asks them to make predictions: "I thought you'd like to revisit this chapter because it seems like such a big moment for the main character. Let's see how we all interpreted this section. What do you think about it? Let me read this part again while

you follow along. The setup, as you recall, is that Beetle, the main character, has been directed by the midwife to buy some items at the market. Beetle has never been there before, and she is overwhelmed by all the new sights, smells, and sounds."

Mr. Graham reads from Chapter 5, then stops after reading, "She sniffed all the spices for free before buying nutmeg and pepper. The hangman was doing a brisk trade in murderer's wash water." To help the students develop the skill of reading for understanding, Mr. Graham has the students think critically about a sentence that might otherwise be overlooked because of lack of understanding. He asks, "What do you think that means? It's not a beheading, but a hanging, so what do you think is going on?"

Jason speaks up, "'Murderer's wash water'? Isn't that just dirty bathing water? Why would anyone want that?"

"Does anyone have any ideas?"

"I guess it's like collecting things, you know, like stamps or rabbits' feet," offers Tran.

Next, Mr. Graham reads a section in which the main character sees an ivory comb at a merchant's table. She loves the comb

but has no money to buy it. Mr. Graham asks, "What do you think will happen? Will she use the money given her by the midwife to buy the comb or will something else transpire?"

Kayleigh states, "I hope she doesn't do that. If she does, the midwife will fire her, and she'll be worse off than she was before."

"I think she gonna steal it," calls out Deanna.

Mr. Graham continues to prod the students' thinking: "What makes you think that she would do that? Is there anything in her character that makes her out to be either a thief or irresponsible? Can you show that to me in the text?"

Here, Mr. Graham has asked students to match their predictions with the character's actual behavior so that they learn that predictions need to be linked to previous knowledge of events and actions. Then he continues reading and stops to help students focus on the key to this section: the development of the main character.

Reading Development in Adolescence

Reading instruction is needed just as much in the middle grades as it is in first grade. Each year the range of materials and purposes for which students read expands. By the middle grades, reading is a part of every subject, but the types of materials and their formats vary considerably. So, too, the purposes and expectations for how students use the materials in learning and sharing their ideas are varied. Students need to read widely, learn a variety of strategies to help them navigate different types of texts, and develop a critical stance to what they read. The more they read, the more they build their knowledge of the world and expand their vocabularies. Recent studies of the reading done by middle and secondary students highlights the importance of teachers helping students expand the sophistication of their choices of fiction and develop interests in informational genres (Renaissance Learning, 2012). According to the report, of the top 40 books chosen by sixth-, seventh-, and eighth-grade students, all were fiction, and for most of these, the average readability was at the 5.2 grade level using the new CCSS readability guidelines. It is hard for students to mature as readers if they don't read more challenging materials. Teachers have an important responsibility in helping students to expand their reading range and gain the skills that make comprehending more challenging texts possible.

This fact has been highlighted recently with the adoption of the CCSS (Common Core State Standards). A major argument for the standards was the fact that for students to be successful beyond high school in college and in work settings, they need higher levels of reading skills than most high schools require. An analysis of texts and workforce materials identified a significant gap between high school and post-high school materials (see Appendix A, CCSS). Over the last 30 years the difficulty of books and materials for adolescents has declined, while those at the adult level have not. The CCSS developers argue that public education needs to accelerate the levels of materials students read to prepare them for adult reading.

Compounding this problem is the reality that even with the current expectations of reading development, 69 percent of eighth graders are not able to read grade-level materials proficiently when tested on the National Assessment of Educational Progress (NAEP, 2009), the only current measure that provides an assessment of reading development across all of the states. Despite many efforts to improve reading achievement, the data show little change over the 40 plus years the assessment has been used. As a result of this reality and the importance of literacy for school success, several recent reports have championed the need for more attention to adolescent literacy development and the expansion of instruction across the content areas.

Providing middle level students with expert reading instruction is essential also because reading is part of learning across the curriculum, and specific reading skills and strategies are needed in many different subject areas. Middle level readers have increasing demands placed on them to become flexible and competent in reading a much broader range of materials than was required in earlier grades.

Both the new CCSS and existing state standards include a range of areas of reading expected during the middle school years. The CCSS are clear about reading being important for learning by including two sets of standards, one for literary and one for informational reading. Even the title of the standards makes the point, "CCSS in English Language Arts & Literacy in History/Social Studies, Science, and Technical Subjects." Middle grade teachers need to work together across discipline boundaries to ensure that students continue to develop their skills as readers; the goal won't be achieved by the language arts or reading teacher assuming the full responsibility for reading development.

Adding to the complexity of reading instruction in the middle grades is the changing structure of this level of schooling. Many schools are organized into content departments, so students move from teacher to teacher, which creates challenges to educators' efforts to provide flexibility in time and integration of reading and writing with content-area learning. When students have multiple teachers and the curriculum becomes very content intense, aspects of good reading instruction often are overlooked. This chapter provides a framework for thinking about what needs to be taught and examines how different classrooms are organized so students can have the opportunities to learn that they deserve.

CCSS

• CCSS Overview

Developing Knowledge and Skills

Given the wide range of reading development needed during the middle years, classroom instruction must be carefully planned so that all aspects of reading can be included. As a teacher, you will want to ensure that you provide students with the experiences and guidance they need to become mature readers. The sections that follow present an overview of nine components to include in your reading program.

Regular Opportunities to Read a Variety of Genres

Reading is not a single activity, but one that is complex and that changes according to the situation, purpose, and type of text. For students to develop as flexible readers, they should be given a variety of purposeful reading opportunities each day. Whenever possible, teachers should provide more than one text on the same topic so students can develop a deeper understanding of how genre, structure, and point of view vary. In the middle grades, students can be introduced to a broader range of fiction genre including utopian/dystopian novels, historical novels, and science fiction as well as classic short stories. The CCSS also highlight some historical writings that are part of our American heritage in the expectations for middle grades reading materials. As one thinks of how to structure teaching of particular pieces, it is good to think more broadly—to combine pieces of fiction with informational texts and visual or graphic displays whenever possible. As they read varied texts that explore similar ideas and become more aware of the numerous options writers have in how they develop and express their ideas, students will become more critical as readers. It is also important to guide students' attention to the features of particular types of texts and text structures; informational texts, in particular, deserve analysis because these are not as familiar to many students. Teachers can model and guide students in adapting their reading strategies to their purposes and materials. Skimming headings and skipping from one chapter or section to another can be an appropriate strategy to use when reading for specific information. Reading and rereading two or three times is an important strategy when trying to understand and appreciate a poem or to analyze an author's subtleties. Some of the various purposes that students have for reading different texts include the following:

- Reading for personal enjoyment and stimulation of imagination
- Developing an understanding of how people deal with conflict and growing up
- Wanting to read what one's friends and teachers are reading
- Learning new content by using a variety of resource materials, news magazines, newspapers, and electronic texts
- Appreciating and enjoying poetry, humorous word plays, and cartoons
- Following directions in procedural texts that enable one to perform tasks
- Grappling with texts for specific problem-solving and learning activities
- Reflecting on values and religious beliefs

One of the most important kinds of reading is self-selected, independent reading. It is clear that students who read widely have a great advantage over students who do not read much or who never engage in self-selected reading. Cunningham and Stanovich's (1998) article, "What Reading Does for the Mind," makes a strong case for wide reading. The article summarizes data from various studies indicating that relying on oral input to learn is just not adequate. An analysis of the vocabulary load of various books and television programs demonstrates that even preschool children's books have a more sophisticated range of vocabulary than adult television shows. Students will never encounter the words and concepts they need to succeed in the professional world if they do not read. When middle level students have been shown this data, many have become convinced of the importance of their continued independent reading. They need to understand, as we do, that it is through engagement in a great deal of reading in varied types of text materials that we encounter the concepts and forms of written discourse needed for life. Teachers have an important role in helping students select more challenging texts as part of their reading experience. They must keep reading!

Daily Reading at the Appropriate Instructional Level

Finding a balance between appropriately challenging reading materials and those that students can handle independently is part of each teacher's task. Students will improve in their reading when they have instructional-level materials that both challenge and reward them. If reading materials are too difficult, students cannot apply their skills to extend their proficiency. If materials are too easy, they do not need to apply their skills; thus, finding the instructional middle is essential. This is the zone in which students can develop as readers. Even so, situations in which students must deal with materials that are too easy or too hard will still occur. Students need some easy materials so that they can gain pleasure from reading and move comfortably through texts.

In whole-class instruction, many students also will be faced with materials that are above their instructional level. In spite of these situations, support mechanisms are available and should be used to assist students. Some of these support mechanisms include the following:

- Pre-reading activation of knowledge and vocabulary under teacher or adult guidance, which might involve viewing videos to set the context and build knowledge
- Audiotapes/CDs of texts or sections of the texts
- Use of buddy or partner reading to give students low-stress settings to practice reading
- Assistance from older or adult readers who can serve as coaches
- Adapted, easier texts on the same topic

Integrating Reading and Writing

Both reading and writing develop better when they are taught as companion tools for learning about and expressing ideas. Integrating units of content instruction with language arts skill development provides a rich context in which to help students learn. With more extensive units, teachers have time to develop students' background knowledge and to help them formulate questions and expand their interests. Thus, the instruction can be personal and focused. Reading more deeply on a particular topic helps students to gain control of the ideas and learn the vocabulary and concepts more fully than a quick covering of curriculum often provides. As a student's knowledge of a topic increases, the student becomes more able to write about it with a sense of confidence and perspective. Examples of situations that encourage integration of curriculum and reading and writing are included in this chapter, both in the opening vignette and later as we explore organizational options for teachers. Additional options include the following:

- Science fairs, history fairs, family history projects, and other events put on by a class, school, or larger organization that encourage projects for which students, working as individuals, pairs, or small groups, choose topics, conduct research, and create exhibits. All language arts are integrated when students engage in these types of inquiry and sharing.
- Addressing broad questions, as in the Great Books Program (Plecha, 1992) and the Paidea program (Adler, 1982), with groups coming together after reading to discuss key issues and topics raised. After rich discussions, students can write their own points of view on one of the questions raised. They might begin by using a graphic organizer to help them compare and contrast ideas raised or to identify a theme statement and then list examples and details that support their perspective.
- Inquiry projects in which students frame their own areas of inquiry around current problems and questions in their world and then go about answering the questions they raised. Sharing the results of their inquiries becomes a community event, so students need to present their findings in visual, written, and oral formats (Pearson, Cervetti, & Tilson, 2008).
- Research projects that are connected to larger units of study. The PARCC assessment consortium has provided an instructional model that suggests teachers should develop four large units each year and that students should do an individual research project connected with each unit. By engaging in research on a regular basis, students can become proficient in this important type of reading and in communicating their results.

CCSS

- Writing 10: Range of Writing

Instructional Conversations

Developing Strategic Reading

Various types of texts and tasks can provide models for teaching specific strategic behaviors. To help students develop these strategies, you need to incorporate them in your planning for each part of the text lesson: before, during, and after the instruction as you help students *Anticipate, Build knowledge,* and *Consolidate* (ABC) what they learn. You need to explain and model for students how to use the strategies and the benefits that come from them. Then students can apply the specific strategies or make modifications that fit their own styles and preferences within the general ABC framework as they learn.

ANTICIPATING Students need to learn some simple strategies to use before reading that will assist their learning. First, they need to learn the importance of establishing purposes for reading. Remind students repeatedly that they can read texts in different ways and that the manner in which they read a text should grow out of their purpose for reading. Review several purposes for reading:

- Skimming a text or scanning some kind of reading material to see what it contains
- Reading for enjoyment
- Reading to learn how to do something
- Reading to remember facts and ideas
- Reading to understand an author's argument and reasoning

Second, show students how to survey or preview the materials to determine both the external and internal features of the text. Explain to students that visual clues and signal words are features provided as aids to make comprehension easier. External features include visual clues such as chapter and section headings, changes in typeface and font size, and illustrations and charts. Internal features include signal words that point to the text's structure. "Once, before anyone can remember," for example, signals the beginning of a fictional narrative. "Characteristics of ____" indicates a descriptive frame; words like *compare, similar, in contrast,* and *unlike* are associated with compare/contrast organization. Words and phrases such as *consequently, therefore, because of,* and *as a result of* indicate the use of a cause-and-effect pattern. Headings and subheadings also help readers identify the text structure. The more students attend to these signals from authors, the more they can comprehend the intended messages of the texts they read and have the ability to summarize important information.

Finally, students need to learn how to activate what they already know about the topic. Remind them that they will better understand what they read if they can connect it to what they already know both about the topic and about the way in which it is presented. Some ways to activate prior knowledge are the following:

Paired Brainstorming

- Brainstorming (Students can individually, in pairs, or in groups make lists of what they already know and then group these items into categories.)
- Surveying visuals (pictures, maps, diagrams, cartoons, video clips) associated with the topic to stimulate memory and help develop images that include setting and characteristics
- Writing out a list of questions they want answered
- Predicting what they expect will be in the text and writing a "possible" table of contents

BUILDING KNOWLEDGE While reading, students add to what they know and deepen understanding as they construct meaning from the text ideas by doing the following:

- Making and confirming predictions
- Identifying main ideas and supporting information
- Summarizing and drawing inferences

- Generating questions
- Visualizing
- Making connections
- Self-monitoring their progress
- Reflecting on an author's purposes and voice
- Checking accuracy of sources
- Comparing various texts on the same theme or topic

As students read increasingly challenging texts, they need to keep notes of the important ideas and questions they have. The easiest way to do this is to mark on the text itself. However, that is often not possible. Students can learn to save the ideas and images encountered in reading by taking notes and creating outlines in journals, writing on sticky notes, and creating graphic organizers. Some students like to create mind maps of the evolution of ideas, using drawings and illustrations to highlight ideas. Writing and drawing require active thinking and processing and help students encode information in long-term memory as well as to create memory aids to help retrieve information later.

CONSOLIDATING NEW UNDERSTANDING   After students complete a text, they can review the whole and create a summary for themselves, generalize from the ideas, consider the text in relation to its purposes and content, make connections to other texts and their own experiences, participate in group sharing or writing experiences, identify themes and create interpretations of literary pieces (essential to the enjoyment and appreciation of literature), and reconstruct the major ideas of informational texts. This is also when students can think critically about the ways the authors have developed their themes and messages, compare and contrast sources, and evaluate the evidence supporting important arguments and conclusions.

Through the Lens of the CCSS

Developing students' active engagement in their reading makes possible the kind of close, analytic reading described by and assessed in the CCSS. The behaviors highlighted in the standards include reading closely to determine what the author says explicitly, determining the central ideas or themes, analyzing how ideas and events develop and interact, and examining the structure of texts and how point of view and purpose shape content and style.

This kind of careful reading and attention to the fine points of authors' style mean that teachers need to spend some time modeling for students and engaging them in thinking through short, dense texts. The standards for integration of knowledge and ideas ask students to take their close reading skills to the next level and compare and contrast texts, analyzing how authors address similar topics and support their ideas. The standards are demanding of students and focus on a more intense style of reading than most middle grade students are accustomed to. Students are most likely to rise to these expectations if they are given engaging and interesting texts with which to develop their skills. The selection of materials and foci for the units of study are important in helping move students to deeper, more thoughtful reading.

Engaging in Inquiry

As part of the CCSS, students are also expected to learn how to engage in inquiry projects and research. As they use their language skills in exploring new ideas, they have a real opportunity to make use of a wide variety of resources. Students develop their own thinking in these real and important

By the middle grades, instruction focuses on content area reading and helping students to develop a structured approach that will help them with formal school work.

CCSS Standards for ELA 6–12 Key Ideas and Details, Craft and Structure and Integration of Knowledge and Ideas

Key Ideas and Details

1. Read closely to determine what the text says explicitly and to make logical inferences from it; cite specific textual evidence when writing or speaking to support conclusions drawn from the text.
2. Determine central ideas or themes of a text and analyze their development; summarize the key supporting details and ideas.
3. Analyze how and why individuals, events, and ideas develop and interact over the course of a text.

Craft and Structure

4. Interpret words and phrases as they are used in a text, including determining technical, connotative, and figurative meanings, and analyze how specific word choices shape meaning or tone.
5. Analyze the structure of texts, including how specific sentences, paragraphs, and larger portions of the text (e.g., a section, chapter, scene, or stanza) relate to each other and the whole.
6. Assess how point of view or purpose shapes the content and style of a text.

Integration of Knowledge and Ideas

7. Integrate and evaluate content presented in diverse formats and media, including visually and quantitatively, as well as in words.
8. Delineate and evaluate the argument and specific claims in a text, including the validity of the reasoning as well as the relevance and sufficiency of the evidence.
9. Analyze how two or more texts address similar themes or topics in order to build knowledge or to compare the approaches the authors take.

pursuits. These applications of research and thinking skills and abilities are not only made in language arts classes but across the curriculum. Students need to develop their abilities to do the following:

- Identify good issues to research
- Ask good questions
- Seek appropriate sources of materials and evaluate their quality
- Synthesize ideas from multiple sources of information
- Use electronic media as a resource in learning—in seeking information, organizing it, and presenting ideas to others
- Create written, visual, or oral presentations to share findings

The Writing Workshop

At some point in the middle grades, schools often develop the more formal aspects of writing research papers and reports. This is where the teacher can provide a great deal of structure and guidance, because it may be the first time such formal work has been required in which students need to show footnotes or references and develop a bibliography. Establish explicit guides for students and clear timetables for the work. You might have the students track their research and turn in weekly journal entries indicating what has been done during the time allocated so that you and the student ensure that things move forward at an appropriate pace. When there are questions or issues, conduct conferences with the students on their progress. This process of developing students' research skills is an example of where teachers can carefully scaffold the initial two components of good instruction: demonstration and immersion and attention to detail. Because the research takes some time to complete, you are preparing students for work they will be expected to do more independently in high school. Middle schools can help students to become more familiar with the research and writing process by giving added research opportunities with guided practice. The middle grades are where the CCSS also position the development of many of these skills.

Common Core Writing Standard 7, Grades 6–8
Research to Build and Present Knowledge
Sixth grade: 7. Conduct short research projects to answer a question, drawing on several sources and refocusing the inquiry when appropriate.
Seventh grade: 7. Conduct short research projects to answer a question, drawing on several sources and generating additional related, focused questions for further research and investigation.
Eighth grade: 7. Conduct short research projects to answer a question (including a self-generated question), drawing on several sources and generating additional related, focused questions that allow for multiple avenues for exploration.

Strategies for Building Vocabulary

In the middle grades, students regularly encounter words in texts that they never hear in oral communication. Therefore, they must learn to attend to these new terms and have strategies to remember them. Vocabulary plays a crucial role in content learning because terms convey key concepts, and even familiar words often take on different and specific meanings. For example, consider the word *angle*. It means one thing in mathematics; in social studies, it has another meaning, as in "What was the government's angle on the incident?"; and in general use, it can be either a verb or a noun (e.g., "the stream angled through the woods" or "he loved angling in the stream").

There are many ways in which teachers help students develop their language facility. A key to students' continuing vocabulary development in the middle grades is increasing their understanding of the ways in which words are formed and also how words enter the English language. When students become sensitive to identifying new words that they perceive as important, the chances of their being interested in words and retaining the ones they select are higher (Blachowicz & Fisher, 2009). Encouraging students to look for words outside of the classroom also is an important component in their developing sensitivity to words. Beck and McKeown (1983) found that the most significant component of their rich vocabulary instruction program was the word wall. Almost incidentally at first, one of the teachers made bulletin board space and encouraged students to post examples of the new words they were learning in class. This factor alone significantly improved the students' learning. Making vocabulary learning interesting and giving students ownership are two key ingredients of successful activities. As you plan your approach to vocabulary development, keep in mind several important components. Just playing games with words, for instance, is not enough. Nor is doing spelling and vocabulary worksheets. Table 14.1 identifies six basic elements of a good vocabulary program.

TEACHER MODELING OF INTEREST IN LANGUAGE By keeping a small set of books about language growth and development on your desk and reading about words periodically, you help to build students' inquisitiveness about language. Books by Richard Lederer and Bill Bryson are great sources for read-aloud pieces on language. The *Readers Digest*'s regular vocabulary quiz is another easy resource that students (and teachers) enjoy

Table 14.1   Basic Elements of a Good Vocabulary Program
• The teacher models interest in language.
• Students engage in enjoyable word play.
• Students become attentive to new words and self-select words to learn.
• Students learn about the history and growth of English including the nature of words—affixes, combining forms, base words, and derivatives.
• Students develop basic strategies for learning and retaining new content-specific words.
• Students are involved in a great deal of reading that extends their knowledge.

Table 14.2   Valuable Language Resources

Bryson, B. *The Mother Tongue: English and How It Got That Way*. New York: Avon Books, 1990.

Bryson, B. *Made in America: An Informal History of the English Language in the United States*. New York: Avon, 1994.

Lederer, R. *Crazy English: The Ultimate Joy Ride Through Our Language*. New York: Simon & Schuster, 1998.

Lederer, R. *The Miracle of Language*. New York: Pocket Books, 1999.

McNeil, R., & Cran, W. *Do You Speak American?* New York: Harvest Books, 2005.

Rheingold, H. *They Have a Word for It: A Lighthearted Lexicon of Untranslatable Words and Phrases*. Louisville, KY: Saraband Books, 2000.

Winchester, S. *The Professor and the Madman: A Tale of Murder, Insanity and the Making of the Oxford English Dictionary*. New York: Harper Collins, 2005.

taking and then exploring the definitions and uses of the terms. Jokes, too, often involve play with words and can be great starters for talk about language. Table 14.2 identifies some excellent books to keep as resources.

STUDENT ENGAGEMENT IN ENJOYABLE WORD PLAY   Middle level students love to play with words and language. Music, clean rap word games, and jokes are wonderful ways they explore language. Even joke books should be considered for the classroom library. Comics are another favorite source of a very expansive vocabulary. The teacher can have great fun introducing strange and unusual forms of words and enjoying with students sesquipedalian words, portmanteau words, palindromes, and other strange word forms. Two great resources are *Superdupers: Really Funny Real Words* (Terban, 1989) and *A Cache of Jewels and Other Collective Nouns* (Heller, 1991). The book on Americanisms written for English language learners, *English the American Way* (Murtha & O'Connor, 2011) also provides a fun way for classes to explore how culture influences our language.

SELF-SELECTION   Students do better in learning language when they have some control over and choice about what they learn. Studies of students' ability to self-select words they want and need to learn have shown that students are quite good at determining key terms when they are given practice and opportunities to discuss their selections with others (Blachowicz & Fisher, 2009). By first modeling how to notice unfamiliar words, the teacher helps students to realize that this is part of what good readers do regularly. The teacher should then provide opportunities for students to build vocabulary by recording words they find interesting and new, trying to determine meaning from context and word parts, confirming hunches with dictionary or glossary checks, and then sharing their choices with others.

Teach It! 62

Word Origins and Definitions

UNDERSTANDING OF THE HISTORICAL DEVELOPMENT OF ENGLISH   The way our language has grown and changed is fascinating. William and Mary Morris's (1962) *Dictionary of Word and Phrase Origins* still is a great source of information about our language, as is Bartlett's (2003) *Dictionary of Americanisms*. Having small sets of paperback books on language history available in the classroom gives students the opportunity to read and discuss the English language together. The talk about words and language also reinforces the use of new words and words used in new ways.

Students in the middle grades need to have some structured study of words and language, too. At this stage, they should be learning how affixes work, how to use Greek and Latin combining forms, and how to connect derivations with base words. Content-area learning involves a great many specialized terms, so knowing how to look for specialized meanings of common words is also valuable. Table 14.3 provides a list of affixes that students should learn. Two useful books are *Techniques of Teaching Vocabulary* (1971) by O'Rourke and Bamman and the more recent *Vocabulary Their Way* by Bear and colleagues (2009).

Figurative language is also important to highlight and teach, especially for English language learners in need of help in understanding the many expressions of English.

Table 14.3 Affixes

PREFIXES	MEANING	EXAMPLE
Un	not	*un*happy
In	not	*in*correct
Re	again	*re*pair, *re*move
Dis	not or away	*dis*agree, *dis*miss
Pre	before	*pre*school, *pre*pare
Ex	out	*ex*hale, *ex*port
Anti	against	*anti*freeze, *anti*war
Sub	under, below	*sub*way, *sub*marine
Super	over, more than	*super*sonic, *super*man
Com	together, with	*com*plete, *com*munity
Con		*con*nect
Col		*col*lection
Co		*co*operate
Cor		*cor*respond
Mid	in the middle	*mid*day, *mid*summer
Mis	wrong	*mis*behave, *mis*understand

NUMBER PREFIXES	MEANING	EXAMPLE
Mono	one	*mono*tone
Uni	one	*uni*corn
Bi	two	*bi*cycle
Di	two	*di*alogue
Tri	three	*tri*cycle
Deca	ten	*deca*de
Centi	hundredth	*centi*pede
Cent	hundredth	*cent*ury

SUFFIXES	MEANING	EXAMPLE
s-es	plural	clock*s*
s-ing-ed	verb, time	sing, sin
er, est	comparison	late, lat*er*, lat*est*
ly	how done	quick, quick*ly*
ful	full of	peace*ful*
ous	full of	fam*ous*
less	without	use*less*, sleep*less*
ist, ian	one skilled in	scient*ist*, physic*ian*
ness	state of being, having	sad*ness*, sick*ness*
ify, fy	to become, make	magn*ify*, de*ify*
en	make, cause, made of	soft*en*, wool*en*
able	can, able to, deserving	cap*able*, lov*able*
ible		poss*ible*, vis*ible*
tion	action, process	comple*tion*
ion		rebell*ion*
ish	have, quality of	fool*ish*, child*ish*
ment	state of, action	fulfill*ment*
ry, ery, ary	product or action of, place where	bak*ery*, pott*ery*
ize	make, made into	dramat*ize*
ism	practice of, act of	hero*ism*, vandal*ism*, patriot*ism*

Sources: From *Vocabulary Building: A Process Approach* © Zaner-Bloser, Inc. Used with permission from Zaner-Bloser, Inc. All rights reserved.

The elementary *Amelia Bedelia* books (Parish, 1992) and *The King Who Rained* (Gwynne, 1989) offer good strategies for introducing figurative language and helping students become aware of the challenge of our language for English language learners.

<u>**CCSS**</u>

Anchor Standards for Language 6–12, Vocabulary Acquisition and Use (4–6)

Vocabulary Acquisition and Use

4. Determine or clarify the meaning of unknown and multiple-meaning words and phrases by using context clues, analyzing meaningful word parts, and consulting general and specialized reference materials, as appropriate.
5. Demonstrate understanding of figurative language, word relationships, and nuances in word meanings.
6. Acquire and use accurately a range of general academic and domain-specific words and phrases sufficient for reading, writing, speaking, and listening at the college and career readiness level; demonstrate independence in gathering vocabulary knowledge when considering a word or phrase important to comprehension or expression.

LEARNING AND RETAINING CONTENT-SPECIFIC VOCABULARY   Students' self-selection of words they want to learn is an important component of language growth. However, when specific content is being learned, teachers don't want to leave to chance key academic terms that are necessary for students to make sense of the major ideas. Many times these academic or domain-specific terms are new and students need to both see and hear them. It is important that teachers draw students' attention to these words and help them begin to understand how they are used in the specific context. When content textbooks are used, a list of key terms can be developed from words suggested as important. If a textbook is not used, content standards can be used to develop curriculum priorities. In these cases, a helpful guide to checking students' vocabulary knowledge and selecting words for particular attention is Marzano's (2004) book on academic vocabulary. He includes lists of key terms taken from standards in all the academic areas and chunks them by grade levels. He also suggests several activities to help students learn the terms, including keeping a vocabulary journal and playing games with the key words periodically. Good strategies are needed to draw students' attention to specific words and their meanings in the particular context being studied. A few of these are listed below:

- *Chunking and categorizing words.* The teacher provides a list of key terms, and students are asked to chunk them together in groups that fit. Once the groups are made, students give each chunk a label or category. When preparing for the activity, the first step is to create a list of the most important terms that students will encounter in their reading. Next, the teacher ensures that there are at least two or three words that can be chunked together. If there are not, the teacher adds some words from the content that will help students build categories of related words.

- *Possible sentences.* The teacher gives students a list of the key terms that will be in the text and need to be learned. Working with a partner or individually, they try to connect two or three of the words into a sentence. They write these sentences and later share their possible sentences, even though they might be unsure of the real meanings of the words. The activity raises students' awareness of words they will need to attend to as they read.

- *Exclusion brainstorming.* The teacher gives students a list of words that includes both words they will need for the content being studied and some that do not relate to the topic. The teacher asks the students to predict which words do not fit the content. This activity is fun because it shifts the purpose of the task from what students normally get while highlighting new words.

- *Predict-o-gram.* The teacher presents students with a list of words that come from the story they will read. The teacher then asks the students to predict which words relate to the characters, setting, problem, or resolution. Students can use a graphic organizer with four blocks and space to write predictions they make about the story content after they complete the activity of categorizing the terms.

- *Vocabulary word cards*. Vocabulary word cards can be a fun and powerful way for students to build their vocabularies. They select the ten most important words from the unit of study and then create a 3 × 5-inch word card for each. On the front side of the card, they draw a picture to illustrate the meaning of the term. On the back side of the card, they write the word, the central definition, and added information to help them understand how to use the word. This might be a sentence, some synonyms, or phrases in which the word might be found.

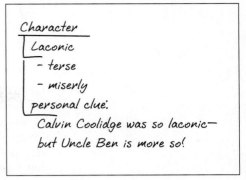

Figure 14.1 Personal Clue

- *Personal clues*. The personal clue approach (Carr, 1985) is also an effective way to learn words in content areas. Words are grouped by the concept they are associated with or by the element or character in a piece of literature. Then students list attributes of the target words and think of one personal association that is the clue they will use to store the terms. For example, when learning *laconic*, one student wrote *terse* and *miserly* and associated them with Scrooge before Christmas. Then, on the second day, the student decided that from his study of American history, Calvin Coolidge was a better choice. On the third day, he added another clue: his New England uncle who hardly ever said more than three words. He had fun finding the right clue for *laconic*—but certainly wasn't laconic in his efforts (see the example in Figure 14.1).

- *Connect two*. Using the list of words being learned, students practice them by creating new and sometimes zany sentences containing either two or three of the new words. Doing this with a partner makes it more enjoyable for students because the sentences, which must respect the definitions of the words, can still be fun, and sharing makes it more enjoyable. Revisiting words is essential for retention.

Students also can use graphic organizers such as concept maps to help them learn new words. The organizer contains boxes or cells into which a question or concept is filled in. For example, a concept of definition map could include questions such as "What is it?" "What is it like?" "What are some examples?" and "What are some attributes?" After creating the web, students can keep expanding them—some draw pictures of the concept, some add antonyms, and others collect sentences in which the term is used—to help deepen their understanding of the term.

Semantic or Concept Web for Upper Grades

WIDE READING   Doing a great deal of reading is a critical way for students to build their recognition of vocabulary and to learn the specific contexts in which words are appropriate. There is no substitute for reading. Studies have shown that direct teaching of specific words can account for only part of the growth in word knowledge needed to develop an adequate vocabulary (Anderson & Nagy, 1991; Beck & McKeown, 1983). When students enjoy reading and are attentive to language and vocabulary, they continue to build their awareness and ability to use an increasingly wide range of vocabulary terms.

In summary, you can guide students in their development of vocabulary sensitivity and curiosity by having them do the following:

- Keep personal records of words new to them or new uses of known words.
- Develop strategies for building meanings for these words.
- Use appropriate visual or graphic organizers to build and retain meanings.
- Practice using new terms in speaking and writing.
- Use resources, especially dictionaries, thesauruses, and glossaries.
- Engage in word play by creating and enjoying jokes, word puzzles, poetry, and games such as Scrabble® and Pictionary®.

Cumulative Semantic Map

- Understand how our language is evolving and how vocabulary grows and changes.
- Keep examples of new words and new usages. (Sports, music, and fashion are areas that keep inventing new words and usage that middle grade students are interested in following.)

The CCSS emphasize the importance of vocabulary development at many places throughout the Reading and Language Standards and specifically in the Language Standards 6–12. Three standards, 4–6, address vocabulary development: Students should be able to determine or clarify meanings of new terms using context, word parts, and references as needed, they should understand figurative language, and acquire and use both general academic and domain-specific words and phrases in reading, writing, speaking, and listening.

Student Self-Reflection

In addition to self-monitoring, which refers to the active checking of one's own thinking while reading, students also become more confident readers when they learn to engage in reflection after completing the text. They learn to think about what they have just read and what is new or different. They also can reflect on their own active thinking processes and how well they have used their energies during reading, asking themselves questions such as: "What did I learn?" "Was I using my energy wisely so I made best use of my time?" and "Did I use the best approach to the reading: visualizing, making a mental map of the text, outlining, or rephrasing as I read?" Adopting a reflective attitude encourages readers to take responsibility for their reading and to realize they can often do more to be effective readers. The teacher can encourage students to improve self-reflection by having them make marginal notes while reading and learning, discuss the process with peers, and keep a journal for self-reflections at the end of reading activities.

Another aspect of self-monitoring is learning to think about the process used in conducting research. Some teachers create guides for students to follow in forming and answering questions about their research: "How did you begin your research process?" "How did you use your prior knowledge as a frame for deciding on what you would need to research?" "How did you compare and contrast different sources of information?" Others have students keep journals of their research process and make notes of what they have done as they go. Another good way to increase students' self-reflection is to use the I-Search Paper model (Macrorie, 1988). In this model, students choose a topic and conduct research on it, but focus most directly on how they go about the process rather than just concentrating on the final paper. They reflect on how they went about their research, what caused problems for them, and what they would do the next time. The strategy creates a more reflective and powerful response to extended learning activities.

Opportunities to Model Fluent and Reflective Reading

The teacher can do a great deal to help students develop an internal model of what fluent reading is like by reading aloud to them on a regular basis. Selecting a variety of material to read helps students understand the beauty and depth of what can be communicated by writers. Contemporary students do not have many opportunities to engage in reflection about reading. Playing good audiotapes or CDs of texts being read can also help students begin to appreciate the sounds of written language read orally. For example, listening to books on tape such as James Joyce's *Dubliners* (2006) and Tony Hillerman reading his own mysteries helps students to gain an appreciation for the varieties of oral readers. This strategy can also help students to think of using their MP3 players and time spent in the car as potential time for listening to good books and poetry.

Reading aloud from interesting material also can be used to model critical thinking engaged in while reading. When reading to students, pay particular attention to reading with expression, asking questions as you read, and responding to the ideas in the text. Comments

Reading Aloud

such as, "That was beautifully described—I can almost see it!" "Did I understand what the author just said?" "That doesn't sound possible to me" and "That reminds me of something else I just learned" are the kinds of reflections students need to use in their independent reading. Modeling such thinking encourages students to evaluate their own habits and can help them build new habits if they do not already have them. You can enhance the power of this thinking aloud by putting some of these "thinking asides" on the board or on strips hanging from the ceiling so that students are regularly reminded of them. Listening to you read aloud in this manner from a wide selection of texts provides students with many benefits, not the least of which are increased interest in print and sensitivity to vocabulary and language use. Think of the power of reading aloud in providing the following:

- A model of fluent reading
- A model of active and reflective reading
- A way to increase their store of knowledge about the world as well as their vocabulary

The amount of time you have with students will vary depending on how the school schedule is organized. Read the Being a Professional Reading Teacher box and think about your preferences.

Fluency Through Repetition

Rereading texts improves students' word knowledge, reading speed, and accuracy while it deepens their understanding of that particular text. Effective methods for incorporating rereading and guided oral reading in the middle level classroom, and thus promoting fluency, include the following:

CCSS

• Foundational Skills 4: Fluency

- Rereading poems and short passages using techniques such as choral reading, two-part reading, and echo reading
- Readers' theater, a technique that involves students in rehearsing and reading aloud their interpretation of a character's lines in passages from a short story
- Self-timing drills, a procedure in which students time themselves or partners in reading and rereading short passages to increase their speed
- An introduction to a variety of new books and genres, giving students short amounts of time to skim through several to see which they like best

Assessment

Assessment is the starting point for good instruction. Students in the middle grades vary significantly in their reading abilities and interests, and, with the increasing range of reading genres and purposes that students this age must handle successfully, there is much teachers need to attend to. Throughout the year, the teacher's job is to monitor what all the students know and can do and to provide supportive instruction. Because this is a challenging task, it is also good to remember that the students themselves can be good assistants in the task of monitoring their knowledge and abilities. In fact, they should be made aware of their strengths and should participate in setting and monitoring their goals throughout the year.

Determining Reading Levels

As a result of the daily reading by students of materials in the classroom, the teacher should have a good idea of their development as readers and can guide them into reading appropriate materials. Determining students' instructional and independent reading levels can be done in a few ways.

INFORMAL READING INVENTORIES   If a reading series is available, one of the easiest ways is to use an Informal Reading Inventory (IRI) provided for the reading program. The IRI contains a series of increasingly difficult reading passages; students are asked to read the passages and then to demonstrate their comprehension by answering a series of questions. If the IRI asks for oral reading of the passages, the guideline is generally that oral reading with 99 percent accuracy and 90 percent comprehension indicates independence with the material. The range for instruction (where your guidance as a teacher supports the reading) is 95 percent word accuracy and 75 percent comprehension. Less success with passages indicates that the material is really too difficult for students to be asked to read. In the language of reading assessment, those texts are at a *frustration level* for students.

ADVANCED INFORMAL INVENTORY   As students mature, teachers also need to find out how well they can read information from more than one source, combine ideas, and learn to think critically about what they read. Teachers need to ask students to compare and contrast two different texts on some appropriate topic. A contemporary news story, two pieces of student writing with different perspectives, editorials in newspapers, and personal letters to the editor all make good content for student thinking. This will provide you with good data as you plan to have students do research (and use the Internet) and engage in extended projects. You can copy two short articles and create a few questions that require students to contrast the pieces, or ask students to write their opinion about the question addressed in the articles, citing references they find useful in the texts.

Another form of an advanced IRI is one that is specific for a content course. The teacher selects passages from the textbook or instructional materials that students read. Questions need to tap the range of reading comprehension tasks—from identifying key ideas, inferring relationships, and understanding specific vocabulary meanings to reading visual information contained in charts, maps, and graphs. This inventory can be completed in a group setting, so it saves much time for teachers.

LEVELED BOOKS   Many districts now have leveled the books they have available according to difficulty, taking into account a variety of features, including vocabulary and concept load, complexity of sentences and redundancy, and layout of the materials. If you have this resource available, you can select a representative set of books at a range of levels and ask students to read short sections. Then, summarize what they have read or have them answer a few of your questions and find their instructional levels this way.

Strategy Knowledge

Another important component of students' reading that needs to be assessed early in the year is their awareness of the strategies they use to read successfully in different kinds of materials and for different purposes. One middle grade teacher begins her year by asking students to fill out a survey of what their strategies are for reading (see Figure 14.2). On it are examples of the kinds of reading tasks teachers in this departmentalized school expect of students. What the teacher and students learned by doing this survey one year was that the students were very "teacher and parent" dependent. Several students responded to the query about how to prepare for a social studies test that would be given on Friday by indicating that they would read over the chapter, maybe more than once, and then ask their mothers to quiz them using the end of chapter questions. When asked how to figure out a difficult mathematics problem, again the response was to ask Mom. Discussing responses to this kind of survey can be a starting place for developing students' awareness of what good readers do.

Another approach is to ask students to indicate what they are aware of doing as they read a challenging short article. Inform students that they can use sticky notes if they want to while reading so they do not forget their thinking or strategies. When finished reading, each student should write a reflection on what he or she did before starting to read, what he or she was conscious of doing while reading, and what he or she did afterward. If students are frustrated by this task, it means that they are not yet fully conscious of what reading is as a strategic behavior and that there is much work for the teacher to accomplish with them during the year to develop a vocabulary for and awareness of reading strategies.

Figure 14.2
Reading Strategies

WHAT DO YOU KNOW ABOUT YOUR STRATEGIES FOR READING TO LEARN?

Your language arts teacher has set up a unit in which you will read novels in groups. Each night you will read one chapter. What strategies work best for you to help you enjoy and understand novels? What will you do?

_____

_____

_____

_____

Your social studies teacher has assigned you a 25-page chapter on Monday. On Friday you will have a test on the material. You are on your own to read and learn. There are lots of headings and boldfaced vocabulary in the text. At the end of the chapter, there are many questions and activities. What will you do this week with this chapter? What is your plan?

_____

_____

_____

_____

Developing a Diagnostic Eye and Ear

One of the most important forms of assessment is what you observe students doing during your ongoing classroom reading activities. During these activities, you will see students engaged with texts and responding to them in a variety of ways. Use all of these typical situations to observe carefully and make notes of what students show about their developing reading abilities. Experiment with ways to record information from these classroom events and build profiles of your students as readers. Many teachers keep a clipboard nearby and focus on two or three students a day, making notes about their engagement in discussions, their responses to specific questions, or their thinking aloud as they read with a group. Other teachers prefer looking at the whole class and recording evidence of students' thinking, no matter who seems to be revealing their strategies and understanding. Writing short sticky notes of these occurrences and noting the students' names on the notes permits you to add these sticky notes to a student folder where a variety of performance indicators are collected along with samples of written work. Another approach is to shadow a particular student for a day; this form of observation helps teachers to create a more complete sense of how the student reads across a variety of situations.

Study Reading

As students enter the middle school years, many find the shift in expectations quite startling. Instead of having teachers guide them through their assigned work, students are expected to know how to read and learn from assigned materials; organize their own study time and come to class prepared; and be able to study and learn a vast amount of information. There are several areas in which teachers need to guide students so they can be successful.

Scheduling Time to Study

Allocating time for study is an important aspect of learning for middle school students. This is a good time to provide students with weekly schedules and to talk through ways to find regular study periods on weeknights and weekends. However, students often are not inclined to listen well to a teacher's recommendations. You can stress the need to study by calling on older peer models. Invite former students from high schools and universities to talk with your students about their study habits. Some students in class might have older siblings who can speak with authority about their strategies for learning. When middle level students hear from older teens they respect, it becomes easier to guide them into more attentive reading and reflecting.

Students need to learn to keep a schedule for their study. You might ask visitors to bring their study plan books with them and show how important it is to develop a study schedule and keep records of assignments and time. Some of your own students might already have some form of study plan book or have parents who have given them planners. This can be a stimulus to help students review each week what they need to be working on and the amount of time they will need to be prepared for all their assignments and projects.

Test Taking

Learning how to study for tests is important—and generally unknown to middle level students. Take time to make a grid for different kinds of study and discuss with students strategies that are effective, noting particularly the advantages of spaced study and repeated rehearsal of new concepts and terms. Practice tests are becoming very familiar—almost too familiar—in states with high-stakes testing. However, making students aware of the nature of those experiences is important. Talk through with the students how they went about answering questions. How did the format of the test influence their strategy for taking the test? When did they read the questions—before or after reading the story or passage? Did they skim through the text if it was fairly long? How did they finally make the decision to answer the questions as they did?

Figure 14.3
Question-Answer
Relationships

In the Book Questions	In My Head Questions
Right There The answer is in one place in the text.	**Author and Me** The reader needs to combine what he/she knows with what is in the text.
Think and Search The pieces of information are all in the text but the reader needs to put them together to answer the question.	**On My Own** The reader needs to use his/her own ideas to answer the question; it is not answered in the text.

Introducing the Question Answer Relation (QAR) strategy (Raphael, 1986) at this point is a good way to help students understand the difference between typical classroom questions that are often of a higher thinking nature and those asked on standardized tests. The QAR approach divides questions into four types: those that can be answered by finding one piece of information (right there), those that require searching the text (think and search), those that require drawing on background knowledge to add to the text (author and you), and those that go beyond information in the text itself (on your own). Standardized tests given to thousands of students must include answers that are available in the text passages themselves. Therefore, according to the QAR terminology, there are no "on your own" questions. All questions have answers that can be found either in a specific location in the text (right there) or by combining bits of information from sections of the text (think and search). See Figure 14.3 for a graphic representation of the QAR model.

Teacher Modeling

Another way to raise interest in and awareness of the cognitive choices readers need to make as they read is to describe your own reading behaviors when you are learning. For example, you might describe how you study for a graduate course you are taking. Show students how you study, and get them to compare and contrast their own habits with yours. A key habit you can reinforce is the need to read the same text sections several times and make notes about what you consider to be important. You may also show them drawings or diagrams you create to help you form a visual image of information. When you show students your own ways of reorganizing information through notes and graphic creations, students can increase their own energy to engage in "study" rather than just looking over materials quickly, as many are likely to do at first.

Metacognition

Middle level students are very pragmatic and seem to always want to know "Why do we need to do this?" They often lack the knowledge of what reading really involves and are unable to describe what they do. Middle school students need to be better informed about what happens when they read and how they can become better readers. They need to develop *metacognition* about their learning, that is, an awareness of how they think. Metacognition involves three basic strategies: connecting new information to former knowledge; developing strategies for thinking; and planning, monitoring, and evaluating how they think (Dirkes, 1985). Activating metacognition can be done in a number of ways.

Active Reading

Students' metacognitive awareness of what good readers do while reading should be developed at this level. Teachers often begin this process by engaging in thinking aloud when they read orally. Using books that have margin notations on them is also a good way to stimulate students' attention toward the kind of thinking that goes on when good readers interact with pieces of text. You might create your own examples by having older students mark up a story or essay that your class is going to read. Go over the notations, and discuss them with the students by asking, "Why do you think this note was made? What would have stimulated this comment? How would you have responded?" Comparing two or three different people's responses to the same article gives students a clearer idea of the wide variety of ways in which people engage with text. Then you can build a list of the kinds of engagements that others have made and begin to use these as thinking strategies for your class; that is, visualizing, connecting to another text or author, marking it as providing an answer to a question, arguing with the text, and so on.

Many good teachers use sticky notes as a way of helping students monitor and develop their thinking as they read. They pose the question, "What kinds of thinking do we do as we read?" To explore their own minds during engaged reading, each student can be given several sticky notes and instructed to use them when ideas, images, and questions come to them while reading. When the group (either the whole class or a small group) is finished reading, the students can compare their notes and begin to understand how different students think about the same text. These different responses can then be categorized, and students can talk about how they think. Extending this activity to explore how the same students read a different kind of text also helps the students extend their understanding of the impact of the text on reading and thinking.

Self-Assessment

Once you have developed students' awareness of how to read and learn from text, they can then regularly include their own self-evaluations of the strategies they use in the work they do. You can do this by asking students at the end of class periods to fill out 3 × 5-inch cards on their class participation and work. You can alter the questions each day you hand out the cards with stems like these:

- What did you learn today?
- How did you learn best today?
- How was your class participation?
- What could you do better to help the class learn?
- What bothers you, or is still unclear?
- What was most interesting to you today?
- What would you like to learn more about?
- What questions do you have?

Begin the next class session by reviewing what the students wrote the day before. This simple process gives students a regular way to think about their learning and to know that the teacher is serious about taking advantage of class time to ensure learning. It also provides the teacher with important feedback on the success of the class sessions.

Learning Logs

Learning logs also give students a vehicle for ongoing self-reflection on their learning. At least weekly, students should be encouraged to review what they have learned that week, what questions they have, and how they have contributed to the class accomplishments. Key concepts and new vocabulary are also important to record in a learning log so that students stay focused on their primary purposes in school. This is serious business, yet it is very enjoyable when each student can keep a record of growth. Too often, students shift attention from learning to social acceptance at this age, and all the ways teachers can use to involve students in knowing and evaluating their own successes can help to balance the intense peer focus these students feel.

Extended Unit Assessment

Units of instruction are another place where student self-reflection is important. Right from the start, students should have a record of what they know and the questions they want to have answered from their study. Keeping this record in the form of a K-W-L chart in students' notebooks means that it will be available when students have completed their units. One teacher also asked students to generate a possible table of contents for the insect report they knew they would write as a culmination of their integrated language arts/science insect study and to make a semantic map of how those topics might be related. All of these pieces were kept in the students' notebooks throughout the unit. At the end of the unit, the teacher asked students to look at their actual table of contents and to compare it with the first one they had predicted would work. The teacher also had the students create a new semantic map and make a comparison with their first one. The teacher asked that the students respond in writing to some questions:

Teach It! 47

Know-Want to Know-Learn (K-W-L)

Teach It! 46

Metacognitive Graphic Organizer

- What surprised you most about your learning?
- How did your first table of contents compare to your final one?
- What did you notice about your semantic maps?
- How do you feel about your learning?

One student responded, "I can't believe how much I learned! I even thought spiders were insects when we started. I learned what that crunchy sound is when you step on an insect—it is the exo-skeleton. I also learned how to create a semantic map and show the relation of body parts and what insects can do." Students also can use personal notes like a sticky notes I-Chart to evaluate their typical responses and thoughts while reading. When they compare their patterns with those of others in their class, they can begin to develop a broader sense of what reading can be and may consciously try to enhance their own thinking.

A teacher's feedback and guidance can help students learn to assess their own development.

Portfolio Evaluation

Portfolios are great tools for student and teacher assessment at this level. These consist of personal collections of illustrative student work annotated to explain how they demonstrate learning or accomplishments. Students can collect examples of their own work that illustrate their best achievements and that also show the areas and goals they still need to work toward. When you have students annotate or add note cards to the pieces in the portfolios, the students' self-reflection is deepened. Be careful to give guidelines and set parameters for portfolios, however, because they can easily get out of hand. Students love to sort and annotate their work and can spend hours creating covers for the portfolios. Space to save the portfolios is also an ongoing concern. So, some clear guidelines about selecting a few pieces each quarter that illustrate both best work and work in progress can make the portfolio process integral to students' learning. Keeping a list of books and articles students have read with a short summary and evaluation can also help them create a lifetime habit. Students need visual records of what they are learning and reading, and the portfolio is a natural aid in helping them to celebrate the results of their efforts.

 Portfolios are an excellent way to document students' literacy abilities and progress. How does the teacher in the video use portfolio assessment to motivate her students and enhance their reading and writing skills?

Teaching All Students

Each year that students grow and learn, their knowledge, skills, learning styles, and strengths and interests become more individualized. Good teaching encourages and

Students in today's classrooms have a diverse range of strengths and needs; effective teachers must consider these factors when planning instruction. What practices in the video demonstrate that the teachers have considered their students' strengths when planning instruction?

nurtures the particular talents and differences in students' learning, so we all must celebrate these increasing variations! Research on multiple intelligences has helped us to understand that variations are natural and need to be considered in organizing for instruction.

Your students will bring with them a wide range of cultural and linguistic abilities. Many students know more than one language and have had experiences in diverse cultural settings. You can enrich your own learning and provide great resources to the whole class by using these opportunities sensitively and well. Therefore, as a teacher, you have real challenges in creating classroom experiences that both meet students where they are and provide opportunities for them to grow as literacy learners.

Identify Strengths

A key to reaching all of your students is being a careful observer, or, to use the term coined by Yetta Goodman (1978), becoming a good kidwatcher. Each day you can observe how your students come into your classroom; you can observe how they interact with their peers; you can listen to what they share; you can watch them as they read; and you can engage them in conversation. It takes just a few moments each day to become attuned to your students. The effort is most valuable. Keeping a notebook page with bits of information gained from informal observations can help you to build a profile of each student that can be useful over time. Then, at an opportune moment, the particular strengths of a student can be called forth. For example, who is good with music and can help to plan the background pieces to accompany the presentations by the novel groups? Who is good at drawing and can illustrate the class book or movie reviews? Who is great at organizing on the computer and can catalogue the independent reading records? Who is a good oral reader or actor and can help others visualize texts they are reading? Some of the less-adept readers and writers may have other strengths that will help them to learn more effectively and also contribute to the group in ways that can enhance their identity with literacy (see the Differentiated Instruction box).

Recognize Students' Cultures

Teachers can help to make all students feel a part of the classroom by ensuring that materials about their cultures and situations are available and by reading from some of these materials. Teachers can also sensitize students to the plights of immigrants and minority students by reading aloud from some stories that represent situations similar to those of students in the school. It is often from ignorance that young teens can seem callous and not caring. When they hear the stories of what others have had to experience, their sense of fairness and empathy can be expanded. Table 14.4 identifies some books that can be good for such read-alouds.

DIFFERENTIATED INSTRUCTION

SIOP®
Sheltered
Instruction
Observation
Protocol®

Learning Journals

Finding out what students know about the content being studied at the beginning of a unit or lesson is important. This is particularly urgent when there are students from a variety of linguistic and cultural groups in the classroom. Yet these are the students who are most hesitant to speak in class and to write out their ideas. An easy way to elicit some of what they know is to have students keep modified Learning Journals in which they record what they are learning on a regular basis. For English language learners, these journals can be places where they can draw and create diagrams and graphic organizers of their knowledge. Rather than insisting that students write in traditional formats, these more visual forms of representing ideas can give English language learners more confidence in activating what they know. A part of their journals can be dual-language lists of key terms. When teachers provide a list of important terms at the beginning of the unit, students can write these in their own journals in both English and their first language. For new terms, teachers can encourage students to copy visual illustrations of the terms from their textbooks or dictionaries or find visual representations they can photocopy.

Table 14.4 Often Unrepresented Voices of Youth

Blohm, J. M., & Lapinsky, T. *Kids Like Me: Voices of the Immigrant Experience.* Boston: Nicholas Bresley, 2006.

Mead, A. *Dawn and Dusk.* New York: Farrar, Straus, & Giroux, 2007.

Na, A. *A Step from Heaven.* Asheville, NC: Front Street, 2001.

Rice, D. *Crazy Loco: Stories by David Rice.* New York: Dial Books.

Schmidt, G. D. *Okay for Now.* New York: Clarion Books, 2011.

Schmidt, G. D. *The Wednesday Wars!* New York: Clarion Books, 2009.

Soto, G. *Baseball in April and Other Stories.* New York: Odyssey Books, 1990.

Walker, R. *Black, White and Jewish.* New York: Penguin, 2001.

Vander Zee, R. *Eli Remembers.* Grand Rapids, MI: Eerdmans Books for Young Readers, 2007.

English language learners bring with them a wealth of knowledge about their own languages and often have the ability to contrast languages in ways that can be helpful to monolingual students in your classroom. Having bilingual or trilingual students in class can be a real asset. Help them to become comfortable talking about these differences in language and culture:

- When you are discussing characters in stories, ask students to reflect on how the same characters' actions would be perceived in their culture of origin. Discuss how the characters would have handled the same situations in their culture.

- Have students act out the behaviors of a character in a story as if the character were from their culture. Compare this with how the same character's actions are depicted by some other students.

- Analyze the language used. Would it be different if it were from another culture? For example, would characters express their emotions as they do in the story you are reading? How would they interact with strangers?

- When reading classic stories, ask whether students from other cultures have stories similar to those you are reading. Do they have the same story in translated form or is the story from their culture (e.g., *Arabian Nights, Aesop's Fables, Cinderella, The Nutcracker*)?

- Make lists of key vocabulary terms, and have students write the same words in their languages. These comparisons can often be the beginning point for discussion of where English has acquired its words.

Teachers can take opportunities to remind students that they live in a world made up of many nations, peoples, languages, and ways of thinking and expressing thoughts and emotions.

- Graph the story structure of pieces you read with the class. Ask someone from another culture to show the structure of a typical tale from their culture. Are they the same? (For example, Athabaskan and Japanese tales often have a less-defined beginning and ending than Eurocentric tales do and can go on and on, leaving more to the reader to determine.)

- Read orally from news that reflects the world as represented by students in your school. Use maps so that the areas they come from become familiar to everyone. Use current events as the texts for some of the reading strategies you model. Often, students from abroad have a better sense of world events than do U.S. students, and their knowledge can be used to expand everyone's perspectives.

Story Maps

Adjusting Teaching for English Language Learners

When students are functioning in a second or third language, they need more time to process what they read and hear and more time to compose their own responses. Even when students have exited from bilingual programs, they have not had time to develop the depth of vocabulary and language usage required by middle school literature and content texts.

The more the teacher can do to support their development of English, the better they will be able to engage fully in class activities and think deeply about content.

There are a few easy ways in which the teacher can support these students' learning within each area or theme. First, brainstorm the key terms you will be using, and check the students' familiarity with them. Create a glossary of the terms that are not known, and put these on a bookmark that students can keep with them while reading and studying. Second, as a way of introducing the writing of an author to students, have some parent volunteers record the first part of a text (a novel or story or a chapter of informational material) so that the students can hear the language and begin to recognize the connections between the oral and written forms.

A third way to help English language learners participate fully is to give them some pre-experiences before the class begins a new area of study. You might hear this referred to as "jump-starting" their thinking and learning. For example, if you are going to have a unit on survival tales and will read some of Gary Paulsen's books, check out a videotape showing the setting of Canada and the northlands so that students can more easily visualize as they read. You might also find some easier books or magazine stories that introduce the same concepts that you will deal with in a novel or informational unit and let students take these home and learn from them before delving into the more difficult class texts. You also might be able to find easier versions of some of the stories you will have students read, and these can be used as advance organizers to prepare your English language learners for the complete version. Many readers do better with texts when they have a good idea of what the content is about; this is particularly the case for English language learners. Help them to discover what works best for them, and then try to provide appropriate scaffolds for their learning.

Organizing for Instruction

Middle grades are just that—in the middle between self-contained elementary classrooms and high schools with their departmental structures. In some schools, grades 5 to 8 are treated much like the earlier elementary grades, in which one teacher has a single class with some special teachers perhaps providing elective courses in foreign language and music or computers for the students. Other schools create teams of students and teachers, so between 80 and 120 students are grouped together with four or five teachers, and the teams stay together for two or three years. Many middle school advocates have supported this model as a way to provide more guidance and create "home groups." Another variant is for students to have the same teacher for two or three subjects—usually language arts, reading, and social studies or a combined reading/language arts block. This core or combined teaching structure helps teachers to know their students more deeply, because they have fewer sections to teach. Yet other schools are totally departmentalized with no groupings, so reading teachers teach four or five different groups of students each day. Any team teaching is done by individual teachers working together. Most new teachers have little say in how the school is organized. It is important that you know what kind of structure your school has in place because it provides the framework within which you have to teach.

There are several options for providing a range of reading opportunities that develop students' strategies and knowledge of reading, some of which are discussed in the following sections. The methods provided are certainly neither exhaustive of how good instruction can be organized nor are they comprehensive, but they provide a number of good options found in schools across this country. Recently, schools have also begun to use block scheduling to provide longer periods of time for students to work within a single content. For middle school teachers the decisions about where reading instruction will be conducted is important; the new CCSS and individual state standards prioritize reading in the content disciplines so all teachers need to be involved. Developing readers and writers can't be the sole responsibility of the reading/language arts teachers.

Yet, finding a balance among curriculum content, reading skills, and the language arts is challenging.

Integrating Content Areas

As one reads about the kinds of reading strategies and skills that middle grade students need to develop, the advantages of teachers either teaming or having students for two or three subjects are clear. Students need to learn to read many kinds of texts and for many purposes. They are more interested and engaged in developing these when they see the concrete and immediate use of them (Guthrie & Davis, 2003). For example, teaching students how to retain new and important vocabulary words is much easier if this instruction is provided when students need to master their history or science content. Helping them learn to read dense textbooks is easier when the teacher can use the students' own content textbooks. Middle graders are very pragmatic and concrete, and the more instruction is directly tied to their specific needs, the more likely they are to attend and process the strategies.

There is so much that needs to be taught that teachers have come up with a variety of ways of organizing the curriculum to meet these wide-ranging aspects of reading. One of the basic issues to be faced is how to balance the reading of literature with reading in informational texts and helping students learn to use reading to learn. A good option is to divide the year into quarters and focus on fictional literature and poetry for two quarters; use a thematic focus concentrating on reading informational texts for the other two quarters, and involve students in reading and evaluating multiple sources and engaging in short inquiry and research projects throughout. This model works well when reading and language arts teachers link with either science or social studies teachers so that students have both the content and the process as high priorities. Within this quarterly organization there are many options for instruction.

In the example of integrated instruction described in the opening classroom story, Rasheed Graham, the language arts teacher, teamed with the social studies teacher, Elizabeth Raphael, so they could develop the deepest learning possible for their students. Mr. Graham had learned in previous years that his students couldn't read the novels he had selected with any depth of understanding unless they had a good foundation of knowledge about the Middle Ages and life in feudal Europe. This came from their work in social studies, where the whole structure of medieval life was explained and students had multiple experiences studying about medieval social structures and economics.

In developing this unit, the teachers began with the state standards and benchmarks in social studies and language arts <http://education.state.mn.us>. In reading/language arts the key standards came from the new CCSS sixth grade standards for reading literature. Mr. Graham knew these standards were essential for his students.

For his part in this integrated unit Mr. Graham had selected a set of novels at different levels of difficulty so his students could engage in small groups and discuss the books together. He had used these literature circles for a few years and felt comfortable having students discuss ideas in small groups. He also knew that his students would be challenged by much of the vocabulary and so had developed some Rate Your Knowledge self-assessment guides for students to use. (The Integrating Across the Curriculum: An Integrated Unit on the Middle Ages and Life in Feudal Europe feature shows an example.) Students complete their assessment of their knowledge of these terms at the beginning of each novel and then keep notes as they build understanding of the terms during the unit. At the end of the unit they return to the sheets to assess their growth.

As Ms. Raphael developed students' understanding of the medieval period in Europe, she used the textbook, videos, and other books and magazine articles so students could build a sense of the social order and life during that period and make comparisons with the way of life they take for granted now. She was grateful that Mr. Graham provided opportunities for reflective analysis of the novels both in discussions and in student writing activities. Students kept vocabulary notebooks that were used across reading and social

Integrating Across the Curriculum
An Integrated Unit on the Middle Ages and Life in Feudal Europe

Put a check by the level of knowledge you have of each word. If you think you really know a term, then either write a few words to define it or draw what it means.

KEY WORDS	UNFAMILIAR	HAVE SEEN	KNOW AND USE	DEFINITION/DRAWING
Scavenge				
Scrawny				
Dung heap				
Midwife				
Apprentice				
Risk-taking				
Haggle				
Ointment				
Merchant				
Herbs				
Self-awareness				

The key social studies standards (MN standards) guiding this unit were:

	STANDARDS	BENCHMARKS
World History, Substrand D. Early Medieval & Byzantium, 400 AD–1000 AD	The student will demonstrate knowledge of Europe during the Middle Ages from about 500–1000 AD in terms of its impact on Western civilization.	1. Students will describe the spread and influence of Christianity throughout Europe and analyze its impact. 2. Students will explain the structure of feudal society and analyze how it impacted all aspects of feudal life.
E, Global Encounters, Exchanges, and Conflicts, 500 AD–1500 AD	The student will demonstrate knowledge of social, economic, and political changes and cultural achievements in the late medieval period.	1. Students will describe the emergence of European states and analyze the impact. 3. Students will identify patterns of crisis and recovery related to the Black Death, and evaluate their impact.

Key Literature Standards & Benchmarks Guiding the Unit (CCSS Standards)

Literature Standards for Reading 6–12: Standards for sixth grade

1. Cite textual evidence to support analysis of what the text says explicitly as well as inferences drawn from the text.
2. Determine a theme or central idea of a text and how it is conveyed through particular details; provide a summary of the text distinct from personal opinions or judgments.
5. Analyze how a particular sentence, chapter, scene, or stanza fits into the overall structure of a text and contributes to the development of the theme, setting, or plot.
6. Explain how an author develops the point of view of the narrator or speaker in a text. Compare and contrast texts in different forms or genres (e.g., stories and poems; historical novels and fantasy stories) in terms of their approaches to similar themes and topics.

studies so they also understood the way their work in both classes overlapped and built a strong foundation for their understanding.

The final projects for this unit also were integrated with grades for both subjects. The students had choices for these: they could develop a character and write a diary or memoir of that person's life over a significant period; they could create a manor and the surrounding community (some did this on their computers and some built three-dimensional displays); or they could research some aspect of medieval life and create a report that was presented to their classmates. In each of the project options, the students followed the guidelines and used the rubrics the teachers had prepared as they worked on the projects and later engaged in self-evaluation.

Teaching Literature

Most elementary students have done much of their independent reading in fiction and can anticipate the basic structures and techniques used in this kind of text. However, in the middle grades, several new genres are introduced, and they can pose problems for readers who are on automatic pilot much of the time in independent-level materials. Science fiction, fantasy, utopia/dystopia, short stories, and stream-of-consciousness pieces are often new to these students. Biography is another genre that is important to teach at this level because it provides a great link for students to the world at different periods of history and to people who have had important influences on the students' own development. Longer, narrative poetry is often given more attention in the middle grades, and students can be involved in dramatic play readings, choral reading, and readers' theater. Some teachers concentrate one unit on novel forms and a second on short stories, poetry, and drama. This is where the developmental continuum from fifth to eighth grades needs to be worked out among the reading and literature teachers so that students continue to learn more about literature each year. Teachers can develop their literature focus in at least three ways: using core novels and literature groups, literature circles, and guided reading and readers' workshops.

CORE NOVELS AND LITERATURE GROUPS   Use a core novel representing a genre you want to introduce with all students to begin the novel unit. Then have students choose from four or five novels you have preselected for their subsequent work in literature groups. By engaging all students in a single novel, you have a good context for introducing and modeling the concepts and strategies you think are important for students to be using independently later. With all students reading the same text, you can also help them develop good discussion skills and courteous behavior. Because a whole class is too large to hold engaging discussions most of the time, you can use a "fishbowl" technique and divide the class into two parts: Half the students sit in the center of the room and participate in oral discussion, and the other half sit around the outer part of the class and write their responses to the questions and flow of ideas and also monitor the participants' discussion behaviors. Use the same inner circle for the whole class period, or, if time permits, shift the roles halfway through the class period and give both groups the opportunity to participate both orally and in written form. By having the outer circle evaluate the participation of the inner circle, there is a record of who has contributed and how the discussion proceeded. Students' written comments also serve as a good way to evaluate their own interpretation of the text and their response to the ideas discussed.

Teach It!   35

Literature Circles

Supporting English Language Learners   Using a single novel also helps students who are English language learners participate more fully in the class. Before the unit begins, a few students or parents can record the novel or the first half of it so that English language learners can hear the sounds of the language and become familiar with the text. The teacher can also prepare special guides for these students so that they can follow the plot, know the characters, and think of questions ahead of class discussion. Some teachers have

Language and Diversity

English sounds different than the written words may suggest. How can students hear correct academic English?

Teach It! 32

Dual-Entry Diary

Writing and Reading Connections

Argue for the importance of writing across units of instruction.

found that giving English language learners mini-lessons before the general class sessions helps them to gain confidence in their understanding of the text; then they can relax and enjoy the discussion of the text during the class periods. Finally, students gain confidence in their ability to contribute to class discussions when the teacher provides time for them to talk with partners before responding in the whole class or fishbowl. Pose a question for the group, then let students turn to their partners to think aloud about their responses, find the words and ways of expressing ideas in English, and get feedback that either modifies their ideas or confirms what they have said. Then open the conversation to the larger group. With this slight modification, many English language learners feel much more confident and comfortable participating in larger class groups. It is also a good model for all students: Think before speaking!

Connecting Writing and Reading   While using a core novel with the whole class, you have the opportunity to model journal writing and use students' own responses to enhance the discussions. Students might need to learn how to respond to literature. Begin by showing your own journal entry for a part of the text the group is reading. Provide labels for the kinds of responses you make: connecting with the text (*this reminds me of . . .*), raising questions (*what does it matter if . . .?*), visualizing (*I see . . . in my mind's eye*), responding emotionally (*I don't like ____ when . . .*), predicting (*I bet this problem will . . .*), and elaborating (*I know at this time in history there were often periods of . . .*). You might need to ask students to use two or three of the kinds of responses in their own journals so that they can develop the various ways of responding and then switch to other forms in the next entry. What you think is easy and automatic might be very uncomfortable for students. Rather than presuming a great deal, it is often better to start slowly and ensure that all students understand the tasks and intent of the journal experiences.

If students have a difficult time writing journal entries, they might do well to partner with another classmate and, between talk and writing, frame their joint responses to the text. You might find it useful to give students sticky notes to jot down their thoughts while they are reading so that they don't lose the ideas that come to them. Then they can return to those notes and elaborate on them as they write in their journals.

Journals can also serve as tools to help students focus on the features of the genre or other important elements of literature that you want to highlight. Students can keep a place in the journal where they record examples of specific literary elements, such as the setting in fantasy or futuristic elements in science fiction. They can also note special phrases or uses of language in the journal and share those later with other students. You can ask students to keep a section of their journals in which they can write new vocabulary items or new ways in which terms are used. If they record the pages on which the words occur, they can begin to see how authors often repeat the same vocabulary in different contexts. Adding drawings of the terms helps many students to enjoy this activity and remember the new words more easily.

LITERATURE CIRCLES   Students tend to discuss books better when teachers are not leading the groups (Almasi, 1995; Hynds, 1997; Raphael & McMahon, 1994; Short & Kauffman, 1995). Many teachers prefer to conduct their literature units by having students self-select the books they read and work in small discussion groups rather than in teacher-led discussions of the same novel. They do their teaching in mini-lessons at the beginning of the class period so that all students can focus on the element the teacher highlights, but within their own texts, and then take on the role of active observers during book discussions led by the students. At times, teachers also serve as facilitators of the students' discussions, but they should not assume the role of "expert."

The nature of the mini-lessons that are used should derive from observations of the students as they are involved in reading and responding and from evaluations of the written work of the students. The major framework that helps teachers to develop the foci for teaching comes also from the standards students should be able to meet.

In both the Minnesota and new CCSS standards, middle grade students are expected to learn to compare how authors and illustrators use text and art across materials to express ideas by employing foreshadowing, flashbacks, color, strong verbs, and language that inspires. Knowing that expectation, Mr. Graham developed the medieval unit using novels and art representing that time period. He selected a set of novels including *The Ramsay Scallop* (Temple, 1994), *Catherine, Called Birdy* (Cushman, 2005), and the *The Midwife's Apprentice* (Cushman, 2012). He added materials that exemplified life in medieval Europe in other artistic forms: books about life in medieval Europe, including *Anno's Journey* (Anno, 1997) and *Castle* (Macaulay, 1982); examples of tapestries from the collection at the Cloisters from the Metropolitan Museum of Art for students to observe; and recordings of Gregorian chants. On the day the unit was introduced, he had music playing in the background and showed slides of the art as he introduced each of the novels. Then he gave students time to look through each of the novels and make a decision about which books they wanted to read. Each student listed his or her first and second choices. From these lists, Mr. Graham could help guide students to appropriate texts; some were much harder than others, and he wanted all students to read somewhat challenging materials but not books they could not handle.

During the unit, Mr. Graham guided students to make comparisons about the techniques used by artists in different media. One of the journal guidelines for the students asked them to locate interesting examples of language used to create pictures of the times and to compare that with other works of art. At specific points in the unit, students compared the plots and literary devices used by the different authors. In these and many other ways the state standards and creative planning combined to develop a stimulating and enjoyable learning experience for the students.

Mr. Graham also created a variety of assignments to focus student learning. Most homework required students to read several pages of text and write two or three questions they wanted their literature circle group to discuss the next day. Because understanding point of view is another standard, some students were asked to keep a journal from the point of view of a character of their choice while doing their reading. Students reading the same novel selected different characters so the impact of the plot and events on them could be recognized. An assignment for another group of students was to take particular scenes and rewrite them from a point of view different from that of the author. This proved a very interesting and challenging task. As a culmination, one group created a short readers' theater production for their novel that required students to take on the personas of the characters in the novel. In all these ways, the focus was on creating engaging and challenging experiences so that the maximum was gained for the time spent reading and discussing the novels.

There are many advantages to having students in literature groups. First, the students' different reading abilities and interests can be accommodated much more easily this way, and all students can participate in the class activities. Assignments can be matched to the students' learning needs; not all able readers have developed the skills and strategies they need and can be focused through specific work. Using multiple texts permits teachers and students to make comparisons among authors and forms of art so authors' decisions and styles can be illustrated. Core vocabulary and concepts are generally repeated in various texts, so students gain a deeper understanding of the basic concepts and can develop better visual images of what they read. Students become resources for each other in very real ways when they are the authorities on particular texts. Speaking clearly, summarizing well, using good examples, and then listening to each other are very real communication skills that can be developed.

GUIDED READING AND READERS' WORKSHOPS There is so much variety in the kinds of reading that students need to develop during the middle years that some group instruction by teachers is necessary. All students need to learn more about how textbooks are structured and the resources they contain. The differences in structures and discourse forms with which students must become familiar require teacher guidance. The various graphic aids and formats also need explanation and some direct attention. Then there is the issue of learning to do research and study independently. The middle years are when these skills become very important for students, and good schools provide a significant

Teach It! 9

Guided Reading

amount of time helping them learn to do research well and to construct reports and presentations. With computers now available in most classrooms, teachers need to provide instruction in the use of both the Web for collecting and evaluating information and the software for creating high-quality reports with digital pictures, imported pictures, and student-created diagrams and charts. For teachers who prefer doing most of their class work in fiction, this means that special segments of each week or a few weeks each quarter need to be devoted to informational reading and study.

Some teachers prefer to structure a portion of their reading program around student-selected individual reading. Atwell (1998) has developed the reading workshop model during which students all read individually in books of their own choosing and keep logs of their reading to use when they conference with the teacher. When students come together to discuss their reading, Atwell characterizes the conversations as a "dining room table" conversation about what each person is reading. Although most of the time students read silently and write individual responses, the teacher brings students together periodically for mini-lessons in which aspects of literature or reading strategies can be explained. Later, students can apply these lesson foci when they engage in their own reading.

Depending on the amount of time the teacher has with students each day, the two components of a rich literacy program can be developed simultaneously or on alternating days and weeks. The two aspects can also be combined if teachers want to direct students' individual reading toward a particular theme or genre. For example, if the class is working on aspects of informational textbooks and scientific articles, then students could do their individual reading in books that include scientific essays, in magazines such as *Science* and *Scientific American* (or student magazines in the areas of science), and in biography. There are many great texts that students can read and use to enlarge their horizons in this more guided reading workshop.

Expository Texts: Thematic Units

Most middle level students enjoy exploring unanswered questions and making school relevant to their own lives. This is easier to do when a class is engaged in a focused group inquiry project or thematic unit of study. Because students are generally much less familiar with informational, expository texts than they are with fiction, providing a stimulating context for the study of such materials is very advantageous. By having the students read several texts on the same topic, you can more easily illustrate the various text structures that are used and can help students to determine the advantages and disadvantages of each. You can also provide activities in which students write using those same structures. Attention to the varieties of forms of informational writing is important, as is the need to make it interesting. Therefore, many teachers have found that developing units around interesting content permits better teaching and learning than other skill-focused instruction. This can be achieved either by creating units with content teachers (in departmental structures) or by integrating reading and content when you teach both to the same students.

One model for integrated units developed by Michigan educators uses a key question as the focus for each unit, such as "Can the American dream be achieved?" In collecting the resources students will read, they use a planning grid to ensure that multiple perspectives on the issues are presented and that a wide variety of literature, both fiction and nonfiction, is included. See the example in Figure 14.4 of the resources for one unit.

Essays and Biography

When teachers do not feel comfortable creating more extended units around themes or content topics, they can still provide guided instruction to help students handle informational reading. Contemporary magazines for middle school students contain much excellent writing and are good sources for reading development. *Cobblestones*, *Calliope*, *Faces*, *National Geographic World*, and *Boys' Life* magazines are great sources of articles.

THE AMERICAN DREAM UNIT OVERVIEW				
Thematic Statement: Personal goals and choices are influenced by our own values.				
Focus Question: Is it still possible to achieve the American Dream?				
Project: Persuasive Paper: Is the American dream still achievable for me?				
Selection	**Genre**	**Perspective**	**Diversity**	**Period**
The Grapes of Wrath	novel/realistic fiction	negative	Lower-class Anglo-American	1930s
The Great Gatsby	novel/realistic fiction	negative	Upper-class Anglo-American	1920s
"I Have A Dream"	speech	positive	African American	1960s
"Maya Angelou"	poem	positive	African American	1990s
"An American Dream"	magazine	positive	European	1990s
"Charlie Two Shoes & the American Dream"	magazine	positive	Asian	1950s
"Is the American Dream Still Alive?"	magazine	positive	Mexican-American	1990s
"False Gold"	magazine	negative	Lower-class America	1990s

Figure 14.4 Thematic Unit Overview

Collecting a variety of biographies, both long and short, is another way of providing texts that permit the teacher to guide students toward reading more deeply in this genre. The different ways in which biographies are structured provide the opportunity to focus on organization and can be linked to students' writing of a biography later. Teachers can provide a good comparative study of how biographers represent the lives and accomplishments of well-known figures by structuring assignments so that students read and compare encyclopedia-type sketches and then read more in-depth book treatments of the same person. When more than one full-length biography is available, even more critical analysis is made possible, and students find it engaging. They easily become excited (and sometimes indignant) at how people are represented. Good questions analyzing the author's purpose, context, and perspective are natural outcomes of this investigation.

Drama and Choral Reading

One of the most interesting aspects of written language is hearing it read and performed orally. Middle level students also love these kinds of activities. Some teachers allocate two to three weeks during the year for the production of a play or choral reading and having students perform before audiences. These dramatic events can comprise science and social studies content as well as literature units. There are Web sites specifically devoted to readers' theater scripts for teacher use. This makes including this oral form of reading (and rereading for fluency) much easier for busy teachers.

For English language learners, opportunities to participate in rehearsed oral language productions or even oral reading of poetry helps to instill a sense of the sounds of the English language that can last a lifetime. Regular opportunities to memorize or at least reread and rehearse language provide valuable patterns that English language learners can rely on and build from later.

Nurturing a Learning Community

As you plan instruction to include all that is important for middle grade students to learn, consider some of the options suggested in Figure 14.5 for a weekly schedule covering the varied components of reading that need to be included. These can shift over the course of the semester; however, you need to use your time wisely, and attention to planning will always pay off. Note the allotted time for whole-group activities, small groups, and individual work and reflection.

Adolescents' Identity and Motivation

Reaching and teaching young adolescents takes special consideration. Students at this period in their lives are going through enormous changes; one day they might seem like they are adults and very much in control, and the next day the same students behave as if they are children, definitely in need of adult structure and guidance. Younger adolescents also feel tremendous pressures from their peers. They want to be accepted and part of the peer group of those they admire. Often, this drives young teens away from adults and family, and teachers have to build their trust to create open, safe classrooms where students will engage fully.

Adding to the normal developmental changes that middle level students go through, our current culture inundates students with information and options—a sort of food court mentality. Everything students do involves choice, from what kind of milk to drink to which brand of French fries they want to eat. Even the cereals they eat in the morning

Figure 14.5 Weekly Schedule

Monday	Tuesday	Wednesday	Thursday	Friday
Class focusing in whole group (10 min.) Share independent reading and viewing	Class focusing in whole group (5—10 min.) Teacher shares own reading	Class focusing in whole group (5—10 min.) Reflect on goals for week	Class focusing: teacher reads orally and thinks aloud—model use of target goal	Class focusing teacher/students share vocabulary
Teacher-guided lessons: reading and writing strategies attention to detail (30 min.+) & Small group and individual reading & writing activities: guided practice and independent work	Individual silent reading and writing (15—20 min.) & Partner/small group work (5—10 min.) Teacher conferences	Small group discussions (10—15 min.) and journal reflections Teacher observation of discussion—some participation Individual reading and writing (15 min.)	Teacher-guided lessons: focus reading or vocabulary strategies (10—15 min.) Individual work reading, writing, and research (10—15 min.)	Small group discussions (10—15 min.) journal reflections Individual work
Reflecting/ writing/planning ahead (5—10 min.)	Reflecting/ thinking ahead (5—10 min.)	Reflecting/ thinking ahead (5—10 min.)	Reflecting/ thinking ahead	Reflecting/ writing/ thinking ahead (1—10 min.)

might be their own selected favorites, chosen by no other family member. They become accustomed to having life tailored to their specific interests and preferences. This has real implications for their response to classroom activities. Choice needs to be a part of what is provided in terms of materials, groups, and learning activities. Children who are given choices outside of school expect them in school, too.

Readers' Theater exercises can be incorporated into all areas of the curriculum; this is a popular technique with young people.

Young students live in a world that is ever changing and somewhat frightening to them. They look for classrooms that are safe and that respect their needs and interests. The teacher can do a great deal to make classrooms predictable and orderly simply by having clear routines and ways of engaging that students can anticipate. For instance, when students have several teachers each day, they often get confused about what kinds of participation each considers acceptable. Explaining how you want students to behave—when they have to raise their hands, when they can interrupt each other, when they can move around the room, and how they should interact in small-group activities is helpful. Putting the rules on a chart that can be displayed regularly makes everyone feel more comfortable. In addition, the clearer you make your expectations for the work students will do and how they will be evaluated, the more likely it is that students will relax and participate actively.

The humor, compassion, and idealism of young students are also wonderful attributes of this stage. They respond well to teachers who bring in humor, give them an opportunity to laugh, and encourage their fun sides. Many middle grade students find meaning by being able to work with younger students, and some classes make it a regular practice to build buddy programs with primary classrooms so that the middle level students serve as mentors and helpers for young children.

Finally, students at this stage need to see the relevance of the activities they are asked to do. The more learning can involve real inquiry about topics of concern to them, the more likely students are to become engaged. Beane (1991) advocates that middle school students themselves determine the units that they study. Being clear about the goals and purposes of class activities and how they relate to the students is important. Establishing a safe climate where students can ask questions, engage in extended inquiry, and express their own ideas and conclusions is a foundation to their learning.

Beamon (2001) suggests that adolescents learn best when activities are interactive and purposeful and include meaningful engagement. The five circumstances that make this most likely are as follows:

1. Adolescents do something that makes sense in a larger context, such as confronting real-life issues and problems.

2. Their personal initiative and energy are moved into action through meaningful involvement with relevant and current content.

3. Their cognitive and affective capabilities are challenged, such as when connections are made between difficult content and its application to personal experience.

4. They can draw on a variety of resources in the learning environment, including personal experience, the local community, and the Internet.

5. Their knowledge and understanding are substantively broadened or deepened.

Engage Students in Twenty-First Century Web-Based Inquiry Projects

Children often come to middle grades with considerable skills in using electronic media. They are often motivated by opportunities to develop new media skills and share their

CCSS

- Informational Text 7: Variety of Media

learning using technology. The ThinkQuest Project, sponsored by Oracle Education Foundation (ThinkQuest.org), is one organization that stimulates such use of technology in addressing real problems. The ThinkQuest Project is constructed so students choose an educational topic that captivates their interest—one that can be investigated from numerous viewpoints, is interdisciplinary, and creates interest by covering multiple academic disciplines—and then create an electronic format that communicates what they learn. As groups of students work with their own questions, they engage deeply in learning about both the content and the way Web sites are set up and how they can be used to communicate meaning. Other groups develop blogs, photo essays, public service projects, and videos.

The Foundation has created an online learning platform that facilitates students' ability to create their own Web sites to share the outcomes of their learning projects. The ThinkQuest project invites teams of students working with a teacher coach to participate in a global competition for the best Web sites. There are clear guidelines for the composition of the teams (3–6 students and a teacher/coach), the selection of the topic and investigation question (12 categories are given from which to select), the process of building a Web site to share student projects and the required components, and a set of criteria that are used for evaluating the projects. Winners receive prizes and some participate in the international competition. The student Web sites are available at <http://library.ThinkQuest.org>.

As part of the Twenty-first Century Project in Orange, Massachusetts, one group of students decided to take on the challenge of creating their own Web site on global warming and ways to protect endangered species. Together with their teacher project advisors, the three girls, Emily, Colleen, and Caroline, carefully read the guidelines for the projects and spent much of their after-school hours engaging in research and in developing their Web site. During the winter, their area of Massachusetts was devastated by an ice storm that left them without electricity for most of a week. There was no heat, which led their teacher, Ms. Fredette, to challenge them with a practical problem: Could they create a portable, small heat source—Heat in a Box? They did, with the support of their parents, and added a most practical component to their project. Their Web site <http://library.ThinkQuest.org/08aug/0428> includes their Home Page, About Us, Global Warming, Climate Change, Environmental Effects, Spreading Disease, Threatened Species, and How to Help. The wealth of Web sites available on the Internet has become a valuable resource for students' learning. When students create their own Web sites, they become much more aware of the nature of these sites and how to use them effectively. They also become active contributors who share the outcomes of their own inquiries and research. See the results of this project and look at the winning Web sites for three divisions: 12 and under, 15 and under, and 19 and under. The winners' projects and reflections of both the students and their teacher coaches are available at <http://library.ThinkQuest.org/>.

Selecting Appropriate Materials

Most new teachers start out the year having to use materials that have already been selected—whether it is a reading anthology/basal series, a literature series, or a curriculum built around novels and thematic units of instruction. If there are classroom sets of novels, informational books, and magazines, these can be great resources for building a rich reading program. You want to make sure you can create a room that invites students into reading and writing. One element of immersion is creating the right environment; the visual statement of a classroom is a powerful one that all students notice. Having books and magazines is important, and ensuring that they are current and of interest is essential, as is displaying them attractively.

Assess what is available to you, and think of any holes that seem apparent. For example, check to see whether multiple levels of reading materials are available so that you can differentiate instruction for your students. Check to see whether fiction, poetry, plays, and readers' theater scripts are handy and that informational materials are in good supply. As you do your own inventory, also check with the school librarian and/or media specialist to see what resources they have for your use. And, of course, talk with the other teachers on your team or in your department so that you can be aware of all the collected materials that are available. Table 14.5 identifies some basic materials you will need to get started.

Table 14.5 Materials Checklist

- Range of core text materials at varying reading levels
- Variety of types of materials (short stories, novels, informational texts, magazines, newspapers)
- Resource materials (how our language grows and changes, language usage and vocabulary, thesaurus, dictionaries)
- Practice materials (print and electronic) including vocabulary supports
- Materials that provide contrasting points of view
- Professional materials for your use and students' use, as appropriate

Given the current attention to the CCSS, a more focused curriculum is also quite likely. You will want to assess areas in which there are ample materials for your use when you want to go in depth and do some lessons that provide attention to detail in practice materials. Some of these might be available for use on computers; make an inventory of all the resources you can locate.

Because it is important that students learn to think critically about their reading, check for ways in which you can help them read from a variety of resources on the same topic or theme. If you have an anthology to use for literature selections, locate two or three pieces that complement or contrast with the core text so you can go beyond a single selection. If you are linking to content areas such as science and social studies, provide both fiction and nonfiction materials that will deepen the units of study and help you guide students into more sophisticated reading of these materials.

A wealth of resources is available for use with middle school learners. The following Web sites provide resources and links to literature discussions in which students can participate:

- The National Council for Social Studies provides a list of Notable Social Studies Books for Young People at <www.socialstudies.org/resources/notable/>.
- The National Science Teachers Association recommends a variety of resources, including books, at <www.nsta.org/recommends/>.
- The International Reading Association provides lists of choice books compiled by teachers, young adults, and children at <www.reading.org/choices/>.
- Many local libraries have Web sites that provide links to online book clubs. Sometimes the libraries themselves sponsor book clubs. In many cases, libraries have partnered with the organization "Chapteraday," which has book clubs for teens as well as adults and covers a broad range of genres. Check out the following links to online book clubs:

    <www.chapteraday.com>
    <www.surfnetkids.com/bookclubs.htm>
    <www.planetbookclub.com>

Involving Parents and the Community

Many parents of middle school students complain that their children no longer want to share with them what happens in school. One middle school decided to create a structure that would bring students and parents together. They initiated the Generations Literature Circle as a voluntary activity and then extended it to become a full part of school life. Parents and students agreed to read the same novel and come together for a book discussion and share their responses to the book. Both groups read and made notes about favorite passages, and both groups developed questions they wanted to ask others about the book. Parents were not to ask those questions of their own children, but could offer them to the whole group. The book discussion replaced part of the parent conference night. It provided a good way for parents to understand the new forms of book discussion being used by the reading and language arts department. As they experimented with the discussions, one class had fun using the inner/outer circle idea. First the students formed the inner circle and discussed some aspects of the book under teacher facilitation. Then the parents took their turn and discussed the same issues. Both groups had a great time gaining a better understanding from the responses of the other generation.

Another exciting community reading event occurred when the mayor of Chicago declared that the whole city would read a book together. The first book that was chosen was *To Kill a Mockingbird*. Since then, a variety of important and ethnically diverse books have been chosen for the ongoing project. These books are being used in many schools as part of the regular middle school literature/social studies curriculum. As a special focus, the middle school teachers in one K–8 building decided to involve the local school council members (the community school board) in a discussion of the book for the year. During the first part of the evening, the council members sat in the inner circle and discussed their responses to the book while the eighth graders listened. Then it was the eighth graders' turn while the adults listened. What a memorable night! And what different perspectives were enabled!

For Review

Middle level students are at a great stage of development—moving from childhood to maturity. They are eager and impatient to find themselves in the world, especially among their peers. Books and good instruction can provide great models and stimulate their best impulses. We as teachers have a great deal we can do to ensure that they develop into their best selves.

This chapter began by laying out the wide variety of literacy skills and strategies students need to develop in the middle grades. Particularly important changes occur at this point in schooling as teachers involve students more heavily in reading informational materials. Students need to become independent in their ability to apply appropriate strategies as they anticipate, build knowledge, and consolidate their learning. Vocabulary development is particularly important because students encounter so many words and concepts that are new to them. In the chapter, several activities that help students develop interest in and curiosity about words and strategies to retain new words for content learning and for their own personal vocabulary enhancement were described. Examples of good references to help teachers and students learn more about the rich nature of our language were also provided.

Because students in the middle grades possess a wide range of reading abilities, the section on assessment provided many avenues through which teachers can determine what students can do and what areas need more attention. These include using informal reading inventories, leveled books, fluency measures, and assessing awareness of text features, vocabulary, interests, and strategy knowledge.

Suggestions for how teachers can help students learn strategies for studying and retaining information from reading and develop their own self-monitoring of their learning were provided. A major component of middle level instruction is expanding the types of texts students read and developing their abilities to use reading and writing to learn new content. When teachers integrate their instruction in units that extend over time, students have more substantial opportunities to think deeply and learn. The importance of students engaging in reading on a regular basis is a theme that continues throughout the chapter. Specific ways to reach all students, including English language learners, were introduced. The chapter suggested ways to organize for instruction with literature and informational texts. These include integrating content learning and reading instruction through thematic units and teaching literature by using core novels and literature groups, literature circles, and guided reading with readers' workshop.

The final section reminds teachers of the importance of organizing and managing a learning community by being sensitive to young adolescents and providing a rich array of materials that they can read with confidence and interest. Knowing students well is the beginning of good relationships and sets the foundation for meaningful instruction.

For Your Journal

1. What do you think is the optimal classroom environment in which to encourage and support middle level students?

2. After reading about different ways to organize classroom instruction, take some time to reflect on which ideas and structures you think you could use most productively. What are the reasons that you selected one over another? Have you seen other ways of organizing that you prefer?

3. Return to the questions in the Anticipation Guide and think about what you can add to your original thoughts. How have your ideas been expanded or altered?

Taking It to the World

1. A pair of eighth-grade teachers added a new dimension to the study of the Bill of Rights by having their students conduct a mock court trial. The issue: A student is accused of humming during the national anthem, a violation of a rule. The teacher faces a loss of job and pension. During a month-long study of the issues, students assembled arguments and witnesses and then argued the case. Because one teacher's spouse is a lawyer, the students did get some assistance in determining exactly how they should argue both sides of the case. Class members served as lawyers, jury, clerks, and witnesses. The students got so involved in their research and legal work that the local newspaper heard about the trial and photographed the final session.

2. Look carefully at the U.S. Constitution's Bill of Rights. Brainstorm with a friend ways you could make a thematic study of the rights practical for your students. What issues in the community could be highlighted?

New Literacies Connections

1. Middle level students love to share their ideas and find out what their peers think. Now it is possible for students to extend these discussions worldwide with some of the good sites that have been established for international book discussions. Search for some of the sites that help students to connect with their peers in other countries.

2. Go to the U.S. Department of Education Web site, Doing What Works <http://dww.ed.gov>. The section on adolescent literacy has a whole set of resources for meeting the needs of readers needing intensive support. View some of the classroom clips and look at the ways teachers are reaching a wide range of students in middle schools across the country.

MyEducationLab™

Go to Topics 5, 7, and 8 (Comprehension, Reading and Writing in the Content Areas, and Assessment) in the MyEducationLab <www.myeducationlab.com> for your course, where you can:

- Find learning outcomes for Comprehension, Reading and Writing in the Content Areas, and Assessment along with the national standards that connect to these outcomes.

- Complete Assignments and Activities that can help you more deeply understand the chapter content.

- Apply and practice your understanding of the core teaching skills identified in the chapter with the Building Teaching Skills and Dispositions learning units.

- Check your comprehension on the content covered in the chapter by going to the Study Plan in the Book Resources for your text. Here you will be able to take a chapter quiz, receive feedback on your answers, and then access Review, Practice, and Enrichment activities to enhance your understanding of chapter content.

- Visit A+RISE. A+RISE® Standards2Strategy™ is an innovative and interactive online resource that offers new teachers in grades K-12 just in time, research-based instructional strategies that meet the linguistic needs of ELLs as they learn content, differentiate instruction for all grades and abilities, and are aligned to Common Core Elementary Language Arts standards English language proficiency standards in WIDA, Texas, California, and Florida.

Models and Strategies for Teaching ESL and for Teaching Reading in the Mother Tongue

Models and Strategies for Teaching ESL and for Teaching Reading in the Mother Tongue

Options for Teaching the English Language Learner
p. 479

The English Language in the Bilingual Education Program
p. 485

Options for Teaching the English Language Learner to Read
p. 495

Mother Tongue Support in the Bilingual Classroom
p. 508

Anticipation Guide

The following statements will help you begin thinking about the topics of this chapter. Answer *true* or *false* in response to each statement. As you read and learn more about the topics in these statements, double-check your answers. See what interests you and what prompts your curiosity toward more understanding.

____ **1.** English language learners can learn English in one year.

____ **2.** It is a waste of instructional time to teach a child to read in the child's mother tongue.

____ **3.** Phonics is the most important component of reading for an English language learner.

____ **4.** Children should always be grouped by level of English proficiency for English as a second language (ESL) lessons.

____ **5.** Children who first learn to read in Spanish or another language have to start over when they learn to read in English.

____ **6.** The teacher should always immediately correct the grammatical errors of English language learners.

____ **7.** Children who have learned to read in their mother tongue have little difficulty learning to read in English.

____ **8.** English language learners should always respond in complete sentences.

____ **9.** Some adolescent English language learners are not able to read in any language.

____ **10.** Students are not learning English if they are not speaking.

____ **11.** Children cannot learn to understand and speak English unless they learn the grammar first.

A Bilingual Teacher in a Bilingual Classroom

Ms. Ortega is a certified bilingual first-grade teacher. Her 23 students speak Spanish as their first language, and their English proficiency ranges from several who have no English at all to a few children who are at a low-to-intermediate level. Her children are ready to learn to read in Spanish, and she is well prepared to teach them. The Spanish reading program she uses is parallel to the English language program used in other classrooms in her school, but it is not a direct translation. She also has a wealth of children's literature in Spanish.

Ms. Ortega begins her morning business in English. "Good morning, boys and girls." "Good morning, teacher," they respond, politely and respectfully addressing her by her title. After several weeks of school, the children can greet their teacher, respond to the roll and lunch count, and understand most classroom routines in English. Morning business is followed by a 40-minute ESL lesson that is characterized by simple dramatized commands, questions, many gestures and smiles, and much laughter.

After recess, the children have whole-class shared reading activities in Spanish with big books. In smaller groups, they dictate language-experience chart stories in Spanish, read them, put the sentences in order, illustrate them, read to each other, and play word games with vocabulary they have used. Independently and in pairs, they will take turns "reading" big books to each other and reading language-experience stories to family members at home.

Some of the children are beginning to associate sounds with letters they recognize, and Ms. Ortega has begun to teach brief focused phonics lessons related to elements that have emerged from their language-experience charts and for which they have demonstrated phonemic awareness in language play activities. They also work in the more structured Spanish reading program with anthologies of stories and some expository text. The program includes more systematic and explicit activities designed to introduce the relationships between sounds and letters in Spanish several weeks into the school year and after they have developed a basic sight vocabulary.

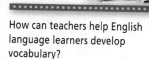

Writing and Reading Connections

How can teachers help English language learners develop vocabulary?

The children in Ms. Ortega's classroom are indeed fortunate. They are in a full bilingual program with a highly qualified teacher who has appropriate instructional materials. She addresses them in English in the parts of her program where they are ready to understand. She consistently devotes 30 to 40 minutes of instructional time each day to ESL, focusing on listening with nonverbal or simple responses at the beginning, with more emphasis on production later.

Her Spanish reading program is analytic or whole-part-whole, with children learning about letter/sound correspondences in the context of words they already recognize. The plentiful authentic literature in her classroom provides for a strong focus on comprehension and motivation.

The vignette also displays how Ms. Ortega presents the elements of the four blocks framework described in Chapter 1: guided reading and writing, self-selected reading, and working with words (Cunningham, Hall, & Sigmon, 2007). She demonstrates reading to her students in the shared reading activities with big books. She works with words in the brief focused phonics lessons that emerge from meaningful reading and writing activities. She provides guided practice both in the shared reading of big books and in the dictation and reading back of dictated language-experience charts. The children extend their reading practice in reading shared books to each other and language-experience charts to family members. They will soon begin to write in Spanish as an outgrowth of their LEA activities.

The purpose of this chapter is to examine the teaching of reading in the mother tongue and also the teaching of ESL as it relates to the teaching of reading and writing. The audience for the chapter is threefold: bilingual teachers who will teach reading and writing in a language other than English, teachers of English language learners whose mother tongue instruction will be conducted by a paraprofessional or other staff members under the teacher's supervision, and all teachers of English language learners who teach ESL.

Options for Teaching the English Language Learner

There are two basic categories of instructional programs for teaching English language learners. These categories are presented in terms of the generic K–8 school program for them; the specific questions of second language and reading instruction are treated later in the chapter.

Teach Them in English

English-only options for teaching English language learners exist in several forms and for many reasons. In some cases, the numbers of children who have a non-English language in common at a grade level are small, and it is not feasible to offer a program of mother tongue instruction. A lack of trained teachers and mother tongue instructional materials may exacerbate this situation. Political considerations constitute another reason for providing only English language instruction, such as in California and Arizona, where statewide ballot propositions largely discourage or make difficult the use of mother tongue instruction and mandate the use of what is characterized as structured immersion in English. But there are many limitations in teaching English language learners only in English, as you will see.

IMMERSION INSTRUCTION   One approach to second-language acquisition is *immersion*, sometimes called *structured immersion* (see Figure 15.1). Immersion instructional programs are focused on intensive English instruction during the first year, although it is well documented that children need more than one year to master enough English to learn academic subjects and reading in English (Thomas & Collier, 1997).

ESL instruction is the most important element in an immersion approach to teaching English language learners. Their academic instruction in reading, mathematics, science, and social science is also conducted in English, although English language learners gain little from this instruction. They do not understand or speak English, nor can they read in English at a sufficient level of comprehension. In some cases, support in the mother tongue is provided by a paraprofessional or parent volunteer. For example, that adult might sit down with the English language learners to assist them in understanding a lesson the teacher taught earlier in English and in completing independent work.

What is often called a *submersion* approach is a variation on structured immersion, and it is truly a sink-or-swim approach. Although most educators do not advocate its use, the submersion approach is often observed as the default methodology in working with English language learners. Non–English-speaking children are simply thrown to the mercies of a teacher, classmates, and instructional materials in English, with no concessions to their language or cultural needs. This sometimes occurs for political reasons. But many times it is simply a reflection of the school's inability to respond to the needs of a small number of non–English-speaking children who have a less common mother tongue.

Lambert (1975) contrasted additive and subtractive education programs for second-language learners. In an *additive program*, children add a new language and its accompanying culture to their mother tongue and culture, along with a positive self-image. Stritikus (2006) concluded that additive programs view linguistic and cultural diversity as an asset to be valued.

The Common Core Standards in English Language Arts that have been referred to throughout this book also apply to English Language Learners. The groups responsible for the standards, the National Governors Association Center for Best Practices and the Council of Chief State School Officers, write:

> "[We] strongly believe that all students should be held to the same high expectations outlined in the Common Core State Standards. This includes students who are English language learners (ELLs). However, these students may require additional time, appropriate instructional support, and aligned assessments as they acquire both English language proficiency and content area knowledge."

—© Copyright 2010. National Governors Association Center for Best Practices and Council of Chief State School Officers. All rights reserved <http://www.corestandards.org/assets/application-for-english-learners.pdf>

Figure 15.1 Model Program Structures for Meeting the Needs of English Language Learners.

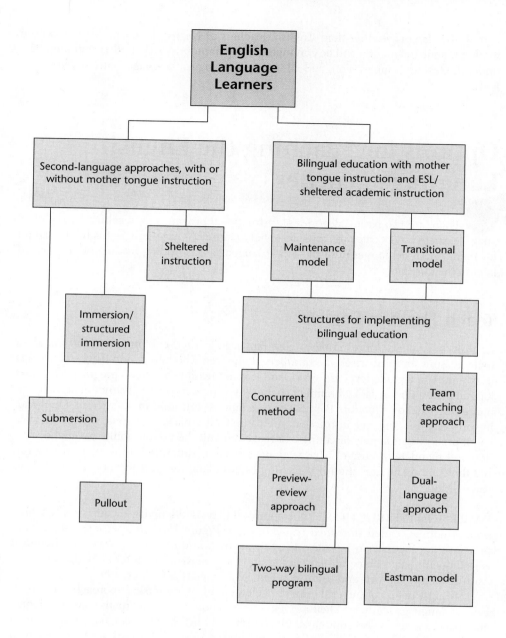

In a *subtractive program*, English and its accompanying culture are substituted for the mother tongue and culture, often leading to low self-esteem, low academic achievement, increased dropout rates, and other negative consequences. Immersion programs are of the subtractive type.

Several major principles guide teachers' understanding of how to provide the best context for learning in general and for learning in a second language. Cummins (1986, 1989) describes two levels of language proficiency that demonstrate the need for high-level proficiency in the second language before academic instruction is provided in the second language. He describes *basic interpersonal communications skills* (BICS) as those that permit English language learners to carry on a simple conversation in the new second language, and they appear to be proficient. But a higher level of language proficiency, *cognitive academic language proficiency* (CALP), is required for the student to learn to read in the second language or, for example, to learn the commutative principle of addition in mathematics. Cummins concludes that a threshold of language proficiency in the mother tongue must be reached for the student to attain academic proficiency in the mother tongue and later in a second language. This threshold is seldom met in programs of immersion in English.

STRUCTURES FOR PROVIDING ESL INSTRUCTION   The most common pattern for providing English language instruction is that in which the teacher in the self-contained classroom provides all instruction, including ESL. Another common pattern is the pullout program. ESL teachers have their own classrooms, and for periods of 40 to 60 minutes, they pull children out of their self-contained classrooms for ESL instruction and then send them back. In semidepartmentalized and departmentalized intermediate or junior high schools, usually at the fifth- or sixth-grade level and above, one teacher might have responsibility for teaching ESL to all English language learners.

Unfortunately, not every teacher is well prepared—or perhaps prepared at all—to teach ESL. An advantage of a pullout program is that a specialist can be very effective in providing this important instruction and will usually have high-quality materials for this purpose.

The pullout approach also has several disadvantages. Children miss instruction in the regular classroom, depending on the hour during which they are absent. English language learners are singled out as "special" or "different" when they leave for ESL instruction, which often has negative consequences. Pullout programs are usually organized according to homogeneous groups in that the ESL teacher will pull beginners from several classrooms for a period of instruction, then intermediate learners from several classrooms, and so on. Even in the self-contained classroom, the teacher should consider teaching the English language learners as a single group, regardless of their proficiency. As you will see later in this chapter, there are advantages to having children at several levels of English language proficiency during ESL/language development lessons, including capable English speakers.

SHELTERED ENGLISH INSTRUCTION, SDAIE, AND SIOP®   *Sheltered English instruction* is a very powerful approach for working with English language learners, but it is an intermediate approach. It is designed to follow an initial second-language acquisition program that takes students from non–English speaker status to that of intermediate speaker of English.

In California, sheltered instruction is sometimes called Specially Designed Academic Instruction in English (SDAIE) (CATESOL, 1992). A more recent model of sheltered instruction is called the Sheltered Instruction Observation Protocol (SIOP®) (Echevarria, Vogt, & Short, 2013).

Sheltered instruction is therefore an important second-language component of all education programs for English language learners, whether they have been in bilingual education or in an English immersion program. It constitutes, however, a submersion approach when used, or misused, with beginning speakers of English. We examine sheltered English instruction later in this chapter.

 Dr. MaryEllen Vogt describes sheltered English instruction and the SIOP model in this video. What advantages and disadvantages of both approaches have you learned?

Teach Them in the Language They Already Speak

The *Lau v. Nichols* decision (see Chapter 2) did not mandate bilingual education as a remedy, but school districts soon found that it was one of the few ways to ensure that English language learners had equal access to education, that is, education in their mother tongue while they learned English. In most bilingual education programs, children learn to read and write, and also to study the other subjects of the academic curriculum—mathematics, social science, and science—in their mother tongue. Simultaneously, they learn English as a second language, a process that typically takes two to five years or more (Thomas & Collier, 1997). As the result of a transition process called *positive transfer of skills*, children can then do in English what they have learned to do in their mother tongue (August et al., 2006; Baker & Sienkewicz, 2000; Cummins, 1981). The knowledge that English language learners have in their mother tongue, they will also have in English. Furthermore, once a child is able to read in his or her mother tongue, learning to read in English as a second language is a relatively smooth and effortless process—the child learns to read only once. When children do not have the opportunity to learn academic subjects in their mother tongue, they obviously fall behind in those subjects during the period of time they are learning English.

The underlying principles of bilingual education are as follows:

- Teach English language learners to understand and speak English as a second language.
- Teach the academic subjects, including reading and writing, in the mother tongue while the children are in the process of learning to understand and speak English.
- Transition the children from mother tongue academic instruction to English language instruction in a sheltered mode when they have attained an intermediate level of English.

Because of the lack of instructional materials and a shortage of trained bilingual teachers in many languages, non–Spanish-language bilingual education programs are less common and usually are limited in scope.

In *Preventing Reading Difficulties in Young Children*, Snow, Burns, and Griffin (1998) endorsed the efficacy of teaching children to read in the mother tongue wherever possible before teaching them to read in English. A major five-year developmental study conducted by Thomas and Collier (2002) provides additional evidence to support this point of view. Although many mother tongues were represented in their study of over 210,000 students in five school districts in Texas, Oregon, and Maine, most of the students were Spanish speaking. Thomas and Collier found that one-way or dual-language bilingual enrichment programs that were 90:10 or 50:50 (the ratio of mother tongue instruction to English instruction) were the only programs in which students reached the fiftieth percentile in both languages and in which there were the fewest dropouts. Children whose parents refused bilingual education programs, because they insisted on English-only instruction, had much lower achievement. The strongest predictor of English language achievement in the study was the amount of formal mother tongue instruction. Thomas and Collier found that the highest achievement in bilingual education programs was associated with those that offered a natural learning environment in school, with rich oral and written language in both the mother tongue and English, problem solving, group student activities, media-rich learning, challenging thematic units, and use of the students' bilingual and bicultural knowledge to access new knowledge.

In a major meta-analysis of studies about the language and literacy development of language-minority students, The National Literacy Panel on Language-Minority Children and Youth published a report in 2006. Their conclusions paralleled those of the National Reading Panel (2000). First, they concluded that phonemic awareness, phonics, fluency, vocabulary, and text comprehension instruction were major factors in the development of literacy. They did, however, recommend that more focus be placed on working with particular phonemes that do not exist in their mother tongues.

Second, they found that although language-minority children were able to keep pace with their English-speaking classmates in the development of word recognition skills, they fell behind in comprehension and writing. They attributed this to the lower level of English language proficiency among these students.

Third, they concluded that children's oral proficiency and reading ability in their mother tongue can be used to facilitate the development of literacy in English as a result of the positive transfer of skills, a finding similar to that of Snow et al. in *Preventing* Reading Difficulties (1998) cited earlier.

Fourth, they concluded that there is a hierarchy of skills in English that must be attained before children can be successful in reading comprehension in English, and that individual differences among children are a significant factor in this development. They further concluded that for language-minority children in special education programs, developing sight word reading and holistic learning strategies might be more effective in teaching them to read and write.

Fifth, they concluded that most assessment tools used with language-minority children are not effective in measuring their individual strengths and weaknesses. They also found little evidence of the effect of sociocultural variables on the development of literacy, except for the positive effect of home language experiences.

TRANSITIONAL VERSUS MAINTENANCE MODELS OF BILINGUAL EDUCATION

There are two underlying philosophies about how to conduct programs of bilingual education: transitional and maintenance. In the more common *transitional model*, children learn English as a second language. They learn their academic subjects, including reading and writing, in their mother tongue, and they make the transition to English language academic instruction in a sheltered mode when they have reached an intermediate level of English, usually between the late second grade and early fourth grade. The major goal of the transitional program is to produce a monolingual, monoliterate, and monocultural child who temporarily uses his or her mother tongue as a vehicle for learning. Children in transitional bilingual programs usually continue their academic studies only in English after the onset of transition to English, although they sometimes receive continuing support in their mother tongue from a paraprofessional, as needed.

In the *maintenance model*, the process is the same up to the point of transition. After the children begin academic instruction in English, they continue to receive periodic lessons in their mother tongue in all subject areas. The major outcome of the maintenance program is a bilingual, biliterate, and bicultural child who is able to function easily and comfortably in two languages and cultures.

STRUCTURES FOR ORGANIZING PROGRAMS OF BILINGUAL EDUCATION

Within the transitional and maintenance models, there are several structures for grouping children and for assigning teachers and paraprofessionals that can be used in either model.

Concurrent Method   One approach that is often used intuitively is called the *concurrent method*. The teacher says everything twice, once in the children's mother tongue, perhaps Hmong, and once in English, assuming there is only one non-English language in the classroom and the teacher is bilingual. When the teacher is not bilingual, a bilingual paraprofessional may fill that second role, basically serving as an interpreter. It is a time-efficient approach with an uncomplicated structure. It is also very ineffective. English language learners begin to tune out the English, which they cannot understand well or perhaps at all, and they listen only to their mother tongue. If they do learn some English as a part of the process, they learn it in terms of their mother tongue. The outcome is a compound bilingual child with two interdependent language systems. The result is a lifetime of unconscious translation from one language to another, a process that takes precious time, especially on examinations such as the SAT, the GRE, or the important high-stakes tests that are now required in almost all states. This approach also promotes *code switching*, the unconscious mixing of vocabulary and syntactical structures from two languages.

Team Teaching   The team-teaching approach is quite different. Two teachers, one bilingual, the other usually not, work together in the same classroom. They work independently, but when they teach, each teaches the entire class. The primary advantages of this approach are to provide outstanding language and cultural models to the children and to reduce the number of proficient bilingual teachers needed.

Dual Language   The dual-language model resembles the team-teaching model in that there are two teachers, one bilingual, the other usually not, but in separate classrooms. The monolingual English-speaking teacher teaches English as a second language and academic instruction in English for those in the two classrooms who are ready for it. The bilingual teacher teaches the academic subjects to the English language learners in the mother tongue and also teaches the other language as a second language.

The advantages of the dual-language model are that both teachers are working in a language of comfort to them and the children are learning English and their academic subjects from teachers who are good models. Unlike the concurrent method, they are not learning English in terms of their mother tongue, but rather are developing as coordinate bilinguals with two independent language systems. The major disadvantage is that the English-speaking and non–English-speaking children are rarely working together because their needs are very different. It is important for English language learners to associate with English speakers because they learn English from those children as well as from their teacher. They can avoid the fossilization or stopping-in-place that can occur when children are separated from native and capable English-speaking peers. It is also important for groups of children from different languages and cultures to associate with each other to avoid ethnic, linguistic, and cultural isolation.

Preview-Review Mode   The preview-review model is very complex, but it resolves some of the shortcomings of the other models. Two teachers work together as in the team-teaching and dual-language models: one bilingual, the other usually not. One teacher provides a preview of the lesson to the entire group in one language, and the other teacher then teaches the main body of the lesson to the entire group in the other language. Each teacher then reviews the main lesson with his or her language group after the main body of the lesson. The order of use of the languages is reversed in that subject area the next day. The children in whose language the main body of the lesson is not to be presented listen to a preview in their mother tongue. They also review the lesson in their mother tongue after the lesson is presented in their second language.

For example, two teachers, one bilingual and the other monolingual, teach a mathematics lesson. The bilingual teacher might conduct a 10-minute preview of the lesson in Korean for all children. The monolingual teacher would then teach the core of the lesson to all of the children in English, probably for 30 to 40 minutes. Both teachers would then review the lesson in English and Korean, respectively, with children dominant in those languages for about 10 to 15 minutes. They would reverse the order the next day. The children always have the best possible model of both languages, and they are mixed for part of the lesson. The model also reduces the number of scarce bilingual teachers needed.

Eastman Model   The Eastman model (Krashen & Biber, 1988) of the Los Angeles Unified School District also effectively alleviates the problem of isolating students from each other at the elementary level. Spanish-speaking students are organized for mother tongue instruction in reading, the language arts, and academic areas of the curriculum during the morning, along with a program of ESL. English-speaking students are similarly organized for reading and academic instruction in English in the morning. In the afternoon, Spanish-speaking students are mainstreamed with English-speaking students in art, music, and physical education, which are conducted in English. As Spanish-speaking students gain English proficiency after two or three years, they begin to receive sheltered academic instruction in English in the more concrete areas of the curriculum, such as mathematics and science. Social studies in English is introduced later.

Two-Way Bilingual Education   The two-way bilingual education program has a different goal from mainstream bilingual education. It is used where two language groups of parents want their children to learn—and learn in—another language. Usually, one group of children will be native Spanish speakers learning English as a second language and academic subjects in Spanish. But another group of English-speaking students is in the classroom because their parents want them to learn Arabic and learn in Arabic. The program goal is additive in that each group learns the language and culture of the other group. The Eastman model is an effective organizational structure for conducting a two-way bilingual education program.

The English Language in the Bilingual Education Program

Teaching ESL is the underlying base of programs established to meet the academic needs of English language learners. It is the major element of the full bilingual education programs in which the mother tongue is used for academic instruction while children develop sufficient proficiency in English to benefit from academic instruction in English.

Second-Language Acquisition

Regardless of whether children learn to read and write in their mother tongue, they clearly must learn to speak and understand English. In fact, it is not possible to address literacy for English language learners without considering the close links that must exist between the teaching of reading and writing and the teaching of ESL. Those links are rooted in the constructivist or whole-part-whole approaches that underlie effective practice in both.

At this point, we examine the contrast between constructivist and reductionist models of instruction. A *constructivist* view of instruction focuses on the construction of meaning, using what the child already knows and combining it with new knowledge, concepts, and skills to be integrated. It is learner centered and highly contextualized; these are important factors in working with students from diverse backgrounds, who are often at risk of failure. The factor of background knowledge is well recognized as being a key to success in reading and writing, especially in reading comprehension. English language learners have no lack of background knowledge, but there is often a discontinuity between the background knowledge they have and the knowledge assumed by the texts they will use in learning to read and reading to learn. Within the constructivist view, language acquisition is embedded in function. Skills are taught in a meaningful context, not in a rigid, artificial, isolated, and fragmented way. There are several approaches to second-language instruction that reflect the constructivist view; they are in the communicative category.

The foundation for communicative approaches to second-language acquisition is based on concepts, theories, and hypotheses that have converged around the interaction of constructivist notions about making meaning, including Vygotsky's (1978) zone of proximal development. Conversely, *reductionist* models, or skills-based models, focus on the disassembly or fragmentation of curricular elements so that isolated skills and concepts can be mastered within a linear paradigm. Traditionally, most students have studied a second language, whether English or a foreign language, using such grammar-based approaches as the grammar-translation and audiolingual methods. These are reductionist or skills-based approaches that move learners from part to whole.

COMMUNICATIVE-BASED APPROACHES   The results of research have changed educators' conceptions of how a second language is acquired and how this acquisition is best promoted in the elementary and secondary classroom. There has been a major paradigm shift away from these grammar-based approaches to language learning and toward those called *communicative*, which are also consistent with meaning-based or constructivist approaches to literacy (Crawford, 1994a; Crawford, 2003).

Several important hypotheses underlie current practice in most communicative approaches to second-language acquisition (Krashen, 1982). In his input hypothesis, Krashen concludes that growth in language occurs when learners receive comprehensible input, or input that contains vocabulary and structure at a slightly higher level than what they already understand. The input hypothesis reflects Vygotsky's zone of proximal development. The context of the input provides clues to maintain the integrity of the message. According to the input hypothesis, a grammatical sequence is not needed. The vocabulary and structures are provided and practiced as a natural part of the comprehensible input that the child receives, much as the process occurs with infants acquiring their mother tongue. Krashen (1981) relates the input hypothesis to the silent period, the interval before speech in either the mother tongue or second language in which the child listens to and develops an understanding of the language before beginning to produce language.

Krashen's (1991) updated input hypothesis includes what he calls "comprehensible input plus 1" or "CI + 1." It is an "aspect of language the acquirer has not yet acquired but that he or she is ready to acquire" (p. 409). The CI + 1 is a new element to be learned in what the teacher has already made comprehensible. It is contextualized, not isolated, and it may include academic language or other new elements, such as a new language structure. In his acquisition-learning hypothesis, Krashen highlights the difference between the infant's subconscious acquisition of the mother tongue and the conscious learning of a second language of the secondary student of French. Students acquire language subconsciously, with a feel for correctness. Learning a language, by contrast, is a conscious process that involves knowing grammatical rules. The infant, of course, is almost always successful in acquiring communicative competence, whereas the secondary school foreign language learner is usually not (Crawford, 1994a; Crawford, 2003).

Gee (1992) elaborates Krashen's concept of acquisition to add a social factor reflecting Vygotsky's "zone of proximal development" and also the concept of approximation.

> *Acquisition is a process of acquiring something subconsciously by exposure to models, a process of trial and error, and practice within social groups, without formal teaching. It happens in natural settings that are meaningful and functional in the sense that acquirers know that they need to acquire the thing they are exposed to in order to function and that they in fact want to so function.* (p. 113)

According to Krashen's (1982) natural order hypothesis, grammatical structures are acquired in a predictable sequence, with certain elements usually acquired before others. He concludes that the orders for first- and second-language acquisition are similar but not identical. He does not, however, conclude that sequencing the teaching of language according to this natural order or any grammatical sequence is either necessary or desirable.

Krashen's (1982) related *monitor hypothesis* describes how the child's conscious monitor or editor serves to make corrections as language is produced in speaking or writing. Several conditions are necessary for the application of the monitor:

- Time to apply it, a situation that is not present in most ordinary oral discourse, especially in classroom settings
- A focus on the form or correctness of what is said, rather than on the content of the message
- Knowledge of the grammatical rule to be applied

These conditions serve to illustrate why so few children or adults learn to understand and speak a foreign language in a grammar-translation or audiolingual foreign language course in the secondary school or university.

In his affective filter hypothesis, Krashen (1982) concludes that several affective variables are associated with success in second-language acquisition. These include high motivation, self-confidence and a positive self-image, and, most important, low anxiety in the learning environment. It is therefore important that teachers avoid high-pressure instruction and especially humiliation of students who are acquiring English.

OTHER BASIC PRINCIPLES   Results from research have led to other major changes in educators' conceptions of how a second language is acquired and how this acquisition is best facilitated in the classroom, one of which is the obvious similarity between primary- and second-language acquisition. In both, primary- and second-language learners form an incomplete and incorrect interlanguage (Selinker, Swain, & Dumas, 1975), with most children moving through similar stages of development in this incomplete language.

The role of correction is also similar in both primary- and second-language acquisition. *Approximation* is a related process in which children imitate more proficient English speakers in all of the dimensions of language, oral and written, and test hypotheses about it. Approximation underlies oral and written language in that children are acquiring new understandings and skills within the context of authentic wholes. Children demonstrate behaviors in which they approximate the language behavior of their English models, growing closer and closer to their levels of proficiency. In his view of successive approximation, Holdaway (1979) describes the process as one in which Vygotsky's adults and more capable peers, that is, teachers and proficient English-speaking students, use information in the output from children's responses to construct, adjust, and finally eliminate the scaffolding that facilitates progress in learning.

Terrell (1982) and Krashen and Terrell (1983) conclude that correction should be viewed as a negative reinforcer that will raise the affective filter and the level of anxiety among English language learners. When errors do not interfere with comprehension, correcting them has no more place in the ESL program than it does when infants acquire their mother tongue. Caregivers might expand incorrect or incomplete forms, such as "me go" or "Kitty gots four feets," and say "Yes, you go" or "Yes, Kitty has four feet." There is little evidence, however, that this expansion has any positive effect. Errors are signs of immaturity, not incorrectness; they will disappear naturally as a part of approximation in the developmental process of language acquisition (Crawford, 1994a; Crawford, 2003).

These similarities between primary- and second-language acquisition are not consistent with either the grammar-translation or audiolingual approach. Children learning their first language do not rely on grammatical rules or on systematic acquisition of vocabulary. With its emphasis on early production instead of a silent period, on correct production instead of an acceptable though immature and incomplete interlanguage, and on grammatical sequence instead of function and communicative competence, the audiolingual approach bears little resemblance to the way primary or second languages are successfully acquired.

Finally, age is an important factor in second-language acquisition. Collier (1987) examined the relationship between the age of English language learners and their acquisition of a second language. She found that those who entered the second-language acquisition program at ages eight to eleven were the fastest achievers. Those who entered the program at ages five to seven were the lowest achievers, and they were one to three years behind children from eight to eleven years of age. Children who entered at twelve to fifteen years of age had the most difficulty acquiring the second language. She projected that they would need from six to eight years of classroom instruction to reach age-level norms in academic achievement.

Collier (1989) later analyzed other research on age and academic achievement in the second language and found that children who had academic instruction in the mother tongue generally required from four to seven years to reach national norms on standardized tests in reading, social studies, and science and as little as two years in mathematics and language arts, including spelling, punctuation, and grammar. She also found that children from ages eight to twelve who had at least two years of schooling in their mother tongue in their home country needed from five to seven years to reach the same levels of achievement in second-language reading, social studies, and science and two years in mathematics and language arts. Young children with no schooling in their mother tongue in either the home country or the new host country needed seven to ten years of instruction in reading, social studies, and science. Adolescent children with no ESL instruction and no opportunity for continued academic work in their mother tongue were projected, for the most part, to drop out of school before reaching national norms, regardless of whether they had a good academic background or interrupted schooling.

Instructional Strategies for Second-Language Acquisition

The implications of Krashen's hypotheses and of related similarities between first- and second-language acquisition are that approaches to second-language acquisition should do the following:

- Provide comprehensible input
- Focus on relevant and interesting topics instead of grammatical sequences
- Provide for a silent period without forcing early production
- Avoid correction
- Maintain a low level of anxiety

There are approaches to second-language acquisition that meet these criteria. The communicative approaches most appropriate for elementary and secondary classrooms are the total physical response method and the natural approach.

THE TOTAL PHYSICAL RESPONSE METHOD   Asher's (1982) total physical response (TPR) method is an important communicative approach in the initial stages of second-language acquisition. The TPR method provides for comprehensible input, a silent period, and a focus on relevant content rather than on grammatical form. The focus of TPR is on physical responses to verbal commands such as "Stand up" and "Put your book on the desk." Because little emphasis is put on production, the level of anxiety is low.

Lessons can be given to small groups or an entire class. In the beginning, the teacher models one-word commands. This is done first with a few children to introduce new vocabulary and structures, then with the entire group, then with small groups of children, and finally with individual children. For example, the teacher says, "Sit," and then models by sitting down. Later, the teacher issues the command without modeling. As the children's levels of language increase, the teacher begins to use two- and three-word commands, such as "Stand up" and "Bring the book."

The children demonstrate their understanding by physically carrying out the commands. The order of commands is varied so that the children cannot anticipate which is next. Old commands are combined with new ones to provide for review. Whenever the children do not appear to comprehend, the teacher returns to modeling. After a silent period of approximately 10 hours of listening to commands and physically responding to them, a child then typically reverses roles with the teacher and begins to give those same commands to other children. It is important for the teacher to maintain a playful mood during classroom activities.

Using physical responses as a strategy of instruction in the bilingual classroom can help to reduce the anxiety ESL students might feel about the need to "perform."

The TPR approach can be extended to higher levels of proficiency by using the technique of nesting commands. The teacher might say the following:

> Jamal, take the book to Svetlana, or close the door.
> Noriko, if Jamal took the book to Svetlana, raise your hand.
> If he closed the door, stand up.

A high level of understanding is necessary to carry out such commands, but no oral production is needed. Parents of young children will recognize that their infants can understand and carry out such commands long before they begin to speak themselves.

THE NATURAL APPROACH   Terrell's (1977) original concept of the natural approach provided for three major characteristics:

- Classroom activities were focused on acquisition, that is, communication with a content focus leading to an unconscious absorption of language and a feel for correctness, but not an explicit knowledge of grammar.
- Oral errors were not directly corrected.
- Learners could respond in the target language, their mother tongue, or a mixture of the two.

Krashen and Terrell (1983) later added four principles that underlie the natural approach to language acquisition:

1. Comprehension precedes production, which leads to several teacher behaviors: teacher use of the target language, a focus on a topic of interest to the children, and maintenance of the children's comprehension.

2. Production emerges in stages ranging from nonverbal responses to complex discourse, with children able to speak when they are ready and speech errors not corrected unless they interfere with communication.

3. The curriculum consists of communicative goals, with topics of interest comprising the syllabus, not a grammatical sequence.

4. Activities must result in a low level of anxiety, a lowering of the children's affective filter, which the teacher accomplishes by establishing and maintaining a good rapport.

Terrell's (1981) natural approach is based on three stages of language development: preproduction (comprehension), early production, and emergence of speech.

Ms. Ortega, the teacher in the bilingual classroom in the chapter-opening vignette, uses the natural approach. The curriculum of her ESL program is made up of themes that are supported by large-format posters and charts, big books, and concrete objects in the classroom. She also uses the four blocks approach to organizing her reading program that is described in Chapter 13 (Cunningham et al., 2007), but her program is a five blocks approach. She has added ESL as an important fifth reading/language arts area of the curriculum.

The Preproduction Stage   In the preproduction stage, topical, interesting, and relevant comprehensible input is provided by the teacher in a close parallel with Asher's TPR approach. The teacher speaks slowly, maintaining comprehension with gestures. Children may respond with physical behaviors, shaking or nodding their heads, pointing at pictures or objects, and saying yes or no. It is important that input is dynamic, lively, fun, and comprehensible. Crawford (1994a) provides an example in which the teacher uses a pet turtle and says,

This is a turtle. It is four years old. Is it green? Who wants to hold it? [Hand to child.] Who has the turtle? Does Tran have the turtle? Yes, he does. Does Rosa have the turtle? No, she doesn't.

This basic input can be repeated with other objects in the classroom, such as large-format posters and illustrations (Crawford, 1994a). Crawford suggests that each child in the group be given a different illustration, and the teacher provides input:

Who has a picture of an airplane? Yes, Olaf, you do. Is the airplane large? Olaf, give your picture to Zipour. Who has a picture of a boat? Yes, Nicole has a picture of a boat.

These examples include three primary preproduction techniques of using TPR strategies, TPR strategies accompanied by naming objects, and pictures.

The required responses include movement, pointing, nodding or shaking the head, and using the names of other children in the group. Remember that nodding the head for an affirmative response and shaking it for a negative one are not appropriate in all cultures; it is the converse in Albania, for example. Children might also have to learn these nonverbal behaviors. Because the emphasis at this stage is on listening comprehension, verbal responses in the mother tongue are also acceptable. This might be a problem if the teacher cannot understand the children's mother tongue, but children usually find a way to help the teacher understand.

Classroom props allow for relevant expansion of this and subsequent stages of the natural approach (Crawford, 1994a; 2003). Any manipulative or concrete object is helpful, including flannel boards and puppets. Large colorful illustrations, such as those in big books, are also very helpful. Sources of free color illustrations include calendars (outdated or otherwise), travel posters, large posters available from textbook and trade book publishers, and colorful illustrations in the annual reports of many large corporations, which are often available on request through announcements in major business magazines.

The Early Production Stage   In the stage of early production, the child begins to produce one-word utterances, lists, and finally two-word answers, such as "big dog" and "in house." Some of the latter, such as "me want" and "no like," are grammatically incorrect or incomplete. According to Crawford (2003), teachers should view these responses as immature, not incorrect. In the presence of good models, these errors will disappear in time, just as they do among infants developing their mother tongue at home.

Several types of questions can be used to elicit one- and two-word responses that are within the reach of children as they move into the early production stage:

Question Format	Illustrative Question
Yes/no	Do you like hamburgers?
Here/there	Where is the picture of the cat?
Either/or	Is this a pen or a key?
One word	How many dogs are there?
Two word	What fruits are in the picture?

As in the preproduction stage, these strategies should be integrated into activities that permit a variety of responses, ranging from physical responses from those not ready for production, to brief oral responses from those who are. As the children begin production, conversations should increasingly require one-word responses. Within the same conversation, the teacher can address questions calling for longer responses to those children who are ready. Teacher questions and commands here are in italics, and student responses are in brackets [ ]:

> *Kjell, show us your picture. What is in Kjell's picture?* [A sandwich.] *Yes, it is a sandwich. What is on the sandwich?* [Ketchup.] *Is there an apple on the sandwich?* [No. Laughter.] *What else is on the sandwich?* [Meat, mayonnaise.] *How does it taste?* [Good.] *What do you like with a sandwich?* [Cookies. Soda.] *I like chips with mine.*

The Emergence of Speech Stage During the emergence of speech stage, children begin to produce structures that are richer in vocabulary, longer and more complex, and more correct. This production proceeds from three-word phrases to sentences, dialogue, extended discourse, and narrative, strategies that are also helpful in teaching standard American English to speakers of African American Vernacular English. At this stage, Terrell (1981) recommends such activities as games, group discussions, preference ranking, skits, art and music, radio, TV, pictures, filmstrips, readings, and filling out forms. An example of a chart that incorporates preference ranking is provided by Crawford (1994a) (see Figure 15.2). After surveying the children about their preferences for pizza toppings and recording them, the teacher uses the survey results in Figure 15.2 to ask questions at different levels, each directed at a particular student and designed to elicit a response that reflects that student's stage of English language development. Teacher questions are in italics, and student responses in brackets [ ]:

> *Does Sofik like pizza?* [Yes.] *What kind of meat does Sofik like?* [Sausage.] *How many like tomato on their pizza?* [Three, Margarita, Nguyen, and Petra.] *How much does Abdul like pizza?* [He doesn't like it.] *Which children like the same kind of pizza?* [Sofik and

Figure 15.2 Second-Language Preference Ranking Chart

Name	Favorite Pizzas					
	Cheese	Sausage	Pepperoni	Tomato	Anchovy	Mushroom
Margarita	X			X		X
Sofik		X		X		
Abdul						
Nguyen	X		X	X		
Petra		X		X		X

Petra.] Is there a topping that no one likes? [Yes.] What is it? [Anchovy.] How do we know?
[Nobody wants anchovy.]

Not only is the chart a valuable source of comprehensible input, but the process of gathering the data for the chart is also. In addition, children begin to read each other's names and the words for popular foods in English.

Wordless picture books can also be used as a stimulus for the production of language at the emergence of speech stage. In an article that addresses struggling upper-grade readers, Ho (1999) describes strategies that will also be very effective for English language learners. After a brief book talk with the teacher, a small group of students creates a short text for a wordless book. One student member of the group records the text, although a paraprofessional or parent volunteer might fill this role when the students' writing abilities make this difficult. This is of even more value when two or three groups of students independently create their own text and then share it with the other groups.

BUILDING VOCABULARY WITH READ-ALOUDS AND OTHER STRATEGIES In addition to building a working vocabulary for everyday communication, English language learners also need to develop the academic language necessary for working and reading in the content areas of the curriculum. Nagy and Townsend (2012) point out the efficacy of morphological word study of words with Latin and Greek roots. These words are particularly useful to Spanish-speaking English language learners, as their own language contains many words with roots of the same origins. In addition, words with these origins tend to reflect the higher levels of vocabulary found in academic language.

Reading Aloud

The importance of read-alouds was demonstrated in Chapter 12. Collins (2005) found evidence that read-alouds were also a potent aid to the development of vocabulary among young English language learners, especially when rich explanations about new words were provided. In a related study of read-alouds done by parents at home and teachers at school, Roberts (2008) found that read-alouds in either the mother tongue or English produced vocabulary gains among preschool children. We can add that when these read-alouds are done with big books, then illustrations provide an important context to the process.

Wessels (2011) shared a vocabulary development strategy for English language learners called *Quilts* that builds on the three-part ABC lesson planning structure that underlies this book. Within the anticipation, reading to build knowledge, and consolidation phases, the strategy focuses on assessing of background knowledge, connecting known vocabulary to new vocabulary (perhaps across languages), providing for practice, ensuring multiple exposures to new vocabulary, and addressing higher level knowledge.

In the anticipation phase of the lesson, the teacher provides a sheet of chart paper folded to create boxes. In groups of three to four, the children write the word for their group in their mother tongue or English in a box. Then they write something about the word, or if they can't do that, they illustrate its meaning with a drawing. They discuss the word within their small groups.

In the reading-to-build-knowledge phase of the lesson, they stop reading when they encounter one of their words and, referring to the quilt, discuss their reactions to the word. In the consolidation phase of the lesson, the students write a definition of the word on a sticky note and put it on the quilt. They then discuss the new words as a larger group. The quilt remains available for future referral.

SHELTERED ENGLISH INSTRUCTION FOR INTERMEDIATE-LEVEL ENGLISH SPEAKERS When English language learners have reached an intermediate level of English proficiency, they are ready to move from academic instruction in their mother tongue to academic instruction in English by using sheltered English instruction, a model that provides extensive support for comprehension. Sheltering strategies in the content areas of the curriculum add substantially to the knowledge and contextualized vocabulary that students need as a base for reading comprehension as they read and think in any language (Krashen, 1985). These strategies are consistent with the philosophy of communicative approaches to second-language acquisition, and they additionally provide access to academic areas of the curriculum in such a way that communication is maintained. Sheltered

Figure 15.3 Classifying Cognitive Level and Contextual Support of Language and Content Activities According to Cummins's Framework

	Cognitively undemanding	Cognitively demanding
Context enhanced	Art lesson Playing kickball Conversation about lunch Playing a board game Singing a song	Mathematics lesson using manipulatives Conducting a science experiment about evaporation Making a map of the schoolyard Watching the news on television
Context reduced	Beginning reading skills Talking on the telephone Listening to the news on the radio Reading a set of instructions	Responding to higher-order reading comprehension questions Participating in a debate on capital punishment Taking the SAT or the GRE

Source: *English learners: reaching the highest level of English literacy* by Garcia, Gilbert G. Reproduced with permission of INTERNATIONAL READING ASSOCIATION in the format Republish in a book via Copyright Clearance Center.

English strategies are also very appropriate in providing support for teaching Standard American English to speakers of African American Vernacular dialect.

Cummins (1981) provides a set of intersecting continua that are very useful for conceptualizing the issue of balancing the complexity of curriculum content with demands on language proficiency (see Figure 15.3). The vertical continuum extends from cognitively undemanding to cognitively demanding—ranging, for example, from a conversation about what students ate for lunch on the cognitively undemanding side to a third-grade mathematics lesson about the distributive principle of multiplication on the cognitively demanding side.

Cummins's intersecting horizontal continuum extends from context embedded to context reduced, ranging, for example, from a science lesson on classification taught with concrete manipulatives on the context-embedded side to an abstract lecture/discussion about the principles of democracy on the context-reduced side. Sheltered instruction in English is most effective in subject areas of the curriculum that can be presented concretely, such as mathematics, science, art, music, and physical education. Although certain aspects of social studies can be taught concretely, such as geography and map skills, so many abstract concepts are taught that English language instruction in this area might well be delayed until students acquire additional English proficiency, especially if expository text in English is an important source of knowledge for the children.

The purpose of a sheltered instruction approach to the core curriculum in English is to provide a focus on context-embedded activities, ensuring that comprehensible input is provided while treating increasingly cognitively demanding aspects of the core curriculum. The Los Angeles Unified School District (1985) prepared a set of English-language teaching strategies that provide the necessary scaffolding in content areas for intermediate English language learners. Recommended strategies for teachers include the following:

- Simplify input by speaking slowly and enunciating clearly.
- Use a controlled vocabulary within simple language structures.
- Where possible, use cognates and avoid the extensive use of idiomatic expressions.
- Use nonverbal language, including gestures, facial expressions, and dramatization.

- Use manipulatives and concrete materials, such as props, graphs, visuals, overhead transparencies, bulletin boards, maps, and realia.

- Maintain comprehension with gestures, dramatization, illustrations, and manipulatives.

- Check understanding by asking for confirmation of comprehension; by asking students to clarify, repeat, and expand; and by using a variety of questioning formats.

Teachers of English language learners can take two additional steps to ensure good communication with students as they teach: They should face the children, not the blackboard, when teaching; and male teachers should ensure that moustaches are trimmed so children can see the upper lip.

Schifini (1985) recommends a focus on student-centered activities, especially at the secondary level, where lecturing and textbook use predominate. Richard-Amato and Snow (1992) provide valuable strategies for content-area teachers of English language learners. For mainstream teachers, they recommend providing a warm learning environment, recording lectures and talks for later review, rewriting some key parts of text material at lower levels, asking native-English-speaking students to share notes with English language learners, and avoiding competitive grading until students have achieved sufficient English proficiency to compete successfully with native speakers.

It is clear that many of these strategies are nothing more than effective teaching practices, but their absence is very damaging to English language learners who are struggling to learn mathematics, science, and social studies in English when they have reached an intermediate level of English proficiency.

Several other strategies provide scaffolding for English language learners in specially designed academic instruction activities in English. The highly contextualized interactions that take place in cooperative learning can make the difference between what Krashen (1985, 1991) describes as submersion, or sink or swim, and sheltered instruction, the type of scaffolded subject-matter instruction just described. Cooperative learning is most effective when, in the words of Vygotsky, more capable peers—that is, stronger speakers of English—are included in groups with English language learners at various levels.

Bauer and Manyak (2008) provide several strategies for enriching language instruction for English language learners at this intermediate stage, each stressing a focus on making input comprehensible. These strategies including the following: having instructional conversations about observations that children log about topics such as weather or the activities of a goldfish or a frog in an aquarium—what they mean; discussing cognates in two languages on the classroom word wall; and talking about a story they have read or heard from a read-aloud. The focus is the theme of the conversation, not the correctness of the grammar.

 The video describes the components of the SIOP model and provides examples of teachers implementing its principles. Which aspects of the SIOP model do you feel are most important for English language learners?

SHELTERED INSTRUCTION OBSERVATION PROTOCOL   The Sheltered Instruction Observation Protocol (SIOP®) (Echevarria et al., 2013) is a carefully organized professional development model that incorporates strategies you have seen in this chapter and previous chapters:

- *Preparation*: lesson planning, content objectives, instructional materials
- *Building background*: integrating student background knowledge and developing academic vocabulary
- *Comprehensible input*: teacher speech presentation strategies and multimodal techniques
- *Strategies*: scaffolding instruction and promoting higher-order thinking skills
- *Interaction*: encouraging elaborated student speech and grouping students appropriately
- *Practice/Application*: activities to extend student learning of language and content
- *Lesson delivery*: delivering lessons that meet teaching objectives
- *Review/Assessment*: teacher review of key language and content concepts, assessment of student learning, and feedback to students

A SIOP® lesson plan incorporates all of these elements. This model is designed for English language learners, but you can see how it would be very effective with speakers of African American Vernacular English and with any student struggling with language and literacy. As a framework for planning and teaching effective lessons, it highlights best teaching practice for all children.

All of these sheltered strategies build background knowledge that supports the reading comprehension of English language learners as they begin to read expository text in their new second language. When instruction in the mother tongue precedes the sheltered instruction in English, their background knowledge is much richer.

Grammar as Part of the Curriculum?

According to Crawford (1994a), teachers who would advocate teaching the first-person present indicative tense to a seven-year-old English-speaking child in a primary school classroom would be incredulous at the suggestion that a parent teach the same concept to a three-year-old at home. Of course, both children can use the tense correctly, neither as the result of instruction. It is clear that second-language acquisition programs should be based primarily on content, not on grammatical sequence.

A communicative second-language curriculum is usually organized around a set of topics to ensure the introduction of new vocabulary and concepts of interest and utility to the children. Needed language structures emerge and are acquired naturally within the context of topical lessons. Some communicative curricula include grammatical sequences as a subcategory.

Terrell (1981) suggests that the initial content should be limited to ensuring that students understand the following:

- Commands for classroom management
- Names of objects in the classroom
- Colors and description words for those objects
- Words to describe people and family relationships
- Descriptions of children and their clothing; school areas and activities
- Names of objects in the school that are not in the classroom
- Foods, especially those eaten at school

Later in the acquisition process, topics of interest to children would include the children's families, their homes and neighborhoods, their favorite activities, and experiences they have had. They also enjoy discussing their preferences about food, colors, television programs and films, and other aspects of their lives.

Linking ESL Instruction and Literacy

There is a close link between literacy and the acquisition of a second language that becomes apparent when, as a part of the natural approach, key words are written on the board in the second language, especially for older children who are literate in their mother tongue (Terrell, 1981). This corresponds to the key words to reading approach (Veatch, 1996; Veatch et al., 1979). In the early production stage of his natural approach, Terrell indicates that children may express themselves quite appropriately in one- or two-word utterances as they begin to acquire a second language. According to Crawford (1994a), it is altogether appropriate that children also begin to read key vocabulary that they have expressed for their teacher to write for them. They may later produce lists of related ideas, such as foods to eat at the school cafeteria, words that describe a favorite friend, or things to do after school. These topics and this output reflect the oral language common in the early production phase of Terrell's natural approach to language acquisition, output that is well suited for children to dictate for their teachers to record and for the children to read later.

Most bilingual teachers who teach reading in the mother tongue recognize that students' motivation to begin reading and writing in English early is strong. Although it is most beneficial for students to learn to read and write in their native language (Cummins, 1986, 1989; Krashen & Biber, 1988; Snow et al., 1998), where possible, teachers can begin an early introduction to literacy in English to take advantage of that motivation. The key vocabulary and language-experience approaches should be used with caution to ensure that the second-language acquisition program does not evolve into an English literacy program presented before the student is ready. Being able to read and write in the mother tongue is always the most desirable base from which to establish literacy in English later because of the positive transfer of literacy skills to English.

As English proficiency increases, the key word approach to reading may give way to the language-experience approach described in Chapter 5. It is important that the teacher accept the language that the children use in their initial dictations. There will be incomplete sentences, missing words, and inappropriate vocabulary, but this represents the stage at which they are working in their new second language, and correction will only serve to dampen enthusiasm and diminish active participation.

Language Experience with English Language Learners

As mentioned earlier, big books are an excellent source of large-format illustrations for ESL lessons. Later in the process, teachers will find that many children benefit from read-alouds in their new second language, especially when these are based on the background knowledge that children have already acquired as a result of lessons using the illustrations in these big books. The big books that are of most value will be very predictable and have repetitive elements.

Shared Reading

Other early second-language reading and writing activities that are useful in the emergence of speech stage of the natural approach include the creation of vocabulary cards, with a word in English and an accompanying illustration from a magazine or by the student. These can be used for word games, including some that begin to focus on beginning sounds; this is especially productive for students who are already learning to read in their mother tongue. Children can also use their vocabulary cards for building word banks, student dictionaries, and word walls. Many children will be anxious to begin writing in their new second language. Simple poetry forms, such as the cinquain (see Chapter 10) and diamante, are useful structures for their initial attempts.

Form Poems

In their efforts to use the mother tongue of children in their classes, teachers sometimes provide cards with a vocabulary word in the mother tongue on one side and in English on the other. They also often provide bulletin boards in the two languages, and search out children's books with text in English on one side of the page and in the mother tongue on the other side. Although these efforts are laudable, such practices lead children to approach their new language of English through their mother tongue instead of directly. Vocabulary cards in English are a good practice, but a picture on the other side is a better choice than the word in the mother tongue. Teachers can and should provide bulletin boards in both languages, but not with both languages represented on the same bulletin board. For example, a science bulletin board can be provided in English on one side of the classroom, and the same bulletin board in the mother tongue can be placed on the other side of the room. Providing the same literature in English and the mother tongue has many advantages, but it is better provided in two separate books. Children will learn their new second language of English better if they do not approach it through the mother tongue.

Options for Teaching the English Language Learner to Read

There are two major options for teaching English language learners to read; these correspond to the two major categories of programs: English only and bilingual education.

In English

In an English-only instructional program, the children necessarily have to learn to read in English. This is not a positive approach, but it is often the only option when a mother tongue reading instruction program cannot be offered because of a very small number of children with a common non-English language, a lack of appropriate personnel and materials, or political considerations.

Assuming that an ESL program is offered beginning in kindergarten and extending into the primary grades, the English language learners should not be placed in a formal and systematic English reading program before they have any proficiency whatsoever in English. The reading program is not an appropriate place for beginning ESL instruction, which should instead focus on understanding and speaking. When reading in English is included at the beginning stages of instruction in listening comprehension and speaking English, the ESL program all too often evolves into a phonics- and text-based reading program instead of an ESL program, with very negative results in terms of both language acquisition and reading. According to Lenters (2005), "one cannot read with comprehension a language one cannot speak and comprehend."

As children gain vocabulary in English in their ESL program, they will be interested in writing the words they learn, and they will begin to learn to read them, too, especially if they are learning to read in their mother tongue at the same time. A complete treatment of teaching the English language learner to read in English is provided in Chapters 12 and 13 in two dimensions: (1) the very positive process of teaching the English language learner who has first learned to read in the mother tongue and who has also reached the intermediate level of proficiency in understanding and speaking English and (2) the less desirable, but sometimes necessary, process of teaching reading in English to an English language learner who has not learned to read in the mother tongue and/or who has not reached the intermediate level of English-language proficiency.

Finally, some families will insist that their children learn to read and write only in English, even though the children do not speak or understand that language. Often, the parents themselves can express that desire only in their mother tongue. A few parents might even believe that the purpose of using the minority language for literacy is to maintain speakers of that language in an inferior social position. In this case, teachers need to demonstrate respect for the mother tongue, and they need to assure the children and their families that they will also have the opportunity to learn to speak, read, and write English. In addition, they need to reinforce the idea that children learn to read and write only once and that learning to read and write in another language, such as English, later is a relatively simple transfer process that is well supported in research. Finally, teachers need to reinforce the idea that reading is *comprehension*, not just pronouncing or "reading" sounds. Nonetheless, some parents still insist on English only, and most schools accept that parental decision.

In the Mother Tongue

A fundamental precept of literacy for children who are English language learners is that they learn to read and write more rapidly and more effectively in their mother tongue than they will in a second language that they learn later. The first important and authoritative position taken on this issue was at a UNESCO conference (UNESCO, 1953), in which it was concluded that children learn better to read in a new second language if they first learn to read in their mother tongue. This conclusion has been corroborated by many investigators in subsequent years. Saville and Troike (1971) reported that once a child has learned to read, transferring that ability to another language is not a difficult matter. Modiano (1968) found that Maya children in Mexico learned to read more rapidly in their mother tongue of Quiché than did Maya children who learned to read in their second language of Spanish. Subsequently, the children who had initially learned to read in their mother tongue read better in Spanish than those who first learned to read in Spanish. Through succeeding years, the evidence consistently indicates that children learn to read most effectively in their second language by first learning to read in their primary language

(Cummins, 1986, 1989; Krashen & Biber, 1988; National Reading Panel Report, 2006; Snow et al., 1998; UNESCO, 1953).

Cummins's (1986, 1989) linguistic interdependence hypothesis indicates that what students learn in two languages is interdependent. This common underlying proficiency (CUP) (Cummins, 1981) forms the basis for positive transfer of skills. Children have knowledge and skills that they have learned in their mother tongue, and they can use them in the second language. They do not have to learn this knowledge and these skills again. In fact, it is axiomatic that children learn to read only once. They can transfer reading and writing skills to their new second language, just as adults do when they study a foreign language. Cummins indicates that CUP explains why children who have attended school in their country (and language) of origin tend to demonstrate higher achievement in English later than do children who lack that experience. These principles lead to the counterintuitive, but inescapable, conclusion that success in English-language proficiency is closely related to students' learning of reading, writing, and academic concepts in their mother tongue (Collier, 1989; J. Crawford, 1989; Cummins, 1989; Hudelson, 1987; Krashen, 1985; Krashen & Biber, 1988; Ramírez, 1991).

Language policy is a factor of great importance in literacy for children. Clearly, children learn to read and write most quickly and most effectively in the mother tongue. Many factors must be taken into consideration, however, before that decision is made (Crawford, 1995). For example, if skilled bilingual teachers are available, if children speak a minority language for which there is a well-developed written form, and if there are instructional materials in that language, the children can be given instruction in their mother tongue. If this is not the case, then the teacher can consider using the language-experience approach in English, as described in Chapter 5 and also later in this chapter.

If children speak a language for which there is not a well-developed written form, such as Hmong, then they must be taught to speak and understand English and later to read and write in English, probably using the language-experience approach and simple predictable literature in English. If bilingual teachers are not available, then even the presence of instructional materials will not be sufficient to permit mother tongue instruction. The school can also prepare a literate speaker of the minority language as a paraprofessional who works under the supervision of a fully trained teacher who is not proficient in the mother tongue of the children.

In the case of a program of bilingual education, the children will have the opportunity to learn to read in their mother tongue. If a bilingual program is provided for that population, children who speak another non-English language will likely be placed in an English-only approach instead.

In the case of Spanish and other languages that use the Latin or Roman alphabet, there is a close correspondence between literacy skills in English and these languages and therefore much transfer of skills from reading in the mother tongue to English:

- The letters of the alphabet in Spanish are almost without exception identical to those of English, except for a few diacritical markings, such as the tilde (~) in Spanish.
- The left-to-right and top-to-bottom directionalities of the languages are the same.
- The concept of print and the alphabetic principle operate in the same way.
- Most consonant sounds and some vowel sounds are the same.
- There are significant similarities in vocabulary because of the many cognates that exist between English and Spanish (Manyak & Bauer, 2009; Montelongo, Hernández, & Herter, 2011a, 2011b). Some, however, are false cognates, such as *actual*, which means "real" in English and "present" or "current" in Spanish.
- Reading comprehension and organization skills are the same. When a child has learned to read in Spanish, these skills do not need to be learned a second time.

You can think of your own experiences in studying a foreign language. There were many new vocabulary words and grammatical elements to learn, but you did not have to learn to read and write again.

Teaching Children to Read in Spanish

Most English language learners in American schools speak Spanish at home, and almost all formal programs of bilingual education are conducted in Spanish (Fradd & Tikunoff, 1987). According to the National Center for Education Statistics (2009), 21 percent of students enrolled in American schools were non-English speaking, and 72 percent of those spoke Spanish at home. In most areas, it is only in Spanish that a wide range of instructional materials are accessible and that sufficient certified bilingual teachers are available to conduct such a program. Therefore, this section of the chapter is devoted to the teaching of reading in Spanish to these children.

As you have seen, the reading and writing processes in English and Spanish have a common alphabet and similar writing conventions. A major difference between English and Spanish is in the regularity of phoneme/grapheme relationships. In English, they are very irregular and inconsistent, especially with respect to the vowels, but in Spanish, they are very regular and consistent, especially with respect to the vowels.

Given this difference, one might expect that reading methodologies in Spanish would focus on phonics to take advantage of that regularity, and many do. But Latin American educators have found that children who learn to read using decoding as their only word recognition skill fall short in comprehension, just as occurs in English reading. Their reading is characterized as *silabeando*, that is, reading syllable by syllable. Their focus is on oral reading accuracy and speed, with little or no attention to comprehension or enjoyment. This is often observed in children who have learned to read in Spanish in Latin America.

A great variety of approaches for teaching reading in Spanish is available, just as there is in English. Table 15.1 summarizes those approaches.

These approaches range from those that are highly synthetic to those that are whole-part-whole, even including what is characterized as constructivist or whole language in English. A balanced approach in the whole-part-whole tradition provides for a strong, well-rounded program that is characterized by the following:

- Extensive read-aloud activities to build background knowledge and vocabulary in the mother tongue
- Use of the key words to reading approach, the language-experience approach, and shared reading of authentic literature at the beginning stages to introduce the concept of print for children who do not have a rich print environment in the home
- Phonemic awareness activities emerging from vocabulary in children's background knowledge and from LEA charts and shared literature experiences
- An inductive whole-part-whole strategy for teaching phonics, with elements emerging from words the children have acquired in the activities just described
- Use of authentic literature in Spanish to serve as a basis for teaching reading comprehension
- Extensive and early opportunities for writing

Application of these strategies in Spanish is similar to that in English, with the exception of phonics, which is addressed later. These key instructional activities also represent the four blocks framework presented in Chapter 1 and, beyond the beginning stages of reading instruction, they should be augmented with the many highly effective strategies described throughout the book.

METHODOLOGIES FOR TEACHING READING IN SPANISH   "He read slowly, spelling out each syllable and murmuring it quietly, as if with great relish, and when he'd mastered the whole word, he would repeat it in one breath." In *The Old Man Who Read Love Stories*, a prize-winning novel written by a Chilean author about an elderly man who lives in the rain forest of Ecuador, Luis Sepúlveda (1989) has described very accurately the way too many Latin American children read as the result of the syllabic approach to reading

Table 15.1 Major Approaches for Teaching Reading in Spanish

CATEGORY OF APPROACH	METHODOLOGY	CHARACTERISTICS	CITATION
Part-whole	Alphabetic (alfabético)	Letter names taught first; sequence of vowels, consonants, syllables, words, phrases, and sentences	Barbosa Heldt (1971) de Braslavsky (2006)
	Phonetic (fonético)	Focus on sounds; sequence of vowels, consonants, syllables, words, phrases, and sentences	Barbosa Heldt (1971) de Braslavsky (2006)
	Syllabic (silábico)	Focus on syllables; sequence of vowels, consonants, syllables, words, phrases, and sentences	Barbosa Heldt (1971) de Braslavsky (2006)
	Onomatopoeic (onomatopéyico)	Focus on auditory associations between sounds of letters and natural sounds of the environment, such as the /s/ as the whistle of a fireworks rocket; sequence of vowels, consonants, syllables, words, phrases, and sentences	Barbosa Heldt (1971) Torres Quintero (1976)
Whole-part-whole	Everyday vocabulary (palabras normales)	An analytic approach in which words are broken into syllables, then into sounds, and then reassembled	Barbosa Heldt (1971) Rodríguez Fuenzalida (1982) Rébsamen (1949)
Global	Whole word (global)	Sequence of words and sentences, with little or no phonics	Barbosa Heldt (1971) de Braslavsky (2006)
	Generated words (palabras generadoras)	Sequence of sight words, syllables, and sounds; use of these elements to create new words, phrases, and sentences	Hendrix (1952) Barbosa Heldt (1971)
Eclectic	Eclectic (ecléctico)	Combination of sight word development and phonics; typical of basal reader programs in English and Spanish	Barbosa Heldt (1971)
Constructivist	Whole language (lenguaje integral)	Focus on literature and authentic text; similar to whole-language focus in English; phonics taught implicitly and when need demonstrated (not explicit and systematic)	Freinet (1974) Solé (1992) Goodman (1989) Arellano Osuna (1992) Salmon (1995)

instruction used in almost every country in the region. It is not uncommon to find the use of similar methodologies in the United States, often in the hands of bilingual teachers who themselves were educated in Latin America, perhaps even trained as teachers there. These approaches have many limitations when used in isolation; their best use would be as an ancillary word attack skill program to use with high-quality children's literature. But as in reading English, children who read in Spanish need to employ all cueing systems in support of their word recognition efforts: the semantic, syntactic, and pragmatic systems, as well as the graphophonic system.

ISSUES RELATED TO THE SOUND SYSTEMS OF SPANISH AND ENGLISH   The sequence in which Spanish phonics is introduced is different from that of English. It begins with vowel sounds because they are few in number and regular (see Table 15.2). Consonants follow in an order that reflects their frequency and regularity. Few word recognition problems appear in reading in Spanish, but there are several difficult points in Spanish, as in English, in which one letter represents several sounds. These are often observed in the invented spelling of children, as seen in Figure 15.4.

The invented spelling in the student's work presented in Figure 15.4 is very typical of children who write in Spanish, and it is also consistent with Gentry's phonetic stage (Gentry, 1981), where there is substitution of incorrect letters with similar or the same

Phonics and Phonological Awareness

Why is the sequence of teaching word recognition skills in Spanish different from English?

Teach It!

Refer to the Teach It! appendix at the end of the book for further activities you can use to reinforce concepts discussed in this chapter.

Inductive Phonics Lesson

In a simple three-step inductive lesson structure, the first step of auditory discrimination serves to verify students' phonological awareness of the sound stated in the objective of the lesson (see the figure below). If the students are not successful in this first step, substitute phonological awareness activities for the second and third steps of the lesson, such as those described in Chapters 5 and 11. If the students are successful, as they usually will be in the first grade, proceed to the second stage of the lesson, which is to verify that the students can already read the sight words used in the first stage of the lesson and also indicate that they recognize the letter and its position in the words.

The third stage, that of associating the sound with the letter, is the key step in the lesson. The students who can correctly pronounce the letter or syllable indicated in the objective in unknown words in the association stage should be able to use that skill to recognize and pronounce that sound in the same position in other unknown words.

Many of the children will be able to state a rule or generalization when asked how they know how to pronounce the target sound in the unknown word. A six-year-old's rule might be a statement that he or she remembered other known words with that letter in the same position, thought about how it sounded in those words, and pronounced it that way in the new word. The purpose of the extra stimulus question ("If that word is 'cola,' what is this word? 'Bala.'") is for the teacher to provide the part of the word that is not the subject of the lesson objective—only the initial syllable /**ba**/ is of interest.

This model lesson is inductive in that you ask questions that lead children to think about what they already know about sounds, letters, and words. You do not tell or explain. Many children will not be able to state a rule or generalization at the beginning of this type of inductive lesson, although most will be able to correctly pronounce the target element in the words. But after a number of lessons, increasing numbers of children will be able to formulate a rule. These generalizations will be remembered and applied more easily if they are derived by the children. If you provide them in a direct instruction activity, then the child must rely on memory to recall the rule later. When children learn to derive their own rules, they can transfer this ability to new unknown words. They can also transfer this generalized ability to English.

The instructional time required for the model lesson presented in the figure should be about five minutes, certainly less than ten minutes. Most instructional activities in beginning reading in Spanish should focus on comprehension through shared reading and, later, in small-group lessons in which children are reading in a directed or guided reading mode.

Figure 15.4
Invented Spelling in Children's Writing in Spanish

Inductive Phonics Lesson (Spanish/English)

Spanish lesson plan	**English version of Spanish lesson plan**

Spanish lesson plan

Objetivo: pronunciar el sonido inicial de palabras nuevas que empiecen con la sílaba /ba/

Etapa de discriminacíon auditiva (verificar conciencia fonémica)

Les voy a decir tres palabras. Escuchen bien.

    bajo   baño   bate

¿Cómo se parecen? ¿Qué tienen en común?

¿En qué parte de cada palabra se encuentra este sonido?

Les voy a decir tres otras palabras. ¿Cuál no pertenece a este grupo?

    ballena   mesa   barra

¿Cuál es diferente? ¿Por qué? ¿Cómo es diferente? ¿En qué parte?

¿Qué otras cosas pueden ver en el salón que empiecen con el mismo sonido?

Etapa de discriminación visual

Vamos a leer tres palabras.

Levanta la mano si quieres leer la primera palabra.

    bajo, baño, bate   Muy bien, etc.

¿Cómo se parecen estas tres palabras?

¿En qué parte de las palabras se encuentra la letra?

Etapa de asociación

Ahora quiero que lean algunas palabras nuevas. ¿Quién quiere tratar de leer la primera palabra nueva? ¿Cómo sabias leeria?

    bala   base   barra   ballena

Si esa palabra dice "cola" ¿qué dice esta palabra? "Bala."

    cola

English version of Spanish lesson plan

Objective: pronounce the initial sound of new words that begin with the syllable /ba/

Auditory discrimination stage (confirm phonemic awareness)

I'm going to tell you three words. Listen to them carefully.

    (short) (bath) (bat)

How are they alike? What do they have in common?

In what part of each word do you hear this sound?

I'm going to tell you three more words. Which one doesn't belong with the others?

    (whale) (table) (bar)

Which is different? Why? How is it different? Which part is different?

What other things in the classroom can you see that begin with the same sound?

Visual discrimination stage

Let's read these three words.

Raise your hand if you want to read the first word.

    (short) (bath) (bat [baseball])

How do these three words look the same?

In what part of these words do you see that letter?

Association stage

Now we're going to read some new words. Who wants to read the first word? How did you know how to read it?

    bala   base   barra   ballena

If that word is "cola," what is this word? "Bala."

    cola

---

pronunciation. The word *castillo* is spelled *castio*, which yields the correct pronunciation of the word, but not the correct spelling. In the words *paresio* and *isieron*, the student substituted the letter *s* for *c*, again yielding the correct pronunciation of the word, but the wrong spelling. In addition, the silent *h* of *hicieron* was omitted. There is much confusion between the sounds of *b* and *v* in Spanish, both being pronounced similarly to the /b/ in English in the initial position and like /v/ in English when between vowels, resulting in the very typical substitution of *v* for *b* in *estava*.

Finally, there is a grammatical error that reflects a troublesome issue even for some adults. The conventions of Spanish require that the sequential repetition of a sound be avoided. Therefore, *y hicieron* should be written as *e hicieron* to avoid the repetition of the *y* (and) and the <u>*hi*</u> in *hicieron*, both of which carry the same sound (in Spanish, *y* followed by *hi* would sound like two English long *e* sounds in succession).

We have already discussed the issue of positive transfer of skills, that a reading skill or concept acquired in the mother tongue doesn't have to be taught again in the second language of English. Yopp and Stapleton (2008) provide evidence from a review of research

Table 15.2 Sequence of Phonics Generalizations in Spanish

INITIAL SOUNDS	FINAL SOUNDS	WORD ENDINGS
a	a	os
e	e	as
i	o	diminutives
o	augmentatives	
u	d	verbs -ar
	l	verbs -er
m	n	verbs -ir
t	s	
l	r	Substitution of initial
p	z	consonants
n		
d	i	Substitution of final
s	u	elements
f		
r	CONSONANT BLENDS	Medial diphthongs
b		
g (soft)	br	Compound words
ll	cr	
c (hard)	dr	Verb endings
j	fr	
y	pr	Homonyms
h (mute)	tr	
ch	bl	Prefixes
z	cl	
qu	fl	Suffixes
g (hard)	gl	
c (soft)	pl	Homographs
gue, gul		
güe, güi		Grades of adjectives
x (medial)		
		Syllabication

and from their own work that phonemic awareness in Spanish transfers to English. They provide a variety of activities and book resources that support the kind of language play that leads to phonemic awareness in Spanish and that transfers to English.

Phonics lessons in Spanish should be drawn out of vocabulary from key words to reading lessons, language-experience approach lessons, and the shared reading experiences of children. The words used in the lessons should be within the children's sight vocabulary, moving from the whole (word) to the part (element to be taught) and back to whole (word) again. Because of the nature of Spanish, elements are frequently syllables in the form of CV (consonant/vowel).

INSTRUCTIONAL MATERIALS IN SPANISH The variety of instructional materials for reading in Spanish is almost as rich as that in English. These include formal reading programs, authentic children's literature, and electronic resources, including the Internet.

Print Resources   Most major publishers that provide an English reading program also offer a parallel program in Spanish. These programs would be fairly characterized as basal, although some have anthologies of original literature instead of contrived basal reader stories or decodable text. The best programs have children's literature from the Spanish-speaking world or children's stories written in Spanish by native Spanish-speaking authors. In both of these cases, the quality of Spanish language and the cultural appropriateness should be evaluated carefully.

Most Spanish programs also contain authentic children's literature translated from English. It is important to consider carefully the quality of translation and the cultural appropriateness of these selections. The best programs also offer selections of authentic Spanish-language literature translated to English for their English versions, a demonstration of their respect for the literary traditions of both languages and cultures. A major strength of programs with parallel literature selections in two languages is that students who read a selection in their mother tongue as part of their mother tongue reading program have a powerful source of background knowledge when they later read an English version of the same story.

There is also a wealth of children's books and big books available in Spanish. The teacher who wishes to use authentic literature for a Spanish reading program instead of anthologies or basal readers will find the constantly expanding series of books on recommended children's literature in Spanish prepared by Schon (2000) to be an invaluable resource. She later published a compendium of children's books in Spanish with themes from around the world (Schon, 2001, 2002). Her final review of children's literature in Spanish was published in 2009 (Schon, 2009).

Electronic Resources for English Language Learners and Their Teachers   There are Web sites that provide support to English language learners and their teachers, both in the areas of English language development and in Spanish. For example, an international school Web site registry provides the home pages of schools around the world that are interested in establishing relationships such as pen pal arrangements with other schools (Greenlaw, 2001). These have the advantage of allowing English language learners to correspond in their developing second language of English with students in other countries who are also studying English, probably as a foreign language. In addition, they may have opportunities to correspond in their shared mother tongues. One site registry is found at <http://ppi.searchy.net/>. Teachers should carefully supervise this activity.

A valuable Web site for the teacher who is searching for outstanding children's literature in Spanish is the Barahona Center for the Study of Books in Spanish for Children and Adolescents, established by the late Isabel Schon, who was cited earlier for her books on this topic. The center's Web site can be found at <http://www.bibliolib .net/detail/1509/barahona-center-for-the-study-of-books-in-spanish-for-children-and-adolescents.html>

Children Who Struggle Learning to Read in the Mother Tongue

Reading recovery has proven to be a very effective intervention strategy for children who experience reading difficulties in English (see Chapters 1 and 12). An authorized Spanish-language version of reading recovery, called *Descubriendo la Lectura*, has also been developed (Escamilla & Andrade, 1992). It follows the pattern of diagnosis and intervention of the original program, but in Spanish. Several adaptations to language and culture were necessary, including the need to locate children's literature in Spanish. The resulting

program includes more than 300 books at 20 different levels of difficulty, with about 20 books per level.

A Spanish diagnostic survey for the identification of students includes six observational tasks: (1) letter identification, (2) a word test, (3) concepts about print, (4) writing vocabulary, (5) dictation, and (6) running records of text reading. Procedures generally parallel those in the English language program, including the rereading of familiar books, a running record of the new book from the previous day, writing, rearranging a cutup story, and introducing a new book. The program is designed for first graders in the lowest 20 percent of the class after one year of reading instruction in the regular classroom.

In a national study of *Descubriendo la Lectura*, Escamilla et al. (1998) found that the program had a very positive outcome with Spanish-speaking second and third graders, with more than 90 percent of students at each grade level scoring above average on Spanish text reading. On the SABE, a standardized achievement test in Spanish, more than 75 percent of students at each grade level met or exceeded the average score.

Assessing the Oral Language Proficiency and Reading Proficiency of English Language Learners

Assessing the language and reading outcomes of English language learners is accomplished in a manner similar to assessment for English speakers (Kame'enui et al., 2001). A number of measures of English language proficiency are used for placement of students in bilingual education programs or programs for English language learners, depending on their levels of achievement (see Table 15.3). In general, they measure the language production of children in English, including vocabulary, syntactical complexity, and auditory discrimination/pronunciation. State and local school district authorities typically establish criteria for the reclassification or identification of children whose English proficiency has advanced sufficiently for mainstream placement

The World of Reading

My 24 First Graders Speak 14 Different Mother Tongues: What Can I Do?

An increasingly common scenario in American classrooms is the presence of children who speak many different home languages. A bilingual education program usually cannot be provided for most of them for the following reasons:

- The teacher is not proficient in more than one of the languages, if that.

- Reading materials are not available in the languages.

- It would not be feasible to provide reading instruction in several languages, even with a proficient teacher and adequate materials.

- There might not be enough children with a common language at a grade level to support a full bilingual education program.

When many children at a grade level have a common language and are scattered among several classrooms, it might be possible to gather all of them into a single classroom. This is especially desirable if there is a teacher who can teach them in their mother tongue or if a paraprofessional or parent volunteer can provide mother tongue support to lessons taught in English. Usually, these children will be taught only in English in an immersion program. Because English is the only language common to most students, they acquire basic interpersonal communication skills rather quickly. Formal reading instruction is usually delayed, although children can work with key words and the language-experience approach early in the process of acquiring English. Shared big books also provide excellent comprehensible input in English, as well as an early introduction to the concept of print and much valuable background knowledge.

Table 15.3 Assessment Measures for Spanish-Speaking English Learners

TYPE OF MEASURE	NAME OF MEASURE	SUBTESTS	ELEMENTS MEASURED	SOURCE OF MEASURE
English language Grades K–12	Basic Inventory of Natural Language (BINL)	N/A	Oral language production, language dominance, fluency, syntax, vocabulary, structural complexity	Pearson
English-language development All LEP	California English Language Development Test (CELDT)	Listening and speaking Reading Writing	Oral language (one-on-one) Reading Writing	CTB/McGraw-Hill
English language Grades K–5	Language Assessment Scales (LAS)	N/A	Auditory discrimination, vocabulary, phoneme production, sentence comprehension, oral production of English and Spanish	CTB/McGraw-Hill
English language Grades K–12	Bilingual Syntax Measure I and II (BSM)	N/A	Syntax, language dominance, second-language level, maintenance of first language	Pearson
English language (or other language) (observation rating scale) Grades 1–12	SOLOM	N/A	Comprehension, vocabulary, fluency, pronunciation, grammar	San Jose USD
English and Spanish language For NCLB Grades 1–12	Stanford English English Language Proficiency Test (ELP, SEP)	Listening, speaking, reading, writing	Listening, speaking, reading, writing	Pearson
Spanish reading (normed test) Grades 1–12	Aprenda 3: Prueba de Logros en Español	Sonidos y letras	Phoneme matching, letter identification, letter/sound correspondence	Pearson
		Lectura de palabras	Word matching with picture, word identification	
		Lectura de oraciones	Sentence match with picture	
		Vocabulario	Synonym matching, defining words in context	
		Comprensión de lectura	Reading comprehension of riddles, modified cloze tests, comprehension questions	
Spanish reading (normed test) Grades K–8	Comprehensive Tests of Basic Skills	Reading	Word attack, vocabulary, reading comprehension	CTB/McGraw-Hill

in regular classroom programs of instruction, although usually with extra support from a paraprofessional or other speaker of the mother tongue at the beginning of the transition process.

There are also several widely used standardized or normed tests of Spanish reading proficiency that usually parallel similar tests in English (see Table 15.3). The results of these tests are often used to evaluate the progress of groups of children or the effectiveness of programs, but they are not very useful to teachers in identifying the levels of children for assignment to instructional groups or levels of textbooks.

In contrast, the informal reading inventory (IRI) serves the same function in Spanish as it does in English. It is an authentic measure of reading accuracy and comprehension, and the outcomes that it yields in Spanish, as in English, can be used to place children in reading groups and textbooks with some confidence (see Chapters 11 and 13 for

DIFFERENTIATED INSTRUCTION

SIOP®
Sheltered
Instruction
Observation
Protocol*

Teaching Older Children Who Are Preliterate

It is not uncommon for teachers of older English language learners from other countries to observe that a few of these students lack literacy skills. Some have been in refugee camps without educational services, others have been working to contribute to family income, and still others have lived in very rural or isolated areas where attending school was not possible because of the great distance to the school and inadequate transportation. Many indigenous children from Latin America leave school because instruction is only provided in Spanish, which they might not speak well, if at all. There are communities of speakers of Zapotec, Mixtec, Maya, Quechua, and many other indigenous languages living in the United States. Their Spanish might be very limited.

Other English language learners have had very limited school experience and have left school, either for the reasons just cited, or occasionally because of the poor quality of education. According to Schifini (1996), many have large gaps in instruction in the primary grades, and they struggle as nonreaders in the higher grades. Schifini recommends several strategies for meeting the needs of these older preliterate English language learners:

- Develop a print-rich classroom environment that reflects student interests, including advertisements, brochures, bumper stickers, comics, drawings, magazines, murals, newspapers, photos, postcards, posters, recipes, and examples of their own work.

- Include native language print in the classroom environment.

- Use reading and writing workshop strategies and shared reading and literature studies.

- Use read-aloud activities for access to the core curriculum not available through reading.

- Use writing activities such as quick-writes to connect students to background knowledge.

- Provide shared book experiences with predictable and patterned books that are of standard textbook size and have mature story lines.

- Use collaborative chart stories, language-experience charts, and other forms of shared writing.

In their SIOP model, Echevarria et al. (2013) recommend additional sheltered instruction strategies effective with preliterate older English language learners:

- Use graphic organizers, such as Venn diagrams, timelines, flow charts, and semantic maps, especially for reading in content areas of the curriculum.

- Use scaffolding techniques, such as paraphrasing or restating students' responses, and think-alouds.

discussions of using the IRI in English). Some major publishers with Spanish-language reading programs provide IRIs for them.

Teachers can also construct their own IRIs by selecting passages from basal readers or anthologies to represent each grade level, just as is done in English. Teachers should verify the levels of the passages by using a readability graph for Spanish (Crawford, 1995) (see the Assessment box). As in constructing an IRI in English, the teacher should ensure that the content of each passage in Spanish corresponds to background and cultural knowledge that the child has in Spanish. With a passage selected for each grade level and four comprehension-level questions developed for each passage, the teacher can employ the same process and accuracy and comprehension criteria for Spanish as for English, as described in Chapters 11 and 13. The IRI in Spanish yields frustration, instructional, independent, and capacity levels, just as it does in English and with the same criteria.

Readability measures are often misused, and the teacher should be aware of their limitations. These measures assess only surface structure features of language, and they ignore the level of content and the background knowledge required of children. Teachers should carefully judge the content of passages they select for inclusion in IRIs for the children they will assess. Finally, teachers are often tempted to rewrite text, changing sentence length or vocabulary to raise or lower readability levels. This is a dangerous practice that should be avoided. A readability graph should be used only as a rough measure and never as a tool for writing to a level.

Spanish Readability Graph

Number of syllables	1.0	1.5	2.0	2.5	3.0	3.5	4.0	4.5	5.0	5.5	6.0	6.5
220												4.3
218												3.8
216												3.3
214											5.3	2.8
212									9.7	7.2	4.8	2.3
210									9.2	6.7	4.3	1.9
208									8.7	6.3	3.8	1.4
206							13.1	10.7	8.2	5.8	3.4	1.0
204							12.6	10.2	7.8	5.3	2.9	
202							12.2	9.8	7.3	4.8	2.4	
200					16.6	14.1	11.7	9.2	6.8	4.4	1.9	
198					16.1	13.6	11.2	8.8	6.3	3.9		
196					15.6	13.2	10.7	8.3	5.8	3.4		
194					15.1	12.7	10.2	7.8	5.4	2.9		
192					14.6	12.2	9.8	7.3	4.5	2.4		
190			19.0	16.6	14.2	11.7	9.3	6.8				
188			18.6	16.1	13.7	11.2	8.8	6.4				
186	23.0	20.5	18.1	15.6	13.2	10.8	8.3	5.9				
184	22.5	20.0	17.6	15.2	12.7	10.3	7.8	5.4				
182	22.0	19.6	17.1	14.7	12.2	9.8	7.4	4.9				
180	21.5	19.1	16.6	14.2	11.8	9.3	6.9	4.5				
178	21.0	18.6	16.2	13.7	11.3	8.9	6.4	4.0				
176	20.6	18.1	15.7	13.3	10.8	8.4	5.9	3.5				
174	20.1	17.7	15.2	12.8								
172	19.6	17.2	14.7	12.3								
170	19.1	16.7	14.3	11.8								
168	18.7	16.2										

Number of sentences

Approximate level of readability

Instructions:

1. Count the first 100 words in the sample.

2. Count the number of sentences in the 100 words, rounding to the nearest tenth of a sentence.

3. Count the number of syllables in the 100 words.

4. Look for the number of syllables in the left column of the graph. Trace to the right to find the number of sentences. The number at the foot of that column is the approximate grade level of the passage.

5. If the text consists of more than a few pages, take samples from every three pages and compute the mean for each variable.

6. If the proportion of sentences to syllables for each 100 words does not appear on the graph, then the readability of the passage cannot be determined.

Source: Crawford, A.N. (1985) Formula y grafico para determinarla comprensabilidad de textos del nivel primario en castellano. *Lectura y Vida 6*(4), 18–24.

Permission to copy with credit to the author.

Mother Tongue Support in the Bilingual Classroom

Monolingual classroom teachers who are unable to teach in their students' mother tongue might be able to use the services of a paraprofessional who can provide this support. Those paraprofessionals' services can extend from follow-up mother tongue support of lessons taught in English by the teacher to instruction provided in the mother tongue under the close and careful supervision of the teacher.

Vignette of a Nonbilingual Teacher and a Bilingual Paraprofessional in a Bilingual Classroom

There are 26 third-grade children in Room 14. Of the 26 native Spanish-speaking children, 11 have made the transition into English reading. Ten continue reading instruction in Spanish while receiving ESL instruction. They will make the transition to English reading within a few weeks or months as they become ready. Five new arrivals to the United States speak only Spanish.

Their teacher, Mr. Scott, is a certified elementary school teacher, but he does not speak Spanish. He is a very good teacher, and he provides all ESL and English reading instruction. But the Spanish reading program is conducted by Ms. Morales, a part-time paraprofessional and university student who plans to become a bilingual teacher. She is occasionally assisted by two Spanish-speaking parent volunteers who read to the children and tell stories from their childhood.

Today, Ms. Morales is teaching a reading lesson from an anthology of stories in Spanish, part of a reading program in English and Spanish that Mr. Scott is also using with the English-speaking students. Ms. Morales begins by introducing new vocabulary that students will encounter in the guided silent reading they will do in a few minutes. In addition, she helps them to construct a semantic map so that they can share background knowledge they have about the topic of the story: a young girl who lives in the Amazon forest of South America. She guides their silent reading with higher-order questions from the teacher manual and additional questions she has formulated herself. After today's lesson, during which they read the first half of the story, the children will write predictions about how the story might end when they complete it the next day. In the meantime, Mr. Scott is teaching a word analysis lesson to the English-speaking students on the other side of the room, which will be followed by a similar literature lesson from the English version of the same anthology that Ms. Morales uses in Spanish.

Mr. Scott meets daily with Ms. Morales to help her plan instruction, to answer questions about how to use the teacher's manual for the Spanish reading program, which is provided in both English and Spanish for his convenience, and to assess children's progress in Spanish reading. As they teach in parallel through the morning, he observes and monitors her activities. She also assists in parent conferences when needed.

Mr. Scott and Ms. Morales have molded themselves into a highly effective team, both making indispensable contributions to the language and reading development of the children in the classroom. She gains much from his extensive teaching experience as they plan instruction for the next day and, on a longer-term basis, for future days, weeks, and months. At the same time, he gains insights from the valuable background she has in the children's mother tongue and their culture.

Although the two are usually teaching parallel to each other, Mr. Scott is able to supervise Ms. Morales's work from his teaching station in the classroom, and he periodically walks

The help of bilingual classroom aides is extremely beneficial in the ESL/ELL classroom, but it is important that the teacher and the aides carefully coordinate their instruction so the messages to the students are consistent.

around the classroom to encourage and reinforce the work of the children in both groups. Although he does not speak Spanish, he finds that he is able to understand much of what is occurring in her lessons.

The parallel structure of the English and Spanish anthologies from the third-grade reading program they use has many advantages. The teacher's manual for the Spanish part of the program has English and Spanish instructions on opposite sides of the teaching manual, so Mr. Scott can quickly determine the students' progress in their lessons. In addition, they will eventually read in English the stories they are now reading in Spanish. Their prior experience with the stories and the background knowledge developed will constitute an important part of scaffolding their comprehension as they move into reading in their new second language.

Supervising the Paraprofessional Who Teaches in the Mother Tongue

It is a challenging task for monolingual teachers to supervise the instructional activities of bilingual paraprofessionals. Teachers should first model for their paraprofessionals in English the teaching manner, approaches, and strategies that are to be employed in Spanish or another language. Teachers should then observe their paraprofessionals, assessing the effectiveness of their modeling. Even though teachers might not understand the paraprofessionals' words, the teachers' knowledge of what is being taught should support good communication. A major emphasis of teachers should be to impress on paraprofessionals the importance of building up the children's self-concepts and of avoiding harsh words, which can undo the effects of even excellent teaching.

At an operational level, there should be outstanding communication between the teacher and the paraprofessional. They should meet in the morning to plan before school and again before the paraprofessional leaves at the end of the day, discussing the activities of the day and planning for lessons to follow. Because the teacher and paraprofessional complement each other so well, the development of mutual respect between them is important. The teacher has skills and knowledge about teaching, and the paraprofessional contributes vital communication skills and cultural knowledge.

Many bilingual paraprofessionals are university students who are in varying stages of teacher preparation programs. They are highly motivated to become teachers, proud of their abilities to manage two languages and two cultures, and anxious to assume leadership in their own classrooms as soon as possible. As they approach and then enter their own student teaching experience, many are able to teach parallel to the regular teacher with careful supervision.

Some paraprofessionals exhibit those same language and cultural skills, but they view their paraprofessional role as their final career goal. They are often members of the local community who might have minimal academic preparation and training as instructional aides. It is perhaps among the members of this group that teachers who do not share the language and culture with the paraprofessional must exercise their most careful judgment. Because they are not trained teachers, their strategies in interacting positively and constructively with children must be carefully monitored. And since the supervising teacher often does not understand what the paraprofessional is saying to the children, it will be important to note the tone of the paraprofessional's voice and the children's reactions.

 The teachers in this video discuss methods to welcome and include bilingual parents in the classroom and in the school community. What benefits do the teachers identify for schools, and for families, when bilingual parents are involved in their child's learning?

Parent Volunteers

Parent volunteers can be an important support to the nonbilingual teacher in the bilingual classroom. An important aspect of preparation for literacy in the mother tongue and English later is oral language development in the mother tongue. Family resources in the form of stories from parents, grandparents, and extended family can make a major contribution to this part of the program. Teachers can invite these adults into the classroom to tell stories to the children that can be used as a source of content for language-experience stories, for example.

Family Literacy

What is the role of parent and family volunteers in working with English language learners?

McQuillan and Tse (1998) describe strategies for extending these storytelling experiences into the English language. The narratives that teachers, parents, grandparents, and other sources use constitute comprehensible input in the hands of an expert storyteller. The children are exposed to rich vocabulary and their background knowledge on a variety of valuable topics is enhanced.

McQuillan and Tse indicate that students begin to write and tell their own stories as their own language production flourishes. When stories are related in English, the children's second language, students should be allowed to listen to stories in that target language without concerns about understanding everything. They should focus on the main ideas. Four steps then follow: (1) telling a short and simple version of the story; (2) revising the story by retelling it with different characters or settings, extending the story beyond its original ending, and narrating the story from the point of view of another character; (3) creating a class story, which might involve considerable negotiation among the children; and (4) creating individual or small-group stories and books.

While McQuillan and Tse are most concerned about using the process to provide comprehensible input in English, the same strategies can be used to provide a stronger base of vocabulary and background knowledge in the mother tongue. In addition, this permits parents, grandparents, and other members of the extended family to play a valued role in the classroom. Finally, it validates and reinforces the value of the mother tongue and culture.

For Review

In this chapter, we examined the teaching of reading in languages other than English and also the teaching of English as a second language (ESL) as it relates to the teaching of reading. The chapter addressed three audiences: bilingual teachers who are capable of teaching reading and writing in a language other than English, teachers of English language learners whose mother tongue instruction will be conducted by a paraprofessional or other staff members under the teacher's supervision, and teachers who are responsible for teaching ESL.

There are various structures and models for teaching English language learners. One major direction is English only, that is, teaching ESL and also teaching all academic subjects, including reading, only in English. This is popularly known as immersion or structured immersion, and there is no evidence to indicate that it is an effective approach. The alternative is known as bilingual education. It consists of an ESL program as in the other approach, but academic instruction is provided in the children's mother tongue during the two to three years that are required for learning English sufficiently to support academic instruction (CALP), as opposed to a conversational level (BICS). There is substantial research support for this approach, although its application is highly political.

ESL is the major component of both immersion and bilingual education approaches. There are many approaches and methods for teaching ESL, but the natural approach is well supported in the literature. It resembles most closely the language environment of the child

learning the mother tongue, a process almost always successful. It is based on themes rather than on grammar. Its major features are the provision of comprehensible input, the avoidance of correction, the acceptance of immature language structures at the beginning, a silent period during which children respond with gestures instead of producing language, and the maintenance of a low anxiety level in the classroom.

The natural approach consists of three stages: preproduction (comprehension), early production, and emergence of speech. During the intermediate stage that follows, children are ready to begin academic instruction in English, but in a sheltered or supported mode. Vocabulary development in English is an important part of the sheltered English (SIOP) process.

The focus of this chapter was on teaching reading in the mother tongue rather than in English. Children learn to read only once. For children who learn to read in their mother tongue, there is a positive transfer of skills from mother tongue reading to the second language: English.

Learning to read in Spanish is not greatly different from learning to read in English. Teaching word recognition skills is easier in Spanish because of the regular correspondences between sounds and letters in Spanish, but it is slightly different because Spanish is a highly syllabic language. Children tend to learn syllables instead of the sounds of individual letters.

Most major publishers provide Spanish language reading programs that are parallel to their English language programs. In addition, there is ample children's literature in Spanish, some originating in Spanish and some in the form of translations from English. Because of a lack of materials in most other languages, it is uncommon to find reading programs except in Spanish, especially beyond the first or second grade.

Many teachers who do not speak their students' mother tongue find themselves in a bilingual classroom nonetheless. They are usually provided with a bilingual paraprofessional who conducts the mother tongue instruction under the teacher's supervision. It is important for each teacher to develop a strong spirit of teamwork in which the paraprofessional benefits from the professional training and experience of the classroom teacher, who in turn benefits from the language and cultural skills of the paraprofessional.

For Your Journal

Find a classmate who did not speak English on arrival at the school or spoke English as a second language, but who speaks English now. Interview this person about his or her experiences in learning English and learning to read. If you have ever traveled to a foreign country and did not speak or read the language, what did you do to adjust? Discuss the feelings you might have had if you had experienced this as a child.

Taking It to the World

You should now have a very clear idea of the challenges facing English language learners in their new classrooms. If you were the parent of a six-year-old child and you were to move to Croatia, describe the language and reading program you would want for your child. What additional information would you need before making a final decision?

New Literacies Connections

1. Yahoo.com provides a primitive translation Web site where children can cut and paste text to be translated to and from English and Spanish, as well as French, Portuguese, German, and Italian. The resulting translations are only fair in quality, but it is an interesting and revealing exercise for children. Visit the Web site <http://babelfish.yahoo.com/> and experiment with it for yourself. How might you be able to use this site when teaching?

2. Kids Net is a multilingual Web site with multiple language translations provided. Visit Kids Net at <www.kidsnet.au> and explore for yourself. Why might this site be a valuable resource in the multilingual classroom?

MyEducationLab™

Go to Topic 11 (English Language Learners) in the MyEducationLab <www.myeducationlab.com> for your course, where you can:

- Find learning outcomes for English Language Learners along with the national standards that connect to these outcomes.
- Complete Assignments and Activities that can help you more deeply understand the chapter content.
- Apply and practice your understanding of the core teaching skills identified in the chapter with the Building Teaching Skills and Dispositions learning units.
- Check your comprehension on the content covered in the chapter by going to the Study Plan in the Book Resources for your text. Here you will be able to take a chapter quiz, receive feedback on your answers, and then access Review, Practice, and Enrichment activities to enhance your understanding of chapter content.
- Visit A+RISE. A+RISE® Standards2Strategy™ is an innovative and interactive online resource that offers new teachers in grades K-12 just in time, research-based instructional strategies that meet the linguistic needs of ELLs as they learn content, differentiate instruction for all grades and abilities, and are aligned to Common Core Elementary Language Arts standards English language proficiency standards in WIDA, Texas, California, and Florida.

Appendix A

Addressing the Common Core State Standards

Reading Standards for Literature	Key Ideas and Details	Chapter Seven Chapter Nine
	Craft and Structure	Chapter Three Chapter Seven
	Integrate Knowledge and Ideas	Chapter Seven Chapter Nine Chapter Twelve Chapter Thirteen Chapter Fourteen
Reading Standards for Informational Text	Key Ideas and Details	Chapter Eight
	Craft and Structure	Chapter Eight
	Integration of Knowledge and Ideas	Chapter Eight Chapter Nine Chapter Twelve Chapter Thirteen Chapter Fourteen
Reading Standards: Foundational Skills	Print Concepts	Chapter Four
	Phonological Awareness	Chapter Three Chapter Four
	Phonics and Word Recognition	Chapter Three Chapter Five Chapter Twelve
	Fluency	Chapter Six Chapter Twelve Chapter Thirteen
Writing Standards	Text Types and Purposes	Chapter Ten
	Production and Distribution of Writing	Chapter Ten
	Research to Build and Present Knowledge	Chapter Eight Chapter Ten Chapter Thirteen Chapter Fourteen
Speaking and Listening	Comprehension and Collaboration	Chapter Seven Chapter Eight Chapter Twelve Chapter Thirteen Chapter Fourteen
	Presentation of Knowledge and Ideas	Chapter Seven Chapter Eight Chapter Twelve Chapter Thirteen Chapter Fourteen
Language Standards	Conventions of Standard English	Chapter Three
	Knowledge of Language	Chapter Three
	Vocabulary Acquisition and Use	Chapter Six

Appendix B

Teach It! Instructional Activities

Codruța Temple, *State University of New York at Cortland* and

Jean Wallace Gillet

Contents

Overview

These lesson plans follow the order of their presentation in the text. They are designed for implementation by preservice teachers or by teacher education students in a practicum setting. They include a wide variety of activities featuring oral language development, emergent and beginning reading skills and concepts, reading comprehension, writing, and vocabulary development. Each of the activities is discussed in detail in the text.

Most of the featured lessons are intended for small group instruction within a regular classroom, and most can be readily adapted for individuals or larger groups, including whole classes. They provide opportunities for preservice teachers to practice instructional planning, lesson implementation, and classroom management while helping students develop critical language and literacy skills.

Each lesson plan includes a statement of objectives, stating what the activity is intended to teach or develop; a list of necessary materials, which should be gathered beforehand; and an estimated duration, or length of the lesson. Most lesson plans also include a list of suggested variations or extensions, which can be used to provide variety in subsequent lessons and to extend and enrich the learning experience. These can themselves become subsequent lessons, guided practice activities, or independent learning activities.

Each of these lessons can easily be modified to meet the individual needs of the preservice teacher, the supervising teacher, and the students in the classroom. Group size can be adapted and procedures and instructions can be modified to fit the needs and abilities of the students. Each activity is specific to one or more fundamental literacy skills, but each is also generic in that it can be productively retaught by changing the literature selection, writing stimulus, discussion props, and so forth. Each activity is one that preservice teachers should be familiar with and able to implement in the classroom.

Guidelines for Lesson Planning

- Plan every lesson ahead of time. Your mental preparation will enable you to present your lesson with skill and confidence. Planning ahead ensures that all necessary materials are at hand, allowing you to focus more on the students than on yourself.

- Select lessons to implement based on students' learning needs, not on your interests, strengths, or time constraints. Every lesson has an instructional purpose; knowing it will increase your confidence and enthusiasm.

- Collect and check all materials, supplies, and equipment beforehand. Missing markers, a mislaid book, or a burned-out overhead projector bulb can sabotage the best lesson.

- Be a positive language and literacy role model. Use precise, correct language, model enthusiasm for reading and literature, and show your enjoyment of learning.

- Reinforce positive behavior and effort by specifically drawing attention to what students did, rather than using empty praise. Point out when students use a strategy, attempt something difficult, or persist when having difficulty.

- Whenever possible, allow students choices, even if the range of choices is narrow. Having choices increases students' feeling of ownership and empowerment. Encourage diversity in answers to questions, ways to show comprehension, and choices of literature.

- Encourage and foster personalization and creativity. Show that you value students' attempts to relate what they are learning about to their own lives and experiences.

- Be prepared to handle interruptions, schedule changes, and the unforeseen with poise. No lesson ever unfolds exactly as planned, and an unexpected outcome can be even better than the planned outcome! Each lesson is a journey, and the "getting there" is as important as the destination.

- Evaluate each lesson you teach, even if your evaluation is only a brief self-reflection. If possible, jot down a few notes about what went well and what you'd do differently another time in a personal journal. Self-evaluation is one key to improving your teaching.

Reading Activities for Emergent and Beginning Readers

1. Reading Aloud

Objectives: To develop children's ability to comprehend written language; to raise children's awareness of the structure of different types of texts; to expand children's vocabulary; to encourage enthusiasm for literacy

Materials: An age-appropriate book

Duration: 10–15 minutes

1. Prepare to read the book.
   a. Read the book through yourself before you read it to the children to decide whether it is suitable for your class.
   b. Decide how you want to read it—with humor, with drama, with questions to whet curiosity.
   c. If there are voices to bring to life, decide how you want to make each one sound.
   d. If you decide to stop reading to ask for predictions or for discussion, decide where the stopping places should be.
   e. If there are any words or ideas that will be unfamiliar to the children, make a note to pronounce them carefully and explain them to the children.
   f. If the book has illustrations large enough for the children to see, practice reading the book through while you hold it in front of and facing away from you, where the children will be able to read it.
2. Prepare the children.
   a. Make sure the children are seated comfortably where they can see and hear you.
   b. Remind the children, if you need to, of the behavior you expect of good listeners: hands to themselves, eyes on the teacher, and ears for the story.
3. Read the title.
4. Show the children the cover of the book, ask them what they know about the topic, and ask them to make predictions about what will happen or what they expect to find out in the book.
5. Turn to the title page. Read the author's name and the illustrator's. Talk about what each contributed to the book. Remind the children of any other books they know by this author or this illustrator.
6. As you read the book through the first time, ask for comments about what is going on and for predictions about what will happen.
7. Follow up the reading with a whole-class discussion about the book.
8. Read the book a second time through, taking more time to look at the illustrations and to talk about characters, their motives, or other things you and the students find interesting about the book.
9. Leave the book available to the children in the library corner, and encourage them to read it later during scheduled time in the reading center or between other activities. The children might especially enjoy taking turns reading it to each other.

2. Dialogic Reading

Objectives: To develop children's oral language and concepts about print

Materials: An age-appropriate book

Duration: 10–15 minutes

A. Dialogic reading for younger children (PEER)
   1. Prompt the child to name objects in the book and talk about the story.
   2. Evaluate the child's responses and offer praise for adequate responses and alternatives for inadequate ones.
   3. Expand on the child's statements with additional words.
   4. Ask the child to repeat the adult's utterances.
B. Dialogic reading for older children (CROWD)
   While reading the book to the child, ask the following types of questions:
   1. Completion questions. Ask the child to supply a word or phrase that has been omitted. (For example, "I see a yellow duck looking at ____.")
   2. Recall questions. Ask the child about things that occurred earlier in the book. ("Do you remember some animals that Brown Bear saw?")
   3. Open-ended questions. Ask the child to respond to the story in his or her own words. ("Now it's your turn: You say what is happening on this page.")
   4. Wh- questions. Ask what, where, who, and why questions. ("What is that yellow creature called? Who do you think Brown Bear will see next?")
   5. Distancing questions. Ask the child to relate the content of the book to life experiences. ("Do you remember when we saw a yellow duck like that one swimming in the lake? Was it as big as this one?")

3. Morning Message

Objectives: To help emergent readers develop familiarity with written language; to focus attention on words

Materials: Chart paper

Duration: 15–20 minutes

1. Tell students that as a class you will write two or three things about your morning, such as the date, the weather, and anything that makes the morning special.
2. Invite students to suggest a sentence. Repeat the sentence.
3. Ask students what word you should write first. Ask what letter it should begin with and whether it should be an uppercase or a lowercase letter. Have a volunteer come forward and write some of the letters of the first word for you. Continue until you have written the complete sentence.
4. Read the sentence, pointing to each word. Have students read the sentence as you point to each word.
5. Repeat steps 2–4 to write two or three additional sentences.

6. Write some of the words that are often repeated on separate pieces of thick paper and tape them to the bottom of the chart or on the chalkboard.

7. Invite a student to come forward, pick one of the pieces of paper, and read the word on it. Then have the student find the same word in a sentence. Have her read the sentence aloud, then place the word on top of the same word in the sentence. Finally, ask the student to read the sentence again with the word in place.

8. Repeat step 7 for all of the words written on pieces of paper.

9. Have all of the students read the lines of text with you as you point to each word.

10. Have students choral-read the whole text.

11. Have students echo-read the text.

12. Invite different groups of children to read the morning message.

13. Ask individual children to come forward and point to any words they can read in isolation. Bracket each word with your hands as the child reads it, so the surrounding words cannot be seen. If the child is successful, write the word on a piece of thick paper and have the student add it to her word bank for later practice.

4. Language Experience or Group Dictated Story

Objectives: To help emergent readers develop oral language fluency, print directionality, concept of word, sight word recognition, and phonemic awareness

Materials: An object, shared experience, favorite song or book, or other stimulus for the dictation; large chart tablet or 24 × 36-inch paper on easel or chalkboard; large marker

Duration: 10–30 minutes; additional time for follow-up activities listed below

1. Select a group of 4–10 children to participate.
2. Select and prepare a stimulus for dictation: for example, an interesting concrete object, classroom pet, familiar story for retelling, or recent classroom event.
3. Invite participants to gather close to the chart paper. Introduce the activity by explaining that they will talk together about the stimulus and create statements about it that you will write for them on the chart paper. They will learn to read the sentences for themselves by rereading them together and pointing to the words.
4. Invite discussion of the stimulus, encouraging students to describe, narrate, and add verbal details. If necessary, ask open-ended questions like "What else do you notice?" "What else do you remember?" or "What happened after that?"
5. Ask for volunteers to contribute sentences for the dictation.
6. Write students' sentences verbatim, allowing changes or additions. Print neatly and clearly in large letters, with clear spaces between each word. Limit the account to 5–7 sentences.

7. Read the completed story expressively and at a natural pace, pointing to each word as you read.
8. Reread the story chorally several times until students have memorized it. Continue pointing to each word. (Keep up the pace so the reading sounds natural, not word by word.) If students have trouble memorizing the whole text, divide it into sections of two or three sentences each.
9. Invite volunteers to come to the chart and recite a part or the whole story while pointing to each word. Continue until each student who volunteers has read the story individually.
10. Point to individual words and invite students to identify the words, reading from the beginning to the target word if necessary.

5. Language Experience with Authentic Children's Literature

Objectives: To help emergent readers develop oral language fluency, print directionality, concept of word, sight word recognition, and phonemic awareness; to stimulate interest in and engagement with children's literature

Materials: A culturally appropriate piece of children's literature; chart paper or chalkboard; large marker or chalk

Duration: 15–30 minutes

1. As a stimulus for a language-experience dictation, conduct a read-aloud of a piece of children's literature that is culturally appropriate for your class.
2. During the read-aloud, share the illustrations in the book and ask questions about the unfolding story.
3. Have the children dictate their brief version of the story.
4. Accept the dictations of the children as stated, regardless of any cultural affectations, as long as other children do not suggest changes. However, spell the words correctly irrespective of students' pronunciation.
5. Make sure the children have many opportunities to read the text in a shared reading mode as the dictation is recorded and after the children's rendition of the story is completed.
6. Optionally, follow up with some of the activities suggested for the Language Experience or Group Dictated Story.

Follow-Up Activities for Group Dictated Story

- Repeat choral and individual reading and pointing on subsequent days until all students can read the story fluently and point accurately.
- Create an exact copy of the story on another sheet of chart paper. Cut the sentences or lines apart. Place in a center for students to reorder the lines and compare to the original.
- Copy each sentence onto a sentence strip. Have volunteers hold up each strip in correct order. (These can also be used for independent practice with a hanging pocket chart.)
- Create exact copies of the story on copy paper. Duplicate several copies for each participant. In different lessons,

students can paste copies on construction paper or in journals and illustrate them, cut lines and sentences apart and put them in correct order, cut sentences into phrases and put them in correct order, and use sentences for handwriting practice.

- Have students find individual words they recognize in isolation and begin building individual word banks with known words on cards. Students should sort and review word banks daily.
- Have students sort words in their word banks in a variety of ways: matching beginning sounds, number of syllables, alphabetical order, and so forth.
- Select one or several familiar words beginning with consonants. Using individual letter cards or magnetic letters, show students how to "make and break" the words by removing the initial letter or sound and substituting another, creating new words. (Change THAT to HAT, PAT, RAT, and CAT; MATCH to PATCH, BATCH, and SCRATCH; MAKE to TAKE, RAKE, FAKE, and LAKE.)
- Have students write known sight words using magnetic letters on cookie sheets, individual letters cut out of sandpaper, wallpaper scraps, or felt, glue and sand or glitter, pipe cleaners, heavy yarn, macaroni letters, mini-marshmallows, dried beans, and so forth. (The more ways they practice making the same words, the more automatic these words will become!)
- Begin personal dictionaries by folding eight to ten sheets of paper vertically and stapling in the fold to create individual books. Have students write a letter at the top of each page (group infrequent letters like q, u, x, y, and z with others) and begin collecting mastered sight words in their dictionaries.

6. Big Book Lesson

Objectives: To help emergent readers develop familiarity with book language patterns, print directionality, concept of word, sight word recognition, and phonemic awareness

Materials: A big book of your choice; for follow-up activities, a Word Hider (index card), sentence strips, pocket chart

Duration: 10–30 minutes; additional time for follow-up activities listed below

1. Display the big book, closed, on an easel or display stand (so your hands are free). Invite students to gather close enough to the book so everyone can clearly see the print.
2. Read the title, pointing to the words, and encourage students' observations about the cover art. Invite predictions of what the book might be about or what might happen based on the title and cover.
3. Open to the title page and read the author's and illustrator's names, pointing to the words. Be sure everyone knows what the author and the illustrator did. Make connections to other familiar books by the author or illustrator, if appropriate.
4. Read the first page fluently and expressively, pointing to the words. Comment, or invite student comments, on the illustrations. Review previous predictions and have

students revise or confirm predictions based on what is now known.

5. Repeat this step with each page, or several pages at a time, depending on the length and complexity of the text and the illustrations. Continue pointing to the words as you read. Continue inviting new or revised predictions as the story unfolds.
6. As you near the story's conclusion, invite final predictions of how it will end. Read to the end of the story.
7. Invite students' comments about the story and illustrations. Encourage them to talk about characters or story parts they liked, appealing illustrations, and so forth. You may wish to go back to particular illustrations to reexamine them, looking for details, or just for enjoyment.

Five-Day Plan for Using a Big Book

Day 1: Follow the preceding plan for the first reading. Goals for this lesson include introduction to the story, forming and revising predictions based on illustrations and unfolding plot, perusal of illustrations, and general enjoyment of the book activity.

Day 2: Either reread the story in its entirety, pointing to the words, or echo-read the story with students. (You read a sentence or two, pointing to the words, then students repeat verbatim or "echo.") At relevant points, stop to discuss predictions made during previous reading, and help students verbalize how they arrived at those predictions. Reexamine illustrations, this time for features overlooked the first time, details of colors, borders, and so forth. If appropriate, compare this book to familiar others by the same author or illustrator.

Day 3: Reread the story, inviting students to "chime in" or read along with you (choral-read) as desired. Some may be more ready to do so than others. Predictable lines, repeating refrains, and rhyming elements will support choral reading. Continue pointing to the words as you read. Emphasize comprehension in this lesson; ask questions about the story events, characters, setting, and so forth, inviting students to use both the text and illustrations to find information and justify their answers.

Day 4: Reread chorally, encouraging all students to read with you as much as they can. Many will have memorized the story by now. (If many are still unable to choral-read it, break the story into sections to work on.) Emphasize "word work" in this lesson. Point to and have volunteers identify selected words. Use the Word Hider (index card) to cover selected words, have students read from the beginning of the sentence and identify the hidden word; uncover to confirm. See how many times students can find the same word on the same and subsequent pages, find other words with the same beginning sound, or match words to familiar words on the word wall.

Day 5: Reread chorally, letting your voice "fade" so students are reading more independently. Have volunteers come forward to read one or more sentences, pointing to the words as they read. Distribute sentences on sentence strips and have students put them in order in a pocket chart. Have students act out the story and/or do related art, cooking, or other extension activities to enrich the literary experience.

7. Making Individual Small Books

Objectives: To provide students with small easily read books they can read independently at school and home

Materials: Two sheets of $8\frac{1}{2} \times 11$ plain paper for each student, supply of old magazines with colorful illustrations, scissors, glue, markers, stapler

Duration: 15–30 minutes, depending on number of students participating

1. Prepare a blank book for each student by placing two sheets of paper together, 11-inch side at top, folding vertically down the middle. Staple vertically in the fold, creating a book about $5\frac{1}{2} \times 8\frac{1}{2}$ with front and back covers and six inner pages.
2. Select a group of six to eight students. For larger groups, another adult is needed to assist students. Give each student a magazine, or magazine pages with colorful pictures, and scissors.
3. Select a group of eight or fewer students. If the group is larger, have another adult available to assist students. Gather around a work table where supplies have been placed.
4. Show students a premade model book: A magazine picture has been cut out and glued to each of the six pages of a book, and an adult has labeled the picture underneath with a simple phrase or sentence: "The dog is jumping," "A box is round," "A red apple," and so forth.
5. Assist students in choosing a picture and gluing it to the first page. Have them continue to complete the remaining pages. Using a marker, write the student's dictated sentence or phrase neatly and clearly under each picture. Have students copy a title onto the cover, print their names, and if desired write or draw on the back cover.
6. Assist each student in reading the entire book and practicing it so each can read his or her book fluently to the group or class during sharing time.

Variations: Give each book a theme and a title: Things That Are Round, What Is Square? (shapes); Red Is Everywhere, Things That Are Blue (colors); Animals All Around, Outdoors, We Can Play (various play activities); What Starts with B? (initial letters/sounds); It's Spring! (seasons or holidays), Foods We Love.

8. Modified Reading Recovery Lesson

Objectives: To help emergent readers develop oral language fluency, print directionality, concept of word, sight word recognition, and phonemic awareness

Materials: Individual copy of a short, predictable, clearly illustrated "little book" at Guided Reading levels A–D or Reading Recovery levels 1–8 for each participant

Duration: 10–15 minutes, depending on length and difficulty of text

1. Select one to three emergent readers to participate. (If more than one, have students take turns during the following steps.)
2. Preview the book by reading the title, encouraging student/s to examine the cover illustration and predict what might happen or what the book might be about.
3. Guide student/s in looking at the illustration on each page, naming objects and/or describing the picture, and if necessary modeling expanded oral language by repeating students' remarks in expanded form (S: "A dog." T: "Yes, there's a dog. It's a brown dog.")
4. Read and point to an important word or phrase, or repeated phrases, on each page as you examine the illustrations. (T: "Here's the word *dog*.") In this way you smooth the way for the reader/s to read each page independently.
5. Return to the first page and invite the student/s to read each page as independently as possible. Provide assistance on unfamiliar words, and encourage the student/s to use the picture, beginning sounds, and sentence context to attempt unknown words. Point out strategies you observe the student/s using: "You were smart to go back and read that sentence again when you got stuck," "I saw you get your mouth ready to say the beginning sound," or "You did what good readers do when you looked at the picture."
6. Choral-read the book with the student/s one or more times to gain familiarity with the sound of the sentences being read smoothly.
7. Invite student/s to read the whole book one more time with less teacher support. Encourage the student/s to reread the book several times independently at school and/or at home for fluency.

9. Guided Reading

Objectives: To develop effective strategies for processing novel text at increasingly challenging levels of difficulty; to develop students' ability to read silently

Materials: Multiple copies of leveled books

Duration: 5 minutes prior to reading; time necessary to complete reading and to respond to the story

1. Select a group of 4–6 children who are reading at about the same level.
2. Introduce a new text at students' instructional level. Encourage the students to converse about the text, to ask questions, and to build expectations.
3. Have the children read the entire text, or a unified part of it, to themselves silently (or softly in the case of younger readers). Allow them to ask for help when needed.
4. While the students are reading, observe their problem-solving strategies and provide assistance by suggesting other suitable strategies.
5. After the reading, involve the children in responding to the story through such activities as writing, discussion, paired reading, or sharing personal responses.
6. For subsequent guided reading sessions, regroup the children in accordance with outcomes that you have observed and assessed.

10. Guided Reading and the Four Blocks Approach

Objectives: To develop effective strategies for processing novel text at increasingly challenging levels of difficulty; to develop children's ability to read silently; to increase children's writing fluency; to teach word study skills in a meaningful context

Materials: Multiple copies of leveled books; optionally, a big book; chart paper for whole-class word study activities

Duration: 40–60 minutes

A. Working with small groups
   1. Follow steps 1–4 of the Guided Reading strategy as described earlier.
   2. Have the students respond to the story in writing. Suggest writing prompts that are appropriate to students' level of writing development.
   3. Follow the writing block with 10–15 minutes of self-selected reading time. Help students select texts at their independent reading level.
   4. Teach word study skills tailored to the needs of the children in the group.
B. Working with the whole class
   1. Make the text accessible to all students with multiple readings involving read-aloud, shared reading, and paired reading.
   2. Have the students respond to the story in writing.
   3. Follow the writing block with 10–15 minutes of self-selected reading time. Help students select texts at their independent reading level.
   4. In the last block, do word study with the whole class, with all students working on the same skills, or, if possible, teach appropriate skills in smaller groups.

11. Shared Reading

Objectives: To develop comprehension by modeling comprehension strategies; provide guided practice in using comprehension strategies

Materials: Fiction or nonfiction book students will read together

Duration: 10–30 minutes depending on length of book and size of group

1. Select a text for students to read. A big book can be used with younger readers.
2. Select two or more comprehension strategies to demonstrate; for example, organizing prior information before reading, predicting story outcomes, creating good questions, visualizing scenes, self-monitoring comprehension, making inferences about information not directly stated, using context to understand new words, identifying and clarifying difficult parts, or summarizing.
3. Preview the book with students; examine the title and cover illustration, predict what the topic of the book might be or what might happen in the story, and look at each page, examining illustrations and pointing out important words.
4. After previewing, read the text to or with students, depending on how well they can handle the text. Students can read predictable or repeated parts, echo-read or choral-read, or alternate reading with you.
5. While reading, "think aloud" to model effective reading: Pause to wonder or predict what might happen next, tell what a part reminds you of, wonder about word meanings, demonstrate how to use word parts or context to figure out new words, identify and reread difficult parts, and comment on illustrations. Emphasize the strategies you selected beforehand. For example, if you selected visualizing, think aloud about how you are imagining the setting, characters, and action; if you selected inferring, demonstrate making an inference from several related facts or ideas. Model what good readers do as they read.
6. Invite students' comments and predictions about the text. Ask and invite thoughtful questions.
7. Reread the text in its entirety to "put the pieces together" and experience the material as a whole. With greater familiarity, students may be able to read more of the text themselves.
8. Make the text available for students to reread independently.

Word Study Activities

12. Phonemic Segmentation with Elkonin Boxes

Objectives: To develop phonemic awareness and ability to segment phonemes in words

Materials: Elkonin boxes (series of connected squares) drawn on paper or sentence strips: two boxes for words with two phonemes, and so forth; "counters" such as poker chips or dried lima beans for the student to move; letter cards or magnetic letters

Duration: 5–10 minutes

1. Select a word with 2–4 phonemes (for example, *to*, *cat*, *trip*) to segment. Use the Elkonin box with the appropriate number of spaces. Say the word, then say the word phoneme by phoneme; as you say each phoneme, push or place a counter into a box. Have the student watch as you do this. If necessary, repeat.
2. Have the student copy what you did: Say the word, and then say each sound while pushing the counters into the boxes. If an error occurs, stop the student by placing

your hand over his or hers and modeling again, saying, "Watch again. Now you try." Repeat until the student can segment the phonemes and place the counters correctly.

3. Repeat the process with another word. You may choose another word with the same number of phonemes (*to, in, at*) or proceed to a word with one more phoneme (*in, pin, spin*).

4. When the student has mastered segmenting the phonemes and moving the counters, begin using letter cards or magnetic letters instead of counters, placing the letters in the boxes. (Keep letters representing digraph sounds together; for example, *that* has three phonemes, and the letters *th* are placed together in the first box.)

5. When the student has mastered moving the letters into boxes, you can remove the boxes altogether and continue practicing using just the letters.

13. Working with Names to Teach the Alphabet

Objectives: To develop knowledge of the alphabet

Materials: Pieces of cardboard, a box

Duration: 5 minutes

1. Write each child's name on a piece of cardboard and put all the names in a box.
2. Each day draw out a name, call the child forward, and interview her (about favorite pastimes, pets, games, etc.).
3. Then put the child's name on the bulletin board and explain that this word is a name.
4. Point to the letters in the name, reading left to right.
5. Have the children count the letters.
6. Call attention to the first letter of the name. Have students notice that it is a big letter. Explain that all names begin with a big letter. Show them the lowercase letter as well. Ask if anyone else has that letter in their name. Write other names that contain the letter on the chalkboard.
7. Repeat the activity every day with another child's name.

14. Beginning Sounds Picture Sorting

Objectives: To develop phonemic awareness, ability to distinguish among several different beginning sounds, and ability to categorize pictures of objects with the same beginning sound

Materials: Set of commercial beginning sounds sorting cards, or teacher-made cards with clear pictures of common objects, six to eight of each of two or more initial consonant sounds; pocket chart

Duration: 10–15 minutes

1. Preselect two or more beginning consonant sounds that are clearly different; begin with two contrasting sounds, and add more as students gain familiarity with the procedure. Select pictures of objects with these beginning sounds.

2. Gather a group of 4–10 students in front of the pocket chart.
3. Hold up each card and have students name each object. Be sure all students can name each object accurately.
4. Place one card for each sound at the top of the pocket chart. Tell students they will name the object on each card and place each card below the picture that begins with the same sound.
5. Mix up the remaining cards. Hold up each one and have students name the object chorally. Give each successive card to a different student. Have the student come to the chart, say a "sorting sentence" naming the two objects such as "Basket starts like baby," and place it in the correct column.
6. As each card is added to a column, have students name all the objects in that column chorally to check that they all have the same beginning sound.
7. When all pictures have been correctly sorted, have students name all the objects in each column one more time to reinforce the beginning sound. You may leave the cards near the pocket chart for students to sort independently as time allows.

Variations: Place one example of each sound at the top of the pocket chart. Distribute the remaining cards to students. Have students holding a card beginning with one sound come to the chart, say the sorting sentence, and place their cards in a column. Repeat with the other sound(s). Or dispense with the pocket chart: Have students line up next to each other, all the students with cards beginning with the same sound in one line. Have them name all the objects with the same beginning sound chorally.

15. Word Sorting

Objectives: To learn to discern patterns of similarity among words with similar sound, spelling, grammatical, or meaning patterns

Materials: Word cards with printed words that share a particular feature; pocket chart

Duration: 5–15 minutes, depending on number of words to sort and size of group

1. From a word wall, sight word banks, spelling list, or other source of words recognized at sight, select 2–4 features to contrast (for example, different beginning consonants, beginning blends, short or long vowel patterns, or parts of speech) and 4–6 words that share the same feature for each category. When introducing a new feature, or with struggling readers, contrast only two features at one time.

2. Review all the word cards with students; hold each up and have them identify the word chorally. Discard any words not recognized quickly.

3. Select one word from each group to represent the feature; read it and place it at the top of the pocket chart. Words sharing that feature will be placed below it in vertical columns. Point out the critical feature: "Let's find all the words that begin with the same sound as ball," "... have

the same vowel sound as run," "… mean more than one," or "… are adjectives, words that describe things."

4. Mix up the remaining cards and hold each one up, having students read it aloud. Have volunteers come forward to place the word in the correct column and say the "sorting sentence"; for example, "Men means more than one man" or "Pretty is an adjective."

5. When all words have been correctly sorted, have students read each column chorally beginning with the example word.

6. Leave the example words displayed, remove and mix up the cards, and leave them near the pocket chart for independent sorting.

Variations: Have students sort their word banks and create their own individual sorts on the floor or table in front of them, using the example words you give them. Have students create their own individual sorts using word bank or word wall words, and let others guess the common feature. Have students sort their spelling words and write the words in categories as a practice exercise.

16. Word Hunts

Objectives: To develop children's ability to make connections between the spelling and the pronunciation of words

Materials: Chart paper

Duration: 10–15 minutes

1. Select a short rhymed poem and write it in large print on a piece of chart paper.
2. Read the poem to the children.
3. Read it a second time with the children reading along.
4. Have the children reread the poem in partner groups.
5. Ask the children what they notice about the words at the end of each line. Elicit examples of rhyming words.
6. Tell the children you want to go on a word hunt for two words that don't rhyme. Thinking aloud, select two words that don't rhyme and, on another piece of chart paper, write them as the headings of two columns.
7. Tell the students to copy the columns and the headings into their notebooks.
8. Organize the class in pairs.
9. Tell the children that each pair has to find as many rhyming words as they can that match the top word in each column. The words can be new ones that they think of, words from the word walls, and words in the poem.
10. Have the pairs share the words they have found.
11. Talk about what makes words rhyme.

17. Making and Breaking Words

Objectives: To develop phonemic awareness and ability to segment onset (beginning sound) and rime (the rest of the word without the beginning sound)

Materials: Magnetic letters or letter cards for students (metal cookie sheets for magnetic letters, and "letter holders"

[sheet of paper folded 2 inches up from bottom and stapled vertically to create three or four pockets for letter cards] are helpful but optional); a large set of letter cards for demonstration

Duration: 10–15 minutes

1. Preselect two to four common phonograms that can become several different words by changing the initial consonant; these are often called "word families." Examples are *-an*, *-am*, *-to*, *-ock*, *-in*, *-ake*, *-ike*, and *-ill*. Preselect letters for these phonograms and the beginning sounds.
2. Select a group of students. Each student needs a set of letters or cards to make the phonograms and the necessary beginning letters. Gather around a table so students can manipulate letters.
3. Use large letter cards on the table or in a pocket chart to demonstrate. Put up the letters necessary to make a word such as *man*. Then remove the *m* and substitute another letter, such as *p*. Ask students to read the new word, *pan*.
4. Have students repeat the procedure themselves, using the magnetic letters or letter cards. Have them say the initial word, then say the new word as the initial letter is substituted. On the display set, again remove the initial letter and substitute another such as *r*, this time asking, "What word did I make this time? That's right, *ran*. Use your letters to make *ran*."
5. Continue until all real words have been made. (Avoid creating nonsense words like *zan*.)
6. Using the demonstration letters, quickly "make and break" all the words in one word family and have students read each word. Then have students use their letters to quickly make the words as you call them out. Repeat with the other word families used.

18. Making and Using Word Banks

Objectives: To develop sight word recognition

Materials: Index cards cut in half or pieces of thick paper or cardboard; a box or a zip-lock plastic bag

Duration: 5 minutes

1. Once a student has demonstrated that she can read a word out of context, write that word on a piece of thick paper and have the student put it in her word bank (a box or plastic bag that contains all the sight words a student has learned).
2. Have students practice reading the words in their word banks every day in one of the following ways:
   - By reading them to a partner or a parent volunteer;
   - By grouping the words into categories (e.g., animals, things, actions);
   - By grouping all the words that begin with the same letter;
   - By doing "word hunts," that is, looking for the same words in a children's book.
3. Have each student read the words in his or her word bank to you every week or every ten days. If a child cannot read a word correctly, put it in a special envelope inside the

word bank. Have students practice reading the words in the special envelope. When a word is read correctly, add it to the word bank.

19. Word Wall Activities

Objectives: To develop automatic (sight) recognition of words

Materials: Large bulletin board or wall space for display of word collections, with room to add 5–10 new words per week; blank word cards or sentence strips; heavy black and/or colored markers

Duration: 2–3 minutes to introduce each new word; 10+ minutes for a daily review of all words

1. To create a word wall of high-utility sight words, select 5–10 high-utility or frequently occurring words per week that students can recognize; begin with the simplest, like *I, a, the, is, am,* and so forth, and continue adding words weekly as students encounter them over and over in reading and writing. Divide the word wall space alphabetically; use letter cards to create spaces so words can be added with others beginning with the same letter.
2. To add a new word, print the word in large neat letters on a letter card. Hold up the card and "say-and-spell" the word aloud: "Good. G-O-O-D. Good."
3. Have students say-and-spell chorally, clapping as they say each letter. Repeat if students had difficulty.
4. Print the word on the board, or trace each letter with your finger, spelling aloud as you go. Say the word again.
5. Have students print the word or trace the letters with their fingers on desktops, the floor, or the back of their other hand, spelling the word aloud as they write/trace and repeating the whole word.
6. Have students "help you" find the letter category the new word goes in, and attach it to the word wall. Say-and-spell it again in unison. Quickly review all the words in that letter category.
7. Review at least some of the word wall words daily; point to the word and say-and-spell chorally. Have students practice "reading the wall" independently throughout the day.

Variations: Instead of, or in addition to, sight words, word walls can be made of word families (*-ike, -op,* etc.); beginning consonants, blends, and digraphs; vowel patterns; plurals; synonyms and antonyms; parts of speech (adjectives, prepositions, etc.); unusual words; subject-area words (math, science, health, history, etc.); holidays; sports; music; homophones; contractions; base words with their derivational forms; prefixes and suffixes; words with related Latin and Greek bases (*bio-, tele-, graph,* etc.); and words from a particular work of literature.

20. Analytic Phonics Lesson

Objectives: To help students learn to recognize new words by analogy to similar known words; to help develop phonemic awareness

Materials: Chalkboard, chart paper, or transparency, or letter cards and pocket chart, or magnetic letters and cookie sheet

Duration: 5–10 minutes

1. Select a word students know that can become several different words by changing the initial consonant, or have a student suggest a word they know to make new words from.
2. Write and say the word. Then say, "If I know _____, I know _____" while you remove or cover the initial consonant or cluster and replace it with another. (For example, "If I know ship, I know slip.") Repeat the process while the students say, "If I know _____, I know _____."
3. Repeat with the other initial letters to continue making new words. Invite volunteers to come forward to move the letters and make new words while saying the sentence as above.
4. Have students practice with a partner making and reading new words using letter cards or magnetic letters.

Variations: Have students write all the new words they can make from one known word. Add words to the word wall as needed. As students are able to recognize the new words at sight, have them add them to their individual word banks. Have students use the new words in oral and written sentences. Add new words to personal dictionaries.

Vocabulary Activities

21. "Word Conversation" for Primary Grades

Objectives: Introduce students to new vocabulary; help students learn the pronunciation, meaning, and use of new words

Materials: A fiction or nonfiction book to read aloud to students; chalkboard or chart paper

Duration: 5–10 minutes for each new word taught; sufficient time to read the book aloud

1. Select a book featuring rich use of language to read to the class or group. Select one to three unfamiliar words to teach. Read the book to the group or class.
2. After the reading, print the new word on the board. Point to it as you put the new word into the context of the book by using the word in a sentence about the book; for example, "In this story (*Best Friends* by Steven Kellogg), Kathy wishes Louise would get a contagious disease so Louise could come home. Say that word with me: *contagious.*" Point to the word as children repeat it.

3. Give a one-sentence definition of the word in terms the students can understand: "*Contagious* means that an illness is catching; you can catch it from someone else."

4. Give an example or two that children will be able to understand: "Colds are contagious; you can get a cold from someone else if that person sneezes or coughs near you and you breathe in the germs. Chicken pox is very contagious; if one child in a family gets it, usually the other children get it soon afterward."

5. Ask children to provide their own examples of the word: "I got chicken pox from my best friend in kindergarten." "When I got pinkeye I had to stay home because I was contagious for one day."

6. Have students echo as you say the word and its meaning again: "*Contagious* means that an illness is catching."

Extensions: Add the new word to a poster, bulletin board, "new word" word wall, or other display of interesting vocabulary words. Have students make up and act out brief skits to demonstrate the word's meaning. Have students write the new word and illustrate it. Have them add their illustration to individual vocabulary books they create and add to systematically. Designate it the "Word of the Day," and see how many ways students can use the word in meaningful sentences. Add the new word as a bonus word to the weekly spelling list.

22. Semantic or Concept Web for Upper Grades

Objectives: To learn specific meanings of synonyms and to categorize synonymous words by connotative meanings or shades of meaning

Materials: List of synonyms or words related by meaning; chalkboard, overhead transparency, or chart paper

Duration: 10–20 minutes, depending on number of synonyms and size of group

1. From a word wall, thesaurus, student writing, reading material, or other source, select a group of words sharing a common meaning; for example, these words relate to the concept of "more than enough": *plenty, excess, ample, lavish, copious, plethora, surfeit, myriad, superfluous, profuse.*

2. Write each word, pronounce it, and brainstorm with students what each one means. Provide several good context sentences to help them determine specific meanings.

3. Help students generate several categories into which the words can be sorted; for example, these words may suggest *many, enough,* and *too much.* Create a web on the board, transparency, or chart paper with circles or boxes that are large enough to write all the words in that category inside it. (Students often make their circles too small.) Or have students fold a sheet of paper to create the required number of boxes: in half for two, thirds for three, or quarters for four. They label each folded section and list the words in it that fit that category.

4. Have students sort the words into their appropriate categories; for example, "many" may include *lavish, ample, myriad, profuse, copious,* and *plethora*; "enough" may include *plenty* and *surfeit*; and "too much" may include *excess* and *superfluous.*

5. Have students come up with their own context sentences that illustrate the meanings of each word.

23. Connect Two

Objectives: Help students learn new vocabulary by predicting meanings of and relationships among key terms from a selection prior to reading

Materials: List of key terms from a selection to be read by students

Duration: 5–15 minutes depending on number and familiarity of terms selected

1. Preview a selection students will read. Collect five or more key terms from the selection, including technical vocabulary and unusual or unfamiliar uses of known words. List them on the board, a transparency, or duplicated worksheets.

2. Explain that all of the terms are used in the selection, and thinking about them before reading will help students recognize and understand them when they encounter them in the text. Pronounce each word.

3. Pair students and have each pair select two terms and use them together in a meaningful sentence. Sentences should, if possible, reflect what students think the words mean or how they are related.

4. Have students write their sentence for each pair of words and, if desired, draw a sketch to accompany it. Then have each pair share the sentences and comments about them with the larger group.

Variation: Instead of creating sentences, have students categorize terms they think go together, give each category a title or heading, and explain why they grouped them together when they share.

24. Semantic Feature Analysis

Objectives: To enrich vocabulary; help students relate a new concept to familiar concepts

Materials: Nonfiction text; chalkboard, chart paper, or transparency; marker

Duration: 10–15 minutes

1. Select a concept from a nonfiction text about which students may have limited prior knowledge or experience. Think of several related concepts about which students may know a little more to compare to it.

2. Create a chart on the board, chart paper, or transparency with a vertical (y) and a horizontal (x) axis. On the x-axis, list the new concept and the related concepts; on the y-axis, list several features of the concepts they may share.

3. Prior to reading, engage students in using what they may already know and their predictions to complete the chart. Start with the concepts they may be more familiar with, and ask if each feature is true; if the concept has that feature, mark it with a plus (+), and if the concept does not have that feature, with a minus (–). End with the new concept; students may not know if it has a particular feature but are to predict based on what they already know.

4. Have students complete the reading of the selection. Have them watch for information about the concept that they predicted about.

5. After reading, reexamine the chart. Have them compare their predictions about the new concept to what they learned from the reading, and change the chart as needed. Review what is now known about the new concept.

Fluency Activities

25. Repeated Reading

Objectives: To develop children's reading fluency

Materials: A reading passage of 50–500 words, depending on the child's reading rate

Duration: 10 minutes

1. Find a text (informational or fictional but not poetry or lists) written at the student's instructional level.
2. Sit next to the student in a quiet place, and listen as the student practices reading the text repeatedly.
3. Keep a copy of the text yourself on which you can mark the student's reading errors. (Errors are words that are omitted, or for which other words are substituted, or which are mispronounced. If the student does not say a word, wait 2 seconds and say the word yourself, and count that as an error.)
4. Time the student's reading for exactly 60 seconds; then stop the student, count the total number of words read, and subtract the errors from the total.
5. Have the student practice reading the text several times— preferably until the child reaches the criterion score for his or her grade level. Remember to offer adequate praise each time.

26. Fluency Oriented Oral Reading (FOOR)

Objectives: To develop reading fluency

Materials: Copies of text at students' instructional level

Duration: Three days (10 minutes each day)

1. Assemble a group of students who are at roughly the same instructional level. Provide copies of the text to all the students.
2. *Day 1:*
   - Read the text fluently while the students are following along.
   - Think aloud: call attention to the way you read words in groups and to how you emphasize important words.
   - Briefly discuss the meaning of the text with the students.
   - Echo read the text (you read one sentence fluently and the students read it at the same pace and with the same intonation).

3. *Day 2:*
   - Pair up the students and have them take turns reading the text, each one reading a sentence or a paragraph.
   - Circulate among the pairs and provide help as needed.
4. *Day 3:*
   - Have students come back together in the original group and choral read the text with you.

Extension: Step 4 may be followed by a Readers' Theater activity.

27. Paired Reading

Objectives: To develop reading fluency

Material: Text at the less fluent reader's instructional level

Duration: 5–10 minutes

1. Match up a fluent reader (a parent volunteer, a tutor, or an older student) with a less fluent reader. Instruct the more fluent reader to carry out steps 3–6.
2. Choose a text at the instructional level of the less fluent reader.
3. The more fluent reader reads the text to the less fluent reader.
4. The two readers read the passage several times in unison.
5. The less fluent reader reads the text, while the more fluent reader monitors her reading (corrects the errors by saying the words correctly, has the partner reread a sentence in which a word was misread, models the adequate intonation for a sentence and has the partner try to mimic it).
6. Repeat step 5 once or twice.

28. Readers' Theater

Objectives: To develop students' reading fluency and comprehension

Materials: A fictional text that contains dialogue, preferably among several characters

Duration: 15–25 minutes

1. Make a photocopy of the text you plan to use for readers' theater.
2. Read through the text and mark the parts that should be read by different readers. Create a code for different

readers, such as a capital letter to represent the name of each different character, and a capital N followed by a number for narrator number 1, 2, 3, and so on.

3. Put brackets [ ] around the parts that will be read by each reader, and write in a letter over each section to indicate who should read it.

4. Strike through any parts that do not need to be read. Often "He said," "she replied," and the like, can be eliminated without affecting the meaning.

5. As they prepare to read a fictional text with readers' theater, have the students discuss the setting of the text, who the characters are, and what they are like.

6. Have the students read portions of the text several times in order to read the lines fluently and with the expression called for.

7. Offer coaching, asking the students questions such as,

- "What is your character feeling right now? How do you sound when you feel that way? Should your voice be loud or soft? Fast or slow?"

- "What might your character think about what the other character is saying? How will your character sound then?"

- "What is going on at this point in the story? How is your character reacting to it?"

- "How is your character changing as the story proceeds?"

8. Offer comments and suggestions after each practice reading and invite the students to do the same.

29. Choral Reading

Objectives: To develop reading fluency in a meaningful context

Materials: Poems with a strong rhythmic pattern

Duration: 10–15 minutes

1. Prepare the children to choral-read a text by discussing the circumstances or the context in which it might be said. Ask the children to imagine the situation and to describe the sounds they associate with it. Offer suggestions as necessary.

2. Decide how the poem should be read, for example, by the whole chorus, by individuals, by pairs, or by two alternating sections; in loud or soft voices; rapidly or slowly; melodiously, angrily, giggling, or seriously.

3. Have each student or group of students practice reading their part until they can keep the rhythm perfectly.

4. Have the whole class practice reading the poem in the manner previously agreed on until they sound like a good chorus. Invite and give feedback after each performance.

Comprehension Activities with Fictional Texts

30. Terms in Advance

Objectives: To develop comprehension by recalling and organizing prior information before reading; enable students to predict what a reading passage might be about; familiarize students with key vocabulary and concepts prior to reading

Materials: List of key terms or phrases from the text to be read, chart paper or transparency, marker

Duration: 5–15 minutes, depending on size of group, number of terms, familiarity of terms

1. From a reading passage students are going to read, collect a group of key words and/or phrases that bear importantly on the content of the passage. Try to include both familiar and unfamiliar terms; don't just collect all the hardest or least familiar vocabulary.

2. Display the words on a chart or transparency with space around each one for recording students' ideas of what each term means and/or how it might bear on the passage they will read.

3. If your main goal for the activity is to encourage predictions about what the text to be read will be about, have students hypothesize about ways in which the terms might be related in the story. Optionally, you may allow them to write down their predictions before sharing them with the class. Accept all hypotheses or predictions encouragingly.

4. If your main goal is to introduce new vocabulary, have students dictate or write sentences explaining the meaning of one or more of the terms, or make up sentences that combine two or more of the terms in one sentence.

5. As students read the text and the meaning of various terms becomes clear, modify the chart or transparency to show what each term means in the passage and to reflect new information gained during reading. Alternatively, ask students to compare the story they read to their initial predictions.

31. Directed Reading-Thinking Activity (DRTA)

Objectives: To develop comprehension by recalling and organizing prior information before reading

Materials: Fiction selection; chalkboard, chart paper, or transparency; marker

Duration: 10–30 minutes or longer, depending on length of selection

1. Select a story with a well-structured plot that revolves around a character's attempts to solve a problem or achieve a goal, with a clear resolution of the conflict at the end.

2. Plan from two to five stopping points in the story, where students will stop reading to discuss what they have read

and make predictions about forthcoming parts of the story. Plan the stops just before some major event or piece of information.

3. Explain to students that they will be making predictions, or educated guesses, about what might happen in the story, and they will base their predictions on the title, illustrations, and what they read in preceding sections. They will read up to, but not beyond, the stopping points and will not read ahead. They will justify their predictions based on what they learn as the story unfolds. All predictions will be accepted respectfully by everyone. The process of predicting, not whether their predictions are proved or disproved, is what is important.

4. Have students read the title, examine cover art and initial illustrations, and perhaps the first section of the story. Elicit predictions by asking, "What might happen in this story?" or "What might this story be about?" and "Why do you think so?" Jot down key phrases from different predictions. Have students read the next section to find out and stop at the next stopping point.

5. After each section, have students briefly review what they know so far and new information revealed in the prior section. Review and check predictions that still seem likely or possible. Elicit further predictions about the next section.

6. Repeat this cycle of "review-predict-read to prove" to the end. At the conclusion of the story, briefly discuss with students how they used clues and events to predict the outcome.

Variation: Read the story aloud to the group as a Directed Listening-Thinking Activity, following the same procedures.

32. Dual-Entry Diary

Objectives: To encourage personal responses to literature; to develop writing fluency

Materials: Response journals

Duration: 10–15 minutes

1. Model the technique on the overhead projector or on the chalkboard. Draw a vertical line in the middle of a blank sheet of paper:

   - On the left-hand side, write a passage from the text that students are reading. Explain that you chose to write it down because you found it particularly striking (because it reminded you of your own experience, or because you disagree with it, or because it is unexpected, etc.).

   - On the right-hand side, write a comment about the passage. (Why did you write it down? What did it make you think of? What question do you have about it?)

2. Instruct students to use their response journals as dual-entry diaries and, as they read the text, to pause and make entries. You may choose to assign a minimal number of entries per text.

Extension: If students are reading a longer text, you may collect the dual-entry diaries periodically and write

comments in them. You may also ask students to share some of their entries in a discussion group or use them to structure a whole-class discussion.

33. Instructional Conversations

Objectives: To develop comprehension; to develop critical thinking; to develop conversational skills

Materials: Story or passages from a book

Duration: 30–60 minutes

1. Decide on what the theme or issue for the conversation should be (a real issue that real people might wonder about, one that invites different responses, one to which students can relate and that is likely to engage them).

2. Select a story or passages from a book and have the students (re)read it/them.

3. Explain that you will have a conversation about the text and that everyone is invited to think hard about it and share ideas.

4. Clarify the rules for participation: Students do not need to raise hands; however, they need to listen to each other carefully, be respectful, and wait for others to finish before contributing.

5. Begin the conversation with an open-ended question. Make sure that the students can resort to their background knowledge, interests, and experience to answer it.

6. Keep the conversation loosely focused on the main theme. Do take the time to explore collateral issues raised by students, but tactfully steer the conversation back to the main topic.

7. As the conversation proceeds, explain points that are not clear, provide background information that you notice students do not have, provide new vocabulary that students may need to express their emerging insights in a more sophisticated manner.

8. Ask students to support their ideas with evidence from the text throughout the conversation.

34. Save the Last Word for Me

Objectives: To develop comprehension; encourage thoughtful discussion of a shared text

Materials: 3 × 5 file cards or sheets of paper cut in quarters; 1–4 cards per student

Duration: 10–20 minutes depending on size of group

1. Distribute blank file cards or papers to students.

2. After they have finished reading a selection, have them find a sentence or short section (no longer than a few sentences, or as short as one sentence) in the text that they find particularly interesting, surprising, evocative, or otherwise noteworthy and write the quotation on one side of a card. On the reverse side they write a comment or response: why they found it interesting, what it made them think about, something it reminded them of, and so forth. Older students and those reading longer or more

complex texts can complete several cards in the same way; younger readers or those reading shorter texts can complete one.

3. When completed, ask a volunteer to read his or her selected quotation aloud and call on several other students to comment on or respond to the quotation. Discussion of each other's comments is allowed. After several others have commented, the first student shares his or her written comment on the quotation. No discussion follows; the original writer has "the last word."

4. Another student is selected by the first student or the teacher to repeat the procedure; read the quotation, invite others to comment, then share his or her written comment. In small discussion groups or literature circles, all students may be able to participate; in larger groups or with the whole class, only some will be able to share each time.

35. Literature Circles

Objectives: To develop comprehension; promote thoughtful discussion and interpretation of shared literature

Materials: A shared work of literature (all students in the group read the same text)

Duration: 20 minutes or longer, depending on the group size, degree of experience with the procedure, and students' interest in discussion

1. Assign students participating to read the same text; they may read a short text in one sitting or read a section such as a chapter of a longer work.

2. Convene a group of all the students reading the shared work; for best interaction, group size should not exceed 5 or 6. If more students are reading the same text, create two groups.

3. Assign each student a role for that meeting; see textbook, Table 7.2, for a list of possible roles. The roles most often used include the Questioner, sometimes called the Discussion Director, who creates three or four thoughtful questions about the main events of the selection for the group to discuss; the Quotation Finder, sometimes called the Passage Master, who selects one or more excerpts to practice and read aloud; the Artist, or Illustrator, who illustrates the selection with written captions; and the Word Finder, or Word Wizard, who locates and explains interesting or important words, figurative language, expressions or idioms, and the like, to the group.

4. Monitor the execution of the various roles in the group discussion; model reflective questioning and responding to the text without lecturing or dominating; move the discussion forward when necessary by drawing all students into the discussion, and use literary terms such as *episode*, *climax*, *resolution*, and so forth, as appropriate.

5. If students are reading a longer work in sections, assist them in deciding how far they will read before the next meeting and when they will next meet.

6. Have all students regardless of their role write a summary, response, or other piece in their literature or reading journals about the section just discussed.

7. Rotate the roles so all students participate and have different responsibilities.

36. Shared Inquiry

Objectives: To develop comprehension and critical thinking

Materials: A shared work of literature (all students have read the same text)

Duration: 20–40 minutes

1. Choose a text or part of a text that encourages discussion (that is, one that lends itself to multiple interpretations or raises interesting or even controversial issues) and which students have read carefully.

2. Prepare four or five discussion questions that meet the following three criteria: (1) they are questions that real people would ask in real life; (2) they have more than one possible answer; and (3) they lead the discussion into the text, that is, they invite revisiting the text as a source of evidence in support of possible answers.

3. Write the first question on the chalkboard and invite the students to think about it and briefly write down their answers.

4. Invite students (including reluctant speakers) to share what they wrote. Point out differences between responses and invite their authors and the rest of the class to expand on those differences. Press them to support their views with references to the text and to restate their ideas more clearly if necessary. Do not correct any answer and do not suggest that it is right or wrong. Do not offer your own answer to the question.

5. Use a seating chart to record what each student has contributed.

6. When the discussion of a question has run its course, summarize it based on your notes and ask if anyone has anything to add.

7. Repeat steps 3–6 with each of the discussion questions you have prepared.

Extension: Have students respond to one of the discussion questions in writing.

37. Discussion Web

Objectives: To develop comprehension; promote thoughtful discussion and interpretation of shared literature; help students perceive and understand both sides of a position or argument

Materials: A shared work of literature (all students in the group read the same text)

Duration: 15–30 minutes

1. Assign students participating to read the same text; they may read a short text in one sitting or read a section such as a chapter of a longer work. Text may be fiction or nonfiction.

2. Generate a discussion question that can reasonably be argued from both sides, sometimes called a binary question; for example, "Was it wrong for ____ (story character) to ____ (act in a way that some might consider wrong, but for which he or she had a reason or rationale)?" "Was ____ (story character) ____ or ____ (two opposite or opposing characteristics, like brave/reckless, caring/selfish, or wise/foolish)?" or "Is (or was) it right or wrong to ____ (nonfiction text or subject area issue: secede from the Union, hunt whales, log the rain forest, send Japanese Americans to internment camps, etc.)?" Write the question so students can refer to it as they reflect.

3. Assign students to pairs. Have each pair answer the question from both sides of the argument, listing three reasons, examples, and so forth, to support each side.

4. Combine two pairs to create groups of four. Have students combine their lists so all positions are included. Then have each foursome reach agreement on one side of the argument and prepare to defend it.

5. Have each foursome summarize and defend its work to the larger group.

Extension: When two or more groups take opposing positions, a formal debate can follow. Groups taking the same position can join forces to share arguments and prepare to present them as forcefully and logically as possible, prepare notes, select spokespersons, and if desired conduct research on their position. Establish strict ground rules (no personal attacks, no raised voices, etc.) and time limits for arguments and rebuttal. Have each side briefly summarize its arguments in closing.

38. Debate

Objectives: To develop critical thinking skills; to give students practice in making claims and defending them with reasons

Materials: Chalkboard

Duration: 20–30 minutes

1. Find a binary question (one that has a yes/no answer) that you think will divide students' opinions roughly equally and write it on the chalkboard.

2. Give students five minutes to discuss it freely in pairs or groups of four.

3. Ask the students who believe one answer to the question is right to go stand along the wall on one side of the room, and those who think the other answer is right to stand along the wall on the other side. If there are undecided students, instruct them to stand along the wall in the middle.

4. Explain the ground rules:
   a. Argue politely!
   b. If you hear an argument that makes you want to change your mind, walk to the other side or to the middle.

5. Ask the students on each side to spend 2–3 minutes in their groups to come up with a sentence that states their position and to appoint someone to say that sentence.

6. Begin the debate by asking each team, including the undecided group, to state their position.

7. Invite students on both teams to respond—either with a counterargument/rebuttal or with more reasons in support of one of the positions expressed.

8. Ask for clarifications as needed. Offer an idea or two from the devil's advocate position to liven up the debate. Change sides when you hear a compelling argument. Encourage students to change sides if they are persuaded to.

9. When the debate has proceeded for 10–15 minutes, ask each side to summarize what they have said.

Extension: Ask the students to write down what they think about the issue and why.

39. Value Line

Objectives: To develop critical thinking; to give students practice in making arguments

Materials: A shared text (one that all the students have read)

Duration: 15–20 minutes

1. After the students have read a text carefully, ask a question about it to which the answers may vary along a continuum.

2. Give the students three minutes to write down their individual answers.

3. Stand at one end of the room and announce that you represent one pole, or extreme position, of the argument. State your position.

4. Invite a student to stand at the other end of the room to represent the other pole of the argument. Help her state that position.

5. Invite the students to line up between the two of you. Instruct them to choose a point on the imaginary line between the two poles of the argument that reflects their position on the question.

6. Tell the students to compare their views with those of the students around them to make sure they are standing in the right spots. Encourage them to move one way or another on the value line after hearing others' ideas and to continue discussing their answers until they find a group that shares the same position on the question.

7. Identify three or four clusters of students who seem to represent different views. Invite them to prepare a statement of their position and to share it with the class.

Variation: After step 6, you may want to fold the value line in the middle so that students with divergent views may debate their answers, while students with similar views may be helped to think of additional reasons in support of their position.

Extension: Have students write an argumentative or persuasive essay in response to the question.

40. Story Maps

Objectives: To develop comprehension; help students identify and sequence key story elements and events

Materials: Shared fiction text; story map graphic organizer, with key story elements for students to label

Duration: 10–20 minutes

1. Have students read, or read to them, a well-structured story that has a clear plot line including a well-defined main character; a problem, goal, challenge, or defining event faced by the main character; a series of attempts by the character to solve the problem or achieve the goal, the first several of which are unsuccessful, often referred to as the *rising action*; a final attempt that is successful, although not always as the character expected, forming the climax; and a resolution of the story, in which the character is often changed in some way.

2. Create a simple graphic organizer that labels the major parts of the story and allows students to fill in spaces on a chart, timeline, or flowchart. (There are many different kinds of premade story map graphic organizers available in teacher resource books, textbooks, basal manuals, comprehension kits, and so forth, or you can make your own.) For emergent and beginning readers, divide a sheet of paper into thirds vertically and label the sections *Beginning*, *Middle*, and *End*; students retell the story, then draw a picture to represent each part and write or dictate one or two sentences telling what happened in that part.

3. Have students include important details supporting the plot, including the setting and supporting characters.

4. Allow students to share their story maps by using them to retell the story.

Extensions: Provide students free access to a variety of types of story maps they can complete as they finish a work of fiction. Carefully completed story maps can be substituted for book reports or reviews when students must demonstrate their comprehension of a completed story. They can be shared during oral book reports. When students are writing fiction, completing a story map during the planning stage of the writing cycle helps students plan a complete story before they start and helps them structure their stories. (See "Story Maps for Writing" activity.)

41. Character Clusters and Character Maps

Objectives: To develop comprehension; help students understand characteristics or traits of story characters and relationships among characters

Materials: Shared work of fiction; chalkboard, transparency, or chart paper

Duration: 10–15 minutes

A. Character Cluster
  1. Have students identify the main character in a shared work of fiction. (If a work has more than one central character, create a separate cluster for each main character.)
  2. Create a web graphic organizer by placing the main character's name in a circle in the center of the web. Have students brainstorm characteristics or traits of that character (e.g., brave, funny, a loyal friend, loves wildlife, shy, etc.). Have students select three to five that are most descriptive of that character and write those traits in circles around the center circle, connected to it by lines.
  3. For each characteristic, have students generate examples of the character's words, actions, and attitudes from the story that illustrate that trait. Write these examples in circles that are connected by lines to the trait circles; for example, *brave*: chased away the mean dog, told the truth about breaking the lamp.

B. Character Map
  1. List with students the main and supporting characters in a work of fiction they have read or are reading. Have students identify the main character/s.
  2. Write the names of the main character in a central circle and the supporting characters in circles arranged around the central one. (Leave plenty of writing space between the circles.) Have students briefly describe how the main character feels about the supporting character. Draw an arrow from the main character to a supporting character; along the line, write a sentence that describes those feelings. Repeat for the other supporting characters.
  3. With student help as above, draw arrows from the supporting characters to the main character and to other supporting characters. Along the arrows, write these characters' feelings about each other.

Comprehension Activities with Nonfictional Texts

42. Think-Pair-Share

Objectives: To reflect on and thoughtfully respond to a question and share responses with a peer; encourage reflective thinking and respectful listening; develop comprehension by recalling and organizing prior information before reading

Materials: Students may write their initial responses in journals or learning logs or on scrap paper; otherwise, no materials are needed

Duration: 5 minutes or less

1. Ask an open-ended question—that is, a question that can be answered many ways depending on the opinions,

experiences, predictions, or preferences of the individuals answering it. For example; "What could we do as a class to show our concern for the environment?" "How could this story character have behaved differently so the story had a different outcome?" or "What traits or characteristics make a person a good leader?" Write the question so students can reread it as they think.

2. Have students think, then write in brief form their thoughts in their journals, learning logs, or on scrap paper.
3. After a short interval for writing, have each student turn to a partner and share his or her answers to the questions, taking turns. Remind students to talk to their partners, not read their papers to them, and to listen respectfully and attentively to each other.
4. Have a few volunteers share their thoughts with the larger group or restate their partner's response instead of their own.

Variation: Paired Brainstorming In a situation where students will share factual information, for example before reading expository text when students are recalling and organizing their prior information about the topic, have individuals briefly list the information they already know during the "Think" phase. After a minute or two, each student joins a partner and the two lists are quickly combined during the "Pair" stage. Finally, a few key facts from each pair are listed on the board, chart paper, or a transparency during the "Share" stage. Students can compare what they knew before reading to information they acquire during and after reading.

43. Paired Brainstorming

Objectives: To activate prior knowledge of a topic

Materials: Journals or scrap paper

Duration: 6–10 minutes

1. Announce the topic of the lesson and ask the students to brainstorm (that is, to think of everything that comes to mind) about it and list the facts or ideas on a sheet of paper in 2–3 minutes. Tell them that they may also list questions they have about the topic.
2. When time is up, instruct the students to turn to a classmate and combine their lists.
3. Have volunteers share their ideas and make a master list on the chalkboard, arranging the ideas in categories if possible.
4. Leave the master list on the board and have students compare it to the ideas they have after they have read a text or at the end of the lesson.

44. Anticipation Guide

Objectives: To develop comprehension by recalling and organizing prior information before reading

Materials: Teacher-made anticipation guides, duplicated for each student

Duration: 5–10 minutes to complete the guide prior to reading and again after reading the material

1. Read through the material your students are going to read. Select a number of important facts, terms, and so forth, you want students to remember and understand from the reading.
2. Create a set of statements to which students will respond by agreeing or disagreeing, marking them True or False, or checking the statements they think are true; for example, "There were thirteen southern colonies," "Maple syrup is made by crushing the leaves of the maple tree," or "Only native-born U.S. citizens can become president."
3. Type each statement, preceding each one with a blank on the left side of the paper and following each one with a blank on the right side of the paper. Head the left-side column of blanks "BEFORE" and the right-hand column "AFTER."
4. Distribute the anticipation guides *before* reading or discussing the text material, and have students read and mark each statement true/false, agree/disagree, and so forth, in the BEFORE (before reading) column. (Be sure they understand they are not expected to know all the right answers, just to make an attempt at each item based on what, if anything, they might already know about the topic, and their answers will not be corrected, graded, etc.) Collect the guides and keep them for later. Briefly discuss students' responses to each statement, but do not tell them the correct answer.
5. Read and discuss the text material as you would normally do. After students have thoroughly read and discussed the material, participated in comprehension activities, and so forth, redistribute the original anticipation guides and have students respond to each item, this time marking in the AFTER (after reading) column. These responses should now represent the correct information; therefore, answers in the AFTER column may be checked for correctness or graded. Be sure students understand that their initial attempts were "best guesses," and only their responses after the reading will be checked.
6. Students can fold the BEFORE column under and keep their anticipation guides as a form of class notes or study guides on the topic.

45. Graphic Organizers

Objectives: To help students organize information in text

Materials: Blank graphic organizers for students to fill in before, during, and after reading

Duration: 5–30 minutes depending on length and complexity of text and the graphic organizer used

1. Select or create a graphic organizer that fits the organization of the text: for example, a timeline or sequential flowchart for sequences of events, Venn diagram for comparison/contrast, or web for main and subordinate categories.

2. Have students preview or skim the material to find some of the main topics or categories of information and enter them on the graphic organizer. With textbook material, chapter headings and subheadings often contain this information.

3. Have students attempt to recall and organize their prior information about these topics before reading, and note what they already know in pencil on the organizer. (If they are later disproved, these entries can easily be changed.)

4. As students read, they continue to enter new information they encounter on the organizer: for example, dates and places of historical events, short- and long-term effects of events, biographical information, and other important supporting details.

5. After the reading, have students compare their organizers in pairs or small groups, adding or moving information as needed to make their organizers clear and accurate. They can then be used as outlines for writing or for study guides.

46. Metacognitive Graphic Organizer

Objectives: To develop awareness of text organization; to assist students in self-monitoring their comprehension of non-fiction texts; to help students create a personal guide for reading and study

Materials: Article or textbook chapter

Duration: Varies with the length of the text

1. Have students place the title of the article or chapter in the center of a sheet of paper and then add the major headings as they survey the material.

2. Instruct students to look at the visual information in charts, diagrams, etc. and add key ideas from these to the graphic organizer, under the appropriate headings.

3. Have students read the text and make notes on the graphic organizer or on sticky notes as they read.

4. When they finish reading, instruct students to review the graphic and the notes made and decide whether to (a) revise the graphic (if the actual organization of the text is different from what students initially drew), (b) add subheadings (if several ideas can be grouped under one subheading), or (c) write extended notes to clarify the important ideas (if there are many new ideas). Students may choose to do any or all of these depending on their own learning needs.

Extension: Have students use their graphic organizers to write a summary of the article or chapter.

47. Know-Want to Know-Learn (K-W-L)

Objectives: To develop comprehension by recalling and organizing prior information before reading; organize new information gained by reading and relate it to prior information

Materials: Nonfiction material; chalkboard, chart paper, or transparency; duplicated K-W-L charts

Duration: 10–30 minutes or longer, depending on length of selection and students' prior information

1. Create a K-W-L chart on the board, chart paper, or transparency consisting of three vertical columns; label the left-side column K: What We Know; the center column W: What We Want to Find Out; and the right-side column L: What We Learned. Write the topic at the top. Duplicate and distribute blank charts.

2. Prior to reading, have students write some things they already know about the topic in the K column on their charts. Have volunteers share some of their ideas; record them in the K column on the group chart. Ask direct questions about important information in the passage that no one mentioned.

3. When disagreements occur or when questions arise that can't be answered prior to reading, note these in the W column. Have students generate and write on their charts one question they can't answer; write some of these on the group chart and have students include them on their charts as well.

4. Briefly review with students what they already know and are uncertain about. Read the passage.

5. After reading, review the K column with students; check those ideas that were borne out by the passage; and cross off those that were disproved, writing the correct information in the L column. Review the W column; check those questions that were answered by the passage, writing the corresponding information in the L column. Mark those questions still unanswered with a question mark for further research. Add to the L column any other new information gathered from the passage.

6. Have students reorganize and add to their own charts as you do so with the group chart.

48. What? So What? Now What?

Objectives: To help students organize facts and arguments to prepare to do persuasive writing or speaking

Materials: Blank organizer on board, chart paper, or transparency; duplicated copies of blank organizer for students to complete

Duration: 10–15 minutes

1. Prepare a model organizer for the group to complete on the board, chart paper, or a transparency. Create three columns across the top: label the left-side column WHAT?, the center column SO WHAT?, and the right-side column NOW WHAT? Explain that this chart will help them organize their facts and opinions to write or speak persuasively on an issue they have read about (e.g., environmental pollution, species endangerment, cafeteria recycling, logging of national forest lands, etc.).

2. On the left side of the chart, list factual information students have learned about the topic: for example, "Since 1950, ____ species have become endangered and ____

have become extinct," or "Species are now becoming endangered at an average rate of _____." In the central column, list students' reasons why these facts are important or why others should care about them. In the right-side column, write students' suggestions of actions that could affect or improve the situation.

3. Using the completed group chart, have students compose persuasive essays or speeches presenting the relevant facts, explaining their importance, and urging their audience to pursue a course of action.

Variations: When an issue arises that students care about, complete this chart with them to help them sort out facts from opinions, create persuasive arguments, and determine how they can act on their beliefs. Then follow through as a group on one or more actions to address the situation.

Extensions: Have students organize the information in the L column in categories and construct a web or other graphic organizer of the information. Have students use their K-W-L charts as study guides or as resources for writing summaries and reports. Gather related reading materials and have students research answers to questions still listed in the W column. Follow up with a "What? So What? Now What?" activity to help students determine actions that can be taken based on what they learned.

49. Reciprocal Teaching

Objectives: To model and practice comprehension strategies of summarizing, questioning, clarifying, and predicting

Materials: Nonfiction text; chalkboard, chart paper or transparency

Duration: 15–30 minutes or longer, depending on length and difficulty of text

1. Survey and break the text into segments for students to read; depending on the length and difficulty of the entire selection, segments may be as short as one or two paragraphs or as long as a chapter section. Students can use sticky notes to mark the end of a segment. Create groups of four students each.

2. Read the first segment with students. Then model how to use the four strategies: First, summarize the section in one or two sentences, writing them on the board, chart paper, or transparency; second, ask one or two good questions to be answered by students; third, clarify by identifying the most difficult part of the section (may be a word or phrase, sentence, example, or concept) and explain it or tell how you could figure it out (look it up, check an encyclopedia, use surrounding context, etc.); fourth, predict what the next section might contain based on what you've already read.

3. Assign each student in a group a task for the next section: summarizer, questioner, clarifier, or predictor. (Job cards help students remember what they are to do.) Read the next section with students.

4. After reading, each student is to complete his or her task following your model. Allow time for task completion.

Each student then shares his or her work with the group, starting with the summary statement and ending with the prediction. The group should discuss and amend the summary as needed, use the text to answer the questions, examine the difficult part and add to the explanation, and discuss the prediction.

5. Repeat the teacher modeling of the strategies after reading the next section. Depending on time available and students' success with the procedure, you can continue to alternate teacher modeling and student practice through the remaining sections or have students work through subsequent sections as above, rotating tasks within the group so each student completes a different task each time.

50. Jigsaw

Objectives: To develop comprehension; to provide practice in using comprehension strategies in cooperative learning groups

Materials: Nonfiction text; expert sheets

Duration: 40–60 minutes

1. Before the lesson select a text, divide it into four sections, and prepare four different expert sheets numbered 1–4. The expert sheets are sets of 4–6 questions that will focus students' attention on the most important points in each section. Make sure you include not only recall questions, but also questions that invite higher order thinking.

2. Begin the activity by explaining that everybody will be reading a text and be responsible for learning all the material. Add that each person will become an expert in one part of the text and will teach others about it.

3. Assign students to home groups of four or five members.

4. Distribute copies of the text to all students. Also distribute a different expert sheet to each student in a group. If there are more than four members in a home group, make sure that no more than two students receive the same expert sheet.

5. Have the class read the entire text. Instruct students that finish early to take notes on the section of the text that pertains to their expert sheet.

6. Reassign the students to one of four expert groups based on the number of their expert sheet.

7. Instruct the expert groups to discuss the questions on their expert sheets and take notes on the answers that the group offers to the questions. Encourage the students to clarify the material as best they can. Explain that each person in the group will be responsible for helping the others in their home group understand the material in the section to which the questions on the expert sheet pertain.

8. Circulate among the expert groups to make sure they stay on task and to provide help as needed.

9. When all the expert groups have answered their questions, have students return to their home groups. Each student should take about five minutes to present in the home group what she learned in the expert group. In

addition to explaining the material in her section of the text, the expert should also ask and entertain questions from the group, to make sure everyone learned her piece of the text.

51. ReQuest Procedure

Objectives: To develop comprehension; to provide practice in asking higher order thinking questions as a way of developing principled knowledge of the topic

Materials: Nonfiction text

Duration: 10–20 minutes

1. Select a text you want your students to read using this technique. To model the kinds of questions you want them to ask, read the first paragraph aloud and ask students to read along. Ask 3–4 questions about the paragraph (e.g., "What is the main idea of the paragraph?" "Why might this piece of information be important?"

"How does this new information relate to...?" "How does this compare to...?") and have students answer them.

2. Have one student read the second paragraph aloud while the class and you read along. Have the student who has read aloud ask you questions about the paragraph. Answer those questions by referring to the text as much as possible.

3. Instruct the class to continue to read the text in pairs, paragraph by paragraph, taking turns at reading aloud and reading along. Tell them to stop after each paragraph, ask each other questions about it, and try to answer them as best they can. Encourage them to refer to the text to support their answers.

Variations: (1) When the students are familiar with the ReQuest procedure, assign them to groups of three and have them take turns reading aloud and asking and answering questions. (2) Use the Paired Reading/Paired Summarizing technique, in which the student who reads a paragraph aloud also summarizes it, while the other student asks questions that probe the meaning of the passage and that both students attempt to answer.

Writing Activities

52. Shared Writing

Objectives: To engage students in composing a written text; to raise students' awareness of letter-sound relationships

Materials: Chart paper

Duration: 10–15 minutes

1. Choose a topic that the students are excited about (e.g., a field trip) and discuss it with the class.
2. Gather the students around an easel and ask them to help you write a few sentences about the topic.
3. Have students suggest the first sentence they want to write and have them say it several times so everyone is aware of the words.
4. Ask students to help you write the first word. Ask what the first sound in the word is, what letter needs to be written, etc.
5. Before you repeat step 4 for the second word, explain that you need to leave a blank space between the two words. Demonstrate the blank space by putting a finger after the first word.
6. Continue writing the sentence in this manner, inviting the students to come forward and supply the letters they can. Pronounce the sounds the children may skip and provide letters for them. If a child makes an error in writing, put a piece of correction tape over the error and help the children write the correct letter.

53. Interactive Writing

Objectives: To help emergent and beginning readers and writers explore the writing system in its details

Materials: Chart paper

Duration: 15–20 minutes

1. Working with a medium-size group of students, begin by agreeing on a topic to write about. The topic might be a retelling of a story or a poem or a song, the daily news, or an idea that the class is studying.
2. Ask the children to offer a sentence about the topic.
3. Have them repeat the sentence many times and even count the words to fix them firmly in their minds.
4. Ask the children for the first word; then pronounce that word slowly, writing its letters.
5. Ask for the next word and invite a child up to write the whole word, a few letters, or a single letter. Fill in letters the children miss.
6. Point to the words and have the children read back the text. Repeat this step each time a word is added.
7. To help the children orient themselves to the text and add letters, you may write blanks where the letters should go.
8. Use correction tape to paste over letters that are poorly formed, and write them correctly.
9. As the lesson progresses, teach about words and print (remind children of words they know or almost know,

remind them of spelling patterns they have seen before, remind them to leave spaces between words, and to add punctuation).

54. Pillowcase, or Me in a Box

Objectives: To introduce yourself to students by displaying objects representing aspects of your life; encourage discussion; provide springboard for personal writing

Materials: Pillowcase, bag, box, or similar container; objects representing your interests, family, pets, hobbies, and so forth, in a container

Duration: 5–10 minutes to share and discuss objects; extended time for discussion and/or writing

1. Collect a number of objects that represent things about you to share with students: for example, photos, sports trophy, dog toy, college banner, map, vacation postcards, and so forth. Put them in the container.
2. Explain that the objects you collected tell about you as a person. As you show each object, explain what it represents.
3. Have students write or dictate a few sentences about you based on what they learned.
4. Invite students to collect objects in the same way and tell the group about themselves. Schedule a few talks per day so students know when to bring in their things. (Remind them to get parents' permission before bringing anything valuable or personal to school.)
5. Have students use their collections to help them write about themselves.

Variations: Invite other teachers, the principal, or other school personnel to share in the same way. Have students draw self-portraits, or use a digital camera or school pictures from cumulative files to illustrate their writing. Collect the compositions in a class book. Display them in or outside the classroom. Make a "Students of the Week" bulletin board to display several students' writings at a time until all have been displayed. Create a web graphic organizer as you model this activity; write your name in the center, the objects in circles around it, and words or phrases explaining the objects projecting from the circles. Show how the web can help you organize your writing.

55. The Writing Workshop

Objectives: To familiarize students with the writing process

Materials: Notebooks

Duration: Sessions of 30–60 minutes scheduled at regular intervals over a longer period of time, with time set aside for five distinct activities in each session

1. *Rehearsing.* Have students think of what they might like to write about. You can do this in one of the ways listed below. For a–c, demonstrate how you yourself would settle on a topic.
   a. Have the students brainstorm possible topics. Optionally, have them create a graphic organizer, such as a cluster or semantic web, with the topic listed in the center connected to "satellites" around it.
   b. Have the students interview each other to find a story.
   c. Have the students research a topic before they write about it (by reading about it, by interviewing experts, or by doing an Internet search).
   d. Ask the students to compose one work together as a class before writing their own. This will allow you to help them if they have difficulty beginning.
2. *Drafting.* Have the students set out their ideas on paper, so they can see more of what they want to say about a topic. Tell them not to worry about spelling, punctuation, and handwriting at this stage. Remember to tell the students to write on every other line, so they can make subsequent changes to the draft.
3. *Revising.* Have students consider how their ideas can be stated more clearly. Teach revising skills through the following:
   a. Focused lessons on different aspects of writing, from word-choice issues such as showing, not telling, to composition-related issues such as ways to write strong introductions and closings. In one of the early focused lessons, show students how to use arrows, carets (^), and stapled-on sections to indicate on a draft how it should be rewritten. Remember to demonstrate how you would revise your own draft each time.
   b. Teacher-led conferences with groups or individual students. Ask students questions to help them focus on areas to improve their writing, and provide checklists of things to watch out for.
   c. Peer-led conferences. Put together a checklist of good questions to ask as students conference with each other, such as the following:
      • Did my opening lines interest you? How might I improve it?
      • Do I need more information anywhere? That is, where could I be more specific?
      • Do you ever get lost while reading my draft?
      • Do I stay on topic?
      • Do I come to a good conclusion?
4. *Editing.* Have the students check their revised drafts for spelling, punctuation, run-on sentences, and so forth.
5. *Publishing/Sharing of work in progress.* Choose two or three students to share who are far along in a draft or whose work displays an interesting issue. Different students should share each time. Model giving feedback to the writers and elicit comments from the class.

56. Descriptive Writing

Objectives: To familiarize students with the genre of descriptive writing; provide practice in descriptive writing

Materials: Excerpt from text that is vividly descriptive; paper bag containing a concrete object; journals or writing folders

Duration: 15–30 minutes depending on length of text excerpt and size of group

1. Select a descriptive passage, fiction or nonfiction, to read aloud. The passage should exemplify good descriptive writing.
2. Place an object in a paper bag for students to feel without looking at it. It should be small and light enough to be held in one hand, unusual enough so students may not recognize it instantly, and safe to feel without looking (no sharp edges, points, etc.).
3. Read the excerpt to the group. Invite students' comments about how the author used vivid descriptive language. Discuss the author's use of sensory words and images to create description.
4. Have students take turns silently feeling the object in the bag without looking at it. Caution them not to say what they think it is or what it feels like. After feeling the object, each one is to brainstorm and write in journals descriptive words or phrases to describe the object without naming it. Then they are to use their list of words to write descriptive sentences or a paragraph about the object, again without saying what it is.
5. Have students share their descriptive writing before naming the object.

Variations: Use senses other than touch to explore an object; with eyes closed, have students sniff objects like a sliced orange, blooming flower, cinnamon stick or other edible spice, school paste, ground coffee, pine or eucalyptus branch; listen to environmental or recorded sounds like wind, flowing water, heavy machinery, rain, surf, traffic; or taste safe and edible substances like toothpaste, coarse sugar, dry gelatin powder, baking chocolate, or pickles. Collect, or have students collect, small objects like keys, erasers, shells, bottle caps, or toys, and place one on each desk; give students a few minutes to write a complete description of the object, and then switch objects with someone else and repeat. Have students write what an object reminds them of rather than describing its physical features alone.

57. RAFT (Role, Audience, Format, Topic)

Objectives: To develop students' awareness of genres

Materials: Blank sheets of paper; newsprint

Duration: 40–60 minutes

1. After the students have studied a topic thoroughly, have them brainstorm 4–5 roles of people or characters that have a stake in the issue. Write down the roles on the chalkboard and have each student choose one role.
2. Assign students to groups based on their roles.
3. Explain that each group will write a message expressing their position on the issue.
4. Ask each group to choose an audience for their message out of the roles listed on the chalkboard.
5. Once all the groups have selected their audience, have them decide what format their message will take (a letter, a newspaper editorial, an advertisement, etc.).

6. Allow the groups about 15 minutes to write their message.
7. Have each group share their message with the class.
8. Engage the students in critiquing the messages. (Is the format appropriate for the targeted audience? Is the register appropriate for the audience? Is the message consistent with the characteristics of the role?)

Extension: Distribute the messages to students in the class. Instruct them to adopt the role of the audience and respond to the messages.

58. Story Maps for Writing

Objectives: To assist writers in planning a cohesive story

Materials: Blank story map on board, chart paper, or transparency; duplicated copies of the blank map for students to complete as they plan their stories

Duration: 5–15 minutes

1. On the board, chart paper, or a transparency, construct a story map containing elements similar to the following: Once there was a ____ named ____ who lived ____. He/she wanted ____. So he/she ____, but ____ (so he/she ____, but ____). Then, he/she ____. Finally, ____. So, ____. Leave plenty of space after each sentence starter.
2. Invite students to help you plan to write a story by suggesting elements to go in each blank space; for example, a boy named Sam who lived in a small apartment in the city, who wanted a dog, so he asked his parents … and so forth. Remind students that the story elements they suggest need to fit together to make sense. Select suggestions to write in the blanks that will make a meaningful story. To set off the sentence starters from the rest of the text, use a different color to complete the sentences.
3. Read through the completed story map, showing students where details could be added that would help readers visualize the story. Focus attention on the character's problem or goal, attempts to solve the problem or achieve the goal, and the final resolution of the conflict. Display the group story for students to refer to as they write.
4. Distribute blank story maps and have students generate their own stories, filling in the blanks to create a skeletal story. Allow time to share ideas and completed plans with partners or small groups.
5. Have students write their stories following their story maps. Encourage them to write several sentences or a paragraph after each sentence starter, to discourage them from recopying their maps as completed stories. Allow time for sharing of completed stories.

Variations: Before attempting to write a story solo, allow pairs to create a shared story after participating in the group story. Encourage students to revise, edit, and illustrate their stories, then display or publish them. Collect illustrated stories in a binder and place in the classroom library.

59. Form Poems

Objectives: To familiarize students with structured poems; increase students' awareness of how form and meaning can shape each other in poetry

Materials: Examples of form poems

Duration: 10–20 minutes

1. Show the students an example of a well-written poem that follows the form. (You might need to write this yourself or save it from a previous class.)
2. Discuss the formal characteristics of the poem with the class.

3. Have the students help you create a poem as a group. Discuss each choice they make so they understand the process well.
4. Have individuals or pairs write their own poems.
5. Share several of the poems, and discuss their qualities. Also call attention to the ways in which the poems followed the structure.
6. Talk about why a writer might choose to write a poem structured that way.
7. Make a wall chart in which you feature several of the students' poems; also outline the procedures for writing a poem with the structure in question.

Activities for English Language Learners

60. Language Experience with English Language Learners

Objectives: To help English language learners develop English fluency, print concepts, sight word recognition, and phonemic awareness

Materials: An object, photograph, shared experience, shared literature, or other stimulus; chalkboard, chart tablet, or transparency; marker

Duration: 10–30 minutes; additional time for follow-up activities

1. Select an individual student or a group of English language learners.
2. Select a topic for dictation: an interesting concrete object, classroom pet, familiar story for retelling, recent classroom event, and so forth. Younger students benefit from a concrete or immediate stimulus, whereas older students can talk about past events, friends, families, and other more abstract topics. Encourage students to select topics.
3. Explain that you can write what students say, that they can learn to read what was written, and that learning words in these sentences will help them learn to read and write many other words.
4. Invite discussion of the stimulus, encouraging students to use as elaborated language as they can. Ask open-ended questions that encourage extended answers. If students give brief or incomplete sentences, model elaborated language using their words: S: "Green. Fuzzy." T: "It's green and fuzzy."
5. Ask for volunteers to contribute sentences for the dictation.
6. Write students' sentences, allowing changes or additions. If you want students to learn to read each other's names, include their names in the text. Print neatly with clear spaces between each word.
7. Read the completed story expressively and at a natural pace, pointing to each word as you read.

8. Reread the story chorally several times until students have memorized it. Continue pointing to each word. (Keep up the pace so the reading sounds natural, not word by word.) If students have trouble memorizing the whole text, divide it into sections of two or three sentences each.
9. Invite volunteers to come to the chart and recite a part or the whole story while pointing to each word. Continue until each student who volunteers has read the story individually.
10. Point to individual words and invite students to identify the words, reading from the beginning to the target word if necessary.

Follow-Up Activities for English Language Learners

1. Repeat choral and individual reading and pointing on subsequent days until students can read the story fluently and point accurately. (Older students can reread and point using duplicated copies of the story rather than at a chart.)
2. Copy each sentence onto a sentence strip. Have volunteers hold up each strip in correct order. (These can also be used for independent practice with a hanging pocket chart.)
3. Create exact copies of the story on copy paper. Duplicate several copies for each student. Students can paste copies on construction paper or in journals and illustrate them, cut lines and sentences apart and put them in correct order, cut sentences into phrases and put them in correct order, and use sentences for handwriting practice.
4. Have students find individual words they recognize in isolation and begin building individual word banks with known words on cards. Students should sort and review word banks daily.
5. Have students sort words in their word banks in a variety of ways: matching beginning sounds, number of syllables, alphabetical order, words that are related by meaning, and so forth.
6. Select one or several familiar words beginning with consonants. Using individual letter cards or magnetic letters, show students how to "make and break" the words

by removing the initial letter or sound and substituting another, creating new words.

7. Students can write known sight words using magnetic letters on cookie sheets, individual letters cut out of sandpaper, wallpaper scraps, felt, glue and sand or glitter, pipe cleaners, gel pens, macaroni letters, letters cut from magazines, and so forth. They can also search for known words in newspaper and magazine ads and headlines, and cut them out.

8. Begin personal dictionaries by folding eight to ten sheets of paper vertically and stapling in the fold to create individual books. Have students write a letter at the top of each page (group infrequent letters like *q*, *u*, *x*, *y*, and *z* with others) and begin collecting mastered sight words in their dictionaries.

9. As students' word banks grow, have them construct sentences with word cards.

61. Cumulative Semantic Map

Objectives: To foster vocabulary growth; help students learn meanings of related words

Materials: Large paper chart that can be displayed and added to periodically

Duration: 5–15 minutes each time new words are added

1. Have students begin collecting words that are related by meaning: for example, synonyms, color words, action words, and so forth.

2. Construct a web graphic organizer on the chart, with one or more general categories in the center and related words radiating from them. For example, a cumulative semantic web on temperature words might show HOT and COLD in central circles, with various temperature words attached to them: *burning, boiling, sizzling, blistering, icy, freezing, frigid, polar,* and so forth.

3. As students encounter related words in their reading, or as you encounter such words in literature you read to them, return to the web and have students suggest where such words might be added or where new categories might be entered. For example, a new category of WARM words could be added, to include *comfortable, mild, tepid,* and *lukewarm.*

4. Encourage students to use words from the charts in their writing and to continue to watch for words that could be added to the collection.

62. Word Origins and Derivations

Objectives: To develop vocabulary; teach meanings of bases and affixes to help students figure out meanings of unfamiliar words; engage students in language learning

Materials: Space for word walls, charts, and bulletin board words; paper and markers; resource materials (dictionaries that include word histories, thesauruses, books on idioms, etc.)

Duration: 10–15 minutes several times weekly

1. Encourage students to begin collecting words they need to learn for subject areas and interesting or unfamiliar words they encounter during reading. Have them copy the sentence in which the word occurs, or share the text, so they can practice using context as a meaning clue. Make a word wall or chart of student-selected words, their context sentences, and meanings.

2. Teach vocabulary words in groups that have a shared base or affix; for example, *ex* (out): *exhale, exclaim, expand, exorcise, expectorate, exfoliate, explode, expire; in-/im-/il-* (not): *illiterate, illogical, illegal, illegible, immature, imbalance, impassable, immortal, incapable, inappropriate, inaudible, inconvenient.* Create word families and add new words as students encounter them.

3. Teach the meanings of the Latin and Greek bases or stems that have consistent meanings: for example, *photo* (light), *graph* (write), *mega* (large), *cap* (head), *corp* (body), *ped* (foot), *manu* (hand), *scrib* (write), *retro* (backward), *poly* (many), *phone* (sound), *mono* (single), *bi* (two), *tri* (three), *cent* (hundred). Draw attention to these word parts and their meanings whenever they occur.

4. Avoid having students copy dictionary definitions, which they rarely understand. Instead, have them predict a word's meaning from word parts they know and context sentences before looking it up. Have them write meanings in their own words rather than a dictionary definition.

5. Have students divide word cards into three sections to include (a) the word, (b) its meaning in their own words, and (c) synonyms and opposites. On the back have them draw a sketch that illustrates the meaning, and write a caption for the drawing.

6. Limit the number of new words students have to learn each week; teach a group of related words and have students really learn fewer words rather than superficially memorize a long list.

63. Visualization

Objectives: To develop comprehension; model and practice visualizing or mentally seeing images a writer creates with words

Materials: Shared text; reading journals or literature logs; duplicated copies of the text that students can draw on; sticky notes; pencils

Duration: 5 minutes or less at various points in a text

1. Copy a short (1–2 paragraphs) excerpt of vivid or descriptive text onto the board, chart paper, or a transparency. Explain that you will model what good readers do as they visualize text.

2. Read the passage expressively; as you read it, pause and think aloud by telling students what you are mentally seeing or imagining. Mark the words, phrases, or sentences that are particularly vivid to you. Make a quick sketch in the margin that represents what you are visualizing, and explain what it means to you.

3. Distribute duplicated copies of similar text or portions of a text students are reading together. Read aloud a short

section while students follow along. Have volunteers say what they visualized as you read, following your model. Have all students sketch in the margin as above, or distribute sticky notes and have students sketch on them and place them over or near the appropriate sections. Ask each student to tell briefly what they drew; they do not need to display the drawings because they are a sort of personal code.

4. In later lessons, students can write ("jot") what they are visualizing, using brief phrases, in addition to or instead of sketching. Students may prefer one method over the other; neither one is "better."

Variations: As students read longer or more difficult passages, encourage them to use the "jot" or "sketch" methods independently to help them visualize by making sticky notes available during reading, by having them jot or sketch in their reading journals at the end of each day's reading, and by periodically repeating the activity with different kinds of text. Use visualization in combination with the Think-Pair-Share activity; after visualizing and drawing, each student shares with a single partner and then each pair with another pair. Encourage students to use sketches, drawings, or cutout magazine pictures to illustrate their writing about what they are reading.

64. Using Questions to Teach English Language Learners

Objectives: Vocabulary development; to help students learning English to acquire words, follow directions, and converse with others

Materials: Props to talk about: magazine pictures, picture cards, small objects like keys, toy cars, plastic fruit and other foods from children's kitchen toys, puppets, stuffed animals, and so forth

Duration: 5–15 minutes or longer, depending on students' age, English fluency, and size of group

1. Select a group of students who are similar in English fluency. Gather pictures or props to use.

2. Determine the general fluency level of students and plan the activity to meet their English abilities: preproduction, where students understand a few words but speak little; early production, where students understand simple sentences and produce very short utterances; or speech emergence, where students understand many words and sentences and produce longer, more varied sentences.

3. For preproduction students, use very simple, repetitive sentences accompanied by gesture and sound effects: "This is an apple. Is it red? Yes, it's red. Is it green? No, not green." "Can Maria hold the apple? Yes, she can. Can Nguyen hold the apple? Yes, he can. Can I hold the apple? Yes, I can." "Who has a frog? Juan has a frog. Who has a bird? Irma has a bird."

4. For early production students, use questions that require short answers, including yes/no, here/there, either/or, how many …, what color …, and common prepositions like in/out/under: "Is this a dog or a bird? What color is the bird? Do you like birds?" "Is this the mother or the father? Where is the baby? How many children are there?"

5. For speech emergence students, ask questions requiring longer answers, description, and simple sentences. Use wordless picture books, tell what is happening on each page, and ask students to retell. Read simple versions of stories several times, and have students retell or act out the stories using puppets or a flannel board. Play direction-following games like Simon Says, and have students give each other directions to follow: Stand behind your chair; open and close the door; raise your left hand. Practice naming objects: foods, clothing, tools, vehicles, classroom objects, colors, temperature words, animals, family members, areas of the school and home, and people (teacher, principal, nurse, bus driver).

References

Abedi, J. (2002). Assessment and accommodations of English language learners: Issues, concerns, and recommendations. *Journal of School Improvement 3*(1), 83–89.

Abedi, J. (2004). The No Child Left Behind Act and English language learners: Assessment and accountability issues. *Educational Researcher 33*(1), 4–14.

Abedi, J., Hofstetter, C. H., & Lord, C. (2004). Assessment accommodations for English language learners: Implications for policy-based empirical research. *Review of Educational Research 74*(1), 1–28.

Abedi, J., & Lord, C. (2001). The language factor in mathematics tests. *Applied Measurement in Education 14*(3), 219–234.

Achieve. (2010). *Understanding the K–12 Common Core State Standards in English Language Arts and Literacy in History/ Social Studies, Science, and Technical Subjects*. Washington, DC: Author. Retrieved from http://www.achieve.org/files/ AchievingCCSS-ELAFINAL.pdf

Achilles, C. M. (1999). *Let's put kids first, finally: Getting class size right*. Thousand Oaks, CA: Corwin Press.

Ada, A. F., & Campoy, I. (1998). *Authors in the classroom*. Washington, DC: Del Sol Press.

Adams, M. J. (1990). *Beginning to read: Thinking and learning about print*. Cambridge, MA: MIT Press.

Adams, M. J. (1998). The three cuing system. In J. Osborne & F. Lehr (Eds.), *Literacy for all: Issues in teaching and learning*. New York, NY: Guilford Press.

Adler, M. (1982). The Paideia proposal: Rediscovering the essence of education. *American School Board Journal, 169*(7), 17–20.

Afflerbach, P. (1993). Report cards and reading. *The Reading Teacher, 46*, 458–465.

Alexander, P. A. (1998). The nature of disciplinary and domain learning: The knowledge, interest and strategic dimensions of learning from subject matter text. In C. Hynd (Ed.), *Learning from text across conceptual domains*. Mahwah, NJ: Erlbaum.

Alexander, P. A. (2000). Learning from text: A multidimensional and developmental perspective. In M. Kamil, P. B. Mosenthal, P. D. Pearson, & R. Barr (Eds.), *Handbook of reading research, volume III*. Hillsdale, NJ: Erlbaum.

Alexander, P. A., & Jetton, T. L. (2000). Learning from text: A multidimensional and developmental perspective. In M. L. Kamil, P. B. Mosenthal, P. D. Pearson, & R. Barr (Eds.), *Handbook of reading research: Vol. III* (pp. 285–310). Mahwah, NJ: Erlbaum.

Alexander, P. A., Jetton, T. L., Kulikowich, J. M., & Woehler, C. (1994). Contrasting instructional and structural importance: The seductive effect of teacher questions. *Journal of Reading Behavior, 26*, 19–45.

Allard, H. (1977). *Miss Nelson is missing!* Illustrated by J. Marshall. Boston, MA: Houghton Mifflin.

Alley, K. M. (2008). *Teaching integrated reading strategies in the middle school library media center*. Westport, CT: Libraries Unlimited, a member of Greenwood Publishing Group.

Allington, R. L. (1983). Fluency: The neglected reading goal. *The Reading Teacher, 36*(6), 556–561.

Allington, R. L. (1983). The reading instruction provided to readers of differing reading ability. *Elementary School Journal, 83*, 549–558.

Allington, R. L. (1997). Overselling phonics. *Reading Today, 14*, 15.

Allington, R. L. (2001). *What really matters for struggling readers: Designing research-based programs*. New York, NY: Longman.

Allington, R. L. (2005). *What really matters for struggling readers*. Boston, MA: Allyn & Bacon.

Allington, R. L. (2008). *What really matters in response to intervention*. Boston, MA: Allyn & Bacon.

Allington, R. L., & Johnson, P. H. (2002). *Reading to learn: Lessons from exemplary fourth-grade classrooms*. New York, NY: Guilford Press.

Allington, R. L., & McGill-Franzen, A. (1989). School response to reading failure: Instruction for Chapter One and special education students in grades two, four, and eight. *Elementary School Journal, 89*(5), 529–542.

Allington, R. L., & Walmsley, S. A. *No quick fix: Rethinking programs in America's elementary schools* (1995, 2007 [preface]). Newark, DE: International Reading Association.

Almasi, J. F. (1995). The nature of fourth graders' socio-cognitive conflicts in peer-led and teacher-led discussions of literature. *Reading Research Quarterly, 30*(3), 314–351.

Anderson, K. L. (2010). Spotlight on the interactive strategies approach: The case of Roosevelt Elementary School. In M. Y. Lipson & K. K. Wixson (Eds.), *Successful approaches to RTI: Collaborative practices for improving K–12 literacy*. Newark, DE: International Reading Association.

Anderson, R. C., & Nagy, W. E. (1991). Word meanings. In R. Barr, M. L. Kamil, P. B. Mosenthal, & P. D. Pearson (Eds.), *Handbook of reading research* (Vol. 2). New York, NY: Longman.

Anderson, R. C., & Nagy, W. E. (1992). The vocabulary conundrum. *American Educator, 16*, 14–18, 44–47.

Anderson, R. C., & Pearson, P. D. (1984). A schema-theoretic view of basic processes in reading. In P. D. Pearson (Ed.), *Handbook of reading research*. New York, NY: Longman.

Anderson, R. C., Wilson, P. T., & Fielding, L. (1988). Growth in reading and how children spend their time outside of school. *Reading Research Quarterly, 23*, 285–303.

Andrade, H. G. (2002). *Understanding rubrics*. Retrieved from http:// learnweb.harvard.edu/ALPS/thinking/docs/rubricar.htm

Archambault, J., & Martin, B. Jr. (1989). *White dynamite and the curly kid*. Illustrated by Ted Rand. New York, NY: Henry Holt.

Arellano Osuna, A. (1992). *El lenguaje integral: Una alternativa para la educación*. Mérida, Venezuela: Editorial Venezolana.

Armbruster, B. B., Lehr, F., & Osborn, J. (2001). *Put reading first: The research building blocks for teaching children to read. Kindergarten through grade 3*. Washington, DC: National Institute for Literacy.

Arnold, M., & Lassman, M. E. (2003). Overrepresentation of minority students in special education. *Education, 124,* 230–236, 340.

Asher, J. J. (1982). The total physical response approach. In R. W. Blair (Ed.), *Innovative approaches to language teaching* (pp. 54–66). Rowley, MA: Newbury House.

Ashton-Warner, S. (1963). *Teacher*. New York, NY: Simon & Schuster.

Atwell, N. (1985). *In the middle*. Portsmouth, NH: Heinemann.

Atwell, N. (1998). *In the middle: New understandings about writing, reading, and learning*. Portsmouth, NH: Heinemann.

Atwell, N. (1998). *In the middle: Writing, reading and learning with adolescents* (2nd ed.). Portsmouth, NH: Boynton/Cook.

August, D., Snow, C. E., Carlo, M., Proctor, C. P., Rolla de San Francisco, A., Duursma, E., et al. (2006). Literacy development in elementary school second-language learners. *Topics in Language Disorders, 26*(4), 351–364.

Ayers, W. (1993). *To teach*. New York, NY: Teachers College Press.

Baildon, R., & Baildon, M. (2008). Guiding independence: Developing a research tool to support student decision making in selecting online information sources. *The Reading Teacher, 61*(8), 636–647.

Baker, C., & Sienkewicz, A. (2000). *The care and education of young bilinguals: An introduction for young professionals*. Cleveland, U.K.: Multilingual Matters.

Baker, L., Serpell, R., & Sonnenschein, S. (1995). Opportunities for literacy learning in the homes of urban preschoolers. In L. M. Morrow (Ed.), *Family literacy: Connections in schools and communities* (pp. 236–252). Newark, DE: International Reading Association.

Banks, J. A. (2008). *Teaching strategies for ethnic studies*. Boston, MA: Pearson.

Barbosa Heldt, A. (1971). *Cómo han aprendido a leer y a escribir los mexicanos*. Mexico City, Mexico: Editorial Pax México, Librería Carlos Cesarmán.

Barger, J. (2003). *Comparing the DIBELS Oral Reading Fluency indicator and the North Carolina end of grade reading assessment* (Tech. Rep.). Asheville: North Carolina Teacher Academy.

Barker, C. (2006). *How many syllables does English have?* Retrieved from http://ling.ucsd.edu/%7Ebarker/Syllables/index.txt

Barone, D. (1992). That reminds me of . . . : Using dialogue journals with young readers. In C. Temple & P. Collins (Eds.), *Stories and readers: New perspectives on literature in the elementary classroom*. Norwood, MA: Christopher-Gordon.

Barone, D., Hardman, D., & Taylor, J. (2006). *Reading first in the classroom*. New York, NY: Pearson.

Barthes, R. (1974). *S/Z*. New York, NY: Hill and Wang.

Bartlett, J. R. (2003). *Dictionary of Americanisms*. Hoboken, NJ: John Wiley & Sons.

Bauer, E. B., & Manyak, P. C. (2008). Creating language-rich instruction for English-language learners. *The Reading Teacher, 62*(2), 176–178.

Baumann, J., Kame'enui, E., & Ash, G. (2003). Research on vocabulary instruction: Voltaire redux. In J. Flood, D. Lapp, J. Squire, & J. Jensen (Eds.), *Handbook of research on teaching the English language arts* (2nd ed.). Mahwah, NJ: Erlbaum.

Beamon, G. W. (2001). *Teaching with adolescent learning in mind*. Arlington Heights, IL: Skylight Professional Development.

Bean, L., & Freppon, P. A. (2003, Spring). The nature of children's discussions in a third-grade classroom. *Ohio Journal of the English Language Arts, 10,* 47–55.

Beane, J. (1991, October). The middle school: The natural home of integrated curriculum. *Educational Leadership, 49*(2), 9–13.

Beane, J. (2002). Beyond self-interest: A democratic core curriculum. *Educational Leadership, 59,* 25–28.

Bear, D. R., Invernizzi, M., Johnson, F. L. & Templeton, S. (2009). *Vocabulary their way: Word study with middle and secondary students*. Boston, MA: Pearson.

Bear, D. R., Invernizzi, M., Templeton, S., & Johnston, F. (2007). *Words their way: Word study for phonics, vocabulary, and spelling instruction* (4th ed.). Englewood Cliffs, NJ: Prentice Hall.

Beck, I. L., & McKeown, M. G. (1983). Learning words well—a program to enhance vocabulary and comprehension. *The Reading Teacher, 36,* 622–625.

Beck, I. L., McKeown, M. G., Hamilton, R. L., & Kucan, L. (1997). *Questioning the author: An approach for enhancing student engagement with text*. Newark, DE: International Reading Association.

Beck, I. L., McKeown, M. G., & Kucan, L. (2002). *Bringing words to life: Robust vocabulary instruction*. New York, NY: Guilford Press.

Beck, I. L., McKeown, M. G., & Kucan, L. (2008). *Creating robust vocabulary*: New York, NY: Guilford.

Becker, H. J. (2000). Who's wired and who's not: Children's access to and use of computer technology. *Children and Computer Technology, 10,* 44–75.

Bettelheim, B. (1975). *The uses of enchantment*. New York, NY: Vintage.

Betts, A. E. (1946). *Foundations of reading instruction, with emphasis on differentiated guidance*. Chicago, IL: American Book Company.

Biancarosa, G. (2012). Adolescent literacy: More than remediation. *Educational Leadership, 69*(6), 22–27.

Biemiller, A. (2009). Vocabulary development (0–60 months). In L. M. Phillips (Ed.), *Handbook of language and literacy development: A roadmap from 0–60 months*. [online], pp. 1–42. London, ON: Canadian Language and Literacy Research Network.

Blachman, B. (2000). *Road to the code*. Baltimore, MD: Paul H. Brookes Publishing Company.

Blachman, B., & Tangle, D. M. (2008). *Road to reading: A program for preventing and remediating reading difficulties*. Baltimore, MD: Paul Brookes.

Blachowicz, C. L. Z. (1986). Making connections: Alternatives to the vocabulary notebook. *Journal of Reading, 29,* 643–649.

Blachowicz, C. L. Z., & Fisher, P. (2000). Vocabulary instruction. In M. L. Kamil, P. Mosenthal, P. D. Pearson, & R. Barr (Eds.), *Handbook of reading research* (Vol. 3). New York, NY: Longman.

Blachowicz, C. L. Z., & Fisher, P. (2010). *Teaching vocabulary in all classrooms* (4th ed.) New York, NY: Pearson-Prentice Hall.

Blachowicz, C. L. Z., Fisher, P., Ogle, D., & Watts-Taff, S. (2006). Vocabulary: Questions from the classroom. *Reading Research Quarterly, 41*(4), 524–539.

Blachowicz, C. L. Z., Fisher, P., Ogle, D., & Watts-Taff, S. (in press). *Academic vocabulary across the curriculum*. New York, NY: Guilford.

Bleich, D. (1970). *Subjective criticism.* Baltimore, MD: Johns Hopkins University Press.

Bleich, D. (1975). *Readings and feelings: An introduction to subjective criticism.* Urbana, IL: NCTE.

Bleich, D. (1978). *Subjective criticism.* Baltimore, MD: Johns Hopkins University.

Block, C. C., & Pressley, M. (Eds.). (2001). *Comprehension instruction: Research-based best practices.* New York, NY: Guilford.

Blohm, J. M., & Lapinsky, T. (2006) *Kids like me: Voices of the immigrant experience.* Boston, MA: Nicholas Bresley Publishing.

Booth, D., & Schwartz, L. (2004). *Literacy strategies.* Portland, ME: Stenhouse Publishers.

Bormuth, J. R. (1968, Autumn). Cloze test readability: Criterion reference scores. *Journal of Educational Measurement, 5*(3), 189–196.

Bornstein, D. (2011, May 16). A book in every home, and then some. *New York Times.* Retrieved from http://opinionator.blogs.nytimes.com/2011/05/16/a-book-in-every-home-and-then-some/.

Bos, C. S., & Anders, P. L. (1989). Developing higher level thinking skills through interactive teaching. *Journal of Reading, Writing, and Learning Disabilities International, 4*(4), 259–274.

Bos, C., & Anders, P. (1990, Winter). Effects of interactive vocabulary instruction on the vocabulary learning and reading comprehension of junior-high learning disabled students. *Learning Disability Quarterly, 13*(1), 31–42.

Bradley, L., & Bryant, P. (1985). *Rhyme and reason in reading and spelling.* Ann Arbor: University of Michigan Press.

Brenner, B. (1992). *Group soup.* New York, NY: Viking.

Britton, J. (1970). *Language and learning.* Harmondsworth, England: Penguin Books.

Bromley, K. (1999). Key components of sound writing instruction. In L. Gambrell, L. Mandell Morrow, S. B. Neuman, & M. Pressley (Eds.), *Best practices in literacy instruction* (pp. 152–174). New York, NY: Guilford Press.

Bronfenbrenner, U. (1979). *The ecology of human development.* Cambridge, MA: Harvard University Press.

Brooks, W. M. (2005). Reading linguistic features: Middle school students' response to the African American literary tradition. In B. Hammond, M. E. Rhodes Hoover, & I. P. McPhail (Eds.), *Teaching African American learners to read* (pp. 253–263). Newark, DE: International Reading Association.

Brooks, W. M. (2006). Reading representations of themselves: Urban youth use culture and African American textual features to develop literary understandings. *Reading Research Quarterly, 41*(3), 372–392.

Brown, H., & Cambourne, B. (1990). *Read and retell: A strategy for the whole-language/natural learning classroom.* Portsmouth, NH: Heinemann.

Brown, M. (1947). *Stone soup.* New York, NY: Aladdin Paperback.

Brown, M. (1949). *The important book.* New York, NY: Harper.

Brown, R. (1955). *Words and things.* Garden City, NY: Basic Books.

Bruner, J. (1978). The role of dialogue in language acquisition. In A. Sinclair, R. J. Jarvella, & W. M. Levelt (Eds.), *The child's conception of language* (pp. 241–256). New York, NY: Springer-Verlag.

Buck, J., & Torgesen, J. (2003). *The relationship between performance on a measure of oral reading fluency and performance on the Florida Comprehensive Assessment Test* (FCRR Tech. Rep. #1). Tallahassee, FL: Florida Center for Reading Research.

Buehl, D. (2001). *Classroom strategies for interactive learning* (2nd ed.). Newark, DE: International Reading Association.

Burns, P. C., Roe, B. D., & Ross, E. P. (1999). *Teaching reading in today's elementary schools.* Boston, MA: Houghton Mifflin.

Butler, A., & Turbill, J. (1985). *Towards a reading-writing classroom.* Portsmouth, NH: Heinemann.

Caldwell, J. S. (2002). *Reading assessment: A primer for teachers and tutors.* New York, NY: Guilford Press.

California County Superintendents Educational Services Association. (2011). *Frequently asked questions regarding the Common Core Standards.* Sacramento, CA: Author. Retrieved from http://www.sbsdk12.org/programs/commoncorestandards/common_core_faq.pdf

California State Department of Education. (2009). *English language development standards.* Sacramento, CA: Author.

California State Department of Education. (2009). *Response to instruction and intervention (RTI²)* . Retrieved from http://pubs.cde.ca.gov/tcsii/ch2/responsetointerven.aspx

Calkins, L. (1994). *The art of teaching writing.* Portsmouth, NH: Heinemann.

Calkins, L. (1996). *The art of teaching writing.* Portsmouth, NH: Heinemann.

Campbell, J. (2008). *The hero with a thousand faces.* Princeton, NJ: Bolingen Press.

Carle, E. (1987). *The very hungry caterpillar.* New York, NY: Philomel Books.

Carle, E. (1994). *La oruga muy hambrienta.* New York, NY: Philomel Books.

Carlisle, J. F. (2000). Awareness of the structure and meaning of morphologically complex words: Impact on reading. *Reading and Writing: An Interdisciplinary Journal, 12,* 169–190.

Carlisle, J. F., & Stone, C. A. (2005). Exploring the role of morphemes in word reading. *Reading Research Quarterly, 40,* 428–449.

Carr, E. M. (1985). The vocabulary overview guide: A metacognitive strategy to improve vocabulary, comprehension and retention. *Journal of Reading, 28,* 684–689.

Carr, E. M., & Ogle, D. (1987). K-W-L Plus: A strategy for comprehension and summarization. *Journal of Reading, 30,* 626–631.

Castañeda v. Pickard, 648 F.2d 989, 5th Circuit (1981).

CATESOL. (1992). *Position statement on specially-designed academic instruction in English (sheltered instruction).* Orinda: California Teachers of English to Speakers of Other Languages.

Cazden, C. (2001). *Classroom discourse: The language of teaching and learning* (2nd ed.). Portsmouth, NH: Heinemann.

Chall, J. (1967). *Learning to read: The great debate* (Rev. ed.). New York, NY: McGraw-Hill.

Chin, J. (2009). *Redwoods.* New York, NY: Roaring Brook Press.

Chomsky, C. (1971). Write first, read later. *Childhood Education, 47*(6), 296–299.

Christie, J. (1991). *Play and early literacy development.* Albany, NY: State University of New York Press.

Christie, J., & Roskos, K. (2001). Examining the play-literacy interface. *Journal of Early Childhood Literacy, 1*(1), 59–89.

Christie, J., & Roskos, K. (2009). Play's potential in early literacy development. *Encyclopedia on Early Childhood Development.* Montreal, Quebec: Center for Excellence in Early Childhood Development.

Clarke, L. W., & Whitney, E. (2009). Walking in their shoes: Using multiple-perspectives texts as a bridge to critical literacy. *The Reading Teacher, 62*(6), 530–534.

Clay, M. M. (1975). *What did I write?* Portsmouth, NH: Heinemann.

Clay, M. M. (1985). *The early detection of reading difficulties: A diagnostic survey with recovery procedures.* Portsmouth, NH: Heinemann.

Clay, M. M. (1987). *Writing begins at home: Preparing children for writing before they go to school.* Portsmouth, NH: Heinemann.

Clay, M. M. (1993). *An observational survey of early literacy achievement.* Portsmouth, NH: Heinemann.

Clay, M. M. (1993). *Reading recovery: A guidebook for teachers in training.* Portsmouth, NH: Heinemann.

Clay, M. M. (2000). *Concepts about print: What have children learned about the way we print language?* Portsmouth, NH: Heinemann.

Cleary, B. (1997). *Ramona and her father.* New York, NY: Harper Trophy.

Cloud, N., Genesee, F., & Hamayan, E. (2009). *Literacy instruction for English language learners: A teacher's guide to research-based practices.* Portsmouth, NH: Heinemann.

Clymer, T. (1996, November). The utility of phonic generalizations in the primary grades. *The Reading Teacher, 50,* 3, 182–187.

Coiro, J., & Dobler, E. (2007). Exploring the online reading comprehension strategies used by sixth-grade skilled readers to search for and locate information on the Internet. *Reading Research Quarterly, 42,* 214–257.

Coleman, J. S., Campbell, E. Q., Hobson, C. J., McPartland, J., Mood, A. M., Weinfeld, F. D., & York, R. L. (1966). *Equality of educational opportunity.* Washington, DC: U.S. Government Printing Office.

Collier, V. P. (1987). Age and rate of acquisition of second language for academic purposes. *TESOL Quarterly, 21,* 617–641.

Collier, V. P. (1989). How long? A synthesis of research on academic achievement in a second language. *TESOL Quarterly, 23,* 509–539.

Collins, A., Brown, J. S., & Newman, S. E. (1987, January). *Cognitive apprenticeship: Teaching the craft of reading, writing and mathematics* (Technical Report No. 403). BBN Laboratories, Cambridge, MA. Center for the Study of Reading, University of Illinois.

Collins, J. L. (1998). *Strategies for struggling writers.* New York, NY: Guilford Press.

Collins, M. F. (2005). ESL preschoolers' English vocabulary acquisition from storybook reading. *Reading Research Quarterly, 40*(4), 406–408.

Common Core. (2012). *Common Core Curriculum Maps: English Language Arts.* San Francisco, CA: Jossey-Bass.

Common Core State Standard Initiative. (2010). *Common Core State Standards for English Language Arts & Literacy in History/ Social Studies, Science, and Technical Subjects.* Washington, DC: CCSSO & National Governors Association.

Common Core State Standards, Grade 5, California State Department of Education. (August, 2010). Retrieved from http://www .scoe.net/castandards/agenda/2010/ela_ccs_recommendations .pdf

Conrad, P. (1992). *Pedro's journal.* New York, NY: Scholastic.

Costello, K. A., Lipson, M. Y., Marinak, B., & Zolman, M. F. (2010). In M. Y. Lipson & K. K. Wixson (Eds.), *Successful approaches to RTI: Collaborative practices for improving K–12 literacy.* Newark, DE: International Reading Association.

Council for Exceptional Children. (2007). *Position on Response to Intervention (RTI): The unique role of special education and special education teachers.* Arlington, VA: Council for Exceptional Children.

Cowhey, M. (2006). *Black ants and Buddhists.* Portland, ME: Stenhouse.

Crawford, A. N. (1982). From Spanish reading to English reading: The transition process. In M. P. Douglass (Ed.), *Claremont reading conference yearbook* (pp. 159–165). Claremont, CA: Claremont Reading Conference.

Crawford, A. N. (1993). Literature, integrated language arts, and the language minority child: A focus on meaning. In A. Carras-quillo & C. Hedley (Eds.), *Whole language and the bilingual learner* (pp. 61–75). Norwood, NJ: Ablex.

Crawford, A. N. (1994a). Communicative approaches to second language acquisition: From oral language development into the core curriculum and L_2 literacy. In C. F. Leyba (Ed.), *Schooling and language minority students: A theoretical framework* (2nd ed., pp. 79–121). Los Angeles, CA: California State University, Los Angeles, Evaluation, Dissemination and Assessment Center.

Crawford, A. N. (1994b). Estrategias para promover la comprensión lectora en estudiantes de alto riesgo. *Lectura y Vida, 15*(1), 21–27.

Crawford, A. N. (1995). Language policy, second language learning, and literacy. In A. N. Crawford (Ed.), *A practical guidebook for adult literacy programmes in developing nations* (pp. 9–16). Paris: UNESCO.

Crawford, A. N. (2000). Strategies for teaching reading and writing to English language learners. In J. W. Gillet, C. Temple, A. N. Crawford, S. R. Mathews, & J. P. Young (Eds.), *Understanding reading problems: Assessment and instruction* (pp. 416–453). New York, NY: Longman.

Crawford, A. N. (2003). Communicative approaches to second language acquisition: The bridge to second language literacy. In G. García (Ed.), *English learners: Reaching the highest level of English literacy* (pp. 152–181). Newark, DE: International Reading Association.

Crawford, A. N., Allen, R. V., & Hall, M. (1995). The language experience approach. In A. N. Crawford (Ed.), *A practical guidebook for adult literacy programs in developing nations* (pp. 17–46). Paris: UNESCO.

Crawford, A. N., Saul, E., & Mathews, S. (2005). *Teaching and learning lessons for the thinking classroom.* New York, NY: Central European University Press.

Crawford, A. N., Saul, W., Mathews, S., & MaKinster, J. (2005). *Lessons from the thinking classroom.* New York, NY: IDEA.

Crawford, J. (1989). *Bilingual education: History, politics, theory and practice.* Trenton, NJ: Crane.

Cummins, J. (1980). The construct of language proficiency in bilingual education. In J. E. Alatis (Ed.), *Georgetown University roundtable on languages and linguistics* (pp. 76–93). Washington, DC: Georgetown University Press.

Cummins, J. (1981). The role of primary language development in promoting educational success for language minority students. In California State Department of Education (Ed.), *Schooling and language minority students: A theoretical framework* (pp. 3–49). Los Angeles, CA: California State University, Los Angeles, Evaluation, Dissemination and Assessment Center.

Cummins, J. (1986). Empowering minority students: A framework for intervention. *Harvard Educational Review, 56,* 18–36.

Cummins, J. (1989). *Empowering minority students.* Sacramento: California Association for Bilingual Education.

Cummins, J. (2001). *Language, power, pedagogy: Bilingual children in the crossfire.* Bristol, UK: Multilingual Matters Limited.

Cummins, J., & Corson, D. (1997). *Bilingual education*. Amsterdam: Kluwer.

Cunningham, A. E., & Stanovich, K. E. (1997). Early reading acquisition and its relation to reading experience and ability 10 years later. *Developmental Psychology, 33*(6), 934–945.

Cunningham, A. E., & Stanovich, K. E. (1998, Spring-Summer). What reading does for the mind. *The American Educator*, 8–17.

Cunningham, P. M. (1995). *Phonics they use: Words for reading and writing* (2nd ed.). New York, NY: HarperCollins.

Cunningham, P. M., & Allington, R. L. (1999). *Classrooms that work: They can all read and write* (2nd ed.). Reading, MA: Addison-Wesley.

Cunningham, P. M., & Allington, R. L. (2003). *Classrooms that work: They can all read and write* (3rd ed.). Boston, MA: Allyn & Bacon.

Cunningham, P. M., Hall, D. P., & Defree, M. (1991). Non-ability grouped, multileveled instruction: A year in a first-grade classroom. *The Reading Teacher, 44*, 566–571.

Cunningham, P. M., Hall, D. P., & Sigmon, C. M. (1999). *The teacher's guide to the four blocks*. Greensboro, NC: Carson–Dellosa.

Cunningham, P. M., Hall, D. P., & Sigmon, C. M. (2007). *The teacher's guide to the four blocks*. Greensboro, NC: Carson–Dellosa.

Curtis, C. P. (2000). *Bud, not buddy*. New York, NY: Yearling.

Dahl, K. L., Scharer, P. L., Lawson, L. L., & Grogan, P. R. (2001). *Rethinking phonics: Making the best teaching decisions*. Portsmouth, NH: Heinemann.

Dahl, R. (1998). *Danny, the champion of the world*. Illustrated by Quentin Blake. New York, NY: Puffin.

Damico, J. S. (1991). Descriptive assessment of communicative ability in limited English proficient students. In E. Hamayan & J. S. Damico (Eds.), *Limiting bias in the assessment of bilingual students* (pp. 157–218). Austin, TX: PRO-ED.

Daniels, H. (1994). *Literature circles: Voice and choice in one student-centered classroom*. York, ME: Stenhouse.

Daniels, H. (2001). *Literature circles: Voice and choice in book clubs and reading groups*. Augusta, ME: Stenhouse.

Daniels, H. (2002). *Literature circles: Voice and choice in book clubs & reading groups* (2nd ed.). Markham, Ontario: Pembroke.

Darling-Hammond, L., Pearson, P. D., Schoenfeld, A. H., Barron, B., & Stage, E. K. (2008). *Powerful learning: What we know about teaching for understanding*. San Francisco, CA: Jossey-Bass.

Davis, F. B. (1944). Fundamental factors of comprehension in reading. *Psychometrica, 9*, 195–197.

Davis, F. B. (1968). Research in comprehension in reading. *Reading Research Quarterly, 3*, 499–454.

de Braslavsky, B. P. (2006). *Adquisición inicial de la lectura y escritura en escuelas para la diversidad, Tomo 1*. Buenos Aires: Fundación Perez Companc.

Delpit, L. (1990). Language diversity and learning. In S. Hynds & D. Rubin (Eds.), *Perspectives on talk and learning* (pp. 247–266). Urbana, IL: NCTE.

Delpit, L. (1995). *Other people's children: Cultural conflict in the classroom*. New York, NY: The New Press.

Delpit, L. (1996). Skills and other dilemmas of a progressive black educator. In L. Delpit (Ed.), *Other people's children*. New York, NY: The New Press.

Delpit, L. (2008). Introduction. In L. Delpit (Ed.), *The skin that we speak: Thoughts on language and culture in the classroom* (pp. xxii–xxvi). New York, NY: The New Press.

Dewey, J. (1913). *Interest and effort in education*. Boston, MA: Riverside.

Diana v. State Board of Education of California, Action No. C-7037RFP (N. D. Cal. Jan. 7, 1970 & June 18, 1973).

Dirkes, M. A. (1985). Metacognition: Students in charge of their thinking. *Roeper Review, 8*(2), 96–100.

Dixon, C. N., & Nessel, D. (1983). *Language experience approach to reading and writing: LEA for ESL*. Hayward, CA: Alemany Press.

Dorn, K. J., & Henderson, S. C. (2010). The comprehensive intervention model: A systems approach to RTI. In M. Y. Lipson & K. K. Wixson (Eds.), *Successful approaches to RTI: Collaborative practices for improving K–12 literacy*. Newark, DE: International Reading Association.

Doyle, D., & Han, J. G. (2012). *Measuring teacher effectiveness: A look "under the hood" of teacher evaluation in 10 sites*. New York: 50CAN; New Haven, CT: ConnCAN; and Chapel Hill, NC: Public Impact. Retrieved from http://www.conncan.org/learn/research/teachers/measuring-teacher-effectiveness

Dudley-Marling, C. (1990). *When school is a struggle*. Richmond Hill, Ontario: Scholastic.

Dudley-Marling, C. (2000). *A family affair: When school troubles come home*. Portsmouth, NH: Heinemann.

Duffy, G. G., & Roehler, L. R. (1989). Why strategy instruction is so difficult and what we need to do about it. In C. B. McCormick, G. Miller, & M. Pressley (Eds.), *Cognitive strategy research: From basic research to educational applications*. New York, NY: Springer-Verlag.

Duffy-Hester, A. (1999). Teaching struggling readers in elementary school classrooms: A review of classroom reading programs and principles for instruction. *The Reading Teacher, 52*, 480–495.

Duke, N. K. (2000). 3–6 minutes per day: The scarcity of informational texts in first grade. *Reading Research Quarterly, 35*(2), 202–224.

Duke, N. K., & Bennett-Armistead, V. S. (2003). *Reading and writing informational text in the primary grades*. New York, NY: Scholastic.

Duke, N. K., Caughlan, S., Juzwik, M. M., & Martin, N. M. (2012). Teaching genre with purpose. *Educational Leadership, 69*(6), 34–39.

Durkin, D. (1978–1979). What classroom observations reveal about reading comprehension instruction. *Reading Research Quarterly, 15*, 481–483.

Echevarria, J., Vogt, M. E., & Short, D. J. (2013). *Making content comprehensible for elementary English learners: The SIOP® model*. Boston, MA: Allyn & Bacon.

Edelsky, C. (1982). Writing in a bilingual program: The relation of L_1 and L_2 texts. *TESOL Quarterly, 16*, 211–228.

Eder, D. (1983). Ability grouping and students' academic self-concepts: A case study. *Elementary School Journal, 84*(2), 149–161.

Edwards, P. A., McMillon, G. T., & Turner, J. E. (2010). *Change is gonna come: Transforming literacy education for African American students*. New York, NY: Teachers College Press.

Edwards, S. A., Malloy, R. W., & Verock-O'Laughlin, R. (2003). *Ways of writing with young kids*. Boston, MA: Allyn & Bacon.

Eeds, M., & Wells, D. (1989). Grand conversations: An exploration of meaning construction in literature discussion groups. *Research in the Teaching of English, 23*, 4–29.

Ehrenreich, B. (2001). *Nickel and dimed: On (not) getting by in America*. New York, NY: Owl Books.

Ehri, L. C. (1991). Development of the ability to read words. In R. Barr, M. Kamil, P. B. Mosenthal, & P. D. Pearson (Eds.), *Handbook of reading research* (Vol. 2). New York, NY: Longman.

Ehri, L. C. (1995). Phases of development in learning to read by sight. *Journal of Research in Reading, 18*, 116–125.

Ehri, L. C. (1997a). Learning to read and learning to spell are one and the same, almost. In C. Perfetti, L. Rieben, & M. Fayol (Eds.), *Learning to spell* (pp. 237–269). Hillsdale, NJ: Erlbaum.

Ehri, L. C. (1997b). *The development of children's ability to read words.* Paper presented at the convention of the International Reading Association, Atlanta, GA.

Elkonin, D. B. (1973). USSR. In J. Downing (Ed.), *Comparative reading.* New York, NY: Macmillan.

Elley, W. (1992). *How in the world do students read?* The Hague: The International Association for the Evaluation of Educational Achievement.

Elley, W. (1996). *The IEA study of reading literacy.* Oxford, England: Pergamon.

Escamilla, K., & Andrade, A. (1992). Descubriendo la lectura: An application of Reading Recovery in Spanish. *Education and Urban Society, 24,* 212–226.

Escamilla, K., Loera, M., Ruiz, O., & Rodriguez, Y. (1998). An examination of sustaining effects in Descubriendo la Lectura programs. *Literacy Teaching and Learning, 3,* 59–81.

Farrell, M. M., & Phelps, L. (2000). A comparison of the Leiter-R and the Universal Nonverbal Intelligence Test (UNIT) with children classified as language impaired. *Journal of Psychoeducational Assessment, 18*(3), 268–274.

Farris, P. J., Werderich, D. E., Nelson, P. A., & Fuhler, C. J. (2009). Male call: Fifth-grade boys' reading preferences. *The Reading Teacher, 63*(3), 180–188.

Federal Register. (2006). *Title I—Improving the Academic Achievement of the Disadvantaged; Final Rule.* 34 CFR Part 200, September 13, 2006. Washington, DC: Department of Education.

Fernandez, M. C., Pearson, B. Z., Umbel, V. M., Oller, D. K., & Molinet-Molina, M. (1992). Bilingual receptive vocabulary in Hispanic preschool children. *Hispanic Journal of Behavioral Sciences, 14*(2), 268–276.

Ferreiro, E., & Rodríguez, B. (1994). *Las condiciones de alfabetización en medio rural.* México: CINVESTAV.

Ferreiro, E., & Teberosky, A. (1982). *Literacy before schooling.* Portsmouth, NH: Heinemann.

Fielding, L., & Roller, C. (1992). Making difficult books accessible and easy books acceptable. *The Reading Teacher, 45,* 678–685.

Fisher, A. (2001). *Critical thinking.* New York, NY: Cambridge University Press.

Fisher, D., Frey, N., & Rothenberg, C. 2011. *Implementing RTI with English learners.* Bloomington, IN: Solution Tree.

Fisher, P., Blachowicz, C., & Smith, J. (1991). Vocabulary learning in literature discussion groups. In J. Zutell & S. McCormick (Eds.), *Learner factors/Teacher factors: Issues in literacy research and instruction* (pp. 201–209). Fortieth yearbook of the National Reading Conference. Chicago, IL: National Reading Conference.

Fitzgerald, J. (1993). Literacy and students who are learning English as a second language. *The Reading Teacher, 46,* 638–647.

Fitzgerald, J. (1995). English-as-a-second-language reading instruction in the United States: A research review. *Journal of Reading Behavior, 27,* 115–152.

Flesch, R. (1956). *Why Johnny can't read.* New York, NY: Popular Library.

Foorman, B. R., & Mehta, P. (2002, November). *Definitions of fluency: Conceptual and methodological challenges.* PowerPoint presentation at A Focus on Fluency Forum, San Francisco, CA. Retrieved from www.prel.org/programs/rel/fluency/Foorman.ppt

Fountas, I. C., & Pinnell, G. S. (1996). *Guided reading: Good first teaching for all children.* Portsmouth, NH: Heinemann.

Fountas, I. C., & Pinnell, G. S. (1999). *Matching books to readers: Using leveled books in guided reading, K–3.* Portsmouth, NH: Heinemann.

Fountas, I. C., & Pinnell, G. S. (2001). *Guiding readers and writers: Grades 3–6.* Portsmouth, NH: Heinemann.

Fountas, I. C., & Pinnell, G. S. (2001). *Guiding readers and writers: Teaching comprehension, genre, and content literacy.* Portsmouth, NH: Heinemann.

Fountas, I. C., & Pinnell, G. S. (2001). *Leveled books, K–8: Matching texts to readers for effective teaching.* Portsmouth, NH: Heinemann.

Fountas, I. C., & Pinnell, G. S. (2007). *The continuum of literacy learning grades K–2.* Portsmouth, NH: Heinemann.

Fountas, I., & Pinnell, G. S. (2008). *Fountas and Pinnell leveled books: K–8.* Portsmouth, NH: Heinemann. Retrieved from http://www.fountasandpinnellleveledbooks.com/

Fountas, I. C., & Pinnell, G. S. (2009). *The Fountas & Pinnell leveled book list, K–8+: 2010–2012.* Portsmouth, NH: Heinemann.

Fradd, S. H., & Tikunoff, W. J. (Eds.). (1987). *Bilingual and bilingual special education: An administrator's guide.* Boston, MA: Little, Brown.

Frazier, D. (2007). *Miss Alaineus: A vocabulary disaster.* San Diego, CA: Harcourt.

Freebody, P., & Luke, A. (1990). Literacies programs: Debates and demands in cultural context. *Prospect: Australian Journal of TESOL, 5*(7), 7–16.

Freeman, D. (1978). *Corduroy.* New York, NY: Viking Junior.

Freinet, C. (1974). *El método natural de lectura.* Barcelona, Spain: Editorial Laia.

Freire, P. (1976). *Education: The practice of freedom.* Danbury, CT: Writers & Readers Ltd.

Freppon, P. A. (1987). Radices docere: Teaching roots. *Ohio Reading Teacher, 21,* 20–25.

Friedman, E. K. (2010). Secondary prevention in an RTI model: A step toward academic recovery. *The Reading Teacher, 64*(3), 207–210.

Frith, U. (1985). Beneath the surface of developmental dyslexia. In K. E. Patterson, J. C. Marshall, & M. Coltheart (Eds.), *Surface dyslexia* (pp. 310–330). London: Erlbaum.

Fry, E. (1967). Fry's readability graph: Clarifications, validity, and extension to level 17. *Journal of Reading, 21,* 242–252.

Frye, Northrop. (1951). The archetypes of literature. In C. Kaplan & W. Anderson, *Criticism: the major statements* (3rd ed., pp. 500–514). New York, NY: St. Martin's, 1991.

Fuchs, D., & Fuchs, L. S. (2009). Responsiveness to intervention: Multilevel assessment and instruction as early intervention and disability identification. *The Reading Teacher, 63*(3), 250–252.

Fuchs, L. S., Deno, S. L., & Mirkin, P. K. (1984, Summer). The effects of frequent curriculum-based measurement and evaluation on pedagogy, student achievement, and student awareness of learning. *American Educational Research Journal, 21*(2), 449–460.

Fuchs, L. S., & Fuchs, D. (2008). The role of assessment within the RTI framework. In D. Fuchs, L. W. Fuchs, & S. Vaughn (Eds.), *Response to intervention: A framework for reading educators.* Newark, DE: International Reading Association.

Fuchs, M. L., & Mellard, D. F. (2007). *Helping educators discuss responsiveness to intervention with parents and students.* Lawrence, KS: National Research Center on Learning Disabilities.

Ga'ndara, P. (2010). Overcoming triple segregation. *Educational Leadership, 68*(3), 60–64.

Ganske, K. (2000). *Word journeys.* New York, NY: Guilford Press.

Ganske, K. (2003). *Word journeys.* New York, NY: Guilford Press.

García, E. E. (1991, Autumn). Factors influencing the English reading test performance of Spanish-speaking Hispanic children. *Reading Research Quarterly, 26*(4), 371–392.

García, E. E. (2005). *Teaching and learning in two languages: Bilingualism and schooling in the United States.* New York, NY: Teachers College Press.

Gaskins, I. W. (1998). There's more to teaching at-risk and delayed readers than good reading instruction. *The Reading Teacher, 51*, 534–547.

Gee, J. P. (1992). *The social mind: Ideology and social practice.* New York, NY: Bergin & Garvey.

Gelman, R., & Greeno, J. G. (1989). On the nature of competence: Principles for understanding in a domain. In L. Resnick (Ed.), *Knowing, learning, and instruction: Essays in honor of Robert Glaser.* Hillsdale, NJ: Erlbaum.

Gelzheiser, L. M., Scanlon, D. M., & Hallgren-Flynn, L. (2010). Spotlight on RTI for adolescents: An example of intensive middle school intervention using the interactive strategies approach-extended. In M. Y. Lipson & K. K. Wixson (Eds.), *Successful approaches to RTI: Collaborative practices for improving K–12 literacy.* Newark, DE: International Reading Association.

Gentry, J. R. (1981). Learning to spell developmentally. *The Reading Teacher, 34*, 378–381.

Gentry, J. R. (1989). *Spel . . . is a four-letter word.* Portsmouth, NH: Heinemann.

Gentry, J. R. (2007). *Breakthrough in beginning reading and writing.* New York, NY: Scholastic.

Gentry, J. R. (2008). *Step-by-step assessment guide to code breaking.* New York, NY: Scholastic.

Gersten, R. (1998). Recent advances in instructional research for students with learning disabilities: An overview. *Learning Disabilities Research and Practice, 13*(3), 162–170.

Gersten, R., & Baker, S. (2000). What we know about effective instructional practices for English-language learners. *Exceptional Children, 66*, 454–470.

Gersten, R., & Dimino, J. A. (2006). RTI (Response to Intervention): Rethinking special education for students with reading difficulties (yet again). *Reading Research Quarterly, 41*(1), 99–108.

Gibson, E., & Levin, H. (1975). *The psychology of reading.* Cambridge, MA: MIT Press.

Gillet, J. W., Temple, C., Temple, C., & Crawford, A. (2012). *Understanding reading problems* (8th ed.). Boston, MA: Allyn & Bacon.

Glasswell, K., & Ford, M. P. (2010). Teaching flexibly with leveled texts: More power for your reading block. *The Reading Teacher, 64*(1), 57–60.

Gleitman, L. R., & Rozin, P. (1973, Summer). Teaching reading by use of a syllabary. *Reading Research Quarterly, 8*(4), 447–483.

Goatley, V. J., Brock, C. H., & Raphael, T. E. (1995). Diverse learners participating in regular education "book clubs." *Reading Research Quarterly, 30*(3), 352–380.

Goetze, S. K., Laster, B., & Ehren, B. J. (2010). RTI for secondary school literacy. In M. Y. Lipson & K. K. Wixson (Eds.), *Successful approaches to RTI: Collaborative practices for improving K–12 literacy.* Newark, DE: International Reading Association.

Goldman, S. R., & Rakestraw, Jr., J. A. (2000). Structural aspects of constructing meaning from text. In M. L. Kamil, P. Mosenthal, P. D. Pearson, & R. Barr (Eds.), *Handbook of reading research* (Vol. 3, pp. 311–335). Mahwah, NJ: Erlbaum.

Gollnick, D. M., & Chinn, P. C. (2008). *Multicultural education in a pluralistic society.* Boston, MA: Allyn & Bacon.

Gomes de Matos, F. (2002, Spring). Teaching peace-promoting vocabulary: A new frontier. *Glosas Didacticas.*

Goodlad, J. I. (1984/2004). *A place called school.* New York, NY: McGraw-Hill.

Goodman, K. S. (1967). Reading: A psycholinguistic guessing game. *Journal of the Reading Specialist, 6*, 126–135.

Goodman, K. S. (1986). *What's whole in whole language?* Portsmouth, NH: Heinemann.

Goodman, K. S. (1989). *Lenguaje integral.* Mérida, Venezuela: Editorial Venezolana.

Goodman, Y. M. (1978). Kid watching: An alternative to testing. *National Elementary Principal, 57*(4), 41–45.

Goodman, Y. M. (1985). Kid watching: Observing children in the classroom. In A. Jaggar & M. T. Smith-Burke (Eds.), *Observing the language learner* (pp. 9–18). New York, NY: New York University. Co-published by the International Reading Association and the National Council of Teachers of English, 1985.

Goodman, Y. M. (2006). *Kidwatching.* Retrieved from www.reading.org/downloads/publications/books/bk558-27-Goodman_Kidwatching.pdf

Gordon, D., & Gordon, C. (2007). *The down-to-earth guide to global warming.* New York, NY: Scholastic.

Goswami, U. (2000). Phonological and lexical processes. In M. Kamil, P. Mosenthal, P. D. Pearson, & R. Barr (Eds.), *Handbook of reading research* (Vol. 3). New York, NY: Longman.

Graham, S., & Harris, K. R. (2005). *Writing better: Effective strategies for teaching students with learning difficulties.* Boston, MA: Paul H. Brookes.

Graves, D. H. (1982). *Writing: Students and teachers at work.* Portsmouth, NH: Heinemann.

Graves, D. H. (1983). *Writing: Teachers and children at work.* Exeter, NH: Heinemann Educational Books.

Graves, M. F. (2006). *The vocabulary book: Learning and instruction.* Champaign, IL: NCTE.

Graves, M. F., & Silverman, R. (2010). Interventions to enhance vocabulary development. In R. L. Allington & A. McGill-Franzen (Eds.), *Handbook of reading disabilities research.* Mahwah, NJ: Erlbaum.

Greenlaw, W. (2001). *English language arts and reading on the Internet.* Columbus, OH: Merrill Prentice Hall.

Griffith, P. L., & Lynch-Brown, C. (2002). Owning technology. *The Reading Teacher, 55*, 614–615.

Gronlund, N. E., Linn, R. L., & Davis, K. (2000). *Measurement and assessment in teaching.* Englewood Cliffs, NJ: Prentice Hall.

Guthrie, J., & Ozgungor, S. (2002). Instructional contexts for reading engagement. In C. C. Block & M. Pressley (Eds.), *Comprehension instruction: Research-based practices.* New York, NY: Guilford.

Guthrie, J. T., & Davis, M. H. (2003). Motivating struggling readers in middle school through an engagement model of classroom practice. *Reading & Writing Quarterly, 19*, 59–185.

Gwynne, F. (1988). *A chocolate moose for dinner.* New York, NY: Aladdin.

Gwynne, F. (2006). *The king who rained.* New York, NY: Aladdin Paperbacks.

Haggard, M. R. (1982). The vocabulary self-collection strategy: An active approach to word learning. *Journal of Reading, 26,* 203–207.

Hall, S. L., & Moats, L. C. (1999). *Straight talk about reading.* Lincolnwood, IL: Contemporary Books.

Halle, T., Kurtz-Costes, B., & Mahoney, J. (1997). Family influences on school achievement in low-income African American children. *Journal of Educational Psychology, 89,* 527–537.

Hanson, J., & Graves, D. (1983). The author's chair. *Language Arts, 60,* 176–183.

Harmon, J. M. (1998). Vocabulary teaching and learning in a seventh-grade literature-based classroom. *Journal of Adolescent & Adult Literacy, 41,* 518–529.

Harris, K., & Graham, S. (1996). *Making the writing process work: Strategies for composition and self-regulation.* Cambridge, MA: Brookline Books.

Harris Interactive. (2011). *One in six Americans now use e-readers with one in six likely to purchase in next six months.* New York, New York, Sept. 19, 2011. Retrieved from www.harrisinteractive.com/NewsRoom/HarrisPolls/tabloid/447/ctl.ReadCustom.

Harste, J., Woodward, J., & Burke, C. (1984). *Language stories and literacy lessons.* Portsmouth, NH: Heinemann.

Hart, B., & Risley, T. R. (1995). *Meaningful differences in the everyday experiences of young American children.* Baltimore, MD: Brookes.

Hasbrouck, J., & Tindal, G. A. (2006, 7 April). Oral reading fluency norms: A valuable assessment tool for reading teachers. *The Reading Teacher, 59*(7), 636–644.

Haselhurst, M. (2005). *Hurricane.* Boston, MA: Pearson (Celebration Press).

Hauerwas, L. B., & Walker, J. (2004). What can children's spelling of *running* and *jumped* tell us about their need for spelling instruction? *The Reading Teacher, 58*(2), 168–176.

Heath, S. B. (1983). *Ways with words: Language, life, and work in communities and classrooms.* Cambridge, England: Cambridge University Press.

Heath, S. B. (1986). Sociocultural contexts of language development. In *Beyond language: Social and cultural factors in schooling language minority students* (pp. 143–182). Sacramento, CA: Bilingual Education Office, California State Department of Education.

Heller, R. (1991). *A cache of jewels and other collective nouns.* New York, NY: Putnam Juvenile.

Helman, L. A., & Bear, D. R. (2007). Does an established model of orthographic development hold for English language learners? In D. W. Rowe, R. Jimenez, D. L. Compton, D. K. Dickinson, Y. Kim, K. M. Leander, & V. J. Risko (Eds.), *56th Yearbook of the National Reading Conference* (pp. 266–280). Oak Creek, WI: National Reading Conference.

Henderson, E. H. (1982). *Learning to read and spell: A child's knowledge of words.* Carbondale, IL: University of Southern Illinois.

Henderson, E. H. (1990). *Teaching spelling.* Boston, MA: Houghton Mifflin.

Hendrix, C. (1952). *Cómo enseñar a leer por el método global.* Buenos Aires, Argentina: Editorial Kapelusz.

Henkes, K. (1987). *Sheila Rae the brave.* New York, NY: Greenwillow.

Henkes, K. (1996). *Lilly's purple plastic purse.* New York, NY: Greenwillow.

Henkes, K. (2006). *Lilly's big day.* New York, NY: HarperCollins Children's Books.

Henry, L. A. (2006). SEARCHing for an answer: The critical role of new literacies while reading on the Internet. *The Reading Teacher, 59*(7), 614–627.

Hickman, J. (1979). *Response to literature in a school environment.* Unpublished doctoral dissertation, Ohio State University, Columbus.

Hickman, J. (1981). A new perspective on response to literature. *Research in the Teaching of English, 15,* 343–354.

Hiebert, E. H. (December 2011–January 2012). The Common Core's staircase of text complexity: Getting the size of the first step right. *Reading Today,* 26–28.

Hill, R., Carjuzaa, J., Aramburo, D., & Baca, L. (1993). Culturally and linguistically diverse teachers in special education: Repairing or redesigning the leaky pipeline. *Teacher Education and Special Education, 16,* 258–269.

Ho, D. B. (1999). Using wordless picture books to support struggling sixth grade readers and writers. *The California Reader, 32,* 9–11.

Hoban, R. (1995). *Bedtime for Frances.* Illustrated by Garth Williams. New York, NY: HarperTrophy.

Hoffman, J. V. (1992). Critical reading/ thinking across the curriculum: Using I-Charts to support learning. *Language Arts, 69,* 121–127.

Hohmann, M. (2002). *Fee, fie, phonemic awareness.* Ypsilanti, MI: Highscope Press.

Holdaway, D. (1979). *Foundations of literacy.* Portsmouth, NH: Heinemann.

Holland, S. (2011, March 9). *Duncan: 'No Child Left Behind' creates failure for U.S. schools.* CNN.

Hudelson, S. (1984). Kan yu ret an rayt en Ingles: Children become literate in English as a second language. *TESOL Quarterly, 18,* 221–238.

Hudelson, S. (1987). The role of native language literacy in the education of language minority children. *Language Arts, 64,* 827–840.

Huey, E. B. (1908). *The psychology and pedagogy of reading.* Cambridge, MA: MIT Press.

Hynds, S. (1997). *On the brink: Negotiating literature and life with adolescents.* New York, NY: Teachers College Press.

Individuals with Disabilities Education Act 1997 (Reauthorization). (1997). 20 U.S.C. 1400 et seq.

Individuals with Disabilities Education Improvement Act of 2004. (2004). 108th Congress (2003–2004) H.R.1350.ENR.

International Reading Association. (2001). *Second-language literacy instruction: A position statement of the International Reading Association.* Newark, DE: Author.

International Reading Association. (2009). *Response to Intervention: Guiding principles for educators from the International Reading Association.* Newark, DE: Author.

International Reading Association & National Association for the Education of Young Children. (1998, July). *Learning to read and write: Developmentally appropriate practices for young children: A joint position statement of the International Reading Association (IRA) and National Association for the Education of Young Children* (NAEYC). Newark, DE, and Washington, DC: Authors.

International Reading Association and the National Council for the Accreditation of Teacher Education. (2006). *Standards for reading professionals.* Newark, DE: Author.

International Reading Association and National Council of Teachers of English. (2009). *Standards for the assessment of reading and writing, revised edition.* Newark, DE: Author.

Iser, W. (1978). *The act of reading.* Baltimore, MD: Johns Hopkins University Press.

Ivey, G., & Broaddus, K. (2001). "Just plain reading": A survey of what makes students want to read in middle school classrooms. *Reading Research Quarterly, 36,* 350–371.

Jacobs, H. H. (1997). *Mapping the big picture: Integrating curriculum and assessment.* Alexandria, VA: Association for Supervision and Curriculum Development.

Jacobs, H. H. (2006). *Active literacy across the curriculum.* Larchmont, NY: Eye on Education.

Jenkins, S. (2008). *What do you do with a tail like this?* Boston, MA: Sandpiper.

Jepsen, C. (2009). *Bilingual education and English proficiency: Discussion Paper Series.* University of Kentucky Center for Poverty Research, ED505041.

Jepsen, C. (2010). Bilingual education and English proficiency. *Education Finance and Policy, v,* 200–227.

Johnson-Coleman, L. (2001, May). *Keep on keepin' on: Motivation for the young and young at heart.* Keynote address presented at the annual conference of the International Reading Association, New Orleans, LA.

Johnston, P. (2010). An instructional frame for RTI. *The Reading Teacher, 63*(7), 602–604.

Juel, C. (1988). Learning to read and write: A longitudinal study of 54 children from first through fourth grades. *Journal of Educational Psychology, 80,* 443–447.

Kagan, S. (1994). *Cooperative learning.* San Clemente, CA: Kagan.

Kagan, S. (1997). *Cooperative learning.* San Clemente, CA: Kagan.

Kame'enui, E. J. (1998). The rhetoric of all, the reality of some, and the unmistakable smell of mortality. In J. Osborn & F. Lehr (Eds.), *Literacy for all: Issues in teaching and learning.* New York, NY: Guilford Press.

Kame'enui, E. J., Simmons, D., Cornachione, C., Thompson-Hoffman, S., Ginsburg, A., Marcy, E., Mittleman, J., Irwin, J., & Baker, M. (2001). *A practical guide to reading assessments.* Washington, DC: U.S. Department of Education.

Katzir, T., & Pare-Blagoev, J. (2006). Applying cognitive neuroscience research to education: The case of literacy. *Educational Psychologist 41*(1), 53–74.

Kawakami-Arakaki, A. J., Oshiro, M. E., & Farran, D. C. (1988). *Research to practice: Integrating reading and writing in a kindergarten curriculum.* Champaign, IL: University of Illinois at Urbana-Champaign — Center for the Study of Reading.

Kelly, M. (2000). *Of dreams and new realities: Mexican immigrant women in transition.* Unpublished doctoral dissertation. National-Louis University.

Klenk, L., & Kibby, M. W. (2000). Remediating reading difficulties: Appraising the past, reconciling the present, constructing the future. In M. L. Kamil, P. B. Mosenthal, P. D. Pearson, & R. Barr (Eds.), *Handbook of reading research* (Vol. 3, pp. 545–562). Mahwah, NJ: Erlbaum.

Klingner, J. K., & Edwards, P. A. (2006). Cultural considerations with Response to Intervention models. *Reading Research Quarterly, 41*(1), 108–117.

Klingner, J. K., Soltero-González, L., & Lesaux, N. (2010). RTI for English-language learners. In M. Y. Lipson & K. K. Wixson (Eds.), *Successful approaches to RTI: Collaborative practices for improving K–12 literacy.* Newark, DE: International Reading Association.

Knoell, D. (2010). Selecting and using nonfiction in grades K–12 social studies and science. In K. Gansky & D. Fisher (Eds.), *Comprehension across the curriculum.* New York, NY: Guilford.

Koskinen, P. S., & Blum, I. H. (1986). Paired repeated reading: A classroom strategy for developing fluent reading. *The Reading Teacher, 40,* 70–75.

Koskinen, P. S., Gambrell, L. B., Kapinus, B. A., & Heathington, B. S. (1988). Retelling: A strategy for enhancing students' reading comprehension. *The Reading Teacher, 41,* 892–896.

Kovalski, M. (1987). *The wheels on the bus.* Boston, MA: Joy Street Books.

Krashen, S. D. (1981). Bilingual education and second language acquisition theory. In California State Department of Education (Ed.), *Schooling and language minority students: A theoretical framework* (pp. 51–79). Sacramento: California State Department of Education, Office of Bilingual Bicultural Education.

Krashen, S. D. (1982). *Principles and practice in second language acquisition.* New York, NY: Pergamon Press.

Krashen, S. D. (1985). *Inquiries and insights: Second language teaching, immersion and bilingual education, literacy.* Hayward, CA: Alemany Press.

Krashen, S. D. (1991). *Bilingual education: A focus on current research.* Washington, DC: National Clearinghouse for Bilingual Education.

Krashen, S. D. (1991). The input hypothesis: An update. In J. E. Alatis (Ed.), Georgetown University Round Table on Languages and Linguistics 1991, *Linguistics and language pedagogy: The state of the art.* Washington, DC: Georgetown University Press.

Krashen, S. D. (1993). *The power of reading: Insights from the research.* Greenwood Village, CO: Libraries Unlimited.

Krashen, S. D. (1997). Conflicting claims concerning computers: A comment on Hinkson (1996). *The California Reader, 30,* 16–17.

Krashen, S. D., & Biber, D. (1988). *On course: Bilingual education's success in California.* Sacramento: California Association for Bilingual Education.

Krashen, S. D., & Terrell, T. D. (1983). *The natural approach: Language acquisition in the classroom.* New York, NY: Pergamon/Alemany.

Kucan, L. (2012, March). What is most important to know about vocabulary. *Reading Teacher, 65,* 360–366.

Kuhn, M. R., & Stahl, S. A. (2003). Fluency: A review of developmental and remedial practices. *Journal of Educational Psychology, 95,* 3–21.

Labbo, L. D., & Teale, W. H. (1990). Cross age reading: A strategy for helping poor readers. *The Reading Teacher, 43,* 363–369.

LaBerge, D., & Samuels, S. J. (1974). Toward a theory of automatic information processing in reading. *Cognitive Psychology, 6,* 293–323.

Labov, W. (1970). *The study of non-standard English.* Champaign, IL: NCTE.

Labov, W. (1972). *Language in the inner city: Studies in Black English vernacular.* Philadelphia, PA: University of Pennsylvania Press.

Labov, W. (1973). *Sociolinguistic patterns.* Philadelphia, PA: University of Pennsylvania Press.

Ladson-Billings, G. (2009). *The dream-keepers: Successful teachers of African American children.* San Francisco, CA: Jossey-Bass.

Lamberg, W. J., Rodríguez, L., & Tomas, D. A. (1978). Training in identifying oral reading departures from text which can be explained as Spanish-English phonological differences. *The Bilingual Review/La Revista Bilingue*, 5, 65–75.

Lambert, W. E. (1975). Culture and language as factors in learning and education. In A. Wolfgang (Ed.), *Education of immigrant students*. Toronto: O.I.S.E.

Landrum, J. (2001). Selecting intermediate novels that feature characters with disabilities. *The Reading Teacher*, 55, 252–258.

Langer, J. (1990). The process of understanding: Reading for literary and informative purposes. *Research in the Teaching of English*, 24, 229–260.

Langer, J. A. (2011). *Envisioning knowledge: Building literacy in the academic disciplines*. New York, NY: Teachers College Press.

Lau v. Nichols, 414 US 563 (1974).

Lehr, F., Osborn, J., & Hiebert, E. (2006). *A focus on vocabulary*. Honolulu, HI: Pacific Resources for Education and Learning.

Lehr, S. S. (1988). Children's developing sense of theme as a response to literature. *Reading Research Quarterly*, 23, 337–357.

Lehr, S. S. (1991). *The child's developing sense of theme: Responses to literature*. New York, NY: Teachers College Press.

Lems, K., Miller, L. D., & Soro, T. M. (2010). *Teaching reading to English language learners: Insights from linguistics*. New York, NY: Guilford.

Lennon, C., & Burdick, H. (2004). *The Lexile Framework as an approach for reading measurement and success*. Durham, NC: MetaMetrics.

Lenters, K. (2005). No half measures: Reading instruction for young second-language learners. *The Reading Teacher*, 58, 328–336.

Leslie, L., & Caldwell, J. (2005). *Qualitative reading inventory* (4th ed.). Boston, MA: Allyn & Bacon.

Lester, H. (1986). *A porcupine named fluffy*. Boston, MA: Houghton Mifflin.

Lester, H. (1993). *Tacky the penguin*. Boston, MA: Houghton -Mifflin.

Leu, D. J., Coiro, J., Castek, J., Hartman, D. K., Henry, L. A., & Reinking, D. (2010). Research on instruction and assessment in the new literacies of online reading comprehension. In C. C. Block & S. Parris (Eds.), *Comprehension instruction: Research-based best practices*. New York, NY: Guilford Press.

Leu, D. J., Zawilinski, L., Castek, J., Banerjee, M., Housand, B., Liu, Y., & O'Neil, M. (2007). What is new about the new literacies of online reading comprehension? In L. Rush, A. Berger, & J. Eakle (Eds.), *Secondary school reading and writing: What research reveals for classroom practices* (pp. 37–68). Chicago, IL: NCTE/NCRL.

Levi-Strauss. C. (1970). *Structural anthropology*. Garden City, NY: Basic Books.

Lipson, M. Y., Chomsky-Higgins, P., & Kanfer, J. (2011). Diagnosis: The missing ingredient in RTI assessment. *The Reading Teacher*, 65(3), 204–208.

Loban, W. (1976). *Language development: Kindergarten through twelfth grade*. Urbana, IL: National Council of Teachers of English.

Los Angeles Unified School District. (1985). *Strategies for sheltered English instruction*. Los Angeles, CA: Author.

Lourie, P. (2011). *The manatee scientists: Saving vulnerable species*. Boston, MA: Houghton Mifflin Harcourt.

Luke, A. (2000). Critical literacy in Australia: A matter of context and standpoint. *Journal of Adolescent and Adult Literacy*, 43(5), 448–461.

Luke, A., & Freebody, P. (1999). A map of possible practices: Further notes on the four resources model. *Practically Primary*, 4, 2.

Luria, A. R. (1976). *Cognitive development: Its cultural and social foundations*. Cambridge, MA: Harvard University Press.

Lyon, G. (1995). Research initiatives in learning disabilities: Contributions from scientists supported by the National Institute of Child Health and Human Development. *Journal of Child Neurology*, 10(Suppl. 1), S120–S126.

Macrorie, K. (1988). *The I-Search paper revised*. Portsmouth, NH: Boynton/Cook.

Mandler, M. J., & Johnson, N. S. (1977). The remembrance of things parsed: Story structure and recall. *Cognitive Psychology*, 9, 51–91.

Manyak, P. C., & Bauer, E. B. (2009). English vocabulary instruction for English learners. *The Reading Teacher*, 63(2), 174–176.

Manzo, A. V. (1969). The ReQuest procedure. *Journal of Reading*, 13, 123–126.

Marsh, G., Friedman, M., Welch, V., & Desberg, P. (1981). A cognitive-developmental theory of reading acquisition. In G. MacKinnon & T. Waller (Eds.), *Reading research advances in theory and practice*, volume 3. New York, NY: Academic Press.

Marshall, E. (1994). *Fox and his friends*. Illustrated by James Marshall. New York, NY: Puffin.

Martinez, M., Roser, N., & Strecker, S. (1999). "I never thought I could be a star": A readers' theatre ticket to reading fluency. *The Reading Teacher*, 52, 326–334.

Marzano, R. J. (2004). *Building background knowledge for academic achievement: Research on what works in schools*. Alexandria, VA: ASCD.

Marzano, R. J., & Pickering, D. J. (2005). *Building academic vocabulary: Teacher's manual*. Alexandria, VA: Association for Supervision and Curriculum Development.

Mayer, M. (2002). *Beauty and the beast*. Illustrated by Mercer Mayer. New York, NY: Macmillan.

McCafferty, S. G., & Iddings, C. (2001). *Carnival: Putting a round peg in a square hole*. Paper presented at the meeting of the National Reading Conference, San Antonio, TX.

McEwan-Adkins, K. (2006). *Raising reading achievement in middle and high school: Five simple-to-follow strategies*. Thousand Oaks, CA: Corwin Press.

McGee, L. M., & Richgels, D. J. (2003). *Literacy's beginnings: Supporting young readers and writers* (3rd ed.). Boston, MA: Allyn & Bacon.

McKee, J., & Ogle, D. (2005). *Integrating instruction: Literacy and science*. New York, NY: Guilford.

McKenna, M. C., & Kear, D. J. (1990, May). Measuring attitudes toward reading: A new tool for teachers. *The Reading Teacher*, 43(9), 626–639.

McKeown, M. G., Beck, I. L., & Blake, R. G. K. (2009). Rethinking reading comprehension instruction: A comparison of instruction for strategies and content approaches. *The Reading Teacher*, 62(5), 383–386.

McKissack, P. C. (1997). *Ma Dear's aprons*. New York, NY: Alladin.

McLaughlin, M., & Vogt, M. (1996). *Portfolios in teacher education*. Newark, DE: International Reading Association.

McMurrer, J. (2008). *NCLB Year 5: Instructional time in elementary schools: A closer look at changes for specific subjects*. Washington, DC: Center for Educational Policy. Retrieved from http://www.cep-dc.org/displayDocument.cfm?DocumentID=309

McPhail, E. P. (2005). On literacy and liberation: The African American experience. In B. Hammond, M. E. Rhodes Hoover, & I. P. McPhail (Eds.), *Teaching African American learners to read* (pp. 9–23). Newark, DE: International Reading Association.

McQuillan, J., & Au, J. (2001). The effect of print access on reading frequency. *Reading Psychology, 22,* 225–248.

McQuillan, J., & Tse, L. (1998). What's the story? Using the narrative approach in beginning language classrooms. *TESOL Journal, 7,* 18–23.

Mehan, J. (1979). *Learning lessons.* Cambridge, MA: Harvard University Press.

Mesmer, E. M., & Mesmer, H. A. E. (2008/2009). Response to Intervention (RTI): What teachers of reading need to know. *The Reading Teacher, 62*(4), 280–290.

Meyer, K. E., & Reindl, B. L. (2010). Spotlight on the comprehensive intervention model: The case of Washington School for Comprehensive Literacy. In M. Y. Lipson & K. K. Wixson (Eds.), *Successful approaches to RTI: Collaborative practices for improving K–12 literacy.* Newark, DE: International Reading Association.

Modiano, N. (1968). Bilingual education for children of linguistic minorities. *American Indígena, 28,* 405–414.

Moffett, J. (1976). *Teaching the universe of discourse.* New York, NY: Holt, Rinehart & Winston.

Moffett, J., & Wagner B. J. (1991). *Student centered language arts K–12.* Portsmouth NH: Boynton/Cook.

Montelongo, J. A., Hernández, A., & Herter, R. J. (2011a). Identifying Spanish-English cognates to scaffold instruction for Latino ELs. *The Reading Teacher, 65*(2), 161–164.

Montelongo, J. A., Hernández, A. C., & Herter, R. J. (2011b). Using cognates to scaffold context clue strategies for Latino ELs. *The Reading Teacher, 64*(6), 429–434.

Moore, J., & Whitfield, V. (2009). Building schoolwide capacity for preventing reading failure. *The Reading Teacher, 62*(7), 622–624.

Morris, A. & Hevman, K. (1989). *Bread, bread, bread.* New York, NY: HarperCollins.

Morris, R. D. (2005). *Case studies in beginning reading.* New York, NY: Guilford.

Morris, R. D. (2005). *The Howard Street tutoring manual* (2nd ed.). New York, NY: Guilford.

Morris, R. D., Blanton, L., Blanton, W. E., Nowacek, J., & Perney, J. (1995, November). Teaching low-achieving spellers at their "instructional level." *Elementary School Journal, 96*(2), 163–177.

Morris, R. D., Nelson, L., & Perney, J. (1986). Exploring the concept of "spelling instructional level" through the analysis of error types. *Elementary School Journal, 87,* 181–200.

Morris, W., & Morris, M. (1962). *Dictionary of word and phrase origins.* New York, NY: Harper & Row.

Morrow, L. M. (2003). *Organizing and managing the language arts block.* New York, NY: Guilford Press.

Morrow, L. M., & Gambrell, L. (2004). *Using children's literature in preschool: Comprehending and enjoying books.* Newark, DE: International Reading Association.

Moskal, M. K., & Blachowicz, C. (2006). *Partnering for fluency.* New York, NY: Guilford Press.

Moustafa, M. (1997). *Beyond traditional phonics.* Portsmouth, NH: Heinemann.

Moustafa, M., & Penrose, J. (1985). Comprehensible input PLUS the language experience approach: Reading instruction for limited English speaking students. *The Reading Teacher, 38,* 640–647.

Murtha, S. M., & O'Connor, J. A. (2011). *English the American Way: A fun ESL guide to language and culture in the U.S.* Glen Ellyn, IL: Research and Education Associates.

Murray, D. (1985). *A writer teaches writing.* Boston, MA: Houghton Mifflin.

Muth, J. (2003). *Stone soup.* New York, NY: Scholastic.

Nagy, W. E., & Anderson, R. C. (1984). How many words are there in printed school English? *Reading Research Quarterly, 19,* 304–330.

Nagy, W. E., Anderson, R. C., & Herman, P. A. (1987). Learning word meanings from context during normal reading. *American Educational Research Journal, 24,* 237–270.

Nagy, W. E., Anderson, R., Schommer, M., Scott, J., & Stallman, A. (1989). Morphological families and word recognition. *Reading Research Quarterly, 24,* 262–282.

Nagy, W. E., García, G. E., Durgunoglu, A. Y., & Hancin-Bhatt, B. (1993). Spanish-English bilingual students' use of cognates in English reading. *Journal of Reading Behavior, 25,* 241–259.

Nagy, W. E., & Scott, J. A. (2000). Vocabulary processes. In M. L. Kamil, P. Mosenthal, P. D. Pearson, and R. Barr (Eds.), *Handbook of reading research, volume III.* New York, NY: Longman.

Nagy, W. E., & Townsend, D. (2012). Words as tools: Learning academic vocabulary as language. *Reading Research Quarterly, 47*(1), 91–108.

Nathan, R., Temple, F., Juntunen, K., & Temple, C. (1988). *Classroom strategies that work: An elementary teacher's guide to process writing.* Portsmouth, NH: Heinemann.

Nathenson-Mejia, S. (1989). Writing in a second language: Negotiating meaning through invented spelling. *Language Arts, 66,* 516–526.

National Assessment of Educational Progress. (2011). *Reading Report Card, 2011.* Retrieved from http://nationsreportcard.gov/reading_2011/nat_g4.asp.

National Assessment Governing Board. (2008). *Reading framework for the 2009 National Assessment of Educational Progress.* Washington, DC: U.S. Government Printing Office.

National Association of School Psychologists (NASP). (2006). *The role of the school psychologist in the RTI process.* Bethesda, MD: Author.

National Center for Education Statistics. (1999). *Digest of education statistics, 1998.* Washington, DC: U.S. Department of Education.

National Center for Education Statistics. (1999). *The condition of education.* Washington, DC: U.S. Government Printing Office. Retrieved from http://nces.ed.gov/programs/coe/

National Center for Education Statistics. (2000). *Elementary and secondary education: An international perspective.* Washington, DC: U.S. Department of Education. Retrieved from http://nces.ed.gov/pubs2000/2000033.pdf

National Center for Education Statistics. (2006). *National assessment of educational progress: The nation's report card.* Washington, DC: U.S. Department of Education.

National Center for Education Statistics. (2009). *The condition of education: Participation in education.* Alexandria, VA: U.S. Department of Education.

National Center for Education Statistics. (2009). *Parent and family involvement in education.* Retrieved from http://nces.ed.gov/programs/coe/2009/section4/indicator30.asp

National Center for Education Statistics, National Assessment of Educational Progress [NAEP]. (2009). *The nation's report card.* Washington, DC: U.S. Department of Education.

National Clearinghouse for English Language Acquisition. (2011). Retrieved from http://www.ncela.gwu.edu/files/uploads/9/growingLEP_0809.pdf.

National Institute for Literacy. (2008). Retrieved from http://www.nifl.gov/nifl/facts/facts.html.

National Literacy Panel on Language–Minority Children and Youth. (2006). *Developing literacy in second–language learners: Report of the National Literacy Panel on Language–Minority Children and Youth* (D. August and T. Shanahan, Eds.). Mahwah, NJ: Erlbaum.

National Reading Panel Web site. (2003). *Reports.* Retrieved from http://www.nationalreadingpanel.org

National Reading Panel. (2000, December). *Teaching children to read: An evidence-based assessment of the scientific research literature on reading and its implications for reading instruction.* (Reports of the Subgroups). Washington, DC: National Institute of Child Health and Human Development, National Institutes of Health.

NEA [National Education Association]. (2004). *NCLB: The intersection of access and outcomes.* Washington, DC: Author.

Nessel, D. D., & Jones, M. B. (1981). *The language-experience approach to reading.* New York, NY: Teachers College Press.

Neuman, S. B., & Celano, D. (2001). Access to print in low-income and middle-income communities: An ecological study of four neighborhoods. *Reading Research Quarterly, 56,* 8–28.

Neuman, S. B., & Celano, D. (2010, November). Roadblocks on the information highway. *Educational Leadership, 68*(3), 50–53.

Neuman, S. B., & Celano, D. (2012, Fall). "Worlds apart" One city, two libraries, and ten years of watching inequality grow. *American Educator, 36*(3).

Newkirk, T. (2012). How we really comprehend nonfiction. *Educational Leadership, 69*(6), 29–32.

O'Leary, D. (2002). *2002 widening achievement gap.* Tucson, AZ: League of Latin American Citizens (LULAC).

O'Rourke, J., & Bamman, H. A. (1971). *Techniques of teaching vocabulary.* Menlo Park, CA: Benjamin/Cummings Publishing Company.

Ockey, G. (2010). *Assessing English language learners' silent reading.* Chicago, IL: Annual Convention of the International Reading Association.

OECD. (2010). *PISA 2009 results: What students know and can do—student progress in reading, mathematics and science* (Vol. 1). Retrieved from http://dx.doi.org10.1787/9789264091450-en

Office of English Language Acquisition (OELA). (2004). Retrieved from http://www.ed.gov/print/programs/sfgp/index.html

Ogle, D. (1986). K-W-L: A teaching model that develops active reading of expository text. *Reading Teacher, 40,* 564–570.

Ogle, D. (1991). The know, want to know, learn strategy. In N. Muth (Ed.), *Children's comprehension of text: Research and practice* (pp. 22–23). Newark, DE: International Reading Association.

Ogle, D. (2000). Make it visual: A picture is worth a thousand words. In M. McLaughlin & M. Vogt (Eds.), *Creativity and innovation in content area teaching.* Norwood, MA: Christopher-Gordon.

Ogle, D., & Beers, J. W. (2009). *Engaging in the language arts: Exploring the power of language.* New York, NY: Pearson.

Ogle, D., & Blachowicz, C. (2001). Beyond literature circles: Helping students comprehend informational texts. In C. C. Block & M. Pressley (Eds.), *Comprehension instruction: Research-based best practices.* New York, NY: Guilford Press.

Olson, M. W., & Gee, T. C. (1988). A review of story grammar research. *Childhood Education, 64*(4), 302–306.

Organization for Economic Cooperation and Development. (2009). *Programme for International Student Achievement: PISA 2009 key findings.* Retrieved from http://www.oecd.org/pisa/pisaproducts/pisa2009/pisa2009keyfindings.htm

Osborn, J., Lehr, F., & Hiebert, E. H. (2003). *A focus on fluency.* Honolulu, HI: Pacific Resources for Education and Learning. Retrieved from http://www.prel.org

Owocki, G., & Goodman, Y. (2002). *Kidwatching: Documenting children's literacy development.* Portsmouth, NH: Heinemann.

Palincsar, A. S., & Brown, A. L. (1986). Interactive teaching to promote independent learning from text. *The Reading Teacher, 39,* 771–777.

Palmer, F. R. (2001). *Mood and modality.* New York, NY: Cambridge University Press.

Parish, P. (1992). *Amelia Bedelia.* Illustrated by Fritz Siebel. New York, NY: HarperCollins.

Patterson, E. (1984). *Language, letters, and learning.* Lecture at Hobart and William Smith Colleges, Geneva, NY.

Pattison, D. (2012). *Common Core ELA activities.* Little Rock, AR: Mims House.

Pearson Education. (2012). *Common core standards.* New York: Pearson. Retrieved from http://commoncore.pearsoned.com/index.cfm?locator=PS11Ta

Pearson, P. D. (1985). Changing the face of reading comprehension instruction. *The Reading Teacher, 38,* 724–738.

Pearson, P. D., & Anderson, R. C. (1985). A schema theoretic view of the learning to read process. In P. D. Pearson, R. Barr, & P. Mosenthal (Eds.), *Handbook of reading research: Volume 1.* New York, NY: MacMillan.

Pearson, P. D., Cervetti, G. N., & Tilson, J. L. (2008). Reading for understanding. In L. Darling-Hammond et al., *Powerful learning: What we know about teaching for understanding* (pp. 71–111). San Francisco, CA: Jossey-Bass.

Peck, J. (1989). Using storytelling to promote language and literacy development. *The Reading Teacher, 43,* 138–141.

Peer-Assisted Literacy Strategies (PALS) Series. (2010). Retrieved from http://smu.edu/education/readingresearch/interventions/pals.asp

Perfetti, C. A. (1985). *Reading ability.* New York, NY: Oxford University Press.

Perfetti, C. A. (1992). *Reading ability.* New York, NY: Oxford University Press.

Pilkey, D. (2000). *Captain Underpants boxed set.* New York, NY: Scholastic.

Pinnell, G. S., Bridges, L. B., & Fountas, I. C. (1999). *Matching books to readers: Using leveled books in guided reading.* Portsmouth, NH: Heinemann.

Pinnell, G. S., & Fountas, I. C. (1998). *Word matters.* Portsmouth, NH: Heinemann.

Pinnell, G. S., & Fountas, I. C. (2001). *Leveled books for readers, grades 3–6.* Portsmouth, NH: Heinemann.

Pinnell, G. S., Pikulski, J. J., Wixson, K. K., Campbell, J. R., Gough, P. B., & Beatty, A. S. (1995). *Listening to children read aloud: Oral fluency.* Washington, DC: National Center for Education Statistics, U.S. Department of Education.

Pittelman, S. D., Heimlich, J. E., Berglund, R. L., & French M. P. (1991). *Semantic feature analysis: Classroom applications.* Newark, DE: International Reading Association.

Plecha, J. (1992). Shared inquiry: The Great Books method of interpretive reading and discussion. In D. Temple & P. Collins (Eds.), *Stories and readers: New perspectives on literature, the elementary classroom* (pp. 103–114). Norwood, MA: Christopher-Gordon.

Policy Almanac.org. (2002). *Almanac of policy issues.* Retrieved from http://www.policyalmanac.org/education/archive/literacy.shtml

Pomplun, M., & Omar, M. H. (2001). The factorial invariance of a test of reading comprehension across groups of limited English proficient students. *Applied Measurement in Education 14*(3), 261–283.

Preece, A. (2009). *Reading Liberia: Guidebook for trainers.* Monrovia, Liberia, and Ottawa, Ontario, Canada: We Care Library/CODE.

Pressley, M. (1999). Self-regulated comprehension processing and its development through instruction. In L. B. Gambrell, L. M. Morrow, S. B. Neuman, & M. Pressley (Eds.), *Best practices in literacy instruction.* New York, NY: Guilford Press.

Pressley, M. (2000). "What should comprehension instruction be the instruction of?" In M. L. Kamil, P. B. Mosenthal, P. D. Pearson, & R. Barr (Eds.), *Handbook of reading research* (Vol. 3, pp. 545–562). Mahwah, NJ: Erlbaum.

Pressley, M. (2002). Metacognition and self-regulated comprehension. In A. E. Farstrup & S. J. Samuels (Eds.), *What research has to say about reading instruction* (pp. 291–309). Newark, DE: International Reading Association.

Pressley, M., & Afflerbach, P. (1995). *Verbal protocols of reading: The nature of constructively responsive reading.* Hillsdale, NJ: Erlbaum.

Pressley, M., Allington, R. L., Wharton-McDonald, R., Block, C. C., & Morrow, L. M. (Eds.). (2001). *Learning to read: Lessons from exemplary first-grade classrooms.* New York, NY: Guilford Press.

Pressley, M., Rankin, J., & Yokoi, L. (1996). A survey of instructional practices of primary teachers nominated as effective in promoting literacy. *Elementary School Journal, 96,* 363–384.

Pressley, M., Wharton-McDonald, R., Mistretta, J., & Echevarria, M. (1998). The nature of literacy instruction in ten grade 4/5 classrooms in upstate New York. *Scientific Studies of Reading, 2,* 159–191.

Purcell-Gates, V. (1991). Ability of well-read-to kindergartners to decontextualise/recontextualise experience into a written-narrative register. *Language and Education: An International Journal, 5*(3), 177–188.

Purcell-Gates, V. (1991). On the outside looking in: A study of remedial readers' meaning-making while reading literature. *JRB: A Journal of Literacy, 23,* 235–253.

Purcell-Gates, V. (1997). *Other people's words: The cycle of low literacy.* Cambridge, MA: Harvard University Press.

Purcell-Gates, V., L'Allier, S., & Smith, D. (1995). Literacy at the Harts' and the Larsons': Diversity among poor inner city families. *The Reading Teacher, 48,* 572–578.

Purcell-Gates, V., McIntyre, E., & Freppon, P. A. (1995). Learning written storybook language in school: A comparison of low-SES children in skills-based and whole language classrooms. *American Educational Research Journal, 32*(3), 659–685.

Radcliffe, R., Caverly, D., Hand, J., & Franke, D. (2008, February). Improving reading in a middle school science classroom. *Journal of Adolescent and Adult Literacy, 51*(5), 398–408.

Raffi. (1996). *The more we get together. Raffi sampler.* [CD]. Cambridge, MA: Rounder Records.

Ramírez, J. D. (1991). *Final report: Longitudinal study of structured English immersion strategy, early-exit and late-exit bilingual education programs.* NTIS, 300-87-0156. Washington, DC: U.S. Department of Education.

Ranker, J. (2009). Learning nonfiction in an ESL class: The interaction of situated practice and teacher scaffolding in a genre study. *The Reading Teacher, 62*(7), 580–589.

Raphael, T. E. (1986). Teaching question answer relationships, revisited. *The Reading Teacher, 39*(6), 516–522.

Raphael, T. E. (1998). Balanced instruction and the role of classroom discourse. In J. Osborn & F. Lehr (Eds.), *Literacy for all: Issues in teaching and learning.* New York, NY: Guilford Press.

Raphael, T. E., & McMahon, S. I. (1994). Book club: An alternative framework for reading instruction. *The Reading Teacher, 48,* 102–117.

Raphael, T. E., Goatley, V., McMahon, S., & Woodman, D. (1995). Teaching literacy through student book clubs. In N. Roser & M. Martinez (Eds.), *Book talk and beyond: Children and teachers respond to literature* (pp. 66–79). Newark, DE: International Reading Association.

Rasinski, T. V. (2003). *The fluent reader: Oral strategies for building word recognition, fluency, and comprehension.* New York, NY: Scholastic.

Rasinski, T. V., Blachowicz, C., & Lems, K. (Eds.). (2005). *Fluency instruction: Research-based best practices.* New York, NY: Guilford Press.

Rasinski, T. V., & Padak, N. (2005). *Three-minute reading assessments: Word recognition, fluency, and comprehension.* New York, NY: Scholastic.

Rasinski, T. V., Reutzel, D. R., Chard, D., & Linan-Thompson, S. (2011). Reading fluency. In P. D. Pearson, M. Kamil, E. B. Moje, & P. Afflerbach. *Handbook of reading research, Volume IV.* New York, NY: Routledge.

Read, C. (1975). *Children's categorization of speech sounds in English* (Research Report No. 17). Urbana, IL: National Council of Teachers of English.

Rébsamen, E. C. (1949). *La enseñanza de la escritura y lectura en el primer año escolar: Guía metodológica.* Paris: Librería de la Vda de Ch. Bouret.

Reichle, E. D., & Perfetti, C. A. (2003). Morphology in word identification: A word experience model that accounts for morpheme frequency effects. *Scientific Studies of Reading, 7,* 219–237.

Renaissance Learning. (2012). *What kids are reading: The book reading habits of students in American schools.* Wisconsin Rapids, WI: Author.

Reutzel, D. R., Jones, C. D., Fawson, P. C., & Smith, J. A. (2008, November). Scaffolded silent reading: A complement to Guided Repeated Oral Reading that Works! *The Reading Teacher, 62*(3), 194–207.

Richard-Amato, P., & Snow, M. A. (1992). *The multicultural classroom: Readings for content area teachers.* New York, NY: Longman.

Rickford, J. R. (1999). *African American Vernacular English.* Malden, MA: Blackwell Publishers.

Rickford, R. R., & Rickford, A. E. (1995). Dialect readers revisited. *Linguistics and Education, 7,* 107–128.

Riley, J. (2007). *Learning in the early years.* London, UK: Sage Publications.

Roberts, T. A. (2008). Home storybook reading in primary or second language with preschool children: Evidence of equal effectiveness for second-language vocabulary acquisition. *Reading Research Quarterly, 43*(2), 103–130.

Rodríguez Fuenzalida, E. (1982). *Metodologías de alfabetización en América Latina.* Pátzcuaro, Michoacán, México: UNESCO/CREFAL.

Rosen, M. (2003). *We're going on a bear hunt*. Illustrated by H. Oxenbury. New York, NY: Alladin.

Rosenblatt, L. (1978). *The reader, the text, and the poem*. Carbondale, IL: Southern Illinois University Press.

Roser, N. L., & Hoffman, J. V. (1992, January). Language charts: A record of story talk. *Language Arts, 69*(1), 44–52.

Ross, T. (1992). *Stone soup*. New York, NY: Dial Books.

Rowe, M. B. (1974). Wait-time and rewards as instructional variables: Their influence on language, logic and fate control: Part one—Wait time. *Journal of Research in Science Teaching, 11*(2), 81–94.

Rueda, R. S., August, D., & Goldenberg, C. (2006), The sociocultural context in which children acquire literacy. In D. August & T. Shanahan (Eds.), *Developing literacy in second-language learners: Report of the National Literacy Panel on Language-Minority Children and Youth* (pp. 319–339). Mahwah, NJ: Erlbaum.

Salmon, K. (1995). *Lenguaje integral: Una alternativa para la enseñanza-aprendizaje de la lecto-escritura*. Quito, Ecuador: Abrapalabra Editores.

Samuels, S. J. (2007). Afterword for B. W. Riedel. The relation between DIBELS, reading comprehension, and vocabulary in urban first-grade students. *Reading Research Quarterly, 42*(4), 546–567.

Samuels, S. J., & Farstrup, A. E. (Eds.). (2006). *What research has to say about fluency instruction*. Newark, DE: International Reading Association.

Sanacore, J. (2004). Genuine caring and literacy learning for African American children. *The Reading Teacher, 57*(8), 744–753.

Santa, C. M. (1988). *Content reading including study systems: Reading, writing and studying across the curriculum*. Dubuque, IA: Kendall Hunt.

Saville, M. R., & Troike, R. C. (1971). *A handbook of bilingual education*. Washington, DC: Teachers of English to Speakers of Other Languages.

Scanlon, D. M., & Anderson, K. L. (2010). Using the interactive strategies approach to prevent reading difficulties in an RTI context. In M. Y. Lipson & K. K. Wixson (Eds.), *Successful approaches to RTI: Collaborative practices for improving K–12 literacy*. Newark, DE: International Reading Association.

Scarcella, R. (1990). *Teaching language minority students in multicultural classrooms*. New York, NY: Longman.

Schifini, A. (1985). *Sheltered English: Content area instruction for limited English proficient students*. Los Angeles, CA: Los Angeles County Office of Education.

Schifini, A. (1996). Reading instruction for the pre-literate and struggling older student. *NABE News, 20*, 5–6, 20, 30.

Schlagal, R. C. (1989). Constancy and change in spelling development. *Reading Psychology, 10*(3), 207–232.

Schmidt, G. D. (2011). *Okay for now*. New York, NY: Clarion Books.

Schön, D. (1983). *The reflective practitioner: How professionals think in action*. New York, NY: Basic Books.

Schon, I. (2000). *Recommended books in Spanish for children and young adults, 1996–1999*. Lanham, MD: Scarecrow Press.

Schon, I. (2001). *Los niños y el mundo: Children's books in Spanish from around the world. The Reading Teacher, 54*, 692–698.

Schon, I. (2002). From Pulgarcito to Shakespeare. *Language, 2*, 28–30.

Schon, I. (2004). *Recommended books in Spanish for children and young adults, 2000 through 2004*. Lanham, MD: Scarecrow Press.

Schon, I. (2009). *Recommended books in Spanish for children and young adults, 2004–2008*. Lanham, MD: Scarecrow Press, 2009.

Schon, I., & Corona Berkin, S. (1996). *Introducción a la literatura infantil y juvenil*. Newark, DE: International Reading Association.

Schwartz, R., & Raphael, T. (1985) Concept of definition: A key to improving students' vocabulary. *The Reading Teacher, 39*, 198–205.

Scieszka, J. (2001). *Baloney (Henry P.)*. Illustrated by Lane Smith. New York, NY: Viking Junior.

Scieszka, J. (2005) *Baloney!* New York, NY: Puffin.

Scott, J. A., Flinspach, S. L. & Vevea, J. L. (2011, December). *Identifying and teaching vocabulary in fourth and fifth grade math and science*. Paper presented at the Literacy Research Association Conference, Jacksonville, FL.

Scragg, D. G. (1974). *A history of English spelling*. New York, NY: Barnes & Noble.

Selinker, L., Swain, M., & Dumas, G. (1975). The interlanguage hypothesis extended to children. *Language Learning, 25*, 129–152.

Sepúlveda, L. (1989). *The old man who read love stories*. New York, NY: Harcourt Brace.

Shanahan, T. (2002). *A sin of the second kind: The neglect of fluency instruction and what we can do about it*. PowerPoint presentation at A Focus on Fluency Forum, San Francisco, CA. Retrieved from www.prel.org/programs/rel/fluency/Shanahan.ppt

Shaw, R., & Shaw, D. (2002). *DIBELS Oral Reading Fluency-based indicators of third grade reading skills for Colorado State Assessment Program (CSAP)*. (Tech. Rep.) Eugene, OR: University of Oregon.

Shaywitz, S. E., Escobar, M. D., Shaywitz, B. A., Fletcher, J. M., & Makuch, J. R. (1992). Evidence that dyslexia may represent the lower tail of a normal distribution of reading ability. *New England Journal of Medicine, 326*, 145–150.

Shinn, M. R. (Ed.). (1989). *Curriculum-based measurement: Assessing special children*. New York, NY: Guilford.

Short, K., & Kauffman, G. (1995). So what do I do? The role of the teacher in literature circles. In N. Roser & M. Martinez (Eds.), *Book talk and beyond: Children and teachers respond to literature* (pp. 140–149). Newark, DE: International Reading Association.

Short, K., Harste, J., & Burke, C. (1996). *Creating classrooms for authors and inquirers*. Portsmouth, NH: Heinemann.

Silverman, R. D. (2007). Vocabulary development of English-language and English-only learners in kindergarten. *The Elementary School Journal, 107*(4), 365–383.

Simon, S. (2007, June 1). Teaching kids right from left. *The Los Angeles Times*. Retrieved from http://articles.latimes.com/2007/jun/01/nation/na-kidbooks1

Simpkins, G., Holt, G., & Simpkins, C. (1974). *Bridge: A cross-culture reading program*. Boston, MA: Houghton Mifflin.

Sipe, L. R. (2000). The construction of literary understanding by first and second graders in oral response to picture storybook read-alouds. *Reading Research Quarterly, 35*(2), 252–275.

Skerry, B. (2010). *Face to face with manatees*. Washington, DC: National Geographic Society.

Slavin, R. E., Madden, N., Calderón, M., Chamberlain, A., & Hennessy, M. (2010). *Reading and language outcomes of a five-year randomized evaluation of transitional bilingual education*. Retrieved from http://www.edweek.org/media/bilingual_pdf.pdf

Sleeter, C. E., & Grant, C. A. (1999). *Making choices for multicultural education.* Upper Saddle River, NJ: Merrill.

Sleeter, C. E., & Grant, C. A. (2007). *Making choices for multicultural education: Five approaches to race, class and gender.* Hoboken, NJ: Wiley.

Smith, C. B. (1997). Vocabulary instruction and reading comprehension. *ERIC Digest.* ERIC Clearinghouse on Reading English and Communication #126.

Smith, F. (1973). *Psycholinguistics and reading.* New York, NY: Holt, Rinehart & Winston.

Smith, F. (1986). *Keynote address: How education backed the wrong horse.* Presented at the meeting of the California Reading Association, Fresno.

Snow, C. E., Burns, M. S., & Griffin, P. (Eds.). (1998). *Preventing reading difficulties in young children.* Committee on the Prevention of Reading Difficulties in Young Children. Commission on Behavioral and Social Sciences and Education, National Research Council. Washington, DC: National Academy Press.

Snow, C. E., Tabors, P. O., & Dickenson, D. K. (2001). Language development in the preschool years. In D. K. Dickinson & P. O. Tabors (Eds.), *Beginning literacy with language.* Baltimore, MD: Brookes.

Snowling, M. J. (2000). *Dyslexia.* London, England: Blackwell.

Solé, I. (1994). *Estrategias de lectura.* Barcelona, Spain: Graó Editorial.

Souriau, E. (1955). *Les deux cent milles situations dramatiques.* Paris, France: Flamarion.

Spache, G. (1981). *Diagnosing and correcting reading disabilities* (2nd ed.). Boston, MA: Allyn & Bacon.

Spandel, V. (1996). *Seeing with new eyes.* Portland, OR: Northwest Regional Educational Laboratory.

Spandel, V. (2000). *Creating writers through 6-trait writing assessment and instruction* (3rd ed.). Boston, MA: Allyn & Bacon.

Spandel, V. (2008). *Creating writers through 6-trait writing assessment and instruction* (5th ed.). Boston, MA: Allyn & Bacon.

Spinelli, J. (1990a). *Maniac Magee.* Boston, MA: Little, Brown.

Spinelli, J. (1990b). *Maniac Magee.* New York, NY: Scholastic. Large-print version from Library Reproduction Service, ISBN 0-590-45203-7.

Spolin, V. (1986). *Theater games for the classroom.* Evanston, IL: Northwestern University Press.

Stahl, S. A., & Fairbanks, M. (1986). The effects of vocabulary instruction: A model-based meta-analysis. *Review of Educational Research, 56,* 76–110.

Stanovich, K. E. (1986). Matthew effects in reading: Some consequences of individual differences in the acquisition of literacy. *Reading Research Quarterly, 21,* 360–407.

Stanovich, K. E. (1992). Are we overselling literacy? In C. Temple & P. Collins (Eds.), *Stories and readers.* Norwood, MA: Christopher Gordon.

Stanovich, K. E., & Siegel, L. S. (1994). Phenotypic performance profiles of children with reading disabilities: A regression-based test of the phonological core variable-difference model. *Journal of Educational Psychology, 86,* 24–53.

Stauffer, R. (1975). *The language experience approach to the teaching of reading.* New York, NY: Harper.

Steele, J. L., & Meredith, K. E. (1997). *Critical thinking.* New York, NY: Open Society Institute.

Stein, N. L., & Glenn, C. F. (1979). An analysis of story comprehension in elementary school children. In R. O. Freedle (Ed.), *New directions in discourse processing: Vol. 2. Advances in discourse processes* (pp. 53–120). Norwood, NJ: Ablex.

Sternberg, R., & Powell, J. (1983). Comprehending verbal comprehension. *American Psychologist, 38,* 878–893.

Stevens, R. A., Butler, F. A., & Castellon-Wellington, M. (2000). *Academic language and content assessment: Measuring the progress of English language learners* (CSE Technical Report No. 552). Los Angeles: University of California, National Center for Research on Evaluation, Standards, and Student Testing.

Stoll, D. R. (Ed.). (1977). *Magazines for kids and teens.* Newark, DE: International Reading Association.

Strickland, D. S. (1991). Cooperative, collaborative learning for children and teachers (emerging readers and writers). *Reading Teacher, 44,* 600–602.

Strickland, D. S. (2006). *Balanced literacy: Teaching the skills AND thrills of reading.* Available from Scholastic online: http://www2.scholastic.com/browse/article.jsp?id=4315

Strickland, D. S. (2012, February/March). Planning curriculum to meet the Common Core State Standards. *Reading Today.*

Strickland, D. S., & Feeley, J. T. (1985). Using children's concept of story to improve reading and writing. In T. Harris & E. Cooper (Eds.), *Reading, thinking, and concept development* (pp. 163–175). New York, NY: The College Board.

Stritikus, T. (2006). Making meaning matter: A look at instructional practice in additive and subtractive contexts. *Bilingual Research Journal, 30*(1), 219–227.

Suárez-Orozco, C., Suárez-Orozco, M. M., & Todovora, I. (2008). *Learning in a new land: Immigrant students in American society.* Cambridge, MA: The Belknap Press of Harvard University Press.

Sulzby, E. (1985). Kindergarteners as writers and readers. In M. Farr (Ed.), *Advances in writing research: Vol. 1. Children's early writing development* (pp. 127–199). Norwood, NJ: Ablex.

Sutherland-Smith, W. (2002). Weaving the literacy web: Changes in reading from page to screen. *The Reading Teacher, 55,* 662–669.

Sutton-Smith, B. (1981). *The folk stories of children.* New York, NY: Olympic Marketing.

Tattershaw, S., & Prendeville, J. (1995). *Using familiar routines in language assessment and intervention.* San Antonio, TX: Communication Skill Builders.

Taylor, B., Pearson, P. D., Clark, K., & Walpole, S. (1999). *Beating the odds in teaching all children to read.* Ann Arbor, MI: CIERA. Retrieved from http://www.ciera.org/library/reports/inquiry-1/1-010/1-010.pdf

Taylor, B. M. (2008). Effective classroom reading instruction in the elementary grades. In D. Fuchs, L. W. Fuchs, & S. Vaughn (Eds.), *Response to intervention: A framework for reading educators.* Newark, DE: International Reading Association.

Taylor, B. M., & Pearson, P. D. (2005). Using study groups and reading assessment data to improve reading instruction within a school. In S. Paris & S. A. Stahl (Eds.), *Children's reading comprehension and assessment* (pp. 237–255). Mahwah, NJ: Erlbaum.

Taylor, W. L. (1953). Cloze procedure: A new device for measuring readability. *Journalism Quarterly, 45,* 415–433.

Teale, W. H., & Sulzby, E. (1986). *Emergent literacy.* Portsmouth, NH: Heinemann.

Teale, W. H., & Sulzby, E. (1987). Literacy acquisition in early childhood: The roles of access and mediation in storybook reading. In D. Wagner (Ed.), *The future of literacy in a changing world* (pp. 111–130). New York, NY: Pergamon Press.

Temple, C. (1994, September). The "global method" of Celestin Freinet: Whole language in a European setting? *The Reading Teacher 48*(1), 86–89.

Temple, C. (2000). What can we learn from 15,000 teachers in Central Europe and Central Asia? *Reading Teacher, 54*(3), 312–315.

Temple, C., Crawford, A., & Gillet, J. W. (2009). *Developmental literacy inventory*. Boston, MA: Pearson.

Temple C., & MaKinster, J. (2005). *Intervening for literacy*. Boston, MA: Allyn & Bacon.

Temple, C., Martinez, M., & Yokota, J. (2014). *Children's books in children's hands* (4th ed.). Boston, MA: Allyn & Bacon.

Temple, C., Nathan, R., & Burris, N. (1982). *The beginnings of writing*. Boston, MA: Allyn & Bacon.

Temple, C., Nathan, R., Burris, N., & Temple, F. (1993). *The beginnings of writing* (3rd ed.). Boston, MA: Allyn & Bacon.

Temple, F. (1992). *Tiger soup*. New York, NY: Orchard.

Temple, F. (1994). *The Ramsay scallop*. New York, NY: Orchard.

Temple, F. (1995). *Tonight, by sea*. New York, NY: Harper Trophy.

Temple, F. (1996). *The Beduin's gazelle*. New York, NY: Orchard.

Templeton, S. (1991). Teaching and learning the English spelling system: Reconceptualizing method and purpose. *Elementary School Journal, 92*, 183–199.

Templeton, S., & Morris, D. (1999). Questions teachers ask about spelling. *Reading Research Quarterly, 34*(1), 102–112.

Templeton, S., & Morris, D. (2000). Spelling: Reconceptualizing spelling development and instruction. In M. Kamil, P. B. Mosenthal, P. D. Pearson, & R. Barr (Eds.), *Handbook of reading research* (Vol. 3, pp. 525–539). Mahwah, NJ: Erlbaum.

Terban, M. (1989). *Superdupers: Really funny real words*. New York, NY: Clarion.

Terman, L. (1916). *The measurement of intelligence*. Stanford, CA: Stanford University Press.

Terrell, T. D. (1977). A natural approach to second language acquisition and learning. *Modern Language Journal, 6*, 325–337.

Terrell, T. D. (1981). The natural approach in bilingual education. In California State Department of Education (Ed.), *School and language minority students: A theoretical framework* (pp. 117–146). California State University, Los Angeles: Evaluation, Dissemination and Assessment Center.

Terrell, T. D. (1982). The natural approach to language teaching: An update. *Modern Language Journal, 66*, 121–122.

TESOL. (1997). *Policy statement of the TESOL board on African American vernacular English*. Arlington, VA: Center for Applied Linguistics.

Texas Education Agency. (1996). *Comprehensive biennial report on Texas public schools: A report to the 75th Texas legislature*. Austin: Author.

Texas Education Agency. (2009). Retrieved from http://ritter.tea.state.tx.us/teks/

Tharp, R., & Gallimore, R. (1991). *The instructional conversation: Teaching and learning in social activity* (Research Report 2). Santa Cruz, CA: The National Center for Research on Cultural Diversity and Second Language Learning, University of California, Santa Cruz.

Thomas, W. P., & Collier, V. (1997). *School effectiveness for language minority students*. Washington, DC: National Clearinghouse for Bilingual Education.

Thomas, W. P., & Collier, V. P. (2002). *A national study of school effectiveness for language minority students' long-term academic achievement final report: Project 1.1*. Santa Cruz, CA: Center for Research on Education, Diversity and Excellence.

Tileston, D. W. (2011). *Closing the RTI gap: Why poverty and culture count*. Bloomington, IN: Solution Tree.

Tinajero, J. V., & Nagel, G. (1995). "I never knew I was needed until you called!": Promoting parent involvement in schools. *The Reading Teacher, 48*, 614–617.

Tomlinson, C. A. (2000). *Differentiation of instruction in the elementary grades*. Champaign, IL: ERIC Clearinghouse on Elementary and Early Childhood Education. Retrieved from http://ceep.crc.uiuc.edu/eecearchive/digests/2000/tomlin00.pdf

Tompkins, G. (2000). *Teaching writing: Balancing process and product*. Columbus, OH: Merrill.

Topping, K. J. (1987). Paired reading: A powerful technique for parent use. *The Reading Teacher, 40*, 608–614.

Torres Quintero, G. (1976). *Método onomatopéyico*. Mexico City: Editorial Patria.

Trelease, J. (2006). *The read-aloud handbook* (6th ed.). New York, NY: Penguin Books.

Trieman, R. (1985). Onsets and rimes as units of spoken syllables: Evidence from children. *Journal of Experimental Child Psychology, 39*, 161–181.

Trout, B. (1993, November). Little dogies, lay down. *Highlights for Children*.

U.S. Census Bureau. (2011). *Overview of race and Hispanic origin*. Retrieved from http://www.census.gov/prod/cen2010/briefs/c2010br-02.pdf

U.S. Department of Education. (2000). *Report of the National Reading Panel: Teaching children to read, an evidence-based assessment of the scientific research literature on reading and its implications for reading instruction*. Washington, DC: U.S. Government Printing Office.

U.S. Department of Education. (2001). *No Child Left Behind*. Retrieved from http://www.ed.gov/offices/OESE/esea/

U.S. Department of Education. (2004). *No Child Left Behind: Toolkit for teachers*. Retrieved from http://www2.ed.gov/teachers/nclbguide/nclb-teachers-toolkit.pdf

U.S. Department of Health and Human Services. (2006). *Quick guide to health literacy*. Retrieved from http://www.health.gov/communication/literacy/quickguide/about.htm

UNESCO. (1953). *The use of vernacular languages in education*. Paris: Author.

Urrea, L. A. (1996). *By the lake of sleeping children: The secret life of the Mexican border*. New York, NY: Anchor Books.

Vacca, R., & Vacca, J. (1986). *Content area reading*. Boston, MA: Allyn & Bacon.

Vacca, R., & Vacca, J. (1996). *Content area reading* (5th ed.). New York, NY: HarperCollins.

Valencia, S., Hiebert, E. & Afflerbach, P. (1993). *Authentic reading assessment: Practices and possibilities*. Newark, DE: International Reading Association.

Vasquez, V. (2004). *Negotiating critical literacies with young children*. Mahwah, NJ: Erlbaum.

Vaughn, J., & Estes, T. (1986). *Reading and reasoning beyond the primary grades*. Boston, MA: Allyn & Bacon.

Vaughn, S., & Fuchs, L. S. (2003). Redefining learning disabilities as inadequate response to instruction: The promise and potential problems. *Learning Disabilities Research & Practice, 18*(3), 137–146. doi:10.1111/1540-5826.00070.

Veatch, J. (1996). From the vantage of retirement. *The Reading Teacher, 49*, 510–516.

Veatch, J., Sawicki, F., Elliott, G., Flake, E., & Blakey, J. (1979). *Key words to reading: The language experience approach begins*. Columbus, OH: Merrill.

Vellutino, F. R., & Scanlon, D. M. (2001). Emergent literacy skills, early instruction, and individual differences as determinants of difficulties in learning to read: The case for early intervention. In S. B. Newman & D. K. Dickinson (Eds.), *Handbook of early literacy research*. New York, NY: Guilford Press.

Vellutino, F. R., Scanlon, D. M., Sipay, E. R., Small, S. G., Pratt, A., Chen, R., & Denckla, M. B. (1996). Cognitive profiles of difficult-to-remediate and readily remediated poor readers: Early intervention as a vehicle for distinguishing between cognitive and experiential deficits as a basic cause of specific reading disability. *Journal of Educational Psychology, 88*, 601–638.

Verhoeven, L. (1990, Spring). Acquisition of reading in a second language. *Reading Research Quarterly, 25*(2), 90–114.

Vernon-Feagans, L., Hammer, C. S., Miccio, A., & Manlove, E. (2001). Early language and literacy skills in low-income African American and Hispanic children. In D. K. Dickenson & S. B. Newman (Eds.), *Handbook of early literacy research*. New York, NY: Guilford.

Vogt, M. E. (2000). Content learning for students needing modifications: An issue of access. In M. McLaughlin & M. E. Vogt (Eds.), *Creativity and innovation in content area teaching* (pp. 329–351). Norwood, MA: Christopher-Gordon.

Von Franz, M. L. (1996). *The interpretation of fairy tales*. Boston, MA: Shambala.

Vukelich, C., Christie, J., & Enz, B. (2002). *Helping young children learn language and literacy*. Boston, MA: Allyn & Bacon.

Vygotsky, L. S. (1976). *Thought and language*. Cambridge, MA: MIT Press.

Vygotsky, L. S. (1978). *Mind in society: The development of higher psychological processes*. Cambridge, MA: Harvard University Press.

Wagner, B. J. (1999). *Dorothy Heathcote: Drama as a learning medium*. Portsmouth, NH: Heinemann.

Walsh, D. J., Price, G. G., & Gillingham, M. G. (1988). The critical but transitory importance of letter naming. *Reading Research Quarterly, 23*, 108–122.

Walton, R. (2011). *Bullfrog Pops!: Adventures in verbs and direct objects*. Layton, UT: Gibbs Smith.

Wheeler, R., Cartwright, K. B., & Swords, R. (2012). Factoring AAVE into reading assessment and instruction. *The Reading Teacher, 65*(5), 416–425.

Wheelock, A., & Dorman, G. (1988). *Before it's too late: Dropout prevention in the middle grades*. Boston, MA: Massachusetts Advocacy Center and Chapel Hill Center for Early Adolescence.

Whipple, G. (Ed.). (1925). *The twenty-fourth yearbook of the National Society for the Study of Education: Report of the National Committee on Reading*. Bloomington, IN: Public School Publishing.

White, E. B. (1980). *Charlotte's web*. New York, NY: Harper Trophy. (Original work published 1952)

Whitehurst, G. J. (1994). *Dialogic reading for parents: Headstart, K, and pre-K* (available from G. J. Whitehurst, State University of New York at Stony Brook, Stony Brook, NY 11794–2500).

Whitehurst, G., & Lonigan, C. (2001). Child development and emergent literacy. *Child Development, 69*, 848–872.

Whitehurst, G. J., & Lonigan, C. J. (2001). Emergent literacy: From pre-readers to readers. In S. B. Neuman & D. K. Dickinson (Eds.), *Handbook of early literacy research*. New York, NY: Guilford Press.

Whorf, B. L. (1964). *Language, thought, and reality* (J. B. Carroll, Ed.). Cambridge, MA: MIT Press.

Wiggins, G., & McTighe, J. (2005). *Thinking by design, expanded edition*. Washington, DC: Association for Supervision and Curriculum Development.

Willems, M. (2003). *Don't let the pigeon drive the bus!* New York, NY: Hyperion.

Williams, S. (1991). Classroom use of African American language: Educational tool or social weapon? In C. Sleeter (Ed.), *Empowering through multicultural education* (pp. 199–215). New York, NY: State University of New York.

Wilson, J. (2005). *The relationship of Dynamic Indicators of Basic Early Literacy Skills (DIBELS) Oral Reading Fluency to performance on Arizona Instrument to Measure Standards (AIMS)*. Tempe, AZ: Tempe School District No. 3.

Wilson, P. (1992). Among non-readers. In C. Temple & P. Collins (Eds.), *Stories and readers*. Norwood, MA: Christopher–Gordon.

Winsor, P. J. T. (2009). *The language experience approach to literacy for children learning English*. Winnipeg, Canada: Portage & Main Press.

Wixson, K. K., & Lipson, M. Y. (2012). Relations between the CCSS and RTI in literacy and language. *The Reading Teacher, 65*(5), 387–391.

Wixson, K. K., & Valencia, S. W. (2011). Assessment in RTI: What teachers and specialists need to know. *The Reading Teacher, 64*(6), 466–469.

Wolf, M. K., Herman, J. L., Bachman, L.F., Bailey, A.L., & Griffin, N. (2008). *Recommendations for assessing English language learners: English language proficiency measures and accommodation uses: CRESST Report 737*. Los Angeles, CA: UCLA.

Wong, H. K., & Wong, R. T. (2009). *First days of school: How to be an effective teacher* (4th ed.). Mountain View, CA: Harry K. Wong Publications, Inc.

Wong-Fillmore, L., & Snow, C. (2000). *What teachers need to know about language*. Washington, DC: U.S. Department of Education, OERI.

Wood, J. M. (2000). *A marriage waiting to happen: Computers and process writing*. Newton, MA: Education Development Center.

Worthy, J., & Broaddus, K. (2002). Fluency beyond the primary grades: From group performance to silent, independent reading. *The Reading Teacher, 55*, 334–343.

Yopp, H. K., & Stapleton, L. (2008). Conciencia fonémica en español (Phonemic awareness in Spanish). *The Reading Teacher, 61*(5), 374–382.

Young, J. P., & Brozo, W. G. (2001). Boys will be boys, or will they? Literacy and masculinities. *Reading Research Quarterly, 36*(3), 316–325.

Zambo, D. (2007). Using picture books to provide archetypes for young boys: Extending the ideas of William Brozo. *The Reading Teacher, 61*(2), 124–131.

Zarrillo, J. (2010). *Are you prepared to teach reading?* (2nd ed.). Englewood Cliffs, NJ: Prentice Hall.

Zehr, M. A. (2008). *Ten-year anniversary of bilingual education*. Retrieved from http://blogs.edweek.org/edweek/learning-the-language/2008/06/tenyear_anniversary_of_proposi.html

Zemach, H. (1964). N*ail soup*. Chicago, IL: Follett.

Zutell, J. (1999). Sorting it out through word sorts. In I. C. Fountas & G. S. Pinnell (Eds.), *Voices on word matters* (pp. 103–113). Portsmouth, NH: Heinemann.

Zutell, J., & Rasinski, T. (1991). Training teachers to attend to their students' oral reading fluency. *Theory into Practice, 30*, 212–217.

Name Index

Subject Index

Assessment (*continued*)
  authentic, 330. *See also* Kidwatching; Rubrics
  of beginning readers, 341–355
  Common Core Standards and, 21
  of comprehension, 207–210
  differentiated instruction and, 355–357
  for ELLs, 359–362
  of emergent readers, 334–336
  extended unit, 459
  forms of, 25
  in grades K–2, 397–399
  in grades 3–5, 420–421
  high-stakes, 217, 327
  importance of, 324
  in middle grades, 454–456
  monitoring, 357
  observational, of comprehension, 207, 208–209
  outcomes-based, 357
  professional, of teachers, 358–359
  purpose of, 25, 325–327
  in RTI programs, 56–57
  self-assessment. *See* Self-assessment
  Spanish Readability Graph, 507
  of spelling development, 292–294
  terms used in, 333–334
  of word knowledge, 351, 352–353
  of word learning, 173
  of writing, 313–315
Assessment-criterion relationship validity, 333
Association for Library Services to Children, 162
At-risk students. *See also* Struggling readers
  differentiated instruction for, 50–53
  racial/ethnic groups overrepresented in, 58
Attitudes, measuring, 355. *See also* Motivation
Authentic assessment, 330. *See also* Kidwatching; Rubrics
Authentic children's literature, 51
Authentic environmental print, 435
Author
  imitating writing of, 307
  questioning the, in ABC model, 195
Automaticity, 405
Auxiliary verbs, 85

B

Background knowledge, 43
  comprehension and, 12, 186
  ELLs and, 186
  informational texts and, 220–221
  narrative text and, 185
  reading readiness and, 413–414
Balanced literacy, approaches to, 22–26
Balanced reading instruction, 22
  four blocks approach in, 382–383
Barahona Center for the Study of Books in Spanish for Children and Adolescents, 503
Barbara Bush Literacy Foundation, 119

Basal reading programs, 22–23, 406–407
Basic interpersonal communication skills (BICS), 165, 480
Beginning readers, assessment of, 341–355
Beginning reading, 14–15
  research studies on, 18–19
Behavior contracts, 369
Benchmark assessment, in RTI programs, 56
Benchmark School (Media, PA), 395
Benchmarks, in social studies unit, 464–465
Between the Lions (TV program), 167
Bias
  in informational texts, 256, 265
  linguistic and cultural, of standardized tests, 360
BICS (basic interpersonal communication skills), 165, 480
Biculturalism. *See* Cultural diversity
Big books
  for ELLs, 495
  shared reading with, 106–107
Bilingual education, 46–47, 481–484. *See also* ELLs (English language learners); ESL (English as a second language) instruction
  classroom support structures for, 508–510
  English language in, 484–495
  principles of, 482
Bilingual paraprofessionals, 504, 505, 508, 509
Biographies, 468, 469
Black dialect, 48, 89. *See also* African American Vernacular English
Board game, for word sorts, 137–138
Book baggies, 119
Book clubs, 39, 198
Book It! program, 163
Bookmarking, of Web resources, 250
Books
  assessing level of, 391
  big books, 106–107, 495
  classroom-produced, 117
  irreverent, for boys, 63
  leveled, 390–391, 433, 455
  for reading aloud, 152–153, 228
  wordless, 491
Bound morphemes, 291
Boys, as struggling readers, 62–63
  irreverent books for, 63
  print materials for, 62, 63
Brainstorming
  exclusion, 450
  paired, 192
  in writing process, 295
Buddy reading, 40, 194
  for fluency, 155, 156
Building knowledge phase, in ABC model
  grades K–2, 384
  grades 3–5, 409, 410–411, 415–416
  for informational texts, 224–225
  middle grades, 444–445
  for narrative texts, 193–196

C

California Achievement Test, 327
California Young Reader Medal, 40
CALP (cognitive academic-language proficiency), 165, 422, 480
Casteñeda v. Pickard, 46
Casual register, 91
Cause-and-effect charts, 310, 311
Cause/effect idea organization, 233
Caxton, William, 75, 89
CBM. *See* Curriculum-based measurement (CBM)
CCSS. *See* Common Core State Standards (CCSS)
Ceremonial register, 91
Chants
    as response to story, 105
    teaching phonological awareness with, 110–112
    word wall, 135
Chapter graphic organizers, 228–229
Chapteraday, 473
Character clusters, 206
Character maps, 206
Characters
    behavior and rewards of, 271–272
    comprehension, 204
    portraying during read-alouds, 152
    relationships between, 261, 272–273
    as stand-ins for other people, 259, 261
Charts
    in classroom, 116
    for recoding repeated readings, 155
Child development
    milestones in. *See* Developmental milestones
    word knowledge, 125–128
Children's Choices Project, 152
Children's literature
    authentic, 51
    special needs portrayed in, evaluation criteria for, 53
Choral reading, 160–162, 469
Chunking, 126, 450. *See also* Orthographic reading
Cinquains, 309
Clap out words, listening game with, 110
Class size, effect on reading, 52
Classroom environment
    adult volunteers in, 435
    for emergent literacy, 100, 115–116
    language-rich, 167
    literacy-rich, 371, 389–390
Classroom fluency measures, 456
Classroom libraries, 38, 115
    integrated curriculum and, grades K–2, 389, 390
Classroom management, 367–369
    grades 3–5, 432–432
    reading aloud and, 376, 377
Classroom Reading Inventory, 328
Classrooms
    at-risk students included in, 53

books produced in, 117
for grades 3–5, 431, 432–433
libraries in. *See* Classroom libraries
linguistic diversity in, 45–47
literacy activities in
    creating environment for, 37–38
    ensuring student interaction, 38–40
    first week of school, 40–41
    involving families in, 118
    teacher modeling encouraging, 40–41, 143–144
Clauses, in sentences, 80
Close reading, of informational texts, 243
Closed syllables, 73
Cloze procedure, 345, 346
    oral, 422
    scoring of, 346
Clustering, in writing process, 295, 296, 310
Code-centered reading instruction, 18
Code-emphasis primary-grade programs, 405–406
Cognition
    factors affecting reading, 52–53
        in ELLs, 492
    reading instruction and, 17
Cognitive academic-language proficiency (CALP), 165, 422, 480
Cognitive apprenticeships, 115
Coleman Report, 50, 51
Collaboration
    between RTI team members, 58
    in writing process, 296
Collaborative chart story, 422
Collocation, 77
Committee on the Prevention of Reading Difficulties in Young Children, 18
Common Core Curriculum Standards, 417
Common Core Curriculum Standards Map, 417
Common Core State Standards (CCSS)
    argument structure and, 269
    assessment and, 326
    bias in informational texts, 265
    characters' perspectives and, 259
    content-specific words, 167
    described, 21
    ELA grades 6–12 and, 446
    ELLs and, 359
    in emergent literacy, 103
    family literacy, 157
    Foundational Reading Skills of, 352
    good discussion and, 254
    for informational reading, 216, 226, 227, 231
        integration of knowledge and ideas, 240
        key ideas and details, 243
    literacy and, 410–411
    literature comprehension, 203
    for literature discussion, 197

L

Labeling classroom objects, 115, 131
Language
  promoting respect for, 166–167
  social use of
    emergent readers and, 98
    variations in, 89–91
  teacher modeling interest in, 447, 448
  written. *See* Written language
Language charts, 204–205
  in hero cycle exploration, 270, 271
Language competence, emergent readers and, 97
Language diversity, demographics on, 45–46, 45–47
Language Experience Approach (LEA), 50, 51
  for ELLs, 130–131, 394, 421, 422–423
  in emergent literacy, 102
  reading words in context through, 129
  for struggling readers, 130–131
Language knowledge, emergent readers and, 98–99
Language sounds, awareness of, 335
Language-based learning, emergent literacy and, 97–98
Language-rich classroom, 167
Latin, 71
  plural nouns from, 81, 82
  prefixes and suffixes from, 75, 142
  word origins from, 75–76, 142
Lau v. Nichols, 46, 481
LEA. *See* Language Experience Approach (LEA)
League of United Latin American Citizens (LULAC), 47
Learning
  reading for, 15–16
  writing boosting, 316
Learning centers, in classroom, 369, 371–374
  standards included in, 371
  teaching reading and writing through science in, 372–373
Learning community, 37–41
  classroom environment for, 37–41
  educators in, 27–28
  organizing and managing
    in grades 3–5, 430–434
    in middle grades, 470–474
  parental involvement in, 40, 41
Learning journals, 460
Learning logs, 317, 458
Learning place, teachers creating, 366–374
Learning standards, 20–21
Legislation. *See individual legislation*
Lesson plan
  reading aloud in, 386
  sample, 411–412
Lessons
  in K–2 classrooms, 384–385
  daily, planning, 409–410, 409–412
  emergent literacy strategies in, 108–110
  focused. *See* Mini-lessons (focused lessons)

plans for. *See* Lesson plan
  teachable moments in, 385
  think-alouds as, 193, 385
Letter name spelling phase, 125–126, 289–291
Letter-by-letter reading. *See* Alphabetic reading/reader
Letter-to-sound relationships. *See* Phonics
Leveled books, 390–391, 433, 455
Lexile Framework, 345
Libraries/Librarians. *See also* Classroom libraries
  access to, reading achievement and, 60–61
  read-aloud recommendations by, 152–153
  reading encouragement by, 162
Linguistic abstraction, 127
Linguistic diversity, 45–47. *See also* ELLs (English language learners)
  IRI results and, 420
  reading programs and, 52
  standardized testing and, 360, 362
Linguistics, 68
  sounds of language, 69–76
  spelling development, 287–292
  spelling-to-sound relationships, historical oddities of, 292
  syntax, 78–91
  for teachers, 114–115
  vocabulary, 76–78
  word morphology, 73–76
Linguists, 72
List poems, 309
Listening games, for language awareness, 110
Literacy. *See also* Critical literacy; Emergent literacy
  adult, programs for, 119
  celebrating, school participation in, 40
  and content instruction integration, 21
  critical, 12–13
  diversity and. *See* Diversity
  ESL instruction and, 494–495
  of family, child's reading success and, 9–10
  importance of, 4–5
  in middle grades, 440–441
  needs of culturally-diverse students, 43
  new vs. traditional literacies, 16–17
  social contexts of, 35–36
  state standards and, 462
  teaching grades K–2 and, 397
Literacy development
  milestones in, 101–102
  phonological awareness and, 72–73
Literacy history
  of community, 35–36
  of students, 34–35
Literacy play, 115–116
Literacy programs
  for adults, 119
  evidence-based, 57
    principles of, 57–58
Literacy Volunteers of America (ProLiteracy), 119

interest in language, 114–115, 447, 448
    reading fluency, 150, 151
    reading for learning, 228, 457
    teachers and, 40–41, 143–144
    of thinking process, 246
Monitor hypothesis, 486
Monitoring assessments, 357
Monophthongs, 70
Mood, of verbs, 83, 84
Morning message, 131
Morphemes, 74, 292
    bound, 291
    in morphological reading phase, 127
    and reading, 74
Morphologic spelling phase, 291
    word recognition and, 127–128
Morphological reading/reader
    error type in, 350
    teaching, 140–141
Morphology, of words, 73–76
Motivation, 222
    in adolescents, 470, 471
    in grades 3–5, 431
"Mrs. Alphabet," 114
Multidimensional Fluency Scale, 163, 332, 352
Multiple texts, comparing same theme between, 279, 280
Multiple-meaning words, 167
mythos, 258

N

NAEP (National Assessment of Educational Progress), reading level definitions, 5–8
Names
    proper. *See* Proper names
    student. *See* Student names
Narrative, web of, 258
Narrative texts
    with common themes, comparison of, 279
    comprehension of. *See* Comprehension, narrative texts
    hero cycle in, 260–261
    informational texts and, balanced reading of, 249
    informational texts vs., processing strategies for, 234
    interpretation of. *See* Comprehension, narrative texts
    plot elements and, 205
    structure of, thinking critically about, 258–261
        strategies for, 269–275
Nasal consonants, 71
National Assessment of Educational Progress, 21
National Association for Bilingual Education (NABE), 28
National Center for Family Literacy, 119
National Council for the Accreditation of Teacher Education (NCATE), 358
National Council for the Social Studies (NCSS), 473
    read-aloud book recommendations, 152–153
National Council of Teachers of English (NCTE), 27

National Governors Association Center for Best Practices (NGA Center), 21
National Institutes of Child Health and Human Development (NICHD), 18
National Literacy Panel on Language-Minority Children and Youth, 482
National Reading Panel, 22, 331, 347, 482
    reading fluency definition, 149
    reading fluency recommendations, 158
National Science Teachers Association, 473
    read-aloud book recommendations, 152
Natural approach, to second-language acquisition, 488–491
Natural order hypothesis, 486
NCATE (National Council for the Accreditation of Teacher Education), 358
NCSS. *See* National Council for the Social Studies (NCSS)
Negative behavior, 397
New Criticism, 13
New literacies
    defining, 256–257
        critical thinking and, 256–257
    for grades K–2, 391–392
    NRP recommendations, 158
    word recognition and, 140
No Child Left Behind (NCLB) Act
    assessment and, 326, 334, 347, 351
        ELLs and, 359
    balanced literacy and, 22
    bilingual education and, 46
    demise of, 19
    Reading First and, 54–55
    reading fluency and, 150
    standards development and, 19–21
    students with disabilities and, 53
Nonfiction books. *See* Informational texts
Nonverbal communication, culturally responsive, 45
Norm-referenced tests, 327
Notes
    anecdotal, 398–399
    "I Have a Problem," 369, 371
Nouns, 81
Novels, core, 465–466
Number, verbs and, 83, 84
Number prefixes, 449

O

Observational assessments, 207, 208–209
Observations, informal and structured, 330–332, 369, 370, 456, 460
    in comprehension assessment, 355
Old English (OE), 75
One-on-one tutoring, 52
One-Word Picture Vocabulary Test Revised, 352
Online dictionaries, 176

Teachers
  culturally sensitive, 44–45
  introducing self to students, 40
  in learning community, 36–41
  learning place creation by, 366–374
  linguistics for, 114–115
  modeling by, 40–41, 143–144.
      See also Modeling
  portfolios of. *See* Professional portfolios
  professional assessment of, 358–359
  professional development of, 27–28
  role of, 5
      in guiding instruction, 221–224
      in literature circles, 198–199
  self-assessment by, 357–358
  special education and, 53
Teachers of English to Speakers of Other Languages
      (TESOL), 28
  African American Vernacular English and, 48
Teaching reading
  African American Vernacular English and, 48, 49–50,
      420, 488, 490, 492, 494
  changes in, 21
  to ELLs
      in English, 496
      in the mother tongue, 496–498
      in Spanish, 498–503. *See also* Spanish, teaching
        reading in
  finding resources for, 62
  fluent vs. disfluent reading, modeling of, 150, 151
  goal of, 182–183. *See also* Comprehension *entries*
  guided reading. *See* Guided reading
  individualized programs for, 23–24
  literature, 464–468
  in middle grades, reflections on, 453
  recent history of, 16–21
  reciprocal teaching, 244, 245
  teaming in, 462–463
  thematic units, 468, 469
  through science, 372–373
  vocabulary, 166
Teaching vocabulary
  general vs. content-specific, 168–169
  principles of, 166
  strategies for, 169–170
Teaching writing
  in different genres, 306
  to learn, 316–317
  through science, 372–373
Team teaching
  in bilingual education, 483
  for reading instruction, 462–463
Technology. *See* Computers; Internet
Terminology, content-specific, comprehension
      and, 234–236
Terms in advance, in ABC model, 193
Test questions, for ELLs, guidelines for simplifying, 361

Test taking, 456–457
Test-retest reliability, 333
Texas Primary Reading Inventory, 335, 352
Text(s)
  coding of, 194
  comprehension of, 186
  organization of, table of contents and, 229.
      See also Text structure
  predicting usefulness of, 239
  in reader response theory, 185
Text patterns, following, 12, 188
  cultural differences in, 189
Text structure
  informational texts and, 88–89, 220, 225
  organizational methods, 232, 233
  story grammar and, 87–88
Textbooks, spelling, 293
Textual patterns
  comparing, 232
  comprehension and, 185
  graphic models, 233
  types of, 232
  writing own text, 232–233
  writing own text and, 232
Thematic units, 418–419, 468, 469
Themes, for teaching comprehension skills, 204
Think-alouds, 193, 385
Thinking critically. *See* Critical thinking
Think/Pair/Share, 192
Thinkquest Project, 472
Third grade, consolidating primary-grade gains in,
      405–407. *See also* Grades 3–5
Third tier words, 168
Three-cuing system, 331
Tier One/Two/Three words, 77, 168, 235
Topical content knowledge, 221
Total physical response (TPR) method, of second-language
      acquisition, 488, 489
Tracking, grouping without, 430
Trade books
  for grades 3–5, 432
  for independent reading level, 432
Transitional alphabetic readers, 126
Transitional model, of bilingual
      education, 483
Transitive verbs, 84
Twenty-First Century Project, 472
Two-syllable words, word sorting with, 140
  order for, 139
Two-way bilingual education, 484

U

Unrestrictive clauses, 80
Unz English Initiative (California), 47
U.S. Department of Education, 352